WARRIORS OF THE HIMALAYAS

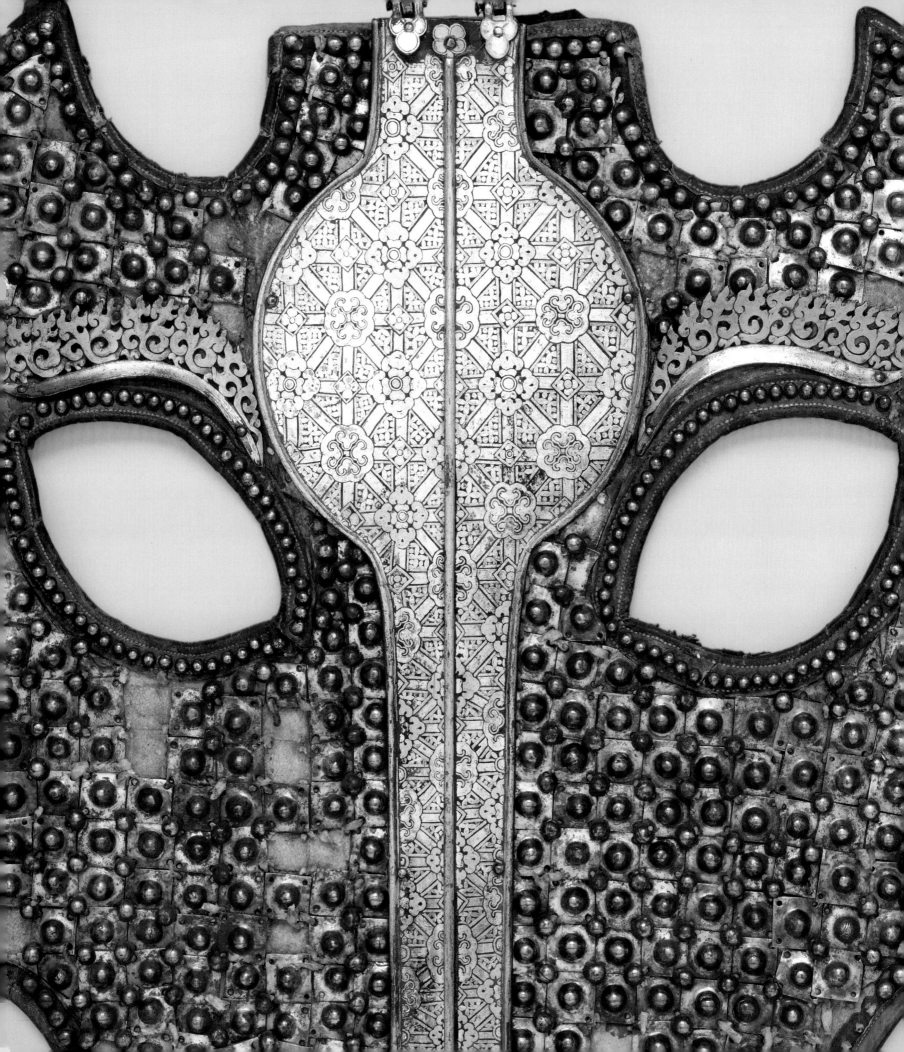

WARRIORS OF THE HIMALAYAS

REDISCOVERING THE ARMS AND ARMOR OF TIBET

Donald J. LaRocca

with essays by John Clarke, Amy Heller, and Lozang Jamspal

The Metropolitan Museum of Art, New York

Yale University Press, New Haven and London

This catalogue is published in conjunction with the exhibition "Warriors of the Himalayas: Rediscovering the Arms and Armor of Tibet," on view at The Metropolitan Museum of Art, New York, April 5–July 2, 2006.

The exhibition is made possible by The Brine Family Charitable Trust.

The exhibition catalogue is made possible by The Carl Otto von Kienbusch Memorial Fund and the Grancsay Fund.

Published by The Metropolitan Museum of Art, New York
John P. O'Neill, Editor in Chief and General Manager of Publications
Gwen Roginsky, Associate General Manager of Publications
Margaret Rennolds Chace, Managing Editor
Margaret Aspinwall, Senior Editor
Bruce Campbell, Designer
Sally Van Devanter, Production Manager
Robert Weisberg, Assistant Managing Editor

Unless otherwise specified, all photographs were supplied by the owners of the works of art, who hold the copyright to the photographs, and are reproduced with permission. Photographs of works in the Metropolitan Museum's collection are by Oi-Cheong Lee (cat. nos. 5, 6, 8–10, 12–19, 21–28, 30, 31, 33–41, 43–48, 50–52, 57, 60–64, 66, 68–70, 74, 75, 77–92, 94, 95, 98, 103–109, 111, 112, 115–124, 127–135), Peter Zeray (cat. nos. 101, 102, 110), and Paul Lachenauer (exploded view of cat. no. 120), The Photograph Studio, The Metropolitan Museum of Art. Additional photograph credits: cat. no. 4, helmet, Donald J. LaRocca; cat. no. 56, Oi-Cheong Lee.

Fig. 6, map by Astrid Fischer, in Valrae Reynolds, *From the Sacred Realm: Treasures of Tibetan Art from the Newark Museum* (Munich, London, New York: Prestel, 1999), p. 6, reproduced by permission of the publisher.

Latin type set in Dante, Univers, and Mantinia. Tibetan fonts are Dedris and Ededris, supplied by Nitartha-Sambhota
Type set by Tina Henderson
Separations by Professional Graphics Inc., Rockford, Illinois
Printed and bound by CS Graphics PTE, LTD, Singapore

Front jacket/cover illustration: Armored cavalryman (cat. no. 46), Tibetan, and possibly Bhutanese and Nepalese, 18th–19th century; iron, gold, copper alloy, wood, leather, and textile. The Metropolitan Museum of Art, New York, Bequest of George C. Stone, 1935 (36.25.25, .28, .351, .476, .583a–c, h–k, .842a–c, .2174, .2461, .2505, .2557); Bequest of Joseph V. McMullan, 1973 (1974.160.10 [saddle rug]); Gift of Mrs. Faïe J. Joyce, 1970 (1970.164.7a, b [boots])

Back jacket/cover illustration: Detail of the pommel plate from a set of saddle plates (cat. no. 111), Tibetan or Chinese, ca. 1400; iron, gold, lapis lazuli, and turquoise. The Metropolitan Museum of Art, New York, Purchase, Gift of William H. Riggs, by exchange, and Kenneth and Vivian Lam Gift, 1999 (1999.118)

Endpapers: Details of lamellar armor (cat. no. 6), Tibetan, possibly 16th–17th century; iron and leather. The Metropolitan Museum of Art, New York, Purchase, Arthur Ochs Sulzberger Gift, 2001 (2001.318)

Frontispiece: Detail of a head defense for a horse (shaffron) (cat. no. 27), Tibetan or Mongolian, 15th–17th century; iron, leather, gold, brass or copper alloy, and textile. The Metropolitan Museum of Art, New York, Purchase, Arthur Ochs Sulzberger Gift, 2004 (2004.402)

Library of Congress Cataloging-in-Publication Data

LaRocca, Donald J.
    Warriors of the Himalayas : rediscovering the arms and armor of Tibet / Donald J. LaRocca, with essays by John Clarke, Amy Heller, and Lozang Jamspal.
        p. cm.
    Catalog of an exhibition at the Metropolitan Museum of Art, New York, Apr. 5–July 2, 2006.
    Includes bibliographical references and index.
ISBN 1-58839-180-9 (hardcover)—ISBN 1-58839-181-7 (pbk.)—ISBN 0-300-11153-3 (Yale University Press)
    1. Armor—China—Tibet—Exhibitions. 2. Weapons—China—Tibet—Exhibitions.
I. Metropolitan Museum of Art (New York, N.Y.) II. Title.
    NK6683.A3T55 2006
    739.70951'50747471—dc22
                                        2005037903

CONTENTS

FOREWORD

The Metropolitan Museum's primary mission of ensuring the preservation and study of its permanent collections and disseminating the results of that research to a wide audience is admirably achieved in *Warriors of the Himalayas: Rediscovering the Arms and Armor of Tibet*. The catalogue and the exhibition clearly demonstrate the benefits that can result when otherwise overlooked portions of the collection become the focus of rigorous curatorial investigation.

In 1936, George Cameron Stone's bequest of nearly four thousand examples of non-European arms and armor brought to the Museum some fifty items of Tibetan armor, weapons, and equestrian equipment, most of which, however, received little attention in the succeeding decades. In 1995, intrigued by the lack of published information on the subject, Donald LaRocca began a thorough examination of this material, which soon led him to search both public and private collections for comparable objects and to begin studying Classical Tibetan. From 2000 onward, his research and the subsequent development of this exhibition were made possible by the support of Kevin Brine and The Brine Family Charitable Trust. Along the way, LaRocca's scrutiny also pinpointed areas of the Museum's collection of arms and armor from Tibet that could be strengthened through carefully selected new acquisitions, which were generously funded by several donors, chief among them Arthur Ochs Sulzberger, a long-time supporter of the Department of Arms and Armor. The result of this dual campaign of research and acquisitions is an exhibition of amazing objects that not only are unfamiliar to the general public, but also until now have been largely unknown even to specialists in the field of Tibetan art and culture. The accompanying catalogue provides the first extensive reference work on the subject, and we expect it will form the cornerstone for further studies in this area for generations to come.

Although centered around the Metropolitan Museum's permanent collection, this exhibition has been fully realized only with generous and invaluable loans from the following institutions: the Royal Armouries, Leeds; the Victoria and Albert Museum, London; the National Museum Liverpool; the National Museums of Scotland; the Pitt Rivers Museum, Oxford; the British Museum, London; the Marischal Museum at the University of Aberdeen; the National Museum of Natural History of the Smithsonian Institution, Washington, D.C.; the Newark Museum, Newark, New Jersey; and Yale University's Beinecke Library, New Haven, Connecticut. To the directors and trustees of these institutions we are indeed grateful for their willing assistance and close cooperation in this project.

This exhibition would not have been possible without the continued generosity of Kevin Brine and The Brine Family Charitable Trust, for which we are extremely thankful. The catalogue was underwritten by The Carl Otto von Kienbusch Memorial Fund and the Grancsay Fund.

Philippe de Montebello
Director
The Metropolitan Museum of Art

ACKNOWLEDGMENTS

This project has taken shape slowly over the past eleven years and would have been impossible without the ongoing help of many individuals and institutions. First and foremost are Arthur Ochs Sulzberger, for very kindly donating the funds that have allowed us to acquire many of the finest and most interesting objects in this catalogue, and Kevin Brine and The Brine Family Charitable Trust, who generously provided the funding that made continued research possible and the resulting exhibition a reality.

I would like to thank Lama Pema Wangdak for first introducing me to the study of Tibetan; Lozang Jamspal for patient guidance in reading and translating various Tibetan texts and for contributing an essay to this catalogue; E. Gene Smith, and the staff of the Tibetan Buddhist Resource Center, for generous and expert guidance concerning Tibetan literature; Greg Hillis, Yankyi Sonam, and Tsering Wangchuk, who taught at the University of Virginia's Foreign Language Institute, and my fellow students in that program during the summer of 2001, for much support and encouragement; Geshe Tenpa Chophel for sharing his time and knowledge, and his fellow monks at Gaden Chophel Ling in Howell, New Jersey, for their kind hospitality; and Annie Bien for many fruitful exchanges about the joys and frustrations of neophyte translators.

A very important debt of gratitude is owed to Amy Heller for answering a steady stream of questions on Tibetan art, language, and culture, and for her essay in this catalogue; Valrae Reynolds for offering important advice particularly in the formative stages of this project; John Clarke for making the collections of the Victoria and Albert Museum available over the years and also for contributing an essay to the catalogue; Jeff Watt and the staff of the Rubin Museum; and the many other Tibetologists who have kindly responded to an endless series of questions. They include Ian Alsop, Lotsawa Tony Duff, Johan Elverskog, David Germano, Michael Henss, Joachim Karsten, Erberto Lo Bue, Dan Martin, Braham Norwick, Hugh Richardson, and Robert Thurman.

For warm hospitality and great assistance in reaching various sites in Ladakh, I am indebted to Tsering Yanskit, Getsul Lobsang Ignyen, Tsering Angmo, Phuntshog Angmo, Tinley Angmo, and the best possible traveling companion, David Kittay.

The staff members of many museums have provided vital assistance in making collections available for study or facilitating my research in other ways: at the Victoria and Albert Museum, in addition to John Clarke, Simon Metcalf (now with the Royal Collections), Donna Stevens, Louise Parris, Marian Kite, and Rebecca Wallace; at the Royal Armouries, London and Leeds, Thom Richardson for access to the collections on many occasions and for freely sharing his notes and opinions, Chris Smith, and Kathy Richmond, and former staff including A. V. B. Norman, Guy Wilson, and Robert Smith; at the Royal Museum, Edinburgh, Jane Wilkinson, Lyn Stevens Wall, Jennifer Scarce, and Charles Stable; at the National Museum Liverpool, Emma Martin, Claire Sedgwick, Sue Barker, Vivian Chapman, Gary Brown, Roger Bailey, and Steve Smith; at the Pitt Rivers Museum, Clare Harris, Julia Nicholson, Tsering Shakya, Jocelyne Dudding, Mandy Sadan, Toby Wilkinson, Gali Beiner, Zena McGreevy, and Claire Freeman; at the Marischal Museum, University of Aberdeen, Neil Curtis and Mike Craig; at the Ashmolean Museum, Andrew Topsfield; at the British Museum, Richard Blurton and Maureen Theobald; at the National Museum of Natural History, Smithsonian Institution, Paul Taylor, Felicia Pickering, and Deborah Hull-Walksi; at Yale University, Ellen Cordes, Robert Babcock, and the staff of the Beinecke Library; at the Academy of Natural Sciences, Philadelphia, Carol Spawn and Eileen Mathias; at the University of Nebraska State Museum, Beth Wilkins; at the American Museum of Natural History, Laila Williamson and Tom Amorosi; at the Field Museum of Natural History, Bennet Bronson; at the National Museum of Denmark, Rolf Gilberg and Christel Braae; at the Peabody Museum of Archaeology and Ethnology, Harvard University, Susan Haskell; at the Horniman Museum, Ken Teague; at the State Hermitage Museum, Saint Petersburg, Juri Miller; at the University of Pennsylvania Museum of Archaeology and Anthropology, Jennifer Lane White; at the National Museum of Ethnography, Stockholm, Håken Wahlquist; and at the Royal Armoury, Stockholm, Nils Drejholt and Lena Rangstrom.

Jeremy Pine can be credited or blamed, depending on one's point of view, for first exposing me to a wide variety of Tibetan arms and armor outside museum collections and thereby inadvertently starting me on this path; and Robert Hales, Tsering Tashi, Namkha Dorjee, Joseph Gerena, and Fabio Rossi should also be thanked for making many other interesting and worthwhile objects available. Julian Freeman, Scott Rodell, and Philip Tom generously shared their personal research and opinions on numerous occasions. Many other individuals have helped in various ways, including Ruth Rhynas Brown, Howard Ricketts, Stephen Wood, Tony Anninos, Jonathan Barrett, James Singer, Cindy Elden, Arthur Leeper, Mehmet Hassan, David Owsley, Ellen Pearlman, Rupert Smith, Friedrich Spuhler, Jill Morley Smith, Jacqueline Simcox, Douglas Wissing, Hugo Weihe, Yamini Mehta, Ann Shaftel, Walter Karcheski, David Alexander, Helmut Nickel, Diki Lhazi Surkhang, Yangchen Lakar, Tsering Choedon, Jampa Tseten Surkhang, and Rigsam Langsur.

Within The Metropolitan Museum of Art, there are many colleagues to thank, including James Watt and members of the Department of Asian Art, particularly Steven Kossak, Denise Leidy, Jason Sun, Maxwell Hearn, Joyce Denney, Anne Boberski, and Jack Jacoby; Barbara Bridgers and the staff of The Photograph Studio including Paul Lachenauer, Peter Zeray, and especially Oi-Cheong Lee, whose superb photographs for this catalogue set a standard for his profession; John P. O'Neill and the staff of the Editorial Department, including Peter Antony, Sally Van Devanter, Robert Weisberg, and especially Margaret Aspinwall, who has been the ideal editor; Bruce Campbell for his design of the catalogue; Linda Sylling for supervising all aspects of the exhibition installation, and Michael Langley for designing the installation; Richard Stone, Pete Dandridge, John Canonico, and Robert Koestler in Objects Conservation, and in the Department of Scientific Research, Marco Leona and Tony Frantz, all of whom rendered useful analysis and advice; Nobuko Kajitani, Florica Zaharia, Midori Sato, and Kisook Suh in Textile Conservation; Grace Brady of the Counsel's Office for sharing photographs and insights from her own visit to Tibet; and Herb Moskowitz, Aileen Chuk, Blanche Kahn, and Willa Cox of the Registrar's Office. Particular thanks are owed to my friends and colleagues, past and present, in the Department of Arms and Armor, who have been very supportive of this project from the outset, including Hermes Knauer and Edward Hunter for their sensitive and skillful conservation of many of the pieces seen here; Stephen Bluto for great attention to the display and storage needs of the same objects; Marilynn Van Dunk, Lara Langer, and Danielle Watson for administrative support; Dirk Breiding who regularly acted as a sounding board for ideas; Bob Carroll who first suggested that I should focus on non-European objects and then beautifully restored the Tibetan pieces acquired before his untimely death; and especially Stuart Pyhrr for his steady toleration and even encouragement of so much exploratory research. I also wish to thank Philippe de Montebello, Mahrukh Tarapor, and the administration and trustees of the Metropolitan Museum for their willingness to support this project.

To my parents for fostering my early interest in history, armor, and museums, including long drives to bring about memorable childhood trips to the Metropolitan Museum; and to my family, Trish, Nick, and Eliza, I am ever grateful for their continued encouragement, love, and support during the long hours of study and many weeks away from home.

Despite such a vast amount of unstinting assistance, the errors and omissions still present are entirely due to the limits of my own knowledge and understanding of the material. The research that went into this catalogue and exhibition remains a work in progress and I hope will be viewed as such.

Donald J. LaRocca

LENDERS TO THE EXHIBITION

A NOTE TO THE READER ABOUT THE USE OF TIBETAN TERMS

In the essays and catalogue entries, many frequently used Tibetan place names, personal names, titles, and other terms are rendered in their generally accepted phonetic equivalents, followed after the first citation by parentheses in which the exact Tibetan orthography is given in italics, transliterated according to the Wylie system.[1] In many other instances, however, particularly where phonetic approximations would be too variable, the Tibetan is given only in Wylie transliteration with no attempt at phonetic renderings. The transliteration system is a necessity because it is the best way to ensure accuracy in citing romanized Tibetan terms and allows them to be pursued further in specialized sources. The general reader, for whom the transliterations may appear awkward or even unintelligible, should feel free to simply ignore them.

Tibetan script is used in addition to transliteration throughout three of the four appendixes because those are intended as reference material for future research and to make them more accessible to native readers of Tibetan. It is hoped, however, that the interested general reader will also find much food for thought by browsing the English passages of these appendixes. In the "Tibetan-English Glossary of Arms and Armor Terms" the head terms are given in transliteration followed in parentheses by the same terms in Tibetan script. The terms are grouped into broad typological categories and within the categories are listed in Tibetan alphabetical order, as they would appear in a Tibetan dictionary.[2]

1. T. V. Wylie, "A Standard System of Tibetan Transcription," *Harvard Journal of Asiatic Studies* 22 (1959), pp. 261–67. The method of transliteration used in this catalogue differs from the Wylie system in two minor ways. Internal capitalization, which Wylie appeared to retain only grudgingly, has been dropped. In addition, following the spirit of Wylie's essay, in which all unnecessary Western typographical conventions should be avoided, the use of hyphens between syllables has also been dropped.

2. For an explanation of the Tibetan system of dictionary order, see Melvyn Goldstein, *Modern Literary Tibetan: A Reading Course and Reference Grammar* (New Delhi, 1991), pp. 40–41.

Fig. 1. Tibet and environs. The shaded portion indicates areas currently inhabited by Tibetans or with strong Tibetan cultural influence. The black outline indicates the political boundaries of the traditional Tibetan government prior to 1959 (map: © Prestel Verlag, Munich)

WARRIORS OF THE HIMALAYAS

REDISCOVERING THE ARMS AND ARMOR OF TIBET

DONALD J. LAROCCA

This exhibition offers the first detailed survey of traditional armor and weapons from the Tibetan plateau. It is based on the concentrations of this material found in The Metropolitan Museum of Art and a small number of other museums, particularly in Great Britain. Until recently these objects—helmets, armor, swords, firearms, saddles, and so on—were seen as following only a few well-recognized styles. When commented on at all, these artifacts have been categorized generally as both archaic and simplistic. However, the emergence during the past ten to twenty years of previously unknown and very early examples has called into question many accepted assumptions about the styles and dating of Tibetan arms and armor. A more careful appraisal reveals a far wider variety of cultural influences and date ranges, as well as styles, types, and materials used, than previously realized or expected. The results of a reexamination of the subject are presented in this catalogue.

The Tibetan plateau, the world's highest, covers an area roughly the size of western Europe and is legendary both for its elevation and its remoteness. It is bordered on three sides by vast mountain ranges—the Kunlun and Karakoram mountains to the north and northwest and the Himalayas to the south—and by the mountains and river gorges of western China on the east. Areas that are culturally Tibetan extend far beyond central Tibet and the current political boundaries of China's Tibetan Autonomous Region (TAR) to include parts of northwestern India, Nepal, Sikkim, Bhutan, as well as parts of Xinjian Uighur, Qinghai, Gansu, Sichuan, and Yunnan provinces of China. The traditional names for Tibet's principal regions are Ü (dbus) and Tsang (gtsang) in central and southwestern Tibet, Kham (khams) in the east, and Amdo (a mdo) in the northeast, the plains of Changthang (byang thang) to the north, and Ngari (mnga' ris) in the west.

Armor and weapons are certainly not among the images usually called to mind when considering the subject of Tibet, which has been identified most closely in recent decades with the pacifism and deep spirituality of the Dalai Lama and the compassionate nature of Tibetan Buddhism. The nuances and beauty of Tibetan culture, religion, and art have been brought to wide audiences through a steady flow of books, exhibitions, and films. The general perception of Tibetan arms and armor, however, stems from only two principal sources: the actual examples brought out of Tibet sporadically since the 1880s, which until now have remained largely unstudied and unpublished, and photographs taken in Tibet in the first half of the twentieth century showing armor and weapons being worn or displayed (figs. 2–8).

These photographs provide rare visual documentation of most of the distinctive types of armor and weapons that form the nucleus of this catalogue and exhibition. Among the earliest are two key photos taken during the Younghusband Expedition, a British military incursion into Tibet in 1903–4 (figs. 3, 4).[1] The weapons shown in them—swords, spears, and matchlock guns—were still in common use in Tibet and were only just then beginning to be replaced by modern small arms. The body armor for men and horses, by contrast, was photographed at the very last moments of its centuries-long history of use for actual defense in battle. Most of the later photos discussed below, still a rich source of information, show Tibetan arms and armor worn as costume in ceremonial contexts.

A summary of the armor and weapons of the Tibetans in 1903–4 was given by Dr. L. Austine Waddell (1854–1938), the medical officer attached to the Younghusband Expedition and the leading British Tibetologist of the time:

A few still wear iron helmets and cuirasses of the type familiar to us in medieval literature, consisting of small, narrow, willow-like leaves about

Fig. 2. Armored infantryman (*zimchongpa*), wearing a Tibetan helmet and lamellar armor and armed with a spear and a sword. Photographed at the Great Prayer Festival in Lhasa, 1943, by Ilya Tolstoy. Ewell Sale Stewart Library, Academy of Natural Sciences, Philadelphia

Fig. 3. Armored cavalryman, wearing a helmet and coat of mail and armed with a spear, sword, and matchlock musket. The horse wears armor on its head, neck, and chest. Photographed in Tibet, 1903–4, probably by L. A. Waddell (photo: after L. A. Waddell, *Lhasa and Its Mysteries* [New York, 1906], facing p. 168)

Fig. 4. Armored infantrymen, wearing Tibetan helmets and lamellar armor and holding wicker shields and matchlock muskets. They are wearing their lamellar armor backward, which suggests that this was a staged photograph or that they were very raw recruits. Photographed in Tibet, 1903–4, probably by L. A. Waddell (photo: after L. A. Waddell, *Lhasa and Its Mysteries* [New York, 1906], facing p. 172)

1½ inch long, threaded with leather thongs. A few also wear coats of chain-mail. The iron helmet of the cavalry was distinguished from that of the infantry, who have a cock's feather, by a red tassel or peacock's feather on the top. The high officers sometimes clothe their horse in armour, a new set of which was captured. The clothing of the horses and saddlery of the leaders was artistic and full of colour, with good carpet saddle-cloth, throat-tassels, and massive bits and stirrup-irons, silver or gold inlaid, mostly from Derge in Eastern Tibet. . . . The weapons of the Tibetan warrior are numerous and picturesque. On his back is slung a matchlock or a modern rifle; in his hand he clutches a long spear; from his belt hangs an ugly long sword, one-edged, with a straight heavy blade. When guns are insufficient to go round, the remaining men carry bows and arrows, the latter of bamboo with barbed iron heads 3 inches long, also slings, and heavy shields, wooden or wicker-work, or hide with iron bosses.[2]

The "iron helmets" Waddell would have encountered were mostly of two kinds: a helmet with a one-piece hemispherical bowl (such as cat. no. 46) and the most typical form of Tibetan helmet, usually made of eight overlapping segments, as worn by the infantrymen in figures 2 and 4 (compare cat. nos. 1, 2, 4, 5). The "cuirasses of the type familiar to us in medieval literature, consisting of small, narrow, willow-like leaves about 1½ inch long, threaded with leather thongs" refers specifically to what may be considered the classic form of Tibetan body armor, known in English as lamellar armor, and in Tibetan variously as *go cha*, *khrab*, or, more precisely, *byang bu'i khrab* (figs. 2, 4).[3] The "willow-like leaves" are the small iron plates (in English lamellae and in Tibetan *byang bu*), which are laced together to form the armor (cat. nos. 1–6). The "chain-mail," just discernible on the cavalryman in figure 3, refers to the meshlike type of armor made up of hundreds or even thousands of small interlocking iron rings (cat. nos. 40, 46). Known in English simply as mail, and in Tibetan as *a lung gi khrab*, most if not all of what was used in Tibet was probably imported from India or the Middle East.

Waddell's photograph of the armored cavalryman in figure 3 and his statement that the "high officers sometimes clothe their horse in armour" provide the only solid evidence for the continued, if limited, use of horse armor in a military context in Tibet up to that time, long after it had gone out of use in virtually all other parts of the world.[4] This highly distinctive form of horse armor was unique to Tibet, and very few complete examples of it have survived to the present day (cat. no. 26). The "saddlery" including "massive bits and stirrup-irons, silver or gold inlaid" (and presumably by extension the saddles themselves), "mostly from Derge in Eastern Tibet," present some of the finest examples of decorated Tibetan ironwork (for example, cat. nos. 112, 130, 135).

In terms of weapons Waddell's list begins with the matchlock, known in Tibetan as a *me mda'* (literally, fire arrow), a simple but reliable type of firearm used in Europe from the fifteenth to the seventeenth century and in Tibet from at least the seventeenth century until well into the twentieth (cat. nos. 99–102). The most obvious feature of the Tibetan matchlock is the pair of long thin prongs, used to prop up the weapon when shooting on foot as opposed to on horseback. In these and other photos the prongs are usually extended straight out when the gun is slung on the back (as in fig. 3) or folded under the stock (as in fig. 4). The long spear (*mdung*), such as that carried by the cavalryman in figure 3, could measure anywhere from 6 to 12 feet in length and typically had a wood shaft reinforced with a coiling iron strap (cat. nos. 75, 76). Beyond the plain fighting spears of this type, a wide variety of decorated ceremonial spearheads have come to light in recent years (cat. nos. 77–84). Waddell's description of the "ugly long sword, one-edged, with a straight heavy blade" could be applied to many of the workaday swords he must have encountered. This ignores, however, the great variety of finely made and elaborately decorated Tibetan swords (*gri*, *ral gri*, or *dpa' dam*), such as those described by the journalist Percival Landon, who also accompanied the expedition, as having "richly worked sword-hilts" (cat. nos. 61–67).[5] Waddell's comment that "when guns are insufficient . . . the remaining men carry bows and arrows" indicates that archery had already been replaced by firearms

Fig. 5. Opposing lines of armored infantrymen (*zimchongpa*), photographed by F. Spencer Chapman at the Great Prayer Festival in Lhasa, 1936. Pitt Rivers Museum, Oxford (1998.157.83)

as the principal projectile weapon, although the bow remained in regular use for hunting and sport (cat. nos. 95–97). He also mentioned slings (sgu rdo or 'ur rdo), a common accessory used by herdsmen and nomads, which made an effective weapon when necessary. Waddell's summary concludes with shields (phub), "wooden or wicker-work, or hide with iron bosses." The wicker or cane shields (sba phub) were of two types, one flat and the other domed, both distinctively Tibetan (cat. nos. 24, 25). The "hide [shield] with iron bosses" describes the characteristic form of shields from India, Nepal, and Bhutan, which would not have been uncommon in Tibet.

The tantalizing but limited glimpse offered by the two Waddell photos is greatly increased just slightly later in the century by a rich source of photographs centering on the ceremonies included in the month-long Great Prayer Festival, or Monlam Chenmo (smon lam chen mo), which was held annually during the first month of the lunar year in the Tibetan capital, Lhasa. This elaborate series of events was well documented in photographs, especially those by Hugh Richardson, who observed some or all of the ceremonies on several occasions between 1937 and 1950, by Frederick Spencer Chapman in 1936, in still photos and film footage shot by Harry Staunton in 1940, and by Brooke Dolan and Ilya Tolstoy, who visited Lhasa in 1942–43.[6] Armor and weapons played an important part in the costume of two groups involved in the festivities: a body of infantry, known as the zimchongpa (gzim sbyong pa), and two detachments of cavalry.

The infantrymen wore lamellar armor and usually the most typical form of helmet, made of eight overlapping segments, and were equipped with a variety of swords, shields, spears, bows, and matchlock muskets (fig. 2).[7] Based on an analysis of the corresponding examples in this catalogue, most of the equipment of the zimchongpa appears to date from the mid-fifteenth to the early seventeenth century, an extremely tumultuous period in Tibetan history.[8] At the time the photographs were taken, the zimchongpa acted as a ceremonial guard troop for the Dalai Lama and the State Oracle on various occasions.[9] Their main performance, however, came toward the end of the Great Prayer Festival and consisted of a sequence of mock combats in which two opposing lines of zimchongpa engaged in verbal exchange, the spokesman from one side proclaiming the victories of his "army" and taunting the leader of the other side, followed by the opposing sides brandishing or discharging their weapons (fig. 5).[10]

Like the zimchongpa, the cavalry had very specific roles to fulfill during the Great Prayer Festival, including a ceremonial review of troops and their equipment and a horseback target-shooting contest.[11] It was the responsibility of various noble families to arm and equip contingents of riders for these events, probably continuing a practice formerly intended for the mobilization of troops in times of need. All of the riders were outfitted with generally the same types of equipment, the quality and condition of which, however, varied widely. The style and type of the equipment suggest that the standards or regulations governing it were established in the seventeenth or eighteenth century. The cavalrymen's armor basically consisted of a steel helmet fitted with textile flaps, a mail shirt, a set of "four mirrors" (four round plates strapped over the chest, back, and sides), and often an armored belt (fig. 6). Their weapons included a matchlock or modern rifle slung over the back, a bandolier with powder and shot for the musket, a spear, a bow worn in a bow case on the left hip, and a quiver of arrows worn at the right hip (fig. 7), all of which can be seen in catalogue number 46. The principal riders, who acted as standard-bearers, wore more elaborate armor and helmet crests. The largest and most decorative crests (fig. 8) were attached by a cord to the rider's thumb, probably to prevent the crest from falling to the ground if it became dislodged from the helmet. The rider in this image also wears what appears to be the most distinctive helmet seen in any of the Great Prayer Festival photos. In addition to the sumptuous crest and very large textile flaps, the helmet itself has a high, stepped bowl, which is decorated on the bowl, brim, and brow with designs of dragons and scrollwork, and has a domed finial of pierced iron just visible at the base of the crest. Unlike most of the helmets worn at this event, which appear to be Tibetan and Bhutanese, this helmet is probably Chinese or Mongolian, perhaps dating from the sixteenth century. It may have been one of the helmets specially issued from the treasury of the Jokhang Temple in Lhasa solely for use in the Great Prayer Festival as mentioned by Hugh Richardson.[12]

As the preceding comments indicate, the seeming paradox of the existence of any, let alone so many, examples of arms and armor from Tibet is no paradox at all when seen in the context of Tibetan history, which included many extended periods of intense military activity. A brief review of Tibetan history from the seventh to the early twentieth century makes this readily apparent.[13] During the Yarlung dynasty, from the seventh to the ninth centuries, Tibet was a powerful and expanding empire and dominated an area stretching from present-day Uzbekistan to western China through trade, politics, and armed might.[14] In contemporary documents, such as the Tang Annals, Tibetan armor and weapons were praised for both their high quality and their great effectiveness: "Their armor is excellent. They clothe their entire bodies in it, except for the eyeholes. Even powerful bows and keen blades can do them little harm. . . . They have bows and swords, shields, spears, suits of armor and helmets. . . . Both men and horses are covered in coats of mail of excellent manufacture."[15] Unfortunately, almost nothing of the armor or weapons from this period appears to have survived, or at least to have been identified as such. The only piece

Fig. 6. Armored cavalryman, wearing a helmet, shirt of mail, set of four mirrors, and armored belt, and armed with lance, bow and arrow, and gun. Photographed by Harry Staunton during the Great Prayer Festival in Lhasa, 1940. Pitt Rivers Museum, Oxford (1999.23.2.67)

Fig. 8. Standard-bearer wearing an elaborately decorated crest, helmet, and breastplate. Photographed by Ilya Tolstoy at the Great Prayer Festival in Lhasa, 1943. Ewell Sale Stewart Library, Academy of Natural Sciences, Philadelphia

Fig. 7. Armored cavalryman seen from the rear, wearing a helmet, shirt of mail, set of four mirrors, and armored belt. This view also shows his musket with a protective cover over the lower half of the stock, a bandolier, and other accessories. Photographed at the Great Prayer Festival in Lhasa, 1943, by Brooke Dolan. Ewell Sale Stewart Library, Academy of Natural Sciences, Philadelphia

in this catalogue tentatively attributed to that era, traditionally referred to as the time of the Three Ancestral Dharma Kings, is a helmet, which is a uniquely important example of its type (cat. no. 8).[16] In the seventh century under the first Dharma king, Songtsen Gampo, Buddhism, which would become the defining aspect of Tibetan culture, was introduced into Tibet. Also at this time the first Buddhist temples were built. The first Buddhist monastery in Tibet, Samye (bsam yas), was built in the 770s by King Trisong Detsen, who later made Buddhism the official religion of the kingdom. In addition, during this time Tibet was in frequent contact with China, the Uighur and other Turkic and Mongol peoples of the steppes, the burgeoning Arab caliphates then spreading into Central Asia, and the kingdoms in northern India and Nepal.

After the fall of the Yarlung dynasty, from the mid-ninth century until the advent of Mongol supremacy in the mid-thirteenth century, authority in Tibet was divided among many noble families and small states, which were frequently at odds with one another.[17] Descendants of the Yarlung dynasty relocated to western Tibet, establishing kingdoms that were instrumental in supporting a resurgence of Buddhism beginning in the eleventh century. During that century and the next, under the patronage of different noble families, various Buddhist sects or schools developed and in turn founded monastic orders throughout the country. In addition to the Nyingma (rnying ma) school, which traces its origins to Padmasambhava, one of the founders of Tibetan Buddhism in the eighth century, other important schools established at that time included the Kadam (bka' gdams), Sakya (sa skya), and Kagyu (bka' brgyud), from which there were several branches including the Phagmodru (phag mo gru), Karma (ka rma), and Drigung ('bri gung). The Gelug (dge lugs) school, which would eventually become the most influential, developed in the late fourteenth century. The larger monasteries gradually became increasingly important, not only spiritually but also as seats of economic and political power.

The thirteenth-century expansion of the Mongol Empire by the descendants of Genghis Khan (d. 1227) led to the conquest of China and the establishment of the Yuan dynasty (1279–1368). Again, few examples of arms and armor can be reliably identified as dating from this period. Among the pieces in this catalogue that can reasonably be attributed to this era or slightly later are an extremely rare multilame helmet (cat. no. 9), an exquisite set of damascened saddle plates (cat. no. 111), a similarly decorated sword (cat. no. 57), and two quivers (cat. nos. 91, 92), the quivers being perhaps the only extant examples of their type. During this period Mongol rulers controlled not only China and Tibet but also Korea, Persia, and Russia, and reached to the edges of Europe. A critical relationship was established at this time between the Mongols and Tibetan Buddhism, beginning with the abbot of Sakya Monastery, Kunga Gyaltsen (kun dga' rgyal mtshan, 1182–1251, known as Sakya Pandita), who was essentially made the representative of Mongol authority in Tibet by Godan, a grandson of Genghis Khan, in 1247. In about 1255 Sakya Pandita's nephew and successor, Phagpa ('phags pa, 1235–1280), became the personal spiritual teacher of Kublai Khan (1215–1294), who within a few years was the first Yuan emperor. Kublai later made Phagpa the official head of his civil administration in Tibet, in charge of the thirteen administrative districts (myriarchies) into which the Mongols divided central Tibet. An elaborately decorated helmet and a coat of plates said to have been given to Phagpa by Kublai Khan are still preserved in Sakya Monastery, Tibet.[18] While other Mongol princes were important patrons of different Tibetan schools, the Sakyapa wielded the greatest temporal power until after the death of Kublai Khan. However, the Yuan emperors following Kublai Khan gradually intervened less in Tibetan affairs, and without active Mongol support Sakya power waned in central Tibet.

In the next and very tumultuous period of Tibetan history, from roughly the middle of the fourteenth century until 1642, power was held by three successive secular dynasties, the Phagmodrupa, the princes of Rinpung (rin spungs), and the kings of Tsang. Most of the armor in this catalogue, including many of the most elaborate and unusual examples, appears to fall, not surprisingly, into this turbulent period: the distinctive examples of horse armor (cat. nos. 26–33), lamellar body armor (cat. nos. 1–7), several examples of leather armor (cat. nos. 34–39), and a remarkably diverse group of helmets (cat. nos. 10–18). By the middle of the fourteenth century, after a period of violent struggle, the preeminent position of the Sakyapa was taken by the secular arm of the Phagmodrupa, a branch of the Kagyu school. The leader of the Phagmodrupa was Changchub Gyaltsen (byang chub rgyal mtshan, 1302–1364), a member of the powerful Lang (rlangs) family, who ruled the Lhokha region south of Lhasa, including the Yarlung Valley. After gaining control of Ü and Tsang, Changchub Gyaltsen abolished many aspects of the Yuan-Mongol administration and instituted a revival of laws, customs, and literature modeled after the practices of the period of the ancient Tibetan kings of the Yarlung dynasty. By the late fifteenth century, after a long rivalry, the Phagmodrupa, who were allied with the Gelugpa, were supplanted by their former ministers, the princes of Rinpung, who were based in Tsang and supported by the Karmapa. In the 1560s the Rinpung were themselves supplanted by their ministers, who established the line of the kings of Tsang, the last native Tibetan secular monarchy, which remained in power for approximately eighty years. Although this was a period of incessant struggle between Tsang and Ü, the Ming dynasty (1368–1644) of China did not actively intervene in internal Tibetan politics. It did, however, expand upon the Yuan practice of patronizing monasteries and conferring titles and bestowing lavish gifts on Tibetan lay and religious officials.[19]

The level of political involvement changed markedly, however, early in the Qing dynasty (1644–1911) owing to renewed military activity by the Mongols in Tibet.

Active ties with the Mongols were reestablished by Sonam Gyatso (*bsod nams rgya mtsho*, 1543–1588), head of the Gelug order, who secured the patronage of the powerful Mongol ruler Altan Khan in 1578 and proselytized with great success in Mongolia for several years. The khan bestowed on him the title of *dalai*, meaning "ocean," in reference to the vastness of his spirituality, combined with the Tibetan term *lama*, for spiritual teacher or guru. As Sonam Gyatso was the third incarnation in the Gelug lineage, the title was conferred posthumously on his two predecessors, making him the Third Dalai Lama although the title had originated with him. After Sonam Gyatso's death in 1588, his reincarnation and successor was identified as the grandson of Altan Khan, Yonten Gyatso (*yon tan rgya mtsho*, 1589–1617), whose installation as the Fourth Dalai Lama solidified the bonds between the Gelug order and their Mongol allies.

Following the death of the Fourth Dalai Lama, armed conflict intensified between the Gelug and rival groups, particularly the Karma Kagyu in Tsang, who were supported by the king of Tsang, Karma Tenkyong (*kar ma btsan skyong*). Eventually, the Fifth Dalai Lama, Nawang Losang Gyatso (*ngag dbang blo bzang rgya mthso*, 1617–1682), turned to Gushri Khan, chief of the powerful Qoshot Mongols, for protection, and after several years of fighting, the king of Tsang and his allies were completely defeated. In 1642 Gushri Khan gave the Fifth Dalai Lama authority over all of Tibet, while retaining for himself the title king of Tibet and settling with his army outside Lhasa. This began the institution of the centralized rule of the Dalai Lamas, a practice that continued, with many vicissitudes, up until 1959. Due in part to Tibetan influence with the Mongol tribes on China's borders, the first Manchu emperor of the Qing dynasty, Shunzhi (r. 1644–61), reestablished ties with Tibet by inviting the Fifth Dalai Lama to Beijing, where he was received with highest honors in 1653. In general the last forty years of the Fifth Dalai Lama's reign were a period of great religious and administrative reform, which, despite border conflicts with Nepal, Bhutan, and Ladakh, was a time of relative peace and stability in Tibet.

By the early eighteenth century, disputes between the Fifth Dalai Lama's regent, Sangye Gyatso (*sangs rgyas rgya mtsho*), and Gushri Khan's successor, Lhabsang Khan, led to violent civil war in which the Dzungar Mongols, a powerful tribe of western Mongols, took the side of the regent. Because of the involvement of the Dzungars, who also posed a potentially serious threat to China, Emperor Kangxi (1662–1722) lent his support to Lhabsang Khan and his allies. Initially Lhabsang Khan was successful, defeating the regent and ruling Tibet as king from 1705 to 1717. In that year, however, Lhabsang Khan was killed and

his Qoshot Mongols decisively defeated in a climactic battle with the Dzungars, who then occupied Lhasa. Within a short time the oppressive methods of the Dzungars led to a popular uprising. In 1720 a combined Qing and Tibetan army drove the Dzungars out and installed the Seventh Dalai Lama, Kalzang Gyatso (*skal bzang rgya mtsho*, 1708–1757), in Lhasa. This marked the end of the Mongols as a dominant military presence in Tibet and laid the foundations for future Qing influence. After a brief civil war in 1727–28, a Manchu garrison was established in Lhasa, and two resident Qing officials, called *ambans*, were also permanently stationed in the capital. After a long period of effective rule by the Tibetan minister Pholhanas (*pho lha nas*), followed briefly by his son Gyumey Namgyal (*'gyur med rnam rgyal*), the Seventh Dalai Lama assumed full administration of the country in 1751. It was also during this period that large, ethnically Tibetan areas of Kham and Amdo, which border China, were incorporated into the provinces of Sichuan, Yunnan, and Qinghai. Under Emperor Qianlong (r. 1736–96) China reached its greatest territorial expansion since the Yuan dynasty, incorporating Chinese Turkestan (Xinjiang Uighur) and Outer Mongolia into the empire. Tibet, however, was treated as an independent protectorate, with no attempt made to convert it into a province during Qianlong's reign.

Objects in the catalogue that reflect the role of the Qing during the seventeenth and eighteenth centuries include a finely decorated helmet (cat. no. 19), two elaborate saddles probably made in China for the Tibetan market (cat. nos. 120, 122), and swords made to be worn suspended from the belt in the Chinese fashion (cat. nos. 65–67). Also from this period or slightly later is the complete set of equipment for a cavalryman, showing the use of mail rather than lamellar armor, and the addition of a musket to the bow and arrow (cat. no. 46). Other than the very limited adoption of some modern firearms, the traditional armor and weapons outlined above remained in use in Tibet up to the early twentieth century.

In 1788, during the reign of the Eighth Dalai Lama, Jampal Gyatso (*'jam dpal rgya mtsho*, 1758–1804), the Gurkhas of Nepal invaded and occupied much of southwestern Tibet. The ensuing war lasted until 1792, when the Gurkhas were driven out by Tibetan troops assisted by a Manchu army. After Qianlong, and for much of the nineteenth century, the Manchus were too preoccupied with internal affairs and the growing involvement of Western nations in China to intervene actively in Tibet. As a consequence, Tibet's war with the Sikhs and Ladakhis (the Dogra War) in 1841–42, a second war with the Nepalese Gurkhas in 1855–56, the Nyarong War fought in eastern Tibet in 1862–65, and finally the Younghusband Expedition of 1903–4 were met without assistance from China. The period of waning Manchu influence in Tibet also coincided with the reigns of the Ninth to the Twelfth Dalai Lamas, all of whom died young enough that Tibet was ruled by regents for virtually all of the nineteenth century, from the death of the Eighth Dalai Lama, in 1804, until the Thirteenth Dalai Lama, Thubten Gyatso (*thub bstan rgya mtsho*, 1876–1933), assumed full spiritual and temporal powers in 1895. The Thirteenth Dalai Lama's reign was the longest, the most active, and, in its later years, the most effective since that of the Fifth Dalai Lama in the mid-seventeenth century.

At the end of the nineteenth century in certain circles of the British government it was feared that the expansion of Russian influence and power in Central Asia would extend, or had already extended, deep into Tibet and thereby pose a threat to the interests of British India. Therefore, in 1903 a mission was authorized ostensibly to negotiate free trade agreements between Tibet and British India.[20] Led by Colonel Francis Younghusband and Brigadier General James Macdonald, the mission was a heavily armed expeditionary force that included approximately three thousand British troops, accompanied by several thousand native laborers who provided support, supplies, and transport.[21] After several failed attempts at negotiations and a few pitched battles, in which the Tibetans suffered disproportionately heavy casualties, the British entered Lhasa on August 3, 1904. Not wishing to be forced into negotiating a treaty, the Dalai Lama fled to Mongolia in advance of the British approach, where he remained until 1906, followed by stays in Amdo and Peking; he did not return to Lhasa until 1909. The British, meanwhile, soon departed, having secured a trade treaty from the government ministers in Lhasa and having failed to find any evidence of Russian complicity in Tibetan affairs. Probably on the occasion of the signing of the treaty, the regent of Tibet, Ganden Tri Ripoche Lozang Gyaltsen Lamoshar (*blo bzang rgyal mtshan la mo shar*), presented Colonel Younghusband and General Macdonald each with a gilded bronze statue of the Buddha.[22] It may have also been at this time that Macdonald acquired a Bhutanese sword of exceptionally fine quality (cat. no. 73). In 1909 Chinese forces invaded eastern Tibet and in 1910 reached Lhasa; the Dalai Lama was forced into exile once again, this time taking sanctuary with the British government in India, where he remained as a guest in Darjeeling. Only the Chinese revolution and the overthrow of the Qing dynasty in 1911 forestalled the invasion and allowed the Thirteenth Dalai Lama to return to Tibet in 1912. In gratitude to his British hosts, the Dalai Lama presented a complete Tibetan horse armor (cat. no. 26) to Sir Charles Bell, his principal host in Darjeeling. He also gave a large and important group of Tibetan objects and works of art to the king of England, George V (r. 1910–36), most of which was then put on long-term loan at the British Museum and the Victoria and Albert Museum. Among these were a lamellar armor and helmet, a sword, two shields, and a saddle said to be that of "the King of Rimpung," a reference to the Rinpung (*rin spungs*) family,

which ruled central Tibet from the late fifteenth until the mid-sixteenth century.[23]

Because the contrast between the traditional arms of the Tibetans and the modern military equipment of the British was so great, the actions of the Younghusband Expedition briefly brought Tibetan arms and armor to the attention of the outside world. Attracted by the distinctive nature and rarity of the material, members of the expedition collected many examples, most of them initially as campaign trophies. The majority, however, soon went directly or indirectly into various museum collections in Great Britain, especially the Victoria and Albert Museum, the Tower of London, the British Museum, the Liverpool Museum, the Pitt Rivers Museum, and the Royal Scottish Museum. Although certainly the most dramatic, the Younghusband Expedition was not the usual or even the first means by which Tibetan arms and armor were collected in the West. The American diplomat and Orientalist William Woodville Rockhill (1854–1914) included several examples of swords, archery equipment, firearms, and equestrian equipment in the far-ranging collection of Tibetan material culture that he assembled for the Smithsonian Institution during expeditions in the 1880s and 1890s.[24] Likewise, the expeditions to China in 1901–4 and to China and Tibet in 1908–10, led by the noted Sinologist Berthold Laufer (1874–1934), were the means by which many examples of Tibetan arms and armor were added to the Field Museum in Chicago.[25] Some examples of arms were also included in the collections gathered by various missionaries working in China and Tibet, the most notable being that of Dr. Albert Shelton (1875–1922), which forms the nucleus of the very important Tibetan collection in the Newark Museum.[26] Other examples acquired by travelers, explorers, researchers, and collectors have continued to trickle into private collections and museums from the 1920s until the present.[27] The core of the holdings of Tibetan arms and armor in the Metropolitan Museum came from the private collector George Cameron Stone (1859–1935), whose extensive collection of approximately four thousand examples of non-European armor and weapons, including some fifty from Tibet, was bequeathed to the Museum in 1935. Stone bought widely from dealers and auction houses, both in the United States and abroad, and also purchased items personally during his travels.[28] A relatively large number of Tibetan works of art and objects of all kinds, often the personal possessions of Tibetan exiles, became available to collectors and museums following the annexation of Tibet by the People's Republic of China beginning in 1948, which resulted in the Fourteenth Dalai Lama being forced into exile in 1959 and the exodus of thousands of Tibetans. Important pieces that can be connected with Tibetan expatriates of this period include catalogue number 126.[29] Of the more unusual and early examples that have emerged since the 1980s, some may have once been pre-

Fig. 9. Column wrapped with armor and weapons in the gonkhang of Phyang Monastery, Ladakh, showing a wicker shield reinforced with iron struts, a spear, matchlock musket, eight-plate helmet, quiver, and parts of a horse armor (photo: the author, 2003)

Fig. 10. Lamellar armor at the temple of the Nechung Oracle, near Lhasa. Photographed by Brooke Dolan, 1943. Ewell Sale Stewart Library, Academy of Natural Sciences, Philadelphia

served as votive objects in Tibetan monasteries and temples, several thousand of which were systematically stripped of their contents and destroyed or significantly damaged by Red Guard units during the Cultural Revolution in the late 1960s.[30]

The fact that such a large quantity and wide variety of armor and weapons survived into the twentieth century, though remarkable, can be explained by the circumstances found in Tibet. Many of the weapons, such as matchlock muskets, swords, spears, and archery equipment, were not outmoded in the Tibetan context and therefore remained in regular use. Although some examples are older or finer than others, objects of these types were still being made on a regular basis. In contrast to this, the lamellar armor and horse armor, some of which was

still being used at the time of the Younghusband Expedition in 1903–4, was as much as four hundred years old or more. The finest examples of these may have been preserved among the heirlooms of the nobility (cat. nos. 30, 31). Through the nineteenth century, much of the more ordinary material was probably kept in armories at regional fortresses (*rdzong*) or maintained by noble families for use by militias or by local levies called up in times of need.[31] This may account for what appear to be inventory numbers on several extant lamellar armors, such as one would expect to find on objects kept in an armory or storehouse context (cat. nos. 4, 5). Of the arms and armor that were photographed in Lhasa in the context of the Great Prayer Festival, that of the *zimchongpa* may have been stored in the *zhol*, the village at the foot of the

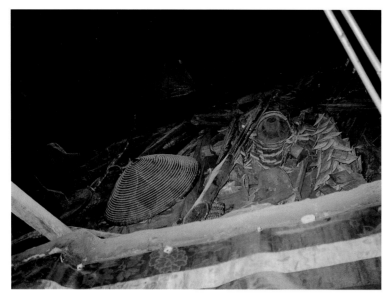

Fig. 11. Votive armor and weapons hung on the walls of the chapel of Hayagriva in Sera Monastery, Tibet, showing a Chinese coat of plates in the center beneath a helmet, a quiver of arrows, and a domed wicker shield (photo: Grace Brady, 1997)

Fig. 12. Another view of the votive arms and armor hung on the walls of the chapel of Hayagriva in Sera Monastery, Tibet, showing several Tibetan lamellar armors, quivers of arrows, and other weapons (photo: Grace Brady, 1997)

Potala Palace in Lhasa, while the equipment of the cavalry, as mentioned earlier, was the responsibility of individual noble families.[32]

Another important way in which historical armor and weapons survives in regions where Tibetan Buddhism is practiced involves the long-standing and widespread tradition of placing votive arms in monasteries and temples. There they are kept in special chapels, known as gonkhang (*mgon khang*), which are dedicated to guardian deities (*mgon po* or *dharmapala*) (fig. 9). The importance of arms in the iconography of these gods, who are seen as the fierce defenders of Buddhism and its followers, is discussed by Amy Heller in "Armor and Weapons in the Iconography of Tibetan Buddhist Deities." The significance of the gonkhang as a place of worship and protection is discussed from a Buddhist perspective by Lozang Jamspal in "The Gonkhang, Temple of the Guardian Deities." The great Tibetologist René de Nebesky-Wojkowitz described the gonkhang as "mostly regarded as the holiest room of a temple."

> *Its entrance is often guarded by stuffed wild yak, leopards, etc. . . . who act as messengers and guards of the protective deities. The* mgon khang *is usually a dark room, lit only by a few butter-lamps burning in front of the images, which represent various chief* dharmapalas *and the particular guardian-deities of the monastery. Most of these images are scarcely visible under the numerous ceremonial scarfs which have been draped over them. On the walls hang painted-scrolls depicting the* dharmapalas *and their retinue. These* thang ka *are usually kept covered by a piece of cloth, which is only removed when a ceremony takes place in the* mgon khang. . . . *The pillars of this chapel are decorated with masks, representing the angrily contorted faces of the various* dharmapalas. *In the corners of the room lean bundles of ancient arms which were used for a long time in warfare and, having in this way acquired magic qualities, they were presented to the temple. They are supposed to be the most effective weapons of the guardian-deities.*[33]

In the narrative of his trip to Tibet in 1881–82, Sarat Chandra Das (1849–1917) mentioned armor or weapons in the gonkhang of the monasteries of Dongtse, Samding, Ramoche, and Samye.[34] Waddell also noted armor in the gonkhang he saw in Gyantse, in the Jokhang in Lhasa, and nearby at the monastery of the Nechung Oracle. In the Jokhang, the most famous temple in Lhasa, he described seeing the figure of the guardian deity Palden Lhamo "surrounded by hideous masks with great tusks and by all sorts of weapons—antediluvian battle-axes, spears, bows and arrows, chain armour, swords of every shape, and muskets, a collection of which gives her shrine the character of an armoury."[35] Some sixty years after Das, Brooke Dolan also visited Samding and noted in his diary: "On the top of fourth level of the monastery is a large room hung with armor and weapons of which much is, or may well be, 18th century Mongolian. There are many suits of link-mail and round casques, also ancient spears and great swords. Many of the weapons, however are more recent and of Tibetan origin."[36] And nearly forty years after Waddell, Dolan visited the temple of the Nechung Oracle (fig. 10) and wrote in his diary: "On the wooden pillars, which support a shallow tiled roof surrounding the courtyard, are suspended suits of mail and iron casques worn by Mongol or

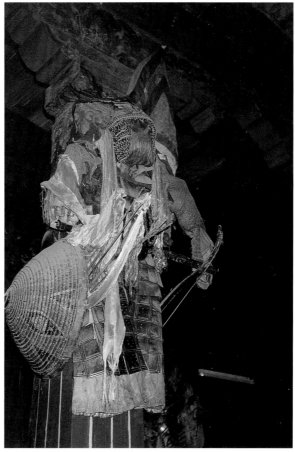

Left: Fig. 13. Panoply of armor and weapons on a column in the main assembly hall, Drepung Monastery, Tibet, showing a Tibetan eight-plate helmet, lamellar armor, coat of mail, set of four mirrors, and armored belt, plus a bow, quiver, and wicker shield (photo: Michael Henss, 1982)

Right: Fig. 14. Another panoply of armor and weapons on a column in the main assembly hall, Drepung Monastery, Tibet, showing a Tibetan helmet, Chinese coat of plates, sword, wicker shield, bow, and quiver of arrows (photo: Steven Kossak, 2001)

Left: Fig. 15. A view of the column wrapped with armor and weapons in the gonkhang of Phyang Monastery, Ladakh, showing the plates of the helmet hanging to the left, a quiver, and parts of a horse armor made of textile and reinforced with iron bosses (photo: the author, 2003)

Right: Fig. 16. Votive arms draped with offering scarves on a column, Hemis Monastery, Ladakh, showing a variety of Indian and Tibetan weapons (photo: the author, 2003)

Fig. 17. Votive armor and weapons mounted on a column in Lamayuru Monastery, Ladakh, showing a Tibetan lamellar armor, several Indian swords, and other weapons (photo: the author, 2003)

played inside out), like that on the walls of the Hayagriva chapel in Sera (fig. 11), and the domed wicker shield, again like those in Sera (compare cat. no. 25). In Ladakh there are also several interesting assemblages of arms and armor in the gonkhang of various Tibetan Buddhist monasteries, including Phyang (figs. 9, 15), Hemis (fig. 16), Likir, Lamayuru (fig. 17), and elsewhere.[40] While the votive arms in the gonkhang of Tibet appear to be mostly Tibetan, Mongolian, and Chinese in origin, those of Ladakh are a mix of Tibetan, Mongolian, Indian, and Middle Eastern, depending probably on the location of the monastery.

The panoplies of arms in Phyang, in particular, have several points of interest. In addition to a typical eight-plate helmet (now in pieces), a spear, a matchlock gun, bow cases, and quivers, they include flat, round wicker shields reinforced with iron struts and fragments of a horse armor made of textile reinforced with iron bosses. Two animal hides, one possibly a horsehide, are also wrapped around the columns. With the exception of a few shields now found in various collections (see cat. no. 24), this type of shield and this form of horse armor are otherwise known only through examples found in the ruins of Tsaparang, capital of the ancient kingdom of Guge in western Tibet, which was conquered decisively in the seventeenth century by the kingdom of Ladakh.[41] The gonkhang is considered the oldest temple in Phyang Monastery and is thought to have been built during the reigns of the Ladakhi kings Tsewang Namgyal (r. 1535–75) and Jamyang Namgyal (r. ca. 1580–90). The arms in the gonkhang are said to have been captured around that time from invading Hor forces, a branch of the Mongols.[42] Therefore, the Tsaparang-Phyang shields, and particularly the horse armors, constitute an important group because of their historical context and rarity of type. Moreover, they suggest what may be learned from the few groupings of votive arms that have remained intact and relatively undisturbed in gonkhang settings.[43]

The materials and techniques used to decorate arms and armor from Tibet cover a broad range, from the very simple to the extremely elaborate. Metalwork of differing types is present on the majority of examples in this catalogue, often uniting the crafts of blacksmith, goldsmith, silversmith, and sculptor, and involving the use of iron, silver, gold, and copper alloys. Leather, after iron, is the most important component and is used for several types of armor, both as the defensive plates that make up the armor and for the lacing that holds the plates together. It also appears in bow cases and quivers, equestrian tack, shields made of hide, and various other accessories. Leatherworking techniques include painted and tooled leather and appliqués, and it is seen as a foundation material or lining made from patterns of cut and sewn leather. In addition, surface decoration on leather can simulate the appearance of lacquer techniques and occurs in this form most

Tibetan warriors one hundred or five hundred years ago. I was flabbergasted at the suppleness of the chamois-leather connecting the links."[37]

A significant array of armor and weapons of various types can be seen in the chapel of Hayagriva (*rta mgrin*) in Sera Monastery, including several lamellar armors, a coat of plates, helmets, round wicker shields, bows and bow cases, and quivers with arrows (figs. 11, 12).[38] Panoplies of arms and armor are arranged at the tops of columns in the main assembly hall of Drepung Monastery (figs. 13, 14).[39] In the first of these groupings (fig. 13), there can be seen a helmet of the eight-plate type, a lamellar armor mounted over a shirt of mail, a set of four mirrors, and an armored belt of the same types seen in the Great Prayer Festival photos (for instance, figs. 2, 6) and in this catalogue (for example, cat. nos. 5, 44, 45). On the second panoply (fig. 14) the most distinctive features are the Chinese coat of plates (inadvertently dis-

often on bow cases and quivers but also on some types of leather armor and other items (for example, cat. nos. 36–38, 94). Wood is used most visibly for gunstocks and less noticeably as the core material for most sword scabbards and for some types of sword grips. Textiles, including embroidered silks and brocades, also play an important part as decorative coverings and trim, particularly on saddles and tack. Stiffened panels of silk brocade are also attached to the ends of sleeves and the hems of some Tibetan lamellar armors (cat. nos. 2, 3). Bhutanese helmets, such as those worn at the Great Prayer Festival (see figs. 6, 7), were refitted in Tibet with upturned flaps of colorful fabric (see cat. no. 46). Fabric is also used on Chinese armors as part of the neck defense attached to the rim of a helmet and as the outer covering of armor of the coat-of-plates type. Ray skin, a seemingly exotic material for the Tibetan plateau, often occurs as the covering for sword grips, particularly in eastern Tibet, and has a long history of being used for this purpose in Japan and China. Tiger and leopard skin reportedly covered quivers and possibly bow cases.[44] Turquoise, coral, and lapis lazuli are treasured components of Tibetan jewelry of all kinds and are also important features in the decoration of arms and armor. Turquoise and coral are among the key decorative elements of swords. One stone is usually set in the center of a sword's pommel, while others are set singly, in pairs, or in groups of three on the scabbard mounts (for instance, cat. nos. 63, 66, 67). They are also found, although less frequently, on saddle plates (cat. no. 111) and helmets (cat. no. 14). Cane, a humble material frequently used in basketwork, is the primary component of most Tibetan shields (cat. nos. 24, 25).

The techniques most often employed to decorate objects made principally of iron include engraving, inlay, and damascening with gold and silver, pierced work, chiseling, and embossing.[45] These techniques can be used alone, but are more frequently combined. All, except inlay and damascening, are also commonly seen on silver. A detailed discussion of Tibetan ironworking traditions is found in "A History of Ironworking in Tibet" by John Clarke.

Engraving consists of incising a design into a metal surface using punches, chisels, or other specialized engraving tools. Inlay involves inserting gold or silver wires into the grooves engraved into the surface of the iron for that purpose. True inlay, however, is rarely found on Himalayan ironwork (cat. no. 41). Closely related to inlay, but far more common, is the technique called damascening (more recently also referred to by the generic term "overlay"), which is done by scoring or crosshatching an iron surface with a pattern of fine lines, usually within the borders of an engraved design. Gold and silver foil or, very often, individual wires of gold and silver are then laid over the cross-hatching and rubbed with a burnishing tool to adhere the precious metal to the iron ground. Wires laid side by side and properly

burnished produce the effect of a continuous sheet of gold or silver. Damascening is the technique employed on nearly every Tibetan iron object decorated with gold and silver, and it is represented by many examples in this catalogue. It is frequently used both on the smooth and relatively flat or slightly curved surfaces offered by helmets, spearheads, or stirrups and on intricately pierced and chiseled surfaces, such as those found on sword fittings, saddles, and horse harnesses. In addition, other types of Tibetan objects that utilize the same form of decoration include pen cases, cup cases, and door fittings (cat. nos. 113, 114). The cross-hatching pattern on the iron ground is often visible to the naked eye, particularly where the gold or silver has worn away, and is always visible under magnification, making it possible to differentiate between damascening and mercury gilding. Mercury gilding, also called fire gilding, is a technique frequently used for applying a thin layer of gold to objects made of silver, bronze, or copper alloys, but it does not appear to have been used on Tibetan objects made of iron before the late nineteenth or early twentieth century (cat. no. 124). In mercury gilding, a paste (called an amalgam) is made from gold and mercury. This is applied to a ground that has been coated with a thin layer of copper or copper sulfate. The surface is then heated until the mercury evaporates, which causes the gold to adhere to the ground. In a less common variation on this technique, a layer of silver is damascened over an iron ground, and then mercury gilding is applied over the silver. This technique is found on only one helmet and a few saddles and related pieces in the catalogue, which, however, are Chinese or appear to be strongly influenced by Chinese styles (cat. nos. 19, 118–121).

Simple pierced work can be found on relatively flat sheets of iron, such as those seen on some horse armor, sword mounts, and other decorative fittings (cat. no. 30). Often, however, it is coupled with chiseling and damascening, as mentioned above. In the case of saddle plates in particular, it is skillfully employed to create an illusion of depth through intricately overlapping figures and scrollwork (for example, cat. nos. 112, 120, 134). Chiseling, often but not always used in conjunction with pierced work, is essentially carving in iron to create decorative patterns. Some of its best examples are found on the most elaborate sword hilts, saddles, and stirrups (for example, cat. nos. 56, 122, 127). Embossing refers to the technique of hammering a sheet of metal over a form, or from the back, to raise up the general shapes of a design, which are then finished from the front by chasing (engraving and chiseling). Embossed silver and copper plaques are found on sword scabbards (cat. no. 65) and gunstocks (cat. nos. 99, 100), usually in silver, and on saddles, sometimes in silver but usually in copper (cat. nos. 116, 125).

The degree of ornamentation and the range of symbols found on Tibetan arms and armor can vary considerably, but generally the same decorative motifs found on other Tibetan objects and works of art, such as furniture, ritual implements, sculpture, and paintings, are seen on arms and armor. While these motifs can have deep symbolic or iconographic significance, on secular objects they usually serve simply as protective and auspicious symbols, and as signs of Buddhist piety.[46] Of the material in this catalogue, the greatest variety of ornament usually appears on saddle plates, probably because they offer more surface area for decoration than many other types of objects, and because elaborate saddles, when well decorated, were recognized as objects of considerable status (fig. 18). The most prevalent form of decoration on objects of all types consists of a wide variety of scrollwork (*pa tra*), which can range in appearance from leafy tendrils (*shing lo*) to stylized clouds (*sprin ris*) to flame patterns (*me ris*).[47] Scrollwork can be used as the sole design feature, but it more often serves as the background for other motifs, particularly dragons (*'brug*). Perhaps the single most frequently used motif, dragons are prominently featured on saddle plates, the fittings of sword scabbards, on helmets, in the surface decoration of leather armor, bow cases and quivers, and elsewhere. Three-dimensional dragon heads, usually chiseled in iron but also sometimes cast in iron, brass, and even silver, are also a ubiquitous feature of Tibetan, Mongolian, and Chinese stirrups (cat. nos. 127–131). Nearly as popular as the dragon is a type of monster mask known in Tibetan as *tsi pa ṭa* or by its Sanskrit name *kirttimukha*, which is sometimes found on early sword hilts (cat. nos. 55, 57) but more often occupies a central position on saddle plates (for example, cat. nos. 112, 116).[48] It is typically represented by a frontal image of a disembodied leonine mask with flaming eyes and bared fangs. A pair of hands floats beneath the mask and holds writhing snakes or tendrils. This symbol is found throughout Tibet, China, India, and Indonesia, where it is used as a sign of good fortune and to ward off evil. A closely related motif has a very similar mask, but it is joined to the body of a winged creature, which represents the *khyung*, better known by its Sanskrit name, *garuda*, a mythical bird that protects against serpents and illnesses (cat. no. 125). Other important and frequently encountered motifs come from the group known as the Eight Auspicious Symbols (*bkra shis rtags brgyad*), which consists of the endless knot (*dpal be'u*), lotus (*pad ma*), umbrella (*gdugs*), conch shell (*dung*), wheel (*'khor lo*), victory banner (*rgyal mtshan*), vase (*bum pa*), and golden fish (*gser nya*). These can appear individually or in groups, as central design features or as subtle accents on virtually any type of Tibetan object, from the most humble utilitarian item to the most elaborate ritual object or painting. Also frequently used is a motif depicting a flaming jewel or jewels (*nor bu me 'bar*), which generally takes one of three forms: three distinct orbs representing the Three Jewels (*dkon mchog gsum*); a cluster of elongated shapes representing the Precious Jewel (*nor bu rin po che*) or Wish-Fulfilling Jewel (*yid bzhin nor bu*); and a single flaming jewel or flaming pearl (*mu tig*). It is usually centrally

placed on saddle plates (cat. no. 122) but also appears on helmets (cat. no. 14), on sword fittings (cat. no. 65), and even on firearms (cat. no. 100). The Three Jewels, a fundamental symbol of Buddhism, signify the Buddha, his teachings, and the community of believers. The Precious Jewel or Wish-Fulfilling Jewel, part of a group of emblems known as the Seven Jewels of Royal Power (*rgyal srid rin chen sna bdun*), symbolizes abundance and prosperity. The single flaming jewel or flaming pearl, a variation of the Wish-Fulfilling Jewel, is often seen in conjunction with dragons and can also symbolize purity. Other popular individual motifs such as the thunderbolt (*rdo rje* or *vajra*, cat. no. 44), the swastika (*g.yung drung*, cat. no. 23), and the whirling emblem (*dga' 'khyil*, cat. no. 43) can form the center of a decorative pattern or be incorporated into an overall scheme of ornament.

A less common but highly evocative type of decoration on armor and weapons is the use of lettering, which is sometimes found on helmets (cat. nos. 12, 16), shields (cat. no. 25), and, in at least one instance each, a sword (cat. no. 55) and a spearhead (cat. no. 77). This usually takes the form of Lantsa (also called Ranjana), an ornamental alphabet derived from ancient Indian scripts, which is used for sacred texts and individual symbolic letters called seed syllables (*sa bon* or *bija*). On a few examples the more conventional Tibetan script, *dbu can*, is also incorporated into the decoration or as an inscription (cat. nos. 16, 45, 80, 90), which in one rare instance includes Tibetan and Mongolian script (cat. no. 85). Less common motifs also occur, such as the dry skull (*thod skam*). A symbol associated with ritual offerings to the wrathful deities, it appears on three objects in the catalogue, a spearhead, gunstock, and gun barrel (cat. nos. 78, 103, 105).

Historical texts on the subject of Tibetan arms occupy a small niche in Tibet's vast literary tradition. They fall into the genre known as *brtag thabs* (analytical methods), which comprises texts devoted to the appraisal, examination, and appreciation of material relating to the arts, ritual objects, and secular culture.[49] Chapters on armor, helmets, swords, archery equipment, saddles, and stirrups are scattered through a handful of these texts, dating from the fifteenth century onward. What appears to be the earliest manuscript to include all of these topics dates from the sixteenth century (fig. 46) and exists in several versions, which, however, vary considerably in their states of completeness. An attempt to reconstruct something approaching a critical edition of the relevant chapters from these different versions appears in the appendix "Excerpts from *A Treatise on Worldly Traditions*."

Our understanding of the creation and development of traditional Tibetan arms is hampered by the fact that, unlike the armor and weapons from areas such as Japan, the Middle East, and Europe, Tibetan arms are not inscribed or stamped with any marks or signatures that might tell us where and when they were made or who their

Fig. 18. Dundul Namgyal (George) Tsarong (*dram 'dul rnam rgyal tsha rong*) outfitted for his role as a *ya sor*, one of the commanders of the feudal cavalry, during the Great Prayer Festival in Lhasa. Part of the elaborately pierced and chiseled pommel plate of his saddle is visible below his left arm. Photograph by Heinrich Harrer, late 1940s (photo: © The Ethnographic Museum of the University of Zürich [VMZ 400.07.23.022])

makers were. Therefore, lacking information indicative of distinct schools or centers of production, the examples in this catalogue have been grouped into broad categories according to type. Within these categories a rough chronology has been attempted based almost entirely on considerations of form and style, supported in a few instances by carbon-14 analysis. Attributions of place and date that result from such a survey can only be provisional at best. It is hoped, however, that by creating even so tentative a framework for this body of material, the variety, complexity, and merit of armor and weapons from Tibet may begin to be appreciated as yet another facet of that rich and enduring culture.

1. The context of the expedition is outlined later in this introduction. For detailed discussions, see esp. Allen 2004, French 1995, Waddell 1905, and *Younghusband* 1999.

2. Waddell 1905, pp. 168–69. Waddell states in his preface (p. vii) that nearly all of the photographs in the book were taken by him personally. Unfortunately, the present whereabouts of Waddell's original papers and photos, if they survive, are unknown.

3. For a listing of Tibetan terms, refer also to the appendix "Tibetan-English Glossary of Arms and Armor Terms."

4. Horse armor may still have been in use in the Sudan at this time. See Spring 1993, pl. 9 and pp. 33–39.

5. Quoted in Allen 2004, p. 106.

6. For the photographs by Richardson, Chapman, and others, see Harris and Shakya 2003. For detailed discussions of the ceremonies and the roles of the armored infantry and cavalry, see Richardson 1993 and Karsten 1983. See Tung 1996 regarding Dolan and Tolstoy. A synopsis of the use of historical arms and armor in the Great Prayer Festival is given in LaRocca 1999a.

7. The elaborate pennons and plumes seen on the helmets of many of the *zimchongpa* have parallels on the helmets of warriors and guardian deities depicted in Tibetan art. It should also be noted that, for whatever reason, the *zimchongpa* who are armed with muskets wear helmets that are consistently without plumes.

8. Regarding this period, see the brief outline below in this introduction, and for the dating of the arms and armor attributed to that era, see the individual catalogue entries and the appendix "Radiocarbon Dating Results."

9. On the term *zimchongpa* and their duties, see Richardson 1993, p. 39.

10. Richardson (1993, pp. 40–44) describes these events in detail and identifies them as taking place on the 24th day of the festival, known as Casting Out the Votive Offering for the Great Prayer (*smon lam gtor rgyag*), in front of the Jokhang Temple. According to Brooke Dolan, who also recorded the event in his diary, this was done three times, first by bowmen, then by those with muskets, and last by spearmen. See Tung 1996, pp. 161–62, and Dolan's unpublished journal, vol. 3, pp. 46–48, entry for February 3, 1943, Archives, Academy of Natural Sciences, Philadelphia. Richardson (1993, p. 41) described the sequence slightly differently, as the bowmen, followed by those armed with swords and shields, then the musketeers. Chapman's photos include the most complete series of the opposing lines of *zimchongpa*, with images very clearly showing the spearmen, musketeers, and swordsmen, and another in which the weapons are not clear, but which may show the archers (Archives, Pitt Rivers Museum, Oxford, 1998.131.605–.610, and in color 1998.157.83–.84).

11. Richardson described the review of troops, or Trapchi Tsisher (*gra phyi rtsis bsher*), as taking place on the 23rd day of the festival, and the target-shooting contest called the gallop behind the fort, or Dzonggyap Shambe (*rdzong rgyab zhabs 'bel*), on the 26th day. See Richardson 1993, esp. pp. 34–37, 44, 56–57; Karsten 1983, passim. In addition to Richardson's and Karsten's description of the horseback target-shooting, see also the very informative first-person account by Tsipon Shuguba (*rtsi dpon shud khud 'jam dbyangs mkhas grub*, Shuguba 1995, pp. 31–32), who was a contestant in 1923.

12. Richardson 1993, p. 34.

13. For extensive information on Tibetan history and culture, see the following sources, on which this outline is based: Beckwith 1993, Goldstein 1999b, Reynolds 1999, Shakabpa 1967, Smith 1996, Snellgrove and Richardson 1995, and Stein 1972.

14. For a detailed study of the period of the Tibetan empire, see Beckwith 1993.

15. As quoted in Stein 1972, p. 62. Examples are also given in Beckwith 1993, esp. pp. 110–11, with references. See also Demiéville 1952, esp. pp. 373–76; Laufer 1914, esp. pp. 252–57.

16. The Three Ancestral Dharma Kings (*chos rgyal mes dbon rnam gsum*) were Songtsen Gampo (*srong btsan sgam po*, r. 620–50), Trisong Detsen (*khri srong lde btsan*, r. 755–ca. 797), and Ralpachen (*ral pa can*, r. 815–38). The helmet attributed to Songtsen Gampo that was included in the exhibition catalogue *Trésors du Tibet: Région autonome du Tibet, Chine* ([Paris, 1987], cover illus. and fig. 25) is actually a Buddhist ritual crown of much later date. Excepting the fragments recovered by Aurel Stein (British Museum, MAS526, 567, 592, 610, 611, 616, 621), the only body armor apparently to have survived from this era is an extraordinary lacquered leather armor of the type used by the Yi or Lolo peoples in the southeastern corner of the Tibetan plateau (Yunnan Province in southwestern China), which has been C-14 dated to the 8th–10th centuries; it is illustrated in Anninos 2000, p. 110, figs. 12, 13.

17. For an overview of military events in Tibet from the end of the Yarlung dynasty to the beginning of Mongol rule (10th–13th centuries), see Petech 1983.

18. Illustrated in *Buddhist Art of the Tibetan Plateau* (Hong Kong, 1988), pp. 284–85; LaRocca 1999a, p. 124 and fig. 21. While the helmet may possibly date from the Yuan period, the coat of plates appears to be later. Published photographs of the coat of plates show it mistakenly displayed inside out. Another helmet and armor, also identified as "given to the leader of the Sakya sect by the Yuan emperor," are illustrated in *Clothing and Ornaments of China's Tibetan Nationality* (Beijing, 2002), p. 3. These are a lamellar armor and an eight-plate helmet of the type seen in the present catalogue, e.g., cat. no. 4.

19. For the high point of Ming interaction with Tibet, during the reign of the emperor Yongle (r. 1403–24), see Watt and Leidy 2005.

20. Regarding the Younghusband Expedition, see esp. Allen 2004, French 1995, and *Younghusband* 1999.

21. The majority of the troops were from the Gorkha, Pathan, and Sikh units of the British Army in India. For a breakdown of the personnel involved in the expedition, see Gulati 2003, esp. p. 242. His overall discussion (pp. 224–302) is revealing in that it is given from the perspective of an Indian military officer.

22. For the Buddha given to Younghusband, see French 1995, pp. 400–401, and for both, see Allen 2004, p. 294. Macdonald's Buddha was bequeathed to the Marischal Museum, University of Aberdeen, in 1931, along with other objects obtained during his military service in Tibet and Africa. I am very grateful to Neil Curtis of the Marischal Museum for making available for study lists of the material and the Tibetan pieces in the collection.

23. I am very grateful to Simon Metcalf for researching this gift and for providing a copy of the original list, entitled "List of Presents to T. M. The King and Queen, from The Dalai Lama, 28 June, 1913." Among the twenty total lots, the descriptions of the arms and armor, quoted here in full, are as follows: "8. A Tibetan Sword, as still used by the Khambas, who are the most warlike of the Tibetans and live in S.E. Tibet. Was probably made in Derge. . . . 16. A Tibetan saddle with trappings, called the saddle of "Rimpung gyalpo" the saddle of the King of Rimpung. This King ruled at Rimpung, (about three days march, N.E. of Gyantse) some five hundred years ago before the era of the [current] Dalai Lama. On this saddle the first Dalai Lama is said to have ridden into Lhasa. His immediate successors did so also, and for the last two hundred years the saddle has been kept in the Potala at Lhasa as a national relic. (This is the most important of the gifts from the Dalai Lama.) . . . 17. A Coat of Tibetan Armour with steel helmet. This kind of armour is no longer made, but it occasionally worn at national festivals. . . . 18. Two old Tibetan leather shields with silver bosses." Lots 8, 16, and 17 were recorded as lent to the British Museum. Unfortunately, at the time of this writing, their whereabouts were unknown. According to Berthold Laufer (1914, p. 290,

n. 3), the Tibetan armor given by the Dalai Lama to the king was the one illustrated as plate 3 of the British Museum's *Handbook to the Ethnographical Collections* (London, 1910). However, since the publication of this booklet preceded the date of the gift by three years, the Tibetan armor illustrated there cannot be from the gift group listed above.

24. See Rockhill 1891 and Rockhill 1895 for examples acquired during his travels, most of which are now in the collections of the National Museum of Natural History, Smithsonian Institution, Washington. I am very grateful to Felicia Pickering of the NMNH for facilitating my study of these objects. Rockhill's published comments about the provenance and the use of this material remain extremely valuable. For the details of Rockhill's career and his travels, see Wimmel 2003.

25. See Laufer 1914. I am very grateful to Julian Freeman for sharing with me his notes and photographs of the Tibetan edged weapons in the Field Museum.

26. For the Newark Museum's Tibetan collection, see Olson 1950–71 and Reynolds 1999. Regarding Shelton's career, see Wissing 2004. I am greatly indebted to Valrae Reynolds for making the Newark collection available for study, and for help with many questions relating to Tibet.

27. Random examples of Tibetan arms have entered many U.S. museum collections this way, including the University of Pennsylvania Museum of Archaeology and Anthropology, the Peabody Essex Museum in Salem, the Peabody Museum of Harvard University, the University of Nebraska State Museum, and others.

28. Several Tibetan pieces from Stone's collection are included in Stone 1934. For a brief biography of him, see LaRocca 1999b.

29. A prime example is the Tibetan collection, including arms and armor, in the National Museum of Denmark, Copenhagen, formed by Prince Peter of Denmark during his fieldwork with the Tibetan expatriate community in Kalimpong, India, in the late 1940s and early 1950s. See Jones 1996.

30. On the effects of the Cultural Revolution in Tibet, see Shakya 1999, esp. p. 420; Smith 1996, pp. 541–62.

31. For his personal observations on the regional militias in Tibet in the late 19th century, see Das 1902a, pp. 88–89, 91, 95–96.

32. I am grateful to Hugh Richardson (personal communication, June 27, 1997) for these suggestions and other helpful information.

33. Nebesky-Wojkowitz 1975, pp. 401–2.

34. Das 1902a, pp. 87, 149, 170, 245. In the text, however, Das repeatedly misinterpreted *mgon khang* as *gong khang*, meaning "upper room." Phonetically the two terms are almost identical.

35. Waddell 1905, pp. 229, 370 (quoted passage), 382.

36. Entry for December 8, 1942, published in "Across Tibet: Excerpts from the Journals of Capt. Brooke Dolan, 1942–43," *Frontiers* (Academy of Natural Sciences, Philadelphia), 2 (1980), p. 6.

37. Dolan diary, vol. 2, p. 147v, entry for January 12, 1943, Archives, Academy of Natural Sciences, Philadelphia.

38. I am very grateful to Robert Hales, Grace Brady, and José Cabezón for providing me with images of this material. The coat of plates in figure 11 is similar to that in Sakya Monastery (mentioned in note 18) and is probably Chinese, 17th–18th century.

39. Images of these were kindly provided by Michael Henss, Grace Brady, and Steven Kossak.

40. For invaluable assistance in the study of this material during a visit to Ladakh in the summer of 2003, I am greatly indebted to Lozang Jamspal, Tsering Yanskit, Getsul Lobzang Yignyen, Tsering Angmo, Phuntshog Angmo, Tinley Angmo, and David Kittay.

41. For the horse armor and shields, see *Guge* 1991, vol. 1, pp. 212–26; vol. 2, color pls. XC, XCI, and black-and-white pls. CXXVIII–CXXXI, CLIX. The horse armor and one of the shields of the same type from Tsaparang appear in *Xizang wen wu jing cui—A Well-Selected Collection of Tibetan Cultural Relics* (Beijing, 1992), nos. 15, 16, where they are dated as 11th–16th century. They were also included in the exhibition catalogue *Tesori del Tibet* (Milan, 1994), nos. 19, 21 (illus. in color). The same shield, or a very similar one from the same group, is included in *Xizang bo wu guan—The Tibet Museum* (Beijing, 2001), p. 48, where it is dated 10th–11th century.

42. *The Guide to the Monastery at Phyang* (n.p., n.d.), p. 22. Francke (1999, e.g., pp. 81, 108) also mentioned several instances of the Ladakhi kings capturing, or being given as tribute, armor and weapons, both from the Mongols and from the kingdom of Guge.

43. It is uncertain how many gonkhang in Tibet survived the Cultural Revolution intact, but it was probably a small minority. A recent photo of the gonkhang in Deyang Monastic College, Drepung Monastery, for instance, clearly shows that both the arrangement of arms and most of the arms in it are relatively new (*Zhaibung Monastery* [Beijing, 1999], n.p.). Even in areas unaffected by the Cultural Revolution, recent changes have sometimes been made. For instance, the weapons lining the wall of the gonkhang of Matho Monastery in Ladakh are all relatively modern Indian reproductions.

44. See the appendix "Tibetan-English Glossary of Arms and Armor Terms: III. Archery Equipment and Projectile Weapons, Other than Firearms," under *stag dong*.

45. On these techniques, see 'od zer 1989 and Dagyab 1977. Decoration on iron is traditionally divided into three basic categories: engraving on a flat or smooth surface (*'jam tshags*), raised engraving (*'bur tshags*), and pierced engraving (*dkrol tshags*). On these, see 'od zer 1989, pp. 44–47; Dagyab 1977, vol. 1, p. 48. The techniques are also discussed in Rauber-Schweizer 1976, esp. pp. 138–39. The spelling *tshags*, rather than *tshag*, follows 'od zer 1989; Tashi Namgyal; and *dung dkar* 2002, p. 1691.

46. For further information on the symbols mentioned here, see Dagyab 1995 and Beer 1999.

47. Another Tibetan name for the scroll motif appears to be *shing lo sprin ris* (literally, tree leave cloud design); 'od zer 1989, p. 61.

48. There are many spelling variations of the Tibetan name for this term, most of them apparently based on phonetic equivalents. It appears in 'od zer (1989, p. 46) as *dziH pa tra*; in *Zhaibung Monastery* ([Beijing, 1999], n.p.) as *rdzi par*; and as *zipak* by Tony Anninos (in Kamansky 2004, p. 102; also with several other variations listed in the glossary, p. 338). The spelling *tsi pa ṭa* has been adopted here since it is confirmed in reliable Tibetan dictionaries, such as *bod rgya* (p. 2186) and Goldstein 2001 (p. 846).

49. Martin 1997, p. 233.

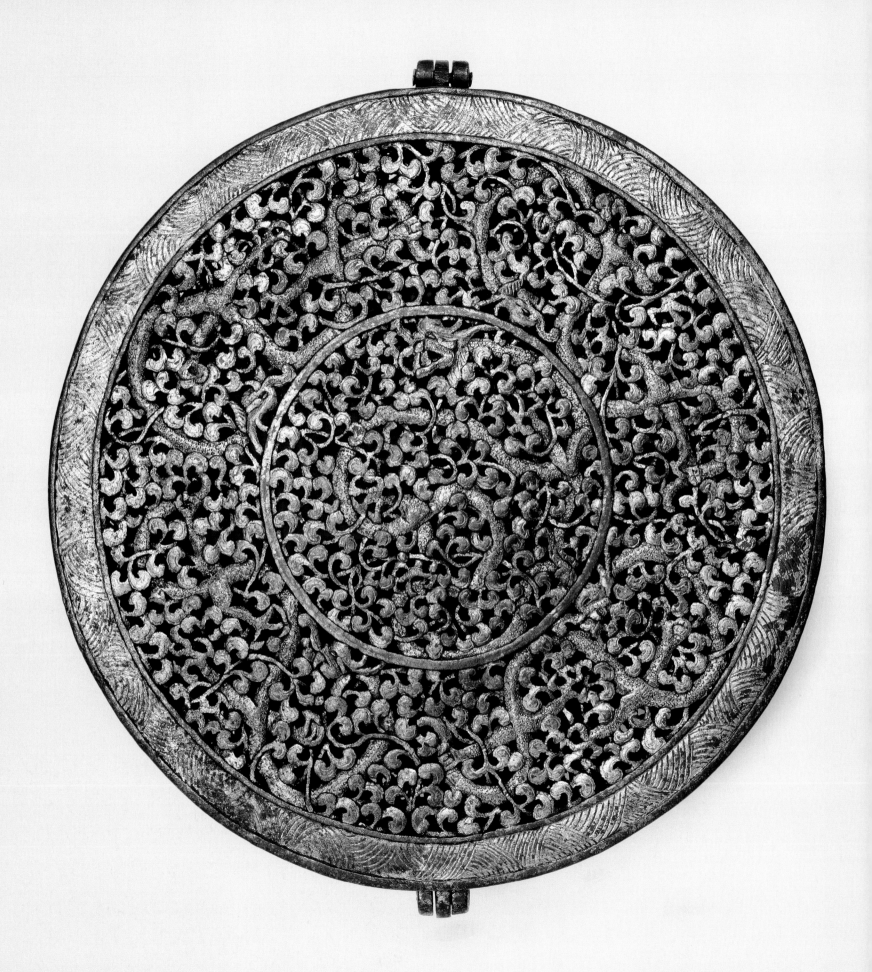

A HISTORY OF IRONWORKING IN TIBET: CENTERS OF PRODUCTION, STYLES, AND TECHNIQUES

JOHN CLARKE

THE EARLY PERIOD, 7TH–12TH CENTURIES

Both Arab and Chinese sources attest to the brilliance and precociousness of Tibetan metallurgy during the first two and a half centuries of the Tibetan empire (7th–mid-9th centuries). The same mastery Tibetans displayed in their gold work was also evident in their manufacture of armor and shields and construction of iron suspension bridges. The Tang Annals from the start of the ninth century tell us that in battle both noblemen and their horses wore strong and fine mail armor that completely covered them, leaving only eye holes.[1] This was evidently a well-established technology even by the early seventh century, as is revealed by a Tibetan gift to the Tang court in 638 of a suit of mail made in gold links.[2] Knowledge of mail was probably borrowed by Tibetans from the Sasanians, and this type of armor is shown clothing the first Sasanian king, Ardashir (r. 226–40), and his son Shapur (r. 241–72) on stone reliefs of the period.[3] Though there is evidence that the Tibetans imported arms in this period from Central Asia and Sogdia, it is clear that their own industry was sophisticated and was producing arms in its own right. This evidence comes in the form of a seventh-century Arab reference to a gift of one hundred mail coats and a tenth-century reference to a type of shield that was well known as a Tibetan product.[4] Between the seventh and ninth centuries the expansionist Tibetan empire was engaged in almost continuous warfare on its Chinese and Central Asian frontiers. This must have necessitated a huge arms production, of which we get only tiny glimpses. When a joint Tibetan-Arab army was defeated in 801 by the Chinese forces, twenty thousand suits of armor were taken, and even allowing for a percentage of these being Arab, one begins to understand the numbers involved.[5] We also know that the Tibetan emperor

(*gtsan po*) traveled with an entourage that included armorers.[6] Additionally the Tang Annals tell us that even in peacetime, as in eastern Tibet until the 1950s, all men carried swords. During these centuries Tibet was also able to span some of its most fearsome river gorges with chain suspension bridges a thousand years in advance of that technology's introduction in the West. Chinese pilgrims en route to India found such bridges in use in the early sixth century in the Himalayan regions from Gilgit (Pakistan) to Uddyana (modern Swat in Pakistan), and there is another reference to one on the Upper Indus River in 646.[7] It is still uncertain whether the technological innovation came from China, as some scholars suppose, or from Tibet whose terrain certainly gave the most need for its use.[8] We do know that by the eighth century iron suspension bridges had been constructed by the Tibetans across two tributaries of the Mekong River on the southwest Chinese border and on the Upper Yangtze River.[9]

But when might Tibet's iron technology have been imported and from where? China is recognized as having developed a wrought iron technology as early as the sixth century B.C.[10] Records of the Han dynasty talk of iron mines, foundries, and workshops producing iron goods for export as lying east of the Tian Shan mountains in Central Asia, an area from which in the ninth–twelfth centuries we know iron weapons were exported to Tibet.[11] In fact in this area of modern Xinjiang two iron-mining and smelting sites of the Han period have been excavated in Lop County, and others in Kuqa County and Minfeng County, respectively.[12] And a fourth-century Buddhist traveler recorded the use of coal to smelt iron in Xinjiang.[13] But though Chinese technology was evidently advanced at an early period, there is no direct evidence that this was the source of Tibet's knowledge.

Tibetan conquests from the seventh century in Central Asia and Transoxiana or Sogdia, the area between the Oxus and Jaxartes rivers, brought them into contact not only with Chinese but with Sogdians

Fig. 19. Top view of cat. no. 113, cup case, eastern Tibetan, 15th century. Wrought iron and gold, H. 2 in. (5 cm), Diam. 6⅛ in. (15.6 cm). Victoria and Albert Museum, London (IM.162-1913)

and Turkic peoples who had their own sophisticated metallurgical industries.[14] The sphere of Tibetan control during some periods coincided with a wide arc of western and Central Asia known for its iron and steel production while even during times when this was not the case they received trade goods from the same places. The area just referred to encompassed much of present-day Iran, parts of Afghanistan, and the area between the Amu Dar'ya (Oxus) and the Syr Dar'ya (Jaxartes), also known as Transoxiana (the former Sogdia). Here, in present-day Uzbekistan, whole urban districts were occupied by armorers and jewelers in the tenth–twelfth centuries,[15] while Ustrūshana, a Sogdian state east of Samarqand, and the Fergana basin were both important ironwork production centers.[16] The Sogdian cities of Samarqand and Bukhara probably also manufactured iron and steel weapons that were exported to Tibet.[17] We know that by the early eighth century, the Sogdians, having probably borrowed the technology from the Sasanians, were manufacturing mail armor and offered suits of the material as gifts to the Tang court in 718.[18] These may also have formed part of the export arms production going from Sogdia to Tibet. The Sasanians may themselves have developed knowledge of steelmaking from contacts with northern India.[19] As no early Tibetan weapons survive that could be metallurgically tested, it is impossible to know whether Tibetans had the use of steel during their early centuries of greatness. But as steel swords were certainly available through trade with Sogdia and Fergana they almost certainly used them, and many steel blades are known from Central Asia from the late first millennium until the arrival of Genghis Khan in the early thirteenth century.[20]

After the sixth century the Sogdians and Sasanians became traders along the overland routes to China and would have encountered Tibetans who for long periods controlled both routes.[21] But there is an even more direct way in which the iron and steel weapon technologies of Sasania and Sogdia might have reached Tibet and enabled it to develop its own arms industry at an early date. The collapse of the Sasanian empire in the mid-seventh century and the more strictly Islamizing 'Abbasid takeover of Sogdia in the mid-eighth, together with Tang China's loss of Central Asia to the Tibetans, also in the mid-eighth century, are likely to have led to many skilled craftsmen seeking new patrons. The newly emergent Tibetan empire would have offered many opportunities and in the towns of Central Asia and of Tibet itself there may have been a multicultural mix of skilled Sasanian, Sogdian, Chinese, and Turkic iron and silversmiths who brought and established new technologies.[22]

The other peoples who were heavily involved with arms production and trade with the Tibetans were the Turkic peoples and especially the Karluks, allies of the Tibetans during the eighth and early ninth centuries, whose zone of settlement and control coincided to some extent with the area of Central Asian metalworking referred to above.[23] The Karluks (Tibetan gar log), originally a federation of three tribes, were noted by Islamic geographers as producers and exporters of iron artifacts and weapons to Tibet and China.[24] By the ninth century they were based in Central Asia to the north and east of the Tian Shan mountains though other groups had pushed farther west and established themselves in Fergana and Tukharistan in the Upper Oxus basin. And it was from centers of iron production nearest the northern edge of Tibet, across the Tarim basin on the northern Silk Route between Kuqa and Aksu, that weapons were exported to China and Tibet.[25] The centers, described in Arab geographies of the tenth and twelfth centuries, were Barman or Bakhwan, a town near Aksu, where excellent iron goods were made, and Farman, which had markets for arms traders.[26] There is evidence that iron was supplied to the Karluks by the Kirghiz, who were involved in iron mining in the Tian Shan mountains.[27] The arms traded here probably included the long thin swords similar to the Carolingian or Frankish swords in Europe.[28]

The routes by which arms entered Tibet during the eighth–ninth-century period may have been the traditional one along the Tarim River from Kuqa to Lop Nur then down to the Tibetan military base at Miran and skirting the Tsaidam basin over the Changthang (byang thang), or the northern plains of the Tibetan plateau, to Lhasa. It would also have been possible for the Tibetans, by following the Tarim River westward from Lop Nur, to have communicated directly with their Turkic allies even while the Chinese were occupying the four garrison cities of Central Asia from 692 to 792.[29]

There is almost no definite evidence of the possible origins of the fine ironworking techniques used in Tibet. It may, however, be worth considering the close association of the village of Horpo (hor po) in Derge (sde dge) with skills such as damascening and pierce-work. The name of the village itself may offer clues to the origins of such techniques in eastern Tibet or even in Tibet as a whole. Immediately to the northeast of Derge Horpo also lay the area of the five Hor tribes (hor ser khag lnga) in the area of Nyarong (nyag rong).[30] From as early as the seventh century, the word hor in Tibet has been used to describe Mongolia and its peoples, usually referring to the Uighur or occasionally the Oghuz, a Turkic people living on the Syr Dar'ya.[31] There were Uighurs in Gansu, an area adjacent to northeast Tibet,[32] and when the Uighur kingdom of Kocho finally collapsed in 1284, its king fled to Yongchang in neighboring Gansu.[33] One wonders if these facts could be related to a legend of Horpo that the village was founded in the thirteenth century by survivors of a defeat in battle. The link with Horpo might also have been through the Oghuz, who in the tenth–twelfth-century period controlled the area around Kuqa from which iron weapons were exported to Tibet. We also know from later, early eighteenth-century, accounts that a number of Mongol peoples, notably the Kalmuks and the Buriats, were skilled in the damascened decoration of ironwork.[34] It is therefore possible, though unproven at present, that the fine metalworking tradition of eastern Tibet was established as the result of contact with Mongolia and/or Turkic Central Asia.

There are very few surviving pieces of pre-fifteenth-century iron inlaid with gold or silver. A probable thirteenth-century iron helmet or drum inlaid with silver decoration from northeastern Iran in the Khalili Collection, London, underlines the importance of Iran as one of the most likely locations for the development of such skills.[35] Inlay in silver and copper on brass or bronze had, in the mid-twelfth century, first become a major feature of eastern Iranian metalwork, where it represented a cheaper substitute for scarce silver.[36] Such inlaying skills could have been spread, or further developed, during the early Mongol Empire through the forced transference of captured craftsmen during the reigns of Ögödei (1229–41) and Möngke (1251–59). During this period artisans, including Iranians and Chinese, were redistributed to established craft-working centers such as Yanjing (today's Beijing), Besh Baliq (capital of the Uighur kingdom), and others including one in the northern foothills of the Tian Shan mountains and another in Transoxiana.[37] The ethnic mix of craftsmen from all over the empire, which included armorers and gold- and silversmiths, resulted in a period of artistic and technical innovation. This would have provided a fertile period for the further development of a technique such as overlay, or damascening, combining as it does the skills of the blacksmith and the goldsmith. The possible adoption or development of these skills during the late thirteenth century in Beijing, under the tutelage of the Nepalese craftsman Anige, is discussed below.

The Organization of Ironworkers, 13th–19th Centuries

By the thirteenth century monastic institutions in Tibet had started to become wealthy and would already have been the major patrons of craftsmen that we know them as in the twentieth century. The consistent early twentieth-century pattern of metalworkers being settled in groups near monasteries, and sometimes paid a retaining fee by the monastic authorities, offers a strong clue to patronage systems in those earlier centuries. This is certainly the type of organization seen in the nineteenth century at Tashilhunpo (bkra shis lhun po) Monastery in southern Tibet, which was then served by a craft-working village of Tashikitsel (bkra shis skyid tshal), one mile south of it. In 1882 Sarat Chandra Das noted that the village contained clerks, painters, and other artisans who received an allowance from the monastery.[38] Up until the mid-seventeenth century, when Tibet was politically unified

under the Fifth Dalai Lama, power lay not only with the monasteries but also with regional secular authorities who would have similarly required craftsmen to provide tools, vessels, and weapons. In Bhutan until the 1950s this same system operated, each district governor or dzongpon (rdzong dpon) keeping his own group of metalworkers and paying them a small retaining fee. Hence economics dictated that craftsmen gathered near monasteries or local rulers. Metalwork made in Tibet was also exported to China. The Chinese Ming Annals of 1587 say that helmets, armor, knives, and swords as well as bronze Buddhas and "pagodas" were made in Tibet by its various rulers. These are described as tribute, a euphemism for trade items in this context.[39]

But during the building of the Potala between 1642 and 1694, thousands of craftsmen of all kinds were required and were organized in a guild system, each set of workers forming a zokhang (bzo khang, literally, house of craftsmen). A permanent building called the Dodzhol Palkyil ('dod zhol dpal 'khyil) at the foot of the Potala itself was built to house the guilds of the metalworkers, wood-carvers, and clay statue makers.[40] The aim of the organization was to make the best craftsmen available for government work for a specified period each year; by the twentieth century this was typically two to three months. During the twentieth century each group of metalworkers had its own zokhang, and among these was that of the ironworkers who numbered about fifteen in the 1940s and who made door clasps, locks, keys, and the corners of boxes. Over the last three centuries such craftsmen will have made much of the ornamental ironwork that the visitor sees today on the great monasteries and palaces of Lhasa such as the Potala and Norbuligka palaces dating from the seventeenth to the twentieth century. No arms had been made there in living memory, though they might well have been produced in the workshop before the establishment during the late nineteenth century of the arsenal just west of Lhasa. Officers on the British military expedition of 1904 noted that by then there were two Muslim artisans at the arsenal. For the previous ten years these men had been copying Martini-Henry rifles and making trips to Calcutta to take back raw materials required.[41]

The Iron Bridge Builder, Tangtong Gyalpo

One exception to our general lack of knowledge of the history of ironworking in Tibet is the life of the enigmatic fifteenth-century engineer saint Tangtong Gyalpo (thang stong rgyal po), also known as Chakzampa (lcags zam pa), "Iron Bridge Builder," who lived between 1385 and 1464.[42] Inspired, according to one source, by being refused a ferry passage due to his eccentric appearance, he began a career as a builder of iron suspension bridges, carrying forward what we have already seen was an ancient Tibetan technology. He is credited with the creation of fifty-eight iron

Fig. 20. Iron chain suspension bridge at Duksum, Tashigang (*bkra shis gang*), eastern Bhutan, built by Tangtong Gyalpo, early 15th century. The walkway was probably formed from wooden slats, which no longer exist. Lines of multiple chains forming the sides and path supports are secured within the massive stone gatehouses at either end (photo: the author, 1998)

chain bridges, of which about eight were in Bhutan, over a hundred boat ferries, and a number of temples, stupas, and monasteries throughout the region. All of these can be seen in the Buddhist context as pious works done to benefit others, and his biographies show him very much as a Tantric yogi or Mahasiddha, a being possessing supernatural powers or *siddhi*.[43] Several of the saint's bridges survive even today in Tibet and include Chakzam (*lchag zam*) and Chungriboche (*chung ri bo che*) on the Tsangpo (*gtsang po*) River and Lundrubshang (*lhun grub shangs*) near Reting (*rva sgreng*) Monastery.[44] The saint's one remaining intact bridge in Bhutan spanning a small river at Duksum in eastern Bhutan (fig. 20) shows how the construction utilizes a number of parallel chain links secured in massive stone gatehouses at each end. At Nyangodruk (*snyan go drug ka*), once a main link between Lhasa and the Yarlung Valley, a now-destroyed bridge had a span of between 150 and 250 meters using five major stone supports of up to 15 meters in diameter.[45] We know that the saint used local blacksmiths to assist him in forging the chains required, as he did at Chusul (*chu shul*) ferry, his first bridge, in 1430.[46]

To gather the iron for one of his most famous bridges over the Tsangpo at Chuwori (*chu bo ri*), also the site of his main monastery in central Tibet, Tangtong Gyalpo traveled to western Bhutan in 1433–44. The iron he collected was forged into seven thousand links by a team of eighteen blacksmiths from five villages near Paro (*spa gro*), one of which, Woochu or Woo (*bye 'u chu* or *bye 'u*), is still the home of blacksmiths, including a sword smith.[47] These links, together with other gifts, were taken in fourteen hundred loads by the people of Paro across the Tibetan border to Phari (*phag ri*).[48] A nearly contemporary figure, the

Seventh Karmapa Chödrak Gyatso (*chos grags rgya mtsho*, 1454–1506), perhaps inspired by Tangtong Gyatso himself, carried out his own program of iron bridge building in Tibet, and it is probable that the technology continued to be used sporadically until fairly recent times.[49]

DERGE AND YONGLE IRONWORK OF THE EARLY 15TH CENTURY

The ironworking skills centered in eastern Tibet, especially at Derge, are strikingly reflected in a group of iron ritual objects dating from the late fourteenth to the early fifteenth century and exquisitely damascened with gold and silver in a style that blends Chinese and Tibetan idioms. The earliest dated pieces are a ritual hammer and an ax, the latter in the Museum of Fine Arts, Boston (fig. 21, right). The ax is inscribed with the reign mark of the emperor Hongwu (r. 1368–98), while other related pieces may also be assigned a late fourteenth-century date (fig. 22).[50] A few pieces show much later, possibly sixteenth-century, features.[51] However, it is objects bearing the reign marks of the emperor Yongle (r. 1403–24), or those stylistically associated, that make up the majority of the dated group. These include a ritual fire spoon at the Museo di Arte Estremo Orientale in Milan (fig. 23);[52] a set of mace, ax, and chopper with an associated incense burner at the Cleveland Museum of Art;[53] and a mask, two ritual fire spoons, and a *khatvanga* (ritual staff, fig. 24) at the Metropolitan Museum.[54] The signature features of the style include sinicized versions of the lotus or peony seen in profile, geometric wire damascening of interlocking fret patterns, bands of *ruyi* heads,[55] and floating clouds. Both the style of motifs and the workmanship, with its fine and minute detailing, point to Chinese craft production. The fluidity of the cloud designs on the edge of the fire spoon in figure 23, for example, speaks of true Chinese draftsmanship. A defining stylistic feature common to the whole group is the precisely damascened design of extended wire spiral (figs. 23, 24). This Chinese motif was developed from the running-scroll form seen abundantly on Yuan dynasty porcelain.[56] Other elements, sometimes found in combination, are more characteristically eastern Tibetan, most notably the dense overlapping pierced scrollwork, as seen on the Metropolitan's two fifteenth-century saddles (cat. nos. 111, 112), combined with sinuous dragons with long bodies. Still others, such as the interlocking fret, are more widely found on other Tibetan metalwork and furniture.[57] We must further note that the wire spiral design is found both on sinicized iron objects and on ones that have no definite Chinese stylistic elements. Where then is the most likely place of manufacture for a stylistic blend featuring such high-quality objects?

Recent research has made it clear that during the fifteenth century there was a very large output of Sino-Tibetan ritual art in several

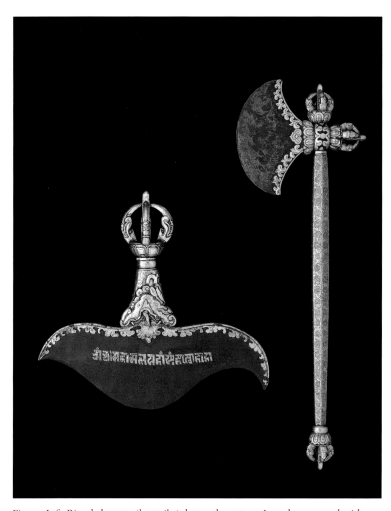

media. The ironwork being discussed shares many of the same stylistic features as woven and embroidered religious textiles and bronze images of the Yongle and Xuande (r. 1426–35) reigns and with Sino-Tibetan style *tangka* (scroll paintings) of the later fifteenth and early sixteenth century.[58] These features point to China and probably Beijing as the most likely place of manufacture. There is every likelihood that this varied production, including the iron ritual objects, was made to act as diplomatic gifts from the Chinese emperor to high-ranking Tibetan spiritual leaders or to mark visits by them to the court. The style both of the paintings and of the related bronzes is a skillful blend of Tibetan and Chinese features that is evidently the result of a long-established tradition, apparently begun in the later thirteenth century by the Nepalese master painter and sculptor Anige (1244–1306).[59] The Sino-Tibetan style established by Anige and his successors, which included his two sons, evidently survived in use into the early sixteenth century, though Chinese elements gradually came to predominate in both sculpture and painting.[60] There is in fact a direct link between the bronzes and the ritual ironwork in the form of the squared puffy Chinese faces that are found both on the Yongle images and on the *khatvangas*.

Could Chinese craftsmen also have produced the ritual iron objects with reign marks guided by Tibetan lamas resident in Beijing? Given a continuity of worship at Buddhist centers in China, such influence could have continued throughout the Ming. One well-known center of Tibetan Buddhist teaching in Beijing was the Temple of Great and Mighty Benevolence which Protects the Dynasty in the northwest corner of the old city. This temple, which housed a number of important Tibetan monks and is associated with the series of late fifteenth- and early sixteenth-century "Tibetan" paintings already mentioned, was under imperial patronage and remained a center of Tibetan Buddhist practice and teaching throughout the Ming dynasty (1368–1644).[61] Like the textiles, paintings, and bronzes, the iron pieces also speak of a well-established and mature craft tradition. Is it not possible that a production of iron objects, including weapons, was also begun in China under Anige in the late thirteenth century? We know that when he was made Head of the Imperial Manufactories in 1278, among the groups of ancillary workers he controlled were blacksmiths. It is quite possible and even likely that a production of ritual objects, including iron pieces, might have been begun at this time. That inlay on iron was produced in the late thirteenth century in China is shown by the existence of a Yuan dynasty iron passport (*paiza*) bearing an inscription in the script developed by Phagpa ('*phags pa*), hierarch of the Sakya (*sa skya*) order, who ruled Tibet for the Mongols as ally and vassal.[62] It is also possible that the shoulder or knee defense decorated with a gold and silver *qilin* (cat. no. 47) belongs to this century.[63] The late fourteenth-

Fig. 21. *Left*: Ritual chopper (*karttrika*), late 14th century. Iron damascened with gold and silver, 9⅛ in. (23.2 cm). Museum of Fine Arts, Boston, Charles Bain Hoyt Fund (1987.256). *Right*: Ritual ax (*parasu*), reign mark of the emperor Hongwu (1368–98). Iron damascened with gold and silver, 16⅞ in. (43 cm). Museum of Fine Arts, Boston, Charles Bain Hoyt Fund and Anonymous gift (1987.93) (photo: © 2006 Museum of Fine Arts, Boston)

Fig. 22. *Vajra* "water" knife, late 14th or early 15th century. Iron damascened with gold and silver, L. 9½ in. (24 cm). Private collection. The name derives from the wavy line of its blade along the top edge of which are depicted stylized waves. Flames shoot from the jaws of the makara, a mythological water monster

Fig. 23. Ritual ladle for the Fire Offering ceremony, reign mark of the emperor Yongle (1403–24). Iron damascened with gold and silver, L. 15⅜ in. (39 cm). Museo di Arte Estremo Orientale e di Etnografia, Milan. The workmanship, seen especially in the smoothly swirling clouds, points to production by a Chinese craftsman. The handle may be a later addition

Fig. 24. Ritual staff (khatvanga), Yongle period (1403–26). Iron damascened with gold and silver, L. 11⅛ in. (28 cm). The Metropolitan Museum of Art, New York, Promised Gift of Florence and Herbert Irving (L.1993.69.5)

and early fifteenth-century objects could then be seen as a continuation of a long Sino-Tibetan craft tradition located in China itself but drawing on Tibetan religion and its iconographic content.[64]

We must also ask if it is possible that, in view of the closeness of ties between the Sakya order (with their Mongol overlords) and the Derge kings during the thirteenth and early fourteenth centuries, Derge craftsmen themselves might not have been present in the imperial atelier. The fervent long-standing support of the order by the kings of Derge had begun during the first half of the thirteenth century when Zhonu Dorje (gzhon nu rdo rje), the firstborn son of the royal family, who was a monk, became the pupil of the Sakya religious leader, Kunga Gyaltsen (kun dga' rgyal mtshan, 1182–1251), also known as Sakya Pandita. Two generations later the second son of the royal line, Sonam Rinchen (bsod nams rin chen), became the attendant of the even more famous Phagpa, who obtained for him the position of Chiliarch of Doe mey (mdo smad), known more usually as Amdo (northeastern Tibet), which meant that he ruled over a large section of east and northeast Tibet.[65] Given the known presence of Tibetan and Nepalese craftsmen in Beijing, especially during the reigns of emperors who were strong supporters of Tibetan Buddhism, such as Qianlong (r. 1736–96), in the later period, it would not be surprising if in the early fifteenth century, the similarly devout Yongle had arranged for Derge ironsmiths to work in the imperial workshops in order to produce the ritual objects he required. This situation would fully explain the coexistence of a strongly eastern Tibetan style of metalwork with reign marks and Chinese features.

In terms of patronage there is evidence that the diplomatic and religious context of much of the ironwork lies in gift giving between the early fifteenth-century Chinese emperor Yongle and some of the most important Tibetan religious and secular leaders of his day. Yongle combined a genuine enthusiasm for Tibetan Buddhism with political and diplomatic aims. By inviting such Tibetan dignitaries to the court, he formed political links that were cemented by the bestowal of titles, seals, and gifts. Of greatest importance at this time were the Three Kings of the Dharma, who represented the three most powerful orders: Deshin Shekpa (de bzhin gshegs pa, 1384–1415), the Fifth Karmapa; Kunga Tashi Gyaltsen (kun dga' bkra shis rgyal mtshan, b. 1349), the thirty-second abbot of Sakya; and Jamchen Chojey (byams chen chos rje shakya ye shes, 1352–1435), the representative of the Gelugpa leader Tsongkhapa.[66] During both Yongle's reign and the succeeding one there was a constant stream of missions and gift givings on both the Tibetan and Chinese sides, often involving gifts of scriptures, religious images, and sometimes ritual objects. Chinese missions, bearing presents, were sent to Tibet in 1410 to invite the Sakya leader and in 1408 and 1413 to invite Tsongkhapa.[67] Altogether, images and texts were sent from China to

Tibet at least six times between 1408 and 1419.[68] We also know that in 1424 before his death Yongle sent a eunuch envoy to what could be seen as his tributaries in Nepal and Tibet carrying images of the Buddha, robes for monks, and ritual objects and utensils.[69] In the opposite direction, large numbers of Tibetan diplomatic missions were also visiting the Chinese capital during the 1430s; in 1430 itself there were two groups of 580 and 542 Tibetans, and in 1436, 691 Tibetan men were recorded as visitors.[70]

There are reasons, however, for singling out the Fifth Karmapa Deshin Shekpa as of particular significance in relation to the iron ritual objects. It is likely that in 1409 he returned from a visit to the Chinese court, made in 1407 to perform memorial services for the emperor's parents, bearing gifts from the emperor that may have included such ritual objects.[71] The present head of the Karmapa order confirms that by tradition the emperor Yongle gifted six *khatvangas* to Deshin Shekpa at the time of his visit.[72] The Karmapa believes that the *khatvanga* currently in the British Museum (1981.0207.1) is one of this group, while a number of other examples have passed through sale rooms.[73] For gifts to important Tibetan leaders such as the Karmapas and to mark such politically significant occasions, Yongle is known to have commissioned specifically appropriate ceramics, such as Monks Cap ewers and stem bowls, and probably also these wonderfully worked iron ritual objects.[74] The style of the Yongle reign mark on a hammer sold in 1997 is so close to that of one of the impressed marks on a porcelain piece made in the same reign that it may have been directly copied and certainly implies familiarity with the atelier producing the ceramics.[75]

There are, however, a number of objects, including the Metropolitan Museum's fifteenth-century saddle plates (cat. no. 111), that show fewer elements of Chinese style, and it may prove to be the case that this Sino-Tibetan material comprises both objects made in China and a separate group made in Tibet, which share some common stylistic features. In most cases the extended wire spiral scroll is a key linking feature, found on both potentially "Chinese" and "Tibetan" pieces. In the case of the saddle, the abundant use of inset stones also suggests a possible Tibetan production point. It may prove to be the case that such "Tibetan" pieces were made in eastern Tibet for monastery authorities or local rulers such as the king of Derge. Present-day informants from Derge Horpo maintained that former generations were required to fulfill part of their tax obligation to the Derge king by going to the capital, Derge Gonchen (*sde dge dgon chen*) and making metal objects there for his government.[76]

It is possible that just as the painting style developed by Anige was reexported to Tibet via craftsmen trained in the imperial atelier, as seen in the early fourteenth-century murals at Shalu (*zhva lu*)

Monastery, a sinicized style of ironworking created in China could have influenced eastern Tibetan craftsmen and resulted in a new production there that mixed Chinese and Tibetan features.[77] Such a situation could have occurred through Derge craftsmen returning from a period working in the imperial atelier or through the copying of Chinese imperial pieces in Tibet at the behest of a figure such as the Karmapa hierarch, as that order retained monastic centers in Kham (*khams*), or even more likely through the Sakya abbot Kunga Tashi Gyaltsen, the recipient of gifts from Yongle. The closeness of links between the Derge court and the Sakya order would have made the commissioning of ritual objects from local Derge ironsmiths an easy matter. This type of scenario is suggested by the existence of an evidently misunderstood imperial inscription of the ritual ax held by the Cleveland Museum.[78]

Style in Ironwork, 13th–19th Centuries

The dating of fine-quality ironwork from Tibet is tentative at present. Among the factors that may be used for dating are comparisons of the evolution of key motifs, such as the dragon and lotus, in Chinese art and their allied reflections in the Tibetan arts. Substantial amounts of Chinese textiles in the form of out-of-fashion dragon robes, uncut woven-to-shape garments, and bolts of silk and silk brocade had reached Tibet since the eighth century both as diplomatic gifts to important religious and secular leaders and through trade.[79] The combinations of clouds, dragons, and scrolling foliage that become so popular in Tibet from the fifteenth century onward are in fact found together on the dragon robe cloth that was used in Tibet to make dance costumes, religious hangings, *tangka* mounts, and the clothes of noblemen. Types of metalwork, such as saddles, are also not infrequently decorated with the combination of stylized rocks and standing waves (*li shi*) design at the bottom edge of dragon robes. Dragons with long sinuous bodies and four claws, one of which is opposed to the others, are characteristic of the early fifteenth century and feature on door fittings from monasteries such as Sera (*se ra*) (fig. 25) and Drepung (*'bras spungs*), where they are combined with the delicate overlapping scrollwork of the period. Such dragons closely mirror in form those on contemporary Chinese textiles.[80] The same style of dragons and scrolling foliage is beautifully demonstrated by the teacup case (fig. 19 and cat. no. 113) and by two saddles (cat. nos. 111, 112) in this catalogue and exhibition. Pierced scrollwork entwined with lotuses and writhing dragons continued to be an immensely popular decoration down to the twentieth century and is found on saddle plates, pen cases, teacup cases, and door clasps. By the later sixteenth and early seventeenth century, dragons on Tibetan

Fig. 25. Gold-damascened iron doorplate at Sera Monastery, ca. 1419. Both the dragons and the scrollwork link stylistically with those on saddles at the Metropolitan Museum (cat. nos. 111, 112) and the teacup case at the Victoria and Albert Museum (fig. 19 and cat. no. 113) (photo: the author, 1993)

Fig. 26. Gold-damascened iron doorplate on the main assembly hall at Nechung Monastery near Lhasa, ca. mid- to late 17th century. Nechung was built by the Fifth Dalai Lama (1617–1682). The five clawed dragons and swirling clouds reflect Chinese brocades of the late 16th and early 17th centuries (photo: the author, 1993)

Fig. 27. Pierced iron grill damascened with gold, part of the door of the funerary chapel of the Eighth Dalai Lama (1758–1804), Potala Palace, Lhasa. Probably made by blacksmiths from the Dodzhol Palkyil, or government workshop, in Lhasa, ca. first decade of 19th century (photo: the author, 1993)

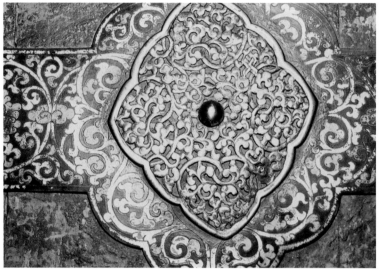

Fig. 28. Pierced and damascened iron doorplate on the main assembly hall of Mindroling Monastery. This door fitting dates either from the founding of the monastery in 1677 or from its rebuilding in 1736. It displays the rather stiff, symmetrical scrollwork found on ironwork from the 18th century onward (photo: the author, 1993)

metalwork appear to closely follow new Chinese models, probably inspired by newly imported brocades. A doorplate from the Nechung (*gnas chung*) complex within Drepung Monastery (fig. 26) shows many of the same features as are found in Chinese woven or embroidered textiles of the Wanli period (1573–1620).[81] By now dragons had lost some of their fierceness and have a playful quality. They display larger heads with bulging foreheads and small eyes and, most

characteristically of all, five evenly spaced claws that are arranged like a Catherine wheel. In the case of the doorplate just described, dragons fly through Chinese-looking swirling clouds reinforcing the idea that they were a direct borrowing from Chinese art. Scrollwork of the sixteenth–seventeenth centuries (see cat. nos. 118–120) tends to show more elongated, snakelike tendrils that intertwine with other design elements. A later version of the typical fifteenth-century small, bifurcating scroll form continues into the nineteenth century and is seen on a doorplate from the Mindroling (*smin grol gling*) Monastery (fig. 28). By this time the scroll had become more spaced out, formal, and symmetrical with reduced areas of overlapping. By the nineteenth century the dragon in Tibet was often depicted as a tame, pet-like creature, as shown on the screen to the funerary chorten of the Eighth Dalai Lama (fig. 27) in the Potala Palace.

Centers and Products in the 19th and 20th Centuries

The great ironworking centers of Kham lay on the traditional border with China, which has fluctuated during the last two centuries as a result of insurrection and warfare between local kingdoms, the central Tibetan government, and China. The foremost metalworking area, the principality of Derge, was able to remain virtually independent until 1909, when China intervened in a succession dispute, deposed the king, and installed a Chinese governor. Since 1955 Derge has been part of the province of Sichuan, lying just outside the border of the Tibetan Autonomous Region. Although Derge is also noted for its copper, silverwork, and casting industries, in the opinion of both Western travelers and local Tibetan metalworkers, the quality of its ironwork was probably supreme within Tibet.[82] As a principality Derge consisted of twenty-five districts (*rdzong khag*), with Horpo, whose origins have been discussed, the foremost metalworking area with a village of the same name at its center. It was here that the skills of damascening, or overlaying silver, gold, and copper (*'jam tshag*), onto the surface of iron was most fully developed. It was also famous for pierced iron decoration (*lcags dkrol*) and at that time Horpo was renowned for pierced saddles and pen cases. In the late nineteenth and early twentieth century Derge saddles, sword blades, scabbards, and knives were prized throughout Tibet, and at the end of the nineteenth century a Derge sword could fetch the equivalent of $150 to $200, a huge sum at that

time.[83] Other products of Derge Horpo included knives, stirrups, bridles and bits, tinder pouches, and teacup cases. The round beer flasks damascened with auspicious emblems and dragons in gold, silver, and copper were made here and in Chamdo (*chab mdo*) to the southwest. Derge Gonchen, the capital of the principality, was also a center of production, and teapots, guns, swords, spears, inlaid saddles, and other ironwork poured from it.[84] To the south of Derge, along the Yangtze (*'bri chu*), lay the important ironworking village of Derge Poyul (*sde dge dpal yul*), its products being very similar to those of Horpo, and like Horpo it was particularly well known for its tinder pouches. Forty miles down the Yangtze lies Apishang,[85] known for its ritual objects and swords, where the skills of piercing and inlaying iron are still continued today (fig. 29). According to the opinions of both nineteenth-century scholar-explorers such as William Woodville Rockhill and twentieth-century informants from eastern Tibet, there was a definite hierarchy in the quality of products emanating from the towns of Kham. Derge stood at the top with Lithang (*li thang*) and Dayap (*brag g.yab*) under it and Chamdo at the bottom.[86] Farther to the southwest lay Dayap in Gonjo (*go 'jo*) state, noted for copper, silver, and ironworking. A small district within Dayap called Sholong (*zho long*) was known for its inlaid ironwork, and during the 1935–45 period there were about six people there making ornate saddles, gun barrels, locks, tinder pouches, and knife cases.[87] Other places known for their manufacture of swords and knives in Kham included Azho on the Le'chu, and Newa,[88] while in Somo state, one of the semi-independent tribes to the east of the Sino-Tibetan border, there were skilled sword smiths and gunsmiths who manufactured most of the guns in use throughout eastern Tibet.[89] Though the large-scale use of pierced and inlaid ironwork tailed off after the Chinese occupation of Tibet in 1950, the skills have not been lost entirely. At Horpo the main products today are large 12-inch-long steel daggers and shorter 6-inch versions for women. These have brass pommels and are cased in silver sheaths. At Apishang,

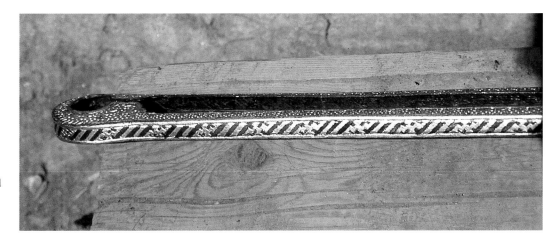

Fig. 29. Iron frame for the bottom half of a sword scabbard damascened with gold and silver, in production in Apishang, near Derge (photo: the author, 2003)

harness mounts enlivened with simple silver inlay, tinder pouches, decorated iron sword scabbards, and swords are still ordered (fig. 29), though ironwork is a small element of a larger production in copper, silver, and brass.

Production today, as in the last century, is carried out throughout the whole Kham region within villages and small towns and mostly in, or near, the houses of the craftsmen. Many metalworkers are part-time craftsmen and have a main job, most commonly farming. In the past demands for metalwork often competed with farming, and this led to the women and children in a family taking over farm duties at the busiest times while the men produced metalwork. But where there is a large family it has sometimes been possible for one or more brothers to be full-time craftsmen. The skill of Chinese metalworkers was also widely recognized throughout the borders of eastern Tibet, and in the late nineteenth century, itinerant Chinese blacksmiths made all the ironware for the nomads of the Kokonor area in northeast Tibet. This included saddles, knives, swords, matchlocks, kettles, and bowls.[90]

RAW MATERIALS AND TECHNIQUES

By the early twentieth century, most of the iron required in central Tibet was imported from India, but there were iron deposits in eastern Tibet at Chamdo, where smelting was also carried out, and in the Thangla (*thang lha*) mountain range on the Tibetan borders of Qinghai.[91] Wrought iron was also exported from Nepal to Tibet at the end of the eighteenth century and from Bhutan during the first half of the nineteenth century.[92] Tibetan former government officials also confirm that iron ore was one of the taxes in kind expected from iron-rich areas, and as there seems to have been no mining in western Tibet, we must assume this applied to eastern Tibet and specifically to the Chamdo area controlled by the Tibetan government.

The shaping of both wrought iron and steel requires a variety of differently sized and weighted hammers with variously shaped ends, depending on what type of surface is being worked. The largest hammers, *tho ba chen po*, are used at the start of the process when the most force is required. Hammers with rounded ends, *tho ba chung ba* or *tho ba ngo che*, allow rounded bowl shapes to be raised, while smaller, lighter hammers are used for more delicate work.[93] Most processes involving carving, stretching, flattening, rolling, and bending require iron to be heated to a red heat before it can be worked. When it is at this temperature the metal can be bent and rolled to create complex shapes. Decoration by piercing and incising or chasing the surface is carried out when the metal is cool by means of punches and chisels (*gzong*) in combination with hammers. There are three generic types of punches. For modeling, punches with square, oval, or round ends are used to raise shapes, and for overall decoration of the surface, dapping punches with patterned ends such as a circle or half moon are used. The effect of scales on the dragons' bodies on the iron teacup case (fig. 19 and cat. no. 113) is made by this type of punch, for example.

Fig. 30. Machete blade in production at Woochu in western Bhutan, 2000. The blacksmith is Phago, the last sword maker in Bhutan (photo: the author, 2000)

Lastly "tracer" punches are used to create a different overall background effect: a blunt roughened punch end will make a dull surface, while a flattened polished end will produce a shiny surface. For lines, a "running" punch (*kha gri gzong*) with a chisel-like end is used.

The blacksmiths of Kham were famous for pierced iron decoration (*lcags dkrol* or *tshan phug*) usually in combination with overlapping, bifurcating scrollwork. The actual piercing was carried out after the scrolls were formed, using a chisel with a sharpened edge (*sho gzong*). There is also evidence that simple hand-operated mechanical devices were being used in eastern Tibet at the end of the nineteenth century to pierce iron.[94]

The other process for which the skilled ironworkers of Kham were particularly renowned was the overlaying of wrought iron with gold and silver, or damascening.[95] In this technique, said to be called *bcad sgrigs* (?), the surface of the iron is roughened by cross-hatching with a ridged punch and the softer metals are applied either as thinly beaten sheets or as wires. These are then beaten carefully down over the cross-hatching, ensuring that the top surface is flat and that the gold, silver, or occasionally copper is gripped by the cross-hatching beneath.[96] This technique is distinct from inlaying, in which a section of the host metal is removed and the inserted softer metal filling the space created is gripped by a cut that widens toward the bottom.[97] Wrought iron, which is almost free of carbon and manganese, has a remarkable resistance to corrosion, which is essential when it is to be overlaid with other metals.[98] An effect that is the same as mechanically overlaid gold may be simulated by fire or mercury gilding, which appears to be a late technique in relation to iron and is mostly seen on objects from the nineteenth century onward. On virtually all Tibetan flat inlaid ironwork, larger decorative emblems are outlined with a visible chased line that defines and emphasizes them against a surrounding plain surface. Some contemporary craftsmen effect this chasing after the inlaying has been carried out (fig. 29). Sometimes scrollwork and emblems have chased lines within them, running parallel to and echoing the outer boundaries. But intricate geometric wire patterning or other small designs are laid out on a rough surface without any defining lines. The early fifteenth-century Sino-Tibetan pieces are also distinguished by a skillful modeling of the iron, seen to advantage on the makara handles of ritual choppers (fig. 22) or the *tsi pa ṭa*, or Face of Glory, on sword hilts.

It is crucial for the blacksmith to be able to visually differentiate between the colors the iron progresses through as it is heated in order to know when to begin particular operations. The three key colors are, progressively, red hot, white hot, and welding hot, and these include a range of subtler shades ranging from red/dark gray to purple/red then white/yellow.[99] In order to be able to see the changes easily, workshops were situated belowground, something attested to during the nineteenth century in Lhasa, where they are described as lying beneath shops facing onto the street, and in eastern Tibet, where they might also be separate structures."[100]

The production of steel, an alloy of iron containing up to 1.7 percent carbon, required for swords, gun barrels, or toolmaking, similarly demands the ability to see color changes. In Tibet during the nineteenth century, swords were made by welding together two different types of steel in the form of rods lying side by side in a hairpin pattern. Later polishing of the finished blade revealed this "hairpin" design to form a decoration.[101] The shaping and working of a steel tool or weapon rendered it hard and brittle; it was therefore necessary to temper or heat it periodically, a process that reduced the hardness of the metal but made it tougher. It was finally heated to a red heat before a final cold tempering by quenching in cold water or oil, causing long crystals to grow in the structure, thus greatly toughening the steel. Nowhere is the gap between the old, long-held skills and the present-day ones more noticeable than in sword making. In eastern Tibet today members of the "younger" generation (under sixty) generally do not have the skills to properly temper swords and instead produce an iron sword blade intended only for show. But surviving members of the older generation, though retaining the skills, are not asked to practice them, as they are too costly or the craftsmen have themselves retired. Much cheaper steel daggers and swords are, however, still forged from steel automobile suspension springs. These are made both by Tibetans and by Chinese metalworkers from Yunnan who are settled in towns such as Kandze (*dkar mdzes*), Chamdo, and Derge. In Bhutan the knowledge of how to temper daggers, knives, and swords is retained in the village of Woochu near Paro (*spa gro*) (fig. 30).

1. Demiéville 1952, p. 180, n. 373.

2. Heller 1998, p. 103.

3. Demiéville 1952, p. 374. Mail armor is also depicted on the later reliefs at Taq-i Bustan, where it is worn by Khusraw II (590–628).

4. Dunlop 1973, pp. 303–4.

5. Ibid., p. 309.

6. Heller 1998, p. 100.

7. Needham 1971, pp. 197–98.

8. Ibid., p. 197.

9. Backus 1981, pp. 36, 78, 96; Needham 1971, pp. 198, 200.

10. From this time onward, small blast furnaces were being used to create wrought iron using the fining process by which brittle, unworkable cast iron was turned into workable wrought iron through the burning off of its carbon while in a molten state.

11. Zeki Validi 1936, p. 35.

12. Wagner 2001, pp. 111–12.

13. Ibid., pp. 7–8.

14. By A.D. 661 Tibetan armies had had penetrated to the junction of the Karakoram and Pamir mountains in the west, where they subdued Gilgit for the first time, and at periods in the 8th century Tibetan troops were found as far west as Fergana and Samarqand, afterward maintaining commercial exchanges with these areas.

15. Bosworth and Asimov 1998–2000, pt. 2, p. 36.

16. Le Strange 1930, p. 488; Craddock and Lang 2003, pp. 245–46; Wagner forthcoming, pp. 203–4. Sites of crucible steel blast furnaces from the 9th to the 13th century have been discovered at Eski Achsy and elsewhere in the Fergana Valley (Uzbekistan).

17. Beckwith 1977, p. 101.

18. Demiéville 1952, p. 373.

19. Lang, Craddock, and Simpson 1998, pp. 7–10; Craddock and Lang 2003, pp. 243–44. A Sasanian sword of the 6th century at the British Museum (WA 135747) was found to be of crucible steel. We also know that the Sasanians imported Indian steel from the 3rd to the 5th century A.D. and used it to make such famously high-quality swords.

20. Lang, Craddock, and Simpson 1998, p. 12.

21. Tibet controlled the northern Silk Route itself across Central Asia from 787 to 842.

22. Carter 1998, p. 37.

23. Sinor 1990, p. 296. The connection of the Turkic populations of Central Asia to ironworking was already established by the 6th century, and the historian Menander remarked that the Turks often offered iron to visitors to their lands to advertise their mining resources.

24. Zeki Validi 1936, pp. 33–36; *Encyclopedia of Islam IV*, pp. 658–59: Chinese *Ko lo hu*, Persian *Khallukh*, early Arabic *Kharlakh*.

25. The Kuqa area had passed from Tibetan control in 790–860 to Karluk control and was finally, by the 11th century, settled by the Tokuz Oghuz, or Nine Clans, one of the tribal groups of the Orkhon Turks.

26. Zeki Validi 1936, p. 35. Al-Idrisi has Djermac for Farman; Jaubert 1975, p. 490; also Minorsky 1937, p. 295. Barman may be another form of Bakhwan given in al-Idrisi (also called in Tibetan *par ban*, in Chinese *Pa huan*); see Jaubert 1975, pp. 491–92.

27 Sinor 1990, p. 297.

28. Beckwith 1977, p. 101; Pyhrr, LaRocca, and Ogawa 2002, p. 44.

29. I wish to thank Philip Denwood for this idea and bringing to my attention the article Zeki Validi 1936.

30. Rockhill 1895, p. 277: Kangsar, Mazur, Beri, Chu wo, and Chango. Roerich 1931, p. 333: the 19th- and 20th-century collective usage of the term *hor* in Tibet also meant the nomadic tribes of mixed origin living to the north of central Tibet, where travelers such as Roerich discerned Mongolian, Turkish, and even Iranian elements. These were the Nub Hor, the western Hor, to distinguish them from the five eastern Hor tribes in Kham.

31. Sinor 1990, p. 271.

32. Yoshinobu 1983, p. 94.

33. Sinor, Shimin, and Kychanov 1998–2000, p. 203.

34. Uray-Köhalmi 1989, pp. 187–89.

35. Alexander 1992, pp. 64–65, n. 24.

36. See Allan 1982, pp. 14–17, for discussion of inlay in the Islamic world.

37. Komaroff and Carboni 2002, p. 63.

38. Das 1904, p. 277. At this village in the 20th century there was a mixture of these monastery-paid workers, a central government guild, and private workers, and among them were many metalworkers. See Clarke 2002, pp. 116–17.

39. Moore 1995, p. 17.

40. For a full account, see Clarke 2002, pp. 122–25.

41. Waddell 1906, pp. 170, 427. They had locally made lathes for boring gun barrels and English saws, files, and other tools.

42. Aris 1979, p. 185; also Dudjom Rinpoche 1991, vol. 2, p. 76, for other versions of life dates.

43. Aris 1979, pp. 185–88. Tangtong Gyalpo was also a discoverer of hidden religious texts and a *gter ston* (treasure finder), and is linked to rituals carried out to prolong life (*tshe sgrub*), which are still performed today in Bhutan. In order to finance his program of bridge building, he is said to have raised a touring operatic troupe, also creating the dance dramas called *a ce lha mo* (Lady Goddess), which are still performed in Tibet today.

44. Chan 1994, pp. 453, 561, 863.

45. Ibid., p. 379.

46. Weldon and Singer 1999, p. 184.

47. Aris 1979, p. 188, has bye 'u.

48. Local tradition in Paro maintains that two local sources for the iron were mines at khes nyes and ge mi na above Woochu itself.

49. Thinley 1980, p. 83.

50. For the hammer, see sale cat., Christie's, Amsterdam, October 23, 1991, lot 165; and a chopper of the same date at the Museum of Fine Arts, Boston (fig. 21, left). Also see Thurman and Weldon 1999, nos. 59, 60, 65.

51. *Rituels tibétains* 2002, p. 149.

52. Zwalf 1985, pl. 307; Clarke 2004, p. 24, no. 13.

53. Huntington and Bangdel 2003, figs, 108, 156, for a related *phur pa*. The incense burner is Cleveland Museum 1983.154; see Watt and Leidy 2005, pp. 81–82, pl. 32.

54. The mask is Metropolitan Museum of Art L.1994.23; the ritual fire spoons, MMA L.1993.477.1.1a, b, and L.1993.477.1.2; and the *khatvanga*, MMA L.1993.69.5 (fig. 24). The fire spoon L.1993.477.1.1a, b is inscribed *da Ming Yongle nian shi* (bestowed during the Yongle era of the great Ming), and the *khatvanga* is inscribed *Yongle nian zhi* (made in the Yongle era), supporting the idea of such objects as diplomatic gifts. See Watt and Leidy 2005, pp. 73–81, pls. 27, 29, 30.

55. The *ruyi* is an ancient Chinese symbol of authority based on the form of a sacred fungus.

56. Mikami 1981, pp. 65–67, 72, 76, 203, 205–6.

57. Gluckman 2004, p. 83.

58. A group of early 15th-century embroideries depicting Buddhist deities, including two with Yongle reign marks, held in the Jokhang Temple in the center of Lhasa, together with others of the Xuande period, may be regarded as another related group of objects made in China as gifts intended for Tibet. A number of slightly later paintings, which are dated from between 1474 and 1516, show a similar cross-cultural blend to the bronzes and textiles, though they represent a later stage of its stylistic evolution. These feature Sakya order tutelary and protective deities and are associated with centers of Tibetan Buddhism in Beijing. The Sakya subject matter and the dating of several paintings to the year, month, and day of the reign suggest that they were made for specific rituals or to mark the visits of high lamas of the same order. Although Tibeto-Nepalese stylistic traits may weaken over time, both paintings and bronzes faithfully adhere to Tibetan iconography, suggesting guidance from Tibetan lamas in residence at temples, though production itself may have been executed by Chinese craftsmen in associated workshops. For bronzes, see

Weldon 1996; for textiles, see Henss 1997, pp. 26–39; for paintings, see Lowry 1973; Kidd 1975; Kerr 1991, pp. 100–101; Tokya-Fuong 1997, p. 30; and sale cat., Christie's, Amsterdam, November 19, 1997, lot 9.

59. Jing 1994, pp. 66–70. This artistic prodigy who was invited to the Mongol court in 1263 rose rapidly to become head of the Supervisorate in Chief of All Classes of Artisans in 1275, a role in which he commanded more than three thousand artisan households producing mainly painting and bronze sculptures, though woven textiles and works in lacquer also formed part of the production.

60. Weldon 1996, pp. 67–68. By the reign of Yongle the bronze religious images still reveal a partial Tibeto-Nepalese physiognomy and the careful attention to jewelry and ornaments that are typical of Nepalese bronze casting, yet they show none of the love of ancillary detail such as the use of inset stones, lion throne supporters, or animals adorning the mandorlas at the back of images that are so typically Tibetan, and the flowing robes worn by the figures are Chinese in conception.

61. Kerr 1991, pp. 100–101.

62. Komaroff and Carboni 2002, p. 69.

63. Another possible 13th- or 14th-century piece is a damascened helmet at the Royal Armouries Museum, Leeds; see Peers 1992, p. 6. An armor said to have been given by Kublai Khan to Phagpa during the second half of the 13th century and preserved in Sakya Monastery appears stylistically to be later; see LaRocca 1999a, p. 124.

64. It must be noted that a small body of purely Chinese style damascened iron dating from the late Ming and Qing (17th–19th centuries) shows the Chinese adoption of the technique and its continuation into later periods. Objects in this group include a flute (1983.0128.1), a lock (1905.1115.61), and two boxes (1878.1230.955, OAr 6653) at the British Museum, and at the Victoria and Albert Museum, a brush pot (M302-1912).

65. Kolmas 1968, pp. 28–30.

66. Henss 1997, pp. 32–33.

67. Karmay 1975, p. 80.

68. Ibid., p. 79.

69. Tsai 2001, pp. 187–88.

70. See Karmay 1975, pp. 74–99; Henss 1997, pp. 32–35; Watt and Leidy 2005, p. 81. There were at least thirteen delegations between Tibet and China during the Yongle reign, including those to secular figures which have not been described in detail here. During this decade there were also Tibetan requests for permission to settle in Beijing, which were granted on several occasions

71. Richardson 1998, p. 344.

72. Communication from Nik Douglas in 2004, and with thanks to him and Amy Heller for this reference.

73. Sale cat., Christie's, Amsterdam, October 23, 1991, lot 165; sale cats., Christie's, New York, March 23, 1997, lot 108, and September 17, 1998, lot 98; Thurman and Weldon 1999, pp. 136–39.

74. Watt and Leidy 2005, pp. 34–35, pls. 5, 6. The stem cup in pl. 6 bears a Xuande reign mark (1426–35).

75. Sale cat., Sotheby's, London, April 24, 1997, lot 122.

76. Clarke 2002, pp. 119–20. This type of corvée labor, called lag khral (hand tax), was widespread in Tibet, and though the production of metal objects as tax items was highly unusual, it was not unknown and was followed in the Sakya principality in southern Tibet, one of whose sister monasteries was Derge Gonchen.

77. See Vitali 1990, pp. 105–12, for discussion of the Yuan murals at Shalu.

78. Watt and Leidy 2005, pp. 77–78.

79. Cammann 1952, pp. 172–73; Gluckman 2004, p. 73.

80. Hong Kong 1995, pp. 199, 209.

81. Ibid., pp. 203, 281.

82. Teichman 1922, p. 171; Ronge 1978, p. 145.

83. Rockhill 1895, p. 712.

84. Sandberg 1906, p. 157.

85. On older maps and according to some senior craftsmen, Apishang is also called Apinang.

86. Rockhill 1891, p. 2; Rockhill 1894, p. 358, Clarke 1995, vol. 1, p. 163.

87. Clarke 1995, vol. 1, p. 165.

88. Rockhill 1894, p. 330.

89. Ainscough 1914, p. 11.

90. Rockhill 1891, p. 81.

91. Lo Bue 1981, p. 58; Clarke 1995, vol. 1, pp. 267–68.

92. Lo Bue 1981, p. 59.

93. Rauber-Schweizer 1976, pp. 144–45, has sbub tho for a hammer with two rounded ends, lag tho che ba for a hammer used for less delicate work, and mthar tho for a hammer used for fine work.

94. Bonvalot 1891, vol. 2, p. 15.

95. The term "damascening" is sometimes also used to refer to the pattern-welded steel blades of swords from the Middle East.

96. Rauber-Schweizer 1976, pp. 138–39.

97. Ibid.

98. Untracht 1975, p. 34.

99. Rauber-Schweizer 1976, pp. 115–16.

100. Bonvalot 1891, vol. 2, p. 150. A French explorer, Bonvalot described a forge he visited at Lagong in eastern Tibet in the last decade of the 19th century: "By a low door we descended to an underground forge, four posts supporting the sloping roof by which the light enters and the smoke escapes. Someone is kneeling between two goatskin bellows which he works alternately with either arm. The old man is bare to the waist and looks like a denizen of the lower regions."

101. Smith 1960, pp. 8–9.

ARMOR AND WEAPONS IN THE ICONOGRAPHY OF TIBETAN BUDDHIST DEITIES

AMY HELLER

Tibetan representations of male protector deities frequently present them dressed from head to foot in helmet and armor, brandishing a sword, and carrying several other different weapons, ready to defend the Buddhist doctrine and its proponents.[1] These guardian deities represent the epitome of vitality and strength and are depicted in armor to emphasize their invincible nature. Their portraits in sculpture and paintings are some of the most remarkable creations of Tibetan art owing to the extreme ardor and energy they manifest to defend Tibetan religious traditions. How and why did the Tibetans create these deities? To answer this question, we will examine here some examples of these deities and their unique weapons as well as the development of their cult in Tibet over the centuries.

The concept of Buddhist deities represented as warriors was inherited from Indian Buddhism as it was progressively introduced to Tibet during the seventh and eighth centuries. The guardians in Indian Buddhism were often depicted as highly muscular athletes wearing loincloths and wielding weapons or carrying shields. Armor was not frequently represented on guardian deities in India at this time. The Tibetans did not rely exclusively on the Indian models of representation of these deities but were also influenced by Buddhist iconography from Central Asia and Tang China, where the guardians of the four directions were already sometimes shown in armor. In fact, because the Tibetans' civilization prior to Buddhism was centered around warrior deities, they were very receptive to the concept of Buddhist guardian deities in armor.

THE ANCIENT TIBETAN WARRIOR DEITIES

Even before Buddhist teachings were introduced into Tibet during the seventh–eighth century, Tibetan esteem for warriors was high—to such an extent that the sovereign, the Tsenpo (*btsan po*, literally, the mighty one), was regarded as a powerful divine warrior. We may interpret his title to mean that he was the supreme warrior, of divine origin, who made manifest his deified nature by his superior qualities as warrior and leader of men. Many ancient Tibetan documents of the eighth–ninth century describe the Tsenpo with his sacred helmet (*dbu rmog*) and his divine radiance (*byin*), the two principal outward signs of his valor and his invincibility. "The Tsenpo is a god who became the sovereign of men, due to his power derived from the great radiance of his sacred helmet. That is why all the kingdoms under the sun, south, north, west, and east, all obeyed his orders and all have been conquered."[2] This incandescence is the source of his military valor and prowess (*byin gyi dgra thabs*), "the radiance which is the means to vanquish the enemy."[3] The sacred radiance of his helmet is the emblem of his power, rendering him a "supernatural warrior" constantly assured of victory. In the Lhasa treaty inscription of A.D. 822, it is said of the Tsenpo, "Subduing external enemies through knowledge of the arts of war, they increased the extent of their dominion. Through the ever-increasing might of their helmet, their wise order was immutable. . . . Thus each and every inhabited region without exception did not fail to revere the mighty helmet and the excellent customs of the supernaturally wise divinity the Tsenpo."[4] At present, there is a reminder of this ancient sacred helmet in the helmet (*dbu rmog*, literally, venerable helmet) worn by the special protector deities such as the State Oracle of Tibet.[5]

The Tsenpo was believed to be a human manifestation of divine presence who first appeared on earth as he descended from a sacred mountain. His personal guardian deity was identified with a sacred mountain that it was his duty to defend as a "sacred precinct."[6] Territorial

Fig. 31. Begtse, 18th–19th century. *Tangka*, pigment on cotton, 30 x 20 in. (76.2 x 50.8 cm). Newark Museum, Dr. Albert L. Shelton Collection, purchase 1920 (20.268)

defense and expansion was not merely political policy. It was the sacred duty of the Tsenpo to expand the Tibetan territory and create vassal states whose tribute would ensure prosperity:

*The Tsenpo came from the land of the gods to be the ruler of men. His was a good religion which never varied; he had great power and his radiance (*byin*) was like the sky, that is why the kingdom has grown, and the sacred helmet has always been mighty. . . . Making the dominion firm for ever by the successsion of his sons; making the populace happy by his orders, conquering the external enemies by the sacred or glorious military strategy (*phyi'i dgra 'dul ba'i byin gyi dgra' thabs*).[7]*

Also, the Tsenpo was considered guarantor of social justice and the well-being of the Tibetan people. Thus the cult of the Tsenpo was practiced to ensure the stability of the empire and the royal government as well as to preserve the divine order. Belief in an afterlife led to elaborate funeral rituals for the Tsenpo and great ministers and generals, which included burial in tombs with food, utensils, jewelry, garments, armor.[8] These rituals were accompanied by the sacrificial burial of live horses in elaborate saddles and tack—sometimes as many as a hundred—for the horse was the symbol of the success of the warrior: his friend in this life and a guide in the afterlife.[9] The Tsenpo achieved their sacred goals, for from the mid-seventh to the mid-ninth century, the clout of Tibetan military power was feared throughout much of Asia. The Tibetans created a strong empire with garrisons stretching from Ladakh to Sichuan as well as throughout the Silk Route oases from Dunhuang to the Pamirs and the Karakoram Range. Their renowned metallurgical skills contributed to their success in war, both for the manufacture of weapons and armor and for strategic advantages such as the eighth-century construction of iron chain suspension bridges to transport troops and goods, a technology not found in the West for nearly another thousand years.[10]

The Tsenpo as warrior was the core of the religion and the Tibetan empire. The earliest representations of the Tibetan Tsenpo were painted during the mid-eighth–mid-ninth-century Tibetan occupation of Dunhuang, where there are many mural paintings of the Buddha with a cortege of royalty. Dunhuang ceremonial scenes show the Tsenpo represented as supreme sovereign among many kings, all dressed in long robes. The Tsenpo was often depicted with, suspended from his waist, his sword, regalia of five or six knives, and two crossed knives.[11] Leopard pelts and tiger-skin trim on garments were a sign of the Tsenpo's success in battle.[12]

Unfortunately, in the extant mural paintings, there are no representations of the Tsenpo in armor and helmet. Yet literary descriptions help us understand how they were dressed for their exploits. For example, in the *Tibetan Chronicle,* which was written in the mid-eighth century and preserves the genealogy and exploits of the Tibetan dynasty from earliest traditions until the reign of Trisong Detsen (*khri srong lde btsan*, r. 755–ca. 797), there is the following request by a vassal to his sovereign, extolling his exclusive possession of miraculous weapons:

*Yes, I will dare [to battle], if you in turn give me the treasures of the gods: the magical lance which attacks alone (*mdung rang 'debs*), the sword which cuts on its own (*ral gyi rang gcod*), the armor which clothes [the body] on its own (*khrab rang gyod*), the shield which repulses [arrows] on its own (*phub rang bzur*). You will give me the power of these great magical possessions, then I accept to fight.[13]*

The significance of magical armor of this type is that the wearer would be instantly and effortlessly clothed in armor and therefore instantly protected and ready for action. The advantage of weapons that act independently is obvious, as is a shield offering effortless protection. This key passage helps us understand how the Tsenpo and his warriors were equipped.

The *Tibetan Chronicle* later (line 262) describes ten armors and two swords as sacred objects that a vassal gave to his king to show allegiance (*sku rten du khrab bse' sna bcu dang ldong prom gyi ral gri mdor cod gnyis gsol to*). The word describing the material of the armor is *bse*, which is variously translated as "leather" or "rhinoceros hide," and may refer specifically to decorated leather, which characterizes the leather from which most armor is made.[14] Although *bse* is a word whose signification has varied over time, it probably refers to leather lamellar armor, or armor of small leather plates laced together, which is the way Tibetan armor is described in the ninth-century Tang Annals.[15] At Samye (*bsam yas*) Monastery in central Tibet, in a late eighth-century stone sculpture of the Buddhist god Vaisravana, god of wealth and also the guardian of the North, the deity is depicted wearing a breastplate of rows of small plates (fig. 32). This may be the earliest extant example of a Tibetan sculpture of a deity wearing a breastplate. A mural painting of Vaisravana made during the occupation by Tibetan troops along the Silk Route near Dunhuang, dating from the early ninth century, shows a slightly later lamellar armor with a skirt made of sewn-together plaques covering the legs (fig. 33).

The French Sinologist Paul Demiéville studied the ancient Chinese armor terms in the Tang Annals and differentiated those for lamellar armor and for mail armor, both of which were described as worn by Tibetans; mail armor was also described as covering horses.[16] Moreover, Demiéville stated that Tibetan armor was worn over a silk or leather undershirt.[17] Recent research on Tibetan manuscripts written in Dunhuang during the Tibetan occupation has revealed the ancient Tibetan terminology for the silk undershirt, *dar gyi beg tse.*

Fig. 32. Vaisravana, late 8th century. Stone, H. approx. 11⅞ in. (30 cm). Samye Monastery, Tibet (photo: the author, 1986)

Fig. 33. Vaisravana, late 8th–early 9th century. Wall painting, H. approx. 70⅞ in. (180 cm). Anxi Yulin cave 25, Dunhuang (photo: after Duan Wenjie, ed., *Dunhuang shi ku yi shu. Yulin ku di 25 ku, fu di 15 ku [zhong Tang]* [Nanjing, 1993], pl. 150)

The garment was so important a component of the complete armor that later the term became the name of one of the major Buddhist protective deities.[18]

In extant Tibetan manuscripts written during the eighth–ninth-century Tibetan occupation of Dunhuang, there is documented a new use of weapons: Buddhist protective charms that have prayers surrounded by drawings of daggers, the *vajra*, ritual scepters, swords, and hooks. In this context, these are all weapons of protective and ritual function. As Buddhism was altering Tibetan society, by the late tenth century the ideal of the Tsenpo as sacred warrior was changing into the ideal of a ruler in devout service to Buddhism and in close relation to the increasingly powerful Buddhist clergy. Rather than expanding the Tibetan empire, the kings sponsored the founding of monasteries and massive projects of translating Indian Buddhist texts into Tibetan. Thus the cult devoted to the Tsenpo as sovereign warrior deities gradually transformed into the veneration of the Buddha assisted by protective deities who ensured the survival of the Buddhist teachings.

TIBETAN DEVELOPMENT OF WARRIOR ICONOGRAPHY

During the period of translating texts from Indian ritual anthologies, Tibetans followed the Indian Buddhist models of protective deities

Fig. 34. Helmet (ca. 14th century, iron with silver damascening), a set of four mirrors, fragments of a lamellar armor, and pieces of horse harness. Shalu Monastery, Tibet (photo: the author, 1999)

although some holding swords or bows and arrows are depicted as hunters, wearing Tibetan robes instead of armor. The practice of the cult of the wrathful protective deities was restricted to those who had received special initiations, and in the monasteries access to the chapel for their worship was restricted. Visually, these warriors are some of the most impressive creations in Tibetan iconography. The chapel interiors are often painted black and the representations of warriors outlined in gold with little pigment infilling, which gives a very dramatic effect. In the Gongkar Monastery in central Tibet, the theme of Vaisravana and his attendants was again a subject, this time in the late fifteenth-century

dressed in short dhotis made of animal hides. Innovative descriptions of wrathful defender deities were written by Tibetan lamas in the thirteenth century during antagonism between various monastic schools that led to armed combat in efforts to gain territory and economic and political prominence. These wrathful deities were regarded as family protectors and as emanations of the major deities of Buddhism; they might also be local mountain gods, who, as territorial defenders, were potentially represented as wrathful warriors, always armed and often wearing armor. As of 1247, the political relationship between Tibet and the Mongols was initiated, and it was the Mongols who would soon organize the administration of China under their reign as the Yuan dynasty (1279–1368). The Mongol armies were renowned fighters. Armor was sent to the Tibetan monasteries of Shalu and Sakya, which had political relations with the Yuan; some is conserved to this day. One example, the helmet in figure 34, has decoration damascened in silver that recalls Chinese *ju'i* motifs. The monks of Shalu regard it as a relic of the early fourteenth century, an item of tribute during a period of reconstruction at Shalu when there were Chinese and Mongol artists at the monastery.[19] According to local documents, the mural paintings in the entrance chapel of Shalu were painted in 1306, during this period of remodeling,[20] and in one representing Vaisravana and his eight attendant cavaliers, one of the attendants is dressed in full lamellar armor, including a Tibetan-style helmet (fig. 35).

The earlier models of armor worn by Vaisravana and the guardians of the directions probably fused with armor actually seen or used in Tibet during the Yuan dynasty, which led to the creation of Tibetan iconographical models for wrathful male protector deities in armor,

Fig. 35. Detail of a wall painting depicting Vaisravana and his eight horsemen, ca. 1306–10. H. of detail approx. 9⅞ in. (25 cm). Shalu Monastery, Tibet (photo: Lionel Fournier)

mural paintings by Kyentse (*mkhyen brtse*), one of the most famous painters in Tibetan history.[21] In one mural a cavalier wears a Tibetan helmet and an armor made of interlocking Y-shaped scales and carries a round shield dramatically decorated with the mask of a fierce guardian deity (fig. 36).[22]

The liturgies for the wrathful protective deities wearing armor became more developed during the thirteenth–fourteenth century. Let us examine, for example, the description for Begtse (*beg tse*) written by an early fourteenth-century teacher at Shalu: "You the youth of *bse*, whose body has the red color of rituals of power, your hair is always

Fig. 37. The oracle of the deity Balung Choje, photographed at Yongning by Joseph F. Rock in 1928 (photo: National Geographic Image Collection)

Fig. 36. Kyentse, wall painting depicting one of Vaisravana's eight horsemen, late 15th century. H. of detail shown approx. 9⅞ in. (25 cm). Gongkar Monastery, Tibet (photo: the author, 2005)

tied back, you wear copper armor (*zangs kyi beg tse*), you carry a copper knife in your right hand, you carry a heart and lungs in your left hand, your body gleams with shine and radiance (*byin pa*). . . ."[23] Later in the same ritual we read: "You the protector who wears the copper armor (*zangs kyi beg tse*), your red hair is always tied back, on your body you have the copper breastplate (*zangs kyi ral kha*). You have copper arrows and copper bow in [a quiver] of tiger skin (*zangs mda' zangs gzhu stag chad brgyan*). In your right hand you wield the sharp copper knife (*zangs gri rnon po*), in the left you hold the spear of red leather (*bse mdung dmar po*)." In comparison with the iconography of *beg tse* seen in an eighteenth-century Tibetan painting, there is close correspondence between the weapons and armor described and the artistic representation of the principal deity (fig. 31). The major distinction is the entourage of the deity, which grew over time to include not only eight young men wielding knives, but also twenty-one armored warriors.

Fig. 38. Mahakala with Lhamo and attendants, dated by inscription 1292. Stone. Collection of Lionel Fournier (photo: Lionel Fournier). Lhamo with her scorpion-handle sword is depicted at the lower right

disks worn by the deities (fig. 37). The large and heavy helmet worn by the oracle is a symbol of the supernatural powers manifest in the medium during a trance, when the medium is possessed by the protective oracular deity. The weight of such a helmet is so great that assistance is needed to put it on, but the oracle then wears it with great aplomb during his trance. The physical force of such trances is tremendous, for the oracles repeatedly perform feats such as twisting iron swords with their bare hands. Such exertion is inevitably followed by an extreme state of exhaustion and collapse. The power attributed to the oracle and the protective deity in armor and helmet manifested through the oracle gradually led to recognition of this deity as one of the two principal protective deities of the government.

The Glorious Goddess Lhamo is the other principal protective deity of the Tibetan government. Lhamo is a wrathful deity who is female. Her cult was introduced to Tibet from India, where she is associated with Mahakala, one of the major Indian Buddhist protective deities. The earliest extant representation of Lhamo is found on a stone statue inscribed with a dedication after it was carved in 1292 (fig. 38). At the center we see Mahakala, the epitome of an Indian protective deity, who is represented as a stout, robust creature. His grimace emphasizes his fangs and ferocious expression. He is crowned and adorned with much jewelry and is essentially dressed in bone ornaments and a short loincloth of tiger skin. He holds a club and a skull cup, and he crushes a Hindu deity underfoot. He is surrounded by several attendants, three fierce male protective deities and Lhamo. She is without armor, nude save for bone ornaments and a short skirt. A female wrathful deity whose weapons and powers have made her protector deity of the Dalai Lama and the Tibetan government, she is depicted carrying an Indian ritual scepter (*khatvanga*), a lance, a skull cup, and a very special sword that has a scorpion handle. In Tibetan medical and religious traditions, the scorpion is esteemed for both its curative and its coercive powers. The holder of a sword with a scorpion hilt is a wielder of power, immune to the venom of the scorpion and even capable of using the scorpion as a weapon in addition to the sword blade. The scorpion sword thus reminds us that in Tibetan Buddhism weapons are conceived not just for their potential for violence against enemies, but also for the intent of their aggressive characteristics in defense of Buddhism against enemies.[24] Yet, since the enemies of the Buddhist doctrine are any and all pernicious elements that prevent good concentration and ethical behavior, these weapons and the deities who wield them ultimately represent the Buddhist ideal of mental discipline, the taming and pacification of the mind for the benefit of humanity.

The arms and weapons of Tibetan warrior deities were subject to the same metamorphoses over time as Tibetan society itself. The military and expansionist ideals promoted by the Tsenpo to bring well-

As of 1642, the Fifth Dalai Lama had reorganized the Tibetan government with Lhasa as capital and his role as the supreme secular and religious authority in Tibet. He codified rituals for deities as protectors of the government, as the institution of theocratic government was developing its protocol, which included a new emphasis on the cult of certain oracle deities who were dressed in elaborate helmets and armor as they gave pronouncements for the policies of the state for the coming year. As may be seen in a 1928 photograph of an oracle in Yongning, there is a strong resemblance between some oracle helmets and the helmets seen in depictions of the wrathful deities and also between the "breastplate" worn by the oracles and the similar pectoral

being in a terrestrial paradise were replaced by the Buddhist ideals of compassion, serenity, and liberation from suffering. To achieve these goals, the individual must seek to conquer the obstacles of ignorance, passion, and delusion. The metaphor of the sword, for example, is to cut through the clouds of ignorance. This is how Tibetans conceive their warrior deities, who wear armor and wield their weapons to protect and preserve Buddhist teachings.

1. This essay concentrates on the iconography of protective deities as developed in Tibet principally by adherents of the Buddhist religion. Some Tibetans also practice the Bon religion, in which the role and iconography of protective deities are largely analogous with Buddhism. The cult devoted to mountain deities is common to both religions as practiced in Tibet.

2. This quotation is from a manuscript from Dunhuang, Bibliothèque Nationale de France, Paris, Fonds Pelliot tibétain, no. 216, as well as a Tibetan inscription carved in stone ca. A.D. 816 at the tomb of one of the Tibetan kings. It is cited in Ariane Macdonald, "Une lecture des Pelliot tibétain 1286, 1287, 1038, 1047 et 1290: Essai sur la formation et l'emploi des mythes politiques dans la religion royale de Srong btsan sgam po," in *Études tibétaines dédiées à la mémoire de Marcelle Lalou* (Paris, 1971), pp. 338–39.

3. Richardson 1985, p. 88.

4. Richardson (1985, pp. 109–11) discussed the terms of this treaty signed between Tibet and China in A.D. 822, of which the text was carved on a stone stele that still stands today in front of the Potala in Lhasa.

5. Nebesky-Wojkowitz 1975, p. 411.

6. These deities identified as protectors of mountains are represented as armed warriors, dressed either in armor or in Tibetan robes. Eventually their cult was integrated into Tibetan Buddhist practices.

7. This quotation is from the tomb inscription stele of Trisong Detsen (*khri srong lde btsan*), ca. A.D. 816, ll. 3–6, as translated in Richardson 1985, pp. 86–87, 88–89, with amendments by the author.

8. Armor segments were excavated from Tibetan tombs in northeast Tibet, in what is now Qinghai Province; they are illustrated as drawings in the research published by Xu Xinguo, chief archaeologist and deputy director of Qinghai Province Archaeological Institute, Xining, "A Conclusion [An Analysis] of Gold and Silver-Plating Vessels Found in Tubo Tombs in Dulan belong to Sogdi System," *Zhongguo Zang Xue / China Tibetology*, no. 4 (1994), pp. 31–45.

9. The sacrificial burial of one hundred horses at the tomb of the great general is discussed in the old *Tibetan Chronicle* (BNF Pelliot tibétain, no. 1287, ll. 264–74). In recent excavations, Chinese archaeologists studied an 8th-century Tibetan tomb with eighty-seven horse skeletons arranged in five trenches in front of the tomb in Dulan, now in Qinghai Province. See Xu Xinguo, "An Investigation of Tubo Sacrificial Burial Practices," edited and translated from Chinese by Susan Dewar and Bruce Doar, *China Archaeology and Art Digest*, no. 3 (December 1996), p. 15; Amy Heller, "Some Preliminary Remarks on the Excavations at Dulan," *Orientations* 29 (October 1998), pp. 84–92; and Amy Heller, "Archeology of Funeral Rituals as Revealed by Tibetan Tombs of the 8th to 9th Century," in Matteo Compareti et al., eds., *Webfestschrift Marshak: Ērān ud Anērān. Studies Presented to Boris Ilich Marshak on the Occasion of His 70th Birthday* (electronic version, Buenos Aires, 2004), http://www.transoxiana.com.ar/Eran/Articles/heller.html (print version, Venice: Cafoscarina, forthcoming).

10. For the history of Chinese bridge construction and the strategic advantage gained by the Tibetans due to their metallurgical skills, see Backus 1981, p. 28 and n. 79.

11. See Dunhuang cave 159 for paintings of the Tsenpo and his entourage with such garments, for example as illustrated in Duan Wenjie et al., eds., *Les fresques de Dunhuang*, vol. 15 of *5000 ans d'art chinois* (Brussels, 1989), pls. 110–12.

12. See Dunhuang cave 231 for mural paintings of the Tsenpo and entourage, a tiger-skin cloak and leopard pelt draped over the Tsenpo's garments, and a long sword suspended from the waist, reaching below the knee. In the same cave, another person of the royal entourage has a wide lapel of leopard pelt and crisscrossed short knives retained in the belt, with several pointed implements suspended from the waist. Cave 360 has a painting of the Tsenpo with a sword in scabbard draped from a leather strap with metal plaques over his shoulder; the sword hangs at knee level, and the pommel of the sword is clearly delineated. In cave 454, the Tsenpo again has tiger-skin trim on garments and five pointed implements suspended from the belt.

13. *Tibetan Chronicle,* BNF Pelliot tibétain, no. 1287, "'ung nas lo ngam gyis gsol pa / de ltar myi gnang na / lha'i dkor mdung rang 'debs dang / ral gyi rang gcod dang / khrab rang gyon dang / phub rang bzur la scogs pa / 'phrul gyi dkor ched po mnga' ba'i rnams bdag la scol na phod ces gsol to." See Bacot et al. 1946, pp. 97, 124, for Tibetan text and French translation; English translation by the author.

14. See, for instance, the definitions under *bse, bse ko, bse khrab,* and *ko bse* in the *bod rgya*. Rhinoceroses are not indigenous to Tibet; it is probable that this definition was given to refer to the hard and resistant quality of the leather rather than the actual animal, although the Chinese Annals of the Sung dynasty record that the Dali kingdom (modern Yunnan) sent rhinoceros-hide armor as tribute; citation in Schafer 1963, p. 230.

15. Ibid., p. 260.

16. Demiéville 1987, pp. 202–3; also cited in Schafer 1963, p. 260.

17. Demiéville 1987, p. 375.

18. Amy Heller, "Étude sur le développement de l'iconographie et du culte de Begce, divinité protectrice tibétaine" (diss., École Pratique des Hautes Études, IVe Section [Histoire et philologie tibétaines], Sorbonne, Paris, 1992), pp. 23–28.

19. Personal communication during visit by the author to Shalu in 1995, 1996, and 1999.

20. See Vitali 1990, p. 109.

21. See Jackson 1996, chap. 4.

22. Another rider in the same mural wears a lamellar armor with pendant lappets at the base of the skirt, just as actual armors have. I am grateful to Donald LaRocca for pointing out this last feature to me.

23. Written by dpal ldan seng ge, a teacher of Buston (bu ston rin chen grub, 1290–1364, abbot of Shalu), this description was included in a 16th-century ritual anthology compiled by tshar chen blo gsal rgya mtsho, *Beg tse be'u bum (Gnod sbyin Beg gdong lcam sring gi chos skor yongs su tshan ba) / A Collection of Highly Esoteric Teachings for the Propitiation of the Yaska Begtse and His Retinue* (Losar, Himachal Pradesh, 1978), pp. 122–28.

24. Heller 1997.

THE GONKHANG, TEMPLE OF THE GUARDIAN DEITIES

LOZANG JAMSPAL

Most of the ancient swords and armor that once existed in Tibet no longer survive. The majority of what remains has been preserved in gonkhang (*mgon khang*), the temples or chapels specifically devoted to protector or guardian deities. These temples are still found throughout Tibet and in neighboring countries with culturally Tibetan regions, such as Ladakh, Sikkim, Nepal, and Bhutan. Armor and weapons are used in gonkhang to decorate the temple and to show the fearsome dignity of the wrathful deity to whom the gonkhang is dedicated.

In order to remove obstacles and to aid in the accomplishment of personal goals, ordinary people often go to a gonkhang to supplicate a protector deity. It is a popular practice for both Buddhists and Hindus to seek assistance in this way from a protector deity, who is often one of the lower-ranking deities in a greater temple complex. For instance, it is still common for many Hindu men and women to visit the gonkhang devoted to Yamantaka in Spituk (*dpe thub*) Monastery, which is located near the airport in Leh, the capital of Ladakh.

Almost every Tibetan monastery has a gonkhang for a protector deity, who is seen as the overall guardian of the monastery, capable of helping with the accomplishment of goals, and whose presence also protects property from being stolen. People commonly believe that if they act badly or steal from others, especially things belonging to the monastery, the protector deity will punish them. Therefore, in the monastery people often pay more attention to the protector deity in the gonkhang than to the Three Jewels. Buddhists traditionally take refuge in the Three Jewels—Buddha (the Enlightened One), Dharma (his teaching), and Samgha (the spiritual community). In principle, this precludes seeking refuge in any deity, though the Buddha did teach that the practitioner could take refuge in oneself, as described in the following verse:

One is the protector of oneself,
Who other would become the protector?
When oneself is well disciplined,
Then one can achieve a rare protectorship.[1]

Although some thoughtful Buddhists take refuge only in the Three Jewels, the needs of average people have dictated that protector spirits be accorded a place even in the great Buddhist monasteries, where they receive offerings from devoted monks and lay people alike. This reflects the Buddhist practice of integrating local customs and adopting local spirits or deities. Padmasambhava, who introduced Buddhism to Tibet in the eighth century A.D., transformed many aboriginal shamanistic spirits into Buddhist protector deities.

In Tibetan monasteries the gonkhang is considered the place where the protector spirits live. As an illustration of a gonkhang I would like to describe that of Likir Monastery in Ladakh, where I was a novice monk from 1944 to 1949, and where I witnessed many rituals regarding the protector deities during those years. Likir is located in a lovely valley two and half miles long and half a mile wide, surrounded by high rocky mountains topped by snow or glaciers. The monastery is situated on a rocky hill, looming up in the middle of the valley (fig. 39). It is a beautiful place, especially in July and August, but it is very cold in the winter.

The outside of the gonkhang of Likir Monastery is painted the traditional reddish brown with ocher, contrasting with the white paint used on the other buildings, as is typical of Tibetan construction. The inside of the Likir gonkhang is small, approximately 20 by 15 feet (fig. 40), and is arrayed with stucco images of several deities, such as Vajrabhairava, Six-Handed Mahakala together with his retinue, Yama Dharmaraja, Shrikalidevi, and Vaisravana. The main protector of the monastery is *chos skyong bse khrab pa* (literally, dharma protector with rhinoceros-hide armor), who is represented by a small image that was brought back from central Tibet long ago. This statue, made of sandalwood painted gold, is considered very powerful. During most of

Fig. 39. Likir Monastery seen from a hill behind the monastery, July 2003 (photo: Donald J. LaRocca)

Fig. 40. The interior of the gonkhang at Likir, July 2003 (photo: Donald J. LaRocca)

the year the statues of the protectors are concealed by colorful silk curtains, which are opened only during the monastery's annual festival. Many white silk scarves, or *khatas* (*kha btags*), hang from the pillars and railings of the gonkhang, offerings left by villagers and visitors to the monastery. Traditionally women are prohibited from entering a gonkhang, although nowadays this custom has been relaxed, especially in the case of foreign visitors.

The main pillar of the gonkhang is surrounded with ancient swords and guns, as is the custom in many gonkhang. I also recall swords and guns arranged like this in the gonkhang of the *dpe thub khang tshan* (Spituk monastic house) in Tashilhunpo (*bkra shis lhun po*) Monastery in Shigatse, Tibet, where I lived as a monk from 1950 to 1957. Among these were the sword and gun that belonged to Nono Bsodnams of Basgo village, who is regarded as a hero and a great patriot by the people of Ladakh.[2] The gonkhang and the images of protector deities in it are purposely made to have a fearsome appearance to scare wicked people. This way many crimes are prevented simply by a person's fear of the protectors in the gonkhang.

Every morning in the gonkhang the temple manager (*dkon gnyer*) arranges several bowls of freshwater offerings (*yon chab*) in addition to butter lamps (*mar me*), offering cakes (*gtor ma*), and incense (*spos*). Following this he consecrates the offerings with incense smoke while repeating the mantra OM AH HUNG three times. Next the temple manager chants for several hours, accompanied by the sounds of a ritual drum, bell, and cymbals. Also, for special purposes or on special days, offerings are made with food, drinks, lamps, flowers, burning incense, drums, cymbals, and trumpets, with chanting of ritual prayers by a group of monks or by a single monk.

SUPPLICATIONS: *BSKANG GSO* AND *'PHRIN BCOL*

There are two types of supplication: *bskang gso* (amending and restoring) and *'phrin bcol* (supplication for help). *bskang gso* is a very colorful ceremonial ritual to propitiate the guardian deities, which involves elaborate offerings of *gtor ma*. The monks conduct the ritual chants and play musical instruments, including drums, cymbals, bells, trumpets, and *rgya gling* (a type of trumpet), almost like a concert. This *bskang gso* ritual is performed once a year in the gonkhang of Likir Monastery and involves many monks. Special *gtor ma*, which will last one year and are called *lo gtor*, are made during this time. Then the caretaker monk of the gonkhang, using the *lo gtor* offerings, performs a reduced version of the *bskang gso* daily at three or four in the morning.

People will sometimes ask a monk to perform the *'phrin bcol* supplication to the deity in the gonkhang before they conduct important business or for similar situations. Shorter and with less elaborate offerings than *bskang gso*, this ritual is performed for the general achievement of success or removing of obstacles. People individually or as a group can request that this ritual be done by the caretaker of the gonkhang, who may either perform the ritual alone or invite other monks to participate.

THE *GTOR MAR MA*

The *gtor mar ma* (offering cakes decorated with butter) have different shapes and colors for each deity. The butter ornaments can be very elaborate depending on the skill of the *gtor ma* makers and the time involved. In the *bskang gso* ritual Vajrabhairava's *gtor ma* is placed in the center of the altar; next to it on the right is the *gtor ma* of Mahakala, then those of other deities, and last that of *bse khrab pa*. To the left of Vajrabhairava's *gtor ma* is that of *dam can chos rgyal* (literally, pledge holder dharma king), followed by others, with the last being the *gtor ma* of Neser Jowo chenpo (*ne ser jo bo chen po*). The preparation and placement of the *gtor ma* for these rituals must be learned by observation, which is called *mthong ba brgyud pa'i nyams len* (traditional practice by watching). The substances used in the preparation of the *gtor ma* for the *bskang gso* ritual are *rtsam pa* (flour of parched barley), *chang* (fermented liquor usually made of barley), butter, *'bri mog* (a kind of herb root that grows in the mountains, which is boiled in ghee and used to dye the *gtor ma*), and *bdud rtsi ril bu* (ambrosia pills, which are made of substances that represent the "five types of flesh" [*sha lnga*] transformed into ambrosia by the meditation mantra).[3]

From this point on I would like to focus on two deities, *chos skyong bse khrab pa* and Mahakala (see figs. 41, 42). The first, *bse khrab pa*, is the principal protector of Likir Monastery. Although some traditions hold that he came from India, there is no evidence to support this belief. In addition he is always portrayed in the dress of an ancient Tibetan warlord rather than in Indian costume. Mahakala was popular in India and Nepal for as many as a thousand years before being introduced into Tibet. He is usually depicted in Indian dress. Generally people seem to consider a deity who originated in India as higher in rank than indigenous Tibetan deities. In Likir Monastery during the *bskang gso* ceremony, people commonly assume that they are mainly propitiating *bse khrab pa*, but since Mahakala is ranked as the highest protector deity, the part of the ritual devoted to him comes first, followed by that for

Fig. 41. Dorje Setrap (*rdo rje bse khrab*) tangka, Tibetan, 19th century. Ground mineral pigment on cotton, 26¾ x 16¾ in. (68 x 42.6 cm). Collection of Shelley and Donald Rubin (P1999.13.4) (photo: Himalayan Art Resources [HAR 845], www.himalayanart.org)

the other deities, with the ritual for *bse khrab pa* almost last except for one local deity whose ritual the monks do at the end.

CHOS SKYONG BSE KHRAB PA, THE DHARMA PROTECTOR WITH ARMOR OF RHINOCEROS HIDE

The following passages give some glimpse of the meaning of the ritual chants used in propitiation of *chos skyong bse khrab pa*:

Everything turns into emptiness; from the state of emptiness in front of me there arises a red lucid ocean of blood. Upon this ocean, from the seed-syllable E in the center of a blazing blue-black dharmodaya *(source of all phenomena), arises a sun disk upon a lotus, and upon it the body of the obstacle enemy (dgra bgegs). Upon this there is the seed-syllable HRI, which transforms into a great club marked by letters HRI. From it rays of light spread, subjugating all harmful enemies; the rays of light then return. The rays of light transform into the great royal spirit* bse khrab pa. *The complexion of* bse khrab pa *is red; he has three round red eyes. He has fearsome wrinkles gathered between the eyebrows. His teeth and fangs are white like a snow mountain, pressing upon the lower lip. From the club in his right hand an emanation army spreads. His threatening left hand, upon the chest, holds a lasso (zhags) to tie obstacle enemies. Under his left arm he carries a blazing red spear (mdung dmar) with a billowing flag. Upon his head is a helmet made of hide (bse rmog), adorned with a victory banner and martial flags made of silk. He wears a red silk garment (tsi ber) and upon it armor made of hide (bse khrab). At the waist he wears a beautiful quiver of leopard skin (stag gdong gzig shubs) and sword (ral gri). He is mounted on an excellent bronze-colored horse with a saddle and bridle trimmed with silk chevron pendants; an excellent horse adorned with armor of hide (bse khrab) to its white fetlocks and jewels at the top. For amusement he is accompanied by a tame red rooster.*[4]

Then the propitiators chant with melody in meditation, saying:

Rays of light spread from the seed syllable at the front of my heart, [inviting] from the natural place the chos skyong *deity together with his retinue. [Say] VAJRASAMAJA; thus one should visualize the arrival.*

From the divine sublime palace, and
The red boulder resembling a wrathful monster,
The great wild king bse khrab pa,
Together with the retinue, please come here.[5]

Say JAH HUNG BAM HO and think of the visualized image deity and the wisdom deity as non-dual.

*In the state of emptiness, who is not different from the Lord Amitayus and unmoved, but manifested as furious body to tame the wicked ones; I bow down to this Red Spirit (*bse khrab pa).[6]

MAKING OFFERINGS OF WEAPONS TO THE PROTECTOR

During *lo gsar* (new year celebration) propitiators offer the deity *bse khrab pa* a horse, a yak, and a dog, which are named as *mgon rta, mgon g.yag, mgon khyi*, respectively. They also make offerings of weapons and various instruments. In this way some swords and guns were deposited in the temple of the protector deity.

HUNG
With this magnificent club made of sandalwood
Brought from the Malaya forest of India,
To tame the three doors[7] *of the demons*
That spread as an army of millions,
*I offer this to the hand of the great Dharma Protector (*chos skyong).

Please accept this, then
Please crush and destroy into dust
The obstacles and hating enemies
Of the jewel of teaching [of the Buddha], and
Of me, the propitiator, together with their army,
Please do this enlightened action.

This lasso, made of material mixed with human hair,
Praised for binding instantly the army of wicked enemies,
I offer this to the hand of the great Dharma Protector.
Please accept this, then
Tie and bind them,
Please act to destroy them.

This sword, made of iron, endowed with sharpness and well tempered,
With flapping streamers of glimmering red silk beautifully dangling,
Afflicting the heart of the evil allied ones,
I offer this to the hand of the great Dharma Protector.
Please accept this, then
Eliminate them [the evils] and destroy [those who do harm].

By merely touching, it can destroy even Mount Sumeru,
This bow and arrow, the integration of skillful means and wisdom,
The weapon piercing all who do harm
I offer this to the hands of the great Dharma Protector.
Please accept this, then
Grind them to dust, and destroy [the evildoers].

This blazing sword of wisdom, tearing the eggshell of ignorance,
Beheading the evil which hates the Buddha's teaching and living beings,
I offer this to the hands of the great Dharma Protector.
Please crush into dust and destroy
The obstacles and hating enemies
Of me, the propitiator, together with their armies.
Please do this action.[8]

Religious Dances ('chams) of bse khrab pa

Likir Monastery has a *mdos mo che* festival once a year in the wintertime on the twenty-seventh, twenty-eighth, and twenty-ninth days of the twelfth lunar month of the Tibetan calendar, during which various *'chams* (religious dances) are performed.[9] On the twenty-eighth day the *'chams* of *bse khrab pa* is performed. The dancer costumed as *bse khrab pa* is accompanied by his retinue of six emanations. Carrying a sword and a lasso in his hands and brandishing the sword, *bse khrab pa* dances. The audience pays respect and honor to him and asks him to bring favors through his spiritual dancing. Some parts of *bse khrab pa*'s retinue are played by novice monks. In this way, during the 1940s, I participated in the *bse khrab pa 'chams* and was able to experience the dance as a member of the deity's retinue.

Divination by Means of bse khrab pa

Virtually all the monks and lay people of the Likir valley have sought the advice of *bse khrab pa*, the chief deity of the gonkhang. Especially when the monks cannot reach a decision on an important issue, they ask the advice of the protector *bse khrab pa*. I witnessed several cases of this. In one instance, in 1948 during the India-Pakistan War, the monks of Likir Monastery heard that Pakistani insurgents would attack Ladakh. Six months before the soldiers arrived at Likir, the monks had to decide where they should hide the monastery's valuable ritual objects in order to protect them from possible theft by the insurgents. They asked *bse khrab pa* whether they should hide them inside or outside the monastery. To do this the monks wrote the words "inside" and "outside" on strips of paper, folded them, and put them inside balls of dough of equal size, which were placed in a Chinese porcelain vessel with a long handle at the bottom. Holding this long handle, the abbot of the monastery made a circling motion until one of the balls flew out of the vessel. The monks would accept the word inside that ball as the deity's decision. On this occasion the *brtag ril* (rounding divination) gave the answer as "inside." The monks then hid the very precious religious objects inside the monastery in a chamber below the gonkhang. Although Pakistani insurgents remained at the monastery for about two months, they never found the chamber, and so the religious objects that had been hidden according to the rounding divination of the monastery's protector, *chos skyong bse khrab pa*, were preserved intact.

The Six-Armed Mahakala (mgon po phyag drug pa)

From the earliest period when protector deities were worshipped in the monasteries of Tibet, the deity Mahakala (also called *nag po chen po* or *mgon po* in Tibetan) was the principal protector deity. From his

Fig. 42. Mahakala *tangka*, Tibetan, early 18th century. Distemper on cloth, 83⅜ x 57¾ in. (211.8 x 146.7 cm). The Metropolitan Museum of Art, New York, Purchase, Florance Waterbury Bequest, 1969 (69.72)

Tibetan name *mgon po* (literally, guardian), the term gonkhang (*mgon khang*) was derived, literally meaning "house of Mahakala" or "house of the guardian." This became the term for all temples of protector deities. Mahakala is still respected as the oldest deity in Tibet and is considered an emanation of Avalokiteshara, the deity of compassion. The formula for the meditative evocation of Mahakala is as follows:

OM SVABHAVA SHUDDHA SARVADARMA SVABHA SHUDDHO' HAM

From the state of emptiness rises the syllable HUNG, and inside that a protecting mandala, and from inside this rises a dreadful and great cemetery, from which there rises the syllable PAM, and from that rises the universal lotus. Upon it, from the syllable RAM arises a cushion blazing like the sun; upon it is the white syllable GAM, which melts into light, and from it rises the white elephant-headed, three-eyed Lord Ganesha. With his right hand he is eating a radish with its leaves, which symbolizes the essence of the earth; in his left hand is a mongoose vomiting jewels. Ganesha is lying down, adorned with silk and jewels; from his mouth, pores, ears, and other bodily openings jewels rain forth. Upon him, from the syllable HUNG, there rises the hooked knife with a vajra handle (rdo rje gri gug) marked by a blue-black HUNG. Then rays of lights spread out from it eradicating all the wicked enemy obstacles. Worshipped by all the noble ones, it benefits sentient beings [Buddhas and Bodhisattvas]. Then the rays of light are absorbed within the vajra-handled hooked knife. Through the transmutation of this, the Six-Armed Lord of Intuition Mahakala is quick to respond and fulfill all the wishes of living beings. His complexion is very black, like the cloud at the end of the eon. With one face and six arms, gazing wrathfully with his three round red eyes, his mouth is open, showing fanglike teeth and his rolling tongue, inwardly agitated showing his furious power and his face with a severe smile. The hairs of his dark brown moustache and eyebrows, and the hair on his head are standing up. His forehead is anointed with a drop of sindhura. On his crown sits Akshobhya Buddha, holding a hooked knife with a vajra handle; his left hand holds a skull cup, which is full of the blood and the flesh of the obstacle enemy. Below the skull cup and sickle, his right hand rests upon the skull. The middle right hand holds a garland of dried skulls; the last right hand vigorously plays the damaru (drum). The second left hand holds a trident; the last left hand holds a black noose. With his two feet that are equal to the power of the three worlds he crushes and suppresses the King of the Demons. His lower garment is a tiger skin which is tied with a belt made of green silk. He is adorned with snakes and a blue snake is tied in his hair. He wears a red ring, an arm ornament of many colors, a white necklace on his breast, yellow bracelets, a green necklace on his throat, white anklets, and a white girdle. All his hands and feet have tinkling garlands. He is stocky with a full belly. His limbs are very strong. He has infinite radiance which is difficult to endure. His head ornament is five dried skulls. He is adorned with a necklace of fifty wet skulls dripping blood, six bone ornaments, and a jeweled crown. He makes dreadful sounds, like thundering HA HA and HUNG PHAT PHAT. Through these sounds he eradicates all the wicked obstacle-making enemies. He sits, leaning on the sandalwood tree, in the middle of the blazing fire of intuition, which is like the fire at the end of the eon.[10]

This visualized image is called "pledged one" (dam tshig pa). When the propitiator invites the wisdom being of Mahakala, the ritual chanting is as follows:

Please get up, please get up from the sphere of reality. Although you [Mahakala] do not move from the state of the pure sphere of reality, you have shown your wrathful body in order to subdue the wicked ones. I [the practitioner] invite the great deity Mahakala. To the blessed Black One, please come, the god who conquers the enemies of yogis, please come, to the Vidyadhara guardians, please come, to the Black Field Protector (Sanskrit kshetrapala, Tibetan zhing skyong nag po), please come.[11]

The practitioner, saying VAJRASAMAJA, visualizes the wisdom spirit absorbed into the pledged image, drawing, or painting, and says:

HUNG
Having made pledges in the presence of Vajradhara, please sit in this blessed place in order to protect the Buddha's teachings. JA HUNG BAM HO dissolve without being two [as pledged and wisdom beings].[12]

A short sample of the supplication of Mahakala:

HUNG
I entertain Mahakala and your retinue,
The Quick Responder, and your retinue. I fulfill the lacking ones and
I also renovate that which is broken. I purge all guilt and all mental enmity.

I entertain lord Mahakala and [your] retinue
With the yak and sheep that have horns of meteors, tongues of
    lightning, thick hairs bursting like black clouds.

I entertain lord Makahkala and [your] retinue with an arrow made of flexible bamboo, which is adorned with the feathers of vultures, a point made of meteoric iron, and which has a moving crown of black silk.

I entertain lord Mahakala and [your] retinue with the red heart of the enemy, pulled out by hand, who is very bad to the teachings of the Buddha, filled with the essence of precious medicinal grain offerings.

I entertain lord Mahakala and [your] retinue with the certain belief in the lama, the embodiment of the Three Jewels and the Lord Quick Responder are no different.

I entertain Mahakala together with your retinue with this infinite red offering cake built up like a mountain, drink and rakta (red drink) filled up like an ocean, actually prepared and emanated by mind.

I entertain you by fulfilling your wish. You should accomplish those tasks that I ask.

When I approach you, do not be distant; when I call you, do not turn a deaf ear; when I propitiate you, do not be indifferent; when I wave at you, do not close your eyes; when I send you somewhere, do not be slow; when I approach you as Lord, do not be overpowering; when I approach you as friend, do not be bad natured; when I approach you as acquaintance, do not be shameless; when I approach you like a mother, do not be hard-hearted; when I approach you like a sister, do not have bad feelings; when I approach you like a servant, do not be distant in your heart.

I give you a reward for your previous actions on my behalf. I give you food for your present actions; and for your future actions I offer you drink. May I fulfill a spiritual wish, please accomplish the activities that I ask.[13]

A popular story recounted by the Tibetan monk Dharmasvami (*chos rje chag lotsawa*, 1197–1264) tells of how he and his elderly teacher were protected by Mahakala from marauding Muslim troops who were pillaging the ruins of Nalanda Monastery in Bihar, northern India, about 1234.[14] Mahakala Natha was for many centuries the protector of the great Nalanda Monastery, where there was a stone statue of four-handed Mahakala larger than human size. During many years of devotion people had applied oils to it, turning it a blue-gray color. The stomach area was worn smooth because people touched their foreheads to this spot to get blessings. The stone image looked like dough made of green peas. Its legend tells that it was self-created, having manifested to Nagarjuna in the Shitavana forest, and was taken to Nalanda. This protector was very popular. When Nalanda was being sacked by Muslim forces, an officer of the invaders personally desecrated the temple altar and ordered his army to destroy the temple and to take all the stone to build a fort in Odantapuri, which was a day's journey on foot from Nalanda. That very evening the officer died of appendicitis, after which the frightened troops did not dare even to go near the temple. In the ruins of the great monastery a few monks remained, along with a very learned monk who was over ninety years old, the great Guru Rahula Shribhadra. Word reached the monks that troops were coming to kill whoever remained in the monastery. The Guru Rahula told the monks to run away, saying, "I am over ninety years old and cannot run." Chaglotsapa Dharmasvami alone remained. His guru scolded him saying, "You crazy Tibetan! All the people ran away; what are you doing here? The Muslims will kill you." To which he replied, "Even if they will kill me, I cannot run away leaving my guru behind." The guru was amazed at his devotion and asked him, "Can you lift me up on your back?" Chaglotsapa lifted the guru on his back and walked around a pillar. The guru told him, "Yes, you can carry me. We will not go far away. I have a plan." Chaglotsapa carried the guru on his back, along with some sugarcane, rice, and important books. They went to the Mahakala temple in accordance with the guru's instructions. While the guru and his disciple were hiding in the gonkhang, about three hundred armed soldiers came and searched Nalanda but found no one. Thus, because of their devotion to Mahakala Natha, the Guru Rahula Shribhadra and Chaglotsapa escaped violent deaths.

This is just one illustration of the belief, still strongly held by many, in the protective powers of the gonkhang and its guardian deities, which are perpetuated through rituals, offerings, and other devotional activities such as those described above.

1. See chapter 12, gatha 4, of the Tibetan text, *chos kyi tshigs su bcad pa* (translated by Gedun Chomphel [*dge 'dun chos 'phel*] [Gantok, 1946]), which corresponds to verse (gatha) 160 of Dhammapada (*Dhammapada*, edited by Bhiksu Dharmaraksita [Delhi, 1977]). The English translations of the Tibetan quoted here are my own.

2. Nono Bsodnams was forced to join the army of General Zorawar Singh to invade Tibet in 1841. The general was killed and most of his army of ten thousand died owing to the severe cold. In the course of the war Nono Bsodnams aided the Tibetans against Zorawar Singh, for which his sword and gun were not confiscated afterward by the Tibetan gorvenment. Alexander Cunningham, who visited Ladakh in 1847 and wrote of its history (*Ladak: Physical, Statistical, and Historical, with Notices of Surrounding Countries* [London, 1854]), was apparently unaware of this story. It is also said that Nono Bsodnams became a confidant of the Seventh Panchen Lama, *bstan pa'i nyi ma* (1781–1853), because of his service to the Tibetan army in the war.

3. The five types of flesh (*sha lnga*) are human flesh (*mi sha*), cow flesh (*ba glang sha*), dog flesh (*khyi sha*), elephant flesh (*glang sha*), and horse flesh (*rta sha*).

4. *chos skyong chen po bse khrab can sgrub thabs rgyas par bshad pa 'phrin las dngos grub kyi bang mdzod*, by brag g.yab blo bzang bstan pa (1683–1739), lithographed edition, India, 1965, fol. 7.

5. Ibid., fol. 9b.

6. Ibid., fol. 12a.

7. The body, speech, and mind.

8. *chos skyong chen po bse khrab can sgrub thabs rgyas par bshad pa 'phrin las dngos grub kyi bang mdzod*, fols. 21b, 22b.

9. The *mdos mo che* is a ceremony wherein an effigy of demons is burned together with thread cross decorations in order to remove obstacles.

10. *dpal ye shes kyi mgon po phyag drug pa'i sgrub thabs gtor ma'i chog ga dang bcas pa 'phrin las gter mdzod*, by Jo nang Taranatha (1575–1635), photo offset of the manuscript, India, late 20th century, fols. 3b–5b.

11. Ibid., fols. 10a–10b.

12. Ibid., fol. 13a.

13. Ibid., fols. 24b, 25b.

14. The Tibetan text *chag lo tsa ba'i rnam thar*, written by ju ba chos dar, was edited and translated into English in Roerich 1959, pp. 90ff.

བྱང་བུའི་ཁྲབ་དང་རྨོག
Lamellar Armor and Helmets

The term "lamellar armor" refers to a type of armor made up of horizontal rows of small overlapping plates joined by leather lacing. The individual plates are referred to as lamella (singular) and lamellae (plural), literally meaning thin plates or layers, from which the adjectival form lamellar is derived. In Tibetan the lamellae are referred to as *byang bu*, a general term for a small label, card, or flat object of rectangular shape. It is used to modify the Tibetan word for armor, *khrab*, giving the term *byang bu'i khrab*, for which the best English equivalent is lamellar armor. The basic features that distinguish lamellar armor from other forms also made up of small plates, such as scale armor or brigandines, are that the lamellae are supported by being laced only to one another rather than to a lining or support material of any kind, and that the rows of lamellae overlap upward. Lamellae were made of rawhide, bronze, and iron. Lamellar armor, in various forms, had an extremely long history over a widespread area, from East Asia to Europe, perhaps originating in the ancient Near East as early as the eighth century B.C. Most of the evidence about its development is provided by archaeological finds, which show that iron lamellae were known in China as early as the third century B.C., in Central Asia probably around the same time, and in western Europe by the fifth or sixth century A.D.[1] Lamellar armor continued to be worn, particularly in parts of Central Asia, through the Middle Ages. The lamellar armor of the Mongols, for instance, was commented on by Western travelers, such as the Franciscan friar Giovanni di Plano Carpini (ca. 1180–1252), who recorded a detailed description in 1247 of the armor he had seen on his travels among the Mongols the previous year.[2]

Given this long period of use over such a widespread geographical area, it is remarkable to note that, other than the late variants used sparingly in Siberia, the armors found in Tibet constitute the only examples of lamellar armor made of iron that do not come from an archaeological context. Equally remarkable is the fact that, having survived above ground virtually nowhere else, lamellar armor from Tibet exists, or existed, in such large numbers, dozens if not hundreds of examples still being extant at the beginning of the twentieth century.

Most Tibetan lamellar armors share several distinct features, which can be outlined here. The body of the armor has the form of a sleeveless robe and is often made from twelve to fourteen rows of lamellae, although the number varies. At present it is not known if there was a standard number of rows, what the true average might be, or if the number is indicative of a certain period, place, or style.[3] The coat has a distinct waist, usually five

or six rows down from the top, the lamellae of that row being bent inward to form a gentle curve. There is sometimes a collar consisting of a single row of shorter lamellae, and this can be lined with leather. Most armors are sleeveless, but some have shoulder defenses formed of several rows of lamellae (described in detail in the entries for cat. nos. 1–3), and one extremely rare example has full sleeves (cat. no. 1). The coat opens down the length of its front; it is closed by braided leather straps and small iron buckles, and a waist belt of the same materials, which seem to have survived on very few examples (see cat. no. 6). The back of the skirt of the armor is split vertically from the bottom row up to the waist by two seams, one at either side.

The individual lamellae are made of iron, which on some armors retain a natural silvery luster while on others they are a russet brown. The lamellae are usually rounded at the top like a fingertip and have slightly rounded corners at the base. Their sizes can vary considerably according to their placement on the armor. As with the number of rows, the size and finish of the lamellae may eventually prove to be indicative of a particular period or place. The larger lamellae are usually located on the torso area of the armor or the lower skirts and can be approximately 7–8 centimeters long by 1.5–2 centimeters wide. Smaller lamellae, near the shoulder openings and on helmets, can be approximately 3–5 centimeters long by 1.5–2.5 centimeters wide. Each lamella is pierced by a series of lacing holes, varying between six and thirteen (the average appearing to be nine), depending on the size of the lamella, its type, and sometimes on its placement. The precise and very effective lacing pattern by which the lamellae are joined together was aptly described and diagrammed by Bengt Thordeman and can be seen well in the interior and exterior details of the armor in catalogue number 6 (see endpapers):

> *The holes at one edge of a lamella cover those on the adjacent edge of the next lamella, and so on. Through adjacent pairs of holes thongs are drawn in a zigzag line in such a way that they appear vertical on the outside of the armour, but diagonal on the inside. Occasionally, even on the same armour, the lacing of the thongs is doubled so that the thongs cross each other on the inside, whereas on the outside they coincide so that their appearance remains unchanged. . . . Thongs are also drawn through the holes at the bottom, which hold the lamellae fast to each other. The thongs are pulled tight so as to form firm but flexible units. The rows, again, are loosely joined to each other, the lower one to the one immediately above; this accomplished by means of a thong which, from a single hole below the*

centre on the lamellae of the upper row, is pulled through the two holes placed in pairs in the upper end of the lamellae of the lower row, which overlaps the lower edge of the row above. The rows thus always overlap from below upwards.[4]

Some armors are trimmed with borders made of a stiff band of silk brocade or other fabric, which is attached around the bottom edge of the coat at the base of the skirts and, if they are present, at the bottom of the shoulder defenses (cat. nos. 2, 3). These borders may indicate armors of higher quality, or that the armors were refitted at some point for a particular occasion. Rather than textile borders, however, the majority of extant armors have a border at the base of the skirts consisting of two layers of leather. The inner layer is made of solid panels of leather, while the outer layer is split in a series of rectangular tabs or lappets (cat. nos. 1, 4–6). Many of these have Tibetan inscriptions in ink or black pigment, usually on the inner layer hidden beneath the lappets, written in a form of *dbu med* (a Tiben cursive script) and including sequences of numbers (cat. nos. 4–6). These may be arsenal or regimental inventory numbers, a suggestion made by H. G. Beasley in 1938, but as of yet the precise meaning of these inscriptions remains unclear.[5] In a few other instances Tibetan characters or numbers are found on other parts of the armors (cat. nos. 3, 4). Some also have as yet unidentified wax seals stamped on their interiors, which may indicate ownership by a particular monastery, fortress, or noble household. These seals have been found not only on armor for man (cat. nos. 1, 3, 9, 44–46), but also on horse armor (cat. no. 32) and archery equipment (cat. no. 96).

Virtually all Tibetan lamellar armors have what would be called "stop ribs" in European armor terminology, the function of which is to stop the point of a weapon from sliding up the lamellae and into an exposed area. These consist of short rolls of leather, about the thickness of a pencil, which are bound with a narrow leather lace in a crisscross pattern. They are attached horizontally at the edge of the top rows of lamellae at either side of the chest, just below the throat, and at the underside of the arms.

Equally distinctive helmets were made to match the lamellar armors and, like the armors, are associated only with Tibet or the Tibetan cultural region. Also like the armors, this type of helmet is constructed of iron plates joined by leather laces. The bowl of the helmet is usually made up of eight arched plates (cat. nos. 1, 2, 4, 5), but there are also examples with sixteen plates (cat. no. 3). The plates are wedge shaped and overlap in an over-under sequence, with four narrow outer plates that have cusped edges, and four wider inner plates that have smooth edges. The side edges of the outer plates usually have two shallow cusps with rounded points, although on some examples the points are much more attenuated. The outer plates also usually have a low medial ridge, while the inner plates are smooth. On some examples, however, the medial ridge of the outer plate is high and

pronounced, and the inner plates also have a medial ridge (cat. no. 3). The outer plates typically have ten lacing holes and the inner plates fourteen, but this can vary. At the bottom edge of most plates there are usually a series of small notches, which probably served as assembly marks. The tops of the inner and outer plates meet beneath the base of a plume finial, which forms the apex of the helmet, and resembles the stem and base of a footed chalice. The plume tube generally has a central lozenge-shaped knop and a flaring funnel-like top. The base is pierced with eight lacing holes arranged in four pairs of two, which are laced to corresponding holes at the tops of the four inner plates. The tops of the outer plates do not have lacing holes, but are slightly stepped to fit snugly under the base of the finial. On complete examples there is a single row of lamellae encircling the base of the helmet bowl, a pair of cheek defenses made of five to seven rows of lamellae, and a flaring nape defense of three rows (cat. nos. 1, 2, 4).

According to the Tibetan author Tashi Namgyal (*bkra shis rnam rgyal*), writing in 1524, the history of lamellar armor in Tibet was divided into three distinct periods (see the appendix "Excerpts from *A Treatise on Worldly Traditions*"). The oldest armor dated from the time of the "Righteous Kings, Uncle and Nephew," which would place it sometime during the Yarlung dynasty, early seventh to mid-ninth century.[6] Armor from the middle period began with the reign of O-sung (*'od srungs*, ca. 842–870), at the end of the dynasty, and continued until the beginning of the reign of the first Phagmodru king, Taisitu Chenpo (*ta'i si tu chen po*), or 1358. The period of new-style armor went from that point up to the time the text was written. The first period, and perhaps the starting point of the second as well, may be seen as conventional divisions in Tibetan historical writing, in which principal epochs served as convenient benchmarks for the introduction of various customs, materials, and technologies. However, the third period, which includes the writer's own lifetime, implies that lamellar armor specifically identified as Tibetan was actively in use at that point and was seen as part of a tradition with a long history in Tibet, even while its past may have been conventionalized to follow the norms of Tibetan historical writing. In a similar fashion, the Fifth Dalai Lama, writing in 1643, said that armor was first brought to Tibet from a district in Kham (*smar khams*) during the reign of the semilegendary ancient king Trigum Tsenpo (*gri gum btsan po*).[7]

Tashi Namgyal also listed a series of characteristics by which he said an expert (*mkhas pa*) should be able to differentiate between the armors of each period, which can be summarized as follows.[8] The lamellae of the armors of the old period are said to be as smooth as polished ice on the outside and like a mirror of white silver on the inside and the iron is said to be mixed with silver. The heads of the lamellae line up like rows of crystal garlands and are smooth and even to the touch. They have a fingernail shape (*sen rgyab*) that is made with a small hammer. The edges of the lamellae are smooth and even and the bottoms are evenly arranged. The lacing holes (*mig*) have smooth inner edges. The color of the iron is glossy, and because the material is equally supple and hard it is proof against cut and thrust weapons. The lamellae of the armor of the middle period are said to be evenly arranged along the top, but the sides and corners are a little sharp. They have a fingernail shape that is made by a chisel, which is a little coarse. The lacing holes are a little narrow. The file finishing is not very well done, but nevertheless the lamellae look pleasing to the eye. The lamellae of the armors of the new period are said to have heads that are rough and not attractive. The fingernail shape is weakly drawn with a chisel. The lacing holes are narrow and rough. The corners or edges are extremely sharp. The color of the iron is blue-black like lead. The finishing is not well done, so that although the lamellae are thin they are nevertheless heavy.

These characteristics appear to be a mix of poetic metaphor and actual observation and should not necessarily be taken literally or as representing a strict chronology of features. They do, however, indicate what their author perceived as a progressive deterioration in both the materials and quality of craftsmanship over time. In applying these standards to extant Tibetan lamellar armor the tendency would be to attribute examples with smoother, more silvery, and finer lamellae to an earlier period and those with darker, simpler, and larger lamellae to a later period. However, the finer armors may be earlier, or they may also represent higher-quality armor of a later period. The cruder armors may be later, or could also be less expensive armors for the rank and file, which tended to be more cheaply made than the armors of high-ranking individuals in many cultures and time periods. This uncertainty is reflected in the results of carbon-14 tests on two Tibetan lamellar armors, one with small, smooth, and finely made lamellae (private collection) and another with larger lamellae that are relatively simple and rough by comparison (cat. no. 6).[9] The tests put the two armors in largely overlapping date ranges: 1416–1649 for the armor with the small lamellae, and 1480–1660 for the armor with the larger, simpler lamellae. Therefore, while this could mean that the finer armor dates to the early fifteenth century and the simpler one to the mid-seventeenth century, it could also mean that the two may simply represent different levels of quality, which could have been made at any point within their respective time frames.

When assessing a lamellar armor, Tashi Namgyal's criteria, judgments based on assessments of quality and style, and any available scientific evidence should all be taken into consideration. Assessments involving quality and style include several features that can be taken into account, some of which follow the general lines laid out by Tashi Namgyal. First, the overall quality of the individual lamellae depends on several characteristics, such as whether their edges are smooth or rough, their contours even and in proportion, whether the plates are completely flat or slightly convex, and what the color and surface finish of the metal itself is like. The lamellae should be looked at for variation in size and whether the variation appears to follow a logical order from row to row, based on the position of the lamellae in the armor, or seems to be random. Also, the lamellae should be checked to see if their quality varies distinctly within the same armor or matches fairly well. Another feature is the pattern of the direction in which lamellae overlap from one row to the next, and whether there is a logic to the overlap pattern, which may seem simple, complex, or haphazard. For instance, the lamellae of all the rows may overlap from the center outward and meet in the center of the back, or overlap left to right, or right to left, all the way around, or have a combination of these patterns. A lamellar armor is also very much dependent on the condition of its leather lacing for its appearance. An armor of modest quality with its lacing intact will present a much better appearance than one of higher quality but with broken, worn, or improperly restored lacing.

One further issue that should be addressed is the tendency in recent years to attribute all lamellar armor from Tibet to the Mongols rather than the Tibetans. The reasons for doing so seem to be based on a premise that can be summarized as follows: Since it is known the Mongols wore lamellar armor of this general type and they were very active in Tibet, all lamellar armor from Tibet must be Mongolian. The acceptance of this assertion is perhaps largely due to the general aura surrounding the military prowess of the Mongols and the desire among collectors, dealers, curators, and historians to connect extant objects with them. When looked at from the Tibetan perspective, however, the evidence for the lamellar armor from Tibet actually being Tibetan, and not Mongolian, seems convincing. First is the fact that these armors survive only in Tibet. If they were Mongolian, one could reasonably expect that at least some examples would be found in other regions in which the Mongols were active, but this appears not to be the case. Second, the armors bear only Tibetan markings on them, such as the written inscriptions on the leather skirts and elsewhere, the incised markings on the iron elements, and the wax seals on their interiors. Third, and perhaps most important, is the fact that in Tashi Namgyal and other similar connoisseurship texts, lamellar armor is not referred to as Mongolian, whereas related material such as swords, saddles, and stirrups, as well as other types of objects such as sculpture and textiles, are routinely separated into classifications according whether they are from Tibet (*bod*), China (*rgya nag*), India (*rgya gar*), or Mongolia (*sog* or *hor*).[10] The lack of this distinction in the Tibetan texts clearly indicates the armor was considered Tibetan and that there were no reservations about describing other things as Mongolian when appropriate. Therefore, there seems no compelling reason to conclude that the iron lamellar armor described in this section is anything other than Tibetan. Several helmets of various types in the next catalogue section, however, do appear to be Mongolian.

1. For detailed discussions of lamellar armor, see Dien 2000; Kubarev 1997; Laufer 1914; Lebedynsky 2001, esp. pp. 187–94; Robinson 1967; Thordeman 1939, esp. vol. 1, pp. 245–84; Yang Hong 1992; Yang Hong 2002. It should be noted that Laufer used the term "plate armor," not lamellar (1914, pp. 258ff.). Lamellar armor, made of bone and of iron, was also used in Siberia, for which see Thordeman 1939 and also Wilson 2000.

2. His description of lamellar armor for man and horse is given in Beazley 1903, in Latin (pp. 89–90) and in English (pp. 124–25); quoted in part in Robinson 1967 (pp. 138–39), and Świętosławski 1999 (pp. 21–22). For many examples of excavated lamellar and depictions of it from this period see Nicolle 1995 and Nicolle 1999.

3. For instance, note the variance in the number of rows of lamellae among the armors included in this catalogue: cat. no. 1, 31 rows; cat. no. 3, 14 rows; cat. no. 4, 11 rows; cat. no. 5, 13 rows; cat. no. 6, 12 rows. This is counting down the front, and not including the collar. Counting down the back there may be one additional row at the top.

4. Thordeman 1939, vol. 1, pp. 245, 248.

5. Beasley (1938, pp. 20–21) commented: "It would seem that these suits, as well as the necessary weapons, were kept in proper armouries connected with the larger monasteries, for on the leather skirts pendant below the actual mail [*sic*] are found Tibetan characters indicating the troops of men to whom they belonged." Beasley's article also includes useful information about the provenance of several pieces now in national collections in Great Britain.

6. The Tibetan is "chos rgyal khu dbon dus" (Burmiok Athing, fol. 27b; British Library Or 11,374, fol. 85a). I am grateful to Gene Smith for clarifying the meaning of this.

7. "bod du khrab kyi thog ma 'di'i dus smar khams nas blangs." Quoted from *Early History of Tibet, gong sa rgyal dbang lnga pa chen po mchog gis mdzad pa'i bod kyi rgyal rabs rdzogs ldan gzhon nu'i dga' ston* (Delhi, 1967), p. 8.

8. See the appendix "Excerpts from *A Treatise on Worldly Traditions*," Burmiok Athing, fol. 27a–b; British Library Or 11,374, fols. 83a–85a.

9. The armor in a private collection is illustrated in *Rituels tibétains* 2002, no. 150, p. 173. The results cited are at 2 sigma, 95% confidence rating. Samples were taken from the leather lacings, which appear to be completely integral and original to the armors.

10. For an example of *sog* and *sog po* and *hor* or *hor pa* to refer to different Mongol groups in relation to types of swords, see the appendix "Excerpts from *A Treatise on Worldly Traditions*," Burmiok Athing, fol. 24b; British Library Or 11,374, fol. 74a–b. Genghis Khan is identified as the king of *hor* in both texts.

1. LAMELLAR ARMOR AND HELMET

Tibetan, 17th century or earlier
Iron, leather, and textile
H. as mounted approx. 65 in. (165.1 cm)
On loan courtesy of the National Museums of Scotland
Royal Museum, Edinburgh (A.1909.406&A)

This armor is distinguished by being made up of twice as many rows as most other lamellar armors, and by being the only example in a Western collection, and probably one of the few in the world, to retain full sleeves. Its helmet is also the most complete and best preserved of the eight-plate lamellar type observed during this study.

The helmet bowl follows the usual design, consisting of eight plates overlapping in an over-under pattern. The four outer plates have two shallow cusps with rounded points on either side and a low medial ridge. The inner plates are smooth. The plume finial has a pronounced lozenge-shaped central knop and a flared funnel-like top. The base of the bowl is encircled by a single row of lamellae, each measuring about 5.5 by 2.5 centimeters. The careful construction of the helmet and its undisturbed condition are demonstrated by the fact that the seven lamellae at the brow are pierced by only ten lacing holes, whereas the rest of the lamellae around the rim have eleven. The eleventh hole, located in the center of each lamella, is necessary for the suspension of the cheek and neck defenses below and, therefore, would be superfluous on the lamellae over the brow.

The cheek defenses consist of five rows of diminishing width and are made up of lamellae measuring 4.5 by 2 centimeters, pierced by eleven lacing holes. There are two horizontally placed leather loops on the fourth and fifth rows of the proper left cheek, and on the fourth row of the proper right cheek. These presumably would have been used in conjunction with a strap or lace to tie the cheek defenses beneath the chin. There is a wax seal on the interior of the bottom row of the proper left cheek (see detail). The same wax seal is also found on the fine Tibetan horse armor (cat. no. 32) that came to the Royal Museum, Edinburgh, from the same source (see Provenance).

The nape defense consists of three rows, which flare out and increase in width from top to bottom. The lamellae overlap outward from the front on either side toward the center in the back of each row. The lamellae of the bottom row measure 4.5 by 1.5 centimeters and have ten lacing holes, while those in the two rows above have eleven. As with the lamellae at the brow, the absence of the central eleventh hole indicates that they were designed to be placed in a terminal row.

A braided leather strap is attached to a loop in the lacing on the interior of the helmet bowl just above the rim at the center of the back. This may be the remainder of the straps by which the helmet was secured to the head. Alternatively, it may be intended for carrying the helmet when it was not being worn, by suspending it from the belt or elsewhere. All of the laces of the helmet are made of a strong, supple, buff-colored leather.

The armor has complete shoulders with full sleeves that extend to cover the backs of the hands to the fingertips. It opens lengthwise down the front and

1, helmet

has thirty-one rows (thirty in the back, having one fewer at the neck) consisting of fifteen rows above the waist in the front, the curved lamellae of the waist row itself, and then fifteen rows below. There is no distinct collar and no stop ribs. Most of the lamellae have nine holes and measure 4 by 2 centimeters, but the number of holes and the size of the lamellae vary slightly depending on placement in the garment. The lamellae of each row overlap away from the front opening and meet at the center of the back. The skirt is split in the back from the hem to the waist by two vertical seams, forming a central panel that widens progressively from top to bottom. The border attached around the base of the skirts is made of two layers of leather. The lower layer is made of solid panels, and the upper layer is split into rectangular lappets. Like the helmet, the laces of the armor are made of a strong, supple buff-colored leather.

The shoulder defenses are made up of eleven rows and reach to the elbow. The top row of each

1

1, detail of seal inside left cheek of helmet

shoulder is perpendicular to the adjacent rows on the chest and back and is laced directly to the holes in the edges of the lamellae at the ends of the first five or six uppermost rows on the chest and back. The lamellae of the shoulders diminish slightly in size, from 3.7 by 2 centimeters in the top row to 3.3 by 1.8 centimeters in the bottom row. The sleeves are laced directly to the bottom row of the shoulder defenses. They have a mitten-shaped extension to cover the backs of the hands and are made of soft leather, which is seamed lengthwise up the center of the inner arm. The outer face of each sleeve is covered with small, closely set iron disks, which resemble buttons and are stitched with leather laces to the sleeve. The edges of the disks are raised, with a sunken hollow in the center pierced by two lacing holes. Many of the disks are now missing. The exterior of the proper left sleeve has the remains of a textile covering between the iron disks and the leather sleeve. There are also the remains of finger loops on the interior of the proper left mitten, showing how it would have been attached to the hand. Very similar sleeves of this rare type, along with other armor parts, were found in the ruins of Tsaparang, the capital of the ancient kingdom of Guge, in Ngari (western Tibet).[1]

Several features seem to suggest that this armor is relatively early in date, perhaps as early as the fourteenth to early fifteenth century. These include the number of rows in the body, nearly double that usu-

ally encountered; the lack of a collar and stop ribs, which seem to be standard features on other armors; and the form of the shoulder defenses, which reach to the elbow, coupled with the full sleeves, which are not found on other armors. Despite the presumed early nature of these features, however, a recent carbon-14 test on a sample from the leather lacing of the body armor yielded a date range of 1630–90.[2] If these results are valid, then, rather than indicators of an early date, the features enumerated may be regional characteristics of armor from western Tibet in the seventeenth century. This would be in keeping with the only other pair of armored sleeves of this type having been found at a site in Guge, which was conquered and apparently abandoned by the mid-seventeenth century. Alternatively, the carbon-14 date may indicate that this is an earlier armor that was re-leathered in the seventeenth century. The helmet, although distinctive, is similar to others attributed to the fifteenth to seventeenth century (compare with cat. nos. 2, 4).

This armor was lent and then sold to the Royal Museum of Scotland in 1908 by F. M. Bailey (1882–1967), an officer during the Younghusband Expedition of 1903–4, who had a long and adventure-filled career in the British Army and the Indian Political Department of the British government.[3] Shortly after the expedition, Bailey became the British Trade Agent in Gyantse, where he was based from 1905 to 1909. During the Younghusband Expedition Bailey maintained a very detailed correspondence with his parents in Edinburgh.[4] The lack of any specific mention of this armor or the horse armor which also comes from Bailey (cat. no. 32) suggests that they may have been acquired by him later, while he was the Trade Agent in Gyantse, rather than during the expedition. Identification of the wax seal, which is found on both the helmet of this armor and on the horse armor, may ultimately reveal their original source.

PROVENANCE: F. M. Bailey, Edinburgh.

PUBLICATIONS: Beasley 1938, pl. IX; Robinson 1967, p. 162 (not illus.).

1. The sleeves are illustrated as part of a complete lamellar armor in Jugoslovenska Revija, Tibet (London, 1981), p. 257; Guge 1991, vol 1, pp. 188–89, vol. 2, pl. CXX.

2. The C-14 test was conducted by the Research Laboratory for Archaeology and the History of Art, Oxford, July 20, 2005. I am very grateful to Jane Wilkinson for arranging this test.
3. See Allen 2004 and, for his later career, Bailey 2002. I am also grateful to Stephen Wood for providing useful details about Bailey's career.
4. British Library, London, Mss Eur/F157/163/164.

2. MINIATURE LAMELLAR ARMOR AND HELMET

Tibetan, possibly 15th–16th century
Iron, leather, and textile
H. approx. 30 in. (76.2 cm)
Royal Armouries Museum, Leeds (XXVIA.18)

This is a finely made lamellar armor with matching helmet, which is remarkable for its high quality, completeness, and for the fact that it the only miniature version of such an armor known to exist. Since the proportions of the armor are not correct for a child, it seems likely that it was made either as a votive object or as a costume for a sculpture in a shrine or temple context. The miniature spearhead and matchlock gun in this catalogue (cat. nos. 79, 103) were probably made for similar purposes.

The construction of the helmet is similar to that of catalogue number 1, the bowl being made of eight plates overlapping in an over-under pattern. The cusps of the outer plates, however, are slightly more pointed. The lamellae encircling the base of the helmet measure approximately 3.5 by 1.5 centimeters and have nine holes each. The cheek defenses consist of three rows each. The nape defense is also made up of three rows, which widen by increasing the number of lamellae in a sequence of fifteen, seventeen, and nineteen from top to bottom.

The armor opens lengthwise down the front and consists of seven rows in front and eight in back, including a short collar row at the top of the back. The waist row is the third row down in the front. The lamellae of the body are relatively long and slender, have thirteen lacing holes and, at 7 by 1.2 centimeters, are comparable to those on some full-size armors.

2

2, back view

The lamellae of the bottom row have twelve lacing holes, the central hole not being necessary, indicating that they were designed to be in a terminal row. The lamellae of each row overlap outward from the center front and meet in the center of the back. On the lower half of the rear of the armor the four rows below the waist are split by the usual two vertical seams, one on either side. There are four stop ribs, one attached across the tops of the lamellae at either side of the top row of the chest and under each arm opening on the sides of the armor. The stop ribs consist of a twinelike cord wrapped in a tubular casing of leather. The core material of the stop rib under the proper right arm extends out of its leather casing toward the rear as an unattached cord approximately 43 centimeters long, the function of which is unknown. There are leather laces at either side of the front seam of the coat at the edges of rows two and three, which may have originally served to tie the coat closed. The shoulders consist of four rows of lamellae, which diminish in their number from top to bottom in a sequence of nineteen, eighteen, fifteen, and thirteen on both sides. To attach the shoulder defenses, the uppermost holes of the central lamellae in the top row of the shoulders are laced to the center holes in the lamellae of the collar row, where they pass over the armhole.

A border of silk, brocaded with metallic thread, is attached at the base of each shoulder defense and along the hem of the armor. It is decorated with a pattern of dragons and flaming pearls among clouds. The silk is edged with green leather piping and backed with buff leather.

PROVENANCE: Gift of Colonel A. M. McCleverty, May 28, 1954. According to family tradition, the donor's father, Colonel James McCleverty, acquired the armor during the Younghusband Expedition.

PUBLICATIONS: Robinson 1967, p. 162, pls. XXVIa, b; Haider 1991, pls. 11a, b.

3. LAMELLAR ARMOR AND HELMET

Tibetan, possibly 15th–16th century
Iron, leather, and textile
H. as mounted approx. 56 in. (142.2 cm)
The British Museum, London (1880-725)
Helmet only in exhibition

This is an armor of very good quality, with a matching sixteen-plate helmet, full shoulder defenses, combined textile and leather borders, very interesting markings, and several unusual and noteworthy features.

The bowl of the helmet is made up of sixteen plates, rather than the usual eight, with eight outer plates overlapping eight inner plates in an over-under pattern. The outer plates have two cusps with distinct points on either side, which almost touch the points of the adjacent outer plates. Both the inner and outer plates have pronounced medial ridges, a feature seldom seen on inner plates. The tips of the ridges at the tops of the outer plates are undercut to make a notch, into which the edge of the base of the plume tube finial is fitted, also an unusual, if not unique, feature. The tops of the inner plates fit under the base. The plume tube finial is itself atypical in form, having two knops shaped like umbrellas and a stepped base. The central knop of the plume tube bears a very small and crude inscription in *dbu can* script with the word *spus* followed by the number 80, the same number that is found on the back of this armor. The term *spus* usually refers to an assessment of quality, but in this case the inscription may simply mean "item number 80."

The rim of the helmet bowl is encircled by a row of lamellae, which overlap in one direction all the way around. This is a different construction, and seemingly less refined, than on the helmets in catalogue numbers 1 and 2, where the lamellae overlap outward in opposite directions from a single lamella at the center of the brow. There are no cheek defenses. The nape defense consists of three rows of lamellae, which overlap from the front to the rear and meet at a central lamella in the back. The lamellae of the helmet measure 5.5 by 1.5 centimeters and are pierced by eight holes in the row around the rim and by twelve holes in the nape defense. A wax seal is found on the interior of the twelfth lamella from the proper right edge on the bottom row of the nape defense.[1] Like the seals found on the helmet in catalogue number 1 and the horse armor in catalogue number 32, this example also has a design of stylized Tibetan letters within a double border. The border on this seal is quatrefoil, however, while borders of the other two are round. Otherwise all three seals are generally very similar.

The armor opens down the center of the front and is made up of fourteen rows in the front and fifteen rows in the back, counting the collar row. The collar is lined with leather. The waist is at the sixth row, counting down the front. There is a buckle attached to the edge of the top row on the proper left side of the chest. The lamellae at the top of the chest measure 7 by 1.5 centimeters, while those from the waist down are slightly smaller at 6.5 by 1.5 centimeters. Most are pierced with twelve lacing holes. At the rear, the eight rows below the waist are split by two vertical seams, one at either side. In the center of the back, three rows down from the collar, there is an iron tag inlaid in brass with the Tibetan number 80 (see detail), matching the number engraved on the helmet. The tag is square with an arched top, made of thick polished iron the same color as the lamellae, and held by a single rivet to a lamella

3, helmet

3, detail of inlaid iron tag on back of armor

beneath it. Exactly the same type of numbered tag is found on the lamellar armor in the Royal Armouries Museum (cat. no. 26).

The shoulder defenses consist of fourteen rows, and they also have an underarm guard made of two rows, a very unusual feature. Laces extend from the ends of several rows, by which the shoulder defense could be tied to the arm, and there is a leather loop at the end of each underarm guard through which the arm would pass. The lamellae of the shoulder defenses are smaller in size, those in the bottom row measuring 3 by 2.5 centimeters, and have nine lacing holes. There is a rectangular panel of woven silk, brocaded with metallic thread, attached to the bottom row of each shoulder defense. The panels are edged with green leather piping and are backed with buff leather or linen. Narrower panels of the same material are attached to the hem of the armor on top of two layers of leather, the uppermost being split into rectangular lappets, and the bottom layer being solid panels of leather. This triple border is also an unusual feature.

The presence of the matching Tibetan inventory number 80 on both helmet and body armor indicates that they were considered a pair in their original Tibetan setting, a fact that has been established conclusively for very few other examples. Other unusual features of this ensemble mentioned above include the sixteen-plate helmet, the presence of medial ridges on the inner plates of the bowl, the form of the plume tube finial, the underarm guards, and the triple hem.

PUBLICATION: Zwalf 1981, p. 124 (illus.).

1. I am grateful to Barbara Willis and Richard Blurton for pointing out the seal, which I overlooked during my brief physical examination of the armor in March 2005.

4. LAMELLAR ARMOR AND HELMET

Tibetan, possibly 16th–17th century
Iron, leather, and textile
H. as mounted approx. 60 in. (152.4 cm)
Pitt Rivers Museum, Oxford (1941.2.126.1, .2)

This is an armor and helmet of good quality, but slightly less so than the preceding examples. The chief differences are that the lamellae are slightly flatter and not as finely finished, they are larger, and they overlap in a different pattern than on the previous examples. Also, the surface is russet brown, rather than silvery iron. The helmet has noteworthy markings on it.

The helmet is very similar in size, form, and construction to the Edinburgh helmet (cat. no. 1), being of the same eight-plate type and having full cheek and nape defenses. The lamellae around the rim of the helmet bowl measure 5.5 by 2 centimeters, have eleven lacing holes each, and, like those on the British Museum helmet (cat. no. 3), overlap in one direction all the way around. The cheek defenses consist of seven rows, the lamellae measuring 3 by 2 centimeters and having eight holes. The nape defense is of three progressively wider rows, the lamellae measuring 4 by 2 centimeters and having eleven holes each. The words *mgon khang shar* are inscribed in large *dbu can* characters on the front of the helmet on the first inner plate to the proper left of cen-ter. The inscription indicates that the armor was kept in the shrine (*mgon khang*) of a guardian deity on the east (*shar*), either the eastern shrine or the east side of a particular shrine. Inscribed in very small *dbu can* characters on the base of the plume tube finial is *shong ba* or *shod ba* (?) followed by the Tibetan number 58 (see detail), which compares with the inscription in the same place on the British Museum helmet (cat. no. 3). The meaning is not clear, but it seems to refer to inventory numbering or storage in an arsenal or fortress before its use in a *mgon khang*.

The armor opens lengthwise down the front and has no shoulder defenses. It consists of eleven rows in the front and twelve rows in the back, including the collar row, which is lined with leather. The waist is the fifth row, counting down in the front. The lamellae are larger than those of the previous armors, measuring 8 by 2 centimeters at the top of the chest, 9.4 by 2 centimeters in the fourth row, and 9 by 2 centimeters in the bottom row. They have nine lacing holes. Unlike the previous armors, the lamellae of this armor do not overlap outward from the front

4, detail of inscription on base of helmet plume finial

and meet at the center of the back. Instead, the lamellae of the top two rows of the chest (which stop at the arm openings) overlap right over left, and the lamellae of all the other rows overlap left over right from the front all the way around the back. The difference in the overlap pattern between this and the previous armors may be an indicator of a later date or a regional style, or reflect a trend toward simplification in armor-making techniques.

4, back view

4, helmet

There are two rows of lamellae over the top of the arm opening, set perpendicular to those on the chest, and attached in the same way as the first two rows of a complete shoulder defense. This feature is also found on other armors without shoulder defenses (see cat. nos. 5, 6). These lamellae measure 3 by 1.5 centimeters and have eight holes each. There are remains of stop ribs at the top of the chest and under each arm. The armor has a detached belt made of a strip of leather with an iron buckle. A rectangular strip of textile with faint traces of Tibetan characters is attached to the proper right side of the chest at the inside of the end of the second row. Two knotted ends of fabric in the center of the second row of the back are probably also the remains of similar textile labels. The back of the armor is split on either side by two vertical seams for the six rows below the waist. A border consisting of two layers of leather is attached to the bottom row of lamellae around the base of the armor. The upper layer is split into rectangular lappets, and the lower layer is made of solid rectangular panels. There are inscriptions written on the lower layer, including

Tibetan characters in the *dbu med* script and numbers. The leather lacing of the armor and the helmet are stiff and relatively brittle in comparison with the previous examples.

The russet brown color of the lamellae does not appear to be a modern coating but seems to be an original surface treatment or a natural patina from generations of storage in a *mgon khang*. The identification of the armor as coming from a fortress,

Phari Jong (see Provenance) may seem at odds with the inscription on the helmet, which clearly indicates that it was kept in a *mgon khang*. However, if the provenance is correct, this suggests that there was a *mgon khang* in Phari Jong, possibly the same shrine room from which L. A. Waddell is known to have obtained a complete one-hundred-volume set of the Kangyur (*bka' 'gyur*).[1] For Phari Jong, see also catalogue number 7.

PROVENANCE: Collected at Phari Jong (*phag ri rdzong*) in Tibet by Major General Sir William Beynon (1866–1955) during the Younghusband Expedition, 1903 (according to Beasley 1938); H. G. Beasley, Cranmore Museum (536), Chiselhurst, Kent.

PUBLICATION: Beasley 1938, pl. V, provenance given in caption.

1. Waddell 1905, p. 98; Allen 2004, p. 71.

5. LAMELLAR ARMOR AND HELMET

Tibetan, possibly 16th–17th century
Iron and leather
H. as mounted approx. 59 in. (149.9 cm)
The Metropolitan Museum of Art, New York, Bequest of George C. Stone, 1935 (36.25.53a, b)

This armor is largely intact but is of poor quality when compared with the preceding examples. It also shows signs of having been remade and repaired in its working lifetime and more recently. The lamellae are relatively coarse, dark in color, and poorly finished, and their sizes are more mixed than on other examples. The pattern from row to row of the direction in which the lamellae overlap is also different from that of the previous armors and may be indicative of its date. This armor is included here to serve as a counterpoint to the others and to emphasize the differences in their quality and condition.

The helmet bowl is of eight-plate construction, like catalogue numbers 1, 2, and 4, and has a similar plume finial with the Tibetan letter *pa* faintly incised on the base of the finial. The lamellae encircling the rim of the bowl overlap in one direction, measure approximately 5.4 by 2.5 centimeters, and have eleven holes. Originally the helmet appears to have had separate ear defenses of four rows, but these are now joined unevenly to the four rows of the nape defense. The nape defense does not flare out in stepped rows, as do those of the helmets in catalogue numbers 1, 2, and 4. The sizes of the lamellae in the ear sections vary but are approximately 5 by 1.5 centimeters and have eight holes. The lamellae

of the nape defense vary more in size and mostly have 8 holes. The overlap is interrupted in random areas from row to row in the cheek and nape defenses, suggesting later repairs or reuse. The Tibetan number 224 or 234 is roughly incised on a lamella in the top row of the proper rear right side of the nape defense.

The armor is made up of thirteen rows front and back plus the collar row. The waist is at the seventh row from the top. It is unusual in having the same number of rows above and below the waist. The sizes of the lamellae and the number of holes vary from 4.5 by 2 centimeters with eight holes in the top row, to 6.5 by 1.7 centimeters with nine holes in the fifth row, to 10 by 1.8 centimeters with thirteen holes in the sixth row, to 7.2 by 2.2 centimeters with nine holes for rows eight through thirteen. The pattern of the direction in which the rows of lamellae overlap is less regular, and different from, the previous armors. The top row in the front follows the pattern seen in catalogue numbers 1–3, the lamellae on the proper right side overlapping left over right, and on the proper left side overlapping right over left, in other words outward from the center. The second row overlaps in only one direction, right over left. The third row overlaps outward from the center.

The next three rows overlap in one direction, but it is left over right. Then from the waist down the sides of each row again overlap in opposite directions outward from the center, as on the armors in catalogue numbers 1–3.

There are two rows of lamellae over the top of the arm opening (as in cat. nos. 4 and 6). These are also irregular in size, measuring between 5 centimeters by 1.5 with nine holes and 4.5 centimeters by 2.5 centimeters with eight holes. In the rear the six rows below the waist are split with a vertical seam, as is usual. There are small stop ribs at the top of either side of the chest and under either arm. The leather borders at the base of the armor are in the usual two layers, but the upper layer is very roughly and unevenly split into lappets. On the proper front left of the lower layer there is a short word written in *dbu med* and the Tibetan number 14. On the proper rear right there are a few words in *dbu med* followed by numbers, including what appears to be *khar pa*, *la byang 1111*, *dpung* (troop?) *162*, and *gang* or *nang 4244* (see detail).[1] The leather laces of the Metropolitan Museum's armor were repaired and in places entirely redone, and seven replacement lamellae were added by Leonard Heinrich at the Metropolitan Museum in January 1963.

5

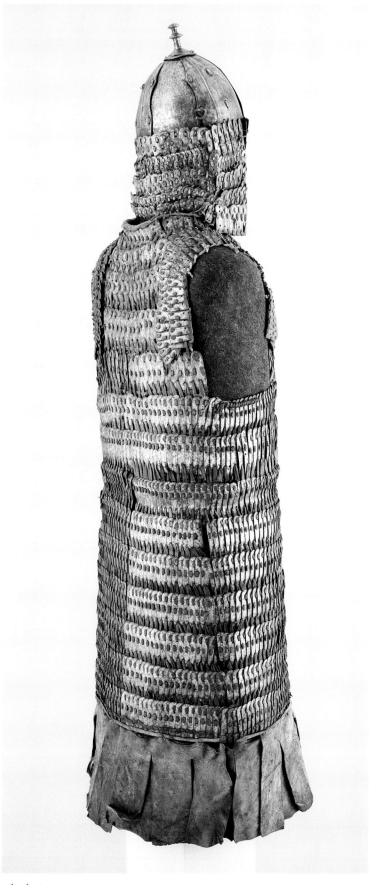

5, back view

5, detail of inscription on leather skirt of armor

The difference in the quality and finish of the lamellae between this armor and the previous ones is immediately apparent. The lamellae of this armor are flatter, have sharper edges, and are dark and uneven in color and texture. This is very different from the silvery color and texture, slightly convex contours, and smooth edges of the lamellae of the other armors, particularly catalogue numbers 1–3. Even the Pitt Rivers Museum armor (cat. no. 4), which appears to resemble this armor closely at first glance, is in fact much more carefully made, cohesively constructed, and stronger and more balanced both overall and in its details. The pattern of the direction of the overlap of the rows of lamellae of the Metropolitan Museum armor seems to fall between the patterns observed in catalogue numbers 1–3, in which the lamellae of the rows overlap outward from the center, and the simpler pattern of the Pitt Rivers

armor (cat. no. 4), in which most of the rows overlap in one direction only. This, coupled with the inconsistency in the size and type of its lamellae, suggests either that the Metropolitan Museum armor is a relatively later and poorly made example or that it is an earlier armor of modest quality, which was carelessly repaired for reuse later in its working lifetime.

PROVENANCE: W. O. Oldman, London; George Cameron Stone, New York.

PUBLICATIONS: Stone 1934, p. 53, fig. 66; LaRocca 1999a, pp. 116–17, fig. 7.

1. I am grateful to Lozang Jamspal for his reading of these characters. This should be compared with a similar inscription on the leather skirt of a lamellar armor in the National Museums Liverpool (56.27.202), which reads in part: *ma* or *la byang 1231, dpung 140, gong sa* (?). The exact meanings unfortunately remain unclear.

6. LAMELLAR ARMOR

Tibetan, possibly 16th–17th century
Iron and leather
H. 38 in. (96.5 cm)
The Metropolitan Museum of Art, New York, Purchase, Arthur Ochs Sulzberger Gift, 2001 (2001.318)

This is a largely intact lamellar armor in relatively good condition, which offers several useful points of comparison with the previous armors in terms of the size and form of the lamellae and the pattern of the direction in which the rows of lamellae overlap.

The armor opens lengthwise down its front, has no shoulder defenses, and consists of a collar row with a sturdy leather lining and twelve rows of lamellae front and back. The waist is the seventh row down from the top, meaning there are six rows above the waist and five below, giving it fewer rows below the waist than the other armors in this study. In the back of the armor the five rows below the waist are split on either side by a vertical seam. The lamellae are made of a bright iron and are relatively flat with some uneven edges, which are not, how-

ever, as sharp as the edges on the other Metropolitan Museum armor (cat. no. 5). The pattern of the direction in which the lamellae overlap is also simpler or seemingly more consistent than that of the latter, but not as simple as that of the Pitt Rivers Museum armor (cat. no. 4). On the present armor the lamellae of the top row overlap outward from the center in opposite directions, the next row overlaps in one direction (left over right), the next three rows each overlap outward from the center in opposite directions, and the last seven rows all overlap in one direction (again left over right). The size of the lamellae generally increases toward the midsection of the armor and then decreases slightly: top row 4 by 2 centimeters, fourth row 8 by 2 centimeters, sixth row 9.8 by 2.3 centimeters, and bottom row 9.2

by 2 centimeters. The lamellae have nine lacing holes each.

There are two rows of lamellae over the top of the arm opening, as in catalogue numbers 4 and 5, which measure 4 by 2 centimeters and have nine holes. There are large and sturdy leather stop ribs on the top row at either side of the chest and under each arm opening. There is a waist belt in the form of a strap of braided leather with an iron buckle, which is attached to the lacing at the center of the back, and a similar strap of braided leather and an iron buckle near the neck at the top of the front. A border consisting of two layers of leather is attached to the bottom row, with the lower layer being solid panels of leather and the upper layer being split into rectangular lappets. The Tibetan numbers 4 (?)

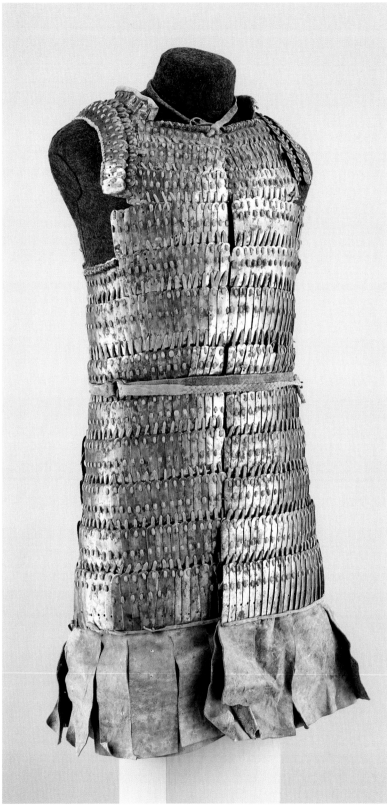

6

6, back view

above 13 are written on the lower layer in the proper right front.

The size and form of the lamellae relate most closely to those of the Pitt Rivers armor (cat. no. 4), while the pattern of the direction of the overlap of the lamellae by rows may indicate that this armor represents a stage between the other Metropolitan Museum armor (cat. no. 5) and the Pitt Rivers armor (cat. no. 4). Carbon-14 testing on a sample from an integral piece of the leather lacing on the interior of catalogue number 6 resulted in a date range of 1480–1660.[1]

1. Results calibrated at 2 sigma, 95% probability; report from the Beta Analytic Radiocarbon Dating Laboratory, March 21, 2005.

7. EIGHT-PLATE HELMET

Tibetan, possibly 16th–17th century
Iron, leather, and textile
H. 8¼ in. (21 cm)
Victoria and Albert Museum, London (528A-1905)

This is a helmet bowl of eight-plate construction with a plume finial and is much like the previous examples, except that it lacks the lamellae defenses for the cheek and neck areas. Its significance in the present context lies in the fact that its provenance is known due to an inscription on one of the plates.

The helmet bowl consists of eight plates, four outer and four inner, overlapping in an alternating over and under pattern. The outer plates have two cusps on each side with slight points, and a raised medial ridge. Each outer plate is pierced by ten lacing holes. The inner plates are smooth and have fourteen lacing holes each. Assembly notches are found on the bottom edge of each plate. The plume tube finial has a central knop and funnel-like top very similar to those on the previous examples. The leather lacing is a recent restoration. Near the upper left cusp of one of the outer plates is the inscription *phag ri* in *dbu can* script followed by the Tibetan number 12 (see detail). A label consisting of a rectangular strip of fabric, on which the Tibetan number 32 is written, is also associated with the helmet.

The inscription identifies the helmet as coming from *phag ri rdzong*, the fortress called Phari Jong, which was occupied by the British without a fight on December 20, 1903, during the Younghusband

7, detail of inscription

7

Expedition. Although strategically located and strongly built, the fort was in abandoned condition. Edmund Candler, a journalist who accompanied the expedition, recorded seeing chambers "filled with straw, gunpowder, and old arms," and went on to describe "rusty helmets, shields, and breastplates . . . made of the thinnest iron plates interlaced with leathern thongs . . . old bell-mouthed matchlocks,

with their wooden rests," much of which was piled in the courtyard.[1] L. A. Waddell similarly described "the courtyard strewn with old lumber, chainarmour, iron helmets, spears, swords, matchlocks, and miscellaneous rubbish."[2] These quotations may describe the circumstances in which the helmet in the Victoria and Albert Museum was originally found.

PROVENANCE: Presumably Phari Jong (*phag ri rdzong*); however, the original accession records of the Victoria and Albert Museum list this helmet, along with lamellar armor 528-1905, as acquired at Gyantse (*rgyal rtse*) Monastery during the Younghusband Expedition, and then purchased in London by the museum.

1. Candler 1905, p. 92.
2. Waddell 1905, p. 98.

ཐོག

Helmets

The principal types of helmets encountered in Tibet have been outlined in "Rediscovering the Arms and Armor of Tibet." These are the eight-plate helmet (see cat. nos. 1, 2, 4, 5, 7) and the helmet with a simple one-piece bowl and upturned fabric flaps, seen so frequently in pictures of the Great Prayer Festival, and usually considered Bhutanese (figs. 6, 7; cat. no. 46). It is only in recent years that there have emerged several other very different types, which represent various important but little-known styles and reflect the involvement of other cultures in Tibet. One example appears to be a very early precursor to the familiar Tibetan eight-plate helmet (cat. no. 8). Three rare styles of multi-plate helmets are represented by examples made up of thirty-one to forty-nine narrow iron lames (cat. nos. 9–13). These probably relate to the helmet styles mentioned by the Tibetan writer Hūṃkaradzaya, who noted the existence of helmets with four, eight, twelve, sixteen, twenty-four, thirty-three, and more lames.[1] Another rare type, probably Mongolian, has a one-piece hemispherical bowl with a cylindrical apex (cat. no. 14). A later and better-known Mongolian helmet style has a stepped bowl made up of two or three fitted conical segments (for example, cat. no. 16). What became the classic Qing helmet style is represented by two early examples from Tibet, which may be late Ming or early Qing (cat. nos. 19, 20). A few of the helmets, however, are so unusual as to have almost no stylistic parallels (cat. nos. 17, 21–23). In terms of decoration, the majority of the motifs are clearly derived from Tibetan Buddhism. This ranges from simple depictions of the Three Jewels (cat. no. 14), to complex arrangements of deities and mantras (cat. no. 16), to an elegant image of Buddha Shakyamuni (cat. no. 19).

1. See Tashi Tsering 1979, pp. 63–64: "bzo dang rnam pa bzhi dang rnam brgyad bcu gnyis gling / bcu drug ma dang nyi shu rtsa bzhi ma / sum cu rtsa gsum la sogs bzo rigs ni."

8. EIGHT-PLATE HELMET

Possibly Tibetan, 8th–10th century
Iron and copper alloy
H. 8½ in. (21.6 cm)
The Metropolitan Museum of Art, New York, Purchase, Arthur Ochs Sulzberger Gift, 2002 (2002.226)

This helmet is important as a possible antecedent to the classic Tibetan eight-plate helmet style and has several interesting constructional features that set it apart from other known examples. The helmet bowl consists of eight slightly convex and arched plates, four narrow outer plates and four wide inner plates, which overlap in an over-under pattern. The sides of the four outer plates are slightly cusped. The plates are joined by four pairs of rivets, which have an iron shank, a conical domed head, and a scalloped washer, the rivet head and washer being a copper alloy. An applied vertical rib of copper alloy is riveted to the center of each of the four outer plates. Each rib has a prominent medial ridge and two pairs of semicircular tabs, through which the rivets pass. Four small plates of copper alloy are located at the top of each inner plate. The lower edge of each of these copper plates has a slight peak and is finely scalloped. There is a conical dome-headed rivet in the center of each plate. A horizontal band of copper alloy forms a rim around the base of the helmet bowl. The band has a raised medial ridge and finely scalloped edges. At the top of the helmet there is a plume finial with a lozenge-shaped knop and a funnel-like top, which is very similar in shape to those found on later Tibetan helmets (compare especially cat. nos. 1, 4, 7). The base of the finial is covered by an applied band of copper alloy. All of the copper alloy fittings are decorated with engraved zigzag, scallop, and geometric patterns.

From a typological standpoint this helmet presents a unique combination of features found on various forms of segmented helmets with riveted construction, which were in use across Eurasia from about the fourth century A.D. onward.[1] The presence of a separate brow band attached to the helmet

8

bowl by four vertical ribs is particularly reminiscent of the *Spangenhelm* type, as is the use of engraved plates of copper alloy, both to reinforce the helmet and to serve as decorative trim. Features that indicate a connection with later Tibetan helmets are the basic eight-plate construction, the vestigial cusped edges of the outer plates of the helmet bowl, and the distinctively Tibetan form of the plume finial. Both the corrosion pattern and the copper alloy trim at the base of the finial show that it is contemporary with the rest of the helmet and not a later addition. This combination of characteristics suggests that

the helmet is early in date and is the result of both Tibetan and Eurasian influence, possibly from around the period of the Yarlung dynasty (7th–9th centuries). This appears to be the earliest extant helmet, and possibly the earliest piece of metal armor, with clearly distinguishable Tibetan characteristics.

1. For examples, see, for instance, Lebedynsky 2001, pp. 190–92; Robinson 1967, pp. 53–57, pl. Ia.

9. MULTI-PLATE HELMET OF FORTY-SIX LAMES

Mongolian or Tibetan, 13th–15th century

Iron and leather

H. 5½ in. (14 cm)

The Metropolitan Museum of Art, New York, Purchase, Gift of William H. Riggs, by exchange, and The Sulzberger Foundation Inc. Gift, 1999 (1999.158)

Other than fragmentary excavated examples, very few multi-plate helmets of this type have survived (see also cat. no. 10), and virtually none in the pristine condition of this one. The general type was in use from eastern Europe through Central Asia by the sixth century A.D. and may have remained in use in Tibet and among the Mongols and other Central Asian peoples as late as the seventeenth century.[1] This helmet is composed of forty-six arched plates, called lames, each of which is pierced by sixteen lacing holes. The upper ends of the lames are overlapped by the edge of the slightly convex disk that forms the top of the helmet. The lames and the disk are tightly joined by a series of five horizontal rows of leather laces and a leather rim at the base of the helmet. In the top two rows a single lace loops through a single hole and over and around each lame. In each of the bottom three rows the lacing pattern is more complex and appears to be done in

the following way. Beginning with a single lame, probably at the center of the back of the helmet, a single lace is threaded through the pairs of holes in the lamellae in a zigzag pattern, passing vertically from one hole to the next on the outside of the helmet and diagonally between the holes in each adjacent lame on the inside. At the last lame the direction of the lace is reversed, and it is threaded through again in the opposite direction, still in a zigzag pattern but this time only passing through the holes in every other lame.

Traces of a badly damaged wax seal, which compares with those on other pieces in the catalogue (cat. nos. 1, 3, 32, 46, 96), were found on the interior leather lacing. Analysis by X-ray fluorescence (XRF) shows that the lames consist of very pure iron, with no discernible trace elements of nickel or other materials.[2] A carbon-14 test conducted on a sample from the interior lacing gives a date range of 1271–

1431.[3] The condition and completeness of the helmet are unparalleled on an iron object of this period and make it one of the most well-preserved iron helmets with such an early date of this or any other type from Tibet or from any culture.

PUBLICATIONS: Gutowski 1997, pp. 24, 28, pl. 9; Nicolle 1999, no. 813g, pp. 317, 488; Pyhrr, LaRocca, and Ogawa 2002, pp. 44–45.

1. Compare the helmet from a 5th-century Avarian grave found at Kertsch in the Crimea, illustrated in Robinson 1967, fig. 29b, and the 8th–9th-century helmet from Balyk-Sook in Central Asia, illustrated and discussed in Kubarev 1997. For the Mongols, see Nicolle 1999, pp. 296–312. The possibility of a 17th-century date for this style of helmet is based on the C-14 dating of the helmet in cat. no. 10.

2. Report, December 10, 1999, of analysis conducted at the Metropolitan Museum by Richard Stone.

3. Results at 2 sigma, 95% probability; test conducted by the Rafter Radiocarbon Laboratory, ref. no. NZA 6399 (July 11, 1996).

9, inside view

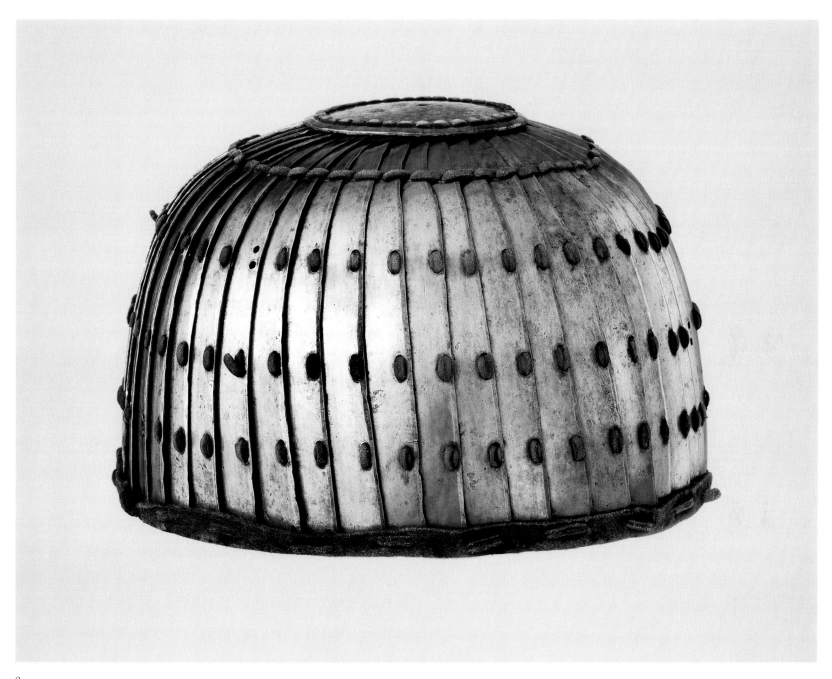

9

10. MULTI-PLATE HELMET OF FORTY-NINE LAMES

Probably Mongolian or Tibetan, 15th–17th century
Iron and leather
H. 8½ in. (21.6 cm)
The Metropolitan Museum of Art, New York, Purchase, Arthur Ochs Sulzberger Gift, 2001 (2001.183)

This helmet is very similar to the previous example, with a few minor differences. There are forty-nine lames (versus forty-six) and each has eleven lacing holes (versus sixteen). The lames are also somewhat more slender and more evenly made, and are longer toward the bottom, making the sides of the helmet straighter and the bowl deeper by comparison. At the top of the helmet there is a slightly convex disk with a simple plume tube (which may be missing from the other helmet). The laces holding the disk were largely missing and have recently been restored. The helmet is held together by four horizontal rows of leather lacing plus a leather rim, as opposed to the five rows on the other, but the lacing technique and pattern are exactly the same as described in the previous entry. On the exterior the lames are covered with a hard blackish layer, which may be an original protective coating of a lacquerlike material or a naturally occurring patination of surface deposits from years of storage in a *mgon khang* or a similar context. A carbon-14 test on a sample from the interior lacing yielded a date range of 1440–1640, meaning it is possible that this style of helmet remained in use later than is generally believed.[1]

1. Results at 2 sigma, 95% probability; tests by the Beta Analytic Radiocarbon Dating Laboratory, sample no. Geta-20221, March 21, 2005.

11. MULTI-PLATE HELMET OF FORTY-TWO LAMES

Possibly Tibetan, Mongolian, or Chinese, 15th century
Iron, gold, silver, brass or copper alloy, and leather
H. 10⅛ in. (25.7 cm)
Royal Armouries Museum, Leeds (XXVIA.158)

This helmet is similar to the two preceding examples in its general form and construction, but it differs enough in several important features that it constitutes a separate style and serves as a link with the helmets of the next multi-plate style, represented by the following two entries (cat. nos. 12, 13). The helmet is composed of forty-two lames, each pierced with ten lacing holes. The exposed left edge of each lame is indented with six cusps, one near the top and bottom and four in succession between them. Each lame has a raised medial ridge, a feature not found on the two previous examples but which does occur on the next two. The left edge of each lame rests against the medial ridge of the adjacent lame. The lames are joined by a row of rivets at the base of the finial and by two horizontal rows of leather lacing. The lacing of the upper row follows the same pattern as on the two previous examples: a lace follows a zigzag pattern, looping vertically through a pair of holes on the exterior and diagonally between the holes in each adjacent lame on the interior, reverses direction at the end, and is laced back through every other lame. Because this helmet has a brim, it is possible to tell that the lacing pattern starts at a lame in the center of the back of the helmet bowl. The lacing of the bottom row consists of a single lace that passes vertically through the paired holes on the outside and diagonally from one lame to the next on the inside. The holes around the base of the bowl are empty but probably once had a leather rim like that on the previous examples.

The helmet has a distinctive and highly decorated plume finial and brim, both of which are made of iron and damascened in gold and silver, and which are attached by brass or copper alloy rivets to the helmet bowl. The plume finial has a central cylindrical shaft with three knops, and a shallow inverted cup as a base. The brim has a scalloped border at its top edge and is turned sharply down. The decoration of the plume finial includes stylized blossoms in octagonal

11

11, detail of brim

compartments, floral scrollwork, and stylized lotus petals. In the center of the brim there is a flaming Sword of Wisdom, a symbol frequently seen in Tibetan art, flanked by scrollwork. The borders of the brim have three motifs often found on Tibetan and Chinese metalwork: a repeat pattern of tight concentric spirals in gold and silver, an interlocking Y pattern representing stylized armor scales, and a repeating wave pattern (see detail). The decoration should be compared with several objects in the exhibition, some of which have been attributed to both China and Tibet: two swords (cat. nos. 55, 57), a saddle (cat.

no. 111), a stirrup (cat. no. 129), a group of harness fittings (cat. no. 133), and two bridles (cat. nos. 134, 135).

That both the plume finial and the brim may be alterations added for ornamental purposes or later reuse is suggested by their lack of any stylistic relation to the workmanship of the helmet itself, and by the fact that they are attached with brass rivets. It seems likely that the finial of a helmet of this type was intended to be attached by leather lacing (as in cat. nos. 9, 10). Also, like the preceding examples the helmet may not have had a brim in its original state. The attachment of a decorated brim and plume finial by brass rivets and the brass trim added to the base of the finial are also very similar to the features on the multi-plate helmets in the following two entries, which are designed to be held together entirely with rivets and not lacing. Lastly, it should be pointed out that the proportions of the helmet bowl are small enough to suggest that it was made for a child or a very young man.

PROVENANCE: Private collection; sold, Sotheby's, New York, September 20–21, 1985, lot 29.

PUBLICATIONS: Sotheby's 1985, lot 29; Peers 1992, p. 45; LaRocca 1999a, p. 115, fig. 3.

12. MULTI-PLATE HELMET OF THIRTY-TWO LAMES

Mongolian or Tibetan, possibly 14th–16th century
Iron, silver, gold, and brass or copper alloy
H. 6¾ in. (17.1 cm)
The Metropolitan Museum of Art, New York, Purchase, Arthur Ochs Sulzberger Gift, 2005 (2005.146)

Despite some losses and damage, this helmet is largely intact and appears to be the most complete example from a small group of rare multi-plate helmets made in this particular style. The defining characteristics of the group are that each lame of the helmet has a raised medial ridge, that the left edge of each lame has an applied brass border as do other parts such as the base of the finial or the edges of the brim, and that all of the components are attached by brass rivets, not leather laces.

This particular helmet is made up of thirty-two arched lames, each of which has a raised medial ridge, the left edge of which has an applied brass border, as stated. The lames are even and well made, and fit together snugly. Each lame is pierced by only five holes, the positioning of which shows that the lames were specifically designed to be riveted, rather than laced, together. The tops of the lames are secured in position by being sandwiched between a flat internal ring made of iron and the base of the

external finial, which are riveted together. The finial is in the form of a hollow hemispherical knob, with a hole in the center, rising from a sloped circular base. There is an applied brass border around the base of the finial. On the front of the helmet there is a short brim with a scalloped upper edge. Both the finial and the brim are decorated with thick damascening in gold and silver. The top of the finial has a series of intertwining scrolls, while the base has a series of eight stylized lotus petals alternating with

12

12, detail of brim

12, detail of finial

floral motifs. In each lotus petal there is a Lantsa character or seed syllable (see detail), partially obscured by corrosion, but including OM, AH, and HUM.[1] In the center of the brim there is a cartouche with an animal in profile, possibly a lion. On the rim of the upper edge of the brim there are a series of five dry skulls (*thod skam*) with tendrils of flames. Three small cartouches on the front edge of the brim were once fitted with copper filigreed settings for stones, of which none of the stones and only one of the settings remain. On the front, back, and both sides of the helmet bowl there are areas that have been made flat by the removal of both the medial ridge and the brass borders of the lames. The remains of iron rivets at these spots indicate that they were intended for applied plaques or decorations of some kind.

Although the helmet has a uniform appearance, is very well made, and appears to be in original condition, it is possible that the finial and brim, the brass rivets, and all of the brass trim are slightly later modifications on this and on the other helmets of this type. Suggestive of this possibility is the fact that on one example (private collection) the interiors of the lames have been sequentially marked with incised Tibetan letters, which probably would have been done so that the helmet could be disassembled and then reassembled, possibly for modifications of the kind suggested here. This could mean that the helmets, if Mongolian, were refitted at some point for use in Tibet.

1. As read by Lozang Jamspal.

13. MULTI-PLATE HELMET OF THIRTY-ONE LAMES

Mongolian or Tibetan, possibly 15th–16th century
Iron, gold, silver, and brass or copper alloy
H. 9 in. (22.9 cm)
The Metropolitan Museum of Art, New York, Purchase, Arthur Ochs Sulzberger Gift, 2001 (2001.53)

The basic construction of this helmet is very similar to that of the preceding example, but differs in its form in that the lames are recurved at the top, rather than arching over to form a bowl. Each lame has a medial ridge, which in this instance takes the form of a sharp upright flange, and the edges of the lames are fitted with an applied brass border. The lames are joined by brass rivets, and each lame is pierced with five rivet holes. The interior edges of the lames are more roughly cut and less well finished than on the previous helmet, on which they are smooth, even, and file-dressed to have a slightly chamfered edge. The finial is in the form of a stepped dome on a straight-sided circular base. It is damascened somewhat crudely in gold and silver with stylized petals and lozenge motifs. The finial fits the bowl poorly, the tops of the lames and the brass edgings having been compressed and slightly distorted to fit within its base. A simple iron brim is attached to the front of the helmet by two brass rivets. A crude brass tab with a ragged front edge is riveted to the top of brim. That the brim was not originally intended for this helmet is suggested by the fact that the flanges of the lames beneath it have not been modified in any way and keep the brim from lying flush against the lames. A crude plume tube is attached to the front of the helmet near the rim to the proper left of the brim. The shape of the helmet bowl is partially distorted, possibly from damage or due to the lames being forced into the finial. Where the brass trim has been dislodged it can be seen that the external edges of the lames have been roughened with a chisel or a file to provide a better gripping surface for the trim. Although very closely related to the previous helmet, and clearly part of the same group, this example is not nearly as well finished or detailed in its construction. The finial, brim, and applied brass borders of this helmet may be later modifications, as suggested in the previous entry.

13

14. HELMET

Probably Mongolian, 14th–17th century
Iron, gold, silver, and turquoise
H. 7½ in. (19.1 cm)
The Metropolitan Museum of Art, New York, Purchase,
Arthur Ochs Sulzberger Gift, 2002 (2002.389)

Helmets with one-piece bowls are very rare in the context of Tibet, China, or Asia in general. This example is made of iron with a natural dark brown patina. The bowl slopes upward at the center to form a short cone, which is closed by a convex finial cap. In the front there is a brim in the form of a short horizontal flange with an ogival edge, which is made in one with the bowl. The front of the brim consists of a separate strip of iron and is riveted at either end to the bowl beneath the flange. Around the bottom edge of the bowl there is a row of nineteen holes, in which five original iron rivets remain. Two of the holes, located directly opposite one another at either side, are square rather than round and were probably intended to secure a chinstrap or a pair of earflaps. A series of blind rivets encircles the bowl just above these holes. The helmet is decorated with a large representation of the Three Jewels motif surrounded by flames on a lotus base, which is damascened in gold on the front, back, and either side. In the center of each of these there are three beaded silver settings for stones, which are missing except for two fragmentary pieces of turquoise that are probably later replacements. The uppermost setting is teardrop shaped, with two circular settings below.

This is an extremely rare and possibly early type of helmet, of which there are few comparable examples. The style, placement, and Buddhist iconography of the decoration are similar to that on a few early helmets attributed to Mongolia. The unusual construction of the brim also appears on some presumably later Mongolian helmets (such as cat. no. 15). The gold decoration combined with the solid construction of the helmet indicate that this was a practical field helmet, but made for someone of relatively high rank. The combination of these characteristics makes this an important piece in terms of reconstructing otherwise unknown aspects of early armor styles in Tibet and Central Asia.

14

15. HELMET

Mongolian, 15th–17th century
Iron
H. 11¾ in. (29.8 cm)
The Metropolitan Museum of Art, New York, Purchase, Arthur
Ochs Sulzberger Gift, 2005 (2005.271)

Like the preceding example, this helmet has a distinctive one-piece bowl, but in this case it is drawn up into a high steep cone, with a stepped profile at the midpoint of the sides that is characteristic of certain Mongolian helmets. Although the cylindrical plume finial at the apex appears to be forged as part of the bowl, it was actually made separately. The helmet has a dark brown patina but was once probably the bright color of polished iron. At the front edge of the bowl there is a short semicircular brim made in the same way as that on the preceding helmet. It consists of a flange made in one with the bowl, and a front piece made from a separate strip of iron that is riveted in place at either end beneath the flange. There are thirteen holes around the edge of the rim for the attachment of a lining or cheek and neck guards. The plume finial is made from a piece of iron rolled into a nearly solid bar, which was attached over the small opening at the top of the cone by dovetail joints and three blind rivets. It appears to have been repaired by brazing at least once in the past; more recently it was broken off entirely and was subsequently restored using modern conservation methods.

The stepped form of the bowl seems to have originated with the Mongols and is echoed in the helmets of many of the cultures upon which they had an impact. The one-piece construction of the bowl is also unusual for a Mongolian helmet, or for an Asiatic helmet of any type. In addition to the stepped bowl, the construction of the brim seems confined to a small group of Mongolian helmets, including that in the preceding entry and a stepped Mongolian helmet in the State Hermitage Museum, Saint Petersburg (N1274).

While many helmets from a Tibetan context show various types of damage, sometimes due to wear, age, or neglect, this helmet has clear signs of damage sustained in battle. Most noticeable among these is a diagonal cut across the proper left side of the bowl, probably made by the edge of a sword or an ax, which is in an area that would be a prime target for a right-handed attacker. There is another smaller diagonal cut on the right rear of the helmet. On the proper right front there is a small dent possibly caused by a projectile, such as an arrow or the pellet from a sling. In addition, there are three larger dents along the rim, which also may have been caused in battle.

15

16. HELMET

Mongolian, 15th–17th century
Iron and gold
H. 7⅝ in. (19.5 cm)
The Metropolitan Museum of Art, New York, Purchase, Gift of William H. Riggs, by exchange, 1999 (1999.120)

This is a distinctively Mongolian style of helmet, one of the few styles that can be recognized conclusively as such, which is represented by a small number of important examples in Russian collections that were collected in Mongolia and Central Asia in the eighteenth and nineteenth centuries.[1] While other helmets of this type are also decorated with Tibetan Buddhist symbols, this particular helmet has the richest and most complex combination of Tibetan iconography found on this or any other style of helmet from Tibet, Mongolia, or China.

In terms of construction, the helmet is made up of three principal sections: a broad brow band, a conical midsection made in two halves, and a short conical top, all of which are joined by internal iron straps and iron rivets. The decoration is damascened entirely in gold. In some forms of damascening the iron ground is crosshatched only within the incised outlines of the decorative patterns. On this example, however, the outer surface of the entire helmet is crosshatched, which is unusual on a large-scale object, even with such densely arranged decoration.

The short top section is encircled by a series of *tsi pa ṭa* or *kirttimukha* masks with long strands hanging from their mouths, which usually represent strings of jewels, but in this case have been suggested to depict jewels, bells, and yak tails.[2] The masks are connected by swags of intertwined tendrils. This motif is often used as a frieze or border decoration in Tibetan architecture and decorative arts, and frequently appears on Chinese helmets decorated with Tibetan Buddhist imagery, particularly those from the Qing dynasty. Below the *tsi pa ṭa* frieze, and forming the border of the next section, there is a row of *vajras* (*rdo rje*). The combination of these two motifs is often used in the decoration of ritual bells (*dril bu*) and other Tibetan objects.

The conical middle section of the helmet features six large oval cartouches, each of which contains a deity surrounded by a mandorla of flames. The center cartouche depicts Yamantaka, literally

"slayer of the lord of death" (*gshin rje'i gshed*), who has the head of a bull and holds a skull cup (*thod phor*) in his left hand and a ritual chopper (*gri gug*) in his right. The other cartouches have images of five female deities called Dakinis (*mkha' 'gro ma*), who wear garlands of skulls and hold implements or attributes connected with their names (see detail), which are given in the Lantsa inscriptions around the base of the helmet (described below). At the top and bottom of the spaces between the cartouches there are twelve circular compartments with protective *bija*, which are seed syllables written in a special stylized script. Around the seed syllables there are a series of inscriptions, written in Tibetan in the *dbu can* script, which identify the protective attributes of the adjacent seed syllables.[3] Starting from the left of the Yamantaka figure, and from top to bottom between each pair of large cartouches, they are as follows: *gza' skar ngan pa srung* (protect against bad planets and stars) and *'dre lnga srung* (protect against the five harmful ghosts);[4] *rlung rta skye pa* (generate good luck) and *bdud gcod srung ba* (protect against destructive demons);[5] *g.yul rgyal ba'i srung ba* (protect victory in battle) and *lha 'dre 'bum gyi srung ba* (protect against 100,000 gods and demons);[6] *lus [stobs skyed] pa* (generate bodily strength) and *tshes grangs ngan pa srung ba* (protect from inauspicious dates);[7] *dbang thang skyed pa* (generate power) and *don grub srung ba* (protect the accomplishment of our goals);[8] *mtshon srung* (protect against weapons) and *phyogs ngan srung ba* (protect against bad turnings).[9]

The brow of the helmet is encircled by a series of mantras in Lantsa characters, including invocations to Yamantaka and to the five Dakinis pictured above.[10] The Yamantaka invocation reads: *Om ya ma/ nta ka hum / phat.* The homage to the five Dakinis, giving their names in succession, reads: *Om vajradakini hum phat / Om ratnadakini hum phat / Om karmadakini hum phat / Om padmadakini hum phat / Om buddhadakini hum phat.* Below this is a phrase often found at the end of sutras: *Ye dharma hetuprabhava*

16, detail

hetu tesan tathagato hyavad tesanca yo nirodha evam vadi mahasramana.[11] This is followed by the mantra *om hum tram hrim* and the concluding supplication *mangalam*, meaning "may it be auspicious."

The symbol in the center of the brow is known as the All-Powerful Ten (*rnam bcu dbang ldan*), a stylized monogram formed from the ten Sanskrit syllables of the Kalachakra mantra.[12] To the proper right of this is a stupa (*mchod rten*), a stylized reliquary that represents the receptacle of Buddha's enlightened mind.

The form of this helmet, the extent of its decoration, and its symbolism indicate that it must have been made for a very high ranking Mongolian follower of Tibetan Buddhism, probably sometime in the period from the Third Dalai Lama (1543–1588) to the Fifth Dalai Lama (1617–1682).

PUBLICATIONS: Thurman and Weldon 1999, no. 76, pp. 166–67; Norwick 2003.

16

1. For examples, see *Musée de Tzarskoe-Selo* 1853, pl. CLXXVI, 1; Arendt 1935, pl. VI.

2. Thurman and Weldon 1999, p. 166.

3. The connection between the seed syllables and the adjacent inscriptions was pointed out by Braham Norwick, who matched them to the seed syllables in Skorupski 1983 and published an article based on his findings (Norwick 2003). A full reading of the Tibetan inscriptions was done by Lozang Jamspal.

4. Skorupski 1983, nos. 83, 84.

5. The first phrase corresponds to the text of no. 95 in Skorupski 1983, but the seed syllable is his no. 98. The second is ibid., no. 87.

6. The first phrase corresponds to the seed syllable to the right, ibid., no. 98, but the seed syllable it accompanies on the helmet is not included in Skorupski and was listed as unidentified in Norwick 2003. The second phrase and seed syllable are Skorupski 1983, no. 62.

7. Skorupski 1983, nos. 93, 84.

8. Ibid., nos. 94, 96.

9. Ibid., nos. 5, 85; however, the meaning for the second is given as "bad places."

10. As read by Braham Norwick, whose careful study of the mantras is included in Norwick 2003; and by Lozang Jamspal.

11. Lozang Jamspal gives the often-found Tibetan equivalent as *chos rnams thams cad rgyu las 'byung / de'i rgyu de bzhin gshegs pas gsungs / rgyu rnams 'gog pa gang yin pa / dge dbyong chen pos de skad gsung.*

12. See Beer 1999, pp. 123–27.

17. HELMET OF EIGHT PLATES

Korean or Mongolian in the Korean style,
possibly 14th–16th century
Iron and leather
H. 5⅛ in. (13 cm)
The Metropolitan Museum of Art, New York, Purchase,
Arthur Ochs Sulzberger Gift, 2001 (2001.181)

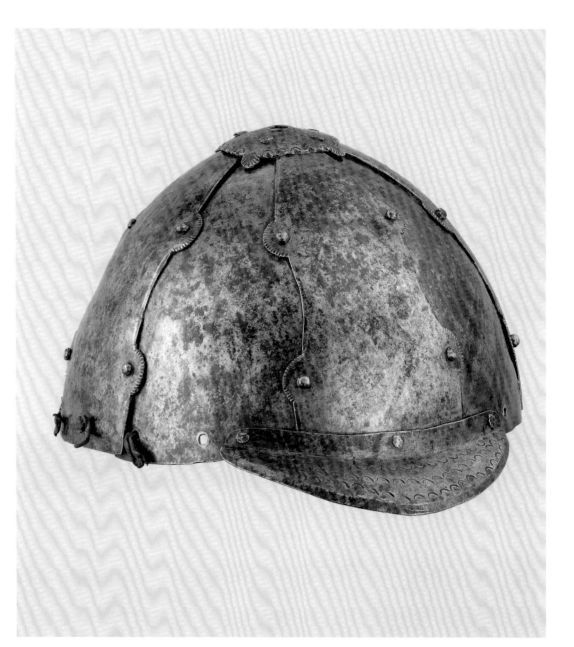

17

Although quite plain, this helmet is of interest for its unusual form, which shows what appears to be Korean influence, and may in fact be Korean, coupled with the likelihood that it comes from Tibet. The link, of course, may be the Mongols, who conquered Korea in the thirteenth century, maintained control of it until the late fourteenth century, and incorporated Korean auxiliaries into Mongolian armies during that period and perhaps much later.

The helmet consists of a low hemispherical bowl made up of eight plates: four outer plates and four inner plates overlapping in an alternating over-under pattern. The outer plates are slightly cusped and have two serrated half-round extensions on either side, where they are attached by dome-headed rivets to the inner plates. Each outer plate has six rivet holes, while each inner plate has eight. There are a series of sixteen holes around the base of the bowl, which appear to have been enlarged with a squared punch during the helmet's working lifetime. There are remains of leather lacing in four of these holes, which probably once served to attach a nape defense of some kind. The finial plate at the top of the bowl is convex and is square with serrated extensions at each corner, cusped edges, and a central hole for a missing plume tube. There is a flat, crescentic brim riveted to the front edge of the bowl. The finial and the brim are decorated with simple incised or punched crescent motifs.

The closest parallels to this helmet are two Korean helmets that have plates of this shape and construction and this form of finial, although they are taller in profile rather than low and round like the present example and appear to be less strongly made.[1]

1. See Boots 1932, pl. 34; Robinson 1967, fig. 85; Yi 1987, p. 94.

18. HELMET

Mongolian or Chinese, 1350–1450
Iron and gold
H. 7½ in. (19 cm)
The Metropolitan Museum of Art, New York, Purchase, Arthur
Ochs Sulzberger Gift, 2005 (2005.270)

Based on the style and technique of its decoration this helmet appears to date from the late Yuan to the early Ming dynasty. Armor that can be reasonably attributed to this period is extremely rare, making this helmet important as a link between earlier Mongolian or Tibetan examples and the elaborately decorated Chinese helmets of the Qing dynasty that followed. The style of the decoration shows Tibetan and Mongolian influence and suggests a date of no later than the first half of the fifteenth century. In addition, the technique of damascening with flat strips of gold instead of gold wire is found on only a few other pieces, such as a pair of stirrups (cat. no. 127), Tibetan or Mongolian, possibly twelfth–fourteenth century; a knee or shoulder defense (cat. no. 47), possibly Mongolian or Chinese, thirteenth–fifteenth century; and an elaborate Mongolian or Tibetan shaffron (cat no. 27), fifteenth–seventeenth century. Also, the placement of a swastika band in the decoration beneath the brim can be seen on a very unusual Central Asian helmet (cat. no. 23), also possibly fifteenth–seventeenth century.[1]

The helmet is heavily decorated with gold damascening and consists of a bowl in two halves topped by a half-round finial with a small knob in its center. The two halves are riveted to an internal iron strap underlying each seam. The finial is also attached by iron rivets. There are fourteen holes along the rim for the attachment of missing nape and cheek defenses. The details of the decoration are lightly engraved in the gold of the damascened areas, not into the iron ground itself. On the front half of the helmet the decoration features a centrally placed flaming mandorla engraved with the image of a seated Buddha. On either side are a lotus on an undulating leafy stalk and a large four-clawed dragon in a vertical S-curve position. On the back half of the helmet two large horizontally placed dragons flank a flaming pearl. Other small motifs are interspersed throughout, including flames, clouds, and auspicious

18

symbols from the set known as the Seven Gems (*nor bu cha bdun*). Borders above and below encircle the helmet and consist of bands with individual lotus and other blossoms in oval scroll cartouches. The bands are edged with a series of cusps and lobed, leaflike finials. There is a short band at the brow with a repeating swastika pattern, which would have been concealed beneath the missing brim (as on cat. no. 23). The finial is decorated with a repeat of the blossoms found on the two bands bordering the main motifs and with narrow gold borders.

Although not readily apparent in the photographs, the iron ground of the helmet has had significant corrosion, which has left a dark brown patina and many losses of gold throughout. The shape of the helmet is somewhat distorted on the proper left side, particularly near the base, but overall it is stable, with many areas of the gold intact and in good condition.

1. A helmet remarkably similar to cat. no. 18 in terms of form, construction, and decoration appeared on the art market in 1995; its chief difference is that it is damascened in silver, rather than gold. A rudimentary line drawing of it was published in Nicolle 1999 (p. 488, fig. 813h). In the course of examining the helmet, Robert Carroll discovered three fragments of paper with passages of Tibetan text printed in *dbu can* script, which were rolled up inside the short plume tube on the helmet's finial. The helmet is currently in a private collection.

18, back view

19. HELMET

Chinese, probably mid- to late 17th century
Iron, gold, silver, and textile
H. 8¼ in. (21 cm)
The Metropolitan Museum of Art, New York, Purchase, Bashford
Dean Memorial Collection, Funds from various donors, by
exchange, 1997 (1997.18)

19

19, detail of brow plate

This helmet is distinctive both for the quality of its workmanship and for the lively character of its engraved and gilded decoration. Because of its overall form and the style of its ornament, it can be considered an early example of helmet types that are usually associated with either the later part of the Ming dynasty (1368–1644) or the more familiar ceremonial helmets of the Qing dynasty (1644–1911).[1]

The helmet is constructed in three basic sections: a spool-shaped finial, a chamfered bowl made in two halves, and a brow band. All of the components are attached by iron rivets. The two halves of the bowl are joined by two internal iron straps and two corresponding external iron struts. A short brim with a faceted edge is riveted to the front of the brow. The brow band has a central peak and two arches over the eye area. A strip of textile riveted along the rim of the back half of the helmet is the remains of a missing nape defense, probably made of fabric reinforced with small iron plates.

The gilding of the helmet's fittings consists of two layers: silver foil burnished onto a crosshatched ground, over which a layer of gold was applied, probably by mercury gilding. This unusual two-stage technique is also found on a saddle and a few other pieces (cat. nos. 118–121). It is a rare alternative to damascening and perhaps implies the lack of the ability or knowledge of mercury gilding directly on iron, the latter technique apparently not being practiced in Asia until much later (see cat. no. 124).

The gilding serves to highlight the crisply engraved ornament, which embellishes the helmet's finial, brim, and brow plate. In the center of the brow is the figure of Buddha Shakyamuni seated on a lotus throne (see detail). The Buddha is flanked by the four *lokapala*, the heavenly guardians of the four directions. Lively dragons, one on each side of a flaming pearl, appear on the finial and brim, a standard motif on virtually all later Chinese ceremonial helmets. Here, however, the design is rendered with a freshness and originality that are unknown on later, more stereotypical examples. Therefore, the innovative nature of the decoration, combined with the skillful construction or the helmet, suggests that this is a very early example of its type. Like some other rare examples of Chinese art, its survival is apparently due to its preservation in Tibet, where it may have been sent from China as a gift or was worn by a high-ranking Chinese officer stationed in Tibet.

PUBLICATIONS: LaRocca 1997, p. 90; LaRocca 1999a, pp. 114–15, 128–30, figs. 4, 33; Pyhrr, LaRocca, and Ogawa 2002, pp. 52–53.

1. I am particularly grateful to Philip Tom and Scott Rodell for advice concerning the development of Chinese helmets under the Ming and Qing.

20. HELMET

Chinese, probably 17th century
Iron and gold
H. 8¼ in. (21 cm)
Courtesy of the Board of Trustees, National Museums Liverpool
(56.27.207)

20

This helmet is extremely similar to the preceding example in its form and general appearance, with a few interesting differences that suggest it may be slightly later in date. The bowl of the helmet is rounded rather than chamfered, and despite having four external struts, it is made in one piece, unlike the previous helmet in which the bowl has two external struts and is made in two pieces. There are several areas in which traces of gold damascening remain, showing that the gold was applied in the conventional manner, again unlike the previous example. The traces of damascening are apparent on the trefoil tabs at the base of the finial, the top edge of the brow band, and the upper edge of the brim. The helmet's very shiny surface is due to over-cleaning in the past. Otherwise, the two helmets are virtually identical in form, construction, and size.

The provenance of this helmet is also interesting, having been collected by John Claude White (1853–1918), a participant in the Younghusband Expedition who was the first Political Officer Sikkim, the British official of the Indian government with local responsibility for Sikkim, Bhutan, and Tibet, serving from 1889 to 1908.

PROVENANCE: Jean Claude White, Sikkim; Castle Museum, Norwich (147.79.928).

21. HELMET

Possibly Iranian or Central Asian, 14th–16th century
Iron and brass or copper alloy
H. 8⅞ in. (22.5 cm)
The Metropolitan Museum of Art, New York, Purchase,
Arthur Ochs Sulzberger Gift, 2001 (2001.162)

The form, construction, and decoration of this helmet present a rare combination of Middle Eastern and Central Asian styles. The eight-plate construction is similar to that of helmets from Tibet, while the applied brass or copper alloy borders are very similar to those on helmets with both Tibetan and Mongolian attributions (cat. nos. 11–13). The peaked shape of the helmet bowl and the raised decoration, however, are strongly reminiscent of helmets depicted in various Iranian Shahnameh manuscripts of the fourteenth and fifteenth centuries.[1] The combination of these features makes it possible that this helmet originated in western Central Asia or Iran under the influence of the Mongols or contacts with western Tibet.

The helmet consists of eight plates, four inner plates and four outer plates, overlapping in an over-under pattern. The outer plates have two cusps on either side. The plates are recurved so that the top of the helmet bowl forms a conical tube. The finial is missing. Both the inner and outer plates are embossed with a series of raised vertical lines with dagged ends, forming an elongated petal motif around the top half of the helmet. A horizontal brow band encircles the base of the helmet. The bottom edge of the brow band has a narrow outward-turned border. The components are attached with iron and brass rivets. The edges of the outer plates of the helmet bowl and the top edge of the brow band are fitted with brass borders, several sections of which are missing. Where the borders are missing it can be seen that the edges of the plates have been scored with a chisel or file, as on the helmet in catalogue number 13. A raised brass disk, perhaps representing the sun, is attached to the center of the helmet at the front. Much of the surface of the helmet is covered with a hard, glossy brown coating that appears to be the remains of an original finish, possibly a type of lacquer. Small traces of bright iron finish are found along some of the raised lines and at the edges where the brass trim is missing, showing that the underlying surface had a pearly silver color.

21

1. For a good survey of comparative examples in terms of general form and style, see Gorelik 1979.

22. HELMET

Western Tibetan or Central Asian, possibly 14th–16th century
Iron, copper alloy, and textile
H. 17½ in. (44.5 cm)
The Metropolitan Museum of Art, New York, Purchase,
Arthur Ochs Sulzberger Gift, 2001 (2001.91)

This is an extremely unusual form of helmet, different in form and style from virtually every other recognized type that was used in Tibet and the surrounding regions. Two similar examples have been published: one photographed in an unspecified location in Tibet, and the other in the Kremlin Armory, Moscow (fig. 43).[1] They may represent a very localized or regional style used in western Tibet or by one of the western Mongol tribes.

The helmet is constructed of eight plates roughly the same size and shape, which overlap in an alternating over-under pattern. The tops of the plates narrow and extend upward to form a tall cylindrical apex, while the lower portions widen and curve out to form the bowl of the helmet. The top is closed by a flat circular plate, its edge turned down at a right angle and cut in a sawtooth pattern. In the center of this plate there is a tall funnel-shaped plume tube, around the base of which there are four knob finials. The base of the bowl is overlapped and encircled by a brow band made of a single strip of iron. On the rear of the brow band there are four star-shaped rivets for securing a nape defense made of textile, small traces of which remain around each rivet. Three empty holes at the front of the brow indicate the original placement of the missing brim. The components are attached by iron and copper alloy rivets. The helmet now has a deep brown patina, but originally it was probably a bright polished iron color.

1. *Tibet* 1981, p. 43, fig. 21, shows the first helmet along with two Tibetan spears, a Tibetan wicker shield, and the remains of a lamellar armor; no location or other identifying information is given. In *Drevnostei Rossiiskago gosudarstva* (Antiquities of the Russian Empire), illustrated by F. G. Solntsev (Moscow, 1849–53), vol. 3, pl. 27, the Moscow example is identified simply as a Mongolian helmet.

Fig. 43. Kremlin Armory Mongolian helmet, after *Drevnostei Rossiiskago gosudarstva* (Antiquities of the Russian Empire), illustrated by F. G. Solntsev (Moscow, 1849–53), vol. 3, pl. 27

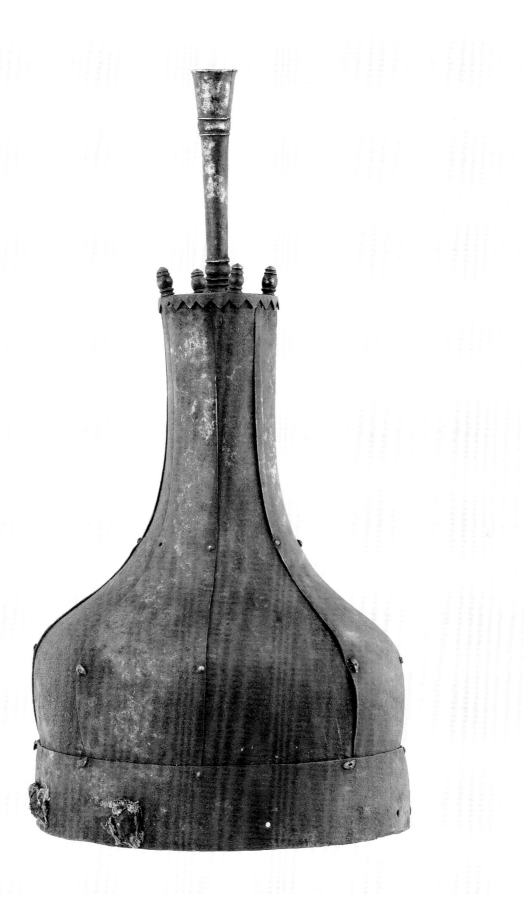

23. HELMET

Tibetan or Central Asian, possibly 15th–17th century
Iron and silver
H. 8 in. (20.3 cm)
The Metropolitan Museum of Art, New York, Bequest of George C. Stone, 1935 (36.25.96)

This helmet also presents an interesting mix of forms, coupled with a highly unusual style of decoration. The bowl consists of four plates riveted to internal iron straps, a form of construction seen in Chinese helmets of the Ming and Qing dynasties. The plume finial is a classic Tibetan type, with two lozenge-shaped knops, one in the center and one at the very top. The base of the finial has been reshaped to fit the top of the bowl. Also, the presence of four unused pairs of holes around the base of the finial shows it to be the type made to be held by laces, rather than riveted in place as it is now. A one-piece iron brim is attached to the front of the bowl by three rivets, and could be Mongolian or Chinese in style. There are a series of twenty-five unused and slightly irregularly spaced holes around the rim of the helmet. The rim has period repairs in two places in the form of internal iron patches riveted in place. A short longitudinal cut on the upper rear of the bowl appears to be damage from a weapon, such as a sword or an ax.

More unusual than the combination of elements is the style of the decoration, which is damascened in silver and is arranged in three bands around the helmet bowl. The top band has a very highly stylized version of a motif otherwise found so often on Chinese helmets, a dragon with clouds and a pearl, repeating four times. In the center of the middle band there is an inverted heart shape surrounded by stylized flames, which appear to be a version of the Three Jewels motif. A Mongolian form of stylized lotus blossom repeats around the rest of the band. The lower band has repeating pairs of reversed scrolls. Beneath the brim, which must be a slightly later addition, there is a rectangular cartouche with five repeating pairs of swastikas, the arms pointing in opposite directions (see detail). The swastika band, which can be compared with that on the helmet in catalogue number 18, was only discovered when the helmet was being conserved in 1999. Despite the seeming simplicity of the decoration, however, the designs are carefully rendered and the damascening is very well done. The style of the decoration suggests the helmet originated somewhere in Central Asia, with influence from both China and Tibet. It was catalogued by George Stone as being from Bhutan.

PROVENANCE: W. O. Oldman, London; George Cameron Stone, New York.

PUBLICATION: LaRocca 1999a, pp. 115–16 and fig. 6.

23, detail of brow of helmet with brim removed

23

སྦ་བ

Shields

Although they have been generally overlooked in the little that has been written on the subject of Tibetan arms and armor, shields were widely used at certain points in Tibetan history.[1] They were invariably round and consist of two basic types: shields made of wicker or cane (*sba phub*), and shields made of leather (*ko phub*). Of these, the cane shields seem to have been made in Tibet, while most if not all of the leather shields appear to have come from India, Bhutan, Sikkim, and probably Nepal. The cane shields have two principal forms: flat (cat. no. 24), and domed or convex (cat. no. 25).

Domed cane shields, as a type, were used over a wide geographical area, from China to the Middle East. In profile the Chinese examples are the most deeply domed, the Tibetan type less so, and the Middle Eastern style only slightly convex. The type culminated, in terms of construction and aesthetics, with Ottoman cane shields of the sixteenth and seventeenth centuries, the best examples of which are finely made and have exteriors that are delicately embroidered in silk and sometimes beautifully painted.[2] Domed cane shields in Tibet can be completely plain or have varying degrees of painted decoration (see, for example, the shield in Drepung Monastery, fig. 14). This type has a small central iron boss and is held by a single handle in the center of the back.

The large flat type of cane shield may have been indigenous to Tibet and perhaps was more prevalent in western Tibet, judging by the examples found there and in Ladakh (see fig. 9). This type has a peaked iron boss in the center from which a series of iron struts radiate. Shields of similar size and shape but with no iron struts may represent another distinct type, or simply a variation of the type.[3] Photographs of the Great Prayer Festival in Lhasa show some flat cane shields, but the domed type seems to predominate.[4] Like the domed shields, the majority of flat shields had a single handgrip in the center of the back.

Leather shields, sometimes made from rhinoceros hide, are hard, strong, and relatively light.[5] They generally have at least four small metal bosses on the exterior, which anchor the handgrips, and sometimes an arm strap, on the interior (see the shield in fig. 16 for a representative example). This general type, from India and elsewhere, was probably used widely in areas along Tibet's entire southern border.[6] There is also at least one example of a wooden shield wrapped entirely in intricately laced leather, which has a Tibetan provenance, but this may be an instance of a locally made, one-of-a-kind type.[7]

1. For instance, Robinson (1967, p. 162) stated, incorrectly, that shields were not much used in Tibet. Also, a brief chapter on shields is included in Gangtok 1981, pp. 105–6, which, however, is the only Tibetan text to do so among those surveyed here.
2. For example, see several shields in the Topkapi Museum, Istanbul; Esin Atil, ed., *The Age of Sultan Süleyman the Magnificent*, exh. cat., National Gallery of Art (Washington, 1987), nos. 98–102 (illus.).
3. See, for instance, the large flat cane shield in a photo by Ilya Tolstoy (Tung 1996, pl. 101), which is trimmed with feathers and does not have metal struts.
4. See Richardson 1993, illus. p. 44.
5. For an example of an Indian shield made of rhinoceros hide and used in Tibet, see Laufer 1914, pl. XXVII, fig. 1. Laufer also referred to the plain, domed style of cane shield as "the national shield of the Tibetans" (ibid., pl. XXVII, fig. 2).
6. For discussions of the various types of trans-Himalayan shields, see Robinson 1967 and Pant 1982.
7. Pitt Rivers Museum, Oxford, 1954.6.133, ex-coll. H. G. Beasley, Cranmore Museum.

24. FLAT CANE SHIELD WITH IRON STRUTS

Tibetan, possibly 14th–16th century
Cane, iron, and brass
Diam. 29⅞ in. (75.9 cm)
The Metropolitan Museum of Art, New York, Purchase, Arthur Ochs Sulzberger Gift, 2001 (2001.55)

This shield belongs to a rare and only recently recognized group, examples of which have been found at Tsaparang in the Ngari area of western Tibet, and in Phyang Monastery, Ladakh.[1] The iron fittings on these shields are extremely similar to those on some types of Tibetan leather arm guards (see cat. no. 35) and on Tibetan furniture, especially leather boxes.[2]

The shield is constructed of a sturdy rod of cane, tightly coiled into a spiral forming twenty-five continuous concentric rings. The rows are joined by being transversely wrapped entirely in thin split cane, except for the outermost ring. The surface of the shield is decorated and reinforced by iron fittings, which are attached by dome-headed nails. The fittings consist of a peaked central boss, from which eight pierced and engraved struts radiate. Four of these terminate in smaller bosses, and four

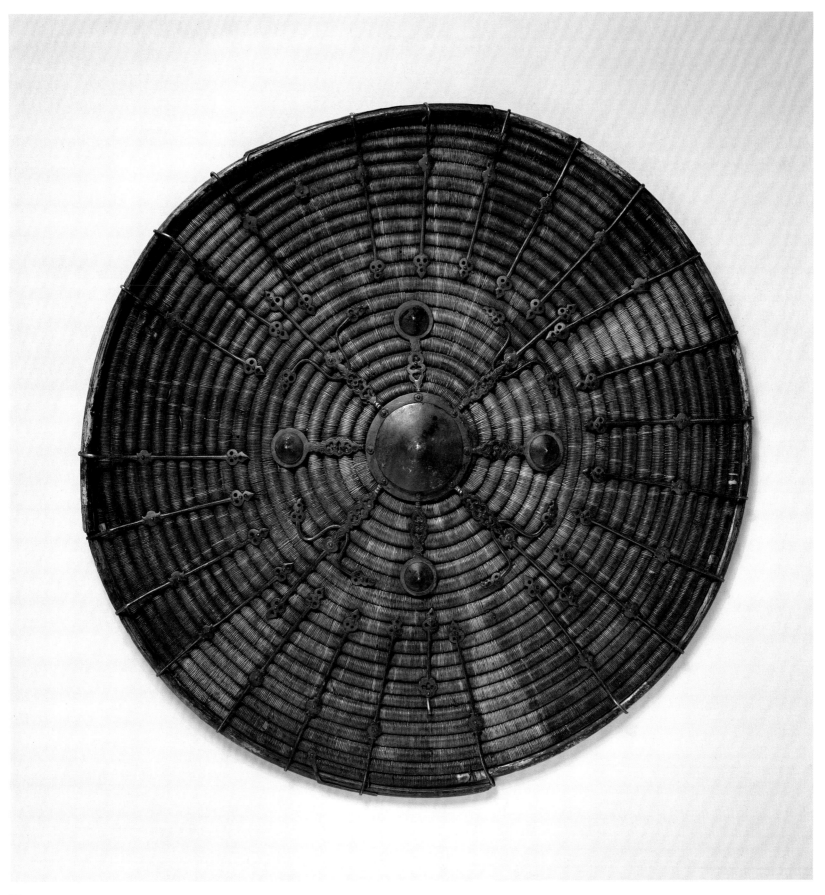

in tridentlike ribs with pierced leaf-shaped finials. A series of twenty-three full and two partial struts, also with pierced leaf-shaped finials, radiate from the rim toward the center. The ends of these struts hook over the rim and are secured by nails to the interior. Two appear to be missing altogether. Many of the nail heads have decorative brass washers. The pierced struts of the four smaller bosses are backed by a plate, possibly tinned or silvered iron or copper, which shows through the piercings. Variegated light and dark patterns on the split caning suggest a sunburst motif over the entire surface of the shield beneath the iron fittings. Two reinforcing strips of plain iron are located along the exterior edge. Three small iron rings are found on the interior, which is otherwise plain.

PUBLICATIONS: LaRocca 2001, p. 83; Pyhrr, LaRocca, and Ogawa 2002, no. 43, p. 46.

1. See "Rediscovering the Arms and Armor of Tibet" and fig. 9 for a discussion and for notes on published examples. A very good shield from this group is also in the Royal Armouries Museum, Leeds (XXVIA.275). Another was published in Gutowski 1997, no. 2.
2. See Anninos 2000, esp. figs. 6–8, 16, 20–24; Kamansky 2004, p. 39 and nos. 57–59, and several other examples therein.

25. DOMED CANE SHIELD

Tibetan, possibly 15th–18th century
Cane, iron, brass, silver, pigments, and leather
Diam. 24 in. (61 cm); H. 10¾ in. (27.3 cm)
The Metropolitan Museum of Art, New York, Purchase, Arthur Ochs Sulzberger Gift, 2005 (2005.145)

Domed cane shields of this type appear in at least one photograph from the Younghusband era (fig. 4), in several scenes of the armored infantry (*zimchongpa*) participating in the Great Prayer Festival in Lhasa, and in *mgon khang* or similar settings (figs. 11, 14).[1]

Like the preceding example, this shield consists of a thick rod of cane, tightly coiled into a spiral, in this instance into twenty-five concentric circular rows, each row being stepped slightly so as to create a dome shape. The rows are completely wrapped with thin split cane, which holds them together. The two outermost rows are covered in thick leather. The remains of four leather laces are threaded through the cane (two in the sixth row and two in the tenth row), which originally must have secured the handgrip, now missing from the interior. In the center of the shield there is a small iron boss held by three brass nails. The boss consists of a short cone on a circular base. It is damascened in silver with stylized petals on the cone and a repeating Chinese coin motif around the base. The surface of the shield is painted red, with six almond-shaped cartouches in black. In the center of each cartouche are traces of what appear to be a Lantsa character (such as can be seen on the shield in Drepung, fig. 14). Between the cartouches there are small wedges of black pointing to the center of the shield. Similar patterns can also be seen on the shields in the photos of the Great Prayer Festival and elsewhere cited above.

1. See, for instance, Richardson 1993, p. 44, in which the majority of the *zimchongpa* carry domed shields, but several also have large flat shields.

25

ཧ་གོ
Horse Armor

Lamellar horse armor made of iron appears to have been in use by the nomadic peoples on the borders of China by the end of the Han dynasty (206 B.C.–A.D. 220) and was in evidence in China itself by the Three Kingdoms Period (220–280).[1] Horse armor with lamellae of similar form and lacing pattern to that found on later Tibetan lamellar armors existed in the Middle East by the early seventh century A.D., as shown by the detailed depiction of it on an often cited sculpture of a Sasanian king at Taq-i Bustan.[2] The Annals of the Tang dynasty (618–906) mention the horse armor of the Tibetans in their overall praise of the strength and beauty of Tibetan armor and weapons.[3] Giovanni di Plano Carpini, writing in 1247, described how the Mongols made iron lamellar armor for men and horses.[4] Many Middle Eastern and Indian illuminated manuscripts include images of horse armor in depictions of the Mongols and their successors in Iran and West Asia in the fourteenth and fifteenth centuries, and of the Mughals in India in the sixteenth century. However, despite this comparative wealth of sources relating to the general type, the specific form of horse armor found in Tibet remains sui generis, a type that exists nowhere other than Tibet, and is known only due to the actual examples coming from Tibet (fig. 3), which are very rare. No example that is actually complete and homogeneous is known to exist, the closest being the armor in the Victoria and Albert Museum, London (included in cat. no. 26), along with two other more composite and less complete examples.[5] The next largest set of matching pieces from a single horse armor is in the Royal Museum, Edinburgh (cat. no. 32). After that it is a matter of individual elements, of which the best available examples in terms of quality and condition have been included here.

The salient features that distinguish Tibetan horse armor are not only the use of iron lamellae, but also their combination with distinctive panels of gilded and varnished leather. The elements of a complete horse armor of the Tibetan type, and their corresponding names in European armor nomenclature, include a head defense, or shaffron (cat. nos. 27–29); a pair of large wing-shaped neck defenses, or crinet (cat. nos. 30, 33); a breast defense, or peytral (cat. nos. 30–32); panels at the sides below the saddle, or flanchards (cat. no. 26); a loin defense in the form of a rectangular panel that lies along the top of the rump from the back of the saddle to the base of the tail and ends in a cloverleaf shape (cat. no. 26), two large panels to protect the flank, thigh, and rump area (cat. no. 32), and a tailpiece covering the back of the hindquarters below the tail (cat. no. 32), which in a European context are collectively referred to as the crupper defense.[6] These will be described in detail under the individual catalogue entries.

The decoration of the leather panels has a lacquerlike appearance but is not true lacquer in the sense of *urushi*. Instead, the effect appears to be achieved through the application of layers of shellac, gold leaf, and a glaze of tung oil.[7] On the best examples the quality of the decoration can be very high. The range of motifs includes a wide array of scrollwork, lotus and other blossoms, dragons and various mythological animals, the Eight Auspicious Symbols, and other Buddhist imagery. The way in which the leather panels are joined together also seems to be unique to Tibetan horse armor. Details of the assembly of the panels, as well as their decoration, will be discussed in the individual catalogue entries.

The only known variation of this type, and it is a significant one, is the horse armor found in Tsaparang, in western Tibet, and in Phyang Monastery, in Ladakh (figs. 9, 15).[8] In this instance the armor consists mostly of textile, reinforced with small iron plates of various shapes and sizes, some of which are the same or closely related to the plates used on the more conventional Tibetan style of horse armor. The neck defenses of the Tsaparang-Phyang type also retain the winglike shape, although they are made in one continuous piece with the peytral. The use of textile, rather than a leather ground, may represent a different regional style, perhaps one more suited to the climate or conditions of western Tibet.

In terms of dating, five separate carbon-14 tests have been made by the Metropolitan Museum on samples from four different elements of horse armor (cat. nos. 27, 30, 31), with the results consistently being from the early to mid-fifteenth century to the mid-seventeenth century.[9] Therefore, this time frame has been adopted here as a working range for dating Tibetan horse armors of the combined iron and varnished leather type. It is also probably no accident that this period coincides closely with the era of the last two secular monarchies in Tibet, the Rinpung (*rin spungs*, 1435–1565) and the kings of Tsang (1566–1641), a period of intermittent strife and at times outright civil war.[10]

The question again arises as to whether these horse armors are Tibetan or Mongolian, the latter attribution having been put forward anecdotally in recent years. As with the lamellar armor, however, there does not seem to be enough definitive evidence to categorically assign this body of material to the Mongols rather than to the Tibetans. Giovanni di Plano Carpini's description of Mongolian horse armor, while extremely useful, shows only that the Mongols used horse armor of this general type elsewhere in Central Asia roughly two centuries before the earliest datable horse armor from Tibet.[11] All of the surviving examples come from Tibet, and not from any of the many areas outside of Tibet associated with the Mongols. The decorative technique of the gilded and varnished leather panels has many parallels in the decoration of Tibetan leather boxes. The only markings found on the interiors of the horse armors consist of either Tibetan letters or wax seals. In addition, the only consistently made carbon-14 tests place these armors in a period of active internal conflict among the secular ruling factions within Tibet. However, it cannot be overlooked that there seems to be no mention of horse armor in the period Tibetan texts such as that by Tashi Namgyal, nor is it depicted in any Tibetan works of art. Given these factors, it seems reasonable for now to retain the original attributions made by the Thirteenth Dalai Lama, Sir Charles Bell, L. A. Waddell, and others, that these horse armors are Tibetan, while not entirely ruling out the possibility that at least some may be Mongolian, pending further research.

1. Brentjes 1996, esp. p. 70; and Yang Hong 1992, pp. 239–43.
2. Nicolle 2002, esp. pls. XIII, 3a–c.
3. References cited in Beckwith 1993, p. 110.
4. Beazley 1967, p. 124.

5. The armor in cat. no. 26 is V&A IM.30&A–J-1933; the others are V&A IM.72&A–J-1910 and IM.73&A–P-1910. The first two are illustrated in Stone 1934, fig. 125.
6. On the European terms, see Pyhrr, LaRocca, and Breiding 2005.
7. Richard Stone and Pete Dandridge, Objects Conservation Department of The Metropolitan Museum of Art, first identified the use of tung oil in this context through examination of the horse armor in the Metropolitan (cat. nos. 30, 31) and in comparison with Tibetan leather boxes in the Newark Museum, kindly lent by Valrae Reynolds for this purpose in 1997. They also suggested that the gold floral designs were applied gold leaf, rather than gold pigments. On the use of gold leaf see the comments in "Leather Armor" below. Recent examination of the Tibetan horse armor in the Royal Museum, Edinburgh (cat. no. 32), by Dr. Anita Quye using FTIR (Fourier tranform infrared) analysis resulted in the identification of layers of shellac beneath layers of tung oil. I am very grateful to Dr. Quye, Katie Simes, and Jane Wilkinson for sharing the results of this analysis.
8. See "Rediscovering the Arms and Armor of Tibet" for the context of these finds and for references. The combined breast and neck defense of the restored horse armor from Tsaparang is illustrated in color in *Tesori del Tibet*, exh. cat. (Milan, 1994), no. 21, where it is dated to the 16th century and incorrectly described as a "sottosella" (saddle rug).
9. Results are given in the individual catalogue entries and in the appendix "Radiocarbon Dating Results."
10. On this period see Shakabpa 1967, pp. 73–90.
11. For Giovanni di Plano Carpini's description of Mongolian horse armor, see Beazley 1967, p. 124.

26. ARMOR FOR MAN AND HORSE

Tibetan or Mongolian, and Bhutanese (helmet only), mainly 15th–17th century
Iron, leather, gold, silver, brass or copper alloy, wood, cane, textile, and yak hair
Victoria and Albert Museum, London (IM.30-1933, IM.30A-1933, IM.30D–J-1933 [horse armor]; IM.72-1910 [saddle]; IM.73O-1910 [reins and bit]), and
Royal Armouries Museum, Leeds (XXVIH.21–22 [crinet pieces of horse armor]); XXVIA.122 [helmet]; XXVIA.157 [lamellar armor for man]; XXVIA.276
[shield]; XXVIB.78, .141, .145 [arrow, quiver, and bow case]; XXVIH.38a, b [stirrups]; XXVIS.298 [sword and scabbard])

This horse armor, except for the neck guards, was given to Sir Charles Bell (1870–1945), the British Political Officer Sikkim, by the Thirteenth Dalai Lama, Thubten Gyatso (*thub bstan rgya mtsho*, 1876–1933) in 1910 in Darjeeling, where the Dalai Lama stayed as a guest of the British government during the Chinese invasion of Tibet from 1909 to 1911. Bell had a deep personal and scholarly interest in Tibet, well beyond the requirements of his professional responsibilities, and developed a lasting friendship with the Dalai Lama. In a letter to the Superintendent of the South Kensington Museum, written from Sikkim on January 15, 1913, Bell commented: "I am sending you on loan a set of old Tibetan armour for a horse and a cavalryman. It was presented to me by the Dalai Lama, and is over 200 years old. Tibetans have, so he informs me, lost the art of making it so

well now-a-days." After listing the pieces involved, he says in the closing: "So far as I am aware there is no other set of such Tibetan armor outside of Tibet as good as this."[1] Bell's comments are particularly interesting in recording that the Dalai Lama seems to have personally identified the horse armor as Tibetan, and as a type of thing that could still be made by Tibetans, although not as well as before. Bell gave the armor to the museum in 1933, perhaps in memory of the Dalai Lama, who died in that year. In the museum register at that time it is described as: "Suit of Horse-armour. Mostly of the 17th century. Presented to the donor by the Dalai Lama in 1910, at Darjeeling, during his flight from Lhasa."[2] The horse armor was put on long-term loan to the Tower of London in the 1960s, and has been displayed at the Royal Armouries Museum in Leeds in its cur-

rent configuration since 1996, with the man's armor and accessories belonging to the Royal Armouries. The neck guards currently with the armor (RA XXVIH.21–22) were added at that time.[3]

The shaffron (V&A IM.30-1933) follows the basic form and construction shared by most Tibetan shaffrons. It consists of a leather ground covered with small square iron plates, which are sewn to the ground by leather laces threaded through a single hole in the corner of each plate. The center of each plate is raised to form a hollow boss, and a detached boss of the same size covers the lacing at the corner of each plate. The eye openings are surrounded by a series of smaller bosses and a narrow piping of shagreen, a pebbled green leather or fish skin (*sag ri* or *nya lpags*). A similar border runs around the outer edge of the entire piece. A rectangular iron plate, which expands to a circular shape in the forehead area, covers the center of the shaffron from top to bottom. This plate has an applied central ridge made of iron with scalloped edges made of brass or a copper alloy. The plate also has an applied outer border of copper alloy. It has a hinged iron poll plate at the top and a similar snout plate at the bottom. These are pierced with broad scrollwork and heavily damascened in gold, and have applied copper alloy borders. On either cheek there is a triangular panel of red leather, which originally would have been covered by a pierced or decorated triangular plate, as on catalogue numbers 27, 28, and 29, which are very similar to this example in basic construction, but with several interesting variations in terms of form, quality, and style. Unfortunately, at some point this shaffron was cleaned with a bead blaster, which has left the metal surfaces with a dull finish and pewter color.

The crinet (RA XXVIH.21–22) consists of two wing-shaped panels, a form that is characteristic of the neck defenses of Tibetan horse armors. Each is made up of a leather ground divided into three concentric sections, the innermost and largest of which is covered with square iron plates of the same type and in the same way as on the shaffron above. Of the two narrow outer borders around it, the inner border is covered with a brocaded textile, which is an unusual treatment, while the outer border is of the more usual gilded and varnished leather, in this case decorated with a simple repeating stylized cloud motif. The edges of the panels are covered with shagreen piping and a close-set series of small iron bosses. On some examples (cat. nos. 30, 31, 33) these small iron bosses are used in attaching separate panels of leather together. On the present example they appear to serve an ornamental function, perhaps suggesting a later date.[4] The reverse sides are unlined, and the Tibetan letter *ka* and a Tibetan number, perhaps 25, are written on the leather ground.

The panels of the peytral (breast defense) (V&A IM.30E–G-1933) and the large side panels of the crupper (V&A IM.30D–F-1933) resemble each other in basic form and construction. The peytrals are made up of five long rows of iron lamellae, with two additional short rows at the top at the shoulder. The bottom and rear edge are bordered with two long rows of narrow gilded and varnished leather

panels, edged with shagreen piping and iron bosses. Attached to the bottom row there are two narrow panels of textile, also bordered with iron bosses. From the lowermost textile row there is a red yak hair fringe and a series of silk lappets. The lamellae of the bottom row are long and narrow, measuring 10.5 by 1.5 centimeters, and are pierced with eleven holes. They have no central hole indicating they were made to be placed in a terminal row. The leather panels of the two halves of the peytral are hinged together where they meet in the center. However, there may be a missing center section of some kind. The side panels of the crupper are made in the same way, consisting of six rows of lamellae, with the same type of borders.

The two flanchards (V&A IM.30I–J-1933) are a pair of oval or bean-shaped flat panels of gilded and varnished leather. They tuck up under, or hang just below, the side edges of the saddle and protect the gap below the rider's leg between the back edge of the flanchard and the front edge of the crupper.[5] Their construction and style of decoration are entirely different from the other parts of the armor and bear no direct relation to it. The flanchards are, however, relatively close in style to the decoration of the leather arm guards in catalogue numbers 36 and 38 and the bow case and quivers in catalogue numbers 93–95.

The loin defense (V&A IM.30A-1933) runs along the top of the rump from the back of the saddle to the base of the tail. It is in two parts, a rectangular section and a hinged end piece in the shape of a three-leaf clover. Each part is built up of three overlapping layers of gilded and varnished leather, each of which has a border of shagreen piping, the inner edge of the piping being followed by a close-set series of small iron bosses.

The tailpiece (V&A IM.30H-1933) has a half-round shape at the top and is straight across the bottom (compare the shape of the tailpiece in the Royal Museum, Edinburgh, cat. no. 32). It is made up of five panels of gilded and varnished leather and two panels of brocaded silk. The upper half consists of one large panel with a half-round shape bordered by two narrow panels that follow its contour. The very top is cut out in a semicircle to accommodate the horse's tail. Hinged to the bottom edge there are two narrow leather panels and below them similarly

shaped panels covered with brocaded silk. All of the panels are edged with the same trim consisting of shagreen piping and small iron bosses that is found on the other pieces.

The saddle (V&A IM.72-1910) has pierced iron mounts, damascened in gold and silver, and is probably Tibetan, seventeenth–eighteenth century. Its pommel plate is very similar in shape and style to the one discussed under catalogue number 119. The stirrups (RA XXVIH.38a, b) are iron damascened in gold, with dragon heads chiseled in relief on either side of the slot for the stirrup leathers. They have been catalogued by Thom Richardson as Mongolian, possibly thirteenth century.

The man's armor has a representative Bhutanese helmet (RA XXVIA.122), probably nineteenth century, with a one-piece hemispherical bowl and cheek and nape flaps made of blue silk brocade. The lamellar armor (RA XXVIA.157) is a very good example, possibly fifteenth–seventeenth century in date. It consists of thirteen rows of lamellae in the front, six above and six below the waist, plus a collar row in the back. The direction of the overlap of the lamellae is extremely consistent, like the armors in catalogue numbers 2 and 3, to which it bears the closest physical resemblance, with the lamellae of all of the rows overlapping outward from the center of the front toward the center of the back. It has full shoulder defenses consisting of twelve rows with a leather border covered in the remains of silk brocade attached to the lowest row, again like the armors in catalogue numbers 2 and 3. Also like the British Museum armor (cat. no. 3), this armor has the same distinctive type of iron tag attached in the center of the third row down on the back, inlaid in brass in this case with the Tibetan number 208.[6] Its presence indicates that these two armors were very likely once kept together in the same armory or arsenal. The quality of the armors and the unusual use of numbered metal tags, where most armors have a numbered strip of cloth, suggest that it was an armory of some importance.

The figure is equipped with a domed cane shield (RA XXVIA.276), very similar to that described in catalogue number 25. At the waist the figure wears a quiver and bow case (RA XXVIB.141, .145) of gilded and varnished leather, which will be discussed under catalogue number 93. It is also equipped with a silver

mounted Tibetan sword (RA XXVIS.298), probably eighteenth–nineteenth century, which is very similar to catalogue number 66.

PROVENANCE: Horse armor (Victoria and Albert Museum, IM.30-1933, IM.30A-1933, IM.30D–J-1933): the Thirteenth Dalai Lama, Thubten Gyatso (*thub bstan rgya mtsho*); Sir Charles Bell. Crinet pieces (Royal Armouries, XXVIH.21–22) and lamellar armor (Royal Armouries, XXVI.157): Sotheby's, New York, September 20–21, 1985, lot 29.

PUBLICATION: Sotheby's 1985, lot. 29 (crinet pieces and lamellar armor only).

1. Archives, Victoria and Albert Museum, kindly brought to my attention by Anthony North and John Clarke. In his biography of the Thirteenth Dalai Lama, Bell (1987, p. 147) gave a slight variation of this comment: "He gave me also a very fine suit of armour for a mounted soldier and his charger, made largely of iron and brown lacquered leather. It was three hundred years old, and people have lost the art of making it so well nowadays."

2. Archives, Victoria and Albert Museum, again provided by Anthony North and John Clarke.
3. The neck guards that were originally part of the armor (V&A IM.30B–C-1933) are described in cat. no. 33.
4. See the comments regarding this form of construction under cat. nos. 30, 31, and 33.
5. They can be seen well in Stone 1934, fig. 125, no. 2. Flanchards of this shape are not necessarily armor per se, but were used to protect the side of the horse from friction from the rider's lower legs and the stirrups.
6. I am grateful to Thom Richardson for pointing out this feature on the Leeds armor to me.

27. HEAD DEFENSE FOR A HORSE (SHAFFRON)

Tibetan or Mongolian, 15th–17th century
Iron, leather, gold, silver, brass or copper alloy, and textile
H. 22½ in. (57.2 cm), W. 24⅞ in. (63.2 cm)
The Metropolitan Museum of Art, New York, Purchase, Arthur Ochs Sulzberger Gift, 2004 (2004.402)

Tibetan shaffrons are relatively rare, the majority having been acquired by museums in the early twentieth century in the aftermath of the Younghusband Expedition. This example is relatively complete, very well made, and by far the most elaborately decorated of those recorded up to this point. In fact, the quality and execution of the damascening rank among the best examples of Tibetan decorated ironwork of this kind.

The shaffron has a flexible leather ground, which is shaped to cover a horse's head from the poll to the nostrils, following the contour of the cheeks and jaw at the sides. A rectangular iron plate that expands to a circular shape above the eye area covers the center of the shaffron from the forehead to the nostrils. An iron poll plate is attached to the top of this plate by two hinges. The corresponding snout plate is missing. There is a triangular iron plate on each cheek. The majority of the remaining exterior surface is covered by small iron plates, most of which are square, and each of which is embossed in the center with a shallow rounded cone. The points where the four corners of the adjacent square plates meet are each covered by a smaller hollow iron boss. These bosses have a transverse interior bar, over which the leather lacing is threaded to sew the bosses to the leather ground, an important method of construc-

tion found on other pieces of horse armor (cat. nos. 26, 28, 30, 31, 33). A continuous piping of shagreen and a row of iron bosses line the exterior edges of the shaffron and the circumference of the eye openings. The bosses lining the exterior edges are attached over a thin strip of red textile. There are two wedge-shaped indentations in the border of the bottom edge to accommodate the horse's mouth and the bit. A subsidiary border consisting of two pieces of gutter-shaped brass or copper alloy covers the leather piping at the border of each of these indentations, and appears to be a later modification. The central plate, poll plate, and cheek plates are densely damascened overall with flat gold and silver wire in a reticular pattern featuring trefoil cloud scrolls (*ju'i*) and lotus motifs in quatrefoil medallions at the intersections of the lines (see detail). The interstices are filled with an interlocked Y-shaped (stylized armor scale) pattern. Above the eye openings there are eyebrows in the form of scrolling flames, which are made of pierced iron, thickly damascened in gold and silver wire, the flames being gold and the base of the eyebrows being silver. The back of the shaffron is largely covered by a thin lining of blue cotton. On the proper right side of the back there are two straps made of braided leather laces, which are attached near the edge of the

leather ground, one above the right eye and the other at the edge of the jaw. The tab end of a corresponding, but now missing, strap or buckle is also located on the top of the proper left at the edge.

A carbon-14 test of a sample from a leather lacing integral to the back of the shaffron resulted in a date range of 1450–1650, which is comparable with the results of tests on catalogue numbers 6, 10, 30, 31, and 34.[1]

1. Results calibrated at 2 sigma, 95% probability; report from the Beta Analytic Radiocarbon Dating Laboratory, March 21, 2005.

27, detail of decoration on proper left cheek

27

28. HEAD DEFENSE FOR A HORSE (SHAFFRON)

Tibetan or Mongolian, 15th–17th century
Iron, leather, and brass or copper alloy
H. 21 in. (53.3 cm), W. 23 in. (58.4 cm)
The Metropolitan Museum of Art, New York, Purchase, The Collection of Giovanni P. Morosini, presented by his daughter, Giulia, by exchange; Bashford
Dean Memorial Collection, Funds from various donors, by exchange; and Fletcher Fund, by exchange, 1997 (1997.242d)

This shaffron is very similar in form and construction to the Victoria and Albert Museum example in catalogue number 26 (IM.30-1933), but is of slightly better quality, more complete, and in better condition. Therefore, only a few of its key features will be described here. The leaf-shaped finial of the vertical rib attached to the central iron panel is very similar to the finial on iron ribs or struts found on Tibetan cane shields (cat. no. 24), leather arm defenses (cat. no. 35), and leather boxes.[1] The scrollwork piercing of the hinged snout plate is large and relatively crude, which is also the case with the scrollwork on most other examples, the notable exception being the neck defenses (crinet) in the Metropolitan Museum (cat. no. 30). The hinged poll plate, which presumably matched the snout plate, is missing. The small bosses around the eye openings are brass or copper alloy, rather than iron. The triangular iron panels on the cheeks are embossed with a simple nested chevron design. The back of this shaffron (see illus.) is characteristic of the type and clearly shows the lacing pattern by which the iron plates on the front are attached. The lacing pattern also shows that the size and positioning of the large central plate and the cheek plates were part of the original design. The Tibetan number 20 is written on the leather ground on proper right side of the back.

PUBLICATION: Pyhrr, LaRocca, and Ogawa 2002, no. 47, p. 50.

1. For comparative examples of iron fittings with finials of this type on Tibetan furniture, see Anninos 2000, pls. 18, 20, 21; Kamansky 2004, nos. 58, 61, 77, and others.

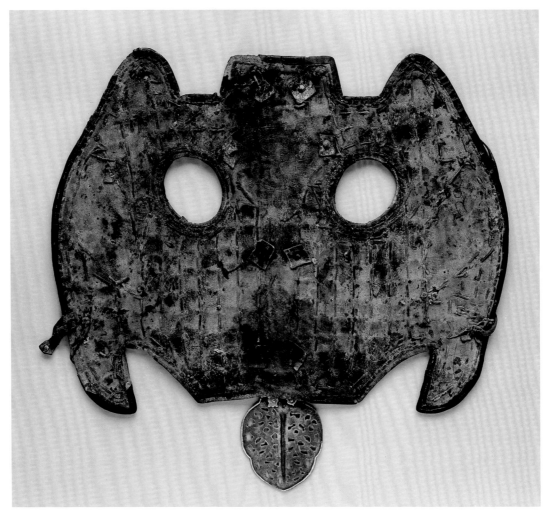

28, back

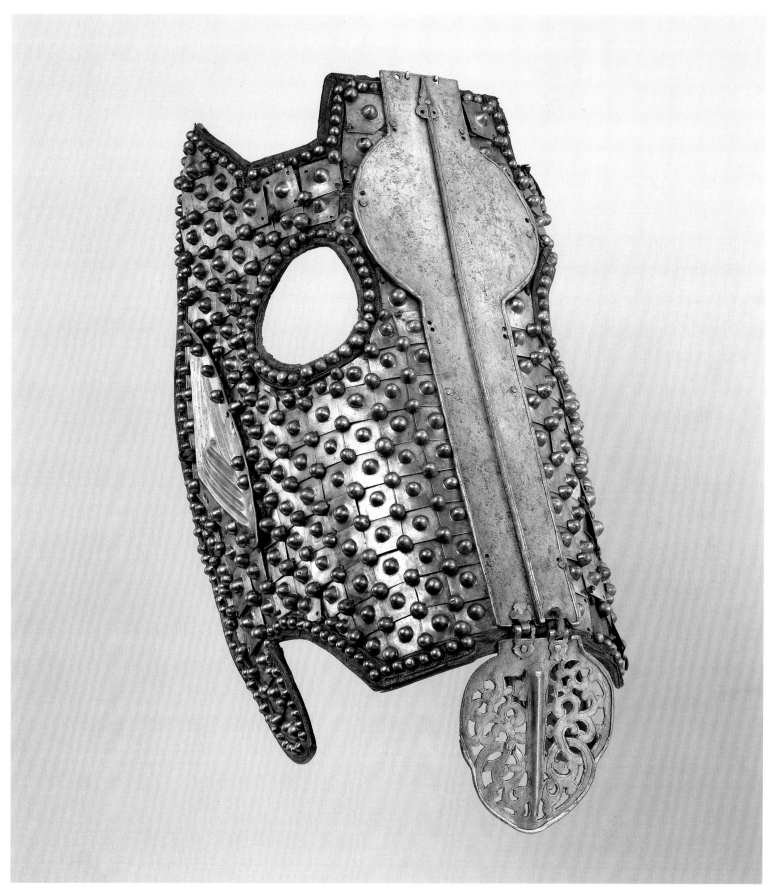

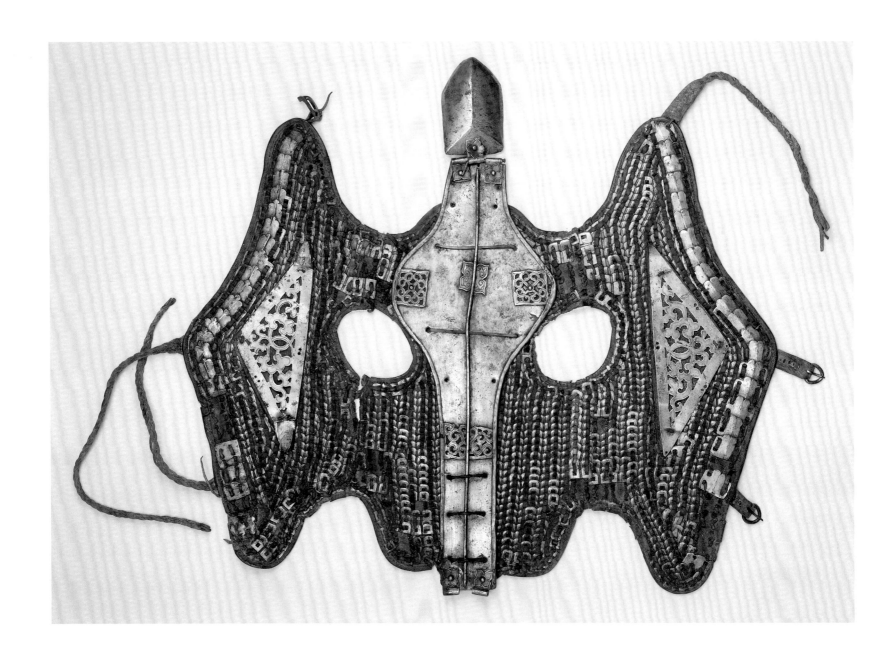

29. HEAD DEFENSE FOR A HORSE (SHAFFRON)

Tibetan or Mongolian, probably 15th–17th century
Iron, brass or copper alloy, and leather
H. 20½ in. (52.1 cm), W. 20¼ in. (51.4 cm)
Victoria and Albert Museum, London (IM.73-1910)

This shaffron shares the same basic shape and principles of construction with the prior examples, but instead of the small square iron plates, its exterior is protected by three different types of iron scales arranged in vertical columns. The first type is a small rectangle with a bilobed top edge, a straight bottom edge, and two square lacing holes separated by a vertical groove. The top edge of each scale overlaps the bottom edge of the scale above, and the left edge of each column overlaps the edge of the adjacent column to its left. The second type of scale consists of half versions of these scales, which are used to fill in the small irregularly contoured areas near the top and bottom edges of the shaffron. The third type of scale is used along each side edge of the shaffron and consists of a larger square scale with a cusped top and four lacing holes.

The large central plate has pierced brass appliquéd plaques and large brass washers on the hinges of the poll plate and snout plate (the latter missing). The vertical rib in the center is crudely made, as are the brass borders around the edges of the central plate. The cheek plates are pierced with simple scrollwork.

On the proper right cheek plate both the top and bottom corners have been damaged and replaced with lighter metal.

The lacing on the back of the shaffron suggests that the central plate and both cheeks have been removed or replaced at some point. The brass trim may also be a later modification. There are two straps with iron buckles on the proper left edge and

two corresponding braided leather straps on the proper right edge. At the two points at the top of the shaffron there is a buckle on the proper right and a corresponding braided strap on the proper left. This apparently complete set of straps and buckles makes it clear how the shaffron would have been strapped to a horse's head, i.e., two straps under the jaw and one over the top of the head at the poll.

30. PAIR OF NECK DEFENSES (CRINET) AND BREAST DEFENSE (PEYTRAL) FROM A HORSE ARMOR

Tibetan or Mongolian, 15th–17th century

Leather, iron, brass or copper alloy, gold, shellac, pigments, textile, and hair

Left neck panel, H. 19½ in. (49.5 cm), W. 22 in. (55.9 cm); right neck panel, H. 19¾ in. (50.2 cm), W. 22 in. (55.9 cm); peytral, H. 19 in. (48.3 cm), W. 24½ in. (62.2 cm)

The Metropolitan Museum of Art, New York, Purchase, The Collection of Giovanni P. Morosini, presented by his daughter, Giulia, by exchange; Bashford Dean Memorial Collection, Funds from various donors, by exchange; and Fletcher Fund, by exchange, 1997 (1997.242a–c)

These three pieces are remarkable for their excellent state of preservation, and rank among the most elaborately decorated examples of Tibetan leather horse armor known, rivaled only by the examples in the next three catalogue entries.[1] The vivid decoration consists of repeating patterns of stylized lotus, peony, and other blossoms in gold, set against alternating reddish orange, black, and maroon grounds. The lacquerlike effect appears to consist of a base layer or layers of pigmented shellac, the gold floral designs in gold leaf, a layer of shellac over the gold leaf upon which the details were painted in fine black lines, and a final coat or coatings of a tung oil glaze.

The neck guards are constructed of three concentric, overlapping bands of strong, stiff leather. The bands are joined firmly together by leather laces, which are threaded through the rows of small hollow iron bosses near the edges of each band. The bosses have a transverse bar on the interior, so a leather lace can be threaded up, over the bar, and back through the same hole in the leather ground below. The edges of the bands are covered with a piping of shagreen, which is sewn with a fine copper alloy wire, rather than thread, in a very precise chain

stitch (see detail). Shagreen piping similar to this was used as edging on most Tibetan horse armor of this type. The fine wire chain stitch, however, is less common, and may have been reserved for the better pieces (it appears, for instance, on cat. nos. 31 and 33).

In the center of each neck guard there is a triangular iron panel pierced with sinuous scrollwork and bisected by a strong, raised medial ridge. The scrollwork is executed with noticeably more skill than that on the previous examples. A varnished red leather ground is visible beneath the scrollwork. On the rear edge of each crinet there are five grommets, covered with shagreen and sewn with copper alloy wire in the same way as the piping.

The next piece appears to be the lower portion of a peytral, and compares very closely in shape to the lower portion of the piece of horse armor in catalogue number 31, also assumed to be a peytral.[2] The shape of its missing upper portion probably also resembled the corresponding part seen in catalogue number 31. It is decorated and constructed in the same way as the neck defenses, consisting of a top section made of three concentric bands of leather with a single row of iron lamellae in the center, and a lower section made of three short bands.

Five small rings along the bottom edge of the lowest band may have been for the attachment of streamers or another form of ornament. Below this there is a border of red fabric with the remains of a fringe of red yak hair.

The backs of all three pieces are covered with a padded linenlike fabric lining, which the pattern of the leather lacing shows to be original and integral to the structure. One iron buckle remains on the back of the proper left neck defense at the top edge, and the remains of a corresponding braided strap can be seen on the proper right. The remains of two flat leather straps on the back of the peytral are very similar to the complete straps on the back of catalogue number 31, and reinforce the assumption that originally it must have had a similarly shaped upper half attached by these straps.

Four separate carbon-14 tests were made on samples taken from these pieces, the first when they were on the art market and three subsequent ones under the auspices of the Metropolitan Museum. The three later tests were very consistent, yielding date ranges of 1435–1640, 1455–1640, and 1457–1665, and were made with samples taken from one of the hard leather bands, one of the leather straps, and the

tung oil glaze.[3] The single earlier test gave a date range of 1161–1406,[4] sparking speculation that all Tibetan horse armors were related to the Yuan dynasty (1279–1368) and the Mongols, but this test result should be discounted as an anomaly given the consistency of the subsequent tests on the same object.

In addition to their elaborate decoration and fine workmanship, these pieces are very strongly made and would have been fully functional as defensive armor. They, and the few examples like them, represent a high point not only in Tibetan armor making, but also in Tibetan leatherwork of any kind.

PUBLICATIONS: LaRocca 1998, p. 78, illus.; LaRocca 1999a, pp. 118–20, fig. 11.

1. Four small, damaged fragments (not shown here) of the same horse armor were subsequently acquired by the Metropolitan Museum (1998.107.1–.4).
2. These pieces were previously published by me as flanchards (see Publications cited in this entry). However, comparison of their construction, form, and placement of the connection straps described in this entry and the next make it more likely that they should be considered peytrals and not flanchards. The asymmetrical contour of the lower bands of the first example is the feature that led to the initial conclusion that it was intended to be worn on the horse's left side as a flanchard.
3. Dates at 2 sigma, 95% reliability; tests made by the Beta Analytic Radiocarbon Dating Laboratory in 1997 and 1998. See appendix "Radiocarbon Dating Results."
4. Test conducted by the Rafter Radiocarbon Laboratory, August 21, 1995; report in Metropolitan Museum Department of Arms and Armor files.

30, detail of right neck panel

31. BREAST DEFENSE (PEYTRAL) FROM A HORSE ARMOR

Tibetan or Mongolian, 15th–17th century
Leather, iron, brass or copper alloy, silver, gold, shellac, pigments, textile, and hair
H. 22½ in. (57.2 cm), W. 25⅝ in. (65.1 cm)
The Metropolitan Museum of Art, New York, Purchase, Bashford Dean Memorial Collection, Funds from various donors, by exchange, 1999 (1999.36)

The techniques of the construction and decoration of this piece are very similar to that described in detail in the previous entry, with a few minor differences. In terms of the style and quality of the decoration, however, while not as vivid as the preceding example, the decoration of this peytral employs a far greater variety of motifs, executed in a more fluid and accomplished style.

Both the upper and lower sections consist of three concentric bands of leather surrounding a central leather panel. The central panel of the upper section has at its center a flaming Wish-Fulfilling Jewel (*yid bzhin nor bu*) on a lotus throne flanked by symmetrical sprays of lush leafy stems and blossoms. The band around this has oval cartouches with pairs of symmetrical scrolls. The next band has a repeating series of stylized clouds connected by wisps or flames. The outermost band has large lotus and other blossoms alternating with symmetrical sprays of leafy stalks, and in the center at the top there is a single flaming Precious Jewel (*nor bu rin po che*) on a lotus throne. On the lower section the decorative pattern of the bands repeats with subtle variations. The central panel features the Right-Turning Conch Shell (*dung g.yas 'khyil*) flanked by large symmetrical lotus blossoms on leafy stalks. From the top to the bottom sections the three important and well-known auspicious symbols—the two flaming jewels and the conch—are placed in vertical alignment down the center of the piece. As with the previous example, all of the sections are bordered with hollow domed bosses and shagreen piping sewn with a fine wire in a precise chain stitch. In this instance, however, the shagreen around the two central panels is sewn with silver wire, while the remainder is sewn with copper alloy wire (see detail). The bottom edge of the upper section, where it is covered by the top of the lower section, is undecorated, even lacking the shagreen and the copper wire stitching.

There are the remains of a red yak hair fringe and three silk lappets at the bottom of the front. On the back, both sections are lined with a padded cotton or linenlike fabric (see illus.). Two flat leather straps join the upper and lower halves loosely together. The remains of the same type of straps are seen on the back of the previous example. There is also a braided leather strap attached to each side edge.

Results of carbon-14 testing give a date range of 1402–1520 and 1574–1626, very close to that of the other horse armor and lamellar armor cited previously.[1]

PUBLICATION: LaRocca 1999a, p. 119, fig. 12.

1. See the appendix "Radiocarbon Dating Results." This piece was tested by the Rafter Radiocarbon Laboratory, August 18, 1998.

31, back

31, detail

31

32. FOUR MATCHING ELEMENTS OF HORSE ARMOR

Tibetan or Mongolian, 15th–17th century
Leather, iron, brass or copper alloy, gold, shellac, pigments, textile,
and hair
A.1909.407A, H. 18¼ in. (46.4 cm), W. 25 in. (63.5 cm);
A.1909.407B–C, H. 29 in. (73.7 cm), W. 30⅛ in. (76.5 cm);
A.1909.407D, H. 24¼ in. (61.5 cm), W. 25¾ in. (65.5 cm)
On loan courtesy of the National Museums of Scotland
Royal Museum, Edinburgh (A.1909.407A–D)

These elements are notable for their good condition and very high quality, indicated by the well-made and carefully assembled lamellae and by the very fine decoration of the gilded and varnished leather lower borders of each piece. The elements consist of a peytral or breast defense (A.1909.407A), right and left crupper panels (A.1909.407B–C) to protect the horse's hindquarters, and a tailpiece (A.1909.407D) to protect the area around and below the tail. They have the same interesting provenance as catalogue number 1, having been acquired in Tibet by F. M. Bailey. Each piece is made up of several rows of iron lamellae with a lower border of gilded and varnished leather, mounted on a layer of felt, with a fringe of red yak hair and textile lappets, and lined with a heavy cotton or linenlike fabric. The overall gold ground of the leather borders suggests that the entire ground may be covered with gold leaf, as opposed to the previous two examples, in which the gold designs appear to be cut patterns of gold leaf.

The peytral (A.1909.407A) has a complete row of lamellae across the bottom, with five shorter rows above this on the right and left, flanking a center section, which is loosely joined to the bottom row by two iron rings. The direction of the overlap of the lamellae is very regular; all of the lamellae on the proper right half overlap left over right, while those on the proper left half overlap right over left, in other words all of the lamellae overlap outward from the center. The rectangular panel of gilded and varnished leather across the bottom is made in three pieces joined by two brass or copper alloy hinges.[1] The panels have a delicately drawn design of a lush, leafy scroll curling back upon itself in a repeat pattern on a gold ground and edged with a row of closely set hollow iron bosses and shagreen piping sewn with copper alloy wire.

32, peytral

The center section consists of a single piece of gilded and varnished leather divided by borders of shagreen piping and hollow domed bosses to simulate two separate concentric bands. The middle compartment is filled with small square plates with raised bosses in the center, like those on the shaffrons in catalogue numbers 26–28. There are attachment straps at the top proper right corner of the main section and the center section, and a corresponding iron buckle on the upper left corner of the main section.

The entire center section appears to have been adapted from another horse armor. The decoration of the leather is different in color and design from that on the lower border of this and the other pieces, and the iron plates in the middle have been filled in an almost haphazard way, including the insertion of a single lamella, giving it the appearance of reused material. Both top corners have been broken off, and the proper left one reattached with iron staples.[2]

The crupper panels (A.1909.407B–C) each consist of seven rows of lamellae, with a matching border of gilded and varnished leather at the bottom. On the proper right panel (A.1909.407B) the lamellae all overlap in the same direction, left over right. At the top there are four braided leather straps, and on the left side there are two straps with iron buckles. On the back there are the remains of a wax seal, a much better version of which is also found on the lining of the tailpiece (see detail). This is the same seal found on the helmet in catalogue number 1, which is also from F. M. Bailey. On the proper left panel (A.1909.407C) the direction of the overlap of the

32, proper right crupper panel

32, detail of seal on tailpiece

32, tailpiece

32, proper left crupper panel

lamellae is much less regular, unlike any of the other panels, although its appearance is otherwise entirely consistent with theirs. At the top it has four iron buckles, corresponding to the straps on the other half, and on its right side there are two straps with iron buckles.

The tailpiece (A.1909.407D) consists of a top row of lamellae in the form of a half circle, with an opening in the center for the horse's tail. Below this there are three rows of lamellae. The lamellae of all four rows are even and symmetrically placed, overlapping outward from the center of each row. The leather panel across the bottom is made in three sections joined with hinges, like that on the peytral. There is one leather strap at the center of the top and two on either side. Those on the sides are presumably for the corresponding buckles on the sides of the crupper panels. The wax seal mentioned above is found on the upper left of the back.

PROVENANCE: F. M. Bailey, Edinburgh (see cat. no. 1).

PUBLICATION: Beasley 1938, pl. IX.

1. The analysis done on the composition of the gilded and varnished leather surfaces of this object by the Royal Museum has been cited in "Horse Armor" above.
2. Two peytrals also made in the same general form, consisting of two loosely joined sections, are found in the Victoria and Albert Museum, London (IM.73I-1910, IM.73H–L-1910).

33. NECK DEFENSES (CRINET) FROM A HORSE ARMOR

Tibetan or Mongolian, possibly 16th–17th century
Leather, iron, gold, shellac, and textile
Each H. 17½ in. (44.5 cm), W. 19⅛ in. (48.6 cm)
Victoria and Albert Museum, London (IM.30B–C-1933)

These neck defenses were originally part of the horse armor given by the Thirteenth Dalai Lama to Sir Charles Bell in 1910, discussed in catalogue number 26. They are remarkable for having tooled decoration, in which the designs are either stamped or carved into the leather to produce images in low relief. The designs are a muted golden color on a red ground.

Each neck defense is made up of three separate panels of leather, the centermost being a solid wedge and the other two forming borders following its contours. The way in which the panels are attached is the same as that described in catalogue number 30, except that in this case the panels overlap from the center out. The panels are bordered with domed bosses and shagreen piping sewn with copper alloy wire, as on catalogue numbers 30 and 31. Both neck defenses are lined with a coarse linenlike fabric. The proper left defense (IM.30C-1933) has two iron buckles on its top edge, while the proper right (IM.30B-1933) has two corresponding braided leather straps.

The center panel of each is decorated with a pair of dragons reaching for a flaming pearl amid stylized clouds and scrolls (see detail). The next panel has a series of animals, each on a lotus throne, separated by sprays of leafy tendrils. The animals include a horse, a hare, a *garuda*, the Wish-Fulfilling Jewel at the peak of the front corner, a bull or ox, possibly a phoenix, and others. The outer panel has a series of twelve oval cartouches containing the Eight Auspicious Symbols alternating with *tsi pa ṭa* masks, *garudas*, dragons, and other creatures.

PROVENANCE: The Thirteenth Dalai Lama, Thubten Gyatso (*thub bstan rgya mtsho*); Sir Charles Bell (see cat. no. 26).

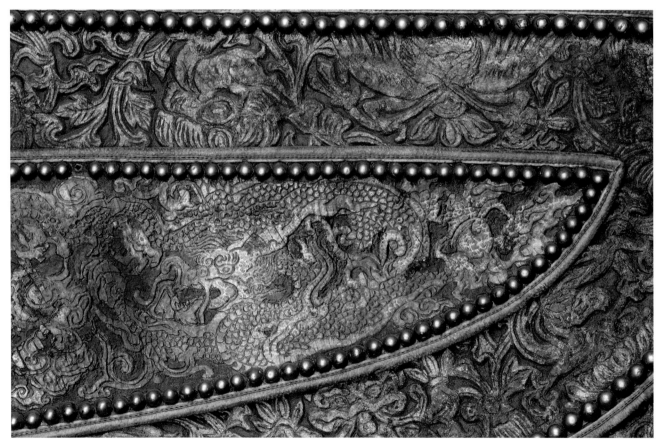

33, detail of right neck panel

33

བསེ་ཁྲབ
Leather Armor

The Tibetan term for leather armor is *bse khrab*, which combines the word meaning tanned leather or rhinoceros (*bse*) with the word for armor (*khrab*). The term *bse*, or *bse ko*, also refers specifically to varnished or dyed leather. Therefore, *bse khrab* is a reference not just to leather armor, but also to armor made of leather decorated in this way, which would apply to the majority of surviving examples.[1] The decorative technique appears similar to that used on leather horse armor, i.e., a combination of pigmented shellac and gold leaf, but with differences in the choice and style of ornament. The use of gold leaf and varnish on leather specifically referred to as *bse* is found in a brief discussion of *bse* in the Tashi Namgyal text.[2]

Unless it is specified as horse armor, the leather armor discussed in this section refers to armor for man. Armor made from leather plates of various sizes and shapes was in use in China and Central Asia from a very early period, with sophisticated examples for man and horse occurring in archaeological sites dating from the Eastern Zhou period (770–256 B.C.).[3] The earliest examples from a Tibetan context may be the remains of armor made of small squares of lacquered leather joined by leather laces, which were found by Sir Aurel Stein at Miran, in a site identified as a Tibetan fort of the eighth–ninth century A.D., on the southern Silk Route in Central Asia.[4] Beyond this there is the seemingly unique lacquered leather armor, carbon-14 tested to the eighth–tenth centuries, which strongly resembles the type of armor that was still being made and worn by the Yi (Lolo) people in southwestern China into the nineteenth century and perhaps up to the early twentieth century, suggesting that this style may have remained current in that region for as much as one thousand years.[5] The 1247 description of Mongolian armor by Friar Giovanni di Plano Carpini also mentions leather armor for man and horse.[6]

However, while examples of leather horse armor from Tibet have been recognized for the past hundred years, virtually no leather armor for man was known to have survived until relatively recently, nearly all of the extant examples having come to light in the past fifteen to twenty years.[7] Based on a limited number of carbon-14 tests, the majority of the examples in this catalogue, like the lamellar armor and horse armor already discussed, appear to date from the fifteenth to the seventeenth century. They include a leather helmet (cat. no. 34) made in the form of an eight-plate iron helmet, an interesting example of leather lamellar armor probably from the southeastern corner of the Tibetan plateau (cat. no. 39), and a series of forearm guards (cat. nos. 35–38).

Of the forearm guards, all of the catalogued examples appear to be for the left arm, suggesting that they were never made in pairs, but were used on the left arm only. They fall into two basic types. The first (cat. no. 35) has applied iron struts, like those on Tibetan shields (cat. no. 24) and furniture, often with ornamental piercings. On this type, the leather is sometimes painted rather than varnished. The second type (cat. nos. 36–38) does not have struts or other applied iron fittings, and the leather surface is entirely covered with gilded and varnished decoration. The same style and technique of decoration are found on a group of bow cases and quivers (cat. nos. 93–95), on some leather flanchards (cat. no. 26), and, in one rare instance at least, on a gunpowder flask (cat. no. 108).[8] On some examples, where the decoration is particularly complex, the ground appears to have been covered entirely in gold leaf, given a reddish or orange tone with pigmented shellac, and then painted, often with densely grouped ornament, in fine black lines. The designs include dragons and other animals or large blossoms in cartouches, intricate scrollwork, and a wide variety of geometric patterns and borders.

1. I am grateful to Tsering Skakya for clarifying these terms.
2. See Beinecke, fol. 52a–b; Burmiok Athing, fol. 30b; British Library Or 11,374, fols. 95a–96b; Gangtok 1981, pp. 238–39 (but not included here in the appendix "Excerpts from *A Treatise on Worldly Traditions*). Although less than a full page in most manuscripts, the *bse* chapter is difficult to interpret because of the widely divergent spellings of several key terms among the four primary versions of the text. However, from the context, it is clear that *bse* refers at least in part to leather suitable for decoration. *Hor* (Mongol) *bse* is said to be the softest and can be rolled like paper. It is described as having a surface so smooth that paint or varnish (*rtsi*) applied to it does not crack or split. Chinese and Tibetan *bse* are also briefly discussed. Gold leaf (*gser shog*) is mentioned repeatedly, and once specifically as a ground (*rgyab*), decorated with applied varnish (*byo rtse*, which seems to be a phonetic variation of *jo rtsi*) in various colors. Also from the context, the term *tshams*, a key part of the discussion, seems to refer to decorated leather boxes. Its closest equivalent may be *hor chams*, found in Das 1902b, p. 1330. Leather armor, however, is not specifically mentioned.
3. Yang Hong 1992, pp. 114–26.
4. Whitfield 1982–85, vol. 3, no. 49, color pls. and pp. 307–8; Robinson 1967, pp. 135–36. According to Amy Heller, fragments of armor from this period or earlier have also been found recently in the Tibetan tombs in Dulan, Qinghai Province, northwestern China (personal communication, May 2005).
5. Anninos 2000, pp. 108–9, figs. 12, 13, where it is suggested that the armor was preserved in a Tibetan temple. For comparable but much later Lolo armors, see Stone 1934, fig. 76. An example in the Metropolitan Museum (20.142), probably 18th or 19th century in date, was described as having been presented as a gift to a French priest by a Tibetan "chieftain" (Ralph Weymouth, letters to Steven V. Grancsay, December 27, 1919, and Bashford Dean, June 2, 1920, correspondence files, Department of Arms and Armor, Metropolitan Museum).
6. Beazley 1967, p. 124.
7. An exception being a very plain leather forearm guard from the Stone collection (MMA 36.25.422; Stone 1934, fig. 67).
8. The similarity of the decorative patterns on arm guards and bow cases was pointed out by Tony Anninos (2000, pp. 109, 112) in relation to Tibetan leather furniture.

34. HELMET

Tibetan, 15th–17th century
Leather, gold, shellac, and pigments
H. 6¼ in. (15.9 cm)
The Metropolitan Museum of Art, New York, Purchase, Bequest
of George Blumenthal and Bashford Dean Memorial Collection,
Funds from various donors, by exchange; Steve and Madeline
Condella Gift and Rogers Fund, 1998 (1998.1)

This helmet imitates in leather the classic Tibetan eight-plate helmet style. The raised areas simulate the overlapping outer plates found on examples made of iron, each plate having a medial ridge and cusps on either side. The helmet has a red ground overall, inside and out, with designs on the exterior in gold, the details of which are painted in fine black lines. The compartments between the raised areas are decorated with two *vajras* (*rdo rje*), a small one near the top and a larger *vajra* draped with stylized swags near the bottom. Between the pairs of *vajras*, on the points of the cusps of each raised area, there is a single Lantsa character or seed syllable, sixteen in all. The characters form the mantra OM, AH, HUM, which repeats five times, ending with a single repeat of OM.[1]

The top of the helmet is pierced by a single hole in the center and four pairs of holes in a circular arrangement, indicating it once had a plume finial. There are twenty-nine holes around the base of the helmet. Two chinstraps consisting of leather laces, possibly later additions, are attached at the front and back of the helmet bowl, crisscrossing toward the back. A single stitched seam is visible on the interior of the helmet, indicating that the bowl was made in two halves. The seam runs diagonally in relation to the placement of the chinstraps, rather than back to front, again implying that the chinstraps were added some time later, but probably still within the helmet's working lifetime. Although decorative and perhaps purely ceremonial, the leather of this helmet is more than strong enough for it also to have been made for practical use.

Results of a carbon-14 test on a leather sample from the interior of the rim gave a date range of

34

1417–1654, placing this helmet within the same period as the lamellar armor and horse armor cited previously.[2]

PUBLICATION: LaRocca 1999a, pp. 114, 117, fig. 2.

1. As read by Lozang Jamspal.
2. Results at 2 sigma, 95% confidence rating; test conducted at Rafter Radiocarbon Laboratory, July 11, 1996.

35. FOREARM GUARD WITH IRON FITTINGS

Tibetan, possibly 15th–16th century
Leather, iron, and pigments
H. 10 in. (25.4 cm)
The Metropolitan Museum of Art, New York, Purchase, Kenneth
and Vivian Lam Gift, 2001 (2001.36)

Other than one example in the Stone collection, leather forearm guards of this type were virtually unknown until relatively recently.[1] It is made of a single panel of hard leather cut in an L shape and curved to fit around the left forearm, which is characteristic of all Tibetan leather forearm guards. The outer surface is painted with designs in red, blue, and beige, with traces of gold, which are badly damaged and hard to read but may include an overall pattern of stylized flames. The engraved and pierced iron fittings are very well made and consist of four vertical struts and an engrailed border, which are riveted directly to the leather ground. The struts have a leaflike finial and cartouches pierced with scrollwork. A single engraved line outlines the edges of all the designs. These fittings compare well with the similar struts used on some types of Tibetan shields (cat. no. 24) and with the iron fittings on Tibetan wood and leather boxes or trunks, especially the leaf-shaped finials. Very few furniture mounts, however, include cartouches pierced with scrollwork and none so fine as on this armguard.[2] The closest comparison, outside of other armguards of this type, is found in the pierced iron scrollwork on the neck defenses in catalogue number 30.

There are two square holes punched through the leather on the right side and two pairs of round holes near the bottom edges on each side, presumably for laces to hold the armguard in place.

PUBLICATION: Pyhrr, LaRocca, and Ogawa 2002, no. 42, pp. 45–46.

1. That example, now in the Metropolitan Museum (36.25.422), is very simple by comparison to this one; it is illustrated in Stone 1934, fig. 67. Others with pierced-iron fittings more similar to the above include two very good examples in the Royal Armouries Museum, Leeds (XXVIA.282, .283). Comparable examples have also appeared on the art market (sale cats., Christie's, London, July 18, 2002, lot 287; April 29, 2005, lot 350).
2. Compare, for example, Kamansky 2004, nos. 69, 77.

35

36. FOREARM GUARD FOR THE LEFT ARM

Tibetan or Mongolian, possibly 15th–16th century
Leather, shellac, gold, and pigments
H. 11⅛ in. (29.5 cm)
The Metropolitan Museum of Art, New York, Purchase, Kenneth
and Vivian Lam Gift, 2001 (2001.35b)

This armguard differs from the preceding example in that it was not made to have iron fittings, and its decoration is varnished and gilded rather than painted. The entire exterior surface appears to have a covering of gold leaf coated with pigmented shellac to give it warm reddish orange and reddish brown colors, and designs painted in fine black lines. The decoration is divided into three registers. At the bottom there is a simple "coin" motif in large scale, with three small circles or pearls on either side. The middle register (see detail), showing very delicate and skillful draftsmanship, has a dense, sinuous

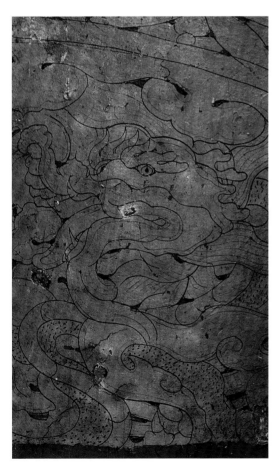

36, detail of decoration

36

arrangement composed of a makara-like dragon and pearl among clouds and leafy scrolls next to a large lotus blossom. The makara-dragon (*chu srin*) is, in fact, among the best examples of figural painting on a piece of Tibetan armor. Between this and the top register there is an interlocked fret or swastika fret border. The top register is filled with a dense and asymmetrical arrangement of leafy scrolls. The armguard is pierced with eight square lacing holes, three on the tab of leather that wraps around the inner arm, three on the opposite edge, and two at the base in the front just to the left of center.

37. FOREARM GUARD FOR THE LEFT ARM

Tibetan or Mongolian, possibly 15th–16th century
Leather, shellac, gold, and pigments
H. 12¼ in. (31.1 cm)
The Metropolitan Museum of Art, New York, Purchase, Arthur
Ochs Sulzberger Gift, 2005 (2005.301.2)

This armguard is slightly broader and heavier than the preceding example and is decorated with the same materials and technique, but the ornament is larger in scale and bolder in its style. It is made of one piece of thick, hardened leather, rounded at the top, narrowing into a tubular form that wraps around the forearm but is open in the back. It is decorated on the upper half in two curved diagonal compartments filled with lush lotus and peony blossoms on a background of leafy scrolls in a golden orange color with detailing in fine black lines, and on the lower half with a large central lotus blossom on entwined leafy stalks in golden orange with black detailing, all on a black ground. The drawing of the leaves is reminiscent of that on the horse armor in catalogue number 30 but on a much larger scale. Like other armguards of this type, the decoration consist of gold leaf covered with an orange-toned shellac and painted with a black pigment, with a clear shellac glaze overall. There are two closely set holes at the bottom edge of the front and two sets of three holes facing each other on the inner edges on the cuff, with three tautly wrapped

37, back view

horizontal rawhide laces running between them. This is the only instance seen so far of what appear to be the original leather straps preserved intact, and it may explain why the piece has kept its shape so well whereas other leather armguards tend to be somewhat flattened or otherwise deformed.

37

38. FOREARM GUARD FOR THE LEFT ARM

Tibetan or Mongolian, possibly 15th–17th century
Leather, shellac, gold, and pigments
H. 11⅛ in. (28.3 cm)
The Metropolitan Museum of Art, New York, Purchase, Kenneth and Vivian Lam Gift, 2001 (2001.35a)

This armguard is made of slightly lighter and thinner leather than the two preceding examples and is marginally smaller in overall scale. The style of its decoration is also different, being clearly linked to the quivers and the bow case in catalogue numbers 93–95. Unlike the three preceding armguards, its lacing holes are all round, rather than square. These minor differences suggest that it may be later in date, or that it represents a distinct variation of the style from the others.[1]

It is made of a single piece of shaped leather, densely covered in varnished and gilded decoration.

Visual examination suggests that, as with catalogue number 36, the entire exterior surface was covered with gold leaf, as opposed to gold pigment, then coated with pigmented shellac to give it a warm reddish brown color, and the designs painted in fine black lines. The bottom third of the armguard is decorated with a central lobed medallion linked to four partial medallions by four smaller medallions, all on a background formed by a netlike pattern of small circles. The central medallion has a compact arrangement of the Eight Auspicious Symbols, while the others are filled with leafy petals. The area above

this is entirely covered by a honeycomb or tortoise-shell pattern and is delineated at the top and bottom by slightly diagonal borders designs of an interlocking fret motif. The leather of the armguard extends in a short tab at the bottom of the left to wrap slightly around the inner arm. This tab sometimes has a separate field of decoration, which on this example consists of three large lotus blossoms set amid leafy scrolls (see detail).

1. An armguard virtually identical to the present one in form and style is found in the Royal Armouries Museum, Leeds (XXVIA.279).

38, detail of decoration on inner-arm tab

39. LEATHER LAMELLAR ARMOR

Eastern Tibet, 15th–17th century
Leather, shellac, gold, and pigments
Laid out flat, H. 33⅝ in. (85.4 cm), W. 55½ in. (141 cm)
The Metropolitan Museum of Art, New York, Purchase, Arthur Ochs Sulzberger Gift, 2001 (2001.268)

Probably originating in the southeastern Tibetan area of Kham, this armor represents a unique combination of influences from the regions to its west and east. The shape and size of the lamellae show the influence of the classic iron lamellar armors associated with central Tibet to the west. The material, decoration, and lacing pattern, however, show the influence of two distinctive styles of leather lamellar armors worn by the Naxi (Moso) and the Yi (Lolo) in Yunnan and Sichuan to the east.[1] Although leather lamellar armors are dated generally to the eighteenth or nineteenth century, a carbon-14 test of this example resulted in a date range of 1440–1640.[2]

The armor has thirteen rows of lamellae, consisting of ten full rows that wrap around the body and three shorter rows that cover the right and left sides of the upper chest and the upper back. There is a large shaped plate of solid leather attached to the top row of the upper back, which has a straight bottom edge and a bilobate top. The lamellae of the waist, in the second full row, are slightly recurved, as they would be in an iron lamellar armor. The lamellae have a hard, shiny, dark red surface, probably from a shellac or a form of varnish rather than true lacquer, and are decorated with floral and leaf designs in reddish gold (see detail). They are pierced by five to eleven lacing holes, depending on placement. Their size averages 8–8.2 centimeters by 2.2–3.2 centimeters wide, which is comparable, although consistently wider, with the lamellae of what seem to be the later iron lamellar armors (compare with cat. nos. 4–6). Most of the lamellae in each row overlap toward the center of the back, but there are several inconsistencies due to later repairs, replacement of lamellae, and relacing.

The lacing pattern differs from that found on iron lamellar armor principally in that the laces connecting the rows run vertically from the top of the lamellae in one row to the top of the lamellae in the rows below, leaving a great deal of the laces exposed,

which is the method used on both Naxi and Yi armors. However, unlike the Naxi and Yi armors, on which the vertical laces are placed side by side, on this example the vertical laces occur only in five groups of three laces side by side, with four widely spaced vertical laces in between the groups. In addition, the large leather plate at the top of the back is a feature otherwise found only on Yi armors.

1. The most detailed discussion of Naxi (also spelled Na-khi and Nahi) armor remains Rock 1955. A very good example of a Naxi armor is found in the Royal Armouries Museum, Leeds (XXVIA.1106). There is no detailed study of Yi (Lolo) armor, but examples in the Field Museum, Chicago, are illustrated in Stone 1934, fig. 76. In addition there is a Lolo armor in the Royal Armouries (XXVIA.161–2) and one in the Metropolitan Museum (20.142).

2. Results at 2 sigma, 95% probability; tested by the Beta Analytic Radiocarbon Dating Laboratory, March 21, 2005.

39, detail of decoration

39

ཨ་ལུང་གི་ཁྲབ་དང་ཁྲབ་སྣ་ཚོགས

Mail and Other Forms of Armor

Mail, a strong and extremely flexible type of armor, is made from hundreds or even thousands of small interlocking iron rings. Although the word "mail" may be encompassed by the general Tibetan terms for armor, *khrab* and *go cha*, there is at least one term referring specifically to it, *a lung gi khrab*, literally, "armor of rings."[1] As a form of armor it appears to have been used in Tibet from a very early date. Texts from the period of the Yarlung dynasty (7th–9th centuries), during which Tibet's empire extended through much of Central Asia, indicate that the Tibetans wore mail of very high quality, although lamellar armor also must have been well known throughout the region at the same time.[2] Whether or how much mail continued to be used in Tibet in the succeeding periods is unknown. It is not mentioned in the armor chapters of the text by Tashi Namgyal written in 1524, in the later versions of the same text, or in the other principal Tibetan discussions of armor found in the texts by Hūṃkaradzaya (dates unknown, but possibly 18th century).[3] The presence of mail in Central Asia in the mid-eighteenth century and its nature as something unusual from an East Asian perspective are well demonstrated by the description of mail armor that had been captured by Chinese troops campaigning in Turkistan as "exotic armor from the foreign land."[4] Its use in Tibet in the early twentieth century is well documented, however, in accounts of the Younghusband Expedition and through the large amounts of it seen in photographs taken of the armored cavalry participating in the Great Prayer Festival during the 1930s and 1940s (figs. 3, 6–8).

These photos show the mail worn in conjunction with a consistent set of equipment that, judging from its constituent parts, probably became the standardized equipment for Tibetan cavalry some time between the mid-seventeenth and the mid-eighteenth century. The mail consists of a short-sleeve shirt reaching to the waist or hips, which in the photos sometimes appears to be little more that a tattered vest. It was worn with a helmet fitted with upturned textile flaps, a set of four mirrors (four iron disks worn over the mail), an armored belt, bow and arrows carried in a bow case and quiver at the left and right hip respectively, a matchlock musket, a bandolier with containers for gunpowder and bullets, and a spear (see especially cat. no. 46).[5]

An ensemble made up of this particular form of helmet, mail, four mirrors, and armored belt was published by George Stone in 1934 as being the typical armor of Sikkim, Bhutan, and Nepal, an attribution repeated by Russell Robinson in 1967.[6] While this may be true, it should be pointed out that the most abundant evidence for its use comes from the photos of the Great Prayer Festival just mentioned, where it was worn by dozens if not hundreds of riders. If the attribution to Sikkim, Bhutan, and Nepal is also true, then this form of armor was being worn throughout the central

Himalayan region. On the other hand, Stone may simply have been repeating an anecdotal attribution, which has since remained unquestioned (see cat. nos. 40 and 46 for further comments).

The term "four mirrors" refers to a type of armor often called by the Persian term *char-aina* or *chahar-a'inah*, literally, "four mirrors." It was widely used in India and Persia, where the plates tended to be larger and squarer or faceted, and in Tibet, where the plates were usually round. The Tibetan name for this type of armor appears to be *me long bzhi*, again a literal translation of the term "four mirrors."[7] The disks are worn on the center of the chest, back, and under each arm, held by leather cross-straps. Most Tibetan examples appear to have been plain disks of polished iron (see cat. no. 46), but those with decoration include the use of engraving and damascening (cat. nos. 43, 44), applied borders (cat. no. 42), and raised inlay (cat. no. 41). The four mirrors should not be confused with the oracle breastplate (*thugs gsal me long*, *thugs kyi me long*, or *me long*), which is an ornate pectoral disk worn by oracles, was used to adorn the images of deities, and is also found on late forms of ceremonial Chinese armor. It is characterized by having an elaborate applied border, a mirror-bright polish, and a seed syllable in the center.[8]

The other forms of armor included at the end of this section (cat. nos. 47–54) present a miscellany of styles, which vary widely in date and material. They are united only by the fact they were preserved in Tibet and are either unique or one of only a few known examples of their particular type. Consequently, most are very difficult to attribute to a particular place or period with any certainty. Nevertheless, like several helmets seen in the previous section, they offer glimpses of armor styles that might otherwise remain completely unknown.

1. Das 1902b, p. 169, under *khrab*. Goldstein (2001, p. 345) also gives the term *lcags long sbrel khrab*, meaning armor of connected iron rings, but this may be a more modern term.

2. For references to the armor used by the Tibetans at this time, see especially Demiéville 1952, pp. 373–76, and his discussion of the interpretation by Laufer (1914, esp. pp. 237, 253–56) of some of the same sources; and Beckwith 1987, esp. pp. 109–11.

3. On this and related texts, see the appendix "Excerpts from *A Treatise on Worldly Traditions*," esp. note 2.

4. *Huangchao Liqi Tushi* (Illustrated Regulations for the Ceremonial Regalia of the Present Dynasty), 1759; reprinted in *Yingyin Wenyuange Sikyu Quanshu*, vol. 656 (Shanghai, 1983), p. 733. I am extremely grateful to Jason Sun and Mike Hearn for providing the translation. The full passage reads: "In the twenty-fourth year of the Qianlong reign, numerous military equipments were captured in the western region campaign, which were stored, by the imperial order, at the Hall of Purple Light to record the military victory. The mail armor is made of refined iron. Both the jacket and the trousers were made of linked iron rings. The jacket has no front opening. The collar is lined with white cloth. It is

donned from the top. The troops in the western region campaign went deep [into enemy territory] and frequently captured such armors, with which they clad themselves as they attacked the rebels. This exotic armor from the foreign land provided humble assistance in the battle. It is respectfully recorded in the volume and attached at the end of the armor and helmet section." The wood-block illustration that accompanies this passage is illustrated in Robinson 1967, fig. 78.

5. Compare the equipment shown in an equestrian portrait of Ayusi, a Kalmuk Mongol cavalryman in the service of the Chinese emperor Qianlong, painted by Castiglione about 1760; see *Splendors of China's Forbidden City: The Glorious Reign of Emperor Qianlong*, exh. cat. (London and New York, 2004), illus. p. 111. His equipment differs only in the style of the helmet and the lack of the four mirrors and armored belt.

6. Stone 1934, p. 53; Robinson 1967, pp. 163–64.

7. I am grateful to Dr. Joachim Karsten for checking for references to this term (personal communication, February 16, 2000).

8. On the oracle breastplate, see Nebesky-Wojkowitz 1975, p. 411.

40. MAIL SHIRT

Possibly Indian or Bhutanese, 17th–19th century
Iron, leather, and textile
H. 35½ in. (90.2 cm)
The Metropolitan Museum of Art, New York, Bequest of George
C. Stone, 1935 (36.25.27)

This is a very good example of the type of mail shirt said to be used not only in Tibet, but also in Bhutan, Nepal, and Sikkim.[1] It is made of alternating rows of riveted and solid rings, has short sleeves, reaches to the hips, and has a short vertical slit in the front and rear. It has a short V-neck and was made to be put on over the head. Especially characteristic is the upright fabric-lined collar, which is made separately from the rest of the shirt. It consists of eleven rows and is attached to the top row of the neck of the shirt by a thin leather lace. It is reinforced and made to stand upright by having a thicker leather thong laced through every other row. The collar is lined on the inside with a faded blue-green cotton fabric and on the outside with a coarse hemplike fabric, which was originally covered by a red fabric, possibly wool, a few traces of which remain.

George Stone treated this shirt as part of an ensemble with a helmet, four mirrors, and armored belt (cat. nos. 44–46), which he described on his original catalogue card as a "suit of Bhutanese armor."[2] He published the ensemble with what appears to be a very similar, but not identical, mail shirt, and described it as typical of the armor of Sikkim, Bhutan, and Nepal.[3]

PROVENANCE: W. O. Oldman, London; George Cameron Stone, New York.

1. Robinson 1967, pp. 162–64.
2. Departmental card catalogue, Department of Arms and Armor, Metropolitan Museum.
3. Stone 1934, pp. 53, 56, fig. 68.

40

41. BREASTPLATE FROM A SET OF FOUR MIRRORS

Possibly Mongolian or Central Asian, 15th–17th century
Iron, gold, silver, and leather
Diam. 8⅝ in. (21.9 cm)
The Metropolitan Museum of Art, New York, Purchase, Rogers
Fund and funds from various donors, by exchange, 2002 (2002.499)

This breastplate was originally part of a set of four matching plates connected by leather straps and designed to protect the front, back, and sides of the torso. Its primary decorative technique is unusual, consisting of raised wire inlay (also called encrustation), in which the wire protrudes slightly above the adjacent iron surfaces, rather than being flush with them, as it would be in typical inlay or damascening. The decoration is rendered with simple lines and features the whirling emblem (*dga' 'khyil*) set in an overlapping stylized blossom, and the coin motif as an outer border. The motifs are typical of Tibetan objects, but the style in which they are done and the use of the raised inlay technique have few immediate parallels. However, the technique is similar to that found on at least one Mongolian-style helmet, suggesting that it comes from an area influenced by Tibetan Buddhism such as Mongolia, or elsewhere in Central Asia.[1]

1. The helmet is published in Nicolle 1999, fig. 813e.

41

42, detail

42. SET OF FOUR MIRRORS

Tibetan or Bhutanese, 18th–19th century
Iron, gold, leather, and textile
Breastplate and back plate, Diam. 8¼ in. (21 cm); side plates, Diam. 7½ in. (19.1 cm)
Royal Armouries Museum, Leeds (XXVIA.159)

The breastplate and back plate of this set are fitted with applied borders of pierced iron, which are damascened overall in gold and decorated with dragons, deer, and birds amid scrollwork. The two side plates are slightly more convex and have no borders. The top edge of each side plate is cut out to accommodate the underarm. The plates have a padded lining with the remains of a textile cover and leather cross-straps. The presence of applied and pierced borders on a set of four mirrors of this type is unusual, their use usually being associated with oracle breastplates. Although somewhat damaged, the pierced work is of good quality. However, the borders are crudely attached by loops of wire passing through five pairs of holes, suggesting that they may be later additions.

PROVENANCE: Sotheby's, New York, September 20–21, 1985, lot 29.

PUBLICATION: Sotheby's 1985, lot 29.

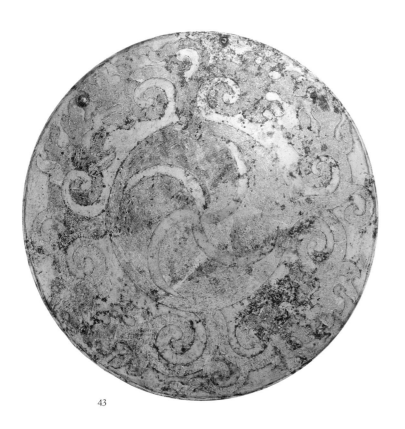

43

43. BREASTPLATE AND BACK PLATE FROM A SET OF FOUR MIRRORS

Probably Tibetan, 17th–18th century
Iron, gold, leather, and textile
Diam. 7⅜ in. (18.7 cm)
The Metropolitan Museum of Art, New York, Purchase,
Kenneth and Vivian Lam Gift, 2003 (2003.331.1, .2)

The breastplate and back plate each consist of a single, slightly concave disk of polished iron with an incised rim. The center of each disk is decorated with a large, circular, four-part whirling emblem (*dga' 'khyil*). From the edges of the emblem four symmetrically arranged, bifurcated flaming scrolls radiate out to the edges of the plate. The outline of the decoration is engraved, the surface within the outline entirely crosshatched, and the crosshatched areas mechanically gilded with gold leaf. Each disk has a full lining consisting of cotton (?) batting sandwiched between two circular pieces of leather, which are stitched together at the edges. Each disk also has a fragmentary pair of cross-straps, made of a woven textile, and a fragmentary double strap at the top,

which identifies these as the breastplate and back plate, rather than side plates. There are fragments of a red silk lining, which once covered the leather lining entirely. Two iron buckles remain on the straps of one (2003.331.1). The other buckles and the remainder of the straps are missing. The lining and the straps appear to be replacements made during the working life of the objects. Originally, there would have been two matching side plates, probably slightly smaller in diameter, which are missing.

The pieces are notable for their very bold and distinctive decoration, which has a clarity and scale that is rarely encountered on armor, or any form of decorative ironwork, from the Himalayas. The only comparable objects in terms of scale and materials would be the iron hardware sometimes found on the doors of more important chapels in Tibetan monasteries and temples. The gilding technique, gold leaf rather than wire damascened on a crosshatched ground, may be indicative of a later date. It also appears to be used, again for the skillful rendering of stylized flame motifs, on two ceremonial Tibetan spearheads in the catalogue (cat. nos. 81, 83), which probably date from the same period as this breastplate and back plate.

44. SET OF FOUR MIRRORS

Probably Tibetan, 18th–19th century
Iron, gold, silver, textile, and leather
Breastplate and back plate, Diam. 8 in. (20.3 cm); side plates,
Diam. 7⅛ in. (18.1 cm)
The Metropolitan Museum of Art, New York,
Bequest of George C. Stone, 1935 (36.25.26)

This set is noteworthy for its completeness, good condition, and precise and distinctive decoration. It consists of four highly polished disks, those for the chest and back being slightly larger than those for the sides. Each disk is decorated at its center with a crossed *vajra* (*vishvavajra* or *rdo rje rgya gram*) within a circle and around the outer edge with a large stylized thunder scroll or fret pattern. At the center of each crossed *vajra* there is a whirling emblem (*dga' 'khyil*). The outlines of the designs are sharply engraved, the designs finely crosshatched, and the surfaces burnished with thin gold leaf. The extreme outer edges of the disks may have been damascened in silver, of which a few traces appear to remain. Each disk is lined with a pad made of textile sandwiched between layers of leather. A well-

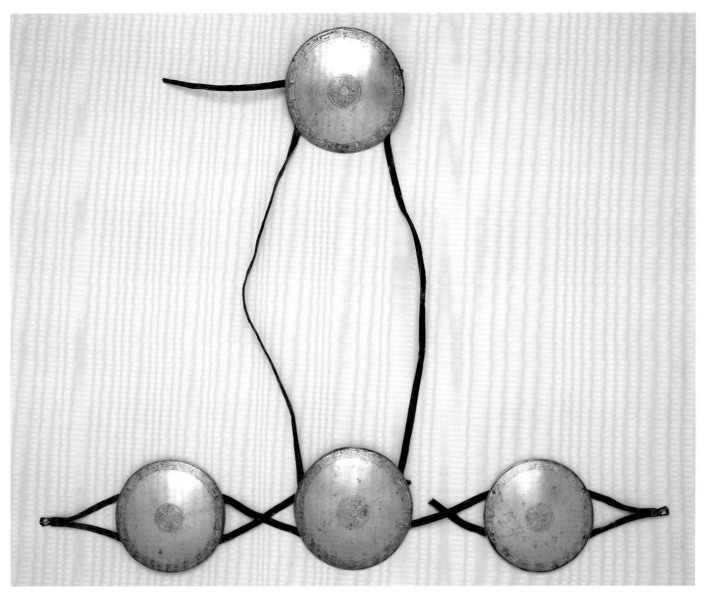

44

preserved wax seal is found on the lining of one of the side plates (see detail). The leather cross-straps are brittle and partially broken off. The V-shaped straps extending from the side plates end in decorated iron buckles.

This set was part of the ensemble described by George Stone as typical of the armor of Bhutan, Sikkim, and Nepal (see above, "Mail and Other Forms of Armor" and cat. no. 40).

PROVENANCE: W. O. Oldman, London; George Cameron Stone, New York.

PUBLICATIONS: Stone 1934, pp. 53, 56, fig. 68; LaRocca 1999a, fig. 29.

44, back plate

44, detail of seal

45. ARMORED BELT

Probably Tibetan, 17th–19th century

Iron and leather

L. 39 in. (99.1 cm)

The Metropolitan Museum of Art, New York, Bequest of George C. Stone, 1935 (36.25.29)

Armored belts such as this are known from a handful of examples acquired in Tibet in the early twentieth century and from the many that can be seen on the cavalrymen in the photos of the Great Prayer Festival taken in Lhasa in the 1930s and 1940s (see above, "Mail and Other Forms of Armor").[1] They share a generally similar form and method of construction, but while some are rectangular and relatively plain, others, like the present example, widen toward the center and have finely made plates. This belt consists of eighty-two plates of a silvery iron color, each of which has a chiseled border and is riveted to three leather support straps that run lengthwise across the interior. There are approximately ten to twenty plates missing from the proper right end, where there are the remains of two leather support straps exposed by the missing plates. The plates overlap from the ends toward the larger central plate, which would be in the center of the

back when the belt was worn. In the center of this larger plate there is a short perpendicular post ending in a knob, which was probably designed to keep any additional belts, worn over the armored belt, from sliding down. At the top of this plate the word *'or* is finely engraved in *dbu can* script (see detail), possibly referring to a place of that name in the district of Nyethang (*snye thang*), southeast of Lhasa in the Yarlung Valley. There are three square iron lugs attached to the ninth plate from the proper left end. At the time of acquisition by the Metropolitan Museum, these had three leather cords, now missing, tied to them. There are the remains of three damaged wax seals on the leather straps of the interior (see detail). For George Stone's attribution of this belt as part of a "suit of Bhutanese armor," see catalogue number 40.

Beasley published a front and back view of an armored belt of this type (possibly now in the

National Museums Liverpool), described it as being from western Tibet, and gave the Tibetan name for it as "Lchacksgi."[2] This may be a semiphonetic interpretation of the Tibetan *lcags sked*, literally, "iron belt."

PROVENANCE: W. O. Oldman, London; George Cameron Stone, New York.

PUBLICATIONS: Stone 1934, pp. 53, 56, fig. 68; LaRocca 1999a, fig. 29.

1. Other armored belts of this type, in varying states of condition, are found at the Victoria and Albert Museum, London (IM.73A-1910, IM.72J-1910, 3083-IS), the Royal Armouries Museum, Leeds (XXVIA.160), the National Museums Liverpool (part of 56.27.203), and the Metropolitan Museum (36.24.28). One example in the Victoria and Albert Museum (IM.72J-1910) has traces of very finely engraved decoration consisting of swirling cloud patterns. The plates of that belt are individually numbered on the interior, both in Tibetan numerals and script.

2. Beasley 1938, pls. X, XI.

45, detail of inscription

45, detail of seal

45, back view

46. ARMORED CAVALRYMAN

Tibetan, and possibly Bhutanese and Nepalese, 18th–19th century
Iron, gold, silver, copper alloy, wood, leather, and textile
The Metropolitan Museum of Art, New York, Bequest of George C. Stone, 1935 (36.25.25, .28, .351, .476, .583a–c, h–k, .842a–c, .2174, .2461, .2505, .2557);
Bequest of Joseph V. McMullan, 1973 (1974.160.10 [saddle rug]); Gift of Mrs. Faïe J. Joyce, 1970 (1970.164.7a, b [boots])

This figure has been assembled based on photographs of the armored cavalry taking part in the Great Prayer Festivals at Lhasa (see "Rediscovering the Arms and Armor of Tibet," esp. figs. 6–8), who wore what appears to be a relatively standardized set of equipment, probably as stipulated by the central government of Tibet from the mid-seventeenth or eighteenth century onward.

The helmet (36.25.25) is a type generally referred to as Bhutanese. It consists of a simple one-piece hemispherical bowl with a finely chiseled and damascened iron plume finial (see detail) and an engraved and damascened iron brim. The plume finial is currently riveted to the bowl, but the paired holes around its base indicate that it was originally intended to be laced in place, rather than riveted, probably to a helmet of a different style than this. The helmet is fitted with ear and neck flaps that have scalloped edges and are made of a brocaded silk with alternating patterns of diagonal stripes and floral designs picked out in gold and silver metallic threads, which appears to be from northern India.[1] The style of the textile fittings is very different from those used on helmets in Bhutan, but is characteristic for this type of helmet as it was worn in Tibet.

The shirt of mail (36.25.476) is very similar to that described in catalogue number 40 with the exception of the collar, which is in poor condition. The four mirrors (36.25.351) were catalogued by Stone as Nepalese and consist of four plain iron disks retaining their full set of original cross-straps. The interiors are lined with textile and have three different wax seals, one of which includes the word *thon* in *dbu can* script (see details). The armored belt (36.25.28) is similar to that in catalogue number 45, but is more simply made. It consists of ninety-eight plates, all of the same length. Attached to the fourth plate from the proper left edge there are two square iron lugs with braided leather straps tied to them, and two corresponding buckles attached to the last plate of the proper right edge. The bow case and quiver

(36.25.2557) are Tibetan or Chinese, nineteenth century, and the bow (36.25.2505) is Chinese, also nineteenth century. The matchlock musket is described in catalogue number 101, the bandolier in catalogue number 106, and the spear in catalogue number 76. For the saddle, see catalogue number 116.

As the Metropolitan Museum accession numbers indicate, this figure is composed almost entirely of elements from George Stone, acquired by him early in the twentieth century. For his attribution of the

helmet and armored belt to Sikkim, Bhutan, or Nepal, see catalogue number 40.

PROVENANCE: W. O. Oldman, London (helmet, armored belt, musket, bow case and quiver, and bandolier); George Cameron Stone, New York (all except saddle rug and boots).

PUBLICATIONS: Stone 1934, pp. 53, 56, fig. 68 (helmet only); LaRocca 1999a, fig. 29 (helmet, bandolier, musket, bow case, quiver, and bow).

1. I am grateful to Joyce Denney for information about the textile.

46, back view

46, detail of helmet plume finial

46, belt

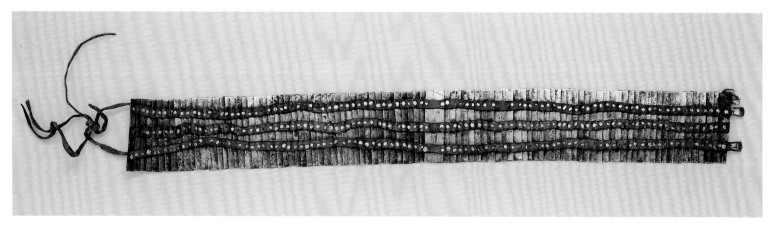

46, inside of belt

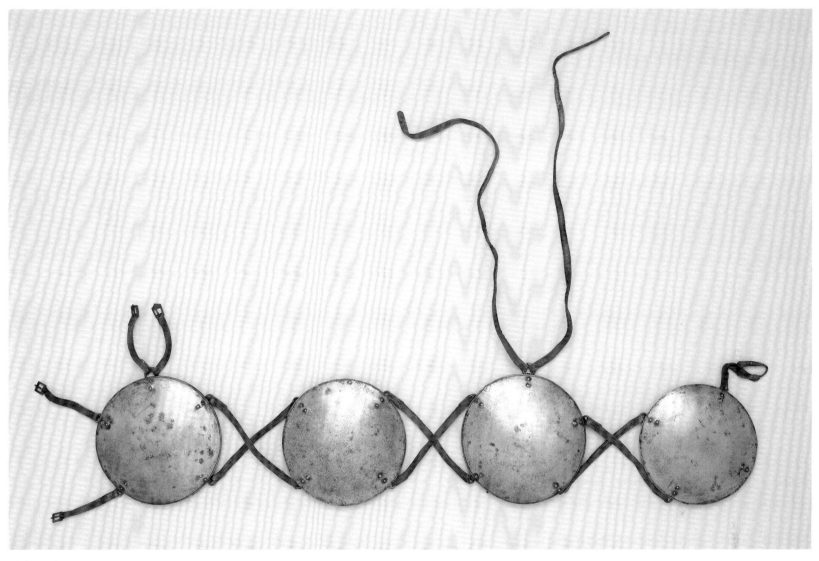

46, four mirrors

46, details of seals

47. KNEE OR SHOULDER DEFENSE

Possibly Mongolian or Chinese, 13th–15th century
Iron, gold, and silver
H. 5¼ in. (13.3 cm), W. 6¾ in. (17.1 cm)
The Metropolitan Museum of Art, New York, Rogers Fund,
by exchange, 1998 (1998.2)

47

This piece is the only one of its kind known at this point, making it difficult to determine its exact function or to attribute it to a particular place or date. It is very well made and consists of a convex rectangular sheet of iron with an applied vertical iron rib riveted at its center. The exterior surface is lavishly decorated with a figure of a *qilin* (a mythological creature combining the characteristics of several animals) in gold surrounded by leafy stalks and blossoms in silver. There is a border formed by a double line of gold around the center compartment and an outer border consisting of a single line of silver. The applied rib is covered in silver and is mounted over a flat base plate covered in gold. The gold and silver decoration is made up of flat strips, rather than wires, laid side by side on the iron ground and burnished together to present the appearance of a continuous sheet. The individual strips are visible under magnification in areas that are worn or damaged. Unlike other iron objects with applied gold or silver, however, there are no visible signs of crosshatching on the ground beneath the decoration, which appears to have been slightly recessed and perhaps roughened with a chisel or engraving tool. The details were picked out in engraved lines and punch marks, done after the gold and silver were in place. The overall exterior surface of the iron is slightly rough, rather than finely polished, and has a dark brown color that is probably the result of natural patination. Around the edges of the interior there are eight raised L-shaped rivets, probably for a support fabric or to attach a lining. The decoration of this piece is similar in style, and possibly in technique, to that found on a ball-headed mace in the Royal Armouries Museum, Leeds (XXVIC.82), which may be Yuan.

The *qilin* was used as a rank badge beginning in the Yuan dynasty (1279–1368) and continued as such through the Ming dynasty (1368–1644), signifying a military official of the first rank, which was the highest of nine possible ranks for military and civil officials. Therefore, it seems likely that this piece was originally part of an extremely elaborate armor for an important military official in the service of the Yuan or Ming emperors.

PUBLICATION: LaRocca 1999a, p. 117, fig. 8.

48, 49. TWO ARMORED ELEMENTS (POSSIBLY FORMING A PAIR)

Tibetan or Mongolian, probably 15th–17th century
Leather and iron
L. 9 in. (22.9 cm), W. 5½ in. (14 cm)
The Metropolitan Museum of Art, New York, Purchase, Arthur Ochs Sulzberger Gift, 2001 (2001.559);
Victoria and Albert Museum, London (IM.73N-1910)

48

49

Based on their form these pieces are suggested here to be knee defenses. They are the only two of their type known and are identical save for a few minor differences. Both share many similarities in terms of materials and construction with the shaffron in catalogue number 29 and were probably made about the same time and in the same region. They consist of nine rows of overlapping scales attached by leather laces to a flexible leather lining that is roughly semicircular in shape with short tablike extensions at either upper corner. The scales have a cusped, fishtail-shaped edge and are pierced by two lacing holes. In the Metropolitan Museum example (cat. no. 48) the center row has five larger scales at the end, while on the Victoria and Albert Museum example (cat. no. 49) the scales of the center row remain the same size. The areas around the edges are filled in with small square scales on the former and with shield-shaped scales on the latter. Square scales of the same shape are also used in this way on the shaffron (cat. no. 29). The principal difference between the two is that the scales overlap in opposite directions, those on the Metropolitan Museum example overlapping downward and those on the Victoria and Albert Museum example overlapping upward. Also, the leather border on the former is made of the same soft leather as the lining, while on the latter it is a harder leather, like that seen on some shaffrons. There is a single leather lace remaining on one of the top tabs of the Victoria and Albert Museum example, and on the lower edge of the Metropolitan Museum example. The Victoria and Albert Museum example is now narrow and flat, but this appears to be from the lining having hardened in this position. The leather of the Metropolitan Museum example is suppler and retains an open shape, suggesting the contour of a knee. Although possibly a pair, the two pieces were acquired more than ninety years apart (by the Victoria and Albert Museum in 1910 and by the Metropolitan Museum in 2001).

50, 51. TWO ARM DEFENSES

Possibly Tibetan, 15th–17th century
Iron, leather, copper alloy, and textile
2000.487.1, L. 12½ in. (31.8 cm); 2000.487.2, L. 10⅝ in. (27 cm)
The Metropolitan Museum of Art, New York, Purchase, Arthur Ochs Sulzberger Gift, 2000 (2000.487.1, .2)

Body armor in Tibet falls into three principal categories: lamellar (iron or leather), mail, and, to a lesser extent, iron scales on leather (such as cat. nos. 29, 48, 49). However, these two arm defenses, not a pair but closely related, fall neatly into none of these categories, and appear to be unique examples of their type. Nevertheless, the details of their construction share a few key features with various types of armor from Tibet, suggesting a relationship of some sort between them.

The first piece (2000.487.1) is for the right arm. It consists of five polished iron panels, each fluted with longitudinal ribs and rimmed all around with a thin border of copper alloy. Within the border, the perimeter of each panel is pierced with a series of holes by which it is tightly stitched to a leather ground by leather laces. Between each panel there is a narrow row of overlapping scales (for a total of four rows). The center of each scale is embossed into a short sharp beak, which overlaps the scale below it to form a sharp ridge filling the gap between each panel. The scales are individually stitched down with leather laces in the same manner as the panels. Four small, well-made hinges connect the panels at their bases. Two small, well-made buckles are located, one each, at the top and bottom outer corner of one end panel. The interior is lined with a plain fabric over which there is a red silk (?) lining. The lining is trimmed with a border or piping of leather. The overall workmanship is crisp and very fine, despite some damage and losses.

The second example (2000.487.2) appears to be for the left arm. It consists of six polished iron panels fluted longitudinally and edged all around with a narrow border of copper alloy. As on the other example, the perimeter of each panel is pierced with a series of holes by which it is tightly stitched to a leather ground. The gap between the panels is filled by a series of overlapping scales, which are fluted in a manner similar to the panels. A single row of scales originally extended in an arch over the top of

the three central panels. The inner arm area is covered by a leather and fabric extension fitted with three double eyelets of iron. There are remains of braided leather laces in the eyelets and corresponding leather loops on the opposite edge. The leather of this area has the remains of brightly colored silk fabric on the exterior. The leather interior, to which the scales and panels are stitched directly, shows no evidence of a lining fabric. A small hinge at the bottom center edge of the center panel suggests an attachment for a missing extension, perhaps for the back of the hand. The workmanship is virtually identical to the example above.

While the form and use of the scales on these two arm defenses is reminiscent of that on some shaffrons (particularly cat. no. 29), the workmanship is much finer. The applied copper alloy borders are also similar to those seen on a few shaffrons (cat. nos. 27–29) and on several helmets (cat. nos. 12, 13, 21), but again the workmanship is much finer. While this comparative material is associated with Tibet, the Mongols, and possibly West Asia, in general the use of plate or mail and plate armguards is associated with India and the Middle East. Therefore, the influences reflected in these arm defenses are likely to have come from the south or west of Tibet.

50, inside

51, inside

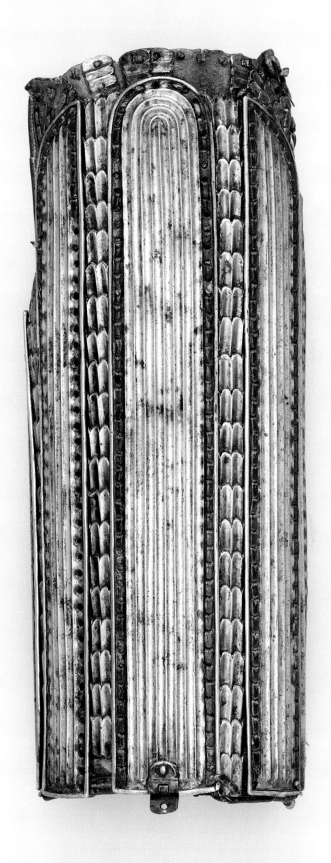

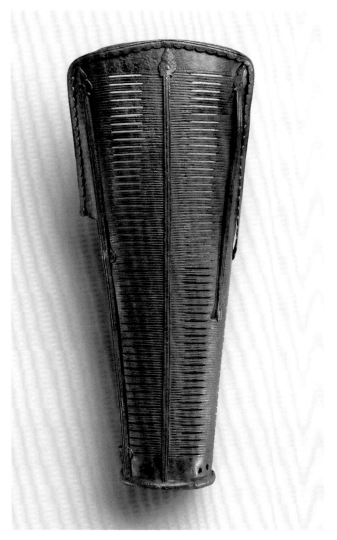

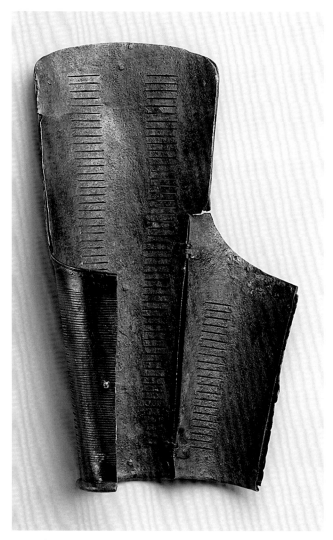

52   52, inside

52. DEFENSE FOR THE LEFT FOREARM

Possibly Tibetan, 14th–16th century
Iron
L. 11¼ in. (28.6 cm)
The Metropolitan Museum of Art, New York, Rogers Fund, 2001 (2001.558)

This arm defense, made entirely of iron, represents a form previously unknown in Tibet or any of the surrounding regions. Its connection with some known types, however, is clearly indicated by the applied vertical struts with trefoil finials, like those found on other armguards, shields, and furniture from Tibet (see cat. nos. 35, 24), and by the scalloped iron border, also found on Tibetan armguards. In addition, the small hinges on the present example are very similar to those on the previous two armguards, suggesting a link between all of them.

The armguard is made of a main plate covering the outer forearm from the elbow to the wrist and a subsidiary plate covering the inner forearm, which, when closed together, fully encircle the lower forearm. The upper portion of the main plate widens toward the elbow and is slightly concave. The subsidiary plate, also concave, is attached to the main plate by two hinges. It is held in the closed position by a pierced lug, which is riveted to the center of the inner edge of the main plate, and which engages a hole in the applied border of the outer edge of the

subsidiary plate. The outer surfaces of both plates are decorated overall with a series of closely set incised horizontal lines, which are pierced by four columns of narrow horizontal slits. The circular opening for the wrist has an outward-turned rim, which is rolled over a thick wire. All of the other edges of both plates have applied iron borders with scalloped inner edges. The scalloping is followed by an inner border consisting of a continuous incised line. The outside of the main plate has three applied vertical iron struts, each of which has a pair of shallow grooves running its entire length and terminates in a trefoil finial. The applied borders and struts are attached by flat rivets.

Various forms of all-metal arm defenses with hinged plates were widely used in India and Persia, where they were called *dastana* and *bazu band*, respectively. Although the present example is different in shape from any of these, the conception and aspects of the construction are similar enough, particularly with the Indian type, to suggest that this forearm defense comes from an area in contact with northern India, perhaps in southwestern Tibet.

53. DEFENSE FOR THE RIGHT ARM

Western Tibetan, North Indian, or West Asian, 15th–16th century
Iron
L. 25 in. (63.5 cm)
On loan courtesy of the National Museums of Scotland
Royal Museum, Edinburgh (A.1907.458)

Various styles of armor made of shaped iron plates joined by small sections of mail were widely used in Turkey and Indo-Persia. This arm defense, while not matching any of the recognized styles, clearly falls into this general category and must have been influenced by them. It was acquired before 1907 from the ruins of a fortress in Leh, the capital of Ladakh, a culturally Tibetan area of northwestern India. It was part of a group of five pieces of armor, including a coat of mail and plate (Royal Museum, A.1907.457) of the type that can still be seen in the Stok Palace Museum in Ladakh. Due to Ladakh's geographical location, the armor and weapons used there often present an eclectic mix of Indian, Tibetan, and Middle Eastern styles, well represented by this arm defense. It is made up of several large plates starting at the shoulder and covering the length of the arm. The gaps in between are filled in with narrower plates and rows of sturdy riveted mail alternating with rows of solid links of mail. There is a round convex plate over the point of the elbow. This arm defense has no exact parallels, being more extensive in its coverage than even the heavi-

53

est Indo-Persian types, but it was probably part of a complete heavy cavalry armor for man and horse similar to those worn by the Turks and the Mamluks in the fifteenth and early sixteenth centuries.

PROVENANCE: Mrs. Lilian le Mesurier, whose husband, Major E. le Mesurier, Political Department, Government of India, held appointments in Sikkim, Kashmir, and Ladakh.

54. ARMORED ROBE

Chinese, 18th century
Textile, copper, and leather
L. 45¾ in. (116.2 cm)
Courtesy of the Board of Trustees, National Museums Liverpool (56.27.204)

This robe again demonstrates the amazing variety of unique or extremely rare types of armor that survived in Tibet and the Tibetan cultural area. It is an example of, or closely based on, a distinctive form of Chinese ceremonial armor of the eighteenth century, of which very few examples appear to exist. It consists of a long, sleeveless tunic that opens down the front and at each side, like a poncho, and is split up the back for about 22 inches (56 cm) from the lower edge. The foundation is a cotton or linen-like fabric lined with red silk on the interior. The exterior is covered with overlapping rows of small shield-shaped copper scales, possibly originally gilded, measuring only 1.7 centimeters high by 1 centimeter wide and having four holes at the top, by which they are sewn to the underlying fabric with a fine thread. The scales running in a line down the center of the back have a slightly embossed central ridge and end in a point. The borders of the robe are covered with woven silk brocaded in metallic threads and having a pattern of large floral blossoms. At the top there is a short collar covered in a woven silk with scroll and leaf patterns.[1] There are three closures on the proper right edge of the front seam consisting of a strip of soft leather rolled into a tube and covered with a sleeve of silk. There is also a single braided silk cord on either side seam to tie the sides below the arm. The robe appears to have been used extensively, showing many signs of wear and repairs, perhaps over several generations.

What appears to be an armored robe of this type is depicted in the *Huangchao Liqi Tushi* (Illustrated Regulations for the Ceremonial Regalia of the Present Dynasty), which was produced in 1759 during the reign of Emperor Qianlong (r. 1736–96) (fig. 44). There it is described as the "armor for the military principal graduate," or *zhuangyuan*.[2]

The robe was identified by H. G. Beasley as being in the Hyslop Collection.[3] This is almost certainly a reference to Captain Hyslop of the 93rd Highlanders, who accompanied J. Claude White on his second trip to Bhutan in 1907.[4]

PROVENANCE: Hyslop Collection; Castle Museum, Norwich (141.79.928).

PUBLICATION: Beasley 1938, pl. VI.

1. I am grateful to Joyce Denney for her efforts to identify these textiles.
2. Reprinted in *Yingyin Wenyuange Sikyu Quanshu*, vol. 656 (Shanghai, 1983), p. 732. Jason Sun explains that the *zhuangyuan* is the first-place winner in the government examination system. I am grateful to him and Mike Hearn for translating the passage relating to this armor, which reads as follows: "By regulation of the dynasty, the armor for the military principal graduate is made of refined copper. It has a red silk lining, red ground with gold borders, and complete rows of copper plates with shell patterns. The two sleeves [also] have copper plates. Below the quadripartite skirt are knitted green ribbons, from which red tassels are suspended, forty in the front and forty in the back."
3. Beasley 1938, pl. VI.
4. See White 1909 for several references to Hyslop, who is included in a photograph with White and various dignitaries from Bhutan and Sikkim, taken in Calcutta in 1906 (facing p. 48).

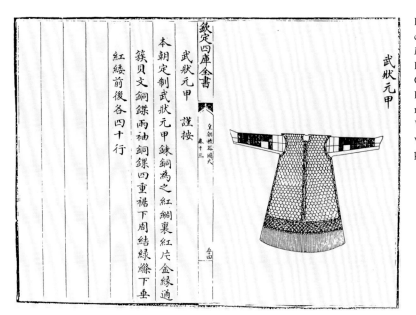

Fig. 44. Armored robe depicted in *Huangchao Liqi Tushi* (Illustrated Regulations for the Ceremonial Regalia of the Present Dynasty), 1759, reprinted in *Yingyin Wenyuange Sikyu Quanshu*, vol. 656 (Shanghai, 1983), p. 732

54

54, back view

རལ་གྲི
Swords

Swords were the primary hand-held weapon in Tibet from at least the seventh century up to the early twentieth. In addition to their utilitarian function, they could also be clear indicators of rank and status, based on their quality or amount of decoration. In some situations, such as among the Khampas of eastern Tibet, the sword was an essential part of male dress and remains an important element of traditional attire. The sword also has rich symbolic significance within Tibetan Buddhism, particularly as the Sword of Wisdom (*shes rab ral gri*), which represents the ability to cut through spiritual ignorance, and is an important attribute of many deities, such as Manjushri (*'jam dpal*). The different styles of actual swords found in Tibet can be distinguished by several basic features, outlined below, which include the type of blade, the form of hilt, the type of scabbard, and how the sword was designed to be worn.

The type of sword blade most frequently found in Tibet is straight with a single edge and an oblique or sloped tip, sometimes called a chisel tip. The shape of the tip varies, and can be a gentle curve, a steep angle, or fairly rounded, this last variation being most similar to swords from Bhutan (cat. nos. 61, 62, 65, 66, 68, 69). The second type of blade is also straight and single edged, but it ends in an acute or attenuated point (cat. nos. 63, 64, 70). This type is frequently found on daggers and short swords, and less so on full-size blades as well. The third type is also straight, but is double edged and has a symmetrical tip. This is found on some very early styles of swords (cat. nos. 55, 57), but also occurs later (cat. nos. 67, 72). The last type of blade is curved and single edged, that is, a saber blade, which is not indigenous to Tibet, most examples being Chinese, Indian, or Middle Eastern (cat. nos. 74, 124).

Another important feature is the pattern of lines and textures, which can be very subtle or extremely clear, that is visible on the surface of a blade. This is also the simplest way to distinguish traditional blades from those made of modern iron or steel, on which these patterns are not present. The effect is created by a technique called pattern welding, which is the combining of different types of iron or steel during the forging process resulting in a particular pattern appearing in the finished blade.[1] The classic pattern seen most often on traditional Tibetan blades consists of a series of gently undulating pairs of lines of alternating dark and light color, which run the length of the blade and meet near the tip (for instance, cat. no. 61). C. S. Smith described this as created by the "side-by-side welding of a nested series of hairpin rods," and it is generally referred to as a hairpin pattern.[2] In Tashi Namgyal and other Tibetan texts the blade pattern appears to be referred to by the term *thur*, and is said to be made by the mixture of male iron and female iron (*pho lcags* and *mo lcags*). The male iron is described as lighter in

color and hard, while the female iron is darker in color and more ductile, a combination that is important in producing a blade that is strong and yet still flexible.[3] From a metallurgical point of view this may indicate that the pale so-called male iron would have a higher carbon content, making it tough and rigid, while the darker so-called female iron would be iron with a lower carbon content, making it more malleable. In addition to male and female iron, the Tibetan texts also mention neuter iron (*ma ning lcags*) and composite iron (*sna 'dus lcags*), all of which have different colors and properties depending how they are tempered.[4] A few other patterns exist, although they are found much less frequently, including one in which the female iron forms series of flattened concentric circles and another in which it appears as a series of separate bands with a slight S-curve, like tiger stripes (cat. no. 65).[5] According to Tashi Namgyal, in addition to *thur* the most important features for assessing a sword blade are referred to as *skra* and *gog*, but the exact meaning of these terms remains uncertain at present.[6]

Tibetan hilts, like most sword hilts, consist basically of a pommel, grip, and guard. The most popular type of pommel is trefoil or three-leaf clover in shape, which is made of sheet iron or silver, and appears to have been used in all parts of Tibet (cat. nos. 61–67). The surfaces are usually chiseled or incised (if iron) or embossed (if silver) with scroll patterns on the front and back and swastika or fret patterns on the sides. Typically there is a single stone, either turquoise or coral, in a bezel setting in the center of the front, and a ring for the attachment of a wrist strap (*dpa' lung*) or a short silk streamer directly opposite it on the reverse. The other primary type of pommel, which occurs mostly in eastern Tibet, is made of a short lozenge-shaped block of iron. It usually has transverse lines of copper inlaid across the front, three small cones of iron on the top, and two holes in the back for a wrist strap (cat. nos. 68, 69).

The grip, particularly with a trefoil pommel, usually consists of a short rectangular wooden core tightly wrapped in silver wire. This type of grip also has a short collar at its base, which matches the pommel in material and decoration. On hilts with the lozenge-shaped iron pommel the wooden core of the grip is usually longer, flares out slightly at either end, and is covered with ray skin. On very simple swords the grip may consist of a rectangular block of wood, or wood wrapped in leather. When this kind of grip is found on a more elaborate sword it may indicate that the grip is a later replacement. A rare form of grip, found on some swords attributed to the fifteenth century, is made entirely of iron and is chiseled and damascened in gold and silver (cat. nos. 55, 57, 60).

The sword guard is mounted at the base of the grip and has the basic function of separating it from the top of the blade and protecting the hand. It should seat the sword firmly in the top of the scabbard when it is sheathed to keep out moisture and dirt. Some forms also present large surfaces for decoration. The most usual type of guard is an oval with cusped edges, which is formed by two trefoils meeting end to end, often used in conjunction with a trefoil pommel and wire-wrapped grip. This type of guard consists of a flat top plate that has deep sides following its contours and is open at the bottom (cat. nos. 61, 65). In a variation of this, the guard is small and rectangular rather than oval, fitting snugly over the opening at the top of the scabbard (cat. nos. 62–64). In another variation, the guard is a circular plate, often of silver, set parallel to the plane of the blade at the juncture between the blade and the grip (cat. no. 66). On eastern Tibetan swords with the lozenge-block pommel and ray skin covered grip the guard is often a simple round undecorated dish with a sloped or chamfered edge (cat. nos. 68, 69). On a few early swords the guard is formed by a collar at the base of the grip, which extends out and curves downward at either side and has large a semicircular flange in the front, also parallel with the plane of the blade (cat. nos. 56–59).

Scabbard fittings can be very elaborate and as such are a visible sign of the wearer's wealth or status. The style of the fittings is in part dictated by the way the sword was intended to be worn, either through the sash at the front of the body or hanging from the left hip. Virtually all scabbards have a wooden core, usually made of two halves, front and back, with a recess shaped to match the outline of the blade. This is glued together and the exposed areas covered in leather or textile. The most typical fitting consists of a U-shaped iron channel covering the scabbard from the very bottom and having arms extending all the way up both sides. This is frequently chiseled or pierced with scrollwork and damascened in gold or silver. The space in front between the arms can be filled with a similarly decorated pierced-iron panel set with stones, or with embossed silver plaques set with stones. The stones are usually turquoise and coral, real or simulated, typically with one at the very base of the U-channel and three on the inset plaque. This style is often found on swords made to be worn in front of the body, thrust through the waist sash at an almost horizontal angle, the hilt to the wearer's right and the blade edge upward in the scabbard. The decoration of the hilt and the lower half of the scabbard are prominently displayed on a sword worn this way (cat. nos. 62, 63). William Rockhill described the best swords of this type as made in Derge (sde dge), in eastern Tibet, and called them "the most highly prized of any in Tibet," being worth large sums of money.[7]

The fittings are slightly different on a sword made to be worn at the left hip suspended by two straps from a waist belt, a style attributed by Rockhill to Chinese influence (cat. nos. 65–67).[8] In this instance, the channel around the edges of the scabbard is often square at the base rather than U-shaped. Alternatively, instead of a channel the scabbard may have an extended silver cap, or chape, at the bottom of the scabbard and a matching collar, or locket, at the top. The front of the chape and locket are often embossed with dragons and foliage, and sometimes set with stones. Between the chape and locket there are two or three horizontal bands corresponding with the fittings for the belt straps. These are also usually set with turquoise or coral. Simpler eastern Tibetan swords can have scabbards covered mostly in leather with various types of silver or gilded copper fittings (cat. no. 69). Scabbards with a single lug on the front a few inches down from the top are designed to be worn vertically at the right hip, in the Bhutanese style (cat. nos. 70, 73).

The traditional history of Tibetan swords is found in three principal texts, all of which offer similar but often varied versions of the subject. In chronological order they are the *rgya bod yig tshang chen mo* (The Great Chinese-Tibetan Compendium) by Palchor Zangpo (*dpal 'byor bzang po*), written in 1434; the *'jig rten lugs kyi bstan bcos* (A Treatise on Worldly Traditions) by Tashi Namgyal (*bkra shis rnam rgyal*) of 1524; and the *brtag thabs padma dkar po'i 'chun po* (Lotus Bouquet of Analytical Methods) of Hūṃkaradzaya, written at a later but uncertain date, which includes two separate sword chapters that differ significantly from each other.[9] The texts divide swords into five principal types, equating each name with a country or people and a legendary origin derived from the purported etymology of its name: *zhang ma*, *sog po*, *hu phed*, *dgu zi*, and *'ja' ral*. Palchor Zangpo is the least equivocal in identifying the countries or peoples to which the swords belong. *Zhang ma* is the sword of China, which spread (*dar*) from the time of the Tang emperor Taizong (r. 626–49).[10] *Sog po* is the sword of the border people (*mtha' mi*), but in the other texts it is simply treated as the sword of the eponymous *sog po*, a branch of the Mongols. *Hu phed* is the sword of the Hor, the branch of the Mongols ruled by Genghis Khan (d. 1227), during whose time this sword spread.[11] The sword of Tibet is the *dgu zi*, which originated in the time of the semi-legendary ancient king Trigum Tsenpo (*gri gum btsan po*). Lastly, *'ja' ral* is the sword of the southern borderlands of Tibet (*lho mon*), which seems to be the only type described as a curved sword (*shang lang*). In the texts each of these five has a subtype, for a total of ten basic types, of which there are many subdivisions, enumerated and named somewhat differently from one text to the next.[12] The texts go on to discuss in brief sections how to differentiate old blades from new, the different types of iron, the different types of tempering and which types of iron these best apply to, and the different methods of polishing and which types of swords of these methods suit best. Rather than technical descriptions, however, the texts seem to be a mixture of practical observation, traditional stories, and literary convention. In addition, the spelling of many key terms can be entirely different within a given text, from one text to the next, and among different versions of the same text, making the meanings of some terms difficult if not impossible to understand with certainty. While these texts often do not apply directly to existing swords from Tibet, they nevertheless contain much that is of interest and worth further study.

1. On pattern welding and Tibetan blades, see Smith 1960, pp. 8–9, and illustrations on the cover, p. xxii, and figs. 5, 6.
2. Smith 1960, p. 8.
3. See Tashi Tsering 1979, pp. 60–61, where the text states that when female iron is lacking the lines can be made in the blade with a chisel. The color and qualities of male and female iron are described in the Tashi Namgyal texts in the appendix "Excerpts from *A Treatise on Worldly Traditions*," for instance, British Library Or 11,374, fols. 76b, 77a; Burmiok Athing, fol. 25a. After tempering, male iron is said to become black and female iron becomes white. The same passage also says that *thur* is made mostly by female iron.
4. For instance, British Library Or 11,374, fol. 76b; Burmiok Athing, fol. 25a; Tashi Tsering 1979, p. 74.
5. Norbu and Turnbull (1968, p. 102) included line drawings of these blade patterns and identified them as "dmar gyi gya [rgya] mtsho phug pa" and "ce rong," respectively. The same illustration identified the hairpin pattern blade as "hgu zi [dgu zi]," but in the traditional sources given in the appendix "Excerpts from *A Treatise on Worldly Traditions*," this is the general name for the type of sword used in Tibet.
6. See, especially, in the appendix "Excerpts from *A Treatise on Worldly Traditions*," British Library Or 11,374, fol. 77b, and Burmiok Athing, fol. 25b: "skra gog thur gsum dbye ba ma shes na / gri rigs 'byed pa'i mig dang mi ldan pas / de bas de yis rnam dbye bshad par bya" (If one does not know how to distinguish the three—*skra*, *gog*, and *thur*—then one will not be able to distinguish sword types by eye. Therefore, differentiating these will be explained).
7. Rockhill 1895, p. 712, where he illustrates three swords collected during his fieldwork and identified as being from Derge (*sde dge*), Dawo (possibly *rta'u*?), and Poyul (*dpal yul*).
8. Ibid. Swords are also worn this way in other surrounding countries, such as India and much of the Middle East, but in eastern Tibet this style probably was directly influenced by Chinese fashion.
9. Details of the published and unpublished versions of these texts are given at the start of the appendix "Excerpts from *A Treatise on Worldly Traditions*."
10. Identified in the Tibetan text as tha'i dzung, who is listed among the early Tang rulers in the same work in the chapter on the dynasties of China (see the chapter "rgya nag gi rgyal rabs" in Palchor Zangpo, p. 105). In the first sword chapter of the Hūṃkaradzaya text, however, *zhang ma* is identified as the sword of zhang zhung (Tashi Tsering 1979, p. 60).
11. The first citation of this sword is spelled *hu phed*, but it appears in other texts as *hu bed*, *hu wed*, and *hu bde*. See the appendix "Excerpts from *A Treatise on Worldly Traditions*," for a discussion and citations.
12. The Palchor Zangpo text names a total of forty-nine sword types and the Tashi Namgyal text fifty-four. According to Hūṃkaradzaya, if the sword types are divided in great detail there are ninety-two types, and in less detail thirty-two types; these can be condensed to eighteen, but the essential six types are *sog*, *zhang ma*, *smug kha shong*, *bod gri*, *khams gri*, and *rgya gri* (Tashi Tsering 1979, p. 61).

55. SWORD AND SCABBARD

Probably Chinese for the Tibetan market, 14th–15th century
Iron, gold, silver, wood, and leather
L. overall 35½ in. (90.3 cm); blade, L. 30 in. (76.2 cm)
Royal Armouries Museum, Leeds (XXVIS.295)

This sword ranks among the most elaborate and artistically accomplished examples of decorated ironwork from China or Tibet. Due to the style and technique of the decoration, particularly the damascening, it has been compared with what appears to be a closely related group of iron ritual objects commissioned during the reigns of the Chinese emperors Hongwu (r. 1368–98) and Yongle (r. 1403–24) for presentation to Tibetan monasteries. One example, a ritual ax, bears the Hongwu reign mark, and the rest, including ritual scepters and fire spoons, have Yongle reign marks.[1] The most prominent shared motif on the pieces in the Hongwu-Yongle group is a repeating design of concentric circles within an undulating line, the spaces between the circles filled with smaller spirals and curls, all damascened in gold wire on a finely crosshatched ground. Versions of this motif continue to appear on Sino-Tibetan and Tibetan damascened ironwork repeatedly over several centuries, including swords, helmets, saddles, bridles, and stirrups (compare cat. nos. 11, 57, 111, 129, 133–135). While it is also appears extensively on the Leeds sword, it is only used there as a minor feature, confined to the narrow borders of the pommel and scabbard. Instead, the principal design elements of the sword include richly chiseled, pierced, and damascened relief ornament that is in many ways more varied and stylistically complex than anything found among the ritual objects of the Hongwu-Yongle group. In addition, the pierced scrollwork, a key feature in the sword's decoration, is entirely absent from the Hongwu-Yongle group. While the sword and these pieces

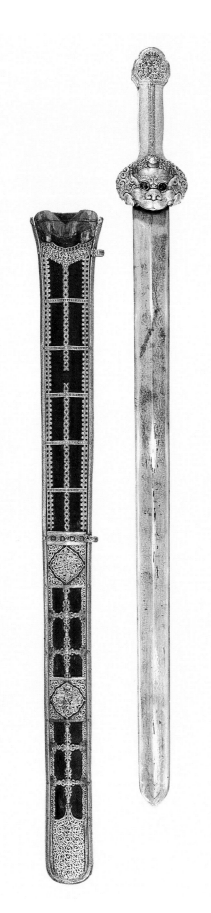

55, detail of hilt and top of scabbard

55, detail of inscription on scabbard

share many techniques, an overall richness, and a high level of quality, there are enough stylistic differences between them to make their exact relationship uncertain.

The hilt is made entirely of iron damascened in gold and silver. Its design centers on the guard, which takes the form of a large three-dimensional *tsi pa ṭa*, or *kirttimukha*, mask, with a mane of billowing scrolls and its mouth fitting over the top of the scabbard (see detail). It is chiseled and engraved in high relief, the open areas stippled with a ring punch, and the lower jaw forming the bottom edge of the back of the guard, clearly indicating that it was conceived to be seen in the round, unlike many sword hilts.[2] The stippling continues over the entire grip, extending like a stylized body from the mask to the trefoil pommel, a ridge flanked by flames in the center of the grip suggesting a spine. The pommel has a dragon on the front and another *tsi pa ṭa* mask on the back, both framed in scrollwork. The sides of the pommel are decorated in fine wire damascening with a double band of the Eight Auspicious Symbols. The sword blade is straight and double edged and shows a faint simulated pattern-welding design of a series of crescents running the length of the blade on either side of the central ridge. The tang does not fit well in the hilt as it is currently mounted, and it has been suggested that the blade is a later Tibetan replacement.[3]

The scabbard, no less elaborate, is encompassed by a damascened iron frame and set with chiseled cartouches of ornament joined by pierced struts. The top of the scabbard has a short curtain of flame-like scrolls that appear to issue from the mouth of the *tsi pa ṭa*. At the center of the scabbard there is a narrow band decorated with a short line of Sanskrit characters (see detail), which have been read as *khadgaratna*, meaning "Precious Sword" (literally, sword jewel).[4] Below this there are two panels of pierced scrollwork with central cartouches featuring pairs of dragons. These panels are connected by struts formed of single and double *vajras*. The chape at the bottom of the scabbard is filled by a dense field of sinuous scrollwork. Two small suspension loops for hanging the scabbard from a sword belt are located on the right edge, one on the frame just below the guard and the other at the end of the horizontal band in the middle of the scabbard.

The *khadgaratna*, or Precious Sword (Tibetan *ral gri rin po che*), is an alternative name for the Precious General (*dmag dpon rin po che*), the last of the Seven Jewels of Royal Power (*rgyal srid rin chen sna bdun*), which are symbolic attributes of monarchy, both spiritual and temporal.[5] The presence of this term on the Leeds sword, therefore, could mean that it was made for presentation to a Tibetan ruler, such as one of the Phagmodrupa, who were the predominant power in central Tibet from 1358 to 1434.[6]

Reflections of this sword, in terms of form, materials, and technique, can be seen in catalogue numbers 56 and 57, and in terms of form and some aspects of construction in catalogue numbers 58 and 59. The possible significance of the differences and points of comparison will be discussed in the following entries.

PROVENANCE: Arnold Lieberman, New York; acquired by the Royal Armouries, 1991.

PUBLICATIONS: Peers 1992, p. 18; T. Richardson 1996; LaRocca 1999a, p. 122, fig. 18.

1. See T. Richardson 1996 for a thorough discussion of this sword, including a detailed physical description and comparisons with the relevant examples of Hongwu and Yongle ritual objects. The ax (fig. 21) is in the Museum of Fine Arts, Boston (1987.93). Other examples with Yongle reign marks in the Metropolitan Museum and the Cleveland Museum of Art are included in Watt and Leidy 2005, pp. 74–79. I am very grateful to Thom Richardson for sharing his notes on this sword and for making it available for study.
2. Much simpler but analogous forms of sword guards, in which the blade emerges from the mouth of a *tsi pa ṭa* mask, are also found frequently on later Chinese and Korean swords up to the 18th or 19th century, for example Metropolitan Museum 36.25.1409, .1456, .1480, .1482, .1484, and .1485.
3. As per Thom Richardson's notes.
4. As read by Braham Norwick in cooperation with Gyatso Tshering in October 1997.
5. On this see Dagyab 1995, pp. 64–83. The other six attributes are the Precious Wheel, Precious Jewel, Precious Queen, Precious Minister, Precious Elephant, and Precious Horse.
6. Shakabpa 1967, pp. 81–86.

56. SWORD GUARD

Tibetan or Chinese, 14th–15th century
Iron, gold, silver, and copper
H. 3⅛ in. (7.9 cm), W. 4¾ in. (12.1 cm)
The Kronos Collections

This sword guard is all that remains of a sword that may have been equal to, or perhaps even more sumptuous than, the sword from the Royal Armouries in the preceding entry. It is exceptional for the precision and crispness of its chiseling, punched work, and damascening, for the height of the relief, and for the balance and cohesion of its overall design. It represents the mask of a fierce guardian deity (*srung ma* or *mgon po*), signified by the third eye, called the eye of wisdom (*dpral mig*), in the center of the forehead, the fiery eyebrows, and the row of bared teeth, including two fangs with small spits of flame on the edges of the mouth above them. The pupils of the eyes are hollow and once may have been filled with stones or other inserts. The surrounding irises are covered in silver, and the whites of the eyes are covered in reddish copper. The inner lip is also covered in copper above the silver damascened teeth and fangs. The remainder of the surface of the front is damascened in gold, and the ground is covered with fine punched work. The top and back of the guard are covered in curls (see illus.), damascened in gold, which are chiseled in low relief across the top of the guard.

The figural relief of this guard is higher than virtually anything else encountered on Tibetan or Chinese decorated ironwork and is more skillfully executed than the relief found on either the Royal Armouries sword or any of the pieces in the Hongwu-Yongle group cited in the previous entry. Also, in terms of overall shape it is more similar to the guards of the next three swords (cat. nos. 57–59) than it is to the Royal Armouries sword. On the Royal Armouries sword the guard is more bulbous and the *tsi pa ṭa* mask forms a distinct mouth, with upper and lower jaws depicted on the front and back of the guard, a style that continues to appear on Chinese swords for several more centuries. The profile of this guard and that of the next three examples, however, are more flat, the upper edges extend more horizontally with a gradual downward slope, and the front of the guard is a vertical half-round flange with no corresponding "lower jaw" on the reverse. Assuming the Royal Armouries sword to be Chinese, early Ming, then this guard and the next three swords may represent Tibetan variations of this style or a style shared in common.

PUBLICATION: LaRocca 1999a, p. 123, fig. 20.

56

56, back view

57. SWORD

Tibetan or Chinese, 14th–16th century
Iron, gold, and silver
L. overall 34⅞ in. (88.6 cm); blade, L. 29½ in. (74.9 cm)
The Metropolitan Museum of Art, New York, Rogers Fund and
Fletcher Fund, by exchange, 1995 (1995.136)

Like the Royal Armouries sword (cat. no. 55), the hilt of this sword, including the grip, is made entirely of iron that has been embossed, chiseled, and damascened in gold and silver (see illus.). In terms of its form and the style of its ornament, however, it is closer to the sword guard in the previous entry (cat. no. 56). The hilt of this sword also has only very small areas of relatively simple punched work, unlike the previous two examples, on which the punched work is extensive and extremely fine. The design of its figural decoration is also simpler, while the geometric and floral motifs are actually more complex. Its guard, like the other two, takes the form of an anthropomorphic mask, but in this instance the features are far more abstracted, consisting only of a pair of eyes and a leonine nose set amid open scrollwork on a black ground. The bottom edge, like that of the previous guard (cat. no. 56), has a border of silver-damascened teeth and fangs. The grip is covered with a netlike reticular pattern, chiseled in low relief, possibly intended to simulate the cord or wire binding of a wrapped wooden grip. The trefoil pommel has a simple *tsi pa ṭa* mask surrounded by foliage.

The top, sides, and back of the hilt, although partly marred by corrosion, are decorated with fine damascening in silver wire. The sides and top of the pommel are covered with the concentric spiral motif mentioned in catalogue number 55 regarding the Hongwu-Yongle group and related examples. It is executed here in fine silver wire and is flanked by narrow thunder scroll borders. The backs of the pommel and grip are divided into compartments of geometric motifs, principally the stylized wave design (*chu ris*). The top and back of the guard are covered with a pattern of lush leafy scrollwork damascened in silver with a few traces of gold.

The blade is straight, double edged, and in cross section a flattened diamond shape, like that of the Royal Armouries sword. It has the remains of a pattern-welding design, in this instance featuring

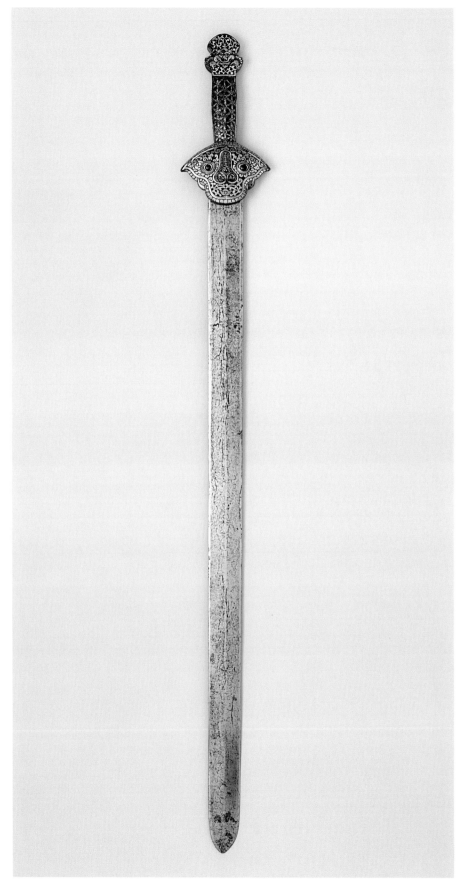

57

57, hilt

57, back of hilt

a series of circles of lighter colored iron along the length of the medial ridge. There are also many dark longitudinal lines in the blade, a feature frequently seen on Tibetan blades, which are evidence of the seams between the layers of iron used in the forging process. Although straight double-edged blades were far more common in China than Tibet, these characteristics suggest that this blade, again like that of the Royal Armouries sword, is Tibetan rather than Chinese.[1]

PUBLICATIONS: LaRocca 1995, p. 77; LaRocca 1996, pp. 15, 42; T. Richardson 1996, p. 99; Lavin 1997, pp. 14–15; LaRocca 1999a, p. 122; Pyhrr, LaRocca, and Ogawa 2002, pp. 47–48.

1. I am grateful to Philip Tom for sharing his thoughts on the blade of this sword and for enumerating its non-Chinese features. It will be included in his forthcoming book on Chinese swords in The Metropolitan Museum of Art.

58. SWORD AND SCABBARD

Tibetan, 15th–16th century
Iron, copper alloy, wood, ray skin, and leather
L. overall 33½ in. (85.1 cm); blade, L. 27⅜ in. (69.5 cm)
Courtesy of the Board of Trustees, National Museums Liverpool
(16.6.05.74)

This sword and that in the next entry (cat. no. 59) are related by the shape of their guards to the detached guard (cat. no. 56) and the Metropolitan Museum sword (cat. no. 57) in the previous entries, and by the form and construction of their scabbards to the Royal Armouries sword (cat. no. 55), although they otherwise differ dramatically from them in terms of material, quality, and state of preservation. They constitute two of only four known examples of an extremely unusual type, characterized by the resemblance to the pieces cited above, and to their unusual combination of materials and construction.[1] The grip and guard of the Liverpool sword are made of wood and leather covered with ray skin, and the bottom edge of the guard is framed with a border of gilded copper alloy. The pommel is a variation of the trefoil type, but has a sandwich construction consisting of two iron plaques, the one in front decorated with simple engraved lines and pierced with a lozenge shape and four circles. The sides and top of the pommel are overlaid with an iron frame pierced and slightly embossed in the form of small crosses, very much like the struts that border the frame on the upper half of the scabbard of the Royal Armouries sword. The blade is single edged and has an oblique tip, but unlike most Tibetan blades it has an offset medial ridge running its entire length. It has been coated with a reddish substance, and a long mantra has been painted over most of its length on both sides in *dbu can* script. Unfortunately, the lettering is now very worn and difficult to read.

The scabbard has the same overall shape as that of the Royal Armouries sword, with the characteristic swelling at the top to accommodate the width of the guard. It also has a similar iron frame around its entire edge, but without decoration except for its cusped interior edge. Also like the Royal Armouries sword, there are two short suspension loops on the right side, one at the top of the scabbard just below the guard and the other at the end of a horizontal

58

band near the center. The scabbard is covered in leather with a band of shagreen down the center. There are three groups of iron and copper bands over the front of the scabbard, at the top, middle, and bottom, which are pierced with scrollwork similar to that seen on some examples of horse armor (for example, cat. no. 30).

The Liverpool museum records concerning the provenance of this sword are somewhat contradictory but still connect it with the Younghusband Expedition. One note states that the sword was "bought from Palhese who got it from the Palha house, Bang-gye-shar, at Lhasa and who says it is more than 100 years old." Another gives the provenance as the monastery at Tsechen. Palhese (*pha lha'i sras*) almost certainly refers to Kusho Palhese, the longtime friend and aide of Sir Charles Bell and a member of the noble Tibetan pha lha family, which had been stripped of its rank and possessions, and some members put to death, for helping Chandra Das reach Lhasa in disguise in 1882.[2] Palhese may have also served as a Tibetan interpreter during the Younghusband Expedition. The second reference is to Tsechan Monastery (*rtse chen dgon pa*), near Gyantse, which was the scene of a hard-fought battle on June 26, 1904, and was subsequently demolished.[3]

PROVENANCE: pha lha family, Lhasa; or Tsechen Monastery, Gyantse, 1904; Sergeant J. Heaney, Younghusband Expedition.

1. In addition to the two swords included here, the other two are a sword in Namgung Monastery, in the Dolpo region of Nepal, and another that passed through the art market in the early 1990s (present whereabouts unknown). I am very grateful to Amy Heller for information about the Namgung sword and to Thom Richardson for informing me about the other example. The Namgung sword has had its hilt replaced, but its blade and scabbard relate closely to the others in this group.
2. McKay 1997, pp. 8, 123–24, 130; Waddell 1905, pp. 8, 9, 203. There is a photograph of Kusho Palhese taken by Sir Charles Bell in 1921 in the Pitt Rivers Museum, Oxford (1998.285.128). I am grateful to Tsering Shakya for additional information about Palhese, and to Emma Martin and Gary Brown for details of the provenance of the sword.
3. Waddell 1905, p. 266; Allen 2004, pp. 207–9, who gives the date as June 28.

59. SWORD AND SCABBARD

Tibetan, 15th–16th century
Iron, copper alloy, ray or shark skin, wood, and leather
L. overall 33½ in. (85.1 cm)
Victoria and Albert Museum, London (IM.290-1907)

For the context and comparative pieces relating to this sword, see the comments on the Liverpool sword (cat. no. 58), which this example resembles very closely in form, materials, and construction. The hilt is made of shaped wood, covered in ray or shark skin. The pommel is made of two iron plaques, the front plaque decorated with simple engraving and pierced by four holes arranged in a square around a central ornamental rivet, which is very similar to the ornamental rivets on the shield in catalogue number 24 and on a Tibetan arm defense in the Royal Armouries Museum, Leeds (XXVIA.282). A strip of copper alloy runs down the front of the grip, is bent to follow the contour of the guard, and ends in a raised teardrop-shaped finial pierced with scrollwork. This finial was probably intended to represent a nose and would have been flanked by appliqués in the form of eyes to make an abstract mask, as on the guard of the Metropolitan Museum sword in catalogue number 57.[1] The bottom of the guard is bordered by a narrow iron strip with a scalloped interior edge, matching the frame around the edge of the scabbard, both of which are very similar to the iron border on the leather arm defense in catalogue number 35. The blade is single edged and has a deeply beveled fuller, a feature not generally found on Tibetan blades. The mouth of the scabbard, however, shows that it was made to receive a single-edged blade of this general profile.

The scabbard is the same shape and construction as described in the previous entry, with differences in the placement and extent of the pierced copper alloy and iron panels. At the very base of the scabbard there is a small border of pierced and raised circles, which are the same form as the pierced strut that runs down the center of the top of the scabbard of the Royal Armouries sword in catalogue number 55. The scabbard retains one suspension loop on the right edge just below the guard, as on catalogue numbers 55 and 58, but the second loop is missing.

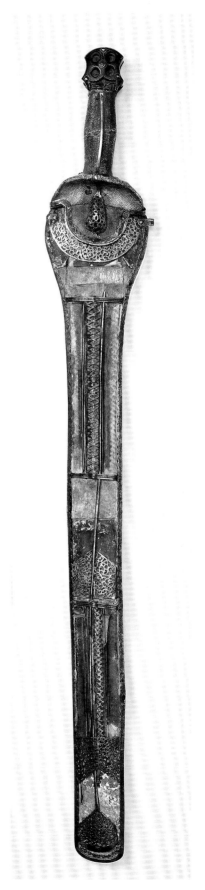

59

In addition to the more obvious aspects of overall shape, materials, and construction, such small details as the style of the ornamental rivet and the scalloped iron borders connect this sword, and by extension the others in the same group, to a greater range of objects from Tibet.

PROVENANCE: Tibet, from the Younghusband Expedition of 1903–4.

1. The similar sword formerly on the art market (cited in cat. no. 58, note 1) has the same type of applied copper alloy band with a nose finial, flanked by eyes to form a mask on the guard.

60. SWORD HILT

Tibetan, Mongolian, or Chinese, possibly 13th–14th century
Iron, gold, and silver
L. 4¾ in. (12.1 cm)
The Metropolitan Museum of Art, New York, Purchase, Bashford
Dean Memorial Collection, Funds from various donors, by
exchange, and Media Marketing Assessment Inc. Gift, 1999
(1999.31)

The form of this sword hilt is rare and possibly very early, but there are no clear parallels for its type. Therefore, until a similar example is found, either clearly depicted in a work of art or excavated in a datable context, it remains difficult to place or date this hilt with any certainty. Nevertheless, it is an early and important example of the lavish use of gold and silver damascening on iron, preserved in extremely good condition. The hilt consists of a contiguous pommel and grip, which are hollow and made of iron in two halves, front and back, brazed together at the sides. The decoration is large in scale and is chiseled in low relief and heavily damascened in gold and silver. On both sides of the pommel there is a large flaming pearl on a lotus base. On the grip, two leafy tendrils or scroll designs run vertically on either side of a central band, which has a gold zigzag pattern on one side and is plain silver on the other. A small collar at the base is decorated on one side with a stylized wave pattern, partly chiseled in relief, and on the other a honeycomb pattern.

60

61. SWORD

Tibetan, 17th–19th century
Iron, silver, gold, turquoise, wood, and textile
L. overall 33 in. (83.8 cm); blade, L. 28¼ in. (71.8 cm)
The Metropolitan Museum of Art, New York, Bequest of George
C. Stone, 1935 (36.25.1464)

This sword is a representative example of the most well recognized Tibetan form, well made, of fairly good quality, and in good condition. The trefoil pommel and the grip collar are made of iron and decorated on the front with a simply chiseled scroll pattern lightly damascened in gold, the open areas in the scrollwork being made with a circular punch. The sides are incised with a fret pattern damascened in silver. There is a single green turquoise in a silver setting in the center of the pommel. The backs of the pommel and grip are undecorated, with a ring in the center of the back of the pommel for a wrist cord or ornamental streamer. The grip is wood wrapped with silver wire. The iron guard is of the double trefoil type with fluted vertical edges but otherwise undecorated.

The direction of the blade in relation to the hilt shows that it was worn in a scabbard (now missing) at the left side. The straight single-edged blade has an oblique tip, a dull gray color, and a prominent hairpin pattern (*thur*) consisting of seven dark lines and six light lines (see detail). This indicates that the core of the blade is made of three folded rods ("hairpins") of dark softer so-called female iron (*mo lcags*), alternating with three folded rods of the harder, lighter-colored male iron (*pho lcags*), with a single rod of dark female iron in the center. The core is surrounded by a frame of the lighter iron forming the back of the blade and the cutting edge. This forging technique is typical of Tibetan blades, in which alternating folded rods of hard and soft iron are combined with the goal of creating a blade that is both strong and flexible. The color and quality of the iron and the number of hairpin lines can vary considerably from one blade to the next. The pattern of fine dots near the center of this blade and the parallel lines at the tip appear to be the result of old corrosion.

PROVENANCE: W. O. Oldman, London; George Cameron Stone, New York.

PUBLICATION: Grancsay 1959, p. 177.

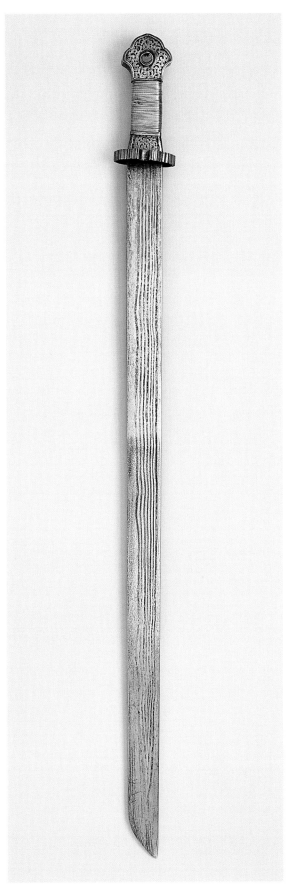

61

61, detail of blade

62. SWORD

Tibetan, 17th–19th century
Iron, gold, silver, coral, and wood
L. overall 31 in. (78.7 cm); blade, L. 26⅛ in. (66.4 cm)
The Metropolitan Museum of Art, New York, Bequest of George
C. Stone, 1935 (36.25.1458a)

This sword is similar in style and construction to the previous example, but the proportions are smaller, the workmanship of the hilt is slightly finer, the blade is of higher quality, is slightly thicker, and was made to be worn horizontally in front of the body with the cutting edge facing up.[1] The iron trefoil pommel and matching grip collar are decorated on the front with a punched and chiseled scroll pattern and on the sides with an engraved fret pattern. There is a single large coral bead, possibly imitation, in the center of the pommel. The iron guard is of the narrow rectangular type with fluted vertical edges. The grip swells slightly toward the center, has two lengthwise indentations in the front, and is wrapped in a fine silver wire.

The straight single-edged blade has a short oblique tip, a very sharp cutting edge, and a pearly silver color. The hairpin pattern is much more subtle than on the previous example, shown only by lines with a slightly different finish. It consists of six polished lines alternating with five lines with a more matte finish, which matches the finish of the rest of the blade, indicating three folded rods of the polished iron alternating with two folded rods of the matte iron, with a single rod of the matte iron in the center. Whether these equate to male iron (*pho lcags*) for the matte finish and female iron (*mo lcags*) for the polished finish, or a different combination, is not known. The blade also appears to have additional laminations at the tip and the cutting edge, suggesting a more complex forging structure.

PROVENANCE: W. O. Oldman, London; George Cameron Stone, New York.

1. The sword retains its matching scabbard, which is not included here, however, because of its condition.

62

63. SHORT SWORD AND SCABBARD

Tibetan, 18th–19th century
Iron, gold, turquoise, coral, leather, and wood
L. overall 27½ in. (69.9 cm); blade, L. 19⅞ in. (50.5 cm)
The Metropolitan Museum of Art, New York, Bequest of George
C. Stone, 1935 (36.25.1466a, b)

The hilt has a trefoil pommel and matching grip collar that are decorated on the front with a simple chiseled scroll pattern and on the sides with a fret pattern, both damascened in gold. There is a setting for a missing stone on the front of the pommel. The grip is a rectangular piece of bare wood. The guard is the narrow rectangular type with fluted vertical edges. The straight single-edged blade ends in an acute point, unlike the oblique tips of the previous examples. It has a simpler hairpin pattern consisting of perhaps four polished and three matte lines (see detail), but the pattern is worn and difficult to read. The top of the blade has a pebbled texture, giving it the appearance of having been damaged by fire.

The scabbard has an iron U-shaped frame, the lower half of which is chiseled with shallow scroll and fret patterns and damascened in gold. The lower half of the front of the scabbard is covered by a similarly decorated iron panel, on which there are three large settings with two turquoise stones flanking a central coral bead. An iron strut extends up from the top of the iron panel and fits under a rectangular collar (locket) at the top of the scabbard. The front of the collar is decorated with matching scrollwork and has the remains of a setting for a missing stone. The other areas of the scabbard are faced with a thin green leather covering.

Provenance: W. O. Oldman, London; George Cameron Stone, New York.

63

63, detail of blade

64. SHORT SWORD AND SCABBARD

Tibetan, 18th–19th century
Iron, silver, turquoise, coral, wood, textile, and leather
L. overall 24 in. (61 cm); blade, L. 16½ in. (41.9 cm)
The Metropolitan Museum of Art, New York, Bequest of George
C. Stone, 1935 (36.25.1462a, b)

This is a good example of a typical late short sword of a standard quality. It has an iron trefoil pommel decorated only with incised lines and a green turquoise set in the center. The grip collar is plain, as is the square guard, save for its fluted edges. The blade is single edged and ends in an acute point. It has a visible hairpin pattern consisting of three polished lines, indicating a single folded rod with a single rod in the center. There are also faint hairpin laminations visible at the tip (see detail). Dark lines and mottled dark areas on the blade represent slag or other inclusions in the structure of the iron, rather than corrosion. The scabbard has a simple U-shaped frame with incised line decoration on its lower half. At the base there is a raised silver knob incised with a swirling leaf design. The lower half of the front of the scabbard is fitted with an embossed silver plaque decorated with raised scrolls and a repeating pearl motif. There are three settings on the plaque with two coral beads flanking a green turquoise. The rest of the scabbard is covered with a painted or stained textile. Rather than a locket there is a band of thick leather at the top of the scabbard. Attached to the back of this is a thin twisted leather cord at the end of which there is a piece of leather tightly braided in the form of an endless knot, which was probably intended as a talisman.

PROVENANCE: W. O. Oldman, London; George Cameron Stone, New York.

64

64, detail of blade

65. SWORD AND SCABBARD

Tibetan, 17th–19th century
Iron, gold, silver, wood, leather, turquoise, coral, and textile
L. overall 39¾ in. (101 cm); blade, L. 33⅞ in. (86 cm)
Royal Armouries Museum, Leeds (XXVIS.187)

This sword was made to be worn at the left side from a waist belt in the Chinese fashion, and has a blade with an unusual and noteworthy pattern-welding design. The pommel is the trefoil type, with a single turquoise in the center, decorated with scrollwork and damascened in gold, as is the matching grip collar. The grip is wrapped in silver wire and has two vertical indentations, as on catalogue numbers 62 and 64. The guard is the double-trefoil type with fluted side edges. The blade is straight and single edged and has an oblique tip. The pattern-welding design features a series of wavy concentric diagonal lines of lighter-colored iron (see detail), resulting in a pattern that has been referred to as *ce rong*.[1] This effect appears to be made from two rods of variegated iron, stacked and folded in thirds during the forging process.

The scabbard has a full-length iron frame with a square bottom, pierced with very simple punched scrollwork and damascened in gold. The top and bottom thirds of the front are covered with silver plaques embossed in relatively high relief with a pair of phoenixes on the top plaque and dragons on the bottom, which are seen in profile and flank a centrally placed setting; in the top setting there is a coral bead and the bottom one is empty. Between the plaques the scabbard is covered by a patterned textile, and on the back by green leather. There is a square iron locket at the top of the scabbard with an incised floral design damascened in gold. Two brackets for the belt straps are attached to the right edge of the scabbard by two horizontal iron bands, which are decorated to match the locket. This type of incised and damascened decoration is also found on the back of the locket of the unusual sword in catalogue number 70. It is also interesting to note that while most swords worn at the side from a waist belt hang with the cutting edge facing down, in this instance the sword fits in the scabbard with the cutting edge up.

65, detail of blade

PROVENANCE: Major A. D. F. White; Sotheby Parke Bernet & Co., London, December 16, 1980, lot. 244.

PUBLICATION: *Antique Firearms, Edged Weapons, Armour, and Militaria, Modern Sporting Guns and Fishing Tackle*, sale cat., Sotheby Parke Bernet & Co., London, December 16, 1980, lot 244.

1. Norbu and Turnbull 1968, p. 102, fig. 8. The term *ce* may be a phonetic version of *bye*, for *bye rong*, meaning something like "divided ravines."

65

66. SWORD AND SCABBARD

Tibetan, 18th–19th century
Iron, silver, wood, textile, turquoise, coral, and leather
L. overall 38⅜ in. (97.5 cm); blade, L. 30⅛ in. (77.8 cm)
The Metropolitan Museum of Art, New York, Bequest of George
C. Stone, 1935 (36.25.1461a, b)

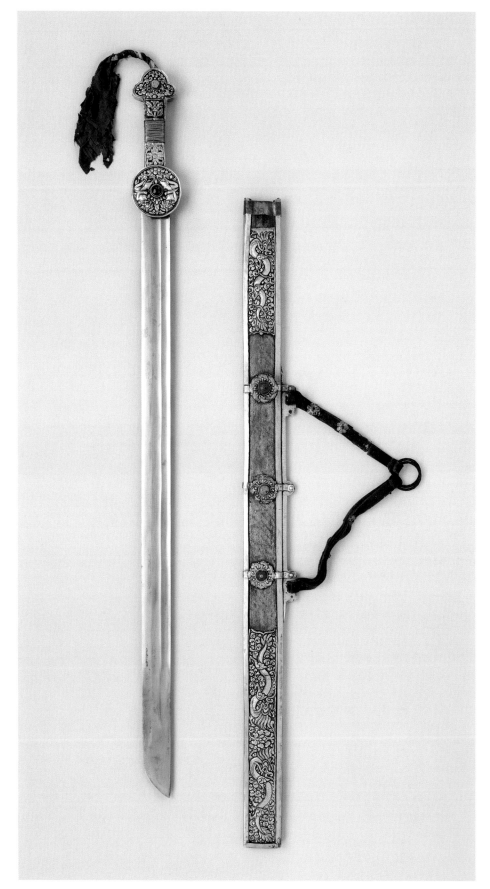

Unlike the previous examples, the hilt and scabbard fittings of this sword are made of silver rather than iron. The pommel is of trefoil shape and has a long base that covers the upper third of the grip. The grip collar covers the lower third, leaving only a short space in the middle, which is wrapped with silver wire. The front of the pommel has a turquoise in the center and is embossed with floral designs, as is the grip collar; the sides and back are plain. There is a tassel consisting of braided strands of red, blue, and yellow silk attached to a ring on the back of the pommel. The front of the guard consists of a silver disk parallel to the plane of the blade, embossed with a pair of animals, possibly snow lions, flanking a central setting, which originally held a coral bead (now missing). The back and sides of the guard are plain. The blade is straight and single edged, with an oblique tip and a short back edge. It has two shallow fullers along its entire length on both sides; there is no evidence of pattern welding; and the blade itself may not be Tibetan or at least was not made in the traditional style.

The frame of the scabbard is also made entirely of silver and has a square bottom. At the top there is a silver plaque embossed in low relief with a single dragon amid foliage, and at the bottom a longer plaque embossed with a pair of similar dragons flanking a lotus. There is a suspension bar along the middle third of the right edge of the scabbard, in the Chinese fashion, which is also made of silver. This is attached to the scabbard by three horizontal bands, each of which has a large floral rosette set with a stone: turquoise in the center rosette and coral in the others. Despite the lavish use of silver, the embossed decoration of this sword is of relatively low quality.

PROVENANCE: Lawton & Co.; George Cameron Stone, New York.

PUBLICATION: Stone 1934, fig. 762, no. 19.

66

67. SWORD AND SCABBARD

Tibetan, 18th–19th century
Iron, silver, copper alloy, turquoise, coral, wood,
leather, and textile
L. overall 33¼ in. (84.5 cm); blade, L. 28¼ in. (71.8 cm)
Victoria and Albert Museum, London (IM.218&a-1927)

Like the two previous examples, this sword was made to be worn at the left side. Overall it is very well made, has silver mountings of high quality, is in extremely good condition, and has a distinctive double-edged Tibetan blade. The all-silver hilt consists of a trefoil pommel with a coral bead in the center, a grip wrapped in silver wire, and a grip collar. The pommel and grip collar are decorated on the front with scroll and *ju'i* motifs embossed in low relief. There is a tassel, made of three braided strips of silk colored yellow (?), blue, and red, which is attached to a ring on the back of the pommel. The sides of the pommel and collar have an engraved

67, detail of blade   67

fret pattern. The guard is the double trefoil type, engraved with cusped lines on the top and with the repeating coin motif on the sides. Below the guard there is a short trilobed langet of copper alloy embossed with a lion or *tsi pa ṭa* mask. The brightly polished blade is straight and double edged, ending in a symmetrical point, and has a noticeable hairpin pattern of perhaps seven lines running most of its length (see detail). This is the only blade of this description encountered during the course of this study, suggesting that the type is relatively rare.

The scabbard has a long locket and chape made of silver with embossed decoration matching that of the pommel and grip collar. The top of the locket has a recessed trilobe area to accommodate the langet. There is a narrow inset oval panel, with a coral bead in its center, in the middle of both locket and chape, which is made of copper alloy and embossed with a scroll and pearl motif very similar to that seen on the silver plaque of the sword in catalogue number 64. The center of the scabbard is covered by leather and is fitted with three horizontal bands, each of which has a large lozenge-shaped rosette; the one in the center is set with a turquoise and those on either side with a coral bead. Attached to the top and bottom bands there are two leather straps, which meet at a ring that is joined by a silver toggle to the sword belt.

The sword came to the Victoria and Albert Museum as the bequest of Lord Curzon (George Nathaniel Curzon, first Marquess Curzon of Kedleston, 1859–1925), who, as Viceroy of India from 1899 to 1905, was the single person most responsible for the conception and authorization of the Younghusband Expedition. It seems likely that the sword was acquired for him in Tibet by one of the members of the expedition, perhaps its commander, Francis Younghusband, himself.

PROVENANCE: Lord Curzon.

68. SWORD

Eastern Tibetan, 18th–19th century
Iron, wood, silver, copper alloy, ray skin, and leather
L. 38⅜ in. (97.5 cm); blade, L. 32⅜ in. (82.2 cm)
The Metropolitan Museum of Art, New York, Bequest of George C. Stone, 1935 (36.25.1460)

Although lacking its scabbard, this is a very good example of one type of sword from Kham, in eastern Tibet. The pommel is a faceted lozenge-shaped block of iron, inlaid across the front with four narrow horizontal bands of brass or copper. There are three short iron cones side by side on the top, the centermost probably being an extension of the tang of the blade. On either side of the center facet at the back of the pommel there are two holes, through which a wrist cord of twisted leather passes. The grip is made of wood, diamond shaped in cross section, which flares out at the top and the bottom. It is covered in ray skin, which has several large white nodules, and is wrapped with a single leather cord in an open spiral. There is a small beaded rim of silver at the top and bottom of the grip. The guard is a round dish of iron with its edge sloped at a forty-five degree angle and a hollow interior, in the center of which there is a lozenge-shaped collar that meets the top of the blade. The blade is straight and single edged and has an oblique tip. The pattern-welding lines are faint, but there appear to be five dark and four light bands, indicating two hairpin rods of darker iron alternating with two hairpin rods of lighter iron and a single rod of the darker iron in the center. Engraved near the top of the blade on the front there are a small whirling motif (*dga' 'khyil*) and a word that possibly reads *lhun* (see detail).[1]

An extremely similar sword was acquired in 1891 or 1892 by William Rockhill, which he identified as made in Poyul (*dpal yul*), once part of the kingdom of Derge and now part of Ganzi Tibetan Autonomous Prefecture in western Sichuan Province.[2] Their chief differences are that the hairpin pattern on the Rockhill sword is a very distinct series of alternating dark and light stripes (six dark and five light), and it retains its scabbard. The Metropolitan Museum's sword is described on George Stone's original catalogue card as coming from the Tibet-Sikkim border, but there seems to be no reason to conclude that it originated in that region rather than in eastern Tibet, particularly in light of the type of scabbard on the Rockhill sword and on the following example.

PROVENANCE: W. O. Oldman, London; George Cameron Stone, New York.

1. I am grateful to both Lozang Jamspal and Tsering Shakya for considering the reading of these characters and suggesting the meanings of "effortlessness" and "spontaneity" as possible appropriate interpretations.
2. Rockhill 1895, pl. 22, fig. 3, and p. 712, National Museum of Natural History, Washington, cat. no. 167301. I am very grateful to Felicia Pickering for making this sword available to me for study.

68, detail of engraving on blade

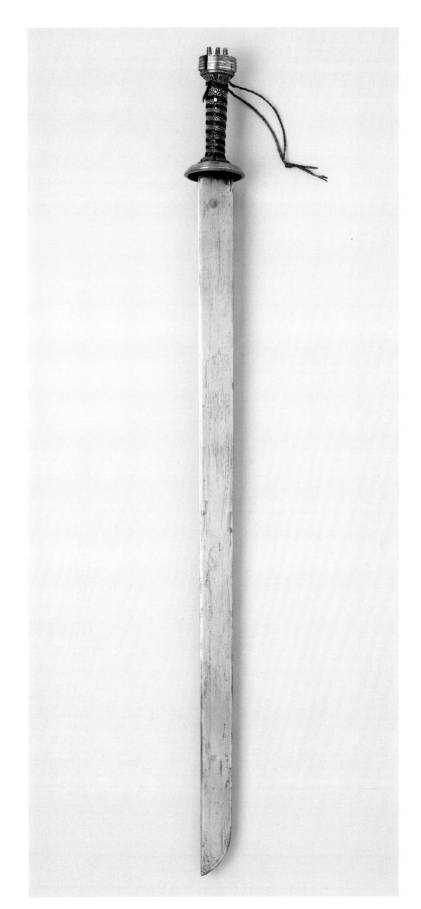

68

69. SWORD AND SCABBARD

Eastern Tibetan, 18th–19th century
Iron, copper alloy, wood, ray skin, leather, turquoise, coral,
and glass
L. overall 38⅜ in. (97.5 cm); blade, L. 31 in. (78.7 cm)
The Metropolitan Museum of Art, New York, Bequest of George
C. Stone, 1935 (36.25.1463a, b)

The hilt is generally similar to that of catalogue number 68 but is more simply made. The pommel is in the form of a faceted, lozenge-shaped iron block with four narrow strips of brass or copper alloy inlaid in horizontal lines across the front. Rather than the usual three iron cones on the top of the pommel, the end of the tang is peened over like a dome-headed rivet. As in the previous example, the back of the pommel is pierced with two holes through which a thin wrist cord of leather passes. The wooden grip is also similarly shaped and is wrapped in ray skin, although with smaller nodules, and it has no top or bottom rims or leather binding. The guard is also the same form—a round, shallow dish with sloped sides and a hollow interior with a lozenge-shaped collar in the center—but it is either roughly forged or has been damaged and repaired on the top. The straight, single-edged blade has an oblique tip and a slightly worn hairpin pattern, which appears to consist of four light lines alternating with three dark lines.

The scabbard consists of a wooden liner covered entirely in dark leather, with a chape, locket, and central band made of copper. These fittings are decorated with low-relief embossing and dense rows of circular and teardrop-shaped settings made of copper wires, which are filled with small pieces of colored glass, chips of turquoise, and coral. There is a single coral bead in the center of the lower half of the scabbard. A narrow leather belt with an iron buckle is wrapped around the upper half.

PROVENANCE: Darjeeling; George Cameron Stone, New York.

70. SWORD AND SCABBARD

Southern or eastern Tibetan, 16th–18th century
Iron, gold, silver, wood, ray skin, and leather
L. overall 33¾ in. (85.7 cm); blade, L. 26¼ in. (66.7 cm)
The Metropolitan Museum of Art, New York, Bequest of George
C. Stone, 1935 (36.25.1465a, b)

This sword shares several features with the two preceding examples, but it also includes certain interesting elements that indicate a Bhutanese influence. The iron pommel is lozenge shaped and hollow, and it is decorated on the front and top with deeply undercut and pierced scrollwork that is damascened in gold and on the back with finely engraved scrollwork, carefully crosshatched only within the lines of decoration and damascened in gold and silver (see detail). There are two holes in the back of the pommel for a wrist cord. The grip is covered in ray skin and is shaped similarly to those of the two preceding swords, that is, lozenge shaped in cross section and swelling slightly at the top and bottom. There is no guard per se, only a lozenge-shaped plate at the base of the grip, which has fluted edges and a collar like that seen on the underside of the dish guards of the two swords above. The blade is straight and single edged and has an acute point, rather than an oblique one. The hairpin pattern is worn, but appears to consist of five lighter lines alternating with four darker ones.

The scabbard is made up of a wooden core wrapped entirely in leather, and it has a raised triple ridge running down its center. The bottom is fitted with a U-shaped frame of relatively thick iron, the front of which is chiseled and pierced with lush scrollwork damascened in gold. In the center of the frame there is another panel, in the shape of an elongated teardrop, decorated in the same way. The back of the frame is engraved and damascened in gold and silver like the back of the pommel. At the top of the scabbard there is a locket, the front of which is pierced and decorated to match the front of the pommel. The back of the locket is engraved with symmetrical scrolls and flowers and damascened in gold and silver. Just below the front of the locket there is an iron staple for a leather strap by which the sword would hang vertically at the wearer's right side in the Bhutanese fashion. Other

Bhutanese features include the shape of the pommel and the fact that its front and top are decorated with pierced work, the shape of the scabbard mounts, and the lack of a guard. On Bhutanese swords, however, these elements are usually made of relatively delicate cast silver, rather than the robust pierced ironwork seen here, which is the type associated with eastern Tibet. It compares particularly well with the ironwork on catalogue numbers 112–14 and with an amulet box (*ga'u*) in the British Museum (OA 1992.12-14.8), which has been called eastern Tibetan, fifteenth century.[1]

PROVENANCE: Darjeeling; George Cameron Stone, New York.

1. Clarke 2004, p. 24, fig. 13.

70

70, detail of back of hilt

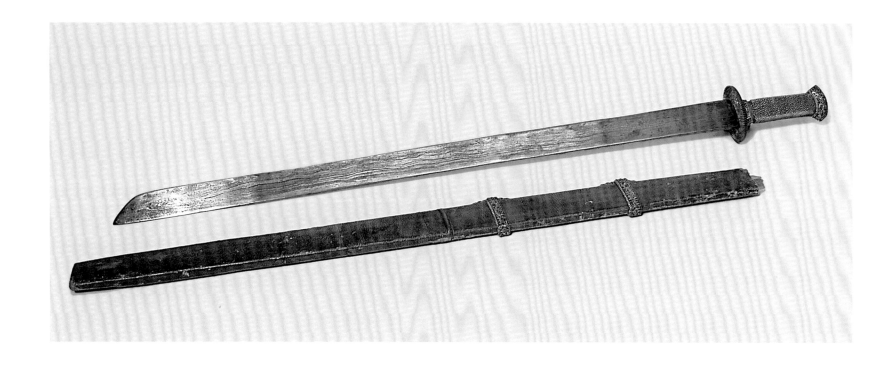

71. SWORD AND SCABBARD

Eastern Tibetan and Chinese, possibly 16th–18th century
Iron, gold, wood, and ray skin
L. overall 39 in. (99 cm); blade, L. 33⅝ in. (85.4 cm)
Pitt Rivers Museum, Oxford (1989.1.1.1, .2)

Although the blade of this sword is typically Tibetan in form—straight and singled edged with an oblique tip—its pattern-welding design is extremely unusual, being one of the most complex and aesthetically accomplished ever seen on a Tibetan blade. Elaborating on the usual series of wavy alternating light and dark lines, the patterns on this blade create an effect resembling eddies and ripples in water in some areas and wood grain in others. In addition, the tips of the hairpin patterns occur at both ends of the blade, near the point, as is usual, but also near the guard (see details). The creation of this blade probably required a combination of bent rods facing in two directions forged between layers of other rods or ingots of variegated iron. The wood-grain effect of the pattern may indicate the use of

the type of iron referred to in the Tibetan texts as "a compound of all sorts," "various types grouped and blended," or simply "mixed iron" (*sna 'dus, sna bsdus 'dres,* or *lcags 'dres*).[1] According to the sword chapter in the Tashi Namgyal text, mixed iron was used to produce "many flowing and swirling designs," a description that would apply well to this blade.[2]

The hilt and scabbard mounts are Chinese, possibly dating from the seventeenth to eighteenth century, and are made of iron, pierced with a design of dragons amid scrollwork and damascened in gold.[3] A very similar Chinese hilt, also fitted with what appears to be a Tibetan blade, can be seen in a photograph of an oracle in Yongning, near the border between Sichuan and Yunnan, taken by Joseph Rock in 1928.[4]

PROVENANCE: Given to the Pitt Rivers Museum by the widow of Major P. C. Hailey, a member of the Indian Political Department who served as Trade Agent in Gyantse from 1933 to 1935.

1. Tashi Tsering 1979, p. 74; appendix "Excerpts from *A Treatise on Worldly Traditions,*" British Library Or 11,374, fol. 76b, and Burmiok Athing, fol. 25a.
2. Appendix "Excerpts from *A Treatise on Worldly Traditions,*" British Library Or 11,374, fol. 76b; Burmiok Athing, fol. 25a: "lcags 'dres pa ni ri mo gya gyu mang."
3. This style of pierced work on Chinese sword fittings is referred to as *loukong* or *gueigong* (see Philip Thom's comments, quoted in "Correspondence," *Arts of Asia* 34, no. 1 [January–February 2004], pp. 23–24). Similar hilts are found on two Chinese sabers in the Metropolitan Museum (36.25.1475a, b, and 36.25.1628a, b).
4. Aris 1992, fig. 7.3.

71, detail of blade, tip

71, detail of blade, midsection

71, detail of blade, near guard

72. ORACLE'S SWORD AND SCABBARD

Chinese and Tibetan, 18th–19th century
Iron, gold, silver, wood, leather, and pigments
L. overall 35⅜ in. (89.9 cm); blade, L. 29⅞ in. (75.9 cm)
Courtesy of the Board of Trustees, National Museums Liverpool (1976.282.3)

The hilt and scabbard mountings of this sword are Chinese, but the blade could be Tibetan or Chinese. The painted decoration on the scabbard was done in Tibet and suggests that the sword was adapted for use by an oracle. In Tibetan Buddhism, oracles are seen as mediums through which various protector deities make prophecies, offer guidance in times of need, and cure illnesses. Oracles wear elaborate ceremonial costumes and are equipped with weapons such as swords, spears, and bows and arrows, which are considered the arms of the deity who takes possession of the oracle. When receiving the spirit of a deity, an oracle enters into a trance, which can include violent fits and unpredictable actions involving the use of his weapons.[1]

This sword has hilt fittings made of iron damascened with thin, tendril-like scrollwork in gold with silver accents on a blued ground. It is composed of an asymmetrical half-round pommel cap, a rectan-gular wooden grip wrapped in leather, a grip collar, and a round guard. There is a transverse hole in the pommel for a leather wrist strap. The blade is straight, double edged, and of flattened diamond shape in cross section, and it has a symmetrical point. There is a series of circles over the length of the blade, which may have been deeply punched as decoration, rather than actually the result of pattern welding.

The scabbard consists of a wooden core covered entirely in dark leather. Its mounts are made of iron and match the decoration of the hilt fittings except that the damascening is in silver with gold borders. The mounts include a locket, a chape, and two hor-izontal bands, which secure a bracket with lugs on the right side of the scabbard for the straps connect-ing to a waist belt. The mounts are typically Chinese in form but more common as fittings for a saber than a straight sword.[2]

The decoration indicating that the sword was probably used as an oracle's weapon is the motif composed of three eyes with fiery eyebrows, which is painted on both sides of the scabbard in the cen-ter, below the locket and above the chape. René de Nebesky-Wojkowitz referred several times to oracle costumes and weapons decorated with what he described as "three torn-out human eyes."[3] The eyes painted on the scabbard of this sword, however, rep-resent the eyes of a fierce protector deity (*mgon po* or *srung ma*) or demon (*btsan*), similar to those found on the sword guard in catalogue number 56.

1. On the subject of Tibetan oracles, see Nebesky-Wojkowitz 1975, esp. chap. 21; and Aris 1992 for several photos of oracles taken by Joseph Rock.
2. For an overview of the fittings on Chinese sabers, see Tom 2001.
3. Nebesky-Wojkowitz 1975, e.g., pp. 412–14.

72

73. SWORD AND SCABBARD

Bhutanese, 18th–19th century
Iron, silver, gold, wood, and leather
L. overall (in scabbard) 34⅞ in. (88.6 cm); blade, L. 27 in. (68.6 cm)
Marischal Museum, University of Aberdeen (ABDUA:56788)

Bhutanese swords are often found in southern and eastern Tibet, and while there are some important shared features, they are nevertheless distinct in form and style from Tibetan swords.[1] This is an excellent example of a Bhutanese sword of higher quality, and it has an interesting provenance, having been acquired in Tibet in 1903 or 1904 by Brigadier General Sir James Macdonald (1862–1927), who was Escort Commander of the Younghusband Expedition.

The hilt has a pommel made of pierced and gilded silver, with designs of a dragon amid scroll-work on the side and top, and a stylized armor pattern consisting of a honeycomb and interlocking Y motif on the other side. The wooden grip has eight shallow flutes and is tightly wrapped in braided silver wire. There is a beaded rim at the top and bottom of the grip, similar to those on catalogue number 68, and a short collar between the bottom rim and the blade, as on catalogue number 70. The bright, silvery blade is straight and single edged and has a steeply angled oblique tip. It has a hairpin pattern either simulated or accentuated by three pairs of straight grooves engraved down the length of the blade and meeting in points near the tip, a technique frequently seen on Bhutanese blades. The edge of the blade, however, is unusual in showing a wavy pattern along its length (see detail), suggesting that the cutting edge may have been made from a separate envelope of pattern-welded iron, applied during the forging process.[2]

The scabbard has a wooden core encased in a three-stage silver sheathing, of which the top and bottom sections are plain. The center section of the front is decorated with a frontal dragon, undulating and vertically aligned amid clouds, skillfully embossed and chiseled in low relief and parcel gilt (see detail).[3] The back has a reticular pattern with whirling emblems at the intersections of the lines and blossoms in the centers of the compartments. At either end of the center section there is a triple

73

border of lotus petals and stylized blossoms. In the middle of the scabbard's top section there is a metal staple for a leather strap (as on cat. no. 70), by which the sword would be hung vertically at the wearer's right side in the Bhutanese fashion.

A few years after Macdonald's death, the items in his collection were divided between the British Museum and the Marischal Museum, University of Aberdeen (where he was a student from 1877 to 1880). The list of twenty-eight items from the "Lhasa expedition 1903/04" includes a "Gilt image of Buddha presented by the Regent of Tibet," and a "Royal sword with silver sheath richly chased."[4] The sword is also described in correspondence and other information as a "royal sword," and a "royal Tibetan sword."[5]

73, detail of scabbard   73, detail of blade

PROVENANCE: Brigadier General Sir James Macdonald; Alice Macdonald.

1. On Bhutanese swords, see Rapten 2001.
2. I am grateful to Julian Freeman for his thoughts on the construction of this blade and on the sword in general.

3. Another very good Bhutanese sword with a scabbard decorated in the same techniques, and in the same style but with different motifs in the central section, is found in the National Museums Liverpool (53.87.73).
4. From the Museum Report, 1931/32, Marischal Museum archives. I am grateful to Neil Curtis for making this material available for study.

5. Correspondence from G. David Knight to Mr. Reid, Hon. Curator, Marischal Museum, December 2, 1932; and on the tags that were attached to the objects when they came to the museum, preserved in the departmental archives, Marischal Museum. The tag for the Buddha reads, "Gilt image of Buddha presented by the Regent of Thibet [*sic*] to General Macdonald when he bade him good-bye at Lhasa in 1904."

74. CURVED SWORD AND MATCHING SCABBARD MOUNTS

Tibetan, possibly 15th–16th century; and Indian (blade only), 18th–19th century
Iron, gold, wood, and ray skin
L. overall 40 in. (101.6 cm); blade, L. 34¼ in. (87 cm)
The Metropolitan Museum of Art, New York, Purchase, Arthur Ochs Sulzberger Gift, 2001 (2001.163.1, .2a–c)

The hilt and scabbard mounts of this sword are excellent examples of finely pierced, chiseled, and damascened ironwork of relatively intricate design. However, they also present a rare and puzzling mixture of form, decorative technique, and style, which makes them difficult to date or place with certainty.[1]

The hilt consists of an asymmetrical half-round pommel, pierced by a transverse hole for a wrist strap, and similar in general shape to the pommel on catalogue number 72; a wooden grip that flares out slightly toward the bottom, is a flattened oval in cross section, and is covered in ray skin; and a guard in the form of a crossbar having tapering arms with trefoil finials and, in the center, upper and lower langets (the narrow vertical flanges). The pommel and guard are decorated overall with finely chiseled and pierced scrollwork damascened in gold. The pierced areas are surrounded by well-defined narrow borders with slightly raised and polished edges, the sunken central channel engraved with a repeating wave pattern (*chu ris*) damascened in gold.

The curved single-edged blade is a replacement made later in the working life of the sword. It is Indian and has a shallow fuller and a single unsharpened shoulder (the ricasso) where the cutting edge ends near the guard, a style known as an Indian ricasso. The blade widens toward the tip, where there is a back edge approximately 12¾ inches long (32.4 cm). Damascened in gold several inches from the guard are a parasol motif and a cartouche with the Islamic invocation "Ya Ali."[2]

The scabbard mounts consist of a locket, chape, and suspension band.[3] The locket and chape are asymmetrical and have a cusped and curvilinear diagonal edge (see illus.). The locket has a recess at the top on either side to accommodate the lower langets of the guard. The suspension band has a circular panel front and back, and a faceted cube on one side, fitted with a suspension ring. The decoration of these elements matches that of the hilt fittings. In addition, the outer sides of the locket and chape each have a single long and sinuous dragon seen in profile. The dragons have delineated striped underbellies and well-rendered heads with flaring jaws, spiked hair, and horns.

Based just on the technique, style, and quality of the pierced ironwork, these fittings would, with little or no question, be attributed to eastern Tibet and dated from perhaps as early as the fourteenth century to no later than the sixteenth. They compare most closely with the decoration of the saddles in catalogue numbers 111 (attributed to ca. 1400) and 112 (attributed to the 15th–17th century), and the cup case in catalogue number 113 (attributed to the early–mid-15th century). The borders on the cup case, in particular, are nearly identical to those on the sword fittings, although the dragons on the cup case are not as precisely rendered.

However, the rare combination of this well-recognized style of decoration with the particular form of the hilt and scabbard mounts makes an attribution more complicated. Cross guards of the general type seen on this hilt were probably used in Tibet and China by the Mongols during the Yuan dynasty (1279–1368) and are similar to styles used by the Mongols and other peoples as far west as Iran from the fourteenth century onward.[4]

Two aspects of the scabbard mounts, however, must also be taken into consideration. First, the form of the locket and chape, particularly the cusped and curvilinear diagonal edge, is not a shape known to have been used by the Mongols, but was well known later in China, however, and is most frequently associated with sabers of the Qing dynasty (1644–1911), although the form may have come into use sometime during the late Ming dynasty (1368–1644). Second is the fact that the decoration of the locket and chape indicates that they were designed for a scabbard that was worn slung from the left hip with the hilt to the back, a method of wearing a sword that was characteristic of the Manchu, founders of the Qing dynasty, but was also in use earlier. Decorated sword fittings invariably have a distinct front and back, usually being more ornate on the side that faces out than on the side worn against the body. On most fittings the difference is pronounced and immediately recognizable, one side being decorated and the other fairly plain. Fittings of higher quality usually have significant decoration on both sides, with one side slightly more ornate, which is the case with this sword. The presence of the dragons on only one side of the locket and chape clearly indicates which side would face out and, therefore, that the scabbard

74, locket

74, chape

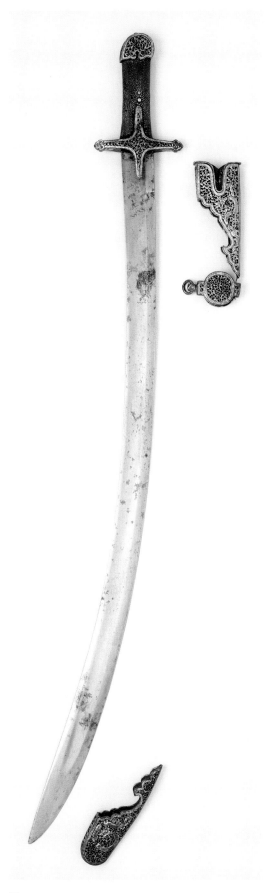

was meant to be worn with the hilt to the rear.[5] How early this style came into use is unknown, but it appears in at least one painting dating from the Yuan dynasty.[6]

The confluence of factors can be summed up as follows: the ironworking style and technique are associated with eastern Tibet, fourteenth–sixteenth century; the hilt type is associated with the Mongols from the fourteenth century onward; the locket and chape are of a form associated with China from the seventeenth century onward, but which could be earlier; and the decoration of the locket and chape indicates they were made for a sword worn with the hilt to the rear, a fashion that may have existed during the Yuan, but became widespread under the Qing. Therefore, balancing the potentially early style of the ironwork and the potentially later form of the scabbard mounts, and considering the variables involved with its other features, a date of the fifteenth–sixteenth century is suggested here for this very distinctive set of sword fittings.

1. I am extremely grateful to Philip Tom and Scott Rodell for sharing their expertise on the development of Asian swords and for much help in considering the dating features peculiar to this sword in particular.
2. I am grateful to Stefano Carboni for reading the inscription and identifying it as Shi'ite. The style of the calligraphy, he feels, dates from the late 15th to early 16th century onward. The parasol mark is found on several Mughal sword blades, including Metropolitan Museum of Art 36.25.1591.
3. Originally there would have been a second, matching suspension band. When acquired, these mounts were fitted to a later scabbard, crudely made and wrapped entirely in a pale ray skin or sharkskin covering.
4. Philip Tom has pointed out, however, that two swords with short cruciform guards and prominent langets were found in the tomb of the Ming emperor Wanli (1573–1620). Personal communication, March 9, 2001.
5. Two similar but somewhat more simply decorated lockets, also for scabbards made to be worn in this style, exist in private collections, proving that the present example is not a one-of-a-kind instance made for a left-handed swordsman, who would wear his scabbard in the conventional direction but on the right hip.
6. The painting is in the Liu Haishu Art Museum, Shanghai, and is published in Ming Deng, *Bai Ma Tushuo—Zhonggou Lidai Minghua Diandu* (Shanghai, 2001), p. 54. I am grateful to Scott Rodell for bringing this to my attention.

74

མདུང་དང་མདུང་རྩེ་དང་མཚོན་ཆ་སྣ་ཚོགས།
Spears, Spearheads, and Miscellaneous Weapons

Tibetan spears (*mdung*) fall into two basic categories: those made for fighting and those designed for ceremonial use. The fighting spears (cat. nos. 75, 76) generally consist of an iron spearhead (*mdung rtse*) mounted on a wooden shaft (*mdung yu* or *mdung shing*), which is reinforced by a spiraling coil of iron wrapped around most of its length. Often there is also an iron ferrule with a short spike at the base of the shaft. The spearhead can be double edged like the blade of a sword, or quadrangular like an elongated spike. Below the head there is usually a faceted or chiseled knop and then a hollow conical socket into which the top of the shaft is inserted. Fighting spears are usually plain, although they can be decorated with tassels (*mdung 'dzar*) or small flags (*mdung dar*). William Rockhill's frequent mention of spears, often in conjunction with swords and muskets, makes it clear that they were still very common weapons at the time of his travels in 1891–92, a fact reiterated by L. A. Waddell just over a decade later in the context of the Younghusband Expedition (see fig. 3).[1] The length of spears varied from about 5½ feet to more than 12 feet. Some were also said to be equipped with a rope (*thag mdung*) so they could be thrown at a target and then pulled back.[2] According to most accounts of the horseback target-shooting contests held during the Great Prayer Festival (see "Rediscovering the Arms and Armor of Tibet"), the armored participants are described as galloping past a series of targets, firing first with the musket and then with bow and arrow.[3] Tsipon Shuguba, however, who took part in the contests in 1923, mentioned that the targets were aimed at with guns, arrows, and then spears.[4] Rockhill also related the following anecdote about the use of spears: "Wang-ma-bum [one of his guides], though passed fifty, vaults on to his horse's back by resting his left hand on the pummel of his saddle and grasping in his right his long lance, its butt end resting on the ground. This is the usual way for an armed Tibetan to get into the saddle, and is a very graceful one."[5]

Ceremonial spears can also be divided into two general groups: those that seem to be intended or modified for use by oracles (cat. nos. 77, 78), and those made for other ceremonial or symbolic uses (cat. nos. 81–83).[6] Except perhaps in the case of miniature votive examples (cat. nos. 79, 80), the spears and spearheads in this second group are not ritual objects per se and are made with the same materials and techniques as the fighting spears. However, their extensive decoration, usually gold and silver damascening, and their unsharpened edges indicate a primarily ceremonial use, the exact nature of which is not known.

Other spearheads included here are Chinese or Mongolian (cat. nos. 86–88), possibly hunting spears, which were used in Tibet, and a unique spearhead socket, which is inscribed in both Tibetan and Mongolian (cat. no. 85). The section concludes with two unusual pieces: an ax head (cat. no. 89), and what is here proposed as a type of chakra (cat. no. 90).

1. Rockhill 1894, pp. 70, 84, 109, 130, 292, 328; Waddell 1905, p. 169. Rockhill bought a spear in Poyul (*dpal yul*), which he kept for his private collection, but its present whereabouts are unknown. It is illustrated in Rockhill 1894, facing p. 170, and described in some detail in Rockhill 1895, p. 713.
2. Norbu and Turnbull 1968, p. 73.
3. For instance, Richardson 1993, pp. 56–57.
4. Shuguba 1995, pp. 31–32.
5. Rockhill 1894, p. 130.
6. The use and appearance of oracle spears are discussed in Nebesky-Wojkowitz 1975, esp. chap. 21.

75. SPEAR

Tibetan, 18th–19th century
Iron, wood, yak hair, and silk
L. overall 74⅝ in. (189.6 cm); spearhead, L. 20⅞ in. (53 cm)
The Metropolitan Museum of Art, New York, Purchase, Arthur
Ochs Sulzberger Gift, 2001 (2001.179a, b)

This is a very good example of a fighting spear, including textile and yak hair attachments that may have been added to adapt it for festival or ceremonial use. The spearhead (*mdung rtse*) is forged from iron and is relatively simple. It has a double-edged blade in the form of an elongated wedge and is of flattened lozenge shape in cross section. At the base of the blade there is a rectangular stem, which ends in a polygonal knop. A hollow cylindrical socket extends from the base of the knop. Streamers of yellow, green, and red silk are knotted to the socket above a tuft or collar (*mdung 'dzar*) of red yak hair. The wooden shaft (*mdung shing* or *mdung yu*) is round in cross section and is reinforced by spiraling strips of iron, which are coiled around the shaft for its entire length. The strips on the upper half of the shaft are half-round in section, while those on the lower half are flat and more roughly forged, suggesting that they are the result of a later repair or alteration. At the base of the shaft there is an iron ferrule, which is roughly forged and consists of a conical socket that extends to form a long quadrangular spike. The purpose of the ferrule is to protect the end of the shaft from damage and to allow it to be planted firmly in the ground when necessary.

76. SPEAR

Tibetan, 18th–19th century
Iron, wood, and leather
L. overall 73½ in. (186.7 cm), spearhead L. 26½ in. (67.3 cm)
The Metropolitan Museum of Art, New York, Bequest of George
C. Stone, 1935 (36.25.1960)
See cat. no. 46 for illustration

This is a representative example of another type of plain fighting spear. The head has a narrow, long spikelike blade that is diamond shaped in cross section, with a simple molding and a square knop chiseled in low relief at the base, which extends into a long conical socket. The wooden shaft has reinforcing iron coil around its upper third. The forging of the spearhead and the coil are relatively rough. The shaft is pierced by three transverse holes, near the top, the middle, and the base, the uppermost having the remains of a leather strap tied to it.

This type of spearhead may be what is referred to by the term *gsor mdung*, derived from the meaning of *gsor* as a type of sharp, narrow blade, or a tool such as an awl, punch, or gimlet.[1] Spears with similar heads can be seen in pictures of the Great Prayer Festival in Lhasa, but the sockets and much of the shafts are covered by furled banners (see fig. 2).[2]

PROVENANCE: W. O. Oldman, London; George Cameron Stone, New York.

1. See the appendix "Tibetan-English Glossary of Arms and Armor Terms: II. Hand Held Weapons," under *gsor mdung*.
2. See also Tung 1980, p. 101.

77. SPEARHEAD

Tibetan, 17th–18th century
Iron, gold, and silver
L. 18¼ in. (46.4 cm)
The Metropolitan Museum of Art, New York, Purchase, Arthur
Ochs Sulzberger Gift, 2001 (2001.180)

This spearhead was probably made for the use of an oracle, or for some other form of ceremony or ritual involving the propitiation of a deity. The blade is relatively flat and double edged, with only a slight medial ridge, and has a rounded tip. Below the shoulders of the blade there is a polygonal knop with ring moldings above and below it. A hollow, conical socket extends from the base of the knop. The base of the socket has a turned, half-round rim. The outlines of the decoration are finely engraved, crosshatched, and damascened in gold on the blade and knop, and in gold and silver on the socket. The blade is prominently decorated on both sides with the syllable *kyai*, in *dbu can* script, and with stylized scrolling flames above and a flaming sword and a trefoil motif below. A simple quatrefoil repeats on the four principal sides of the knop. The socket is decorated on two sides with a trefoil motif above symmetrical leafy scrolls damascened in gold and silver.

René de Nebesky-Wojkowitz identified the terms *rten mdung* and *btsan mdung* for spears used by oracles, and mentioned a specific instance of a *btsan mdung* with a small triangular pennant decorated with the syllable *kyai*.[1] He also cited the example of ritual mirrors or breastplates (*thugs kyi me long*) worn by oracles and decorated with seed syllables (*sa bon*), including *kyai*, which invoke the deity that takes possession of the oracle.[2]

PUBLICATION: Pyhrr, LaRocca, and Ogawa 2002, no. 45, p. 48.

1. Nebesky-Wojkowitz 1975, pp. 414, 415, 438. A square banner decorated with the syllable *kyai* is identified as the flag of the guardian deity Begtse in Heller 1992, p. 485, fig. 5.
2. Nebesky-Wojkowitz 1975, pp. 411. *Kyai* is also an abbreviation for the name of the Tantric deity *kyai* or *kye rdo rje*, also known as Hevajra, and for *kye kye*, a term sometimes used for divine invocation.

78. SPEAR

Tibetan, 17th–19th century
Iron, gold, silver, wood, and pigments
L. overall 53¼ in. (135.3 cm); spearhead, L. 15⅝ in. (39.7 cm)
The Metropolitan Museum of Art, New York, Purchase, Kenneth
and Vivian Lam Gift, and funds from various donors, 2004
(2004.340a, b)

The decoration on the spearhead and shaft indicates that this spear was intended for ritual use, probably by an oracle. The iron spearhead is well forged and is distinctively decorated with dry skulls (*thod skam*) and curling tendrils that may represent stylized intestines (see detail), which are often used as a motif in conjunction with dry skulls. These are among the attributes of the fierce guardian deities and would be appropriate for a weapon intended for the chapel (*mgon khang*) of such a deity, or for an oracle acting as a medium for one.

The spearhead has a long, straight, narrow blade, diamond shaped in cross section, and is probably the type referred to as a *gsor mdung* (see cat. no. 76). It has a faceted square knop at the base of the blade and a short, wide conical socket with a turned, half-round rim. The decoration is carefully rendered with fine engraving and cross-hatching, and damascened in gold and silver. The wooden shaft is circular in cross section and is painted with a design of the body of a scaly dragon coiling around the shaft amid stylized clouds; both the clouds and the dragon are painted in gold on a red ground. A narrow iron band, also damascened in gold and silver, is coiled around the upper half of the shaft and is held in place by a nail at either end. At the base of the shaft there is an iron ferrule consisting of a simple spike, a knop, and a conical socket, to the base of which a crudely made tubular iron extension has been welded. The crudeness of the alteration to the socket and the fact that the body of the dragon continues to the top of the shaft but has no head indicate that the shaft has been modified, perhaps reused from another object, at least once in its working life. Nevertheless, the painting of the shaft is well done, and the quality of the engraved and damascened decoration of the spearhead is very high.

78

78, detail of decoration

79. MINIATURE VOTIVE SPEARHEAD

Tibetan, 18th–19th century
Iron and gold
L. 6⅞ in. (17.5 cm)
The Metropolitan Museum of Art, New York, Purchase, Arthur
Ochs Sulzberger Gift, 2001 (2001.185)

In form and type, this is essentially a miniature version of the previous spearheads, especially catalogue number 78. Although harshly scoured in the past, enough traces of the gold damascened decoration remain to show the designs of curling tendrils, also similar to the tendrils on the oracle spear in the previous entry. This miniature spearhead may have been made as a votive object for a sculpture, a household shrine, or a portable shrine devoted to one of the guardian deities. For other examples of miniature armor and weapons see catalogue numbers 2, 80, and 103.

80. MINIATURE VOTIVE OBJECT, POSSIBLY A SPEARHEAD OR ARROWHEAD

Tibetan, 17th–18th century
Iron, gold, and silver
L. 5¾ in. (14.6 cm)
The Metropolitan Museum of Art, New York, Purchase, Arthur
Ochs Sulzberger Gift, and funds from various donors, by
exchange, 2001 (2001.184)

Although its form is unusual, this object is here suggested as possibly being a miniature spearhead, like the preceding example, or a ceremonial arrowhead of some type. The distinctive shape, however, also suggests that it may be from, or is at least modeled after, the central prong of a *vajra* (*rdo rje*). It has a pyramidal tip and is quadrangular in cross section for its upper half, after which there is a gradual transition into the conical section of the hollow socket. Below the tip the sides are concave, swelling out at the midpoint and then becoming concave

again at the transition to the socket. The decoration is finely done and consists of a dense overall pattern of stylized waves (*chu ris*) damascened in gold, bordered by damascened silver lines that frame the faceted planes of the surface. The last quarter of the socket is bare metal and is pierced at the base by two holes for attachment to a shaft. Also at the base of the socket the Tibetan word *mchod* (offering) is incised in *dbu can* script (see detail), leaving no doubt that it was specifically intended as a votive offering.

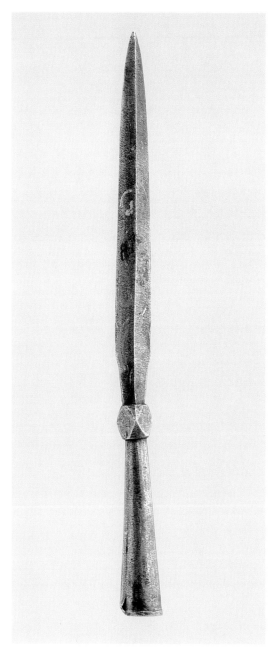

79

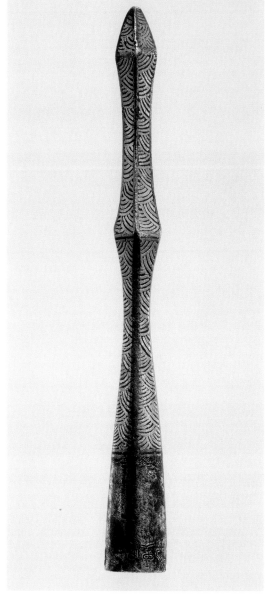

80

80, detail of inscription

178   WARRIORS OF THE HIMALAYAS

81, 82. SPEARHEAD AND FERRULE

Tibetan, 17th–18th century
Iron, gold, and silver
Spearhead, L. 27⅛ in. (68.9 cm); ferrule, L. 13⅝ in. (34.6 cm)
The Metropolitan Museum of Art, New York, Purchase, Arthur
Ochs Sulzberger and The Sulzberger Foundation Inc. Gifts, and
Rogers Fund, 1999 (1999.256a, b)

Although this ceremonial spearhead and ferrule originally may not have been a pair, they are both exceptionally long in comparison to other examples, suggesting that they would have balanced each other appropriately when mounted on a relatively long shaft. Both are very well made, and the spearhead in particular is extensively decorated with damascening in gold and silver. The ferrule is also damascened in gold and silver but to a lesser extent, which is nevertheless noteworthy since ferrules are generally left entirely undecorated.

The spearhead has a straight, gradually tapering blade with a prominent medial ridge on both sides. In cross section it has the form of a lozenge with concave sides, which seems characteristic of Tibetan ceremonial spearheads. The edges of the blade are designed to be blunt. At the base of the blade there is a short, faceted column that swells at the center; a knop in the form a cube with chamfered edges, which is skillfully chiseled with a knot pattern; and a long, slightly faceted conical socket. The decoration of the blade features the Three Jewels in silver, surrounded by flames in gold and positioned on a golden lotus base, with curling flaming scrolls in gold and silver extending up the length of the blade. The spearhead was heavily corroded in the past and appears to have been acid cleaned. The present dark background color is a restoration based on similar examples. The blade is also slightly bent, and one edge has several deep nicks and cuts, indicating that this ceremonial arm may have been pressed into service as a fighting weapon at some late point in its existence.

The ferrule consists of a hollow, conical socket, a square knop with faceted corners, and a solid, four-sided spike with chamfered edges and a blunt tip. Its decoration includes an open pattern of simple quatrefoil blossoms from which rows of circles and straight tabs extend, damascened mostly in silver with a few gold highlights.

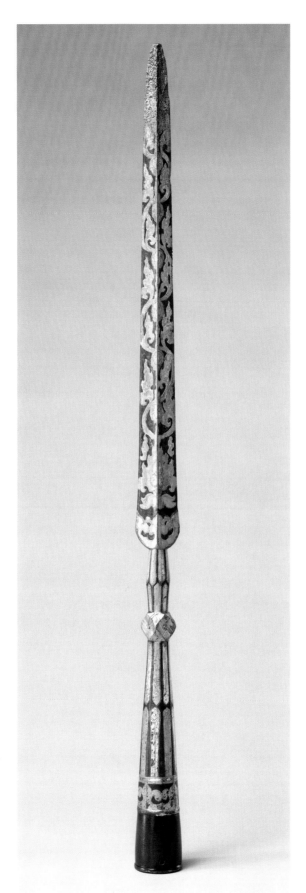

81

82

83. SPEARHEAD

Tibetan, 17th–18th century
Iron, gold, and silver
L. 18⅞ in. (47.9 cm)
The Metropolitan Museum of Art, New York, Purchase, Arthur
Ochs Sulzberger Gift, 1999 (1999.258)

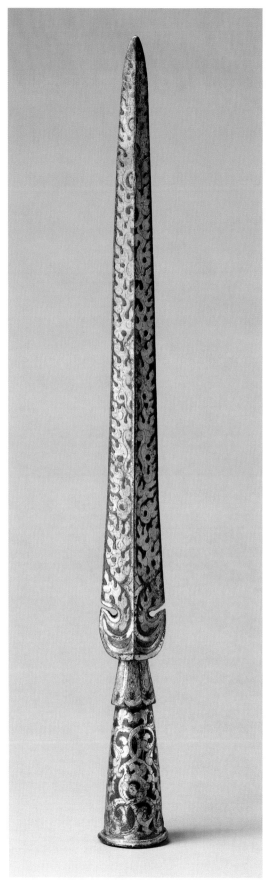

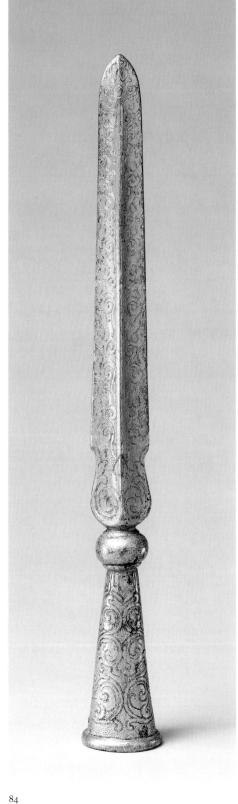

Similar in materials and technique to the previous example, this ceremonial spearhead has a double-edged tapering blade, the edges of which are intentionally blunt, and a prominent medial ridge. There are two teardrop-shaped notches cut out near the base of the blade, one on either side. There is a short, eight-sided conical stem at the base of the blade, and below this a hollow conical socket with a turned rim. The blade is elaborately decorated with a symmetrical pattern of finely incised flames damascened in gold over its entire length. A motif that appears to be a stylized Sword of Wisdom (*shes rab ral gri*) is damascened in silver on the central ridge, surrounded by the flames. The socket has an intricate pattern of curling and overlapping scrollwork, also damascened in gold and silver.

A blade that is very similar in size, shape, and decoration to the one on this spearhead exists in the Los Angeles County Museum of Art (AC 1994.112.1). In this instance, however, rather than a socket, the blade is fitted with a copper handle in the form of a scorpion, making it into a representation of the sword with a scorpion hilt (*ral gri sdig pa can*), which is an important attribute of the fierce guardian deity Begtse (*beg tse*) and others.[1]

1. On the symbolism of the sword with a scorpion hilt, see Heller 1997.

83

84

84. SPEARHEAD

Tibetan, 17th–18th century

Iron and gold

L. 14¼ in. (36.2 cm)

The Metropolitan Museum of Art, New York, Purchase, Arthur Ochs Sulzberger Gift, 2001 (2001.63)

This example is closely related to, but also distinctly different from, the preceding ceremonial spearheads. It is very well forged and consists of a straight double-edged blade with tapering sides, again with the edges designed to be blunt, and a strong medial ridge. In cross section the blade is a lozenge shape with concave sides. At the base of the blade there is a round knop, and below this a hollow conical socket, which has a strong, half-round turned rim. The decoration is crisply engraved and the entire exterior surface of the spearhead finely crosshatched and damascened in gold, including the undecorated areas. The motifs are similar to that of the preceding example, with a symmetrical arrangement of stylized flames running up both sides of the blade and what appears to be a simplified version of the Sword of Wisdom along the central ridge in the midst of the flames. The socket is decorated with a symmetrical pattern of curling scrollwork. The background on the blade and the socket is filled in with finely punched circles.

85. SOCKET FROM A SPEARHEAD OR A CEREMONIAL STAFF

Tibetan or Mongolian, ca. 1607–17

Iron, gold, and silver

L. 11¾ in. (29.8 cm)

The Metropolitan Museum of Art, New York, Purchase, Arthur Ochs Sulzberger Gift, 2005 (2005.301.1)

In Tibet and China sufficiently important documents, seals, and commemorative inscriptions were often written in more than one language, usually Tibetan, Mongolian, Manchu, and Chinese. This socket, however, appears to be the only known piece of ironwork with a dual-language dedicatory inscription in Tibetan and Mongolian. The presence of the two scripts, therefore, suggests that it was originally part of a significant commission or presentation.

The socket is made in a way very similar to those on the spearheads in the preceding entries. It consists of a slightly conical iron tube with three half-round ring moldings, one at the top edge, one in the center, and one at the base. There is a single lap-welded vertical seam running the length of the tube. There are two holes at either side of the top, just beneath the ring molding, for attachment of the missing head, or attachment to the shaft. The upper half of the socket is encircled by a Tibetan inscription in *dbu can* script consisting of eleven horizontal lines damascened alternately in gold and silver. The lower half has fourteen vertical lines in Classical Mongolian, damascened mostly in silver, but with certain words damascened in gold. Both inscriptions are fragmentary due to corrosion of the iron surface.

The Tibetan inscription begins with a short mantra, includes two terms meaning guardians of the Dharma (*chos skyong* and *bstan bsrung rgya mtsho*) and gives the name of the patron or donor (*sbyin bdag*), which begins with Sodnam (*bsod nams*). The term *zo bo* (usually meaning craftsman) appears to be in the last line and may identify the maker, which would be very unusual on a Tibetan object, or it may refer to the making of this piece in a more general sense.[1]

In the Mongolian inscription the donor's name is repeated more clearly, in gold lettering, as Sodnam Ombu Taiji, one of the most powerful noblemen of Inner Mongolia in the early seventeenth century.[2] The inscription is dedicated to Yonten Gyatso (*yon tan rgya mtsho*, 1589–1617), the Fourth Dalai Lama, who was the great-grandson of the Mongol ruler Altan Khan.[3] Yonten Gyatso's reign included periods of armed conflict between rival Tibetan factions and their patrons. During this time Sodnam Obu Taiji may have allied himself with the young Dalai Lama as a military supporter, a relationship to which this enigmatic object possibly bears witness.

1. I am very grateful to Lozang Jamspal for attempting to translate the badly damaged Tibetan inscription.
2. As identified by Prof. Johan Elverskog, to whom I am indebted for his work on the difficult task of translating and interpreting the remains of the Mongolian inscription. These comments and the suggested date of the object are derived from his notes (personal communication, October 15, 2005).
3. For bibliographic information, see Elverskog 2003, p. 195; Mullin 2001, pp. 165–83.

85

86. SPEARHEAD AND STORAGE CASE

Chinese or Mongolian (spearhead) and Tibetan (case),
18th century
Iron, gold, leather, copper, cork (?), and wood
Spearhead, L. 14⅜ in. (36.5 cm); case, L. 15½ in. (39.4 cm)
The Metropolitan Museum of Art, New York, Rogers Fund, 2000
(2000.206a, b)

This spearhead, with its pure form and clean lines, is an excellent example of very refined blade smithing of a quality seldom found on a staff weapon. It has a pearly silver color, with a double-edged blade of flattened lozenge cross section and a distinct medial ridge. The blade has relatively straight sides, which taper into short point. Faint lines parallel with the edges suggest that the cutting edge may have been separately applied during the forging process. From the shoulders at the base of the blade there is a gradual transition into the socket, at the base of which there is a braided ring realistically chiseled in high relief and damascened in gold. Incised just above this is the motif of a stylized mountain flanked by turbulent waves, also damascened in gold, which is a symbol of longevity, sometimes called the Islands of the Immortals, and is frequently found on Chinese decorative arts and, to a lesser extent, on Tibetan objects.[1]

The storage case is made of wood following the silhouette of the spearhead. The exterior is covered in pebbled black leather, and the upper half has an applied copper rim. The lower half is hinged at the top to allow for the insertion of the spearhead. The interior is lined with a thin layer of pliant material, possibly cork. There are two copper hook-and-eye closures near the bottom.

1. An 18th-century ceremonial staff in the Department of Asian Art of the Metropolitan Museum (1986.148) has a concealed spearhead of very similar form to this, but without the decoration.

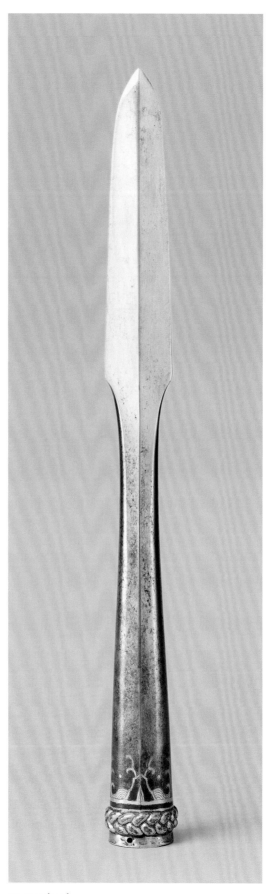

86, spearhead

86, storage case

87. SPEARHEAD

Chinese, 17th–18th century
Iron and gold
L. 14⅞ in. (37.8 cm)
The Metropolitan Museum of Art, New York, Purchase, Arthur
Ochs Sulzberger Gift, 2001 (2001.581)

Despite its heavy surface patina, this spearhead is very similar to the preceding example in terms of the form of the blade and the presence of a braided ring chiseled in high relief. The blade has two shallow fullers, one on either side of the medial ridge, and makes the transition to a straight-sided stem just below the shoulders of the blade. Below this is the braided ring, which is chiseled in higher relief than that of the previous example, and the conical socket. At the base of the socket there is a stepped and deeply chiseled collar with *ju'i* and stylized lotus petal motifs. The spearhead is damascened in gold below the blade and on the socket with very simple designs of the flaming pearl, and above the chiseled collar at the base of the socket with simple versions of the mountains and waves motif, which repeats four times.

A very similar spearhead was formerly in the Metropolitan Museum, catalogued as a seventeenth-century Chinese hunting spear.[1]

1. MMA 16.118.8, gift of Lai Yuan (through C. T. Loo), a complete spear measuring 56¼ inches (142.9 cm). It was deaccessioned and sold at Christie's, London, November 22–23, 1960, as part of lot 176.

87

88. SPEARHEAD

Chinese, 17th–19th century
Iron, gold, and silver
L. 14⅞ in. (37.8 cm)
The Metropolitan Museum of Art, New York, Purchase, Arthur
Ochs Sulzberger Gift, 1999 (1999.259)

The symbolism of its decoration and its purposely blunt edges suggest that this spearhead, although well forged and made of iron, was probably intended for some type of votive or ceremonial purpose. The double-edged blade tapers into a short point. It is relatively flat, and is slightly concave on either side of the strong medial ridge. Below the shoulders of the blade it tapers into a slender socket, which flares out slightly and becomes faceted. The decorative motifs are incised, finely crosshatched, and damascened in gold and silver. On both sides of the blade there are representations of a flaming pearl, a crescent moon, clouds, flames, and a schematic depiction of a constellation consisting of seven stars, in the form of seven circles connected by zigzag lines. On either side of the shaft below the blade there is a lotus blossom in an ogival cartouche. Around the base of the socket there are four auspicious symbols: conch, ingot, coin, and books. The decoration presents an interesting mix of Buddhist symbolism, Taoist symbolism, and general symbols of good fortune typical of Chinese ornament, many of which were also common in Tibet.

Like catalogue number 81, this spearhead has been bent and its edges roughly nicked and cut, suggesting it was reused as a fighting weapon, a purpose for which it appears not to have been designed.

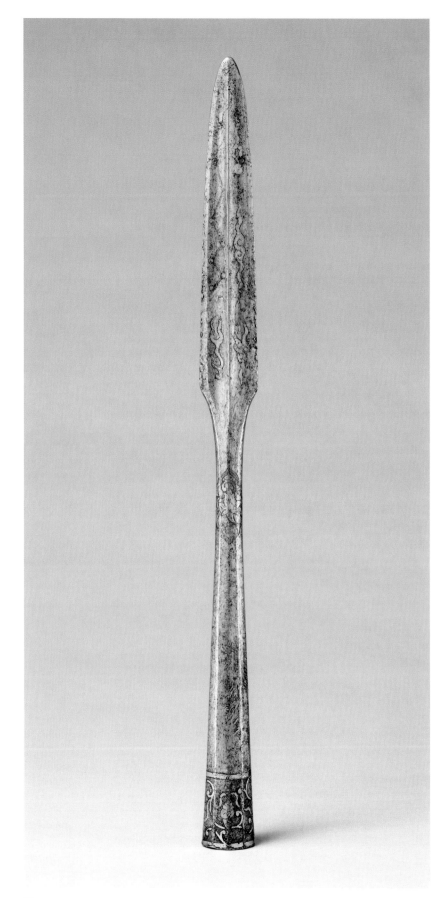

88

89. AX HEAD

Probably Chinese, 15th–18th century
Iron and gold
L. 9 in. (22.9 cm)
The Metropolitan Museum of Art, New York, Purchase, Arthur
Ochs Sulzberger Gift, 2001 (2001.56)

The ax was not a common weapon in Tibet, China, or the Far East in general, but was frequently found in India and from Persia westward. The form of this ax head presents an interesting and unusual mix of styles: the blade is more Chinese in type, while the wavy beak relates to Indo-Persian examples. Likewise, the decorative motifs show various potential influences. The dragon and pearl motif occurs from Persia to China, the cusped lines at the base of the blade are Chinese in style, while the crossed *vajra* motif occurs most frequently on Tibetan objects. The ax head is solidly made of iron and consists of a square socket in the center with a crescentic blade on one side and a wavy beak of lozenge section on the other. An oval aperture for the ax handle vertically transverses the center of the socket. The decoration is inlaid and damascened in gold and consists of a crossed *vajra* motif within a hexagonal compartment on the front and the back of the socket; an undulating triple-clawed dragon and a flaming pearl on each of the four facets of the beak; and a pair of cusped borders on either side of the blade where it meets the collar.

While battle-axes (*dgra sta*) were apparently known in Tibet, they are most frequently found as symbolic weapons depicted in works of art as attributes of guardian deities, or as actual ritual objects.[1] That form, the *vajra* ax (*rdo rje dgra sta*), incorporates *vajra* finials and crossed *vajras*, reminiscent of the crossed *vajra* motif on this ax head, which, however, appears to be a fighting ax rather than a ritual object, and as such is very rare in terms of form and type.

89

1. See, for instance, the Sino-Tibetan ritual ax in the Cleveland Museum of Art (1978.1), illustrated in Watt and Leidy 2005, p. 78, pl. 30.

90. CHAKRA (QUOIT)

Tibetan, 15th–18th century (?)

Iron

Diam. 5½ in. (14 cm)

The Metropolitan Museum of Art, New York, Purchase, Arthur
Ochs Sulzberger Gift, 2003 (2003.467)

This object appears to be the only known example of a chakra (*'khor lo* or *be rdo*) that is clearly Tibetan. The chakra is well known as a symbolic weapon of both Hindu and Buddhist deities and figures frequently as a divine attribute in the literary and iconographic traditions of both religions. As an actual weapon, however, extant chakras are usually associated with the Sikhs of northwestern India, who carried chakras as both symbolic and practical arms through the late nineteenth century, and continue to use them for ceremonial purposes today. This example strongly resembles certain Sikh chakras, which are often decorated in a similar way with religious invocations.[1] In addition, the wear patterns are entirely consistent with an object that has been handled as a chakra would be. Therefore, lacking any signs of fixtures or attachments of any type that might indicate this object was once part of something else, such as a mirror frame, and because of the long Tibetan poem covering its entire upper surface, it is here suggested as a unique example of a chakra from Tibet.[2]

It is made in the form of a flattened ring of silver-colored iron. In cross section the underside is flat and the upper side is chamfered and slopes down from the inner edge of the ring to the outer edge. Both the inner edge and the outer edge are rounded. There appears to be a single lap-weld visible on the underside. The surface of the upper side is engraved with a Tibetan poem, consisting of six lines written in the *dbu can* script, which has been translated as follows: "There is a lake in Rinchen Margang / In which very beautiful lotuses bloom / The face of the lake is smooth as a mirror and shines / In it the sun reflects with golden rays / Seeing that gives endless satisfaction to someone with the eye of wisdom / But for one whose eyes are blind to knowledge, it is not like that."[3]

90

1. Compare, for instance, with the Sikh chakra decorated with verses from the *Adi Granth* (Metropolitan Museum, 36.25.2878), included in LaRocca 1996, pl. 25.
2. An iron chakra made by the Nepalese artist Anige (1245–1306) and used in an imperial procession in China is cited by Anning Jing, "Financial and material aspects of Tibetan Art under the Yuan Dynasty," *Artibus Asiae* 64, no. 2 (2004), p. 218. I am grateful to Steve Kossak and Denise Leidy for pointing out this reference.
3. *rin chen mar sgang yod ba'i [pa'i] mtsho nang du / rab tu mdzes pa'i pad ma rgyas pa bzhin / me long ngos ltar mjam ['jam] zhing 'tshar ['tsher] ba la / nyi ma'i mdangs ldan gser gyi 'od gzer [zer] can / shes rab spyan ldan blta bas ngoms mi 'gyur / rig pa ldongs pa'i myig la de lta min.* Some of the vowel signs along the inner edge have been worn away by handling. I am very grateful to Lozang Jamspal, Gene Smith, and Zenkar Rinpoche Tudeng Nima for checking the transcription, suggesting corrections, and amending my translation of the poem.

འཕོང་སྒྲུབ
Archery Equipment

The archery equipment from Tibet included here consists principally of quivers and bow cases, which are notable for their form, construction, and decoration. Horseback archery was a major component of warfare in Asia, including Tibet, for fifteen hundred years or more, and it provided much of the firepower that made the nomadic peoples of the steppes, from the Huns to the Mongols, feared from Japan to western Europe. The necessity of being able to carry a bow and a quiver of arrows for long distances on horseback, ready for quick use in battle or the hunt, engendered a method of wearing the bow in a sheath or case on the left hip and the quiver on the right hip, both suspended from a waist belt.

One of the earliest types of quivers worn in this way has the form of a long, narrow container, with an open cowl at the top and a flared or triangular base, which can be seen in works of art from China to Iran, dating from the seventh to the fourteenth century. One of the few surviving examples of this type, made of wicker and leather with metal fittings, is discussed in catalogue number 91. In a later stage of development (cat. nos. 93, 94), the quiver was made entirely of decorated leather; the same type of gilded and varnished leather (*bse*) is found on some of the leather arm defenses from Tibet (for instance, cat. no. 38).

In both of these types of quivers the arrows were inserted with the fletchings at the bottom of the quiver and the arrowheads at the top. In the next form of quiver, which overlapped with the others for an extended period, the arrows were held side by side, with the arrowheads and the first third of the shafts inserted in a broad, flat quiver made of a wood frame covered with leather. This type frequently had a matching bow case (cat. no. 95) and was also made of gilded and varnished leather. The bow cases are closed at the bottom, except for a small gap, and cover about one-half

of the bow. Later types, in which the quiver is shorter and the bow case is completely open at the top and bottom, remained in use until the early twentieth century.

The bows used in Tibet ranged from simple wooden bows to composite bows made of wood, horn, and sinew (cat. no. 97). Arrows were made of cane or bamboo, fletched with feathers, and fitted with arrowheads made of iron in various shapes (cat. nos. 96, 98). In terms of traditional Tibetan literature, although Tashi Namgyal is silent on the subject, Hūṃkaradzaya, in his *Lotus Bouquet of Analytical Methods*, included two short chapters devoted to bows (*gzhu*), arrows (*mda'*), and arrowheads (*mde'u*).[1] He mentioned some of the different types of wood used to make bows, the special materials used for the nocks (the notches at the ends of a bow in which the bowstring is held), the merits of different types of arrow shafts, what time of year and from what type of birds to get feathers for the fletching of arrows, and what types of arrowheads to use.

Evocative examples of archery equipment as it was worn and used in Tibet can be seen on the figure of a heavy cavalryman equipped in the manner of the fifteenth–seventeenth centuries in catalogue number 26; on the more lightly armored cavalryman of the eighteenth–nineteenth century in catalogue number 46; and in the various photographs of the armored cavalry participating in the Great Prayer Festival in Lhasa (figs. 6–8).

---

1. The archery chapters of the *brtags thabs padma dkar po'i 'chun po* exist in three published editions (for references, see the appendix "Excerpts from *A Treatise on Worldly Traditions*"), which are, however, highly contradictory in the spelling of many key terms. The end of the chapter on arrows and arrowheads, which is missing from Tashi Tsering 1979, p. 66, can be found in the other two published versions, Gangtok 1981, p. 110, and Lhasa 1990, pp. 244–45.

91. QUIVER

Tibetan or Mongolian, late 13th–15th century
Leather, iron, copper alloy, wicker (bamboo or cane), and wood
L. 32½ in. (82.6 cm)
The Metropolitan Museum of Art, New York, Purchase, Arthur
Ochs Sulzberger Gift, 2001 (2001.65a, b)

This quiver and the following one are the only known extant examples of their type, the basic form of which is depicted repeatedly in works of art from at least the seventh century until the end of the fourteenth century.[1] In none of these sources, however, does the top of the quiver have a round cowl, as on the present examples.[2] The primary dating features of catalogue number 91 are its strongly flared and ribbed body, the fact that it is triangular rather than oval or round in section, and the form of the cowl covering the top. The combination of these elements suggests a date of the twelfth–fourteenth centuries, which is borne out by carbon-14 testing that places the quiver in a date range of 1290–1410.[3]

The complex and well-designed construction of this quiver clearly indicates that it was the product of a long-standing crafts tradition. The wickerlike structure of the body is made of cane or split bamboo, covered in leather, and reinforced by an iron frame. The top is covered by a keyhole-shaped cowl made of a copper alloy, which is closed at the back by a panel of leather and is open at the front for the insertion or removal of arrows. The bottom of the cowl is half round where it joins the body of the quiver, which widens and flares out, ending in a triangular base made of a flat board faced with leather. The cowl is decorated with raised knobs around its rim and bands of raised dots across its base. The middle third of the quiver is faced with plain black leather, framed in iron, and has a peaked medial ridge of iron. The bottom third has six raised longitudinal ribs on either side of the medial ridge, all of which are covered in brown leather. The iron frame, which borders the entire quiver, includes two fixed suspension loops, to which two knotted leather thongs are attached. The frame is decorated with borders consisting of incised double lines and by a series of large dome-headed rivets. The back of the quiver is flat and is faced with plain brown leather. The body of the quiver is slightly convex in profile, that is, curved away from the wearer.

The existence of this quiver and the next present the rare opportunity to study firsthand an important type that was widespread over much of Asia for hundreds of years, but which, until now, has been known only from artists' representations.

1. Compare, for instance, the quiver on the stone relief of a warrior from the tomb of the emperor Taizong (dated to A.D. 637; University of Pennsylvania Museum, C395); the quivers worn by Tibetan cavalry depicted in 8th–9th-century wall paintings in Dunhuang (an example illustrated in Yang Hong 1992, fig. 344); many quivers shown in the Ilkhanid manuscript of Rashid al-Din's *History of the World* (completed in 1306/7; portions in Edinburgh University, the Nour Foundation, and elsewhere); and in miniatures from various Shahnameh manuscripts made late in the 14th century (for example, Elgood 1979, figs. 44, 47).
2. Quivers with this general form, however, including a rounded cowl, can be seen in a Tibetan manuscript with illustrations from the Gesar epic (Thurman and Weldon 1999, no. 79, with references). An earlier and extremely rare quiver of this form, but made entirely of birch bark, is included in the exhibition catalogue *Dschingis Khan und seine Erben: Das Weltreich der Mongolen* (Munich, 2005), no. 58, p. 84.
3. Results with 95% confidence rating at 2 sigma; test by Beta Analytic Radiocarbon Dating Laboratory, March 21, 2005.

92. QUIVER

Tibetan or Mongolian, 14th–15th century
Leather, lacquer or shellac, and wood
L. 30¾ in. (78.1 cm)
The Metropolitan Museum of Art, New York, Purchase,
Arthur Ochs Sulzberger Gift, 2005 (2005.301.3)

Although similar in overall form and closely related in type, this quiver is made entirely of leather, with only a small baseboard of wood, unlike the preceding example, on which the leather is supported by a wicker frame and has fittings of iron and copper alloy. In the present instance the leather has been shaped and molded and has a pebbled brownish black surface over a reddish ground. The round cowl at the top is open at the front and has straight deep sides, which merge into a tubular body that widens toward the bottom and has a flat back. Unlike the preceding quiver, the body does not become triangular toward the base. The quiver is decorated at the top on the front of the tube with applied leather ribs arranged in a lozenge pattern. Below this, approximately in the center, there is a raised *ju'i* scroll of tooled leather coated with a gesso or a lacquerlike material. The bottom half has seven vertical ribs of applied leather. There is a single suspension loop, also made of molded leather, on the top edge at the end of the central scroll design. The corresponding loop, once located near the opening of the tube, is missing. The structure of the cowl and tube of the quiver are formed from a single continuous piece of shaped leather, which has a vertical internal seam running up the center of the front. In addition to the leather ribs that form the decorative patterns and the ribs that form borders around the sides of the tube and the edges of the cowl, at least two other layers of leather have been added over the front of the tube. There are two pairs of small holes on either side edge just below the *ju'i* scroll, one square hole where the second suspension loop would be, and two pairs of small rectangular holes at the midpoint of the upright sides of the cowl. A wooden baseboard is placed at bottom of the tube on the inside. There is an old, slightly diagonal cut approximately 1 inch (2.5 cm) long in the leather surface of the front of the quiver near the bottom front, which was possibly caused by a weapon. The dark pebbled surface that covers the entire quiver may be a heavily crazed layer of shellac or lacquer, including what appear to be faint traces of gold pigment or gold leaf on the surface of the *ju'i* scroll.

The differences in construction between this quiver and the preceding one suggest that this quiver represents a slightly later and more refined version of this extremely rare and early style.

91

92

93. QUIVER

Tibetan or Mongolian, possibly 15th–17th century
Leather, shellac, gold, and pigments
L. 31¼ in. (79.4 cm)
Royal Armouries Museum, Leeds (XXVIB.141)
Part of cat. no. 26

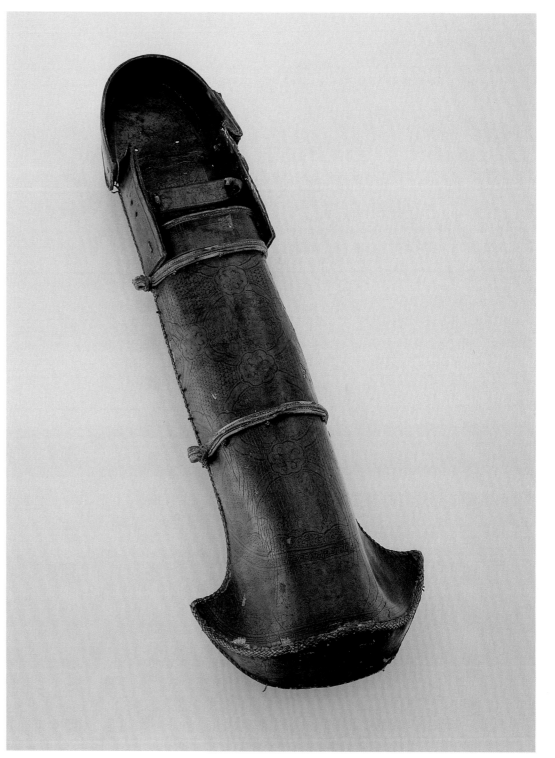

93

This and the following example appear to be the type of quiver to which the term *bse dong* would apply: *bse* in reference to the decorated leather, and *dong* meaning a hollow container, the term used for various types of quivers as well as other tubelike objects. Unlike the quiver in catalogue number 91, which is made of wicker, leather, and metal fittings, quivers of this type are made entirely from shaped panels of stiff leather, the edges of which are sewn together with thin, flat leather laces in a braided cross-stitch. The construction, consisting of six leather sections, is representative of the type: a flat back panel running the full length of the quiver; a convex panel making up the lower half of the front; a cowl or hood, which consists of a double layer with the characteristic crimps or folds on either side; a decorated flat insert covering the interior at the back of the cowl; a horizontal collar that overlaps the seam between the cowl and the front panel; and a plain flat insert for the interior of the bottom half. On some examples the ends of the cowl and the folds on the side are held by brass rivets with long shanks and decorative quatrefoil or rosette washers. This quiver has on the left side two horizontal bands of leather with loops for attachment to a belt. On some examples, however, the space between the bands is filled with a netlike series of leather laces across the middle of the front of the quiver.[1]

The decoration consists of a layer of gold leaf covered with shellac, pigmented in the characteristic reddish brown color, with designs painted in fine black lines. The style and type of decoration are shared by that of the quiver in the next entry.

1. See, for instance, the quiver illustrated in Anninos 2000, fig. 15.

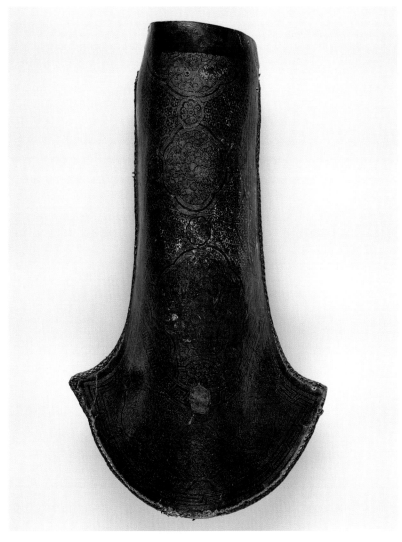

94

94, back view

94, detail of decoration

94. PART OF A QUIVER

Tibetan or Mongolian, 15th–17th century
Leather, shellac, gold, and pigments
L. 18½ inches (47 cm)
The Metropolitan Museum of Art, New York, Purchase, Kenneth
and Vivian Lam Gift, 2001 (2001.37)

This quiver is closely related to the preceding example and, like it, is probably the type referred to as a *bse dong*. Although it is incomplete and slightly damaged, its decoration is among the best found on this type of object. The upper portion, consisting of the cowl and a horizontal band, are missing, as are any suspension straps or other hanging devices by which the quiver would have been suspended from the right side of the wearer's belt. It is constructed with a hard leather body in the form of a tube with a flattened back, flaring out strongly into a crescentic base. This is made up of three shaped panels of leather (front, back, and bottom) sewn together with thin, flat leather laces in a braided cross-stitch. An insert consisting of a single panel of thick leather forms a back panel inside the body of the quiver.

The front and bottom panels are covered with gold leaf and densely decorated with motifs outlined and detailed in black on a red ground and covered overall with reddish brown shellac. The central section of the front panel has three lobed cartouches linked by smaller medallions: in the largest there is a snow lion between a lotus and a peony, surrounded by thick scrolls; in the second there is a large peony and scrolls; the third cartouche is filled with stylized clouds. The cartouches are on a dense field of two distinct diaper patterns: one a honeycomb or tortoiseshell pattern and the other a net of circles filled with interlocking Y's, one of the so-called stylized armor patterns (see detail). The lower, crescentic area of the front panel has three quatrefoil cartouches filled with symbols of good fortune from the Eight Auspicious Symbols (lotus, white conch, umbrella, endless knot, golden fish, wheel, victory banner, and vase) and the Seven Gems (elephant tusks, rhinoceros horn, king's earrings, queen's earrings, coral, ingot, and books). Both areas of decoration are bordered by bands of geometric designs: the swastika fret and the thunder scroll. The underside of the quiver has a central quatrefoil cartouche with a crossed *vajra* motif, set on a simplified diaper-pattern ground. The back of the quiver has a large lotus at the base, which is encircled by a spiraling leafy stalk on a black ground (see illus.).

The decoration, in terms of technique, style, and motifs, is very similar to that found on the leather arm defense in catalogue number 38, as well as the quiver in the preceding entry and the bow case and quiver in the following entry.

95. BOW CASE AND QUIVER

Tibetan or Mongolian, 15th–17th century
Leather, shellac, wood, iron, and gold
Bow case, L. 25 in. (63.5 cm), W. 16½ in. (41.9 cm); quiver, L. 20 in. (50.8 cm), W. 11½ in. (29.2 cm); belt, L. 50¾ in. (128.9 cm), W. 1¼ in. (3.2 cm)
The Metropolitan Museum of Art, New York, Purchase, Arthur Ochs Sulzberger Gift, 2003 (2003.344a–c)

Matching sets of this early type of bow case, quiver, and belt are very rare, there being a few examples in museum collections in Great Britain, mostly collected around the time of the Younghusband Expedition. The bow case (*gzhu shubs*) is a V-shaped sheath of leather, shaped to cover the lower half of a strung bow. It has a wide opening at the top for insertion and removal of the bow, and a narrow opening at the bottom where the end of the bow would protrude slightly. The entire front of the bow case is covered with decoration executed in black lines and golden brown shellac. The main field is framed by two geometric borders of repeating lozenge compartments. The compartments of the outer border are filled with a cross motif and those of the inner border with a swastika motif. The inner border also includes interspersed cloud patterns and concentric scrolls. The ground of the main field is decorated with a honeycomb pattern of repeating hexagons, each of which is filled with a pattern of dots. A large circular cartouche near the center top contains an indistinct figure, possibly a dragon. Below this are two trilobate cartouches, one on either side, which contain a phoenix motif, and between them is a lobed cartouche filled with a repeating lozenge pattern. In each of the three corners of the main field there is a small trefoil cartouche with floral motifs. A domed iron boss in the upper right corner of the bow case is pierced and chiseled with designs of a dragon on a scrollwork ground and a central blossom, all damascened in gold. The boss is encircled by a narrow border decorated with the wave design (*chu ris*), similar to the border on the iron mounts of the curved sword in catalogue number 74 and elsewhere. The stem of the boss is a pierced lug, which protrudes on the back of the bow case and by which it is laced to the waist belt. Eleven dome-headed studs of polished iron line the right edge of the bow case, which is stiffened by an internal frame of six or more layers of hard leather. The back of the bow case is undecorated.

The quiver (*mda' shubs*) is decorated with the same motifs and materials as the bow case. There is a pair of straps in an X pattern across the center of the quiver. The straps are fitted with five domed iron bosses, two large and three small. The larger bosses are located on the two strap ends on the right side. They are the same as the single boss on the bow case, their pierced stems similarly protruding at the back of the quiver. The stem of the upper boss is laced to a ring attached to the waist belt, and that of the lower boss has a subsidiary lacing. The three small bosses are located one in the center where the straps cross and one at each of the strap ends on the left side. They are decorated like the large bosses but with a central whirling emblem (*dga' 'khyil*) and no dragon. Twenty-nine dome-headed iron studs line the outer edges of the front of the quiver, which has an internal wood frame that follows the contours of the outer edges along both sides and the bottom. Inside the opening at the top of the quiver there is a thick cord of padded leather, twisted in a braid pattern, which held the arrows in place. The back of the quiver is undecorated. Two shaped leather tabs on the back were presumably for additional attachment laces.

The leather of the belt is undecorated. It is fitted with three iron mounts, two circular and one rectangular, which have pierced, chiseled, and damascened

95

scrollwork matching that of the bosses on the bow case and quiver. Each of the two circular mounts has a plain pendant iron ring for the laces attaching the bow case and quiver. The rectangular mount has a plain iron hook at one end, by which the belt is fastened.

The shellac on both the bow case and the quiver is darkened to varying degrees, making the decoration hard to read in some areas. There are some small cracks and tears around the bottom edges of the bow case, and the leather on the front of the quiver is partially warped. Otherwise all elements of the set are in fairly good condition and largely intact. The combination of varnished leather and dome-headed iron studs also offers an important parallel to the similar features found on the elements of horse armor seen earlier in this catalogue.

96. QUIVER AND ARROWS

Tibetan, 17th–18th century
Leather, iron, gold, silver, wood, shellac, pigments, cane or bamboo, feathers, and textile
Quiver, L. 18½ in. (47 cm), W. 10⅝ in. (27 cm); arrows, L. 35⅜ in. (89.9 cm)
On loan courtesy of the National Museums of Scotland
Royal Museum, Edinburgh (A.1927.321A–O)

This beautifully decorated quiver is of the same form and construction as the example described in the previous entry, but its style of decoration, both the leather and the metalwork, is very different and suggests a slightly later date. In this instance the designs on the quiver appear to be painted in gold on a black ground, as opposed to being executed in gold leaf with designs painted in black lines. As a result, the decoration has a far more painterly appearance. The surface is divided into several irregularly shaped strapwork cartouches filled with lush scrolling foliage and lotus blossoms with thick petals. A cartouche in the center of the bottom portion features the Wish-Fulfilling Jewel flanked by the wheel and the lotus. The Three Jewels motif appears in a cartouche in the upper half. The cross-straps are painted with over and under concentric scrolls, a motif usually found in damascened ironwork.

The pierced iron fittings, damascened in gold and silver, are also very distinctive. Most prominent are two D-shaped mounts on the right side at the point where the suspension straps would be connected to the quiver, which have a dragon amid scrollwork in gold surrounded by a large beaded border in silver. The same treatment is also found on the pierced iron rim that covers the bottom edge of the quiver. On the lower left end of one cross-strap there is an irregularly shaped iron plaque pierced with a stylized image of a dragon seen directly from above. In addition to this there are two gilded buttons with simple engraved floral decoration.

The quiver is also unusual in having a full set of arrows, which have cane or bamboo shafts fletched with feathers (*mda' sgro*), ivory nocks (*mda' stong* or *ltong ka*), and iron arrowheads (*mde'u* or *mda' lcags*). The arrowheads have several different shapes, including a sharp quadrangular point, a narrow double-edged point like that of a spearhead (these two may be armor-piercing types), a teardrop-shaped head, and a leaf-shaped head (perhaps better suited for hunting). These may correspond to the types of arrowheads referred to in Tibetan as *phag lce* (pig tongue), *khyi lce* (dog tongue), and *mde'i byi'u snying ma* (arrowhead like a bird's heart).[1] It is also notable that the shaft of one arrow is braided with strips of silk in five different colors: pink (possibly faded from red), yellow, blue, white, and green. Arrows adorned in this way are known as a *mda' dar* or *dar tshon sna lnga btags pa'i mda'* (literally, silk arrow or arrow with five various silks attached) and are used in marriage, divination, and long-life ceremonies.[2] Also of interest is the wax seal stamped on the braided silk, which features the design of a conch shell (see detail). This may be the personal seal of a former owner, or it is possibly a variant of the *g.yang sgrub mda' dar*, an arrow used in ceremonies to ensure prosperity, which has a conch shell and silk streamers attached to it.[3]

PROVENANCE: Captain Dalmahoy (member of the 40th Pathans, a regiment that took part in the Younghusband Expedition), given to the museum by Miss Dalmahoy, Edinburgh.

PUBLICATION: LaRocca 1999a, fig. 32, p. 129.

1. See Tashi Tsering 1979, p. 65; and the appendix "Tibetan-English Glossary of Arms and Armor Terms: III. Archery Equipment and Projectile Weapons, Other than Firearms."
2. On the different types and uses of these arrows, see Nebesky-Wojkowitz 1975, pp. 365–68.
3. Ibid., pp. 365–66.

96, detail of seal

96

97. COMPOSITE BOW

Chinese or Tibetan, 19th century
Wood, horn, sinew, and leather
L. 48⅜ in. (122.9 cm)
On loan courtesy of the National Museums of Scotland
Royal Museum, Edinburgh (A.1910.5)

A composite bow refers to a bow made up from a combination of wood, horn, and sinew, as opposed to one made from a single piece of wood or several sections of wood glued together. In the basic construction of a composite bow, which applies to the present example, wood is used for the core of the bow to give it structure; strips of horn are glued to the belly (the side facing the archer when the bow held for shooting), where there is great compression when the bow is drawn; and strips of sinew fibers are glued along the back (the side held away from the archer) to give the bow tensile strength. The sinew is usually covered with a protective and decorative material, often, as in this case, birch bark. In Chinese and probably also Tibetan composite bows, the core may be bamboo as well as wood. The nocks (the notches at the tips of the bow to hold the loops of the bowstring) on this bow appear to be made of horn, but some were also said to be made of special materials such as shell, ivory, gold, and sandalwood.[1]

The grip is wrapped in leather. Bowstrings can be made of twisted fibers of cotton or silk, or sinew. The string on this bow appears to be sinew, which would work well only in a region with a predominantly dry climate like that of Tibet.

PROVENANCE: F. M. Bailey, Edinburgh (see cat. no. 1).

1. See Tashi Tsering 1979, p. 64.

98. WHISTLING ARROWHEAD

Chinese or Tibetan, 17th–18th century
Iron and gold; L. 6½ in. (16.5 cm)
The Metropolitan Museum of Art, New York, Purchase, Edward
C. Dittus Gift, 1999 (1999.32)

Whistling arrows were used in Tibet, but to what extent it is not known.[1] However, there are at least two Tibetan terms for them: *lcags mda' sgra can* (literally, iron arrow with sound) and *lcags sbubs can* (literally, iron [arrow] with a hollow space). This particular example has a flat spade-shaped blade with a low, well-defined central ridge from the tip to the base. At the base there is a hollow chamber of chamfered teardrop shape pierced by four evenly spaced holes, through which the wind would rush when the arrow was in flight to produce a whistling sound. The tang is four-sided and tapers to a dull point. The decoration is damascened in gold and consists of a stylized flaming cloud motif symmetrically placed on either side of the central ridge on the front and back of the blade. A narrow border damascened in gold outlines the edges of the central ridge, the base of the blade, and the base of the whistling chamber. The gold forming the wavy lines of the flame motif and the outlines of the cloud design is slightly raised from the adjacent iron surface, rather than flush with it.

What appear to be whistling arrows with heads similar to this one are included in the woodcut illustrations to the *Huangchao Liqi Tushi* (Illustrated Regulations for the Ceremonial Regalia of the Present Dynasty), which was produced in 1759 during the reign of the emperor Qianlong (1736–96).[2] Also, an arrow with a head very similar in shape to this one, but without a whistling chamber, was acquired in 1891 or 1892 by William Rockhill as part of a set of archery equipment, described by him as Chinese and of the type used in China, Tibet, and Mongolia.[3]

1. See E. McEwen and D. Elmy, "Whistling Arrows," *Journal of the Society of Archer Antiquaries* 13 (1970), pp. 25–26, for the comment, "prior to the last Chinese invasion of Tibet, the monks at Shigatse monastery practiced a form of short range shooting with whistling-arrows."
2. Reprinted in *Yingyin Wenyuange Sikyu Quanshu*, vol. 656 (Shanghai, 1983), pp. 773, 775.
3. Rockhill 1895, pl. 21.

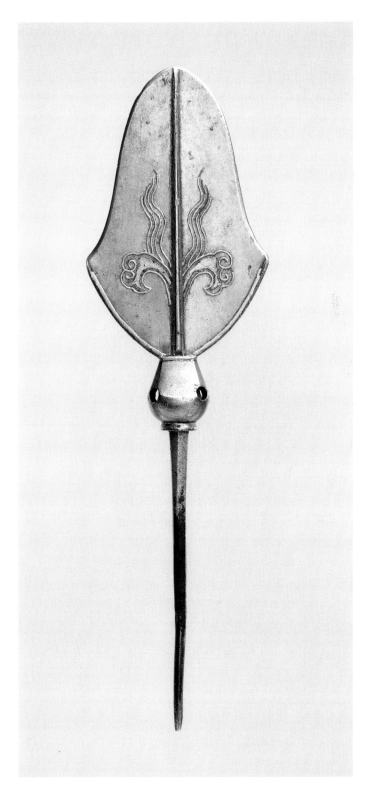

98

མེ་མདའ་དང་མེ་མདའ་ཆས
Firearms and Accessories

Firearms were probably introduced into Tibet gradually during the sixteenth century from several sources, including China, India, and West Asia, as part of the general spread of the use of firearms throughout Asia. The traditional Tibetan gun is a matchlock musket, known as a *me mda'* (literally, fire arrow), which appears to have changed little if at all in its construction and technology between the time of its introduction and the early twentieth century. Its basic components are a tubular gun barrel mounted on a long wooden stock, fitted with the simple matchlock firing mechanism from which the gun takes its name, and, attached to the underside of the fore-stock, a pair of prongs that are used to steady the aim of the gun (compare cat. nos. 99–101).

Matchlock muskets are muzzle-loaders, a type of gun that is loaded by putting gunpowder and a bullet down the muzzle of the barrel and tapping them firmly into place with a ramrod. The barrel invariably has a smooth bore, which means that the interior surface of the barrel is smooth rather than incised with spiraling grooves, called rifling, the feature that distinguishes a rifle from a gun. The barrel flares out slightly at the muzzle, on the top of which there is often a small bead or leaf sight (*tsha kha* or *so kha*). On the right side of the breech (*pho brang*, the chamber for gunpowder at the base of the barrel) there is a small flange with a shallow depression, which is called the priming pan in English and the *rna mchog* (literally, ear) in Tibetan. On the side of the barrel where the priming pan is attached to the breech there is a small hole, called the touchhole (*rdzas khung*, literally, powder hole). The priming pan holds a small amount of gunpowder, which, when ignited, sets off the main charge inside the breech of the barrel via the touchhole, thereby firing the gun. The powder in the pan is ignited by a slow-burning match, as explained below.

The wooden gunstock (*sgum shing*) extends the full length of the barrel, which fits into a long groove hollowed out in the fore-stock. It is secured by leather thongs or copper (occasionally silver) wire wrapped over the barrel and around the stock in three or four places to hold them firmly together. The ramrod (*rdzong thur*, *sim 'big*, or other terms) fits into a slot or hole (*sim khung*) on the underside of the fore-stock, parallel with and beneath the barrel. Behind the breech, the stock widens to accommodate the few parts of the firing mechanism, which on a firearm are referred to as the lock, hence the name matchlock. This consists of an S-shaped arm called a match-holder, cock, or serpentine in English and *me skam* or *me mda'i skam* in Tibetan, which is held in a slot in the stock by a transverse nail so that it pivots in the center. The upper arm extends above the stock through the top of the slot and has a simple set of jaws to hold the end of the match; the lower arm protrudes toward the rear on the underside of the stock and acts as the trigger. There is usually a simple leaf spring inside the stock that presses against the lower arm to keep upper arm in an upright position. Because the slot for the match-holder can weaken the stock, it is usually reinforced on both sides by a flat iron plate called the lock plate. The jaws hold what is essentially a long wick or slow-burning fuse called a match, match cord, or slow match in English and in Tibetan *sbi ti* (spelled several different ways), *bir thig*, or *me len skud pa*. When lit, the end of the match does not burn up, but rather smolders slowly for a long period of time. When the trigger is squeezed up, the jaws are tilted down, putting the smoldering end of the match into the priming pan and igniting the powder in the pan, which fires the charge in the barrel. It is a simple but surprisingly reliable system, with few moving parts, which are easily replaceable or repairable.

The butt of the stock (*bya gzhug*) is generally long, fairly flat, and narrow, resembling both Chinese and certain types of Indian gunstocks in profile. To protect the butt from damage when the musket is rested on the ground there is a butt cap at the end of the stock made of a layer of bone sandwiched between two layers of horn. There is usually a cloth and leather pouch (*bir shubs*) attached to the outer side of the butt, in which the unused match cord is stored. There is also often a decorated leather patch of oval shape attached loosely to a ring on the opposite side of the stock, which is used to cover the priming pan when it is not in use. Nearly all Tibetan matchlocks are also fitted with a leather strap, or sling, by which the gun is carried crosswise on the back. Some gunstocks are protected and reinforced by a covering of leather, which is tightly fitted and stitched in place (cat. no. 102).[1] The lower half of the stock, from the butt to the priming pan, is sometimes also protected by a removable cloth or leather bag (as in fig. 7).[2]

The most noticeable feature of Tibetan matchlocks is the two long, slender prongs, or horns, which are attached to the horn block (the thicker rectangular section of wood on the underside of the fore-stock) by a transverse pin or screw. They usually have metal caps at the top and are made in two halves, the upper half being wood and the lower half often being an actual horn (*ru* or *rva co*), either antelope or gazelle, with a metal band where the halves are joined. It is either from the use of horn or the general hornlike shape that their various names derive, such as *ru kha*, *me mda'i ru*, and *me mda'i rva co*, meaning "muzzle horns" and "gun horns." There is also usually at least one short cross strut between the horns, to keep them from spreading apart. When in use the horns are swung down to rest on the ground and steady the aim of the shooter. When not in use they are generally folded up against the fore-stock with the ends projecting forward well beyond the muzzle.

The decoration found on Tibetan matchlock guns varies, but even the most utilitarian examples generally have some degree of ornament. It is not uncommon to find stocks with applied plaques of pierced or embossed silver, copper, or iron, which range from being relatively simple to fairly elaborate (cat. nos. 99–101). Stocks are more rarely inlaid with bone or painted (cat. nos. 100, 103). The match-cord pouches and pan covers often have appliqués of colored leather or textile and decorative rivets or bosses. The barrels are usually plain except perhaps for some fluting at the muzzle, ring moldings toward the breech, or simple engraved designs. There are, however, some notable exceptions of barrels decorated with gold and silver damascening (cat. nos. 103–105).

The accessories used with a matchlock gun are designed for carrying gunpowder (*me rdzas* or *rdzas*) and bullets (*mde'u*, *rde'u*, or *mdel ril*), which are lead balls or shot, similar to the musket balls used in Europe, rather than bullets in the modern sense. The powder for the main charge (*me mda'i kha rdzas*), that is, the powder put down the barrel, is carried in a flask (*rdzas*

khug) made of hard leather (cat. nos. 107, 108), whereas the powder for the priming pan (*rna rdzas*), which can be a little more finely grained, is sometimes carried separately in a small carved horn (*rdzas rva* or *pho rva*). The musket balls are carried in leather pouches (*mde'u khug*, *mdel khug*, or *mdel shubs*) of different shapes, which are usually of relatively stiff, but not hard, leather and are sometimes decorated with leather appliqués (cat. nos. 106, 107, 110). A bandolier was also frequently used. This is a leather strap worn over one shoulder and across the chest, attached to which there are several individual containers, called chargers, each of which holds enough powder for a single shot. Also attached to the bandolier would be a horn of priming powder and a bullet pouch (cat. no. 106). To make the bullets there were small stone bullet molds (*mdel par* or *rde'u par*), which could be carried in a leather case attached to a waist belt (cat. no. 109).

While early documentation for the use of firearms in central Tibet appears to be lacking before the late seventeenth century, they were recorded in Ladakh at least as early as the reign of King Senge Namgyal (*seng ge rnam rgyal*, r. ca. 1590–ca. 1640), who succeeded in conquering the kingdom of Guge and much of western Tibet, and whose personal skill with bow and matchlock is mentioned in the Chronicles of Ladakh (*la dvags rgyal rabs*).[3] The same source also gives a list of gifts presented by the king to a leading religious figure, which included twenty-five matchlocks, twenty-five spears, twenty-five swords, and fifteen armors.[4] The earliest extant matchlocks in a potentially datable context appear to be those found in the gonkhang of Phyang Monastery in Ladakh, which are said to date from the time of Senge Namgyal's immediate predecessors (see fig. 9). Also, the remains of firearms, probably dating from no later than the 1630s, have been found in the ruins of Tsaparang, the capital of Guge.[5] Firearms appear to have been introduced into Bhutan around the same time. According to a biography of Shabdrung Ngawang Namgyal (*zhabs drug ngag dbang rnam rgyal*, 1594–1651), the first ruler of a unified Bhutan, he was given matchlock muskets, cannon, and gunpowder by a Portuguese emissary in 1635–36; which were said to be instrumental in his subsequent military victories.[6]

In Europe the matchlock was primarily an infantry weapon, but in Tibet and Central Asia it was also used on horseback in the same way as the bow. A relatively early image of this is found among the murals decorating the walls of the Fifth Dalai Lama's Chorten Hall in the Potala Palace, Lhasa, which depict the celebrations held in 1694 to mark the completion of the Potala.[7] In it riders gallop past a target and shoot arrows at it, followed by riders armed with matchlocks, who shoot at the same target as they ride past it. As mentioned previously, a version of this event continued well into the twentieth century as part of the Great Prayer Festival in Lhasa (see fig. 45). Fairly realistic depictions of matchlocks are also sometimes included in paintings of offerings (*rgyan tshogs*) to the guardian deities from the seventeenth century onward.[8] Beyond its obvious military applications, use in festivals, and iconographic depictions, however, the matchlock musket was recognized primarily as an essential possession of pastoralists and nomads for hunting and personal protection, and as such was found throughout Tibet until relatively recently.

1. According to Rockhill (1895, p. 712), the leather was sometimes the skin of a wild ass.

2. Five examples of these bags, collected by William Rockhill, are found in the Smithsonian's National Museum of Natural History, E167299.

3. Francke 1999, pp. 96, 143; Petech 1999, pp. 146ff.; Francke 1914–26, vol. 2, pp. 39 (Tibetan text), 108 (English trans.). It is interesting to note that the term for matchlock in the passage cited in Francke 1914–26 is *glog*, literally, "lightning."

4. The terms are *me mda'* (matchlocks), *mdung* (spears), *ral gri* (swords), and *khrab* (armor), given to stag tshang ras chen, cited in Franke 1914–26, vol. 2, pp. 40, 109.

5. *Guge* 1991, vol. 1, pp. 226–30, vol. 2, pls. CXXXII, CXXXIII.

6. I am very grateful to Gene Smith for pointing this out and for providing copies of the relevant pages of his typescript transliterations from an 18th-century biography of Shabdrung Ngawang Namgyal, *dpal 'brug pa rin po che ngag dbang rnam rgyal gyi rnam par thar pa chos kyi sprin zhes bya ba rgyas pa las nye ba'i gleng gzhi bod kyi skor*, fol. 96r–v; and from an untitled manuscript history of Bhutan compiled ca. 1963 by gnyer chen bgres pa, pp. 56–59.

7. Guise 1988, pp. 58ff.; Liu 1988, pl. 363.

8. In *Rituels tibétains* 2002, no. 66, just to the right of center is a complete lamellar armor seen from the rear with a shield and a matchlock slung across its back; no. 70 includes three armors with three matchlocks in a similar fashion.

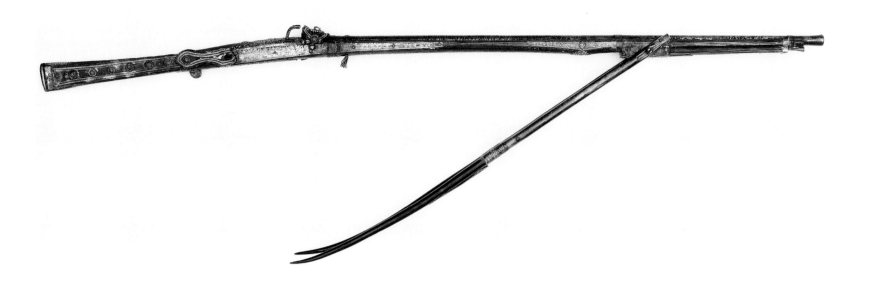

99. MATCHLOCK MUSKET

Tibetan, 18th–19th century
Iron, wood, silver, leather, horn, bone, turquoise, gilded copper, and textile
L. overall 65½ in. (166.5 cm); L. barrel 43¾ in. (111 cm)
Royal Armouries Museum, Leeds (XXVIF.227)

This gun is notable for the overall attention to the details of its decoration, particularly the number and quality of the matching embossed silver plaques attached to its stock. The plaques are embossed in low relief with curling leafy scroll patterns and are attached by silver nails. There are three of them on the underside of the fore-stock; a long trigger panel beneath the lock with a slot for the bottom of the serpentine; narrow panels on either side of the fore-stock just behind the horn block; a long panel behind the breech with a slot for the top of the serpentine (see detail); and a short tablike panel at the base of the butt. The end of the butt is wrapped with a band of silver engraved with the wave motif (*chu ris*), and there is a butt cap made of three narrow layers of horn and bone. The match-cord pouch is faced with red wool, edged with multicolor herringbone trim and shagreen piping, and has six embossed silver rosettes along its front and one on the cover flap. The pan cover is made of similar materials and has an embossed rosette on each side and a turquoise in the center in a gilded-copper rosette setting. Each of the horns has an engraved silver cap at the top and a partially gilded silver band in the center. The top half of the horns are made of wood and the bottom half from actual horn. One horn is reinforced, or has been repaired, just below the center band with a tab of engraved iron.

The barrel is plain, as is often the case, even on guns such as this with very decorative stocks. It flares out slightly at the muzzle and is forged in a twist pattern, that is, a spiraling iron band that has been hammer-welded into a tube, which was a standard way of producing gun barrels. At the base of the breech there is a peep sight, which is an upright half-round flange pierced by a single hole for sighting along the barrel when taking aim. The barrel is lashed to the fore-stock in three places with iron wire.

PROVENANCE: Christie's, London, October 13, 1998, lot 162.

99, detail

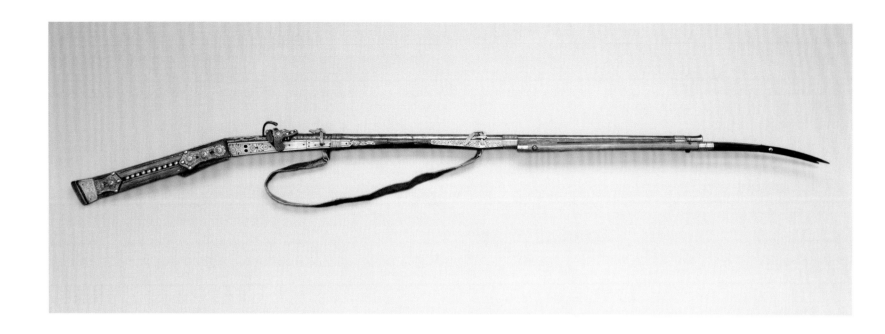

100. MATCHLOCK MUSKET

Eastern Tibetan, 19th–20th century
Iron, wood, silver or copper alloy, bone, leather, and textile
L. 62 in. (157.5 cm)
The Newark Museum, Edward N. Crane Memorial Collection (11.639)

Although this gun closely resembles other Tibetan matchlocks in form and construction, its decoration is very unusual. The standard approach, so well represented by the previous example, involves the application of embossed silver plaques to the stock. In this instance, however, rather than silver plaques, the principal decoration consists of the extensive use of engraved bone plaques and bone designs inlaid into the stock. In addition, the few embossed metal plaques and rosettes on this gun have in the past been identified as white brass but appear instead to be low-grade silver.[1]

Bone plaques engraved with patterns of circles are inset on the side of the stock in place of the more usual iron lock plate; scrollwork and concentric-circle motifs in bone are inlaid into the fore-stock, in the area behind the breech, opposite the lock-plate area, and covering most of the cheek stock (the gun butt on the side opposite the match pouch; see detail). All of the bone appliqués appear to be secured by small wooden pegs. The metal ornament features the Wish-Fulfilling Jewel embossed or cast in low relief on the underside of the horn block (see detail) and plaques with low-relief scrollwork on the sides of the fore-stock. Floral rosettes cast in high relief are found on the leather pan cover and the flaps of the match-cord pouch, which are also decorated with dome-headed tacks. The pouch still contains a length of match cord.

The barrel is plain iron and is lashed to the fore-stock in three places with wire. It flares slightly at the muzzle and has a bead sight. The fore-stock appears to have been repaired or partially replaced at some point. The sling is attached by leather loops tied through transverse holes in the fore-stock and in front of the lock. The horns have metal caps at the end and metal bands in the middle where the wooden upper half is joined to the lower half, which is made of actual horn.

This gun was part of the first group of a large and very important collection of Tibetan objects acquired by the Newark Museum from Dr. Albert L. Shelton (1875–1922), a missionary and medical practitioner who was active in western China and east-ern Tibet from 1904 until his death.[2] He is said to have acquired it in Batang, in Kham (now part of the Kandze Autonomous Prefecture in the western part of Sichuan Province, China).[3]

PROVENANCE: Dr. Albert L. Shelton.

PUBLICATIONS: Olson 1950–71, vol. 5, p. 23 and pl. 15; Reynolds 1999, pl. 8.

1. See Olson 1950–71, vol. 5, p. 23. White brass is copper alloyed with at least 45% zinc. Richard Stone (personal communication) suggests that the mounts may be an alloy of copper, nickel, and zinc, which was frequently used in China and is called *paktong*, the equivalent of so-called German silver or nickel silver in the West. The use of this alloy for ornamentation of Tibetan guns and swords, especially in eastern Tibet, may be more widespread than generally realized. Valrae Reynolds has recently identified the mounts on the Newark gun as low-grade silver (personal communication).
2. On Shelton's career and the growth of the Tibetan collection at the Newark Museum, see Reynolds 1999, pp. 11–21; Wissing 2004.
3. I am grateful to Valrae Reynolds for information on the provenance of this piece.

100, detail of underside of horn block

100, detail of cheek stock

101. MATCHLOCK MUSKET

Tibetan, 19th century
Iron, wood, leather, brass, and copper
L. overall 58¾ in. (149.2 cm); L. barrel 39⅛ in. (99.4 cm); bore .55
caliber (14 mm)
The Metropolitan Museum of Art, New York, Bequest of George
C. Stone, 1935 (36.25. 2174)
See also illustrations in cat. no. 46

This is a good example of a fairly plain but well-made and utilitarian Tibetan matchlock in relatively complete condition. Its fittings consist of a small engraved copper cap at the tip of the fore-stock; a plain brass plate on either side of the fore-stock just behind the horn block, where it is pierced by a transverse hole for a loop to hold the front of the sling; and an iron lock plate on both sides of the stock. Behind the breech is the most decorative feature of the gun—a very simple pierced copper plate (the escutcheon plate) with scrollwork, lions, and a *garuda* motif, which is pierced by a slot for the upper arm of the serpentine (see detail). The match-cord pouch is made of leather and is unusual in having a lengthwise flap that closes over eleven copper rings, which pass through slots in the flap. The plain iron barrel flares at the muzzle and has a bead sight on the top of the muzzle and a peep sight at the base of the breech. The twist pattern of the barrel forging is also faintly visible. The barrel is attached to the stock by two copper bands and five cord wrappings (the latter are restorations). The horns have no metal caps or bands, and the lower halves are made entirely of iron, rather than horn. There are the remains of a barrel plug, which was originally attached by a cord to the horns. Barrel plugs, usually made of a roll of leather or felt with a decorative horsehair tuft, were inserted in the end of the barrel when the gun was not in use to keep out dirt and other debris. The ramrod is missing.

PROVENANCE: W. O. Oldman, London; George Cameron Stone, New York.

PUBLICATIONS: Stone 1934, p. 444, fig. 565, no. 1; LaRocca 1999a, p. 128, fig. 29.

101, detail

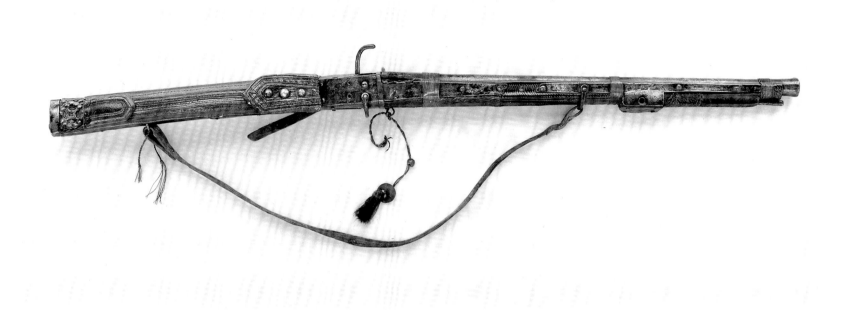

102. MATCHLOCK MUSKET

Tibetan, 17th–19th century
Iron, wood, leather, copper, and textile
L. overall 40 in. (101.6 cm); L. barrel 22¼ in. (56.5 cm); bore .65 caliber (17 mm)
The Metropolitan Museum of Art, New York, Bequest of George C. Stone, 1935 (36.25.2173)

Shorter by 1½–2 feet than most Tibetan match-locks, this gun may have been specifically designed for use on horseback and is roughly the equivalent of a European carbine, which was a shorter version of the musket developed for cavalry use in the seventeenth century. It is also an incredibly sturdy gun, being clad over virtually its entire surface with leather and iron.

The stock is encased from the tip of the fore-stock to the butt cap in a form-fitting leather cover, which was probably stretched over the stock when slightly damp and then stitched in place. The stock is further reinforced with extended iron plates along the sides of the fore-stock, including the sides and bottom of the horn block; longer than usual lock plates on both sides; a trigger plate with a long slot for the lower arm of the serpentine; and, behind the breech, an iron escutcheon plate, which has a long, narrow extension with a leaf-shaped finial (see detail), similar to the iron struts used on cane shields and leather arm defenses (see cat. nos. 24, 35). The upper arm of the serpentine protrudes through a slot in the escutcheon plate. The butt cap is also iron, rather than the usual layers of bone and horn. The match-cord pouch, still containing a length of match cord, is made of leather trimmed with leather piping and has three dome-headed tacks on the cover flap. The only applied decoration consists of a coin motif made of pierced iron backed with red wool, which is attached to the stock on either side just in front of the butt cap. There are also an actual Tibetan coin (a silver *ṭam ka*) and a jade bead hanging on a tasseled cord attached to a ring on the underside of the stock beneath the lock.[1] Two pivoted iron loops for the sling are attached to the underside of the stock.

At .65 caliber, the bore of the barrel is the same as that of several eighteenth-century British carbine models designed for cavalry and light infantry use, although the length of the barrel and overall length of the gun are slightly shorter by comparison.[2] The barrel is securely attached to the stock by three bind-ings of copper wire. It has a bead sight and a peep

102, detail

sight; it flares slightly at the muzzle and is undecorated. The ramrod is also made of iron. The horns are missing or have been intentionally removed.

Most Tibetan matchlocks vary only in their degree of decoration or quality of workmanship; otherwise they would serve equally well for hunting, target shooting, or, if needed, warfare. This gun, on the other hand, was built to withstand particularly rigorous conditions and may have been designed principally for military use.

PROVENANCE: W. O. Oldman, London; George Cameron Stone, New York.

PUBLICATION: Stone 1934, p. 444, fig. 565, no. 2.

1. For this coin, see Olson 1950–71, vol. 5, p. 26, pl. 16, nos. 1, 2.
2. Compare with the measurements of British military carbines given in Blackmore 1961, p. 277.

103. MINIATURE VOTIVE MUSKET

Tibetan, 17th–19th century
Iron, gold, silver, wood, pigments, horn, and leather
L. overall 14⅛ in. (35.9 cm); L. barrel 6¾ in. (17.1 cm); bore .28 caliber (7 mm)
The Metropolitan Museum of Art, New York, Purchase, Arthur Ochs Sulzberger Gift, 2001 (2001.34)

This miniature musket is constructed with the same basic materials and techniques as a full-size Tibetan matchlock musket, and it is one of only a few known Tibetan weapons made as working scale models, in contrast to miniature ritual objects in the form of weapons that are made as pieces of decorative metalwork. It should be compared with the miniature armor and spearhead discussed earlier (cat. nos. 2, 79).

The iron barrel is damascened in gold with four of the Eight Auspicious Symbols (endless knot, golden fish, vase, and lotus) supported by lotus pedestals and set among scrolls on a silver ground (see detail). At the muzzle and the breech there are geometric borders of the thunder-scroll pattern. There is a bead foresight at the muzzle and a priming pan and touchhole at the breech. The barrel is secured to the fore-stock by two leather thongs, which pass over the barrel and through the sides of the fore-stock, emerging through two pairs of holes on the underside of the fore stock where they are knotted and extend to form the sling. The stock is carved from one piece of wood and has a flat paddle-shaped butt with a squared end. The sides of the stock are slightly concave. A slot for the upper arm of the serpentine is cut through the stock at the rear right of the breech, and there is a corresponding long rectangular slot in the underside of the stock for the lower arm, but the serpentine itself is missing. The ramrod and fore-end cap are also missing. The stock is painted overall with yellow designs on a red ground. The decoration features a grinning dry skull (*thod skam*) and a severed head (*dbu bcad*) with flowing hair seen in profile on each side of the butt, joined by scrolling tendrils, probably stylized entrails, which continue over the rest of the stock. A shallow rectangular recess cut into the cheek side of the stock has the remains of a painted inscription in *dbu can* script (effaced and illegible except for partial characters). The horns consist of two slender, slightly curved prongs of actual horn, with a short peg acting as a spacer between them. There is also a wooden barrel plug attached to the sling by a slender leather cord.

The decoration on the stock suggests that this gun was intended for use in a ritual context and not just as a toy or a model. The motifs of dry skulls and severed heads linked by stylized entrails belong to the imagery associated with offerings to, and attributes of, wrathful guardian deities (see cat. nos. 78, 105). Given its size, this miniature gun may have been intended as an offering for a portable altar dedicated to a guardian deity, or perhaps as a votive object in a small household shrine. The inscription on the stock, which may have shed light on its origin or intended use, appears to have been purposely effaced.

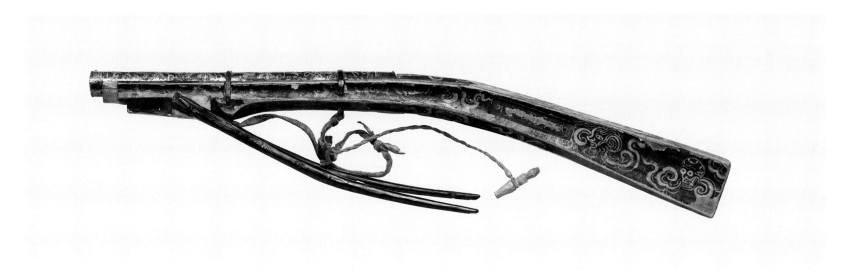

103, left side

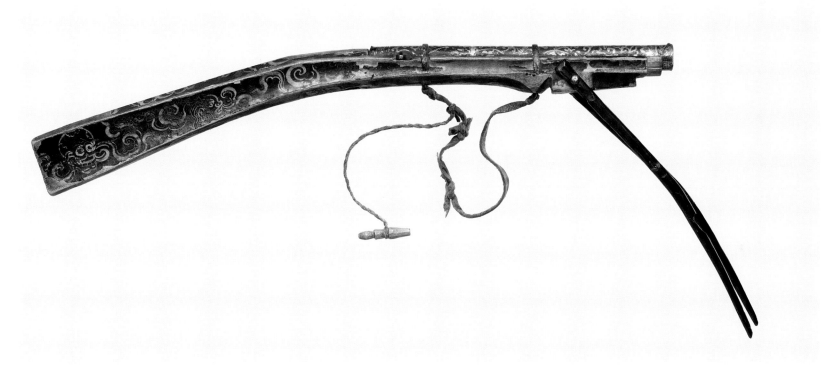

103, right side

103, detail of barrel

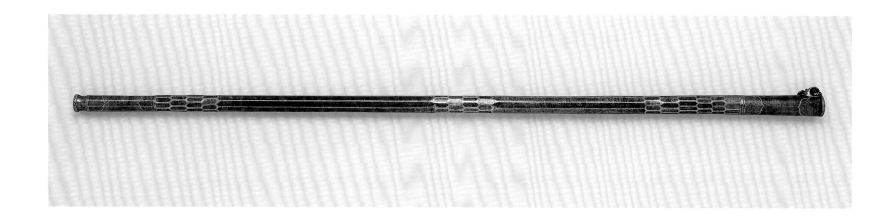

104. MUSKET BARREL

Tibetan, 18th–19th century
Iron, gold, and silver
L. 46⅛ in. (117.2 cm); bore .65 caliber (17 mm)
The Metropolitan Museum of Art, New York, Purchase, Arthur Ochs Sulzberger Gift, 2001 (2001.62)

This is the single most finely made gun barrel known from Tibet. It also appears to be unique in that it bears an inscription positively identifying it as having been made in Tibet, which is contrary to the general belief that all musket barrels used in Tibet were made in India or China.[1] Stylistically the form and decoration of this barrel can be compared with examples from India and Persia, both countries that were well known for producing finely made and richly decorated gun barrels.

The barrel is smooth bore, decorated in seven stages, and made of pattern-welded iron or steel in a twist pattern, sometimes referred as a Damascus barrel. The first stage (at the breech area) is rounded in section, with a slight medial ridge. It is decorated with two ogival or mihrab-shaped cartouches outlined by a fine line of inlaid gold. Engraved within the cartouches there are scrolling foliate vine motifs damascened in gold. The second stage consists of six rows of offset facets or chamfers forming an elongated honeycomb pattern. Each chamfer is outlined by a double border consisting of two finely inlaid lines, the outer line in gold and the inner line in silver. The center chamfer of the bottom row (above the first molding) is inlaid in gold with a Tibetan inscription in *dbu can* characters, which reads *bod brdungs yin*, meaning "forged [or hammered] in Tibet" (see detail). The third and fifth stages are

polygonal in section, with five long undecorated chamfers. The fourth and sixth stages have faceted honeycomb patterns like the second stage, but with only four rows each. The seventh stage is decorated with ogival cartouches, like those on the breech, and has five chamfers. The belled muzzle is decorated with inlaid gold and silver lines, which simulate chamfering, and has a gold bead as a foresight. Ring moldings separate the first and second stages and the sixth and seventh stages. The underside of the barrel is half-round in section for its entire length and has no barrel lugs. There is an arch-shaped peep sight with a central notch on its top edge at the base of the breech. The priming pan consists of a shallow, open bowl with a cusped forward extension. A small node on the extension indicates that it was originally fitted with a pan cover, a feature not typically found on Tibetan gun barrels, but which is not uncommon on Indo-Persian examples. The front edge of the bowl has been repaired.

Writing in 1905, L. A. Waddell recorded that by the late nineteenth century the arsenal in Lhasa included two Muslim craftsmen from India who were producing good copies of the British Martini-Henry rifle, a regulation military weapon.[2] The pattern-welded twist of the barrel, the shape of the muzzle and the priming pan, and the style of the decoration suggest that this musket barrel was also

104, detail of inscription

the work of an Indian or Indian-trained craftsman, probably working in Lhasa during the eighteenth or nineteenth century.

1. Rockhill 1895, p. 713; this has been repeated by subsequent writers on the subject.
2. Waddell 1905, pp. 170, 427.

105. BARREL FROM A CEREMONIAL MUSKET

Tibetan, 17th–19th century
Iron, gold, copper, and silver
L. 29⅛ in. (74 cm); bore .75 caliber (19 mm)
The Metropolitan Museum of Art, New York, Purchase, Arthur Ochs Sulzberger Gift, 2005 (2005.143)

The barrel is smooth bore, round in section, with a flared octagonal muzzle and ring moldings at the muzzle and the breech. There is a copper bead sight at the muzzle and a peep sight at the base of the breech. The priming pan extends out from beneath the touchhole at the right side of the breech. The barrel has a russet brown patina and is decorated along its length with a series of three dry skulls (*thod skam*), engraved and then damascened in gold and silver (see detail). A single curling tendril of stylized flame, done in the same technique, issues from the top of each skull. At the base of the breech there is an ogival cartouche filled with large symmetrical scrollwork, also damascened in gold and silver.

The decoration strongly suggests that this musket barrel was intended for ritual or votive use, dry skulls often being found on objects designed for propitiation of the fierce guardian deities. Similar motifs

of dry skulls and tendrils have been seen on a spear and on the miniature musket (cat. nos. 78, 103). The presence of the motifs on this barrel and the spear suggests that they were either installed as part of the panoply of armor and weapons often found in shines devoted to a guardian deity, or that they were designed for use in a divination ceremony conducted by a high-ranking oracle, such as the State Oracle formerly at Nechung in Tibet.

PROVENANCE: Gérard Labre, France; sold, Hôtel Drouot, March 11, 2005, lot 42.

PUBLICATIONS: *Rituels tibétains* 2002, no. 111, p. 149 (color illus.), lent by Gérard Labre; *Arts primitifs, arts d'Asie: Collection Gérard Labre, arts de l'Himalaya, bibliothèque Annie de Vriese-Jernander, important ensemble d'ouvrages sur l'Extrême-Orient et l'art tribal,* sale cat., Cornette de Saint Cyr, Hôtel Drouot, salle 6, March 11, 2005, pp. 24–25 (color illus.).

105, detail of decoration

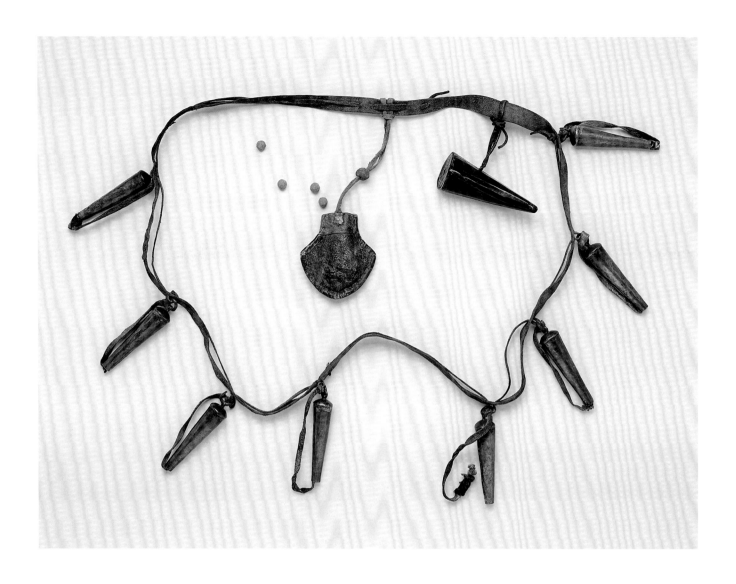

106. BANDOLIER

Tibetan, 19th century
Leather, horn, copper, textile, and lead
The Metropolitan Museum of Art, New York, Bequest of George C. Stone, 1935 (36.25.2461)
See also cat. no. 46

A bandolier was worn over one shoulder and diagonally across the chest and was made to carry gunpowder and bullets. This example has eight chargers, conical copper tubes, each of which would hold a premeasured amount of powder sufficient for a single shot. A continuous leather lace is threaded through a copper ring at the base of each charger, attaching it to the bandolier strap. Each charger is fitted with a wool stopper, which is also attached to the ring by a short strip of leather. A leather bullet pouch contains five round lead bullets, or musket balls, each measuring about 11 millimeters in diameter, and is suspended from the bandolier strap by a knotted leather cord, as is a small priming flask made of horn. This held the gunpowder for the priming pan of the musket. It has a flexible strip of horn running from its base to its tip, which, when squeezed, would open the tip of the horn and allow powder to be poured out.

PROVENANCE: W. O. Oldman, London; George Cameron Stone, New York.

PUBLICATIONS: Stone 1934, p. 91, fig. 116, no.1; LaRocca 1999a, p. 128, fig. 29.

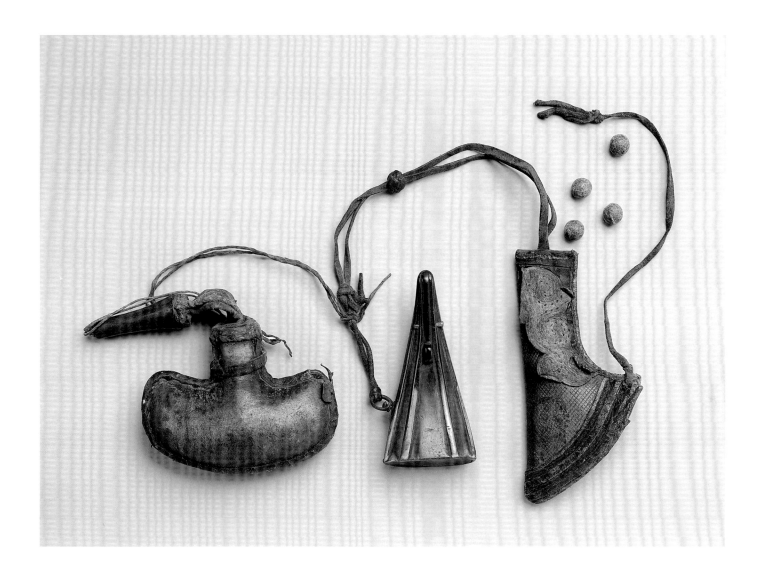

107. BULLET POUCH, PRIMING FLASK, AND POWDER FLASK

Tibetan, 19th century
Leather, horn, lead, and iron
The Metropolitan Museum of Art, New York, Bequest of George C. Stone, 1935 (36.25.2340)

Like the bandolier in the preceding entry, this set would hold the material necessary to load and prime a musket for firing. Unlike the bandolier, the three elements would be worn suspended from a waist belt or tucked into the folds of a garment. The powder for the main charge was stored in the bulbous flask made of hard leather, instead of in the individual chargers of the bandolier. At its top this has a short flexible tube of soft leather with a nozzle made of horn, which is closed by a leather stopper attached to a thin leather string. The nozzle also

acted as a powder measure; inverting the flask filled the nozzle with enough powder for a single charge (i.e., the amount needed to load the gun once). The priming flask, made of horn like the previous example, held the powder for the priming pan. The bullet pouch has an asymmetrical shape characteristic of this type and is made of stiff leather decorated with leather appliqués. By squeezing the sides, the top opens enough to allow the lead bullets to be poured out. This pouch contains twelve round lead bullets, each measuring about 14 millimeters in diameter.

George Stone illustrated the powder flask from this set and identified it by the name *hmam skuk*, which may be a phonetic version of *sman khug*. The more usual term for this type seems to be *rdzas khug*, meaning "gunpowder flask."

PROVENANCE: W. O. Oldman, London; George Cameron Stone, New York.

PUBLICATION: Stone 1934, p. 239, fig. 369, no. 1 (powder flask only).

108. POWDER FLASK

Tibetan or Mongolian, possibly 16th–17th century
Leather, horn, shellac, gold, and pigments
L. 10½ in. (26.7 cm)
The Metropolitan Museum of Art, New York, Bequest of George
C. Stone, 1935 (36.25.2339)

This powder flask is similar to the preceding example, the bulbous type made of hard leather with a flexible leather tube and a horn nozzle. It is noteworthy, however, because the leather is gilded and varnished like that of the arm defenses and archery equipment seen earlier (cat. nos. 36–38, 94, 95). The layout of the decoration is also very similar, with the upper third bordered by a diagonal line of repeating swastikas. Above the border there is a large-scale flora pattern; the decoration in the lower section is too badly damaged to read. The presence of the decoration on a powder flask demonstrates that decoration in this style and technique was in use, at least initially, in the same period as firearms, suggesting that the leather arm defenses and the use of firearms may have overlapped for a time. For comments on George Stone's term for this type of powder flask, see the preceding entry.

PROVENANCE: W. O. Oldman, London; George Cameron Stone, New York.

PUBLICATION: Stone 1934, p. 239, fig. 369, no. 3.

109. BULLET MOLD AND CASE

Tibetan, 19th century
Stone, leather, lead, and textile
Size of assembled mold 1¾ x 1⅝ x 1⅜ in. (4.5 x 4.1 x 3.5 cm)
The Metropolitan Museum of Art, New York, Bequest of George
C. Stone, 1935 (36.25.2459a–c)

The mold consists of two halves and is made to cast two musket balls in lead at the same time. The halves of the mold are incised in Tibetan on the front and back with the numbers 1 and 2, and across the seams with the number 1 on one side and a swastika motif on the other. There are also two lead pegs on the face of one half, which fit into corresponding sockets in the other, to ensure that the halves are properly aligned. The cast bullets measure approximately 12.5 millimeters in diameter. Stone identified the material of the mold as soapstone. It fits snugly into its original case made of dark leather, which has at the top, for attachment to a belt or sash, a narrow leather strap formed into a loop by a braided slipknot. Another mold of this type is found in the collection of the University of Nebraska State Museum, Lincoln (A712).[1]

PROVENANCE: W. O. Oldman, London; George Cameron Stone, New York.

PUBLICATION: Stone 1934, p. 155, fig. 198, no. 2.

1. Accessioned in 1947, it was given to the museum by Edgar Nichols, who had been a missionary to Paan, Sikong, China. It has recesses for casting up to seven bullets and does not have a case. From the same source the university also received a Tibetan matchlock gun (A710), bandolier (A711), and leather bullet bag (A713). I am grateful to Beth Wilkins for this information.

108

109

110. BELT WITH ACCESSORIES

Tibetan, 19th century
Iron, leather, bone, horn, ray skin, copper, silver, textile
The Metropolitan Museum of Art, New York, Bequest of George C. Stone, 1935 (36.25.842a–c)

The belt has five iron mounts pierced with a scrollwork pattern. One mount on each side has a pivoted D-ring from which different accessories are suspended on leather cords. A matching leather needle case (*khab shubs*) and a bullet pouch hang on the left, and a steel and tinder pouch (*me lcags*) hangs on the right. A dagger hangs from a leather strap at the end of the belt opposite the buckle end. Bone dice, copper coins, and braided leather slipknots are strung on suspension cords. The needle case and bullet pouch are decorated with gilded-leather and appliquéd-leather scrollwork. The leatherwork on the bullet pouch is very ornate for this type of object and compares closely with the elaborate appliquéd leather found on a set of saddle pads acquired by William Rockhill, identified by him as from Poyul (*dpal yul*) in eastern Tibet.[1] The tinder pouch has an iron frame with simple piercings. The dagger hilt has a grip made of horn plaques with diamond-shaped iron fittings and an iron pommel cap. The single-edged blade is well made and has an interesting pattern-welding design of symmetrically undulating wavy lines, which is largely unreadable now due to abrasion. The sheath is made of wood covered in iron, with two small panels of ray skin in the center. George Stone listed the source of this belt and accessories as Darjeeling.[2]

PROVENANCE: George Cameron Stone, New York.

1. Rockhill 1894, facing p. 192 (National Museum of Natural History, cat. no. 131049). I am grateful to Felicia Pickering for her assistance in the examination of the saddle set.
2. Object card catalogue, Department of Arms and Armor, Metropolitan Museum.

ক্লু'ক্ত৯খঁব'ৼৼৼৠৢব

Saddles and Tack, Stirrups, and Bridles

The saddles (*sga*) found in Tibet are a mixture of Mongol, Chinese, and Tibetan types and styles.[1] The structure of a saddle consists of a wood frame, called the saddletree (*sga lag* and perhaps *sga khyim*).[2] This is made up of four basic parts: an arch-shaped front and back, called the pommel (*snga ru*) and the cantle (*phyi ru*), connected by a pair of sideboards (*sga gshog* or *sga ldebs*), which are tightly tied together with leather laces. On most Asian saddles the sideboards have short paddlelike extensions, or end-boards (*sga yag*), in the front and back.[3] The section of the sideboards between the pommel and the cantle where the rider would sit is usually covered by a cushion (*sga 'bol*), which is attached by two or four ornamental bosses (*sga 'bor*). A set of saddle rugs (*sga gdan*) was also used, one on the horse's back underneath the saddle and one above, on the seat of the saddle.

The most outstanding components of a Tibetan saddle are the metal plates that cover the outside of the pommel, cantle, and end-boards. Although these plates reinforce the saddletree, they function chiefly as a very visible and often very elaborate form of ornament, and as clear indicators of the rank, status, and importance of the rider. They can be made of copper alloy or silver, but the finest are done in pierced and chiseled iron, usually damascened in gold and silver, and constitute some of the best examples of Tibetan and Sino-Tibetan ironwork of any kind. The use of decorative metal saddle plates originated very early, possibly among the nomadic steppe cultures of Central Asia. Among the earliest complete examples is a set of pierced and gilded bronze saddle plates from a fourth-century Xanbei tomb found in Inner Mongolia.[4] A complete set of gilded silver Liao saddle plates from a tomb dated to 959 shows not only the development of forms but also of some primary decorative motifs, such as dragons flanking a flaming jewel, that continued to be used on Tibetan and Chinese saddles until the twentieth century.[5] The date of the first pierced-iron saddle plates (as opposed to bronze or silver) is not known, but it may have occurred during the Yuan dynasty as either a Mongol or Tibetan innovation. One of the finest and earliest iron examples can be seen in catalogue number III.

The straps that accompany a saddle are referred to as the tack and include the girth or cinch strap (*sga glo*), which is usually plain leather or a woven fabric; a breast strap (*gong* or *gong thag*) across the front of the horse's chest; and the crupper straps (*rmed*), which go over the top of the horse's rump and have a band that passes under the tail. When attached to decorated saddles, the breast strap and especially the crupper often have pierced-metal fittings, which can be equally as elaborate as those of the saddle itself (cat. nos. 121, 124, 133). The same is true for bridles (*srab*), the best of which

can have very delicately pierced fittings and pierced and chiseled work on the exposed sides of the bit (cat. nos. 134, 135).

The most immediately recognizable feature of the stirrups (*yob*) found in Tibet, China, and Mongolia is the nearly ubiquitous pair of dragon heads at the top of the arch, flanking the slot for the stirrup leathers. The stirrups are usually made of iron and can be chiseled in high or low relief, often including pierced work, and may be extensively damascened in gold and silver. They are basically made up of two posts (*rkang*) that form an arch over the foot and a tread (*mthil*) on which the foot rests. Beyond these similarities, however, there is an almost infinite variety in the form, decoration, and quality of stirrups from these regions. The discussion of stirrups in the Tashi Namgyal texts is one of the few chapters that is succinct and unambiguous enough to be quoted in full here. It is interesting not only for its comparison of Mongol, Chinese, and Tibetan stirrups but also for the information it gives about the techniques involved in their decoration.[6]

*There are three types of stirrups, Mongol (*hor*), Chinese, and Tibetan.[7] Mongol stirrups have fine dragon heads and two posts, one on the right and one on the left, which are completely round in section.[8] In terms of shape, the tread is level [or even] and proportionate in size. The decoration is done by gold and silver inlay.[9] On Chinese stirrups the dragon heads are a little less fine. The two posts on the left and right are flat, rather than round. The tread is also a little bit oblong [or concave, like a shallow dish]. They are decorated with gold and silver damascening. There are two sizes of Chinese stirrups, large and small. The smaller are called "queen's treasured stirrups" (*btsun mo gan yob*). Tibetan stirrups are like these smaller Chinese stirrups, but finer and of smaller proportions, and there is less gold and silver damascening.*

*The inlay [and damascening] techniques of the three: Mongol Chinese, and Tibetan. For the type of inlay done on Mongol stirrups, channels are engraved (*dong brkos par*) and by laying in flat strips of gold (*gser leb*) most of the surface is covered with gold. For the gold damascening of Chinese stirrups the iron is finely cut (*btsabs par*, i.e., crosshatched) and by laying in gold wire (*gser skud*) small areas are covered with gold. Tibetan damascening is like that of the Chinese, but in comparison it is a little unsteady (*mi brtan pa*, i.e., less precisely rendered or less durable).*

It should be kept in mind that many extant stirrups do not strictly correspond to these descriptions, perhaps because the writer was familiar with only certain types of stirrups. Nevertheless, the passage is very valuable, especially as it may be the only traditional Tibetan commentary on the subject.

1. Although this is an observation based on the appearance of extant saddles, Tashi Namgyal, writing in 1524, commented that at that time the newer types of Tibetan saddles were based on various Hor (Mongol) and Chinese models (Beinecke, fol. 53a; British Library Or 11,374, fol. 98a; see the appendix "Excerpts from *A Treatise on Worldly Traditions*").

2. *Sga khyim* appears to be the equivalent of *sga lag*, or saddletree, based on its usage in the Tashi Namgyal texts cited in the preceding note.

3. End-boards is suggested here as a translation of *sga yag* to supply the lack of a convenient English term that describes the projecting ends at the front and rear of the sideboards, which extend well beyond the pommel and cantle on many types of Asian saddles, but which are not found on saddles in European or English-speaking contexts. The closest terms in English saddle nomenclature appear to be front jockey and back jockey, but in describing Asian saddles the term end-boards seems clearer and more descriptive as a complement to the term sideboards. The full definition for *sga yag* (*bod rgya*, p. 584) is "sga'i snga ru'i mdun dang / phyi ru'i rgyab nas thon pa'i sga gshog gi sne mo" (The extremities [or tips] of the saddle wings [the sideboards], which extend from the front of the pommel and the back of the cantle of a saddle).

4. *L'Asie des steppes: D'Alexandre le Grand à Gengis Khan*, exh. cat. (Paris, 2000), p. 163, no. 152.

5. Ibid, pp. 182–83, no. 166.

6. Translation based on a comparison of Beinecke, fols. 52b–53a; Burmiok Athing, fols. 30b–31a; British Library Or 11,374, fols. 96b–97b; Hūṃkaradzaya (Gangtok 1981), pp. 239–40; see the appendix "Excerpts from *A Treatise on Worldly Traditions*."

7. The term *hor* can refer to different groups of Mongols or the region and peoples of Turkistan, depending on the time and context. Both *hor* and *sog po* are usually translated as Mongol. It is interesting to note that in the texts cited above Genghis Khan is mentioned in the sword and saddle chapters as the king of Hor.

8. The translation of *gtsang* as "fine" follows Tucci 1959, p. 179.

9. The Tibetan term is *tshags*, which according to the context of the text refers both to true inlay and to damascening. The alternate meanings of *tshags*, relating to strainers, sieves, and the weave of textiles, make sense in this regard in that they involve the type of pattern produced by the cross-hatching utilized in the damascening technique. The English distinction between the two techniques becomes apparent in the description of the decoration of the *hor* stirrups versus those of China and Tibet, further on in the text.

111. SET OF SADDLE PLATES

Tibetan or Chinese, ca. 1400

Iron, gold, lapis lazuli, and turquoise

H. as mounted 9⅞ in. (25 cm)

The Metropolitan Museum of Art, New York, Purchase, Gift of William H. Riggs, by exchange, and Kenneth and Vivian Lam Gift, 1999 (1999.118)

This set of saddle plates represents a high point in the medium of pierced ironwork, equaling or excelling anything of its type so far recorded, including the group of ritual implements bearing Hongwu (r. 1368–98) and Yongle (r. 1403–24) reign marks that were made in the Tibetan style in the Chinese imperial workshops (discussed in cat. nos. 55–57).

The set consists of seven plates, which would cover the pommel, the cantle and the step beneath the arch of the cantle, the front end-boards, and the rear end-boards. The plates are made entirely of iron, approximately 5 millimeters thick, and are decorated chiefly with long, thin four-clawed dragons, seen in profile, which undulate sinuously amid a dense scrollwork ground. The piercing and chiseling of the ironwork were done with great skill. The dragons are chiseled in relatively high relief and are very detailed, with the eyes, eyebrows, ears, horns, makara-like snouts, and curling tongues clearly delineated. The bodies of the dragons are lively and fluid, the limbs muscled, and except for their striped underbellies, entirely covered with precise punchwork. Some of the dragons also have unusual features, such as having the pearl on their outstretched tongues instead of, or in addition to, holding it in their claws in the usual way. On the pommel, two of the dragons grasp their own tails with one of their rear paws, which is also very unusual. Although each plate is made from a single piece of iron, the dragons were cut entirely free from the surrounding framework and can be moved slightly within it. The finely chiseled scrollwork ground is strong but also very delicate. The scroll patterns were undercut to give the appearance of depth and overlapping, in addition to the areas that actually overlap the bodies of the dragons. The iron is damascened overall with gold foil, except where it is covered by stones, and the precision and fineness of the cross-hatching beneath the gold is exceptional. One area on the pommel is decorated with an arc of repeating concentric circles within an undulating line damascened in gold, a feature found extensively on the Hongwu and Yongle pieces cited earlier and on other examples of Tibetan ironwork.

In the center of both the pommel and the cantle a Wish-Fulfilling Jewel motif, made from pieces of blue and green turquoise set in shaped compartments in the iron ground, is flanked by pairs of dragons (see detail; see also back cover). Within the bends of the dragons' bodies there are individual lotus blossoms made in the same way. The outer edges of the plates are bordered by a continuous row of half-round pieces of lapis set in compartments. The center of each of the end-board plates contains a circular motif of flower petals formed of green and blue turquoise (see detail). The dragons and scrollwork on the scabbard mounts of the sword in catalogue number 74 are close to those on these saddle plates in terms of quality, but the former, while extremely good, are two-dimensional by comparison, lacking the high relief and undercutting found on the saddle plates.

PUBLICATIONS: Thurman and Weldon 1999, no. 71, pp. 154–55; LaRocca 1999c, pp. 76–77; Pyhrr, LaRocca, and Ogawa 2002, no. 48, pp. 50–51; Pyhrr, LaRocca, and Breiding 2005, p. 19, fig. 12.

111, detail of cantle plate

III, detail of end-board plate

112. SADDLE

Tibetan, 15th–17th century
Iron, gold, copper, wood, and leather
H. 13¾ in. (34.9 cm), L. 23⅜ in. (59.4 cm), W. 15¼ in. (38.7 cm)
The Metropolitan Museum of Art, New York, Purchase, Arthur Ochs Sulzberger Gift, 2002 (2002.225)

The strength of this saddle lies in the quality and extent of its pierced and chiseled decoration, in particular the figural *tsi pa ṭa* masks worked in low relief in the center of the pommel and cantle plates. These are more artistically accomplished and on a larger scale than virtually any other known example of low-relief ironwork from Tibet or China.

The saddle consists of a complete set of ten matching iron saddle plates mounted on a wooden saddletree. The pommel and cantle are each covered by three plates: a large central plate with an arched border plate above and below. There is a single plate on each of the four end-boards. All of the plates are intricately pierced with a dense scrollwork ground, chiseled, and damascened in gold overall. The *tsi pa ṭa* masks have very distinct and well-articulated features, including fiery eyebrows and lips, leonine noses, fangs, horns, and curly hair. The mask on the pommel plate has a flaming Three Jewels motif on its forehead (see detail), while that on the back has the sun and moon motif on its forehead. The surfaces of the masks are stippled with fine punchwork. Other motifs include the Wish-Fulfilling Jewel in the center of the upper border plate of the pommel and cantle, and undulating, four-clawed dragons in profile, which are found singly and in pairs on each of the plates. The plates are attached to the saddletree by copper nails. Although the plates are somewhat abraded and there are significant areas of old corrosion, the surfaces retain traces of what appears to be an original coating that would have been applied to give the gold a warm reddish tone, which was often favored in Tibet over the natural yellow color of gold.[1] Traces of this coating are also found on the saddle plate in catalogue number 115.

The saddletree is made up of four sections of shaped wood, which are tied together by leather laces (see illus.). The underside of the tree is covered with a facing of original red leather. There are Tibetan characters written in black in *dbu med* script on the leather underneath the bow of the pommel, which read *rdor brag* (see detail). This may be an abbreviation of *rdo rje brag* the name of an important Nyingma monastery in southern Tibet that was badly damaged by the Dzungar Mongols in 1717 and largely destroyed during the Cultural Revolution of the 1960s.[2] Portions of the pommel and cantle facing the seat also have the remains of an old leather covering. Modern red fabric has been glued to the front to the pommel and cantle (as a background for the plates).

Many Tibetan saddles have pierced and chiseled ironwork done in this style, but not of this quality. In the great majority, however, the large central plates of the pommel and cantle are made of another, more easily worked material, often embossed and gilded copper (as on cat. no. 116) and sometimes embossed silver. The present saddle is one of the few examples in which the entire set of saddle plates, including the large plates of the pommel and cantle, has been made in the more difficult pierced ironwork technique. This style of ironwork is usually attributed to Derge (*sde dge*), formerly an independent kingdom and a famous metalworking center in the Kham region of eastern Tibet (now part of Ganzi Tibetan Autonomous Prefecture in western Sichuan Province). It was used not only

112, detail of pommel plate

112

112, underside

112, detail of inscription

for saddle plates, but also for tack and bridles (cat. nos. 133–35), sword fittings, pen cases, cup cases (cat. no. 113), door fittings (cat. no. 114), and ritual objects such as censers.

PROVENANCE: Christie's, New York, March 21, 2001, lot 150.

PUBLICATION: *Indian and Southeast Asian Art*, sale cat., Christie's, New York, March 21, 2001, lot 150, p. 137.

1. Dagyab 1977, p. 49.
2. I am grateful to Lozang Jamspal for suggesting the possible connection with *rdo rje brag*.

113. CUP CASE

Eastern Tibetan, 15th century
Wrought iron and gold
H. 2 in. (5 cm), Diam. 6⅛ in. (15.6 cm)
Victoria and Albert Museum, London (IM.162-1913)

This is an iron teacup case of the type used by wealthy noblemen to protect expensive and fragile Chinese porcelain or jade teacups while traveling. The cup would have been packed inside between wads of yak hair, wool, or felt to cushion it in transit. Attached iron loops allow for the case to be hung from a packsaddle or at the side of a horse. Older craftsmen in eastern Tibet can still remember making such pierced-work cases, which were particularly time consuming, taking seven weeks to complete.

The most striking aspect of this object is the decoration of almost its entire surface with delicate pierced scrollwork through which coil the snakelike bodies of several dragons. The thick and even bifurcating scroll form, which compares closely to the scroll found on two saddles, catalogue numbers 111 and 112, is entirely covered by overlaid gold. One of the Tibetan names for this type of scroll is *krab gdan*, or carpet design, and today it tends to be associated stylistically with eastern Tibet. But its other name, *gtsang dkrugs pa tra*, or Tsang scroll, appears to reveal an unexpected, and perhaps distant in time, cross-regional borrowing from southern Tibet, which is as yet unexplored. Four dragons with open mouths and prehensile snouts are closely integrated into the scroll foliage of the outer circle on the lid, their heads resting against the inner circle as if to support it (see also fig. 19). A further single dragon is found in the lid's inner circle, while four others appear on the sides of the case. The lively, long-bodied dragons with four claws are highly comparable to those found on early Ming dynasty textiles of the first half of the fifteenth century, as well as to those on a door fitting from Sera Monastery built in 1419 (see fig. 25, and see also cat. no. 114). These parallels tend to confirm a fifteenth-century date for the Metropolitan Museum's saddles, which show the same dragons interlaced with nearly identical scrollwork.

John Clarke

113

114. DOOR FITTING

Tibetan, probably 15th–16th century
Iron and gold
L. 10¼ in. (26 cm), W. 3⅜ in. (8.6 cm), D. 3⁄16 in. (4 mm)
National Museum of Natural History, Smithsonian Institution, Washington, D.C. (E420071)

The doors of major shrine rooms and large assembly halls in Tibetan monasteries and temples are often fitted with elaborately decorated metal hardware in the form of cross-straps and large central bosses with ring-pulls. These are usually made of gilded copper or damascened iron, and they are frequently pierced and chiseled in a manner similar to that found on some sword fittings, saddle plates, and other types of pierced ironwork (cat. nos. 74, 111–113). This example, the fragment of a door strap, is exceptional for the quality and depth of its chiseling, which relates very closely to the best pierced-iron saddle plates in both technique and style, but on a significantly larger scale. It features a large, sinuous, four-clawed dragon with a scaly body, densely overlapped by scrollwork and lotus blossoms, and is damascened overall in gold. A door boss worked in a very similar style, which may have come from the same set of door fittings, or one closely related to it, passed through the art market in the 1980s (Sotheby's 1985, lot 30).

PROVENANCE: Tsering Lhungay, Nepal.

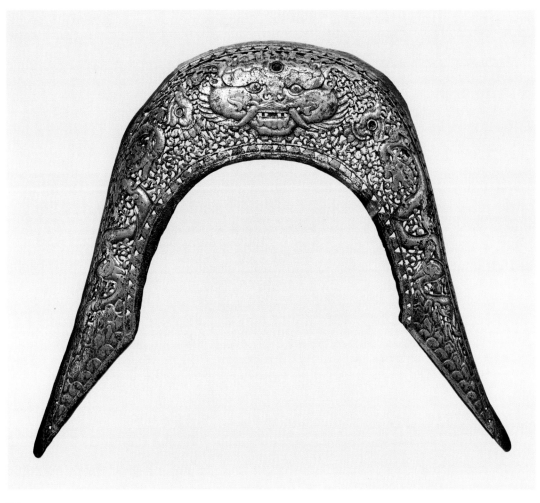

115

face of this pommel plate has the remains of what appears to be an original coating applied to give it the warm reddish tone (*gser mdangs*) that was preferred in Tibet over the natural yellow color of gold.[1]

1. Dagyab 1977, p. 49.

116. SADDLE

Tibetan, 18th–19th century
Iron, gold, copper, turquoise, wood, leather, and textile
H. 15 in. (38.1 cm), L. 23½ in. (59.7 cm), W. 17¾ in. (45.1 cm)
The Metropolitan Museum of Art, New York, Bequest of George
C. Stone, 1935 (36.25.583a, b)
See also cat. no. 46

This saddle represents very well a later but still fairly lavish Tibetan type, which combines pierced ironwork borders with central panels of gilded copper engraved and embossed in very low relief. The borders above the pommel and cantle are decorated with a central *tsi pa ṭa* mask flanked on each side by representations of the Wish-Fulfilling Jewel and pairs of undulating dragons holding pearls, set on a ground of pierced scrollwork. The borders below the pommel and cantle have a Wish-Fulfilling Jewel in the center flanked by a pair of deer and similar dragons. The workmanship of the motifs is stylized and rigid, and the dragons are very simplistic compared with earlier examples. The gilded-copper main panels of the pommel and cantle have a large *tsi pa ṭa* mask in the center flanked by birds and dragons on a scrollwork ground, but the quality of the embossing and engraving is relatively low. The endboards are similarly decorated with matching pierced-iron borders and central copper panels engraved with scrollwork.

The saddletree is original and in good condition, and it is lined with red leather on the underside (see illus.). There are two short leather straps with iron buckles for attaching the girth strap. The red silk damask saddle cushion is probably a replacement made during the working life of the saddle, and it is held by four simple dome-headed copper bosses.

115. POMMEL PLATE FROM A SADDLE

Tibetan, 17th–19th century
Iron and gold
H. 12½ in. (31.8 cm), W. 14⅜ in. (36.5 cm)
The Metropolitan Museum of Art, New York, Gift of The Kronos
Collections, 2005 (2005.41)

This pommel plate is a good example of the later use of relatively complex pierced ironwork on Tibetan saddles. It shows the continuation of the motifs, style, and techniques exemplified by the saddle in catalogue number 112, which was probably made about two hundred years earlier. On the pommel plate, however, the motifs are broader and more loosely rendered, and the relief is much shallower. Nevertheless, in nearly all late saddles of this type the pommel plates are made of copper, embossed in low relief (as in cat. no. 116), rather than the more difficult medium of pierced iron. This pommel plate consists of a single piece of arch-shaped iron decorated over most of its surface with pierced and chiseled ornament. At the center top there is a large *tsi pa ṭa* mask flanked by a pair of hands. On either side of this, running down the arms of the pommel plate, there is a large undulating dragon in profile. At the base of each arm are stylized mountains and waves. There are three circular settings for missing beads of coral or turquoise, one in the center of the forehead of the mask and one on each hand. The mask and dragons are on a ground of pierced scrollwork, bordered above and below by a row of half circles. The decoration is heavily damascened in gold overall. The top edge and the interior are plain iron. Also like the saddle in catalogue number 112, the gold sur-

116

The saddle is outfitted with an associated pair of stirrups (Metropolitan Museum, 36.25.583c, d) and tack consisting of a bridle, breast strap, and crupper (36.25. 583h–k). The tack is decorated with simple pierced and gilded iron fittings, which match one another but not the ironwork on the saddle itself. The presence of a red yak-hair tassel (*snying dom*) on the breast strap indicates that this set once belonged to a government official (see also cat. no. 124).

PROVENANCE: George Cameron Stone, New York.

PUBLICATIONS: Stone 1934, p. 533, fig. 681, no. 5; LaRocca 1996, pp. 13–15, 42, pl. 8.

116, underside

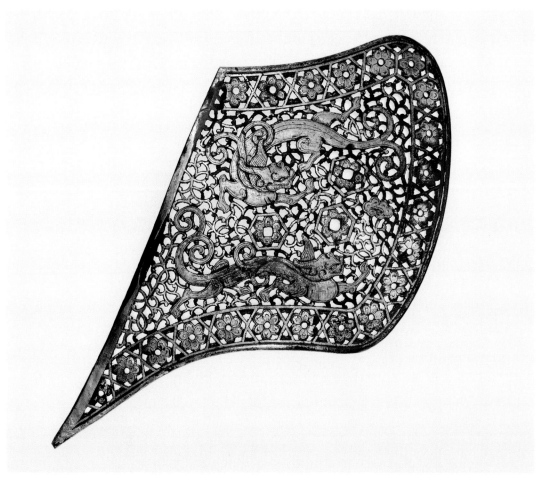

118. SADDLE

Eastern Tibetan or Chinese, possibly 17th–18th century
Iron, gold, silver, copper, leather, wood, and textile
H. 10 in. (25.4 cm), L. 21½ in. (54.6 cm), W. 11½ in. (29.2 cm)
The Metropolitan Museum of Art, New York, Rogers Fund, 1999
(1999.318)

117, proper left end-board plate

117. PAIR OF PLATES FOR THE BACK END-BOARDS OF A SADDLE

Tibetan, probably 18th century
Iron, gold, and silver
H. 4⅜ in. (11.1 cm), W. 8¼ in. (21 cm)
The Metropolitan Museum of Art, New York, Rogers Fund, 1997
(1997.229)

These plates are all that remain from what must have been a fairly elaborate and distinctively decorated saddle. They are notable for their delicate pierced work, their damascening in gold and silver, and the unusual archaic style of the paired dragons on each plate, which are distinguished by a short feline snout, a single horn, a split tendril emerging from behind the head, a long curving body, catlike limbs, and a curling split tail. This type is similar to forms of dragons that occur as early as the Han dynasty and again during the Yuan period, and were

also used in revival styles in the eighteenth century during the Qing dynasty.[1] The thinness of the saddle plates, the relative simplicity and flatness of the scrollwork, which has no undercutting whatsoever, and the regularity of borders consisting of a blossom repeating in hexagonal compartments suggest they belong to the later period, with decoration perhaps influenced by the Qing revival of archaic dragon styles. A saddle with similarly made plates, decorated with repeating blossoms in hexagonal compartments, is in the collection of the Musée de l'Homme, Paris.[2]

1. Compare with the dragons on an ivory plaque in the Metropolitan Museum (19.1909a, b), discussed by Denise Leidy in "Chinese Decorative Arts," *The Metropolitan Museum of Art Bulletin* 55, no. 1 (summer 1997), p. 41, and with examples from the Ming and Ching periods illustrated in Chunfang Li, *Zhongguo wen shi / Chinese Decorative Design*, vol. 1 (Taipei, 1987), figs. II-52, II-79.
2. Tavard 1975, pl. 92.

The previous saddles (cat. nos. 111, 112) represent one of the principal forms found in Tibet, in which the pommels and cantles are large, half-round, and of relatively even height, creating a deep seat in between.[1] This saddle represents another form, one that has a taller narrow pommel with a rounded or pointed top, and a low reclining cantle, creating a much more open seat. The overall proportions of the saddletree in this type also tend to be smaller and narrower.

There are also appreciable differences in the style and technique of the ironwork, although the general choice of motifs and overall appearance are similar. In this instance the pommel features a pair of dragons flanking a flaming jewel or pearl on a scrollwork ground, at the base of which there are stylized mountains and waves (see detail). The cantle plate and the end-board plates have the same dragons and scrollwork ground, with stylized clouds and floral motifs. The tendrils of the scrollwork are longer and much thinner than on the types previously seen, making the ground much more open. The dragons are less serpentine and have simplified features and a single prominent tuft of hair on their heads and tails. The plates have a wide, plain border damascened entirely in silver. On this particular saddle the plates have an additional separate iron border, also damascened in silver. Another important feature is the way in which the gold was applied. The iron ground was finely crosshatched overall and then damascened entirely in silver. The dragons and various other elements of the design were then selectively gilded on top of the silver by mercury gilding, rather than the more usual damascening in gold. This technique was commented on in relation to the helmet in catalogue number 19 and is also found on the pommel plate in the next entry and the saddle in catalogue number 120. The helmet and the later saddle are both Chinese objects that were used in Tibet, while this saddle and the pommel plate (cat. no. 119)

118

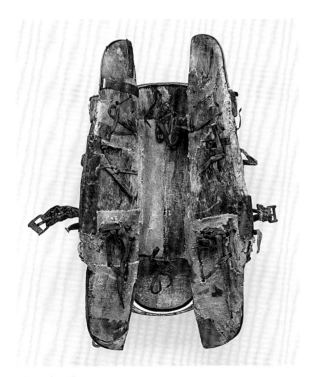

118, underside

118, detail of pommel plate

may be Tibetan or Chinese. This suggests that this particular type of gilding may have been used in China on objects destined for Tibet, or that it is simply a seldom-found gilding technique used in either Tibet or China, probably because of lack of knowledge of how to mercury gild directly on iron.

The front end-boards each have a single iron ring set in a rosette, which forms part of the scrollwork ground. The back end-boards have three such rings, two of which hold a short iron loop with leaf finials, and all of which have traces of damascening. The rings could be used for cords to attach game or other items to the saddle. The loops in the back were for attaching the crupper. In the center of the seat area the saddletree has a rawhide suspension strap that runs from front to back between the pommel and cantle above the seam where the tops of the side-boards meet. There are two braided straps with iron buckles for attaching the girth and two leather loops for the stirrup leathers. Areas of the underside of the tree and the inside of the pommel and cantle are faced with a linenlike fabric. The saddletree has been repaired several times with strips of iron and copper patches, testifying to the length and strenuous nature of its working life.

---

1. This form seems related to Tashi Namgyal's short description of the characteristics of *hor* (Mongol) saddles at the start of his chapter devoted to saddles in Beinecke, fol. 53a; Burmiok Athing, fol. 31a; see the appendix "Excerpts from *A Treatise on Worldly Traditions*."

119. POMMEL PLATE

Eastern Tibetan or Chinese, possibly 17th–18th century
Iron, gold, and silver
H. 10¼ in. (26 cm), W. 10 in. (25.4 cm)
The Metropolitan Museum of Art, New York, Purchase, Bernice and Jerome Zwanger Gift, 2000 (2000.404)

This pommel plate is closely related to the ironwork of the previous saddle. It is slightly larger in scale, but the style and technique are otherwise the same, including the use of the two-stage technique of mercury gilding over damascened silver, as described in the previous entry. The design is also very similar, featuring a pair of dragons flanking a flaming Three Jewels motif on a scrollwork ground with stylized clouds and, at the base, the motif of stylized mountains and waves. The dragons are chiseled free from the scrollwork ground and can be moved slightly. The scrollwork is characterized by its long, thin tendrils, making the framework of the ground very open. The borders are plain and completely damascened in silver. The lower arms on either side of the pommel end in a narrow compartment with a lobed upper border, the ground of which is not pierced or otherwise decorated. These compartments are also a feature of this type of saddle plate, which is found in a vestigial form on the previous saddle and more fully developed on the following two examples.

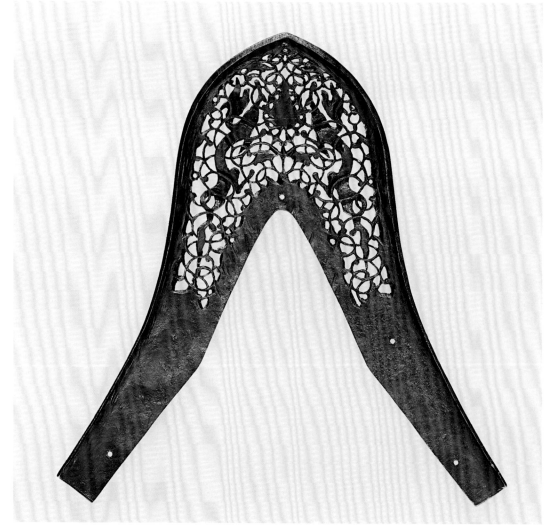

119, back

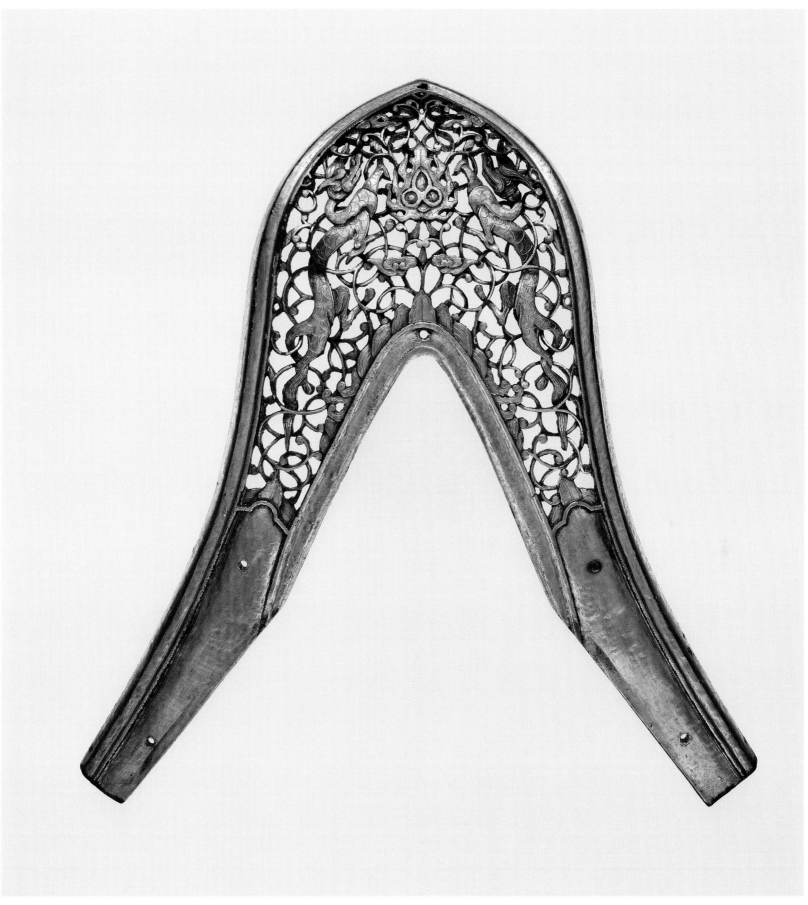

120. SADDLE

Eastern Tibetan or Chinese for the Tibetan market, 17th–18th century
Iron, gold, silver, wood, leather, and textile
H. 10¾ in. (27.3 cm), L. 22½ in. (57.2 cm), W. 11¾ in. (29.8 cm)
The Metropolitan Museum of Art, New York, Purchase, Rogers Fund, and Bequest of Stephen V. Grancsay, by exchange, 1997 (1997.214.1)

This saddle represents another form found in Tibet—Chinese or strongly influenced by Chinese types—and within that form it belongs to a small group of closely related saddles, which may either stem from a single workshop or reflect a specific type developed in one particular region. The saddles in this group, of which this is one of the best examples, share several key features. First is the shape and contour of the saddle plates, particularly the square, reclining, and slightly concave top of the pommel plate. Second are the motifs, chief among which is a single, symmetrical, upright, splayed dragon in the center of the pommel, its head in left profile, holding a flaming pearl in each upraised four-clawed forepaw. The dragons are chiseled free from the scrollwork ground, as are the dragons on the saddle plates in catalogue numbers 111 and 119. Third is the distinctive method of assembly of the saddle plates involving three layers, which becomes apparent only on close examination. This consists of the outer layer of scrollwork with long tendrils deeply undercut to give an appearance of depth. This effect is enhanced by a second layer, which forms a separate subsidiary ground that (where it survives) underlies each saddle plate and consists of an iron grill made up of overlapping half circles damascened in silver to create a stylized cloud pattern. Beneath this, directly on top of the wood, there is a layer of colored fabric. The fourth feature is the use of parcel gilding as described in the previous entries, involving silver

120, detail of pommel plate

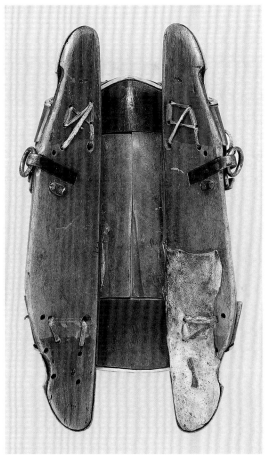

120, underside

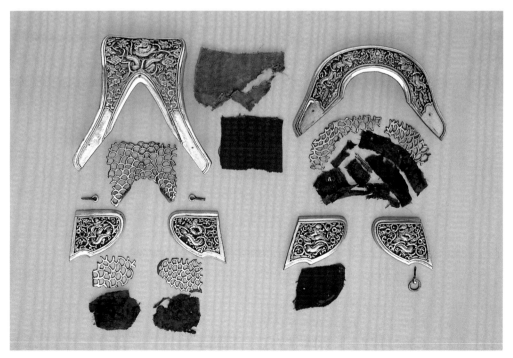

120, saddle plates and underlying layers removed for conservation

damascening of the entire surfaces of the saddle plates, with select design elements being mercury gilded. Beyond these traits there are several other small features, such as the use of plain silver damascened borders on all of the plates, and the inclusion of only a very few subsidiary motifs such as stylized clouds and mountains flanked by waves. The saddle-trees are also similar, having a high seat formed by the arched centers of the sideboards, and characteristic hardware that includes plain but carefully made tablike iron straps and rigging rings for the attachment of the girths or stirrup leathers. The underside of the saddletree of the Metropolitan Museum example is marked in Tibetan with the number 12.

The principal saddles in this group, in addition to the present example, are one in the Musée d'Ethnographie de Neuchâtel, Switzerland (68.4.79.a); another in Drepung Loseling Monastery, India, which is said to have been used by the Fifth Dalai Lama in the mid-seventeenth century; and two examples seen on the art market.[1] In a slight variation, the body of the dragon in the center of the pommel plate is turned more in profile, rather than symmetrically splayed, and the relief is noticeably flatter and the quality of the chiseling slightly lower. Two known examples of this variant include an example in the Royal Armouries Museum, Leeds (XXVH.30), and another seen on the art market. It should also be noted that many of these saddles are missing some or all of the background layers behind the saddle plates due to their having been repaired or altered over the years.

The possible Chinese origin of these saddles is suggested by the presence of the Chinese characters

xià above *shi* chiseled on the interior of the pommel plate and *wàng* on the interior of the cantle plate of the Metropolitan Museum's saddle.[2] The exact meaning of the characters remains unclear, but they may have been added during the making of the saddle plates to signify the rank of the individual for whom the saddle was intended and therefore the extent to which the plates should be decorated.[3]

In light of the purported use of the Drepung Loseling saddle by the Fifth Dalai Lama, it is interesting to note that according to family tradition the Metropolitan Museum's saddle was ridden by the young Gyalwa Tenzin Gyatso during the late 1930s in ceremonies held some time after his identification as the Fourteenth Dalai Lama.[4]

PUBLICATION: LaRocca 1999a, pp. 120–21, fig. 14.

1. See Daoulas 1998, no. 85, for the Neuchâtel saddle, which is called Bhutanese and is mistakenly catalogued as gilded bronze; and Mullin 1996, p. 153, for the Drepung Loseling saddle.
2. The characters were discovered by Robert Carroll, at the Metropolitan Museum, when he was cleaning and restoring the saddle in 1997, and were subsequently read by Oi-Cheong Lee, James Watt, and John Rogers.
3. The Chinese character *wu* is similarly chiseled on the interior of a pommel plate made of gilded bronze and probably 18th-century Chinese that was sold with its matching cantle at Sotheby's, New York, March 26, 2003 (*Indian and Southeast Asian Art*, sale cat., lot 117; mistakenly catalogued as damascened iron), and is now in a New York private collection. A complete saddle with plates in the same style as the Sotheby's examples is in the collection of the National Museum of Mongolian History, Ulaanbaatar, illustrated in Jan Fontein, *The Dancing Demons of Mongolia*, exh. cat., Nieuwe Kerk, Amsterdam (London, 1999), no. 78.
4. Personal communication, June 18, 1997.

121. DECORATIVE FITTING FROM A CRUPPER STRAP

Eastern Tibetan or Chinese for the Tibetan market,
17th–18th century
Iron, gold, and silver
L. 3¾ in. (9.5 cm), W. 1⅝ in. (4.1 cm)
The Metropolitan Museum of Art, New York, Purchase, Arthur
Ochs Sulzberger Gift, 2001 (2001.182)

This fitting is made in exactly the same style and technique as the saddle plates of the saddle in catalogue number 120, and may have been part of the tack that once belonged to this saddle or one of the others closely related to it. It consists of a pierced circular boss with a winglike extension on the right side. The boss is decorated with a dragon in profile on a scrollwork ground. The extension is also pierced and has a broad leafy scrollwork ground. As with the saddle plates, but on a far smaller scale, the dragon is cut free from the surrounding scrollwork and can move slightly within it. The fitting is damascened overall in silver, over which gold was selectively applied by mercury gilding. Behind the scrollwork ground of the boss there is a hemispherical insert of iron pierced in a netlike pattern and damascened in silver, forming a subsidiary ground, again just as with the saddle plates. Based on comparisons with complete Tibetan cruppers, it appears that this fitting would have been mounted at the end of the crupper strap, just above the attachment for the tail loop.

122. SADDLE

Chinese for the Tibetan market, 17th–18th century
Iron, gold, silver, wood, coral, ivory, silk, hair, tin, pigments, and leather
H. including textile 13¾ in. (34.9 cm), L. 27 in. (68.6 cm), W. 14½ in. (36.8 cm)
The Metropolitan Museum of Art, New York, Purchase, Gift of J. Pierpont Morgan, Bequest of Stephen V. Grancsay, Giovanni P. Morosini Collection, presented by his daughter Giulia,
and Gift of Prince Albrecht Radizwill, by exchange, and Nicholas L. Zabriskie Gift, 1998 (1998.316)

In terms of quality and style of workmanship this saddle is extremely similar to some imperial Chinese saddles, such as one owned by the emperor Qianlong (r. 1736–96), which is part of the imperial collections preserved in the Palace Museum, Beijing (G.171546).[1] Most saddles from Tibet, even elaborately decorated examples such as this one, show clear signs of repeated use over several generations, with the result that very few have survived to the present with all of their original components intact. In addition to its very high quality, therefore, this saddle is also exceptional for having all of its original parts, including the seat cover of embroidered silk and the fittings of the saddletree.

Although this type of saddle is often identified as Tibetan, the form of the saddle plates, the style of workmanship, and the type of saddletree, along with the similarity to imperial Chinese saddles, indicate it is more likely to be Chinese, perhaps from the imperial workshops. That this saddle was used in Tibet, however, is demonstrated by the Tibetan letter

122, back view

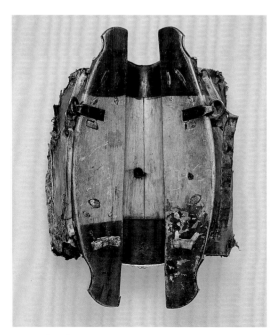

122, underside

ka, which is branded on the underside of the saddle-tree. Tibetan objects were often marked with letters instead of numbers; *ka*, being the first letter of the Tibetan alphabet, would have been equivalent to inventory number 1. The blue color of the saddle cover indicates that it was owned by a lay nobleman, rather than a religious figure, whose saddle would have been upholstered in yellow.[2] Given the quality of the saddle, it must have belonged to a Tibetan nobleman of the highest rank, possibly received as a gift directly from the imperial court.

The saddle has seven saddle plates: a pommel plate, a separate stepped plate beneath the arch of the pommel plate, a cantle plate, and four plates for the end-boards. The plates are made from relatively thick iron, deeply chiseled and pierced, the motifs densely arranged so that the gaps in the scrollwork

are narrow compared to the more open ground of the previous example. The plates are finely cross-hatched and damascened overall with a thick layer of gold foil. In the center of the pommel plate there is the motif of the Three Jewels, consisting of one white and two red beads, possibly ivory and coral, in a flaming aureole setting chiseled in high relief so that it juts out approximately 5 millimeters beyond the surrounding ground (see detail).[3] This is flanked by a pair of dragons, the heads of which are chiseled in equally high relief. The dragons' paws, usually shown prominently, are merged into the scrollwork so as to be almost imperceptible, but they appear to have four claws.[4] The surrounding scrollwork is densely arranged and deeply undercut. As with the previous saddle, the only subsidiary motifs consist of *ju'i*-style clouds and the mountain and waves

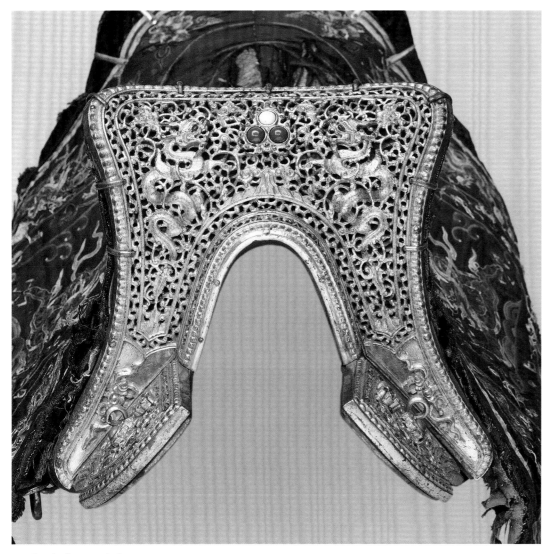

122, detail of pommel plate

plates. It is made of blue silk elaborately embroidered with multicolored silk threads in long and short, satin, couched, and several other stitches, and trimmed with a patterned velvet border. The design features four-clawed dragons with pearls amid clouds, waves, and lotus blossoms. The cover has an inner layer of soft animal hair, perhaps deer or camel, and is lined with a patterned red silk damask.[5]

The saddletree is complete and in good condition. It is painted red beneath the arches of the pommel and cantle and on the underside of the end-boards, except for the rear left end-board, which is lined with red leather. Like the previous saddle, it is fitted with a simple but well-made iron strap and rigging ring on either side for the attachment of the girth or stirrup leathers. In this case, however, in addition to the main strap and ring there are two smaller ones toward the front and rear of the tree, with a horizontal strap and a D-ring suspended between them. The iron straps were coated overall with tin where they came in direct contact with the underside of the silk saddle cover to keep rust from staining the fabric, a further sign of the great attention to detail present in every aspect of this saddle's manufacture.

PROVENANCE: Sotheby's, New York, September 16, 1998, lot 191.

PUBLICATIONS: *Indian and Southeast Asian Art*, sale cat., Sotheby's, New York, September 16, 1998, lot 191; LaRocca 1999a, p. 120, fig. 13.

motif. All of the plates have a pierced chainlike inner border and a beaded outer border. The narrow compartments at the base of the arms of the pommel plate each have a smooth gold ground decorated with the motif of a conch shell and a curling ribbon chiseled in high relief. The cantle plate has the same decoration as the pommel, except for the narrow compartments at the base of the arms, each decorated with the motif of a rhinoceros horn or elephant tusk and a curling ribbon.

The end-board plates each have a single dragon in profile and a single flaming jewel in the form of a red bead, on a pierced scrollwork ground. The setting for the bead and the dragon head are chiseled in high relief, as on the pommel and cantle. The pommel and cantle plates are held by large clips, also damascened in gold, which hook over their upper edges at one end

and are nailed to the saddletree at the other. These clips, the original method by which saddle plates of this type were attached, are often missing from saddles due to their having been refurbished at some point. The end-board plates are held by nails, which were driven in from the underside and their exposed points peened over and dressed to blend with the decoration. The front end-boards have a single iron ring each, while the back end-board plates have three, as is usual. The rings are held by split pins, visible on the underside of the tree. The paired rings on the back end-boards have an iron loop with leaf finials, similar to, but more elaborate than, those on the saddle in catalogue number 118. Virtually all of the nails and other fittings appear to be original and undisturbed.

The saddle cover is attached directly to the saddletree by the same clips as the pommel and cantle

1. The saddle is illustrated in *La cité interdite: Vie publique et privée des empereurs de chine (1644–1911)*, exh. cat., Musée du Petit Palais (Paris, 1996), no. 18, pp. 142–43.
2. I am grateful to Hugh Richardson for pointing this out to me (personal communication, September 30, 1998).
3. The proper right read bead on the pommel and that on the front proper left end-board were made in November 1998 by Robert Carroll, Armorer at the Metropolitan Museum, to replace the missing originals.
4. The claws on dragons are generally carefully delineated on Chinese objects because the number of claws was recognized as an important sign of rank in China. The ambiguity of the claws on this saddle may have been intentional, with the implication that it was more elaborate than was technically acceptable for the rank of its owner by Chinese standards, particularly if it were intended for the Tibetan market.
5. The textile was carefully cleaned and conserved in the Metropolitan Museum by Midori Sato and Kissok Suh, in consultation with Florica Zaharia, Conservator in Charge of Textile Conservation. The catalogue photographs, unfortunately, show the textile prior to conservation.

123. SADDLE PLATE

Chinese or Tibetan, 17th–18th century
Iron, gold, and silver
H. 3½ in. (8.9 cm), W. 4¼ in. (10.8 cm)
The Metropolitan Museum of Art, New York, Purchase, Kenneth and Vivian Lam Gift, 2002 (2002.17.20)

This plate, for the front left end-board of a saddle, is made of thick iron that was pierced, chiseled, and heavily damascened in gold and silver. In the center there is a *tsi pa ṭa* mask chiseled in high relief so that it stands 10 millimeters above the adjacent scrollwork ground of the central compartment. Around this compartment there is a pierced row of *ju'i*-shaped clouds surrounded by a solid outer border. The outer border is damascened in silver, the rest in gold. This plate is similar to those on the preceding saddle, especially in the use of the heavy gold damascening, but the workmanship of the piercing and chiseling is less fine. The *tsi pa ṭa* motif is somewhat unusual for an end-board plate, where most saddles have dragons.

124. SET OF SADDLE, TACK, AND SWORD

Tibetan, probably 19th–early 20th century
Iron, gold, copper, wood, leather, textile, varnish, tin, ray skin, and yak hair
Sword, L. overall in scabbard 35½ in. (90.2 cm), L. of blade 29 in. (73.7 cm); saddle, H. 14½ in. (36.8 cm), L. 25½ in. (64.8 cm), W. 23 in. (58.4 cm); bridle, H. 19 in. (48.3 cm); breast collar, L. 56 in. (142.2 cm); crupper, L. 28 in. (71.1 cm), W. 18¾ in. (47.6 cm); stirrups, H. 6¼ in. (15.9 cm), W. 5¾ in. (14.6 cm)
The Metropolitan Museum of Art, New York, Purchase, Arthur Ochs Sulzberger Gift, 2003 (2003.230.1–.3a–e)

Like the previous example (cat. no. 122), this saddle is remarkable for its elaborate decoration, and is even more so for its state of preservation and its completeness, being one of the few to retain a fully matching set of tack, comprising a bridle, breast strap, and crupper, all decorated with the same distinctively chiseled, pierced, and gilded ironwork and fitted throughout with a sumptuous yellow Chinese silk damask. The workmanship of the stirrups and sword differs slightly from that of the saddle and tack but is similar enough to be in keeping with them. An extraordinary iron seal, which has been suggested as belonging to the Thirteenth Dalai Lama, was also formerly associated with the sword, saddle, and tack as part of the same set.[1] That these pieces belong together as a group is reinforced by the fact that they are the only known iron objects of their type that are mercury gilded.[2] While mercury gild-

124, detail of pommel plate

124, saddle

ing as a technique was common on sculpture and other objects made of copper alloy or silver, iron objects from Tibet and China otherwise invariably have gold applied by damascening or, more rarely, by parcel gilding, in which mercury gilding is selectively applied over a silver damascened iron ground (cat. nos. 19, 118–121). Mercury gilding directly on iron, a technique practiced in Europe from at least the fifteenth century, seems to have been unknown, or at least unused, in Asia and was perhaps not introduced until the nineteenth century or later. Stylistically, the form and decoration of the saddle and the sword are also very unusual and appear to represent a hybrid or revival style, which also points to a late date for the creation of this group.

The saddle (2003.230.2) consists of six saddle plates, a padded seat cushion held by four elaborate bosses, and a wooden saddletree. The saddle plates are densely chiseled, pierced, and engraved in a tour de force of late ironworking in the tradition of earlier saddles such as catalogue number 112. The style is both exuberant and mannered, almost to the point of caricature. The dragons, in particular, are extremely unusual, with long snakelike bodies, bulbous heads chiseled in high relief, and round flat eyes. The dragon in the center of the pommel holds what appears to be a stylized version of the Treasure Vase (*gter chen po'i bum pa*), one of the Eight Auspicious Symbols, over its head. It is flanked by a pair of dragons and phoenixes above the mountain

and wave motif on a dense scrollwork ground. The cantle features a phoenix in the center flanked by dragons. The end-board plates are similarly decorated with dragons, phoenixes, and other birds.

The saddle cushion and the matching textile on the rest of the tack have been described by Nobuko Kajitani as yellow silk damask lined with green damassé, probably nineteenth century, and Chinese. She further observed that the fabric was woven thickly and so was perhaps designed to be used for upholstery rather than clothing; and that the damask was cut from a new bolt rather than pieced together from reused material.[3] The seat cover is held by four large dome-headed bosses of pierced iron decorated in the same style as the saddle plates.

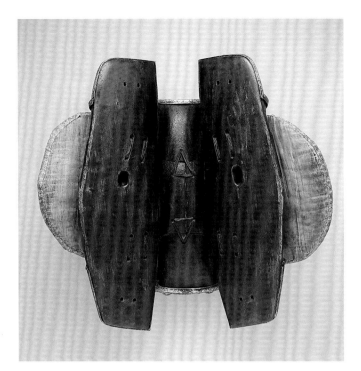

124, underside of saddle

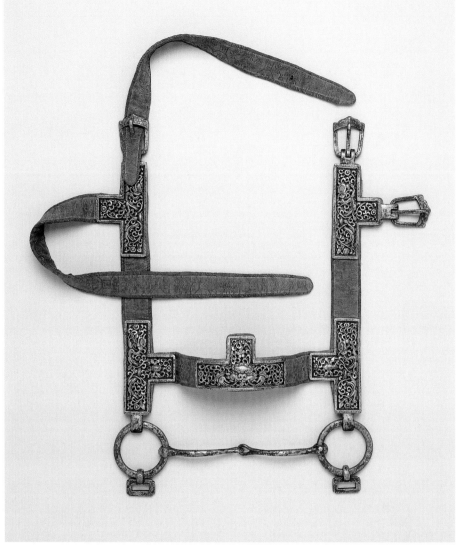

124, bridle

The saddletree consists of four thick pieces of shaped wood and is of the highest quality, being carefully constructed, fitted, and finished. Both the underside and the exposed wood of the upper side were smoothed and coated with a dark reddish black varnish. The leather laces, which tie the pieces of the tree together, are clearly old and show no signs of having been altered or replaced. Only the four laces attaching the seat cushion bosses are more recent.

The bridle (2003.230.3a) consists of an iron snaffle bit (*srab lcags*), which is gilded at its exposed ends and tinned where it would be inside the horse's mouth. It is attached to a headstall (*mthur*), which is made of silk straps fitted with five pierced and gilded iron plaques and three gilded and engraved iron buckles. The bit is composed of a two-piece

snaffle with a large round bit ring (*srab sgor*) at either end. A rectangular slotted iron tab, for the attachment of reins, hangs from each bit ring. The headstall consists of a noseband and two cheek straps with a short secondary strap, attached by two buckles, to go over the top of the head. T-shaped iron plaques are mounted at the juncture of the straps. The plaque in the center of the noseband is slightly curved. The others, mounted at the top and bottom of each cheek strap, are flat. A long strap extends from the side of the proper right cheek strap. A corresponding buckle is attached to the side of the proper left cheek strap. The cheek rings of the bit attach to the headstall by two iron loops, which are made as part of the plaques at the bottom of the cheek straps. The decoration of the plaque on the noseband has

a large *tsi pa ṭa* mask in the center. The decoration of the other plaques features an undulating dragon seen in profile on a scrollwork ground. The plaques at the base of the cheek straps also include a bee chiseled in relief.[4] The plaques are mounted to the textile with small dome-headed copper-capped rivets that function like cotter pins, having split shanks that are bent flat over leather washers on the back, which is the method of attaching the metal fittings to the textile on the following pieces of tack as well.

The breast collar (2003.320.3b) is made up of five silk straps intersecting at two pierced and gilded hemispherical iron bosses. The end of each strap, where it meets the boss, is fitted with a rectangular pierced and gilded iron plaque. The breast strap has

124, breast collar

124, crupper

124, stirrups

124, detail of crupper

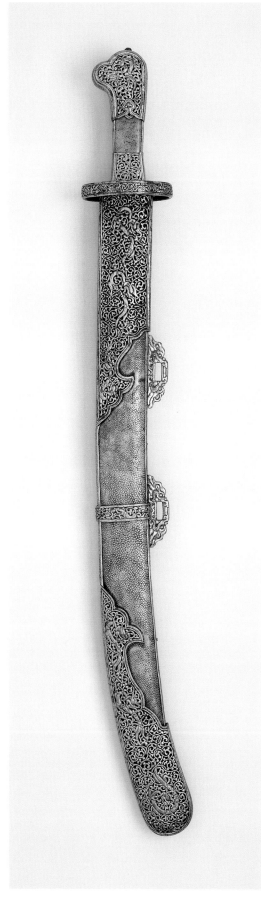

a large tassel in the center (*snying dom*), consisting of a tuft of red yak hair mounted in a pierced and gilded iron bell, attached to the strap by an iron swivel ring.[5] A long strap extends from the top of the proper left boss. A corresponding shorter strap, fitted with an iron buckle, extends from the top of the proper right boss. Extending from the side of each boss there is a single short strap, the end of which is turned over to form a closed loop (probably to engage the girth strap). The decoration of the plaques features an undulating dragon seen in profile on a scrollwork ground. The textile, ironwork, and mounting fixtures match those of the other parts of the set.

The crupper (2003.230.3c) has at its center a prominent boxlike central boss of pierced and gilded iron (see detail), which is backed by a square section of the silk lining rather than the usual padded crupper cushion (*rmed gdan*). From the boss four silk straps project in an X pattern. The straps are mounted with eight rectangular plaques of pierced and gilded iron. There is a decorative silk flap with cusped edges (*rmed 'dzar*) attached to the outer edge of each rear strap. The padded leather band (*rmed hril*) that goes under the tail is attached to the end of each rear strap by a flat iron ring. The boss is decorated with dragons on the top and on two sides, and on the other sides with the Three Jewels motif. The decoration of the plaques features an undulating dragon seen in profile on a scrollwork ground. Silk, ironwork, and mounting fixtures match those of the other parts of the set.

The heavy iron stirrups (2003.203.3d, e) are pierced, chiseled, and, unlike the pieces above, thickly damascened in gold rather than mercury gilded. At the top of the arch of each stirrup there is a horizontal slot for the stirrup leathers. The slot is bordered on either end by a short post and a dragon head (*'brug mgo*) in profile, with the mouth pierced through. The arms of the arch are a flattened triangle in cross section, the interior side being flat and the two exterior sides chiseled with a scrolling foliage motif. The tread is round, has a shallow rim, and is pierced by a cluster of four oval holes with a square hole in the center.

The sword (2003.230.1) has several features, in terms of form, construction, and decoration, that show clear Chinese influence but are not treated in any usual Chinese style. Other features, such as the shape of the pommel and the type of components making up the hilt, are an imaginative combination of Tibetan, Chinese, and perhaps Mongol styles. The sword has highly elaborate mounts of chiseled, pierced, engraved, and mercury-gilded iron. The hilt has a long, asymmetrical pommel, a short grip of polished ray skin, and a prominent collar at the base of the grip, which is made in one with the guard. The front and back of the pommel and collar are decorated in pierced scrollwork. The sides are not pierced, instead being engraved with scrolling foliage. Both sides of the grip are covered by a short, flat iron strap, likewise engraved with scrolling foliage. The guard is a flat oval plate, the edges of which are slightly cusped to form a subtle quatrefoil

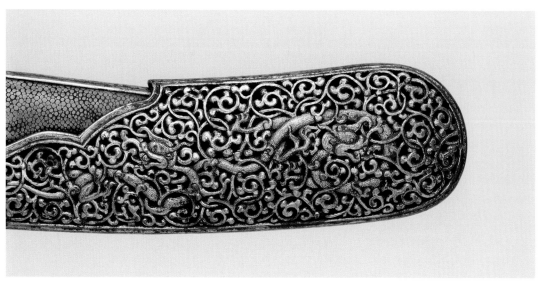

124, sword

124, detail of chape

outline. There is a perpendicular flange or rim approximately ½-inch (1.27 cm) deep around the edge of the guard, forming a shallow dish, with the concavity toward the blade. The top of the guard (facing the hilt) is deeply chiseled with scrollwork. The rim is chiseled with dragons and scrollwork. The bottom of the guard (facing the blade) is engraved with scrollwork. A single large tablike langet emerges from the bottom of the guard on the obverse side and is parallel with the plane of the blade.[6]

The scabbard mounts consist of a long cusped Chinese-style locket, chape, and one suspension band of pierced and chiseled iron, and two deeply chiseled suspension lugs on the top of the scabbard. Scabbards of this form, particularly the rounded style of the chape, did not come into use until the eighteenth century at the earliest.[7] The edges of the scabbard between these mounts are covered by flat iron straps engraved with scrolling foliage (as on the sides of the grip). The other surfaces of the scabbard are covered in polished ray skin (matching that on the grip). The decoration of the front and back of the locket and chape features three regardant dragons amid scrollwork (see detail). The edges of the locket and chape are finished with shallow, recessed borders. The top of the locket has a deeply recessed groove with a raised half-round border, which engages the langet. The suspension lugs are made in the form of a pair of dragon heads, which flank (and face toward) either side of the suspension slot. The scabbard has a thick liner made of a dark wood. The blade is single edged, slightly curved, with an unsharpened back edge approximately 9 inches (22.9 cm) long, and has two shallow fullers running its entire length. While perfectly serviceable and functional, the blade is extremely plain and in total contrast to the hilt and scabbard fittings in terms of quality. The scabbard liner, however, fits the blade very well, and the sword has the proper weight and is well balanced, suggesting that the blade is not a later substitution.

In conclusion, the questions remain as to when, where, and for whom this saddle, tack, sword, and possibly the seal were made. The combination of the extremely unusual style of the decoration and the elaborate and labor-intensive nature of the ironwork suggests that the group was made for an important event and for a very high ranking patron. The use of mercury gilding on the iron should be a key factor in dating the group. Further research needs to be done to establish the earliest date for the use of this technique, specifically on iron, in Tibet, China, or Mongolia, but it probably would not predate the mid- to late nineteenth century and may even indicate a date in the early twentieth. The group may have been created for one of the series of regents who held power during the nineteenth century prior to the reign of the Thirteenth Dalai Lama (ruled politically, 1895–1933), if not for the Thirteenth Dalai Lama himself or the regents who followed him. Alternatively, the sword, saddle, and tack may have been made as part of the costumes in the ancient style worn by presiding lay officials at the Great Prayer Festival in Lhasa. The scale and ostentation of the sword and saddle compare well with that of the oversize ancient-style jewelry worn by officials on these occasions.[8] The textile fittings of the saddle and tack have undoubtedly been refurbished, possibly as late as the early to mid-twentieth century, but using original materials and traditional methods. This is particularly evident in the leather laces and washers on the reverse of the textiles, which are more recent than the silk fabric but are integral to their structure as presently mounted. The yellow color of the silk would seem to suggest that the set was refurbished for use by a religious figure; however, the saddle in catalogue number 126, which was made for a well-known lay government official, is also upholstered in yellow silk, showing that the use of yellow was not strictly confined to ecclesiastics.[9]

1. The seal was sold at Christie's, New York, September 23, 2004 (*Indian and Southeast Asian Art including 20th Century Indian Paintings*, sale cat.), lot 121.
2. To confirm the use of mercury gilding, the sword and bridle were tested by X-ray fluorescence (XRF) analysis in the Metropolitan Museum's Objects Conservation and Scientific Research Departments, the sword by Richard Stone in 2003 and the bridle by Tony Frantz and Diane Lyons in consultation with Marco Leona in 2004.
3. Memo dated May 15, 2003. I am very grateful to Nobuko Kajitani, former Conservator in Charge of Textile Conservation at the Metropolitan Museum, for carrying out a brief examination and test cleaning of the textile and for sharing her observations.
4. The bee is very unusual as a motif and may be an allusion to the Sixth Dalai Lama, Tsangyang Gyatso (*tsangs dbyangs rgya mtsho*, 1683–1706), who was nicknamed the Turquoise Bee (*g.yu sbrang*).
5. Such tassels, hung from the breast strap and the headstall, were signs of rank for both lay and religious officials (see also cat. nos. 116 and 46).
6. Langets are unusual on Tibetan swords, but they do exist, as for instance on the fine Tibetan sword, ex-collection Lord Curzon, in cat. no. 67.
7. I am grateful to Scott Rodell and Philip Tom for clarifying this point and for many other useful observations on the nature and possible dating of this sword.
8. See, for instance, Richardson 1993, pp. 16–17, and the swords worn by the Yaso officials as seen on p. 43. Compare also the elaborate hybrid style sword worn by a Yaso official in a photograph taken by Heinrich Harrer (1992, p. 104 top, figure to the far right).
9. According to Diki Lhazi Surkhang, yellow brocade was used for saddle covers by both lay and religious officials of the highest ranks (personal communication from Yanchen Lakar, November 7, 2005).

125. SET OF SADDLE PLATES

Probably Nepalese, 19th–20th century
Copper and gold
Pommel, H. 11 in. (27.9 cm), W. 15⅛ in. (38.4 cm); cantle,
H. 12⅜ in. (31.4 cm), W. 16½ in. (41.9 cm); front end-board plates,
H. 5¾ in. (14.6 cm), W. 3¾ in. (9.5 cm); back end-board plates,
H. 6¾ in. (17.1 cm), W. 4 in. (10.2 cm)
National Museum of Natural History, Smithsonian Institution,
Washington, D.C. (E420066A–B)

Richly decorated repoussé and mercury-gilded copper, this set is an excellent example of a late and very elaborate version of earlier pierced-iron saddle plates, but made in a more easily workable material. Based on the style and variety of ornament, these saddle plates appear to be Nepalese in origin. The very dense scrollwork ground and the arrangement of the motifs are also reminiscent of the saddle in the previous entry. On this set the pommel features a *garuda* in the center above the Wheel of Dharma (*chos kyi 'khor lo*), one of the Eight Auspicious Symbols (see detail). These are flanked by lotus blossoms, snow lions, leopards, and dragons on a densely lush field of pierced scrollwork. The upper border has the Wish-Fulfilling Jewel in the center flanked by deer, dragons, and phoenixes. The dragons hold a pearl in each of their four paws. In the center of the lower border there is the grouping of objects known as the Five Qualities of Enjoyment (*'dod yon sna lnga*, the mirror, lute, incense, fruit, and silk), which symbolize the five senses, flanked by peacocks and dragons. The cantle has in its center a pair of snow lions holding a jewel tray (*gzhong pa rin po che*) filled with the Seven Gems (*nor bu cha bdun*, crossed gems, coral, king's earrings, queen's earrings, a rhinoceros horn, elephant tusks, and the three-eyed gem above a line of pearl-like jewels), flanked by a pair of half-bird half-human creatures called *kinnara* (*mi'am ci*) and dragons. The upper border has the Dharma Wheel flanked by deer, dragons, and phoenixes. The lower border has the Wish-Fulfilling Jewel flanked by peacocks and dragons. The end-board plates are decorated with very animated undulating dragons on a scrollwork ground. The plates may not be fully finished and show no signs of having ever been mounted on a saddletree.

PROVENANCE: Tsering Lhungay, Nepal.

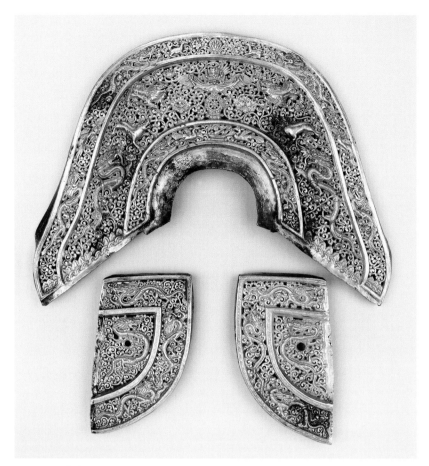

125, pommel plates

125, detail of pommel plate

125, cantle plates

126. SADDLE AND STIRRUPS

Eastern Tibetan, ca. 1930s
Silver, brass, gold, wood, leather, and textile
L. 20 in. (50.8 cm), W. 15 in. (38.1 cm)
The Metropolitan Museum of Art, New York, Purchase,
Arthur Ochs Sulzberger Gift, 2005 (2005.48.1, .2a, b)

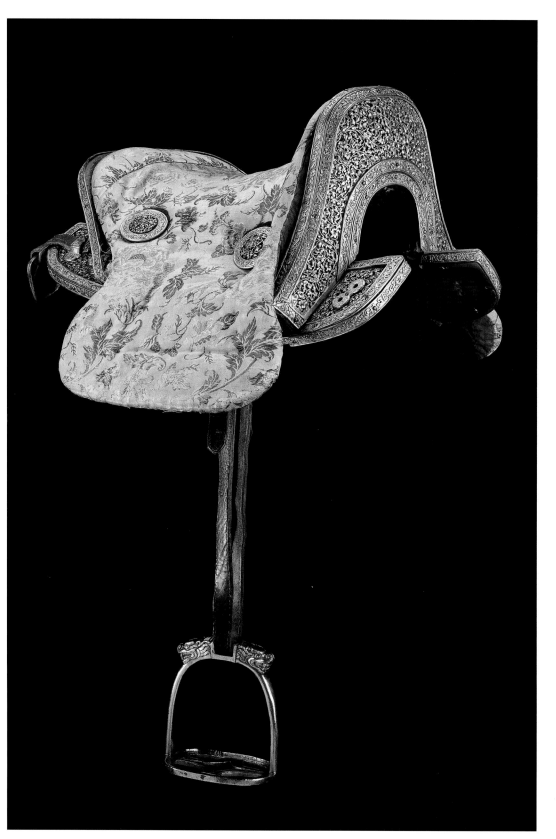

Completely traditional in its form, this luxurious saddle was made in Derge in the 1930s for the Tibetan government official Surkhang Wangchen Tseten (*zur khang dbang chen tshe brtan*, b. 19th century), while he was serving as governor of eastern Tibet. In the early 1940s it was used by his son Surkhang Lhawang Topgyal (*zur khang lha dbang stobs rgyal*, b. 20th century) when he won the *drung 'khor rtsal rgyugs*. This was a ceremonial horseback target-shooting competition held once every twelve years, in which younger government officials had to demonstrate their horsemanship and skill with musket, bow and arrow, and spear. Later the saddle was owned and used on many ceremonial occasions by another of Surkhang Wangchen Tseten's sons, Surkhang Wangchen Gelek (*zur khang dbang chen dge legs*, 1910–1977), who became a senior cabinet minister, or Shapey (*zhabs pad*), and close adviser to the Fourteenth Dalai Lama.[1]

The pommel, cantle, and end-boards are entirely covered with delicately pierced scrollwork cast in silver and set on a ground of bright red foil made of copper with a lacquerlike coating. Each section is surrounded by a gilded-brass border decorated with auspicious symbols set among foliate scrolls and blossoms. The holes for leather laces on the front and back end-boards are bordered with grommets of the same material, as are the brackets for the crupper straps on the back end-boards.

The saddle cushion is covered with yellow silk brocade, which has a strong pattern of large leafy stalks and flowers. The cushion is held by four bosses made in the same way as the saddle plates, with a central scrollwork medallion of pierced silver bordered by a ring of gilded brass decorated with foliage and auspicious symbols. In the center of each medallion there is a stylized butterfly or blossom motif.

The stirrups are relatively simple in their design, with a pair of outward-facing dragon heads flanking the slot for the stirrup leather, round undecorated

126

arms, and an openwork tread pierced with the coin motif. Nevertheless, they are very unusual in that they are solid cast in nearly pure silver, rather than made of the more usual iron or copper alloy.[2]

PROVENANCE: Surkhang family.

PUBLICATION: Giuseppe Tucci, *Tibet: Land of the Snows*, translated by J. E. Stapleton Driver, 2nd ed. (London, 1973), pp. 152–53.

1. I am grateful to Mrs. Diki L. Surkhang and her daughter Yanchen Lakar for much useful information about the history of the saddle and its use, and to John Clarke and Andrew Topsfield. For the Surkhang family, see Dorje Yudon Yuthok, *House of the Turquoise Roof*, rev. ed. (Ithaca, N.Y., 1995). For the *drung 'khor rtsal rgyugs*, see Goldstein 2001, p. 554.
2. Confirmed by XRF analysis carried out by Richard Stone, November 16, 2005.

127. PAIR OF STIRRUPS

Tibetan or Mongolian, possibly 12th–14th century
Iron, gold, and silver
H. 6½ in. (16.5 cm)
The Metropolitan Museum of Art, New York, Purchase, Gift of William H. Riggs, by exchange, and funds from various donors, 1999 (1999.119a, b)

127

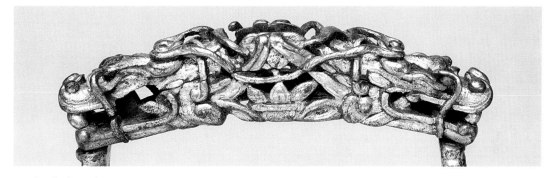

127, detail of crossbar

The key aspects of the style, form, and construction of this stunning pair of stirrups appear to be without precedent and largely without parallel. Like most stirrups from Tibet, China, and Central Asia they have a pair of outward-facing dragon heads at the top. The dragon heads, however, are unlike those seen on any other pair of stirrups in their form and execution, and appear to be Yuan in style at the latest and are possibly much earlier. They are long and narrow and form an almost horizontal crossbar at the tops of the stirrups (see detail). Their chiseling is deeply undercut so that their horns, tendrils, and mouths are fully in the round. The crossbar is made in two halves, upper and lower, which are riveted together, an otherwise unknown form of stirrup construction. The slot for the stirrup leather pierces the crossbar vertically, with a transverse bar in the center of the slot, rather than the usual horizontal slot found on the majority of stirrups. There are two short upper arms, rather than the long post-

like arms found on other examples. The arms flare out into a curved oval that forms the sides and bottom of the tread. These are pierced and deeply chiseled with floral designs. The principal motif on the sides of the treads appears to be a view of the top of the dragon heads as they are seen on the crossbars. The base of the tread is pierced with a reticular grill pattern. The edges have a continuous chiseled border of half-round lobes. The stirrups are heavily damascened overall in gold and silver. Where the silver is slightly worn, particularly on the inner sides of the treads, it appears to have been applied in flat strips, very reminiscent of the technique described by Tashi Namgyal, as quoted in "Saddles and Tack, Stirrups, and Bridles" above.

The date range suggested for these stirrups is purely speculative. Because they are stylistically very unorthodox, as well as extremely lavish, it would be tempting to attribute them to a period as early as the Yarlung dynasty (7th–9th century), except for the fact that it has yet to be demonstrated that damascening in gold and silver on iron was known or practiced at such an early date. A later date, therefore, seems more reasonable. Although the stirrups are difficult to categorize, the quality of the ironwork, the richness of the decoration, and their distinctively atypical style make these very important examples, both as stirrups and as metalwork in general.

PUBLICATION: Thurman and Weldon 1999, no. 72, pp. 156–57.

128

129

128. PAIR OF STIRRUPS

Tibetan, 15th–18th century

Iron, gold, and silver

H. 5⅞ in. (14.9 cm)

The Metropolitan Museum of Art, New York, Purchase, Kenneth
and Vivian Lam Gift, 2002 (2002.220a, b)

Although much simpler in their design and execution than the previous example, the stirrups
here offer two very interesting points of comparison. The features that are reminiscent of the previous pair are the vertical slot for the stirrup leathers
and the reticular oval tread with pierced and curved
sides, although the sides on this pair are much
shorter. The addorsed dragon heads are much more
conventional. They are set close together at the top,
in relatively low relief, and are somewhat soft in
their chiseling. The arms are beaded, which is fairly
unusual, and semicircular in section, the inner faces
being flat. The sides of the tread are pierced with a
symmetrical spray of floral scrollwork. The stirrups
are damascened overall in gold and silver with careful
transitions between the two materials to set off the

different design elements. Although not as dramatic
as the previous pair, these stirrups are nevertheless
typologically and aesthetically interesting in themselves. They also offer a good contrast to the more
conventional form of stirrup found in Mongolia,
China, and Tibet, which has broadly chiseled dragon
heads, simple arms, and a round tread plate, and
which is generally, but incorrectly, assumed to be the
only form of stirrup used in the region.

129. STIRRUP

Tibetan, 15th–18th century

Iron, gold, and silver

H. 4½ in. (11.9 cm)

The Metropolitan Museum of Art, New York, Purchase, Arthur
Ochs Sulzberger Gift, 1999 (1999.257)

Several Tibetan stirrups of this particular type
are known.[1] It is characterized by having the
form of an arch with a peak in the center, above the

slot for the stirrup leather; a pair of addorsed dragon
heads that slope downward following the contour
of the arch; and round smooth arms that merge into
the curved ends of a pierced tread that is rectangular
or a narrow oblong in shape. This example is nicely
made, with well-modeled and deeply chiseled, but
not pierced, dragon heads damascened in gold; the
arms damascened in gold and silver; and fairly intricate silver damascening on the tread consisting of,
on the top of the tread, the Wheel of Law surrounded
by wave motifs and, on the underside, repeating patterns of spirals and concentric circles. The tread has
a slightly down-turned edge, the underside of which
is damascened in silver with a lotus leaf pattern.
This stirrup may correspond to the smaller Tibetan
type mentioned by Tashi Namgyal, cited in "Saddles
and Tack, Stirrups, and Bridles" above.

1. For example, a pair of similar stirrups in the American
   Museum of Natural History, New York (70.2/3496 BC), and a
   pair in the Department of Asian Art, Metropolitan Museum
   (1997.445.1, .2). Of the latter pair, however, the decoration and
   the stirrups themselves may be much later.

130. PAIR OF STIRRUPS

Tibetan, 16th–18th century
Iron, gold, and silver
H. 5⅛ in. (13 cm)
The Metropolitan Museum of Art, New York, Purchase, Rogers
Fund, and Bequest of Stephen V. Grancsay, by exchange, 1997
(1997.214.2a, b)

Although closer in form to the well-known style of Mongolian, Chinese, and Tibetan stirrups still in use in the region today, this pair, with its slender proportions and fine decoration, is earlier than most examples of this type. The dragon heads are chiseled in high relief with deep undercutting and some piercing. At the back of each head, above the slot for the stirrup leather, there is a short post with a flat top, which becomes a characteristic feature of the type. The arms are relatively flat and widen slightly from the top to the bottom, unlike the thicker, usually square arms on later examples. The tread is a flat plate without piercings and is oval, rather than the round form with a deep rim found on later stirrups of this type. The dragon heads are damascened in gold, while the arms are damascened in silver inside and out. The treads are decorated with the interlocked king's earrings motif and a narrow border damascened in silver. These stirrups were acquired with the saddle in catalogue number 120, which was said to have been used by the Fourteenth Dalai Lama.

130

131. PAIR OF STIRRUPS

Tibetan, 16th–18th century
Iron, gold, and silver
H. 6½ in. (16.5 cm)
The Metropolitan Museum of Art, New York, Purchase, Arthur
Ochs Sulzberger Gift, 2002 (2002.136.1, .2)

In terms of form, the deep lozenge-shaped box tread found on these stirrups is very rare. On Tibetan stirrups, one generally sees flat treads that are round or oval or, occasionally, curved and oblong, as in the preceding examples. Stirrups with deep treads of this type are otherwise virtually unknown. Each stirrup consists of an arch in the

131

form of an inverted U, which is attached to the box tread. The tread has a flat lozenge-shaped top and deep sides. The arches are rectangular in section, and at the apex of each arch there is a vertical slot. At either end of the interior of each slot there is a small vertical channel for a crossbar (missing), around which the stirrup leather would have passed. The base of each arch is socketed into the corners of the tread plate and peened over on the underside.

The arches are deeply chiseled in relief with engraved details, leaving only the inner faces of the arches flat. The box treads, in addition to being similarly chiseled and engraved, are also pierced throughout. All of the exterior surfaces are crosshatched and damascened in gold, except for the inner faces of the arches, which are damascened in silver.

A pair of dragon heads flanks the slot at the apex of each arch. The arms of the arches extend from the mouth of the dragons, as is usual. The arms are decorated with a repeating four-petal flower motif on the front and back and an undulating dragon on each side. The top plate of each tread is decorated with the Wheel of Dharma motif (*chos kyi 'khor lo*), which has the whirling emblem (*dga' 'khyil*) in its center and six *vajra* spokes radiating from it. The wheel motif is set in a dense field of pierced scrollwork. The center of each side of the box treads is decorated with a lotus motif flanked by a pair of dragons, all set in a dense field of pierced scrollwork. The bottom edges of the treads have cusped edges.

The construction is unusual in that the arms of arches are peened to the treads, as opposed to the usual method in which the arms are forged in one with the treads, are hammer welded, or form an integral part of a one-piece cast. Also unusual is the arrangement for the stirrup leather, which consists of a vertical slot requiring a crossbar, as opposed to the simple horizontal slot usually found on Tibetan and Sino-Tibetan stirrups.

As examples of elaborately pierced, engraved, and damascened Tibetan ironwork, these stirrups are exceptional for the robust boldness of their decoration, even though they do not compare in terms of finesse with many of the examples included in this catalogue. Instead, they appear to represent a distinct style that depended on strength rather than delicacy for its impact.

132. PAIR OF STIRRUPS

Tibetan or Mongolian, possibly 16th–19th century
Wood, iron, and copper alloy
H. 6 in. (15.2 cm)
The Metropolitan Museum of Art, New York, Fletcher Fund, 2004 (2004.400a, b)

Despite their initial appearance of simplicity in both form and materials, these stirrups are relatively complex and well made in a very purposeful style that shows careful attention to detail and function. Rudimentary stirrups made from bentwood and also carved horn exist as a type and have been identified both as Tibetan and Mongolian.[1] This pair, however, is more finely finished and very unusual in having iron fittings. In addition, the form and construction are similar to that of some of the earliest existing stirrups, showing an amazing continuity of style and leaving the date of these stirrups open to speculation.[2]

Each stirrup consists of a teardrop-shaped bentwood hoop with a short tab at the apex and is partly clad with iron fittings. The wood, possibly maple or birch, is medium brown in color and has a straight, close grain.[3] The iron fittings consist of a faceplate on the front and back, covering the top half of the stirrup from the midpoint of the arms to the top of the tab, which is pierced by a rectangular slot for the stirrup leathers. The outer sides of the arms, between the edges of the faceplates, are each covered by an iron side plate, which is curved to follow the contour of the arms, has a slight medial ridge, and ends in a triangular point. The outside of the bottom of each hoop is reinforced by a narrow flat band of iron, the ends of which are covered by the points of the side plates and secured by a single nail on either side. The faceplates are attached by six dome-headed nails, each with a small copper alloy washer; the outer edge of each washer is decorated with a simple diagonal notch pattern. Each pair of side plates appears to be made of a single continuous piece of iron. A thin edging strip of copper alloy is found at the edges of the faceplates where they overlap the side plates. One edging strip is missing from the right stirrup and three are missing from the left stirrup. The left stirrup can be differentiated from the right by the degree of wear on the points of each side plate. The point of one side plate on each stirrup is worn relatively smooth, while the point on the oppo-

132

133

site side is sharp. Presumably the worn points indicate the side closest to the horse, where they would have become smooth by regular contact with the leather fenders or saddle rug with which Tibetan and Mongolian saddles are typically equipped.

1. For instance, there are three pairs in the American Museum of Natural History, New York, two catalogued as Tibetan (70.0/2113, 70.0/2114) and one as Mongolian (73/484); and a pair catalogued as Mongolian in the Museum für Völkerkunde, Berlin (I.A.2009)
2. Compare these stirrups, for example, with a pair of wooden stirrups sheathed in gilded copper, dating from the Sixteen Kingdoms period (407–436), found in Beipiao, Liaoning Province, which borders Inner Mongolia; illustrated in Watt 2004, no. 41.
3. Turned wood bowls from Tibet and Mongolia are also made of birch and maple and are highly regarded for their grain and texture. I am grateful to John Canonico, formerly in charge of furniture conservation at the Metropolitan Museum, for his opinions of the nature of the wood.

133. FOUR HARNESS FITTINGS

Tibetan, 15th–17th century
Iron, gold, leather, copper
L. 3⅛ in. (7.9 cm) to 2⅛ in. (5.4 cm)
The Metropolitan Museum of Art, New York, Purchase, Kenneth and Vivian Lam Gift, 2002 (2002.17.4, .7, .10, .16)

Harness fittings of this type were used to decorate the leather straps of horse tack of the highest quality, and would have been used in conjunction with saddles such as those in the previous entries and with the two bridles that follow. They are very good examples of fine Tibetan ironwork and relate not only to equestrian equipment but also to the best sword fittings as well as damascened iron ritual objects. The fitting are made of iron, pierced, chiseled, and damascened in gold, and decorated with scrollwork, floral motifs, dragons, *ju'i* scrolls, and the concentric spiral motif damascened in fine lines. The leaf-shaped pendants on two of the fittings retain their original leather lining pad, which is held by small copper rivets.

134. BRIDLE AND MATCHING CRUPPER STRAPS

Tibetan, 15th–17th century
Iron, leather, gold, and textile
Bridle, H. 22 in. (55.9 cm), W. 10 in. (25.4 cm);
crupper, L. 37 in. (94 cm)
The Metropolitan Museum of Art, New York, Purchase, Arthur
Ochs Sulzberger Gift, 2005 (2005.73a, b)

The lavish fittings of this bridle rank among the best examples of pierced and damascened Tibetan ironwork. The delicacy and complexity are particularly noteworthy, and in many ways they are equal to those of the bridle in the following entry, which is one of the best of this type in existence. Ceremonial bridles with pierced ironwork fittings are extremely rare, the vast majority having fittings of gilded copper.

The bridle consists of a headstall, bit, and two lead straps for the reins. The headstall is made up of a foundation of shagreen leather, decorated with a series of elaborate fittings made of pierced and chiseled iron and damascened in gold. The fittings include three large ogival plaques located in the center of the forehead band (see detail) and on the noseband; domed bosses along the length of the leather straps; and four diagonal sections formed of pierced-iron fittings linked together and not backed by straps. The snaffle bit is attached by two large bit rings, each of which has two leaflike projections pierced with scrollwork. The ends of the snaffle and the bit rings are also chiseled and damascened in gold (see detail). The two short leather leads for the reins are attached to the bit rings on either side by chiseled iron toggles, which match the ends of the snaffle bit. The leads are fitted with damascened iron tabs, the proper right one ending in a flat iron ring.

The pierced work of the ogival plaques, the domed bosses, and the extensions of the bit rings appear to be very thin, but the iron is actually relatively thick. The effect is created by the upper layer of scrollwork being finely chiseled and deeply undercut, the thickness allowing for depth and overlap in the designs. Each of the plaques is decorated with a dragon set among scrollwork. In the largest plaque, in the center of the forehead band, much of the dragon's body is overlapped by tendrils of scroll-

134, detail of plaque on forehead band

134, detail of snaffle and bit ring

work that are chiseled entirely in the round. The same is true on all of the larger iron fittings, in which the pierced work has the appearance of two layers due to the skillful undercutting and chiseling.

Although incomplete, the crupper (not pictured) is of interest for its fittings and for the fact that it appears to match the bridle as part of the same elaborate set of tack, rather than merely being associated with it. The crupper consists of shagreen leather strap crossed in an X pattern; the two forward ends are loose (for attachment to the rear of a saddle), and the opposite ends form the padded loop that fits under the horse's tail. Two sets of smaller subsidiary straps are joined to the main straps, and all are decorated with a series of deeply chiseled iron bosses damascened in gold. There are two flaps of red silk brocade at either end of the tail loop, and a square of the same material at the center of the straps, the latter being the lining for the central crupper boss, which is missing.

134

135. BRIDLE

Tibetan, 15th–17th century
Leather, iron, and gold
H. 21 in. (53.3 cm), W. 19 in. (48.3 cm)
The Metropolitan Museum of Art, New York, Purchase, Gift of
J. Pierpont Morgan, by exchange, 1998 (1998.282)

While both the previous bridle and this one are superb examples if their type, of the two this bridle is more refined in its details and more complex in its construction. The treatment of their pierced and chiseled work and damascened decoration also represents subtle but clear differences in style.

The bridle consists of a headstall, snaffle bit, and two braided leather leads for the reins. The headstall is made up of shagreen leather straps comprising a horizontal noseband, a forehead band, which extends around under the jaw, a vertical noseband, and two cheek bands that are connected over the top of the head by the head strap. The headstall is decorated with an elaborate series of pierced and chiseled iron fittings damascened in gold. In the center of the forehead band there is a lobed ogival plaque delicately pierced with a thin serpentine dragon on a scrollwork ground (see detail). To add to the appearance of depth there is a secondary ground behind the scrollwork, which is made of a shaped plate of dark iron damascened in gold with a wave pattern. In the center of the vertical noseband there is a plaque in the form of a *vajra*, pierced and chiseled in low relief, which is decorated with *tsi pa ṭa* masks on either end and a whirling emblem (*dga' 'khyil*) in the center (see detail). There are two rings at the top and the bottom of the *vajra* to which four quatrefoil plaques are attached by narrow stems. The plaques run diagonally from the *vajra*, the two above being linked to bosses on the forehead band and the two below to bosses on the noseband. From the latter two, additional plaques run diagonally in the opposite direction and are linked to bosses on the check bands. Each plaque is decorated with small animals such as birds and rabbits, singly or in pairs, on a scrollwork ground. These plaques also have a secondary ground behind the scrollwork, the same as that described above, as do some of the larger pierced bosses.

At the top of the headstall there is a buckle to fasten the head strap and an iron latch that engages

135

135, detail of plaque on vertical noseband

135, detail of bit ring

135, detail of plaque on forehead band

slots rimmed with iron borders on the strap that runs under the jaw, all of which are damascened in gold. At the bottom the headstall is connected to a bit ring on either side by a chiseled and damascened toggle decorated with a *tsi pa ṭa* mask. Each of the bit rings has two S-shaped extensions, which end in a pierced ogival finial with an embossed whirling motif in its center. The bit rings are chiseled all around with scrollwork and damascened in gold (see detail). Each end of the bit is attached to the bit ring by a toggle similar to that above. The braided leather rein leads are attached to the bit rings by decorated iron tabs linked to a third pair of similarly decorated toggles. Although some of the fittings vary slightly in style and workmanship, overall the quality and degree of finish are very high. In addition, many small areas of the fittings or the borders surrounding them are decorated with geometric patterns and concentric spiral motifs damascened in fine gold lines.

It is of anecdotal interest to note that this bridle was used as a costume prop in the movie *Little Buddha* (1993), in which it can be seen on the horse used by Keanu Reeves in his portrayal of Prince Siddhartha, the historical founder of Buddhism.

PUBLICATION: LaRocca 1999a, pp. 121–22, fig. 16.

Fig. 46. *'jig rten lugs kyi bstan bcos las dpyad don gsal ba'i sgron me zhes grags pa bzhugs so,* by bkra shis rnam rgyal, 1524. Beinecke Rare Book and Manuscript Library, Yale University, fols. 2b (list of contents), 73b (colophon)

Excerpts from *A Treatise on Worldly Traditions, known as the Shining Lamp of Analysis* (*'jig rten lugs kyi bstan bcos las dpyad don gsal ba'i sgron me zhes grags pa bzhugs so*, འཇིག་རྟེན་ལུགས་ཀྱི་བསྟན་བཅོས་ལས་དཔྱད་ དོན་གསལ་བའི་སྒྲོན་མེ་ཞེས་གྲགས་པ་བཞུགས་སོ།), by Tashi Namgyal (*bya 'jam dbyangs bkra shis rnam rgyal*), 1524[1]

This text is essentially a manual of connoisseurship. It outlines the ways in which a wide variety of items could be categorized and assessed according to criteria such as age, place of origin, style, quality, and materials. Chapters are devoted to religious statues, sacred texts, and reliquaries, cymbals, bells, silk fabrics, porcelain, tea, and—of particular interest for the purposes of the present catalogue—swords, armor, helmets, stirrups, and saddles. Several of the same topics are found in a handful of closely related Tibetan texts.[2] Unfortunately, many of these are incomplete, and are partly inaccurate or unintelligible due to spelling changes introduced by later copyists. These texts are also particularly challenging in that they can include a number of technical and archaic terms, some of which can only be provisionally translated, if at all.[3]

The *Treatise on Worldly Traditions* is important because it appears to be the earliest known Tibetan text of this genre to cover such a broad range of topics, and it may have served as the basis for later texts dealing with the same subjects. It is also important in that the accuracy of its contents can be verified, as far as possible, by comparing five extant versions. Of these, however, only the one listed below under number 2 is largely complete.[4]

1. Beinecke Library, Yale University, New Haven, uncatalogued manuscript (see fig. 46). This appears to be the earliest version. It is missing the first folio (including the title) and several other folios throughout, but includes the colophon on the last folio. The entire sword chapter and the first part of the armor chapter are missing.[5]

2. Photocopy made from an original in the library of Rai Bahadur Burmiok Athing (1902–1988), Sikkim (copy provided by Gene Smith). Composed of 42 folios, it is the only complete version in this group. It follows the Beinecke manuscript closely, but with many minor spelling variations and a few missing lines of text. Confirmation of the missing title and the contents of the missing first folio of the Beinecke manuscript comes from this version and number 5 below.

3. British Library manuscript Or 11,374, entitled *rin po che bzo yi las kyi bsgrub pa'i rgyud dang ja dang dar gos chen dang rta rgyud tshugs bzang ngan gyi rtag pa bzhugs so* (The Continuum of Precious Things Accomplished by the Crafts, and the Analysis of the Quality and Forms of Tea, Silk Brocades, and Horse Breeds). The title and introduction differ from those above, but from folio 3 onward this manuscript matches the others until the final folios. It has many spelling differences and random missing lines of text, and it does not include a colophon. A note on the last page states that the manuscript was donated by Sir Charles Bell, June 10, 1933.

---

1. The author is named in the colophon as bkra shis rnam rgyal dpal bzang po (Beinecke, fol. 73b; Burmiok Athing, fol. 42b; and Gangtok 1981, p. 266). The identification with bya 'jam dbyangs bkra shis rnam rgyal was kindly pointed out to me by Gene Smith. The same author is referred to as "Peykoe Tashi Namgyal, a Tibetan scholar who specialized in the art of manufacturing icons and musical instruments," in an article by Rinchen T. Sandhutsang, "Tibetan Porcelain," *Tibet Journal* 7, nos. 1–2 (spring–summer 1982), p. 82. Peykoe refers to the monastery of padma bkod in Metok County, southeastern Tibet, named in the colophon as the place where Tashi Namgyal wrote this work.

2. In addition to those listed, there are also the relevant sections in Tashi Tsering 1979; the text *rgya bod kyi nor rdzas kyi ris brtags shing dpyad pa'i dpyad don yid kyi 'dod 'jo*, which is included in Lhasa 1990, cited in Martin 1997, p. 233; and the chapter on swords in the *rgya bod yig tshang chen mo* (see Palchor Zangpo, pp. 232–39).

3. The difficulty of translating texts of this type is commented on by Gyatsho Tshering in "A Short Introductory Note on Porcelain Cups of Tibet," *Tibetan Studies: Proceedings of the 4th Seminar of the International Association for Tibetan Studies, Schloss Hohenkammer, Munich 1985* (Munich, 1988), pp. 171–75.

4. Above all I am indebted to Lozang Jamspal, who worked patiently and tirelessly to guide me through the reading and provisional translations of these texts over the course of three years. I am very grateful to several individuals for generously bringing the texts to my attention, and in some cases providing copies of them, especially Gene Smith, Amy Heller, Dan Martin, and Nawang Thokmey. Another version of this text once belonged to Giuseppe Tucci, whose comments on its importance are merely echoed here (Tucci 1959). The sculpture chapter of the Tucci version was later discussed in detail by Erberto Lo Bue (1997). Unfortunately, the present location of the Tucci manuscript is unknown. I am indebted to Prof. Lo Bue and Elena Rossi Filibeck for their efforts to locate it.

5. Originally the folios of the Beinecke manuscript seem to have been unnumbered. Small Tibetan numbers, perhaps added by a proofreader, are found just above the *yig mgo* at the start of the front side of each folio. However, what should be folio 21 is numbered 22, which is confirmed by the fact that above the number 22 there is a small notation in *'khyug yig* (cursive script), which reads ༢། གྲང་ཡིན་འདུག ("but seems to be 21"). More recently Western numbers, which do not reflect the correct sequence of the folios, were added in pencil. The folio numbers cited in this appendix refer to the Tibetan numbers, although from folio 22 onward the count is off by one, as the *'khyug yig* notation indicates.

4. Edition published in Gangtok in 1981, included in the *legs par bshad pa padma dkar po'i chun po* by Hūṃkaradzaya (a variant of the text found in Tashi Tsering 1979, with additions). The section entitled *legs par bshad pa pad dkar chos 'bum bsdus pa bzhugs so* (pp. 165–267) includes chapters 1–8, 13–18, and a portion of the same colophon (p. 266) as the Beinecke manuscript. Although some of the opening phrases of the introduction are different, most of the text is copied verbatim, but with some omissions and many spelling differences.

5. Edition published in Thimphu, Bhutan, in 1975. This version consists of 24 folios (less than half of the original text) comprising only the first 7 chapters (out of 18), and does not include the colophon.

The complete table of contents, which appears in all five versions (with some spelling variations), is as follows:[6]

1. *sku gsung thugs rten* (སྐུ་གསུང་ཐུགས་རྟེན་), Receptacles of Body, Speech, and Mind
2. *rin chen yi dpyad* (རིན་ཆེན་ཡི་དཔྱད་), Analysis of Jewels
3. *sil snyan* (སིལ་སྙན་), Large Cymbals
4. *dril bu* (དྲིལ་བུ་), Bells
5. *ting ting shag* (ཏིང་ཏིང་ཤག་), Small Cymbals
6. *gos* (གོས་), Clothing or Silk Cloth
7. *dar zab ling med* (དར་ཟབ་ལིང་མེད་), Fine Silks, Patterned and Unpatterned
8. *dkar yol* (དཀར་ཡོལ་), Porcelain
9. *ja* (ཇ་), Tea
10. *ral gri* (རལ་གྲི་), Swords
11. *khrab* (ཁྲབ་), Armor
12. *rmog* (རྨོག་), Helmets
13. *ras* (རས་), Cotton
14. *bse* (བསེ་), Leather or Rhinoceros Hide
15. *yob* (ཡོབ་), Stirrups
16. *tshags gser sga* (ཚགས་གསེར་སྒ་), Saddles Decorated in Gold
17. *thor bu ba* (ཐོར་བུ་བ་), Miscellaneous Topics
18. *rta dpyad* (རྟ་དཔྱད་), Analysis of Horses[7]

Because the published versions of this text are incomplete or corrupt and the manuscript versions are not readily accessible, the chapters dealing with armor, weapons, stirrups, and saddles, and the colophon are reproduced here in the original Tibetan in their entirety. The Beinecke manuscript has been taken as the most authoritative, with its missing sections supplied by the Burmiok Athing text, with reference to the British Library and Gangtok texts when applicable. All the versions have been closely compared for spelling and content in an effort to ensure that the chapters given here are as complete, consistent, and accurate as possible.

Chapter 10, རལ་གྲི་ (Swords)[8]

རལ་གྲི་ལ་ནི་ཐུབ་ཁྲུངས་གསར་རྟིང་བཏགས། ལྕགས་རིས་ནར་ཐེས་སྐྱ་གོག་ཐུར་གསུམ་དཔྱད། ནང་ཚན་དབྱེ་བ་རྣམས་སུ་ཤེས་པར་བྱ།

[The origins of the five types of swords.] ཐུབ་ཁྲུངས་ལྷ་མ་ཡིན་དང་སྲིན་ འབྲུགས་ཆེ། ལྷ་མ་ཡིན་གྱི་མཚོན་ཆ་རྩལ་[བཙལ་]བར་བརྩམ། དྲག་པོའི་འབྱུང་པོ་ལགས་ན་ མཚོན་ཆ་ཅན། མཐོང་ནས་སྟོབས་ཀྱི་རིགས་ལས་འཕྲོག་ཏུ་ཐིན། འབྱུང་པོ་ཐིང་ནས་ཐོས་ པར་ཚམ་[བརྩམ་]ན་ཡང་། མ་ཐར་ལྕགས་ཀྱི་ལ་བོང་[24b]ཉིན་དུ་སྐྱལ། ལྷ་མ་ཡིན་གྱིས་དེ་ ཉིད་ལས་བརྩམས་ཏེ། སོག་ཀྲུན་རལ་གྲི་བཟུངས་ལས་འོང་འབར་བ། རིག་པ་ཆམ་གྱིས་ ཐམས་ཅད་གཅོད་པ་བྱུང་། དེ་ཉིད་སོག་ཡུལ་ཞེས་བྱའི་ཐ་[མཐའ་]ལ་ལྱངས། མགར་བ་ སོག་པོ་ཐུབ་ཀྲུལ་ཞེས་བྱ་བས། དེ་ལ་དཔེ་བྱས་མང་དུ་བརྩམས་པར་གྲགས། གྱི་ནེ་ལྕགས་ ཀྱི་ལ་བོང་གསེས་[བཟོས་]པས་ན། སོག་པོ་ལྕགས་ལའོ་བརྩོ་བར་གྲགས་པ་ཡིན། རྒྱལ་མོ་ཁྲལ་ པོའི་]ཞན་ཡུལ་བུ་བའི་ལྱང་པ་ར། ཞན་ཟ་ཐྲོ་མོ་[ཞ་ཟ་ཁྲམ་] བྱ་བས་བརྟད་པའི་གྲིས། སྟེད་ཀྱི་གྲི་གུ་གོས་དང་ལྱན་བཏད་བཏད[9] ཐུབ་མེད་གྲི་ལ་མཁས་པར་དེ་ནས་གྲགས། ཞང་མ

---

6. Beinecke, fol. 2b; Burmiok Athing, fol. 2a; British Library Or 11,374 (hereafter, Brit. Lib.), fol. 3b; Gangtok 1981, p. 166; and Thimphu 1975, p. 4.
7. The headings for chapters 17 and 18 are not specified in the list of contents, but are taken from the body of the text itself; e.g., Beinecke, fol. 55b; Burmiok Athing, fol. 32a; and Brit. Lib., fol. 102a: ཐོར་བུ་བ་དང་རྟ་དཔྱད་རྣམས་པ་གཉིས་, the two [chapters], scattered [topics] and the analysis of horses.
8. This chapter is missing from the Beinecke, Gangtok 1981, and Thimphu 1975 versions. The text given here is taken from Burmiok Athing, fols. 24a–27a, in comparison with Brit. Lib., fols. 73b–83b. Where spelling differences occur the former has

generally been followed. Individual Tibetan words in square brackets represent alternate spellings from the latter or elsewhere as noted. Grammatical or spelling corrections, made only when absolutely necessary for clarity, are added in parentheses. The folio numbers in brackets in this section are from the Burmiok Athing text only. Sectional headings in English have been added in brackets.
9. Brit. Lib., fol. 74b, reads སྟེད་ཀྱི་གྲི་གུ་དགུ་གོས་དང་ལྱན་ཅིག་བཏད་, but both readings seem garbled. It should perhaps read སྟེད་ཀྱི་གྲི་གུ་དགུ་གོས་དང་ལྱན་གཅིག་བཏད་, in the sense that the sword could cut through nine layers of silk at once, which is similar to the claims made for the other types that follow.

གས་(གོས་?) ལ་རྫོ་བར་དེ་དུ་ཀྲགས།[10] ཞེན་ཞེས་བྱ་བ་ལྱུང་བའི་མིང་ཡིན་ཏེ། མ་ཞེས་བྱ་བ་ མགར་བ་དགའ་ལ་བྱུགས། དེ་ལ་རྟེ་ཡིག་བྱུང་བ་ལྡང་རྟེ་ཟེར། ཏུ་བེད་ཅེས་བྱ་ཏོར་གྱི་གྱི་ཡིན་ཏེ།[11] ཟིང་གིར་རྒྱལ་པོའི་རིང་ལ་བྱུང་བར་གདའ།[12] ཏུ་[མ་ཏུ་]ཞེས་བྱ་བའི་[བུའི་]གྲོང་ཁྱེར་ཆེན་པོ་ དེར། མགར་བ་ཏུ་བེད་[ཏུགེ་]བྱ་བས་བཟོས་པ་ཡིན། གྱི་དེས་འབྲོང་དུ་དྲུག་ཚམ་ཆོད་ཅེས་ ཟོས། ཏུ་བེད་ར་ལ་རྒྱལ་བར་དེ་ནས་བྱུགས། གྱི་ཟི་བོད་ཡུལ་དབུས་ཀྱི་རལ་གྱི་དེ།[13] གྱི་གུས་ བཙན་པོའི་དུས་སུ་དར་བ་ཡིན། ཡུལ་དབར་དགུ་ཆེས་བྱ་བའི་ས་ཆ་དེར། མགར་བ་མི་ཟི་སྐུན་ དགས་བཏང་བ་ལས།[14] རྩོ་དང་འཛོམ་ལས་གནས་ཀྱི་འདུ་ཐུག་ཆོད།[15] གྱི་ཟི་གནད་ལ་རྫོ་བར་ དེ་ནས་བྱུང་། དེ་ཡིས་སློབ་མས་བོད་དུ་མང་དུ་བྱུང་། བོད་ཡུལ་རལ་གྱི་མོད་པ་དེ་ལྟར་ཡིན། འཛའ་རལ་ཐ་མའི་ཡུལ་དུ་བྱུང་བ་སྟེ། ནས་མཁན་གྱི་མཚོས་རིང་ལ་སྲིད་ཅེས་ཟེར། འཛའ་ ཡུལ་རྫོ་ཡུགས་བྱ་བའི་ནགས་སེབ་(གསེབ་)ན། མགར་བ་ཐགས་[ཐལ་]མགོ་བྱ་བས་བཏང་ པ་ཡིན། གྱི་དེས་སྟོང་ཞིང་དགུ་ཆོད་པས་ན། འཛའ་རལ་ཞིང་ལ་རྫོ་བར་དེ་ནས་གྲགས།

[The characteristics distinguishing old swords from new.] གསར་རྙིང་ ཏུག་[བཏུགས་]པའི་རིམ་པ་འདི་ལྟ་སྟེ།[16] གྱི་རིགས་རྩིང་མ་རྣམས་ཀྱི་མཚན་ཉིད་ནི། བྱར་ནི་ ཏེ་བ་མི་ཡིན་ཅིག་དུ་འདུས། འཕྲེ་བ་མ་ཡིན་ཐ་དད་སོ་སོར་[25a]གསལ། དཔེར་ན་རྒྱ་མཚོ་ ཆེན་པོ་དུས་པ་ལ། ཆུ་སྔུ་འབབ་བ་སོ་སོར་གསལ་བ་བཞིན། ཞིན་ཏུ་རྩིང་མ་ལྱུགས་མའི་རྣམ་ པ་ལ། ཕྱིས་ལ་སོགས་བ་མི་གསལ་ཕྱིད་[ཕྱིང་]བ་ཡོད། དེ་ཡང་ཐོགས་མར་བླུག་སྟེ་བཏུངས་བ

[The five classes or types of iron.] ལྱུགས་རིགས་[རིགས་]པོ་ལྱུགས་མོ་ལྱུགས་ མ་ཟིན་དང་། རྟེས་སྱུག་སྲུ་འདུས་ལྱུ་རུ་ཞེས་པ་བྱ།[18] པོ་ལྱུགས་དཀར་ལ་དར་པོགས་[ཆགས་] ནག་པ་དང་། མོ་ལྱུགས་ནག་ལ་དར་པོགས་དཀར་བ་སྟེ། མ་ཟིན་ལྱུགས་ཀྱི་ནི་སྟོ་ལ་སྐྲ་བ ཉིད། རྟེས་སྱུག་ལྱུགས་ནི་རྩོ་[སྟོ་]ལ་དམར་དམས་ཡོད། ལྱུགས་འདུས་པའི་ནི་རི་མོ་གུ་གུ་མང་ པོ་ལྱུགས་ལྱུགས་དང་མོ་ལྱུགས་རྣ་[བསྟེལ་]མ་སོགས། མ་ཟིན་གང་འཛ་རྫོ་བར་[འདྲེས་] ཞེས་པར་བྱ། སོ་སོར་རྫོ་ཆུང་འཛུན་པར་ཞེས་པར་བྱ། པོ་ལྱུགས་ཀྱི་ནི་རྫོ་མོ་ལྱུགས་མ་ཉེན་ མ ད་ང་།[19] ཕྱུ་རྣམས་ཕལ་ཆེ་[ཞེས་ཆེ་]མོ་ལྱུགས་བྱས་པ་མང་། ཞིན་ཀུང་ཕུང་འབྱུར་པོ་ ལྱུགས་ཡིན་པར་བཤད།

[The four types of hot and six types of cold tempering.] དར་ལ་ཚོ་ དར་གྲང་དར་གཉིས་སུ་དབྱེ། ཚ་དང་ཆུ་སྱུ་ཆུ་སྱུ་དུག་སྱུ་དང་། སྐྱན་སྱུ་བཞི་ཡིན་གྲང་དར་རྩ ད་ང་ཆུ། ཞོ་མ་ཆུ་དང་འཛིམ་འདག་རྗས་སྱེས་དྲུག[20] དེ་ཡང་པོ་ལྱུགས་ཆུ་སྱུའི་ཚ་དར་འབོད

---

10. The preceding two lines are missing from Brit. Lib., fol. 74b.

11. There are various spellings for the name of this type of sword. Burmiok Athing appears to read ཏུ་བེད་, whereas the sword chapter of the *rgya bod yig tshang chen mo*, the earliest text on the subject, uses the spelling ཏུ་ཡེད་ (Palchor Zangpo, pp. 232ff.). These could conceivably be confused if a text were being read aloud to a copyist. Both the spelling ཏུ་ཡེད་ and ཏུ་བདེ་ are used in Gangtok 1981 (for instance, p. 120), while the corresponding lines in the other edition of the same text have ཏུ་ཡེད་ (Tashi Tsering 1979, p. 68). Brit. Lib., fol. 74b ff., uses the spelling ཏུ་བེད་. This is also the spelling in the Das dictionary (1902b, p. 1328), and seems to be the result of an interpretation of a written text, basing the spelling on the perceived placement of the vowel over the second rather than the first letter of the second word. This spelling is probably more common in printed sources now due to its inclusion in Das. The spelling ཏུ་བེད་ is used in the present catalogue because it is consistent within Burmiok Athing and because it is phonetically closer to ཏུ་ཡེད་, which appears to be the earliest version of the term.

12. Burmiok Athing has བདང་, but this may be a misspelling of གདའ་, with the sense of འདུག་ or ཡོང་, while Brit. Lib., fol. 74b, has གྲགས་. Note also the mention of Genghis Khan as king of the Hor-Mongols.

13. Both texts misspell this sword type at its first citation: གུ་ཟི་ in Burmiok Athing and གུ་ཟི་ in Brit. Lib., fol. 75a. In should also be noted that although throughout most of Burmiok Athing this term is spelled གུ་ཟི་, in most other sources it appears as དགུ་ཟི་. Its spellings in Brit. Lib. include གུ་ཟི་, གུ་ཟི་, and དགུ་ཟི་.

14. The spelling of the names of the sword smiths, and the place-names, can vary considerably from one text to the next. For instance, མི་ཟི་ appears as མིག་ཟི་ in Brit. Lib., fol. 75a, and as མིག་ཟེས་ in the *rgya bod yig tshang chen mo* (see Palchor Zangpo, p. 234).

15. The term གནམ་གྱི་འཇུ་ཐག་, sky climbing rope, appears to be a reference to the དམུ་ or དམུ་ཐག་, the sky rope by which the early legendary Tibetan kings returned to heaven. The sky rope of *gri gum btsan po*, who is mentioned a few lines earlier, was said to have been cut during a duel, making him the first Tibetan king to leave his body on earth. See Stein 1972, pp. 48–49.

16. Burmiok Athing has ཏག་པ་ (permanent), but here and in other instances where this term is used it seems that a form of the verb བཏུག་ (to examine) or the noun ཏགས་ (signs) would be more appropriate.

17. The word for thick, མཐུག་པོ་, usually appears as ཐུག་ in Burmiok Athing and as འཐུག་ in Brit. Lib.

18. In Burmiok Athing the name of the fourth type of iron is first spelled རྗེས་སྲུ་, but appears as རྗེས་སྱུག་ thereafter, which is closer to the majority of variations found in the related texts. It is spelled this way in Lhasa 1990, p. 249. In the two Hūṃkaradzaya texts it appears as རྗེ་སྱུག་ (Tashi Tsering 1979, p. 74) and as སྱེ་སྱུག་ (Gangtok 1981, p. 131). In Brit. Lib., fol. 76b, it appears as རྗེས་སྱུག་ and རྗེས་འཇུག་. These terms may be a corruption of སྱེ་བསྒྲགས་, meaning "aggregated," or an abbreviation of རྗེས་སུ་འཇུག་པ་, meaning "to imitate or follow," but the exact spelling and meaning remain uncertain.

19. Here and in other instances, although the text reads གཉེན་ (relative), the sense of the text indicates that the term མཉེན་ (pliable, soft) is intended.

20. The spelling of the terms འཇིམ་འདག་, both of which can mean "clay" or "mud," is a combination taken from both texts. Brit. Lib., fol. 77a, has འཇིམ་སྱུག་, while Burmiok Athing, fol. 25a, has འཇིའས་འདག་. Other terms in this section have been confused due to similar pronunciations. Therefore, in the version given here several lines have been reconstructed using both texts and the sense of the context.

མོ་ལྕགས་ཚྭ་སྣའི་ཚ་དངར་འཕྲོད་པ་སྟེ།[21] སྣ་འདྲེས་ལྕགས་ལ་དྲུག་གི་ཚ་དངར་ཉིད། མ་དྲེས་ལྕགས་ལ་སྣོན་སྣའི་ཚ་དངར་མཆོག མ་ཉིང་ལྕགས་ལ་གྲང་ཆུའི་གྲང་དངར་དེ།[22] རྫེས་སྲུག་ལྕགས་ལ་གྲང་རྫས་གཡོགས་པ་སོགས། དེ་དག་ཐ་དད་སོ་སོར་འཕྲོད་པས་ན། དངར་ལྕགས་མ་བུ་འཕྲོད་པས་རྣོ་ལ་དངར། ལྕགས་ལ་དངར་གྱིས་རྒྱན་པ་ཞེས་སུ[25b] འདོགས།

[The five materials for polishing.] ཕྱིས་ལ་ཀོ་ཕྱིས་ཕྱིང་[འཆིང་(བུ་)] པའི་སྐྱ་ཕྱིས་དང་། དབྱིག་ཕྱིས་ཤིང་ཕྱིས་རྫས་ཕྱིས་རྣམ་པ་ལྔ། ཀོ་ཕྱིས་སྐུམ་སྟེ་ཞང་མ་རྣམས་ལ་མང་། ཕྱིང་ཕྱིས་སྐྱ་བ་ཀུ་ཟེ་རྣམས་ལ་མང་། དབྱིག་ཕྱིས་རྣོ་བ་སོག་པོ་རྣམས་ལ་མང་། ཤིང་ཕྱིས་རྒྱུབ་པ་འཇའ་རལ་རྣམས་ལ་མང་། རྫས་ཕྱིས་ནག་པ་ཧུ་པེད་རྣམས་ལ་མང་། གཞན་དག་ཅི་རིགས་པ་ཡིས་ཤེས་པར་བྱ།

[The three features: *skra*, *gog*, and *thur*.][23] སྐྲ་གོག་ཐུར་གསུམ་དབྱེ་བ་མ་ཤེས་ན། གྲི་རིགས་འབྱེད་པའི་མིག་དང་མི་ལྡན་པས། དེ་བས་དེ་ཡི་རྣམ་དབྱེ་བཤད་པར་བྱ། སྐྲ་རིགས་ཞེས་པ་སྐྲ་རྩེའི་དབྱིབས་ལྟ་བུ། ཤ་སྤུ་གཏོར་བ་ལྟ་བུ་སྐྱུ་བ་ཡོད། གོག་སྐྱུད་[སྐྱུར་] རིགས་ནི་མཐོ་སྨད་ཅན་དུ་འདོད།[24] ཐུར་གྱི་རིགས་ནི་དཀར་ནག་ཁྲ་བོར་བཤད། དེ་ཡང་ལྕུག་ཕྲན་སྒྲིགས་པ་ལྟ་བུར་འབྱུང་། སྐྲ་རིགས་ལ་ནི་གསེག་བརྡར་ཕྱེད་རྒྱུབ་པའི། རྗེས་ལ་ཁ་ཅིག་འདོད་ཀྱང་རྙིང་མ་མིན། བར་རྙིང་མན་ལ་དེ་དག་ཡོང་བ་སྲིད། རྙིང་མའི་སྐྲ་རིས་ལྕུགས་སྲིས་ཁྲད་ལས་བྱུང་།

[The divisions of the seven types of swords.] གྲི་རིགས་དབྱེ་བ་སོག་པོ་ཞང་མ་དང་། ཧུ་པེད་ཀུ་ཟི་འཇའ་རལ་ཤེལ་རྡོ་དང་། མཐིང་ཁྲ་རྣམས་[རྣམ་] པ་བདུན་དུ་དབྱེ་བ་ཡིན།[25] སོག་པོ་ཕལ་ཆེར་རྒྱ་རྩེ་[རྩེ་མོ་]ཆུང་བ་ལ། དཔུང་ཟུར་རྒྱས་པ་རྣལ་མའི་[སྦྲལ་པའི་] ཡ་ཐོད་འདྲ། གཞུང་ཚུགས་ཐང་ཤིང་ལོ་འདབ་དབྱིབས་འདྲ་བ། རྩེ་ནས་སོར་གཉིས་གཞལ་བར་ཕོ་མོའི་ལྕུགས། འདྲེས་མཚམས་ཅུང་ཟད་མ་འདྲེས་མགོ་ལྕོག་ཡོད།[26] དེ་ཡང་ཅུང་ཟད་རྩེ་འཕྱུར་རྣམ་པ་ཡོད། ཞང་མ་རྩེ་མོར་བལ་གྱི་ཁྲར་སོང་བས།[27] རྒྱ་རྩེ་ཆེ་ཞིང་རྩེ་སྣོར་དཔུང་པ་ཞུམ། ལུག་ཆོལ་ཞག་གི་བྲུགས་འདྲ་སྐུམ་བག་ལྡན། རྒྱ་བར་ཞང་ཐེམ་ཞེས་པ་ཡུ་མཚམས་ཉག ཁྱད་པར་རྩེ་ནས་སོར་གསུམ་གཞལ་བ་ན། སེན་སྣོར་ལྟ་བུའི་རྗེས་ཤིག་ཡོད་པ་ཡིན། གཞུང་གི་སྣང་དབྱིག་ཅུང་ཟད་མི་ཚུགས་པའོ། ཧུ་པེད་ནག་པས་སྤྲུལ་ནག་ཐུར་རྒྱུག་འདྲ། རྒྱ་རྩེ་ཆུང་ཞིང་རྩེ་མོ་དཔུང་མགོ་ཞུམ། འཐུག་ལ་རྒྱུབ་པ་[26a] རྩེ་ནས་སོར་བཞིའི་བར། ཐུར་[འཐུད་] མཚམས་སྟག་སོ་འདྲ་བ་མི་འགྱུར་རྟགས།[28] ཀུ་ཟི་ཕལ་ཆེར་སྐྱ་ལ་ལྡིད་པ་སྟེ། ལྕགས་ཀྱི་དབྱུག་པ་སྔོན་པོ་[སྔོན་སྔོན་?] ལྟ་བུ་ལ། ལྕང་རློན་ལྕུག་མ་འདྲ་བར་ལྡེམ་ལྡེམ་བྱེད། རྒྱ་རྩེ་ཅུང་ཡོད་དཔུང་པ་ཞུམ་པ་ཉིད། ཁྱད་པར་དཀྱུ་ཆོགས་སྤྲུལ་རིས་འདྲ་བ་ཡོད། ཁ་ཅིག་མགོ་ལྕོག་བུག་པ་ཅན་ཡང་སྲིད། ཞང་ཐེམ་ལྟ་བུའི་ཡུ་མཚམས་ཉག་པ་ཡོད། སྐོམས་(?) [ཉམས་] མེད་ཤལ་(ཤུལ་?) གོག་དག་ཏུ་འབྲུལ་པ་སྲིད། འཇའ་རལ་རྒྱ་བ་མ་གཏོགས་ཤང་ལང་སྟེ། ཤང་ལང་ལྡན་པ་ཅན་ལ་ཟེར་བ་ཡིན། འཇའ་རལ་ཕལ་ཆེར་ཧྲམ་ཞིང་ལྷོ་ལ་རྒྱུབ། རྒྱ་བ་བཤམ་(གཤམ་) ཕྲ་རྩེ་མོ་དཔུང་པ་རྒྱས། སོ་གཉིས་ཅུང་ཟད་སྲབ་པ་ཞིག་ལ་ཟེར། ཤེལ་རྡོ་སྐྱ་ཞིང་ལྕགས་འདྲེས་རི་མོ་རྩིང་། མཐིང་ཁྲ་སྔོ་ཞིང་ལྕགས་འདྲེས་རི་མོ་ཞིབ།

[Characteristics of the subcategories of the ten sword types.] དེ་ནི་བྱེ་བྲག་དབྱེ་བ་མཚན་ཉིད་ལ། སོག་པོ་སོག་རྗེ་ཞང་མ་ཞང་རྗེ་ཟེར།[29] ཧུ་པེད་ཧུ་གྲོགས་ཀུ་ཟི་ཀུ་བདག་དང་།[30] འཇའ་རལ་རྒྱལ་འཇའ་བཅུ་རུ་གྲགས་པ་ཡིན། དེ་ལས་གྱེས་པ་འོག་ཏུ་འཆད་བཞིན་ལང་[མང་]།[31] དེ་ཡིས་ངོས་འཛིན་བཤད་རྒྱ་[ཙ་]ན། སོག་པོ་ཉིད་ལས་གྱེས་པ་ལ།

---

21. Burmiok Athing has ཚྭ་དངར་ (salt tempering), when the context indicates that it should read ཚ་དངར་ (heat tempering). This same error occurs in the following two lines, again probably because of the similar sounds of the words for salt and heat.
22. Burmiok Athing has དྭང་དངར་, but context indicates it should read གྲང་དངར་, which is the spelling found in Brit. Lib., fol. 77a.
23. སྐྲ་ literally means "hair." In this context it seems to refer to a pattern of fine points or lines in the surface texture of the blade. The meaning of གོག་ here is unclear, but, based on the text, it seems to refer to highs and lows on the surface of the blade of a sword. ཐུར་ can mean "declivity" or "slope," and as ཐུར་མ་, "stick" or "rod." It is in this last sense that is seems to refer to the rods of different types of iron, which are forged together to form a pattern in the blade (pattern welding). They are visible on older Tibetan sword blades as alternating wavy lines of lighter and darker metal, the so-called hairpin pattern.
24. Burmiok Athing has མཐོ་སྨན་, but the correct reading is probably མཐོ་སྨད་, which is supported by the reading མཐོ་དམན་, as found in Brit. Lib., fol. 78a.
25. This list begins with the five classic sword types that are usually found in the Tibetan literature, plus two others that are dropped later in the text when the first five are expanded upon. For the seventh sword type, Burmiok Athing initially has འཆིང་ཁྲ་, but this is later written as མཐིང་ཁྲ་, as it also appears in the Brit. Lib. text (fol. 78a) and which corresponds to the definition, involving the color blue, which follows a few lines down.
26. Using མགོ་ལྕོག་ for the term that is written as འགོ་ལྕོག་ in Brit. Lib,. fol. 81a, and གོ་ཙོག་ and གོ་ལྕོག་ in Burmiok Athing, fol. 25b.
27. Brit. Lib., fol. 78b, reads: ཞང་མ་རྩེ་སོར་བགས་ཀྱི་ཁྲར་སོད་པ།.
28. Brit. Lib., fol. 79a, reads སྟག་པོ་ (male tiger) and Burmiok Athing རྟག་སོ་ (horse teeth). The correct interpretation here may be སྟག་སོ་, apparently referring to a pattern shaped like tiger teeth, which is mentioned elsewhere in the text. But note that རྟག་སོ་ can also refer to a squared zigzag or crenellated pattern.
29. All of the texts agree that the སོག་པོ་ and ཞང་མ་ sword types have སོག་རྗེ་ and ཞང་རྗེ་ as their principal subtypes. However, the spelling of རྗེ་ can vary randomly, appearing, for instance, as སྦྱི་ here in Burmiok Athing, before reverting to རྗེ་ later in the same text.
30. In both instances in this line, དཀུ་ was spelled the conventional way, with the སྔོན་འཇུག་ད་, but this was marked with an "x" by the Tibetan proofreader. This may indicate a preferred spelling, or simply that the proofreader was signaling that this is inconsistent with the rest of the text.
31. Note that from here the text changes from nine to seven syllables per line.

སྤོ་ཞང་ཆེན་སོག་རྒྱན་ཡིན། ཕྲ་ཞིང་སྐྱེ་ལེགས་སོག་ཕྲན་ཟེར། དཀར་ལ་ཐུག་པ་རེལ་ཆོད་ཡིན།[32] སྐྱེ་ལ་སྲབ་པ་སྐྱེ་ངམ་ཡིན། སོག་སྐྱེ་ཞེས་ཀུང་ཁ་ཅིག་འབོད། ནག་ལ་ཐུག་པ་ཏ་ར་ཡིན། ཐུར་ཁྲ་ཁྱུག་པ་སོག་ཕྲན་ཁྱུག ཕྲ་ཞིང་ལྡེམ་པ་སོག་ཕྲན་ལྡེམ། སྐམ་ཆས་ཁྲིགས་དེ་ཐག་ཁྲེས་ཡིན། མགོ་ལྟོག་མེད་ན་སོག་རྫིར་(རྫེར་) འབོད། ཞང་མའི་རྟགས་རྣམས་ཚང་བ་ལ། ཞང་ཐེམ་ཐེམ་དགུ་གོ་ཆོད་ཡིན། རྩུབ་ལ་ཞང་ཆེ་འབྲི་ལྟེ་ཡིན། དཀར་ལ་འཇམ་ན་རྡོ་ཚད་ཟེར། ཕྲ་ཞིང་སྐྱེ་ལེགས་ཞང་ཕྲན་ཡིན། ཐུག་ཅིང་ཐུང་བ་སླུག་ཐུང་གྲགས། གཞུང་བསྲུབ་འདུག་ན་ལྡེམ་ཐུང་ཡིན། ཕྲ་ཞིང་སྲབ་ན་ཕྱིང་ཆོད་འབོད། ཐུར་ཁྱོག་ལི་ན་མེ་ལྕེར་འདོགས། ནག་ཅིང་རྩུབ་[26b]ན་ཞང་རྫེ་ཟེར། ཧུ་བེད་རྟགས་རྣམས་ཚང་བ་ལ། སྟག་སོ་རིང་ན་རྒྱ་བར་གྲགས། སྟག་སོ་ཕྱིར་ལྟ་ཟལ་དཀར་ཡིན།[33] སྟག་སོ་ནང་ལྟ་ཟལ་དམར་འབོད། ཕྱི་ནང་གཉིས་ཀ་ཟལ་ཁྲར་འདོགས། ཐུར་རྣམས་བཅད་བཏུབ་ལྟ་བུར་ཡོད། ཧུ་བེད་རིང་མོ་ཞེས་སུ་ཤེས། ཐུག་ཅིང་ཐུང་ན་ཁས་རྒྱན་[ཁལ་རྒྱལ་]ཡིན། ཐུར་རིང་དགུ་ཐུབ་མིང་དུ་ཆགས། སྟག་སོ་ཉིས་རྩེགས་ཡོད་པ་ལ།[34] ཧུ་གྲོགས་ཞེས་སུ་མཁས་པས་དཔྱད། གུ་ཟེའི་རྟགས་རྣམས་ཚང་བ་ལ། སྒྲ་གོག་ཐུར་གསུམ་འཛོམ་པའི་ཚེ།[35] རྣམ་མཁའ་དགུ་ཆོད་ཅེས་སུ་འདོགས། སྒྲ་རིས་ཅན་དེ་ཤ་ཐོར་ཡིན། ཐུར་ཡོད་སྟོང་སྟེ་ཁྲ་བོར་གྲགས། ཐུང་[ཐུག་]ལ་ཞེང་ཆེ་སླུག་ལེབ་ཡིན། འཇམ་ངར་ཅན་དེ་ལི་རྩ་བྱི།[36] རྩ་བར་ཉ་མིག་སྟོང་རི་ཆེ། ཉ་མིག་རི་[རིང་]མོར་བྲིས་པ་ལ། སྟོང་རི་ཆུང་བར་གྲགས་པ་ཡིན། ལྟག་ཤི་འགྲི་ལྷ་ཞེས་སུ་གྲགས།[37] ཐུར་དམའ་ཆུ་ནང་ཉ་མཆོད་(ཆོད་) ཟེར། ལྟག་ཅན་སྤྲུལ་ནག་ཞེས་སུ་འབོད། མོ་ལྕུགས་ངར་ཡོད་ཅིག་ལ་གྲུབས(འགྲུབ)། སྤྱང་མོ་རྐྱག་འདྲ་ཞེས་སུ་འབོད།[38] ཉ་མིག་ཐལ་ཕྱུག་གཉིས་བྱུང་ན། གུ་བདག་ཅེས་སུ་ཀུན་གྱི་ཤེས། འཇའ་ཡིས་རྟགས་རྣམས་ཚང་བ་ལ། ཤར་འཇའ་ཐུར་ཡོད་སྒྲ་རིས་ཅན།[39] ལྟག་པ་སྒང་ཅན་ཞིག་ལ་ཟེར། ལྟོ་འཇའ་ལྡིང་ལ་སོ་ཁྲུད་སྟོམས། ལྟག་ལེབ་ཐེའུ་རྫེས་ཅན་ལ་ཟེར། བར་གསར་ལྟག་ལེབ་སེ་བདར་ཅན། གསར་རྟུང་ལྟག་སྒང་ཅན་ཡང་ཡིན། རམ་[རབ་]སྒང་རལ་གྱི་བྱ་བ་ཉི།[40] ཐུར་མེད་སྒྲ་རིས་ཅན་ལ་ཟེར། ཤང་རྡོ་ལྟག་ཤིང་ལྟག་ལེབ་ཡིན། ཨ་ལི་ཟེ་[ཛི་]ལ་སྒྲ་ཐུར་མེད། ངར་འབྲུམ་ཟིལ་པ་ཆགས་འདྲ་ཡོད། འཇམ་ཞིང་ངར་ན་ཤང་དམར་ཡིན། འཐུག་ཅིང་རྩུབ་ན་ཤང་ནག་གོ ག་འུམ་ཞེས་གྲགས་པ་ཡིན།[41] རྩ་བར་འཇའ་[འཇབ་]རྩེ་ཁ་སྒྲུར་ཡིན།[42] ཤང་ལང་མི་ལྤགས་གཡང་གཞི་དེ། འཇབ་རྩེ་གཡག་ཧུ་ཁ་ཞིག་ཡོང་། ལྤ་བ་མ་ནི་འཇབ་རྩེ་[27a]འཐུག ཨ་ལོང་མ་ནི་འཇབ་རྩེ་རྡོར་[སྒོར་]། ཅུང་ཟད་འབྲུལ་པ་ཞིག་ལ་ཟེར། སྒྲ་རིས་ཤ་སྤྱུ་སྟོར་འདྲ་ལ། ཐོ་དོ་ལྟག་ཅན་སྐྱེ་ཕྲར་བཞད།[43] ལྟག་ཅན་དམར་ངམ་ཐུར་ཕྲ་བ། དགུ་ཐེམ་ཞེས་སུ་གྲགས་པ་ཡིན།[44] འཐུག་ཅིང་ཤིན་ཏུ་རིང་བ་སྟེ། རྒྱལ་འཇའ་ཞེས་སུ་འདོད་པ་ཡིན། ཤལ་གོག་རྡུ་གོག་རྣམ་པ་གཉིས། འབྲི་གོག་ཁང་དཀར་གཉིས་ཏེ་བཞི།[45] གྲི་རིགས་གང་ལའང་འབྱུང་བས་ན། སྒྲ་ཡིས་རིགས་དེ་གོག་སྐྱུར་ན། ཤལ་གོག་ཅེས་སུ་གྲགས་པ་ཡིན། ཐུར་རིས་[རིགས་]འཇམ་དང་ལྡན་པ་ཉིད། གོག་ཏུ་སྐྱུར་བས་རྡུ་གོག་ཟེར། ཐུར་མེད་འཇམ་པ་གོག་ལ་སྐྱུར། འབྲི་གོག་ཅེས་སུ་བོད་པར་བྱ། ཁང་དཀར་ཅུང་ཟད་ལྟེ་[གྲི་]གྲགས་(དྲགས་?) པས། བདར་བས་ཡང་དུ་བཏོང་[བཏང་]ལ་ཟེར།

[Three aspects of damage to different-quality blades.] སོ་ཡི་ཆག་བྲུམ་[གྲུམ་]སྟོད་ལུགས་གསུམ། གྲི་རབ་ཁ་ཚང་[གཙང་]སླར་ཡང་སོས། གྲི་འབྲིང་སོ་ཆག་འོག་ཏུ་སོ་[གསོ]། འདྲ་བའི་རྣོ་བ་[ཁ་]འབྱུང་བ་ཡོད། གྲི་ཐ་ཐད་བཅད་ཆག་པ་ཡིན། གྲི་རྙིང་གྲོས་ཆོས་འགྲུགས་པར་ནུས།[46] གཞན་ལ་དེ་འདྲ་ཅུང་ཟད་དཀོན།།

Chapter 11, ཁྲབ་ *(Armor)*[47]

ཁྲབ་ལ་གསར་རྙིང་སྟག་[བརྟགས་]པ་དང་། གང་གི་དུས་སུ་བྱུང་བ་བཅད་[དཔྱད]། བྱང་བུའི་རིགས་ལ་ལེགས་པར་དབྱེ། ནང་ཚན་སོ་སོར་དབྱེ་བ་བཞི།

[1. The analysis of old armor versus new.] དང་པོ་གསར་རྙིང་བརྟགས་པ་

32. རེལ་ may be equivalent to རེ་ལྡེ་, meaning a type of shield, which would make the name of this sword "shield cutter." See *brda dkrol*, p. 894, under རེལ་དེ་; and Das 1902b, p. 1190.
33. This line and the preceding one are missing from Brit. Lib., fol. 81a.
34. Using སྟག་སོ་ from Brit. Lib., fol. 81a, rather than རྟགས་སོ་ as in Burmiok Athing.
35. Burmiok Athing has འཛོམ་པ་ (subdue, defeat), but the sense of འཛོམས་པ་ (gather, assemble), as found in the Brit. Lib. text, seems more appropriate.
36. Although both texts read ལི་རྩ་བྱི་, the name for this subtype of དགུ་ཟེ་ should perhaps be ལི་ཙ་བྱི་, which is a place-name for Vaizali in India, and also means "learned" or "brave" (*bod rgya*, p. 2779).
37. Brit. Lib., fol. 81b, reads སྟག་ཤིང་འབྲི་ལྷ་ཞེས་སུ་གྲགས་.
38. This line and the preceding one are missing from Brit. Lib., fol. 81b.
39. Brit. Lib., fol. 81b, reads ཤར་འཇའ་ཐུར་སྒྲ་རིས་ཡིད་འདུ་.
40. རབ་སྒང་ is the name of one of the six districts of Kham, and perhaps indicates where this type of sword was from.
41. ག་འུམ་ or ག་འུ་རི་མ་ is also the name of a wrathful female deity, which may relate to the use of this sword or knife for flaying skins used for ritual purposes, which appears to be described in the following lines.
42. Here Burmiok Athing has འཇའ་རྩེ་; Brit. Lib., fol. 82a, has འཇབ་རྩེ་ (hidden point or tweezers); and then both texts use the form འཇབ་རྩེ་ three times in the next few lines.
43. Brit. Lib., fol. 82b, reads, ཐོ་ལྟོ་ལྕུགས་ཅན་སྐྱེ་ཁྲང་བཞད་.
44. Both texts start the line with འགུ་ rather than དགུ་, but the latter seems more in keeping with the sense of the text. Compare with the ཞང་མ་ type called ཐེམ་དགུ་གོ་ཆོད་.
45. Brit. Lib., fol. 82b, gives the first three as ཤང་གོག་, དངུལ་གོག་, and འབྲི་གོག་. For the last term, Burmiok Athing reads either འགྲི་མགོ་ or འགྲི་མོག་.
46. Brit. Lib. reads གྲི་ཉིད་གྲོས་ན་འགྲུགས་པར་ནུས་, but the exact meaning of both versions is unclear. The sense is perhaps that old blades can be flexed in a way that others cannot.
47. The first part of this chapter is missing from the Beinecke text. The chapter begins with Burmiok Athing, fol. 27a, and Brit. Lib., fol. 83b. The first Beinecke folio (fol. 48a) picks up at Burmiok Athing, fol. 28a, and Brit. Lib., fol. 87a.

ལ། རྙིང་མ་རྣམས་ཀྱི་མཚན་ཉིད་ནི། ཕྱི་ནི་ཁྲག་པ་ཕྱིས་[འཇིབ་] ལྟར་འཇམ། ནང་ནི་དཔྱལ་དཀར་མེ་ལོང་འདྲ། ལྷགས་ལ་དཔྱལ་བསྲེས་ཡོད་ཅེས་གྲགས། ཕྱི་ལ་སེན་རྒྱབ་ཅུང་ཟད་ཡོད། ཤ་ཐུག་ཅུང་ཟད་ལྗི་བ་མང་[ལ]།[48] བྱང་མགོ་ཤེལ་ཕྲེང་བརྒྱུད་འདྲ་ལ། སོར་མོས་ཉུལ་ན་འཇམ་ཞིང་སྐྱོམས། ཐེའུས་བཀུག་པའི་སེན་རིས་ནི། ལྟ་བཟོས་པིར་གྱི་བྲིས་འདྲ་ཡོད། བྱང་ཁ་འབྱམ་[འཇམ་] ཞིང་སྲབ་འཐུག་སྐྱོམས། བྱང་བུའི་འགྲམ་གཉིས་རྒྱུན་སྐྱོམས་ལ། བདར་ཕྱིས་མང་བས་ཁྲོག་[འཁྲོག་] ཅིག་ཡོད། བྱང་བཞམ་(གཞམ་) འགྲིག་ཅིང་སྐྱོམས་པ་མང་ (or ལང་) [ལ]། བྱང་ཟུར་ཅུང་ཟད་ཟླུམ་པ་ཡོད། བྱང་མིག་ཡོ་ཁྲོག་[འཁྲོག་] མེད་པ་ལ། ཡངས་ཤིང་ནང་ནི་[27b] འབྱམས་[འཇམ་] པ་ཡིན། ལྷགས་མདོག་ཞག་ཆེ་ལྷགས་རྒྱུ་མཁྲེགས། མཉེན་འཁྲེགས་སྐྱོམས་པས་མཚོན་ཁར་སྲ། སྐྱིད་པའི་བྱང་བུར་ཉག་སྟོན་པས། དེ་ལ་ཀ་ཙ་སྐྱེད་ཉག་ཟེར།[49] དེ་རྣམས་ཕལ་ཆེར་རྙིང་མ་ཡིན།

[Characteristics of armor from the middle period.] བར་རྙིང་རྣམས་ཀྱི་མཚན་ཉིད་ནི།[50] བྱང་མགོ་འབྲིག་[འགྲིག་] ཅིང་སྐྱོམས་པ་ལ། ཟུར་རྣམས་ཅུང་ཟད་རྣོ་བ་ཡོད། སེན་རིས་གཟོང་གི་བཀུག་པ་ལ། ཅུང་ཟད་སྦོམ་ཞིང་རྩང་[གཙང་] བ་ཡོད་[ཡིན]། བྱང་ཁ་སྲབ་འཐུག་སྐྱོམ་པ་ལ། ཁྲོངས་[འཁྲོངས་] ཤིང་གཙང་ཤ་ཆེ་བ་ཡོད། བྱང་མིག་ཅུང་ཟད་དོག་པ་ལ། མིག་གི་ནང་རྣམས་རྩུབ་པ་སྟེ། བདར་གད་ཅུང་ཟད་མི་ལེགས་ཀྱང་། མིག་གི་བལྟས་ན་མཛེས་པ་ཡོད། གསེར་ཞུན་ཅན་གྱི་རིགས་རྣམས་ལ། བྲུག་གསེར་འབྱུང་སེར་གཉིས་སུ་སྲིད(?)།

[Characteristics of new armor.] ཁྲབ་གསར་རྣམས་ཀྱི་མཚན་ཉིད་ནི། བྱང་མགོ་བཙུམ་[རྩུབ་] ཞིང་ལྟར་མི་མཛེས། སེན་རིས་ཟོང་(གཟོང་) གི་ཕྲ་བར་བྲིས། མིག་རྣམས་དོག་ཅིང་ནང་རྩུབ་པ། ཟུར་རྣམས་མཆོག་ཏུ་རྣོ་བ་དང་། ལྷགས་མདོག་སྔོ་ནག་ཞ་ཉེ་འདྲ། བདར་གད་ཞུན་ཐར་མི་ལེགས་པས། བྱང་ཤ་སྲབ་ཀྱང་ལྗི་བ་ཡིན།

[2. The time periods in which the above types originated.] གཉིས་པ་གང་གིས་དུས་བྱུང་ཚུལ། རྙིང་མ་ཆོས་རྒྱལ་ཁུ་དབོན་དུས།[51] བར་རྙིང་འོད་སྲུངས་རྗེས་ཙམ་ནས།[52] ཏ་སི་ཆེན་པོ་ཡན་གྱི་བར།[53] དེ་ནས་ད་ལྟའི་བར་གསར་མ།

[3. The divisions of the seven main types of armor lamellae.] གསུམ་པ་བྱང་རིགས་སྣ་ནས་དབྱེ། རྒྱ་ཁྲེ་དམར་ཡུ་འབལ་གཡའ་མ། སྐྱ་ཆེན་ལི་དིང་མེ་རུ་བདུན།[54] རྒྱ་ཁྲེ་སྐྱི་ཡི་མཚན་ཉིད་ནི། བྱང་མགོ་ཅུང་ཟླུམ་ཐུང་བ་ལ། སེན་རིས་ཟེ་ལ་ཉེ་ཞིང་ཕྲ། བྱང་ཐ་[མཐའ་] ཤིན་ཏུ་སྲབ་པ་ལ།[55] བྱང་མིག་ཐ་ལ་ཉེ་བར་ཕུག ནང་ཤ་ཐད་སོར་གནས་པ་ལ། ཐེ་[ཐོ་] རྗེས་མི་གསལ་བདར་རྗེས་ལེགས། ལྷགས་རྒྱུ་མཁྲེགས་ཤིང་ཅུང་ཟད་ཁྲོ་[འཁྲོ]། བྱང་ཤས་ཕྲ་བའི་ཉམས་ལྡན་པས། མིག་གིས་ལྟས་ན་མཛེས་པ་ཡིན། དམར་ཡུ་རྣམས་ཀྱི་མཚན་ཉིད་ནི།[56] བྱང་མགོ་ཅུང་ཟད་སྒོར་བ་ལ། འབལ་པས་བྱང་མགོ་ཅུང་ཟད་ཐུང་། རྒྱ་ཁྲེ་ལས་རིང་[28a] འབྲིང་པ་སྟེ། སེན་རིས་ཕྲ་ཞིང་ཅུང་ཟད་ཐོ་[མཐོ]། ནང་ཤ་སྲབ་ཅིང་མཐོ་[ཐེ་] རྗེས་གསལ།[57] ལྷགས་མདོག་དམར་[དཀར་] ཞིང་འོད་ཆགས་པ། ཅུང་ཟད་མཉེན་པའི་རྣམ་པ་ཅན། བྱང་ཤས་ཕྲ་ཞིང་མིག་ཡུལ་མཛེས། འབལ་རིགས་རྣམས་ཀྱི་མཚན་ཉིད་ནི། བྱང་མགོ་གཞན་[གཞལ་] ལས་ཅུང་ཟད་རིང་། སྤྱི་བོ་མཐོ་བར་མངོན་པ་ཙམ[རྩམ]། བྱང་ཞེང་ཅུང་ཟད་ཆེ་ཞིང་རིང་། སེན་རིས་ཡ་ཆག་[ཆག་ས་] བསྐོལ་ནས་བཀུག སྦོམ་ཞིང་མིག་ལ་ཉེ་བ་ཡོད། ནང་ཤ་གཞན་ལས་འཐུག་ལ་བསྙེད། ལྟས་ཆེ་ཟིལ་པ་ཆགས་པ་སྐྱོམས། ལྷགས་མདོག་དཀར་ཞིང་འོད་ཆགས་པ། ཕོ་ལྷགས་མོ་ལྷགས་སྦྱོར་སྟེ་ལེགས། མིག་ངོར་མཛེས་ཤིང་ཅུང་ཟད་ལྗི། མཚོན་གྱི་སྟེང་དུ་ལྷག་པར་སྲ། གཡའ་མ་རིགས་ཀྱི་མཚན་ཉིད་ནི། བྱང་མགོ་ཅུང་ཟད་རིང་བ་

48. Here, as elsewhere throughout the text, ཐུག་ is used for འཐུག་ or མཐུག་. The term ཤ་མཐུག་ is used repeatedly in describing armor lamellae, and probably has the sense of "thick in overall proportion." Compare with the term ཤ་མཐུག་པོ་, meaning "fat" or "a type of thick bamboo" (Goldstein 2001, p. 1090).

49. Lozang Jamspal suggests that the term ཀ་ཙ་ may be an abbreviation of the Sanskrit word *ka ba ca*, meaning "armor." Based on this the phrase ཀ་ཙ་སྐྱེད་ཉག་ may mean "armor (or lamellae) with a notched waist," which makes more sense in this context than the definition "rusty and crooked" given to it by Das (1902b, p. 8). It should be noted, however, that Das cited this same text, or a version of it, as his source.

50. This line is missing from Burmiok Athing, but is found in Brit. Lib., fol. 84b.

51. The Tibetan phrase "In the time of the righteous kings, uncle and nephew" probably refers to the period of the early Dharma kings, which would cover the early 7th to the mid-9th century A.D. I am grateful to Gene Smith for clarifying the meaning of this phrase and those cited in the following two notes.

52. The reference is probably to འོད་སྲུངས་ ('od srungs, 842–870), who was the nephew of the king རལ་པ་ཅན་ (ral pa can) and the son and successor of the apostate king གླང་དར་མ་ (glang dar ma), so that the sequence of epochs can continue without having to include mention of the last.

53. ཏ་སི་ཆེན་པོ་ is a variation of ཏའི་སི་ཏུ་ཆེན་པོ་ (ta'i si tu chen po) in reference to ཏའི་སི་ཏུ་བྱང་ཆུབ་རྒྱལ་མཚན་ (ta'i si tu byang chub rgyal mtshan; 1302–1364), the first of the phag mo gru kings, who came to power in 1358.

54. The spelling of four of the seven types varies slightly from one text to the next. For example, རྒྱ་ཁྲེ་ appears repeatedly as རྒྱ་དྲེ་ (Burmiok Athing, fol. 28a) and as the homophonous རྒྱ་ཡི་ (Brit. Lib., fol. 87b). Yet later both of these texts continue with the spelling རྒྱ་ཁྲེ་, which is the form found in Beinecke from fol. 48a onward. Similarly, དམར་ཡུ་ is the form found in Brit. Lib. and Beinecke, but it first appears repeatedly as དམར་གཡུ་ in Burmiok Athing before that text adopts the spelling found in the other two. Likewise, འབལ་ first appears in Burmiok Athing as འབའ་ and then changes to འབལ་ later in the text. ལི་དིང་ is the spelling in Beinecke and Burmiok Athing. It appears as ལི་དིང་ and ལི་ཞིང་ in Brit. Lib.

55. In most instances where Burmiok Athing has ཐ་, Brit. Lib. has མཐའ་, both meaning "edges" or "borders" in the context of describing the shape and form of the lamellae.

56. According to Hūṃkaradzaya (Tashi Tsering 1979, p. 50), the name of this type, དམར་གཡུ་ (and by extension དམར་ཡུ་), is a misunderstanding of the similar-sounding དམར་ཡུལ་, which derives from དམར་ཁམས་དེ་མོ་, the place in eastern Tibet where, according to him, this type was made.

57. The context suggests ཐོ་རྗེས་, meaning "hammer marks," which are visible on the interior in this instance.

ལ། བྱང་སྤྱོད་གཞན་ལས་ཐུང་ཟད་སྤྱོར། སེན་རིས་དམའ་ཞིང་ཡ་ཆགས་བསྲོལ། འཕལ་གྱི་

སེན་རིས་ལས་ཀྱང་སྤྱོམ། བྱང་བུ་ཕྱི་ནང་ཐད་སོར་གནས། དཔེ་ན་གཡལ་མོ་ངི་བཞིན་ནོ།

ལྷགས་རྒྱུ་ལྷགས་མདོག་འབལ་དང་མ་ཆུངས། ཐར་བཞིན་[ནེན་]མདོག་ཏུ་ལེགས་པ་སྟེ།༥༨

བྱང་བུ་གཞན་ལས་ཆེ་བ་ཡིན། གོན་ལ་[བདེ་]ཡང་ཞིང་སྲ་ཆེན་ཆེ། སྲ་ཆེན་རྣམས་ཀྱི་མཆན་

ཉིད་ནི། བྱང་མགོ་སྟོར་ཞིང་བྱུང་བ་དང་། སེན་རིས་[B 48a]༥༩ ཐུང་ཟད་མགྲོ་བ་ཡོད། བྱང་

ཕ་སྲབ་ཅིང་བྱུ་བུ་སྤྱོམ། ཞིང་ཆེ་དགུས་རིང་ཐུང་ཟད་སྤྱོར། མིག་གི་ཡུལ་དུ་མི་མཛེས་ཤིང་།

བྱང་ཡུག་རིང་བས་གོན་མི་ཤེས་[བདེ་]།༦༠ ལི་ངི་རྣམས་ཀྱི་མཆན་ཉིད་ནི།༦༡ བྱང་མགོ་བྱུང་

ཞིང་སེན་རིས་མགྲོ། བྱང་སྤྱོད་སྤྲོ་ཞིང་བྱུང་སྤྲད་[མ]། བྱང་བུ་སྲབ་ཅིང་བྱུང་ཤ་སྤྱབ། བྱང་

ཡུག་ཐུང་ཞིང་ལྷགས་རྒྱ་མ་ཉེན། ཡ་ཞིང་གོན་ལ་བདེ་བ་ཡིན། མི་རུ་རྣམས་ཀྱི་མཆན་ཉིད་ནི།

ལྷོག་གི་ཁ་བྱང་རིགས་ནས་མཆེད། བྱང་མགོ་སྒུ་བཞི་ཡིན་པ་ལ། ཟུར་རྣམ་སེན་རིས་ཐིག

[ཁྱུང་]ལ་བཀབ། ཉེ་ལ་ཉེ་བ་འབའང་རེ་སྤྱིད། ཕྱི་ལ་ཤུལ་ཤ་ཆགས་པ་དང་།༦༢ ནང་ན་ཐབ་

སོར་གནས་པ་ཡོད།

[4. Classifying the subdivisions of the seven types of armor

lamellae.] བཞི་ལ་ནང་ཚན་དབྱེ་བ་ནི།

[The nine *rgya byi* subtypes] རྒྱ་བྱི་ལ་ནི་དགུ་ཡིན་ཏེ། རྒྱ་བྱི་ཆེན་མོའི་མཆན་ཉིད་

ནི། བྱང་ཡུག་རིང་བྱུང་སོར་བཞི་ཙམ། [BA 28b] བྱང་ཞིང་ཐུང་ཟད་ཆེ་བ་ཡིན། ཆུ་རྫི་རྐྱང་ཞིང་

ཤུལ་ཤ་ཅན། བརྫི་ཞིང་ཡིད་དུ་འོང་བ་ཡོད། འབྲིང་པོ་དེ་བས་ཕྲ་བ་ལ། སྟོང་སྣང་ཞེས་ཞིང་

ཤུལ་ཤ་ཅན། བྱང་བུ་ཡིད་དུ་འོང་བ་ཡོད། ཆུང་བ་བྱང་ཤ་སྤྱབ་པ་ལ། ཕྱི་ལ་ཤུལ་ཤ་ཡོད་པ་ལ།

བྱང་མགོ་རིང་ཞིང་སྒུ་བཞི་ཙམ། [B 48b] ཟུར་ཚག་[ཆག་]ཅུང་ཟད་ཡོད་པ་ཡིན། སྤྲད་ཞེས།

ཁྱུང་ཁས་ཐ་བ་ལ། སྲ་ཆེན་ཆུང་བས་འཛ་བར་གནགས། ཐི་མོ་མགོ་ནི་བྱང་མགོ་རིང་། ཕྱི་བོ་སྤུང་

ལ་ཤུལ་ཤ་སྤུམ། ཤུལ་ཤ་བྱུང་ན་བཟང་བ་ཡིན། ཆེ་མིག་གཉིས་འོག་མཐའ་གཉིས་སྲུ། སྲིད་

ཞག་ཡོད་པ་ཞིག་ལ་ཟེར། ཕུན་བྱུང་འོག་རྒྱན་ཞེས་པ་དེ།༦༣ བྱང་མགོ་ཤིན་ཏུ་རིང་བའི་འོག

སྤྱིལ་རྒྱན་གོ་མ་གབ་པ་དང་། སེན་རིས་ཉིས་རིམ་རྐ་ཆོས་དབུབས། རྒྱལ་མོ་འོག་རྒྱན་ཞེས་པ་ནི།

སྤྱིལ་མིག་འོག་མའི་མིག་ཉིས་སོ། ཆེམ་མིག་འོག་ཏུ་ཕྱུག་པ་ཡིན། ཟུར་རྒྱན་མ་ཞེས་བྱ་བ་ནི།༦༤

མིག་རྣམས་ཟུར་ལ་ཕྱུག་པ་ཡིན། རྒྱལ་མོ་མིག་བཞི་བྱུང་མིག་བཞི། བྱང་བུའི་གཞུང་ལ་སྤྱོས།

བྱས་ཕྱུག༦༥ དད་པོ་གསུམ་ལས་སྤྱེལ་རྒྱུན་ཕྱེ། གཉིས་པ་བཞི་བས་ཕྱེད་ལ་བཅོམས། རྒྱུན་

མི་གསལ་ཞེས་བྱ་བ་ནི།༦༦ བྱང་བུའི་ཞེང་ལ་གསུམ་ཆ་བྱས། མིག་ཅན་ཆ་གཉིས་མིག་མེད་པའི།

གསུམ་ཆ་གཅིག་གིས་མཐན་པ་སྟེ། བྱང་བུ་འབའ་ཞིག་མ་གཏོགས་པ། ཕྱི་ལ་རྒྱུན་བུ་མི་གསལ་

ཡིན། འོག་རྒྱན་ཟུར་རྒྱུན་མིག༌[B 49a] བཞི་བ། རྒྱུན་མི་གསལ་ལ་སོགས་པ་ནི།

[The twenty *dmar yu* subtypes.] དམར་ཡུའི་རིགས་ལ་འབ་བྱུང་བས་ན། སྤྱི་ཡི་

དགས་ལས་དབྱུང་བར་བྱ། དམར་ཡུའི་རིགས་ནི་ཉི་ཤུ་ཡོད། དམར་ཡུ་དངོས་ཀྱི་མཆན་ཉིད་ནི།

བྱང་ཡུག་སོར་བཞི་བྱང་མགོ་སྤྲོ། བྱང་ནས་ཕྱ་ལ་ཤུལ་ན་ཅན། དེ་ལས་བྱིད་བ་ཀྲང་སྤྲུད་ཡིན།

མཆག་དཀར་རྗེ་དང་དེའི་གཡས་གཡོན། ཟུར་གཉིས་གསུམ་ཆར་བཅད་པ་སྟེ། སྐུ་ཆོན་སྤྲ་རིས་

བཅད་འདུ་བའི།༦༧ བྱང་མགོ་རྣང་བཅད་གཅིག་ལ་ཟེར། མཆག་དཀར་སྐུ་ཆོན་གཉིས་ལ་ནི།

[BA 29a] ཤུལ་ཤ་བྱུང་ན་བཟང་བ་ཡིན། མཆོ་ཆེན་བྱང་མགོའི་སྒུ་བཞི་ཡི། ཟུར་བཅག་བྱང་

ཞེང་ཆེ་བ་དང་། རྒྱལ་ཕ་ཐབ་སོར་གནས་ལ་ཟེར། སེན་རྒྱལ་བྱང་མགོའི་སྤྲུག་[སྤྲབ་]པ་དང་།

བྱང་བུའི་ཟུར་ཀྱང་སྤྲབ་ཆགས་པ། སེན་མོའི་རྒྱབ་དང་འདྲ་བ་ཡིན། ཁ་ཅིག་སྒོ་ཀང་ལ་ཡང་

ཟེར། སེན་རིས་ཞིང་[ཞེས་]པ་རྒྱབ་གཞུང་ལ།༦༨ སེན་རིས་ཉིས་བཅུགས་གསུམ་བཅུགས་ཡོད།

---

58. Perhaps related to smelting and refining, ནེན་ཐར, a term that is used at the end of the section "Characteristics of new armor," above.

59. The extant part of the armor chapter in Beinecke begins from here on fol. 48a. The spelling in the Beinecke text is given precedence over the other texts unless otherwise indicated. Its pagination will be indicated by the letter B and the folio number in brackets. The pagination of the Burmiok Athing manuscript will be indicated by BA and folio number in brackets. From this point, alternate spellings given in brackets are generally from the Burmiok Athing version.

60. Burmiok Athing, fol. 28a, and Brit. Lib., fol. 87a, both end this line with བདེ་, rather than ཤེས. The former term is similar to a phrase a few lines earlier (Brit. Lib., fol. 87a) at the end of the of the གཡལ་ type, which describes it as light and easy or pleasant to wear (གོན་བདེ་ཡང).

61. From here Burmiok Athing is missing the next six lines, which comprise the rest of the description of the ལི་རིང་ type and the first line dealing with the མི་རུ་ type. The lines are present in both the Beinecke and Brit. Lib. texts.

62. "Central ridge" or perhaps "shallow recess" are suggested as possible meanings of ཤུལ་ཤ, which from this point on appears repeatedly as a term describing a feature on the exterior of various types of armor lamellae.

63. Here and in several instances རྒྱན seems to be an abbreviation for རྒྱན་བུ (leather

laces), just as བྱང in these texts is usually an abbreviation for བྱང་བུ (armor lamellae).

64. This line and the next are missing from Brit. Lib., fol. 88b.

65. This line and the next three were originally omitted from Burmiok Athing, fol. 28b, but then added in at the foot of the page in 'khyug yig by a Tibetan proofreader.

66. The name of this type, རྒྱན་མི་གསལ (laces not visible), appears in this form in Beinecke and in the 'khyug yig correction of Burmiok Athing. It is given as རྒྱན་མིག་གསལ (lacing holes visible) in Brit. Lib., fol. 88b.

67. This type is called དམར་ཡུ་ཁ་ཆོད in Brit. Lib., fol. 89b, in both Hūṃkaradzaya texts (Tashi Tsering 1979, p. 51; Gangtok 1981, p. 83), and, depending on how the character is read, in Burmiok Athing, fol. 28b. The key difference is the word ཏ (horse) vs. the word སྟ (ax), which could be easily confused in an oral transcription. Both Hūṃkaradzaya versions and the Beinecke text explain the reason for the name, but it is assumed here that the Beinecke explanation, involving a notch like the shape made by an ax cut, is the correct one, and that the substitution of the word horse for ax was a mistake perpetuated by later copyists.

68. Both Burmiok Athing, fol. 29a, and Brit. Lib., fol. 90a, have ཞེས་པ (called), rather than ཞིང་པ (farmer), as found in Beinecke. However, the sense of the text suggests that ཞིང་པ (wide), a term used frequently in the description of the lamellae, was probably intended.

ཁྱི་གཤོག་ཆེ་བ་སྒྲབ་པ་ལ། སྣ་ཞིང་བྱུང་མགོ་ཅུང་ཟད་སྒུང་། ཚེམ་མིག་མཚམས་ནས་སྟོང་སྒུང་ ཞུམ། ཁྱི་གཤོག་ཅུང་བ་དེ་བས་ཆུང་། [B 49b] ཉ་འདུ་བྱུང་མགོ་རིང་ཞིང་སྒུང་། ཉ་ཡི་མགོ་དང་ འདྲ་བ་ལ། བྱུང་གཤམ་ཅུང་ཟད་ཞིམ་པ་ཡོད། ཁྱི་ཞིང་བྱུང་ན་ཉ་འདུ་ཆུང་། གི་ཀར་མཆོག་ ཅུ་རིང་ཞིང་སྒོམ། རྒྱབ་ལ་སྒྱབ་ཅིག་ཡོད་ན་ཡིན། ཁྱི་ཞིང་རིང་ན་དགི་ཀུང་ཡིན། འབབ་ཡིས་ [འབབ་གཡིར་] བྱུང་བུའི་ཟུར་བཞི་བཅད། ཟུར་བཀྲུན་ལྡུ་བུ་ཞིག་ལ་ཟེར། འཕུ་གཡིར་[འབྱུར་ མེད་] བྱུང་མགོ་རིང་བ་ལ། བྱུང་བུའི་གཤམ་ཕྱོགས་ཞིང་ཆེ་བའི། ཟུར་གཞིས་བཅད་པ དག་ལ་ཟེར། དམར་འབབ་འདྲེས་པའི་རིགས་ཆན་ཏེ། ནབ་གི་དྲགས་རྣམས་དམར་ཡུལ་ལ། ཕྱི་ཡི དྲགས་རྣམས་འབབ་དང་འདུ། དམར་ཡུ་ཀྲུབ་མོ་མིག་བཞི་དང་། ཕོག་ཀྲུབ་ཟུར་ཀྲུབ་མི་གསལ ལོ། དམར་ཡུའི་མཚན་ཉིད་ཕྱུར་པ་ལ། རྒྱ་བྱིའི་སྐབས་སུ་བཤད་པ་བཞིན།

[The thirteen 'bal subtypes.] འབབ་ལ་ལ་བྱུང་རིགས་བཅུ་གསུམ་ཡོད། འབབ་ དངོས་བྱུང་ཡུག་ཁྱུང་རེ་ཚབ། བྱུང་ཞིང་ཆེ་ཞིང་བྱུང་ཀྲུབ་ལ། ཤུལ་ག་མངོ་ཚབ་ཡོད་པ་ཡིན། དེ་ལས་ཕུ་ཞིང་བྱུང་པ་ལ། འབབ་ཕྱུན་ཞེས་སུ་གྲགས་པ་ཡིན། ཆུང་དཀར་བྱུང་ཤས་བྱུང་པ་ལ། ཤུལ་ག་མེད་པའི་སྒྲབ་ལ་ཟེར། སྐྱ་འབབ་ཞེས་སུ་གྲག་འབོད། [B 50a] ལ་ལ་འབབ་དཀར ཞེས་ཀྱང་ཟེར། ཆུར་ནག་ཡུག་རིང་ཞིང་[ཞིང་] ཆེ་ཞིང་། རྒྱབ་ག་འབྱུག་ལ་ནག་དམས་ཡོད། [BA 29b] འབབ་ཞིག་མཆོ་ནག་ཆེས་སུ་འདུགས། ཕ་[ནུ] སྐྱ་བྱུང་མགོ་རིང་བ་དང་། ཕྱི་ཕོ སྐྱེ་མོ་མགོ་སྒུར་རྟོ། སེང་མགོ་བྱུང་བུའི་མགོ་ལ་ནི། བབ་ལེའི་ལྡེ་བྱིས་སྒུར་ཡོད་པ་ཡིན། སྐྱ ལྕོག་དང་ནི་སེང་རིས་གཉིས། པོ་བོ་འབབ་དུ་ཡོད་པ་ལ། དམར་ཡུ་སྐྱབས་སུ་བཏང་ལྡུར ཡོད། དུ་སོ་སྐྱེད་པར་ཉག་གསུམ་ཡོད། ཕྱི་སོ་སྐྱེ་པར་ཉག་གཉིས་ཡིན། ལ་ཆེ་ཁོག་སྐྱོག གཡས་གཡོན་དུ། མ་འགྲིག་ཉག་རེ་ཡོད་པ་ཡིན། ཕྱི་མོ་སྐྱེ་ནི་ཞེས་ཆེ་ཞིང་། ཕྱི་པོ་སྒང་ལ གཡས་གཡོན་དུ། འགྱིག་པའི་སྐྱེད་ཉག་ཡོད་ལ་ཟེར། འབབ་ལ་དམར་ནག་གི་ཤ་སེན་ནི། འབབ་འདུ་བྱུང་མགོ་བྱུང་ཞེས་ནི། དམར་ཡུ་ལྡུ་བུ་འདྲེས་ལ་ཟེར།

[The seven g.ya' ma subtypes.] གཡའ་མ་ལ་ནི་རིགས་བདུན་ཏེ། གཡའ་ཆེན བྱུང་ཞེས་ཆེ་ཞིང་ཡིན་[རིང་]། བྱུང་མགོ་ཅུང་ཟད་ཡིད་ཚབ་ལྡུམ། དེ་ལས་བྱུང་ཕ་གཡའ་ཕྲན ཡིན། ཁ་ཅིག་གཡའ་འབབ་ལ་མིད་དུ་འབོད། དངོས་སློ་དེ་བས་བྱུང་མགོ་ལྡུམ། བྱུང་ཡུག་བྱུང

 བ་[B 50b] ཞིག་ལ་ཟེར། བྱང་སྒྲང་ཅུང་ཟད་ཞིམ་པ་ཡིན། བྱང་ཕ་ཕྲི་ནན་སྒྲབ་པ་ཡོན། ལ་ལ མཚོ་དཀར་དག་ཏུ་འདོགས། མཚོ་ནག་དེ་བས་བྱུང་ག་འཕྱུག དིང་ཆེན་བྱུང་བུ་དེ་བས་སྒྲག པེ་ལོ་དེ་བས་ཆེ་མོ་སྒྲུང་། དགར་པོར་ཅན་ནི་འཕྱུམ་ཅན་ཡིན།

[The three me ru subtypes.] མེ་རུ་ལ་ནི་རིགས་གསུམ་སྟེ། མེ་རུ་ཆེ་བ་འབའལ་ཚམ་ ལ། བྱང་ག་བརྟེན་ཞིང་མཛེས་པ་དང་། རྒྱབ་ལ་ཤུལ་ག་ཆགས་པ་ཡོད། དེ་ལས་བྱུང་ཞིང་ཕུ་བ ན། མེ་རུ་ཆུང་བ་ཟེར་བ་ཡིན། གཞན་མེར་ཞེས་པ་ཕིན་ཏུ་བྱུང་། ཞེན་ཅུང་ཤུལ་ག་ཆུང་ཟད ཆགས། གཞན་དག་མེ་རུ་ཀར་བྱུང་ཟེར།

[The three skya chen subtypes.] སྐྱ་ཆེན་ལ་ནི་རིགས་གསུམ་སྟེ། བྱུང་ཞིང་ཆེ་ཞིང་ བྱུང་ཡུག་རིང་། དེ་ལ་སྐྱ་ཆེན་ཟེར་བ་ཡིན། དེ་ལས་ཕུ་ཞིང་བྱུང་བ་ན། སྐྱ་ཕྲན་ཞེས་སུ་འབོད་པ ཡིན། སྐྱ་ཕྲན་གོ་ཅིག་(མགོ་ཕྲོག) ཅེས་པ་ནི། བྱུང་མགོ་རིང་ཞིང་ཅུང་ཟད་སྒུང་། གོང་བས བྱུང་ཞེས་ཅུང་བ་དང་། [BA 30a] སེན་རིས་ཆེ་ལ་ཉེ་བ་ཡིན།

[The three li ding subtypes.] ལི་དིང་རྣམས་[རྣམ་] པ་གསུམ་ཡིན་ཏེ། ཆེ་བ་གོན་ ཁྲབ་ལ་མངགས་[བསྒགས་]ཤིང་། དེ་བས་ཆུང་ན་ཆུང་བ་ཟེར། སྐྱོད་ཁྲབ་དག་[B 51a] ལ་ མངགས་པ་ཡིན། དམར་ཡུ་ལི་དིང་ཞེས་པ་སྟེ། རོ་པོ་ལི་དིང་ཡིན་པ་ལ། བྱང་ཡུག་དེ་བས རིང་བ་སྟེ། བྱུང་སྒྲང་ཞིམ་ཞིང་ཕུ་བ་ཡིན། བར་རྟིང་ཕན་ལ་ཁྲབ་རིགས་ཀྱི། འདྲེ་བ་འདྲེད་ལ་སྐྲ བ་ཡིན། གསར་པ་མགར་བ་མི་ལགས་པས། ཁྲབ་རིགས་འདྲེས་པའི་རིགས་སུ་བཏང་། ཆོན ཀུང་སྐབས་ལས་ཞིག་ཏུ་དཔྱད། གོལ་རྣམས་ལི་དིང་རྟེན་སུ་འགྲོ། དེ་བས་ཅུང་ཟད་སྒྲབ རྒྱས་ཤིང་། བྱུང་མགོ་རྣོ་བར་མཛེན་ཚམ་ཡིན། གོལ་ཆེན་གོལ་རོག་གོལ་ཀུང་གསུམ། བྱུང་བུ ཆེ་འབྲིང་ཅུང་གིས་དཔྱེ།།

Chapter 12, རྨོག (Helmets)[71]

[Helmets: the ten types.] རྨོག་ལ་ལེ་མ་གཞན་མ་དང་། གཞན་ལེ་ཕྲུལ་མང་མི་ཉག རྨོག རྣམ་རྒྱལ་རྨོག་དང་དགར་ལེ་བ་དང་། མཛོ་རྨོག་ཡུར་རྨོག་སྒྱུ་གང་བཅུ། ལི་མ་ལྦུགས རྒྱ་སྒྱུག་ལ་དྭངས། མོ་སྦུམ་ཞིང་ཆེ་པོ་སྦུམ་རྒྱུང་།[72] པོ་སྦུམ་ཅིག་ཟུར་མི་རོ་ལ།[73] པོད་ཟུར་ཅུང

69. While both Beinecke and Burmiok Athing have ནག (black), Brit. Lib., fol. 91a, has དམར (red).

70. All three texts agree on the spelling བབ་ལེ, but the meaning of the term is unclear. It may be a variant of or related to the term བབ་སྟེ, which is defined as a form of decoration sewn on tents (Goldstein 2001, p. 717), or བབ་ཟེབས, a long decorative over-door panel (Goldstein 2001, p. 716).

71. Beinecke, fol. 51a–b; Burmiok Athing, fol. 30a–b; and Brit. Lib., fols. 93b–95a.

72. The term ལི་མ usually indicates bronze, bell metal, or another alloy. It also means "pear," and in that sense it may refer here to a helmet type that is generally pear shaped, especially since the text specifically refers to the material of this helmet as iron, and not bronze or another alloy. It may also be derived from a place-name, such as ལི་ཡུལ, Khotan. The terms མོ་སྦུམ and པོ་སྦུམ are here interpreted to refer to the overlapping segments out of which most types of Tibetan helmets are made. སྦུམ, possibly an abbreviation for སྦུམ་བུ (as was the case with བྱུང and བྱུང་བུ, and རྒྱུན and རྒྱུན་བུ), which has the meaning of a streamer or a long piece of cloth, in this context appears to refer to the various types of long narrow segments of which a helmet bowl was constructed. In this form of construction the uppermost plate, here considered the male segment (པོ་སྦུམ), usually has cusped edges, consisting of two or three peaks and concave

ཀྱུས་ཁ་ཅུང་སྐྱབ། ཏྲེ་ལྷོག་ཀོ་[ཀོང་]བུ་ཀྱུ་དུ་བྱིནས་ཏེ། [74] སྐྱ་[སྐྲ་]བ་གསུམ་དུ་བཅུགས་ལ་ལ། མོ་སྐྲ་ནད་དུ་བྱུད་བཞིན་གསལ། ཞོ་[ཞིལ་]གྱི་བྱུང་བུ་ཅུང་རགས་ཡིན། གཞན་མ་ཡ་ལ་ཅེར་དེ་འདུ་[B 51b]ལ།[75] བོད་ཟུར་ཅུད་ཞེམ་ཁ་ག་ཡེལ་བ། ཏྲེ་ལྷོག་ལྕ་ཉིས་བཅེགས་མད། ལྡགས་མདོག་སྐྱ་ཞིང་གདང་མི་གསལ། ཞོལ་བྱུང་ཞིབ་པ་དག་ལ་ཟེར། ལྡགས་མདོག་ཕྱིས་གསར་ངེས་པར་མེད། གཞན་ལི་ཁ་གཡེལ་བོད་ཀྱུས་ཅེ། སྲུལ་མད་ཅུང་ཅུད་ཁ་དྲུབ་ཅིད།[76] བོད་ཀྱུས་ཏྲི་ལྷོག་ཀོ་བུ་ཀྱུད། པོ་སྲུམ་མོ་སྲུམ་མཉམ་པ་ཡིན། མི་ཉག་རྟོག་ཀྱུན་དེ་འདུ་ལ། ཁ་གཡེལ་དཔུང་ཞེམ་པོ་སྲུམ་ནི། ཡིད་ཀྱི་ཅེ་བ་ཞིག་ལ་གྲགས། རྩམ་ཀྱལ་རྟོག་གི་མོ་སྲུམ་ཞིན། ཅེ་ཞིང་པོ་སྲུམ་ཀྱུད་བ་ལ། པོ་སྲུམ་ཉག་ཟུར་རྟོ་བ་འབྲོང་། མོ་སྲུམ་མཐོངས་[BA 30b]ཆ་རྟོར་མོར་ཡོད། བོད་ཡངས་ལི་མའི་དྲུ་བྱིནས་ལྕ་བྲ། ཏྲེ་ལྷོག་རྒྱུམ་བུ་ཅེ་མོག་ཅན། རྟོག་ཞོལ་ཕིན་ཏུ་རིང་བ་ཡིན། སྐྲ་བ་དགར་ལེབ་དེ་བས་ལེག། མཛེ་རྟོག་པོ་སྲུམ་ཟུར་གཅིག་ཕོད་(འཕོད་)། འདི་ནི་གོང་བས་ཅུང་ཟད་གཡེལ། ལྭུར་རྟོག་ཅུང་ཞིང་དཔུང་ཟུར་ཀྱུས། པོ་སྲུམ་ཟུར་རྩམས་མ་འཕོད་པའོ། སྤུང་གདོང་མི་ཉི་དེ་འདུ་ལ། དཔུང་མགོ་ཞིམ་པ་ཞིག་ལ་ཟེར།

Chapter 15, ཡོབ་ (Stirrups)[77]

[Hor, Chinese, and Tibetan stirrups.] ཡོབ་ལ་ཏྲེ་རྒྱ་བོད་དང་གསུམ། ཏྲེ་ཡོབ་འབྱུག་མགོ་གཅོང་བ་དང་། གསལ་[BA 31a]གཡོན་ཀྲ་གཉིས་སྐྱམས་ལ་ཉི་ལ། ཆུགས་ལ་མཐིལ་སྟོམས་ཆེ་ཀྱུང་རང་། གསེར་ཆགས་[ཆག]དངུལ་ཆགས་[ཆག]དགབ་གིས་སྐྱས། ཀྱུ་ཡོབ་འབྱུག་མགོ་ཅུང་མི་གཅོང་། གསལ་མ་གཡོན་ཀྲ་གཉིས་ལེབ་ཉམས་(མཉམ?)ཡོན། མཐིལ་ཀུན་ཅུང་ཟད་ཀྱིས་བ་སྟེ། གསེར་ཆགས་དངུལ་ཆགས་དགབ་གི་སྐྱས། ཆེ་ཀྱུང་གཉིས་ཡོབ་ཀྱུབ་བ་ལ། བཙུན་མོ་གཏན་ཡོབ་ཞེས་སུ་འབོད། བོད་ཡོབ་རྒྱ་ཡོབ་ཀྱུབ་བ་འདི། དེ་བས་གཙོང་ན་ཀྱུབ་བ་སྟེ། གསེར་ཆགས་དངུལ་ཆགས་ཡོབ་ལ་ཅུང་། ཆགས་[B 53a]གསེར་ཏྲེ་ཀྱུ་བོད་

Chapter 16, སྒ་ (Saddles)[78]

[Hor, Chinese, and Tibetan saddles.] སྒ་ལ་ཏྲེ་སྒ་ཀྱུ་སྒ་དང་། བོད་ཀྱི་སྒ་དང་རྣམ་པ་གསུམ། ཏྲེ་སྒ་ཁྲི་རུ་རྟུ་སྐོམས། སྒ་ཀྱུབ་ཆྲོམ་ཞེས་སྟ་དུ་ཡི།[79] དཔུང་པ་ཅུང་ཟང་ཀྱུས་པ་དང་། སྒ་གདན་བར་དུ་གསེད་[གསང་]འབྱུང་ཡིན། ཀྱུ་སྒ་བན་[བོད་]སྒ་སྟ་དུ་མཐོ།[80] སྒ་ཁྲིམ་ཆེ་ཞིང་ཡངས་པ་ཡིན། སྟ་རུའི་ཟུར་གཉིས་ཞེམ་པ་ལ། སྒ་ཁྲིམ་ཀྱུད་བ་སེ་མ་ལི།[81] བཙུན་མོ་སྒ་ནི་སྟ་རུ་ཅལ། དཔུང་ཟུར་གཉིས་པོ་མཐོན་[ཐོན་]པ་ལ། སྒ་ཁྲིམ་ཆེ་བ་ཞིག་ལ་ཟེར། བོད་ཀྱི་སྒ་ལ་འར་སྒ་ནི། སྒ་ཁྲིམ་ཅུང་ཆེ་སྟ་དུ་ཙོང་། མི་ཉག་སྒ་ནི་དེ་བས་ཅུང་། དེ་ལ་དཔེ་ཀྱུང་[ཆེན་]དཔེ་ཀྱུང་གཉིས།[82] བོད་སྒ་གསར་མ་ཀྱུ་ཏྲེ་ར་ལ། དཔེ་བྱུས་ཅི་རིགས་ཕུང་བར་སྲུང་།

[The materials from which saddles are made.] ཀྱུ་ཏྲེ་ར་སྒ་ལ་སྟེན་མ་དང་། སྒྲ་གོར་ཞོན་ཟ་བོ་ཞིག། གུལ་གོག་དང་ཞིག་ལ་[B 53b]སོགས་པ། ཀྱུ་ཡི་དབྱི་བ་ཅི་རིགས་འབྱུང་། ཁྱད་པར་ཀྱུ་ལ་སོ་སྟེགས་པའི། སོ་སྒ་ཞེས་པ་འདང་འབྱུང་བར་སྲང་། ཀྱུས་ཤུལ་སྟེན་དུ་འགྲོ་ཀྱུད་[སྐྱོད་ཀྱད་]ཀྱི། བང་[སྡང་?]ལ་གཡུང་དུད་ཡོད་པ་མང་། གསེར་གྱི་དུ་བཔགས་ཡོད་སོགས་འབྱུང་། གཞན་ཡང་འབའ་གན་[ཀུན་]འབའ་ཕུན་དང་།[83] འབའ་རེ་འབའ་གཞིན་སྒྲ་ར་ཤིང་། ཅན་དན་དཀར་དམར་ཨ་ཀཱ་རུ། མ་ཤིང་བུ་ཤིང་ཚ་[རུ་]བ་ལས། སྒྲུབ་པའི་རྣམ་གངས་ཤིག་ཏུ་མང་།

[The way in which saddles came about][84] སྒ་ཡི་འབྱུང་ཀྱུལ་བཤད་ཙ་ན།

---

troughs, while the underlying plate (མོ་སྣམ་), or female segment, has plain edges.

73. The term ཉག་ཟུར་ may refer to the cusped edges of the male segments.

74. The term ཏྲི་ལྷོག་ may refer to the negative spaces formed on the surface of the female segments by the opposing cusped edges of adjacent male segments.

75. གཞན་ may indicate a place-name, as may མི་ཉག་, another helmet type.

76. The name of this type, སྤུབ་མང་ (many pleats or folds), implies a helmet made of many narrow overlapping lames.

77. Beinecke, fols. 52b–53a; Burmiok Athing, fols. 30b–31a; Brit. Lib., fols. 96b–97b; and Gangtok 1981, pp. 239–40. For a provisional translation of this chapter, see "Saddles and Tack, Stirrups, and Bridles" in this catalogue.

78. Beinecke, fols. 53a–55a; Burmiok Athing, fols. 31a–32a; Brit. Lib., fols. 97b–102a; and Gangtok 1981, pp. 240–45.

79. In Gangtok 1981 this line begins with ཀྱུ་སྒ་ instead of སྒ་ཀྱུབ་, and in Brit. Lib. the line ends with ཉི་ instead of ཡི་. Both of these variants change the meaning significantly

80. Three of the four texts have བན་ (Beinecke, fol. 53a; Burmiok Athing, fol. 31a; Gangtok 1981, p. 240), in the sense that this is a type of Chinese saddle. Only Brit. Lib, fol. 97b, has བོད་, rather than བན་, meaning Chinese and Tibetan saddles. The term appears again at the end of this chapter.

81. སེ་མ་ལི appears to be the name of a type of saddle, and is repeated near the end of the chapter as a Bon saddle, said by some to be Indian and also called སྒྲོ་རོས་ (Beinecke, fol. 54b; Burmiok Athing, fol. 32a; Brit. Lib., fol. 101a [there called སེ་མ་མོ་]; and Gangtok 1981, p. 243).

82. Beinecke, fol. 53a, differs from the other three here in repeating the words "small example," rather than reading "large example small example."

83. འབའ་ may refer to an area of that name in Amdo, eastern Tibet.

84. Although the story of the origins of saddles according to this text begins in the time of Genghis Khan, wood-frame saddles were widely used in Central Asia from at least the 5th century A.D. onward.

དང་པོ་ངིམ་[ངིང་]་གིར་རྒྱལ་པོའི་དུས། [BA 31b] སྣ་ཡོད་ཏུ་མེད་ཅེས་གྱུང་ཟེར།⁸⁵ དེ་ནས་
སྟེན་སྒྲུག་ཡུལ་དུ་ནི། སྟེན་སྒྲུག་དགར་མ་ཞེས་བྱ་རུ། དེ་ཡིས་རྟ་དགའ་ཚོང་དུ་ཕྱིན།⁸⁶ མདོ་སྨད་རྨ་
ཆུའི་གྱིང་ཁུགས་[ཁུག]་དང་།⁸⁷ བཙོང་[ཙོང་]་ཁ་མཚོ་སྔོན་མཐའ་བསྐོར་བས།⁸⁸ མདོ་བའི་
ཏུའི་དུ་མ་ཉིད། དེ་རྗེས་རྒྱལ་པོའི་ཆིབས་སྣ་བཟོ་[བཟོས]། གོང་དུ་སྐྱེས་པའི་ཞིང་ལ་བྱ།
བཟོ་པོ་གོན་གྱི་[གྱིན་]་མི་ཆོད་ཡིན། བཟོ་ལྷགས་[འདུ]་དཔེའི་བཤད་ཚུན།⁸⁹ ཡ་ཡོད་རྒྱལ་པོ་
འགྱིང་འདུ་དེ།⁹⁰ འགྱིང་པའི་ནང་ནས་འདུམ་པ་ཞིག མ་ཡོད་བཙུན་མོ་བུ་ཁྲིད་འདུ། དེ་ལ་
ཁྱག་པའི་བདེ་ཉམས་ཡོད། ཡུ་མོ་ཡོག [B 54a] གོང་དོག་པ་ལ། དོག་པའི་ནང་ནས་
ཡངས་པ་སྙེད། སེ་གེའི་དཔུང་འདུ་དཔུང་པ་བཏུན། བཏུན་པའི་ནང་ནས་ཕྱུག་[འཕྱུལ]་བ་
ཞིག བྱ་བཞི་ཆོང་དུ་ཉལ་བ་འདུ། ཕྱེལ་ཞིང་[བཞི]་གཟན་བུ་འཕྱུ་བ་འདུ། རྒྱ་བཞི་ཡུར་བར་
དངས་པ་འདུ། སྣ་ཆུན་སྐར་ཕྱུན་ཁར་བ་འདུ། གོང་ཕག་པོ་བར་འཞེན་པ་འདུ། སྲིད་ནེ་ཆུ
པོར་[པོར]་འདུམ་པ་འདུ། སྒྲོ་ནན་སྐྱོ་ལ་འཕུར་བ་འདུ། སྣ་སྦོམ་འབོལ་གྱི་ཆུ་བདོག ཕྱི་སྐྱོམ་
སྟེན་མོའི་ཕལ་མོ་ཡངས། འདོམ་གང་ཁུ་གང་མགོ་གང་དང་། ཁྱད་[འཁྱུད]་གང་ཆགས་[ཆག]་
གང་ཆོང་དུ་ཡོད། བྱ་རྒྱལ་ཁྱུང་གཤོག་ཕྱིང་འདུ་བའི། མར་ན་[སྣ]་སྒྲོག་འདུ་[ཁྱུག]་པ་ཡོད།
ཡར་སྣ་སེ་གེའི་འགྱིང་འདུ་པའི། ཕབས་ཞེས་སེ་སེག་[ཁྱུག]་པ་འདྲིན།⁹¹ སྣ་རིང་མདགས་
པའི་པོ་ཏུ་བདོག མར་སྣ་མགྱོགས་པའི་བང་[དབང]་ཞེས་པ། འཕུལ་བ་བཞི་ནས་[གནས་]་ལ
ཁྱིང་བ་བཞི། ཁྱིང་གཉིས་པ་ལ་འབུར་བ་ཡིན། རྒྱལ་པོ་འདུ་བས་འཛུམ་པ་ལ། ཧུ་(?)
ཕྱབ་འབབས་དང་འདུ་བ་ཡི་[ཡིན]། སྟེན་པོ་ཆེ་བས་ཕེག་ཆེས་ཟེར། དེ་ནི་དེ་ལས་གྱིས་པ
བསླབ། སློམ་སློར་[འབོར]་སྣར་དུ་[B 54b] བཟོས་པ་ལ།⁹² བརྒྱུད་ལྷ་[སྣ]་སྣ་ནི་[ཞེས]།
ཆུམ་[བཅུམ]་གཉིས།⁹³ བརྒྱུད་ལྷ་སྣ་ཞེས་པ་ནི། ཡ་ཡོད་རྒྱང་བ་བརྒྱམ་པ་ལ། ཤིང་ཆོས་ཆེ་ཞིང་

སྟེན་ཆུང་ཆུང་། མི་ཏུ་གཉིས་ལ་མི་ཕྱམས་ཞིང་། དེ་བས་རྒྱང་བ་ཞེས་ཚུམ་[བཅུམ]་ཡིན།
འཛིང་སྣ་ཕྱགས་གཟེར་མ་ཞེས་པ། སློན་པོའི་སྣ་རུ་གྲགས་པ་ནི། ཡ་ཡོད་མ་ཡོད་ཚོམ་པ་གཉིས།
[BA 32a] ཁུ་ཆུང་བཅངས་འདུ་[སྣ]་དུ་བས། ཕྱི་རུ་མཐོ་བ་དག་ལ་ཟེར། འཛིང་སྣ་དམར་པོ་
གྲགས་པ་ནི། ཡ་ཡོད་ཆུང་ཞིང་མ་ཡོད་རྒྱས། སྣ་སློམ་དོག་ལ་ཕྱི་སློམ་ཡངས། གསང་ཕག་འདོ
བའི་གཞུང་དུ་སྒྲ། སྣ་ཡི་ཕག་[ཁ]་ཁལ་དག་དུ་བདག ཡུང་ལ་བུད་རྒྱལ་མཁར་སྟོང་ནི།
ཟི་མ་ཞིང་སྣ་མཁན་གྱིས་ནི། ཁྱུད་འདོན་བྱ་པའི་སྒྲ་དག་ནི། པོ་གྱི་སེ་མ་ལི་ཞེས་པ།⁹⁴ [ག]
ཙིག་རྒྱགས་སྣ་ཞེས་འབོད། སྤོ་རོ་གྱི་སྒྲ་གྱུང་ཟེར། ཏེ་འུན་རྒྱལ་སྣར་[རྒྱགར]་དག
གྲགས་ནས། ཡ་ཡོད་སྟེན་བུའི་མགོ་པོ་འདུ། གྱུ་བཞི་ཤིང་ཆོན་ཆེ་བ་ཡིན། མ་ཡོད་འཛིང་གི་
སྣ་དག་འདུ། གྱིས་མེད་སློ་བུར་གྱིན་དུ་ལངས། གཡུལ་[B 55a] སློང་སྣ་ལ་མགོ་ཞེས་ཟེར། མི་
ཆག་སྣ་ཡི་གནས་ལུགས་ནི། ཡ་ཡོད་ཕྱུས་[དུས]་ཀྱི་མགོ་འཛངས་མགོ། མ་ཡོད་ནོར་གྱི་[གྱི]
གུ་རེ་རྒྱས། སྟེན་པ་པོ་མོ་གཉེན་འབྱེད་འདུ། འཁྱལ་ཁྱིམ་རྣམས་[རྣམ]་པ་གཉིས་[བཞི]་དུ་སྲིད།
རྒྱན་ལ་མ་ཞེས་ལ་[རྣམ་པ]། བཙུག་གཉིས་ཞིང་ཡོད། སྣ་ཡག་རྒྱ་བུའི་གཞུང་འདུ་ལ།⁹⁵ པོ་དོག་ན་སྣར་
ཕྱེད་འདུ་ཡོད། ཡག་སྣ་ས་སུ་ཕྱི་གཉིས་ཀ་ཕུང་། ཕྱི་ཁྱིམ་དུ་ཡི་དུག་མགོ་ཁིའགས། ཡག་བཟང་དབའི་
ཆེན་ཞེས་གྱང་ཟེར། རྒྱང་འདའི་རྒྱང་དག་ཏུ་གྱགས། རོ་སྣ་ཞེས་ལ་རྒྱན་རྒྱལ་ཅན། སྣ་སྣ་ས
དུ་གཅོན་བ་ལ། ཕྱི་དུ་རྒྱང་ཞིང་ཡག་གཞི་ཕྲིམ་[ཕྲེ་བས]། ཁྱག་ཅིང་གཏོག་འཛོལ་རིང་བ་ལ།
འདོ་བ་དུ་བྱམས་པ་ཡིན། མི་ཆེན་སྣ་དུ་མོ་དུ་ཟེར། དེ་དག་ཐལ་ཆེ་རྒྱ་སྒྲག་[བདག]་བ
[ལ]། ཡིན་ཞེས་སྣ་མ་གྱིག་[སློག]་པར་བྱེད། བཙན་སྣ་དག་ལས་ཡ་ཡོད་དམའ། སྣ་ཁྱིམ་ཆེ་ཆུང་
བ་རྒྱའི་བོད་[བས]་སྣ།⁹⁶ དེ་ཡི་ཡ་ཡོད་ཆུང་ཟང་ནལ(?)། གཟར་ཆགས་དག་འདུལ་ཆགས་དག
གིས་སྲས་[སྲས]།།

85. The phrase is literally, "there were saddles [but] there were no horses," which is the opposite of what might be expected. However three of the four texts have the same wording (Beinecke, fol. 53b; Burmiok Athing, fol. 31b; and Gangtok 1981, p. 241). Only Brit. Lib., fol. 98b, has the opposite reading, "there were horses [but] there were no saddles." The apparent contradiction makes sense, however, when taken as providing the reason (the acquisition of ample numbers of horses in Amdo) for the creation of an elaborate saddle for the king, which is then described.

86. Again, Brit. Lib. reads, "went to seek saddles," instead of "went to seek horses," as in the other three texts.

87. The Ma Chu River in Domey, eastern Tibet, which becomes the Yellow (Huang) River in China.

88. The Tsongkha district in Domey, on the shores of Lake Kokonor, here called by its Tibetan name མཚོ་སྔོན་, Blue Lake.

89. This line in Beinecke is only six syllables, rather than the usual seven. The missing word, འདུ་, is found in Burmiok Athing, fol. 31b, and Gangtok 1981, p. 242.

90. From their use in these lines and later in the chapter, it appears that the terms ཡ་ཡོད་ and མ་ཡོད་ refer to the pommel and cantle of a saddle, usually called སྔ་རུ་ and ཕྱི་རུ་.

91. This passage is one of many in which the four texts offer three to four different spellings of a given term. In this instance Beinecke, fol. 54a, and Gangtok 1981, p. 242, have སེ་བག་; Burmiok Athing, fol. 31b, གཟང་བག་; and Brit. Lib., fol. 100a, སྲབ་བག་.

92. The first three words are spelled differently in each of the four texts, the two variations above seeming the most likely. All, however, may be misspellings of སྒྲོ་འབོར་ སྣང་, one of the six traditional districts of Kham.

93. This line is missing from Brit. Lib., fol. 100a. This and the following lines seem to refer to two saddles, one called བརྒྱུད་ལྷ་, and a smaller version of that called ཤེ་ཆུམ་ or ཞེས་བཅུམ་.

94. See note 81 for the mention of སེ་མ་ལི་ as a type of saddle.

95. སྣ་ཡག་ refers to the end-boards, the four projections at the ends of the sideboards of the saddletree, or to the sideboards themselves. ལྷ་སྣ་, mentioned two lines down, refers specifically to the short tips of the end-boards, front and back.

96. This is the line as it appears in Beinecke, fol. 55a, with eight syllables. The other four texts read only ཆུང་བ་, instead of ཆེ་ཆུང་བ་, for the correct number of seven syllables.

སྔར་བྱུང་ *(Colophon)* [97]

བདག་གི་གང་བསགས་རྗེ་སྟེང་ཡོངས་ལ་མཁའ་མཉམ་སྐྱེ་འགྲོ་རྣམས་དང་ལྷུན་ཅིག་ཏུ། ཐོབ་ལ་

ལས་བྱུང་མཐུ་ལས་འདི་བརྩམས་པ་ཡང་ཐམས་ཅད་མཉེན་པའི་རྒྱུ་གྱུར་པོར། གྱུར་ནས་བླ་

མེད་བྱང་ཆུབ་བརྙེས་ཏེ་མཐའ་ཡས་ཤེས་བྱའི་ཚོགས་རྣམས་འཇལ་གྱུར་ཅིག ཅེས་པ་འདི་

ནི་སྟོན་གྱི་ཡི་གེ་རྟིང་ལ་མཐོང་བ་དང་། གཞན་གྱི་དག་རྒྱུན་རྩ་བར་སོན་པ་དང་། མཐོང་བ་རྒྱུད་

ལ་ལས་འོངས་པ་རྣམས་གྱང་བསྟུན་ནས། [98] ནི་སྐྱོལ་བྱེད་ཅེས་པ་གསུམ་ལྷུན་ཤེད་པོ་སྐྱེ་འུ་ལོ་

ཁྱིམ་ (ཁྱིམས་) སྟོང་ཟླ་བ་མེད་གཞན་ཏོར་ཟླ་བ་བརྒྱད་པར་གྲགས་པའི་ཡར་གྱི་ཏོའི་གྲལ་ཚེས་

བཅུ་གསུམ་རྒྱལ་བ་གསུམ་པར་མེད་དུ་འབོད་པ་ལ། [99] པདྨ་བཀོད་པའི་ཚོན་སྟེར་བགྲ་ཤིས་

རྣམ་རྒྱལ་དཔལ་བཟང་པོས་སྤྲ་བ་འདིས་གྱང་རིག་པའི་གནས་མཐའ་དག་ལ་བློ་གྲོས་ཀྱི་

འཇུག་པ་ཅིག་ཅར་དུ་སྐྱེ་བར་གྱུར་ཅིག །[100]

---

97. Excerpted from Beinecke, fol. 73b; Burmiok Athing, fol. 42b; and Gangtok 1981,
     pp. 265–66. The Gangtok version is less complete than the other two.

98. The end of this line and the start of the next read དགུང་ཕུན་ནས in Gangtok 1981.
     Lozang Jamspal points out that in this context this and གུང་བསྟུན, as found in
     Beinecke and Burmiok Athing, would be similar in meaning to གུང་སྒྲིག་པ་ (to match
     or compare) or གུང་བསྒྲིགས (to arrange in sequence).

99. The date is given as the 13th day of the 8th lunar month of the male wood monkey
     year, or 1524. As part of the date, Gangtok 1981 reads མར་གྱི་ཏོ (waning of the moon),
     but the correct reading ཡར་གྱི་ཏོ (waxing of the moon), as found in Beinecke and
     Burmiok Athing, is confirmed by the day being the 13th, which falls in the waxing
     rather than the waning part of a lunar month.

100. The place name, པདྨ་བཀོད, is omitted from the Gangtok 1981 text.

Types and Subtypes of Swords, Helmets, and Armor Named in *A Treatise on Worldly Traditions* (*'jig rten lugs kyi bstan bcos*)

I. Swords: the categories of sword types found in Burmiok Athing, fols. 24a–27a, and British Library Or 11,374, fols. 73b–83b

A. The five principal types of swords
1. སོག་པོ་ (*sog po*)
2. ཞང་མ་ (*zhang ma*)
3. ཧུ་བེད་ (*hu bed*); also spelled ཧུ་ཕེད་ (*hu phed*), ཧུ་བེད་ (*hu wed*), and ཧུ་བདེ་ (*hu bde*)
4. གུ་ཟི་ (*gu zi*) or དགུ་ཟི་ (*dgu zi*)
5. འཇའ་རལ་ (*'ja' ral*)

B. The subtypes of the five principal types of swords
1. སོག་པོ་ (*sog po*)
   a. སོག་རྒན་ (*sog rgan*)
   b. སོག་ཕྲན་ (*sog phran*)
   c. རེལ་ཆོད་ (*rel chod*)
   d. སྐྱ་ངམ་ (*skya ngam*), also called སོག་སྐྱ་ (*sog skya*)
   e. ཧ་ར་ (*ha ra*)
   f. སོག་ཕྲན་ཁྱུག་ (*sog phran khyug*)
   g. སོག་ཕྲན་ལྡེམ་ (*sog phran ldem*)
   h. ཐག་ཁྲེས་ (*thag khres*)
   i. སོག་རྗེ་ (*sog rje*)
2. ཞང་མ་ (*zhang ma*)
   a. ཞང་ཐེམ་ (*zhang them*)
   b. འབྲི་ལྕེ་ (*'bri lce*)
   c. རྡོ་ཚད་ (*rdo tshad*)
   d. ཞང་ཕྲན་ (*zhang phran*)
   e. སྨུག་ཐུང་ (*smug thung*)
   f. ལྡེམ་ཐུང་ (*ldem thung*)
   g. ཕྱིང་ཆོད་ (*phying chod*)
   h. མེ་ལྕེ་ (*me lce*)
   i. ཞང་རྗེ་ (*zhang rje*)
3. ཧུ་བེད་ (*hu bed*)
   a. སྟག་སོ་ (*stag so*)
      1. ཟལ་དཀར་ (*zal dkar*)
      2. ཟལ་དམར་ (*zal dmar*)
      3. ཟལ་ཁྲ་ (*zal khra*)
   b. ཧུ་བེད་རིང་མོ་ (*hu bed ring mo*)

c. ཁས་རྒན་ (*khas rgan*) or ཁལ་རྒལ་ (*khal rgal*)
d. དགུ་ཐུབ་ (*dgu thub*)
e. ཧུ་གྲོགས་ (*hu grogs*)
4. གུ་ཟི་ (*gu zi*) or དགུ་ཟི་ (*dgu zi*)
   a. ནམ་མཁའ་དགུ་ཆོད་ (*nam mkha' dgu chod*)
   b. ཤ་ཐོར་ (*sha thor*)
   c. སྟོང་སྟེ་ཁྲ་བོ་ (*stong ste khra bo*)
   d. སྨུག་ལེབ་ (*smug leb*)
   e. ལི་རྩ་བྱི་ (*li rtsa byi*) or ལི་ཙ་བྱི་ (*li tsa byi*)
   f. སྟོང་རི་ཆེ་བ་ (*stong ri che ba*)
   g. སྟོང་རི་ཆུང་བ་ (*stong ri chung ba*)
   h. ལྟག་ཤི་འགྲི་ལྔ་ (*ltag shi 'gri lnga*), or སྟག་ཤིང་འབྲི་ལྔ་ (*stag shing 'bri lnga*)
   i. ཆུ་ནང་ཉ་མཆོད་ or ཆོད་ (*chu nang nya mchod or chod*)
   j. ལྟག་ཅན་སྤྲུལ་ནག་ (*ltag can sprul nag*) or སྤྲུལ་ནག་ (*sprul nag*)
   k. སྤྱང་མོ་རྒྱུག་འདྲ་ (*spyang mo rgyug 'dra*)
   l. གུ་བདག་ (*gu bdag*) or དགུ་བདག་ (*dgu bdag*)
5. འཇའ་རལ་ (*'ja' ral*)
   a. ཤར་འཇའ་ (*shar 'ja'*)
   b. ལྷོ་འཇའ་ (*lho 'ja'*)
   c. རབ་སྒང་རལ་གྲི་ (*rab sgang ral gri*)
   d. ཤང་རྡོ་ (*shang rdo*) or ཤང་རྡོ་ལྟག་ཤིང་ (*shang rdo ltag shing*)
   e. ཨ་ལི་ཟི་[ཇི་] (*a li zi [ji]*)
   f. ཤང་དམར་ (*shang dmar*)
   g. ཤང་ནག་ (*shang nag*)
   h. ག་འུ་མ་ (*ga 'u ma*) or གའུ་མ་ (*ga'u ma*)
   i. ལྦ་བ་མ་ (*lba ba ma*)
   j. ཨ་ལུང་མ་ (*a lung ma*)
   k. སྐྱ་ཕྲ་བ་ (*skya phra ba*)
   l. འགུ་ཐེམ་ (*'gu them*) or དགུ་ཐེམ་ (*dgu them*)
   m. རྒྱལ་འཇའ་ (*rgyal 'ja'*)
      1. ཤལ་གོག་ (*shal gog*)
      2. རྔུ་གོག་ (*rngu gog*)
      3. འབྲི་གོག་ (*'bri gog*)
      4. རྐང་དཀར་ (*rkang dkar*)

II. Armor: the categories of armor lamellae in Beinecke, fols. 48a–51a; Burmiok Athing, fols. 27a–30a; and British Library Or 11,374, fols. 83b–93b

A. The seven principal types of armor lamellae
1. རྒྱ་བྱི་ (*rgya byi*), also spelled རྒྱ་དབྱི་ (*rgya dbyi*), or རྒྱ་ཡི་ (*rgya yi*)
2. དམར་ཡུ་ (*dmar yu*), also spelled དམར་གཡུ་ (*dmar g.yu*)
3. འབལ་ (*’bal*), also spelled འབའ་ (*’ba’*)
4. གཡའ་མ་ (*g.ya’ ma*)
5. མེ་རུ་ (*me ru*)
6. སྐྱ་ཆེན་ (*skya chen*)
7. ལི་དིང་ (*li ding*), also spelled ལི་ཏིང་ (*li ting*), or ལི་ཐིང་ (*li thing*)

B. The subtypes of the principal types of armor lamellae
1. རྒྱ་བྱི་ (*rgya byi*), nine subtypes
   a. རྒྱ་བྱི་ཆེན་མོ་ (*rgya byi chen mo*)
   b. འབྲིང་པོ་ (*’bring po*)
   c. ཆུང་བ་ (*chung ba*)
   d. སྲེན་མོ་མགོ་ (*sren mo mgo*)
   e. ལྡན་བྱང་འོག་རྒྱུན་ (*ldan byang ’og rgyun*)
   f. རྒྱལ་མོ་འོག་རྒྱུན་ (*rgyal mo ’og rgyun*)
   g. ཟུར་རྒྱུན་མ་ (*zur rgyun ma*)
   h. རྒྱལ་མོ་མིག་བཞི་ (*rgyal mo mig bzhi*)
   i. རྒྱུན་མི་གསལ་ (*rgyun mi gsal*)
2. དམར་ཡུ་ (*dmar yu*), twenty subtypes
   a. དམར་ཡུ་དངོས་ (*dmar yu dngos*)
   b. རྐང་ཐུང་ (*rkang thung*)
   c. མཆོག་དཀར་ (*mchog dkar*)
   d. སྟ་ཆོད་ (*sta chod*)
   e. མཚོ་ཆེན་ (*mtsho chen*)
   f. སེན་རྒྱབ་ (*sen rgyab*)
   g. སྒྲོ་རྐང་ (*sgro rkang*), alternative name for སེན་རྒྱབ་ (*sen rgyab*)
   h. སེན་རིས་ (*sen ris*)
   i. བྱེ་གཤོག་ཆེ་བ་ (*bye gshog che ba*)
   j. བྱེ་གཞོག་ཆུང་བ་ (*bye gzhog chung ba*)
   k. ཉ་འདྲ་ (*nya ’dra*)
   l. ཉ་འདྲ་ཆུང་ (*nya ’dra chung*)
   m. ཤ་རྐང་ (*sha rkang*) or ཤ་རྐང་མཆོག་ (*sha rkang mchog*)
   n. དགེ་རྐང་ (*dge rkang*)
   o. འབའ་ཡེར་ (*’ba’ yer*)
   p. འབུ་ཡེར་ (*’bu yer*)
   q. དམར་ཡུ་རྒྱལ་མོ་མིག་བཞི་ (*dmar yu rgyal mo mig bzhi*)
   r. དམར་ཡུ་འོག་རྒྱུན་ (*dmar yu ’og rgyun*)
   s. དམར་ཡུ་ཟུར་རྒྱུན་ (*dmar yu zur rgyun*)
   t. དམར་ཡུ་མི་གསལ་ (*dmar yu mi gsal*)

3. འབལ་ (*’bal*), thirteen subtypes
   a. འབལ་དངོས་ (*’bal dngos*)
   b. འབལ་ཕྲན་ (*’bal phran*)
   c. ཚུར་དཀར་ (*tshur dkar*), also called སྐྱ་འབལ་ (*skya ’bal*) and འབལ་དཀར་ (*’bal dkar*)
   d. ཚུར་ནག་ (*tshur nag*), also called མཚོ་ནག་ (*mtsho nag*)
   e. ཝ་སྣ་ (*wa sna*)
   f. སེང་མགོ་ (*seng mgo*)
   g. སྟ་ཆོད་ (*sta chod*)
   h. སེན་རིས་ (*sen ris*)
   i. རྟ་སོ་ (*rta so*)
   j. ཁྱི་སོ་ (*khyi so*)
   k. ཨ་རྩེ་ (*a rtse*)
   l. སྲེ་མོ་སྐེ་ (*sre mo ske*)
   m. འབལ་དམར་ནང་གི་ཤ་སེན་ (*’bal dmar nang gi sha sen*)
4. གཡའ་མ་ (*g.ya’ ma*), seven subtypes
   a. གཡའ་ཆེན་ (*g.ya’ chen*)
   b. གཡའ་ཕྲན་ (*g.ya’ phran*), also called གཡའ་འབལ་ (*g.ya’ bal*)
   c. དངོས་སྒོར་ (*dngos sgor*), also called མཚོ་དཀར་དག་ (*mtsho dkar dag*)
   d. མཚོ་ནག་ (*mthso nag*)
   e. དིང་ཆེན་ (*ding chen*)
   f. བེ་ལོ་ (*be lo*)
   g. དཀར་ཐོར་ཅན་ (*dkar thor can*)
5. མེ་རུ་ (*me ru*), three subtypes
   a. མེ་རུ་ཆེ་བ་ (*me ru che ba*)
   b. མེ་རུ་ཆུང་བ་ (*me ru chung ba*)
   c. གཞའ་མེ་ (*gzha’ me*), also called མེ་རུ་རྐང་ཐུང་ (*me ru rkang thung*)
6. སྐྱ་ཆེན་ (*skya chen*), three subtypes
   a. སྐྱ་ཆེན་ (*skya chen*)
   b. སྐྱ་ཕྲན་ (*skya phran*)
   c. སྐྱ་ཕྲན་གོ་ཙོག་ [མགོ་ལྕོག་] (*skya phran go cog [mgo lcog]*)
7. ལི་དིང་ (*li ding*), three subtypes
   a. ཆེ་བ་ (*che ba*)
   b. ཆུང་བ་ (*chung ba*)
   c. དམར་ཡུ་ལི་དིང་ (*dmar yu li ding*)
7a. ཤོལ་རྣམས་ (*shol rnams*)
   a. ཤོལ་ཆེན་ (*shol chen*)
   b. ཤོལ་རོག་ (*shol rog*)
   c. ཤོལ་ཆུང་ (*shol chung*)

III. Helmets: the ten types of helmets in Beinecke, fol. 51a–b; Burmiok Athing, fol. 30a–b; and British Library Or 11,374, fols. 93b–95a

1. ལི་མ་ (li ma)
2. གཞའ་མ་ (gzha' ma)
3. གཞའ་ལི་ (gzha' li)
4. སུལ་མང་ (sul mang)
5. མི་ཉག་རྨོག་ (mi nyag rmog)

6. རྣམ་རྒྱལ་རྨོག་ (rnam rgyal rmog)
7. དཀར་ལེབ་ (dkar leb)
8. མཛེ་རྨོག་ (mdze rmog)
9. ཨུར་རྨོག་ (aur rmog)
10. སྤྱང་གདོང་ (spyang gdong)

Tibetan-English Glossary of Arms and Armor Terms

The glossary is divided into five sections by types of objects. The entries within each section are arranged in Tibetan alphabetical order, as they would appear in a Tibetan dictionary. The definitions given here are quoted or derived from the sources cited in parentheses within or immediately after each definition. Amendments, where necessary, are inserted in brackets. Commentary or definitions without citations are my own.

 I. *Armor (ཁྲབ་) and Shields (ཕུབ་)*

 II. *Hand-Held Weapons (མཚོན་ཆ་), Non-Projectile*

 III. *Archery Equipment (འཕོང་སྒྱུད་) and Projectile Weapons (འཕེན་མཚོན་), other than Firearms*

 IV. *Firearms (མེ་མདའ་) and Accessories (མེ་མདའ་ཆས་); Ordnance (སྒྱོགས་)*

 V. *Equestrian Equipment, including Saddles and Tack (སྒ་ཆས་), and Horse Armor (རྟ་གོ་)*

I. *Armor (ཁྲབ་) and Shields (ཕུབ་)*

kul kar (ཀུལ་གར་), also **kul dkar** (ཀུལ་དཀར་). A kind of shield manufactured in Kul-kar, a place in Tsang: "The shield manufactured at Kul-kar is of superior quality (on account of its superior [materials])" (ཀུལ་གར་ཕུབ་རྣམས་རྒྱུ་ཡི་ཁྱད་དུ་འཕགས།); "As to the Kul-kar shield it costs five *zho* for the best" (ཀུལ་དཀར་ཕུབ་ནི་རབ་ལ་ཞོ་ལྔ་སྟེ) (Das 1902b, p. 30). See also *phub* (ཕུབ་).

ko phub (ཀོ་ཕུབ་). Leather shield (Das 1902b, p. 825; *bod rgya*, p. 1718, both under ཕུབ་).

ko bse (ཀོ་བསེ་). See *bse ko* (བསེ་ཀོ་) and *bse khrab* (བསེ་ཁྲབ་).

kong bzo (ཀོང་བཟོ་). A kind of armor or weapon manufactured in Kong po, a province southeast of Lhasa (Das 1902b, p. 36, under ཀོང་པོ་). See also sec. II, under *kong mdung* (ཀོང་མདུང་).

kor bzo (ཀོར་བཟོ་). A kind of shield of round shape; literally, anything of round make (Das 1902b, p. 37, citing *Rtsii*).

rkang khrab (རྐང་ཁྲབ་). Iron shoes worn along with the coat of mail [i.e., armor]; that part of the armor worn like boots from foot to the knees; greaves (Das 1902b, p. 72).

khyung thur can (ཁྱུང་ཐུར་ཅན་). According to Das, equivalent to *go cha* (གོ་ཆ) and *go khrab* (གོ་ཁྲབ་), armor (Das 1902b, p. 164, citing *Mngon*). Armor or helmet (*bod rgya*, p. 266).

khrab (ཁྲབ་). A general term for body armor. 1: According to Das: shield; buckler, coat of mail. The coat of mail [i.e., armor] used in Tibet and Bhutan is generally made of iron rings or thin disks resembling the scales of fish netted together. Two kinds of *khrab* (ཁྲབ་) are known in Tibet; one is called *a lung gi khrab* (ཨ་ལུང་གི་ཁྲབ་), which is made of iron rings or scales [i.e., mail]; *byang bu'i khrab* (བྱང་བུའི་ཁྲབ་), that made of thin plates or iron foils [i.e, lamellar armor]. There are accounts of coats of mail made of silver and gold for the use of kings. The common quilted cloth armor used in Mongolia and China is called *sring bal khrab* (སྲིང་བལ་ཁྲབ་). In Mongolia it is called *dasa* (Das 1902b, p. 169). 2: Armor (Goldstein 2001, p. 141).

khrab mkhan (ཁྲབ་མཁན་). 1: One who makes or wears armor (Das 1902b, p. 169). 2: Armorer (ETED, p. 352).

khrab gos (ཁྲབ་གོས་), same as *khrab* (ཁྲབ་). Armor (Goldstein 2001, p. 141).

khrab can (ཁྲབ་ཅན་). Having or wearing armor. According to Das: scaled, scaly, wearing a coat of mail [i.e., armor] (Das 1902b, p. 169).

khrab lcibs (ཁྲབ་ལྕིབས་). 1: The lining inside armor (Goldstein 2001, p. 141). See also *lcibs* (ལྕིབས་). 2: The padding or underclothes inside armor (*bod rgya*, p. 275).

khrab chas (ཁྲབ་ཆས་). Armor, or arms, in the sense of including armor and weapons; defined as *drag chas go khrab* (དྲག་ཆས་གོ་ཁྲབ་) in the *bod rgya* (p. 275), which may be equivalent to the English term "arms and armor."

khrab thung ba (ཁྲབ་ཐུང་བ་). A short armor, covering the arms to the elbows and the body to the knees (*dung dkar* 2002, p. 341).

khrab byang (ཁྲབ་བྱང་). Term for the small plates, the *byang bu* (བྱང་བུ་ or lamellae), that make up a traditional Tibetan lamellar armor. Precisely defined in the *bod rgya* as "the lamellae of an armor" (*khrab kyi byang bu* ཁྲབ་ཀྱི་བྱང་བུ་), which is preferable to other definitions, such as "scales on armor" (Goldstein 2001, p. 141) or "armored plate" (ETED, p. 352). See also *byang dgu* (བྱང་དགུ་), *byang bu* (བྱང་བུ་), and *byang bu'i khrab* (བྱང་བུའི་ཁྲབ་).

khrab byang gu (ཁྲབ་བྱང་གུ་). Defined by Das (1902b, p. 169, citing *Rtsii*) as "scales or iron foils used in a coat of mail," but this and *khrab byang* (ཁྲབ་བྱང་) can more accurately be described as terms for the individual lamellae of a lamellar armor. See also *byang dgu* (བྱང་དགུ་), *byang bu* (བྱང་བུ་), and *byang bu'i khrab* (བྱང་བུའི་ཁྲབ་).

khrab byin lus kheb (ཁྲབ་བྱིན་ལུས་ཁེབ). A coat of mail [i.e., armor] for covering the whole body (Das 1902b, p. 169, citing *Rtsii*).

khrab ma (ཁྲབ་མ). 1: Soldiers clad in armor. 2: Archaic for armor (Goldstein 2001, p. 141; *bod rgya*, p. 275). Not specifically a breastplate, as defined in the ETED, p. 352.

khrab rmog (ཁྲབ་རྨོག). Armor and helmet; *khrab rmog 'gyon* (ཁྲབ་རྨོག་འགྱོན), to put on or wear armor and helmet (Goldstein 2001, p. 141). Coat of mail [i.e., armor] and helmet (Das 1902b, p. 987, under རྨོག, citing Jäschke 1881). Not specifically a breastplate and helmet, as defined in the ETED, p. 352.

khrab rang gyon (ཁྲབ་རང་གྱོན). An ancient magical armor that comes on the body by itself (Goldstein 2001, p. 141).

go bkrag (གོ་བཀྲག). Armor (Goldstein 2001, p. 185).

go khang (གོ་ཁང). Armory (Goldstein 2001, p. 185) in the sense of the room or building where arms and armor are kept. See also *go khrab kyi rdzod* (གོ་ཁྲབ་ཀྱི་རྫོད) and *go mdzod* (གོ་མཛོད).

go khrab (གོ་ཁྲབ). 1: Armor (Goldstein 2001, p. 185; *bod rgya*, p. 363); or 2: as defined by Das (1902b, pp. 225–26 citing *Mngon*) in the sense of armor and weapons *go cha dang khrab* (གོ་ཆ་དང་ཁྲབ) and as a coat of mail [i.e., armor] with helmet. See also *go cha* (གོ་ཆ) and *khrab* (ཁྲབ).

go khrab kyi rdzod (གོ་ཁྲབ་ཀྱི་རྫོད) or **go rdzod** (གོ་རྫོད). Armory (Kazi 1919, p. 54), the room or building where arms and armor are kept. See also *go mdzod* (གོ་མཛོད).

go khrab 'khur mkhan (གོ་ཁྲབ་འཁུར་མཁན). Armor-bearer (Kazi 1919, p. 54).

go khrab bgo (གོ་ཁྲབ་བགོ). To wear or put on armor (Goldstein 2001, p. 185). Also cited as *go bgo* (གོ་བགོ) in *bod rgya*, p. 363.

go khrab 'rdung mkhan (གོ་ཁྲབ་འརྡུང་མཁན). Armorer (Kazi 1919, p. 54), the person who makes or repairs armor.

go khrab rmog gsum (གོ་ཁྲབ་རྨོག་གསུམ). The three: weapons, armor, and helmet (Goldstein 2001, p. 185).

go gyon pa (གོ་གྱོན་པ), also **go cha gyon pa** (གོ་ཆ་གྱོན་པ). According to Das, to wear a coat of mail [i.e., armor of any kind]; to put on war dress. Syn.: *go bgos* (གོ་བགོས), *g.yul gyi chas zhungs pa* (གཡུལ་གྱི་ཆས་ཞུངས་པ), *ya lad bgos* (ཡ་ལད་བགོས) (Das 1902b, p. 225, citing *Mngon*).

go bgos pa (གོ་བགོས་པ). The act of equipping or arraying, to equip with armor, or put on harness (Das 1902b, p. 225). See also *go gyon pa* (གོ་གྱོན་པ).

go ca (གོ་ཅ). See *go cha* (གོ་ཆ).

go cha (གོ་ཆ). 1: Armor, harness, gear, implements, tools. Syn.: *ya lad* (ཡ་ལད), *mtshon skyob* (མཚོན་སྐྱོབ), *lus skyob* (ལུས་སྐྱོབ), *lus bsrung* (ལུས་བསྲུང), *lcags gos* (ལྕགས་གོས), *zhub can* (ཞུབ་ཅན), *dra ba can* (དྲ་བ་ཅན), *'khrug gos* (འཁྲུག་གོས), *lcags kyi bgo ba khrab* (ལྕགས་ཀྱི་བགོ་བ་ཁྲབ), *khrab* (ཁྲབ), *rmog* (རྨོག), *mgo skyob*, (མགོ་སྐྱོབ), *rmog zhu* (རྨོག་ཞུ), *lcags zhu* (ལྕགས་ཞུ), *rmog thur* (རྨོག་ཐུར), *khyung thur can* (ཁྱུང་ཐུར་ཅན), *go khrab* (གོ་ཁྲབ) (Das 1902b, pp. 225–26, citing *Mngon*). Additional syn.: *brang g.yogs* (བྲང་གཡོགས), *mtshon sgrib* (མཚོན་སྒྲིབ) (*bod rgya*, p. 364). 2: Weapons (Goldstein 2001, p. 186, def. 2).

go cha gyon pa (གོ་ཆ་གྱོན་པ). See *go gyon pa* (གོ་གྱོན་པ).

go rtsed (གོ་རྩེད). Soldiers attired in the battle dress and weapons of the era of the kings (this occurs during the Great Prayer Festival) (Goldstein 2001, p. 187, def. 2).

go mtshon (གོ་མཚོན). Weapons, arms (Goldstein 2001, p. 187; *bod rgya*, p. 367).

go mdzod (གོ་མཛོད). Armory or arsenal (*bod rgya*, p. 367). See also *go khrab kyi rdzod* (གོ་ཁྲབ་ཀྱི་རྫོད) and *go khang* (གོ་ཁང).

go zhub (གོ་ཞུབ). Archaic term for armor, equivalent to *khrab* (ཁྲབ) (*bod rgya*, p. 367).

go lag (གོ་ལག). Arms, weapons (Goldstein 2001, p. 187; *bod rgya*, p. 368).

glo spir (གློ་སྤིར). Assording to Das (1902b, p. 261, citing *Jig*), name of a kind of shield: "kul dkar phub ni rab la zho lnga ste, glo spir zho re phub skor zho phyed yin (ཀུལ་དཀར་ཕུབ་ནི་རབ་ལ་ཞོ་ལྔ་སྟེ། གློ་སྤིར་ཞོ་རེ་ཕུབ་སྐོར་ཞོ་ཕྱེད་ཡིན)" (the best *kul dkar* shield costs five *zho* and that of *glo spir* costs a *zho* for each disk on it). An alternative to Das's translation of this citation could be, "It costs five *zho* for the best *kul dkar* shield, a single *zho* for a *glo spir* (shield), and half a *zho* for a round shield." In the sense that *glo* (གློ) can refer to things to do with the waist or side, this may indicate a small shield that was hung from the belt when not in use, as was the type of shield known as a buckler in Europe. See also *phub* (ཕུབ).

dgra le (དགྲ་ལེ). A Bhutanese term for shield (Kazi 1919, p. 708). See also *phub* (ཕུབ).

rgyun bu (རྒྱུན་བུ). Laces, string, or thongs of leather (*bod rgya*, p. 578). This is the material with which the lamellae of a Tibetan lamellar armor are laced together. See also *bye rgyun* (བྱེ་རྒྱུན).

lcag (ལྕག). Forepart of a coat of mail (Das 1902b, p. 396, def. 3, citing Schmidt 1841). But note that the wording of Schmidt's definition

(p. 151), "Vorshooss des Panzers," implies a type of apron or frontal skirt. "Panzer" here means "armor," not specifically mail.

lcags khrab (ལྕགས་ཁྲབ་). Iron armor, plate armor (Goldstein 2001, p. 343).

lcags gos (ལྕགས་གོས་). Protective body armor (*bod rgya*, p. 760).

lcags rmog (ལྕགས་རྨོག་). Iron helmet (Goldstein 2001, p. 344).

lcags zhu (ལྕགས་ཞུ་). Helmet or head covering of iron (*bod rgya*, p. 763).

lcags long sbrel khrab (ལྕགས་ལོང་སྦྲེལ་ཁྲབ་). Armor made of iron rings connected together [i.e., mail] (Goldstein 2001, p. 345). See also *a lung gi khrab* (ཨ་ལུང་གི་ཁྲབ་).

lcibs (ལྕིབས་). A shield (Das 1902b, p. 400, def. 3). Compare with *khrab lcibs* (ཁྲབ་ལྕིབས་). See also *phub* (ཕུབ་).

lcog ras (ལྕོག་རས་). According to Das (1902b, p. 401), a piece of cloth put over an iron helmet in a war dance in Tibet. See also *thod* (ཐོད་).

gnya' khobs (གཉའ་ཁོབས་). Defined by Das (1902b, p. 491) as a screen to protect the neck, attached to the helmet. On a traditional Tibetan helmet this would refer to the rows of *byang bu* (བྱང་བུ་, lamellae) laced to the bottom edge of the helmet at the back and sides. On a Chinese helmet this would be the curtain of textile lined with small iron plates, which is riveted to the bottom of the helmet.

thugs gsal me long (ཐུགས་གསལ་མེ་ལོང་). Metal breastplate worn by oracles (Goldstein 2001, p. 497). See also *me long bzhi* (མེ་ལོང་བཞི་).

thod (ཐོད་). According to Nebesky-Wojkowitz (1975, p. 12), a kind of turban made of silks of various colors and wound around a helmet. This may refer to the braided circlet of cloth often seen at the base of the helmet, both in works of art and on actual helmets. See also *lcog ras* (ལྕོག་རས་).

dar 'phru (དར་འཕྲུ་). Flag attached to the apex of a helmet (*bod rgya*, p. 1251). See also *rmog dar* (རྨོག་དར་).

dra ba can (དྲ་བ་ཅན་). Defined by Das (1902b, p. 647, def. 3. citing *Mngon*) as a coat of mail, equal to *go khrab* (གོ་ཁྲབ་). The fact that this term is derived from a word with meanings of "lattice" and "net" may indicate that it does specifically refer to mail, as opposed to other forms of armor. However, the name may simply indicate one of the stylized artistic representations in which armor is frequently depicted by a lattice-like pattern. The *bod rgya* defines it simply as body armor (p. 1314).

rna khebs (རྣ་ཁེབས་). The part of a helmet that protects the ears (Jäschke 1881, p. 312, under རྣ་བ་). See also *rmog gzhol* (རྨོག་གཞོལ་).

spang leb (སྤང་ལེབ་). A type of shield (Das 1902b, p. 797). See also *phub* (ཕུབ་).

pha li (ཕ་ལི་). Shield, buckler (Das 1902b, p. 818). See also *phub* (ཕུབ་).

phub (ཕུབ་). 1: According to Das (1902b, p. 825), armor, shield, plate, or breastplate: *ko phub* (ཀོ་ཕུབ་), a leather buckler; *phub shubs* (ཕུབ་ཤུབས་), the cover of a shield; *phub kyi me long* (ཕུབ་ཀྱི་མེ་ལོང་), the center of the shield [lit. mirror of shield, i.e., the shield boss or umbo]. Note that although Das's definition includes armor and breastplate, the primary meaning for this term seems to be shield. 2: Shield (Goldstein 2001, p. 682; Schmidt 1841, p. 344). 3: Implement to protect against arrows, sword, etc., made of cane, bamboo, and so on (*bod rgya*, p. 1718). See also *glo spir* (གློ་སྤིར་), *dgra le* (དགྲ་ལེ་), *lcibs* (ལྕིབས་), *spang leb* (སྤང་ལེབ་), *pha li* (ཕ་ལི་), *sba phub* (སྦ་ཕུབ་), *re lde* (རེ་ལྡེ་), *bse ko* (བསེ་ཀོ་), and *bse khrab* (བསེ་ཁྲབ་).

phub kyi me long (ཕུབ་ཀྱི་མེ་ལོང་). The round metal boss in the center of a shield (Das 1902b, p. 854, under ཕུབ་; *bod rgya*, p. 1718), and probably not a mirrorlike metal shield (as defined in Goldstein 2001, p. 682). Tibetan shields made of cane often had a round metal boss in the center. Round metal shields, on the other hand, were typical of India and Persia, but not Tibet.

phub dmag (ཕུབ་དམག་). Soldiers equipped with shields (*bod rgya*, p. 1719).

phub rtsed (ཕུབ་རྩེད་). A display of martial skill using a shield (Goldstein 2001, p. 682).

phub shu (ཕུབ་ཤུ་). A covering for a shield (Schmidt 1841, p. 344). See also *phub shubs* (ཕུབ་ཤུབས་) under *phub* (ཕུབ་).

byang khrab (བྱང་ཁྲབ་). Lamellar armor (ETED, p. 352, under *khrab* ཁྲབ་, but there incorrectly described as "chain mail"; Goldstein 2001, p. 731). See *byang bu* (བྱང་བུ་) and *byang bu'i khrab* (བྱང་བུའི་ཁྲབ་).

byang dgu (བྱང་དགུ་). Metal lamellae pierced with nine holes, laced together to make traditional lamellar armor (Goldstein 2001, p. 731). See *khrab byang gu* (ཁྲབ་བྱང་གུ་), *byang bu* (བྱང་བུ་), and *byang bu'i khrab* (བྱང་བུའི་ཁྲབ་). Also called *dgu mig* (དགུ་མིག་, lit. nine eyes), according to Mrs. Diki L. Surkhang.

byang chung (བྱང་ཆུང་). Lamellar armor made of small lamellae (*bod rgya*, p. 1868).

byang bu (བྱང་བུ་). 1: Individual iron plates, or lamellae, of lamellar armor, which are flat, rectangular with rounded corners, and usually pierced with nine to thirteen holes. The term is often mistranslated as "coat of mail" or "chain mail." Defined by Das (1902b, p. 885, citing *Jig* 31) as a coat of mail made of thin circular scalelike iron rings.

While that definition could apply to mail, scale, and lamellar armor, the actual term refers specifically to the lamellae that make up a lamellar armor, and not mail or scale. Note also that Das's definition 2 under *byang bu* refers to an inscription written on a board, which also implies the rectangular shape of armor lamellae. 2: A strip of armor [i.e., a lamella from a lamellar armor] (Goldstein 2001, p. 732).

byang bu'i khrab (བྱང་བུའི་ཁྲབ་). Lamellar armor; an armor made up of lamellae (*byang bu* [བྱང་བུ་]) laced with leather cord into rows, which overlap upward. According to Das (1902b, p. 169, under ཁྲབ་) a type of armor, *khrab* (ཁྲབ་), which is made of thin plates or foils. But note that this appears to be the specific term for a lamellar armor, as opposed to mail or scale.

byang rmog 'thor 'phros (བྱང་རྨོག་འཐོར་འཕྲོས་). Armor that is coming apart (Goldstein 2001, p. 732).

byang zhva (བྱང་ཞྭ་). Iron helmet; Das (1902b, p. 855, citing *Rtsii*) gives the example *lcags kyi byang dgus bzos bas zhva mo* (ལྕགས་ཀྱི་བྱང་དགུས་བཟོས་བས་ཞྭ་མོ་), which can be translated as "a hat made of iron lamellae."

bye rgyun (བྱེ་རྒྱུན་). The leather straps which join strips of armor [i.e., the thin leather laces by which the lamellae, or *byang bu* [བྱང་བུ་], of a lamellar armor are laced together] (Goldstein 2001, p. 737). See also *rgyun bu* (རྒྱུན་བུ་).

brang khebs (བྲང་ཁེབས་). Breastplate (armor) (Goldstein 2001, p. 739).

dbu 'phangs (དབུ་འཕངས་) or **dbu rmog** (དབུ་རྨོག་). A helmet (Das 1902b, p. 911).

sba phub (སྦ་ཕུབ་). Shield made of cane (*bod rgya*, p. 1718, under ཕུབ་). Cane or rattan shield (Goldstein 2001, p. 775). See also *phub* (ཕུབ་).

me long bzhi (མེ་ལོང་བཞི་). Literally, four mirrors. This term appears to describe the type of torso armor found in Tibet that is made up of four polished circular plates. This type of armor was also widely used in India and Persia, where, however, the plates were often faceted or rectangular, and where the armor was known as *chahar ainah*, again literally meaning "four mirrors." See also *thugs gsal me long* (ཐུགས་གསལ་མེ་ལོང་).

rmo yas (རྨོ་ཡས་). Steel helmet; also, perhaps a full coat of mail [i.e., armor] (Das 1902b, p. 987, def. 2, citing *Mngon*).

rmog (རྨོག་). Helmet, armor specifically for the head (*bod rgya*, p. 2156); according to Das (1902b, p. 987, citing Jäschke 1881) the same as *go cha* (གོ་ཆ་), or *go khrab* (གོ་ཁྲབ་); *khrab rmog* (ཁྲབ་རྨོག་), coat of mail [i.e., body armor], and helmet. Syn.: *rmog thur* (རྨོག་ཐུར་), *tshom zhu* (ཚོམ་ཞུ་), *rmog zhu* (རྨོག་ཞུ་), *dmag zhva* (དམག་ཞྭ་) (Das 1902b, p. 987, citing *Mngon*).

rmog dkar (རྨོག་དཀར་). Helmet (Kazi 1919, p. 347).

rmog rgyan (རྨོག་རྒྱན་). 1: The name of an ornament or crest on top of a helmet (*bod rgya*, p. 2156). 2: Banner/standard attached to a Tibetan helmet (Goldstein 2001, p. 836).

rmog stan (རྨོག་སྟན་). A hat worn beneath a helmet (*bod rgya*, p. 2156). Presumably this was a padded cap of some kind, intended to make the helmet more comfortable to wear and possibly adding some additional protection, serving the same function as the padded lining of a European helmet. See also *rmog tshangs* (རྨོག་ཚངས་) and *zhva gdan* (ཞྭ་གདན་).

rmog thur (རྨོག་ཐུར་). The fixture at the top of a helmet, to which the crest or pennant is attached (*bod rgya*, p. 2156). This would correspond to the plume tube or plume holder on European helmets.

rmog thod (རྨོག་ཐོད་). The front of the helmet (*bod rgya*, p. 2156; Goldstein 2001, p. 836). This may possibly signify the small iron brim, which is riveted to the forehead area on many Tibetan, Chinese, and Mongolian helmets.

rmog dar (རྨོག་དར་). Small flag at the top of a helmet (*bod rgya*, p. 2156). See also *dar 'phru* (དར་འཕྲུ་).

rmog tshangs (རྨོག་ཚངས་). The lining or padding inside a helmet (Csoma 1834, p. 257; Schmidt 1841, p. 429). See also *rmog stan* (རྨོག་སྟན་) and *zhva gdan* (ཞྭ་གདན་).

rmog zhu (རྨོག་ཞུ་). 1: Helmet (Goldstein 2001, p. 836). 2: An early style of Chinese hat (*bod rgya*, pp. 2156–57).

rmog zhva (རྨོག་ཞྭ་). Iron helmet to protect the head (*bod rgya*, p. 2156).

rmog gzhol (རྨོག་གཞོལ་). Protective ear flaps on a helmet (Goldstein 2001, p. 836). See also *rna khebs* (རྣ་ཁེབས་).

rmog ril (རྨོག་རིལ་). A type of hat, or a helmet (*bod rgya*, p. 2157; Goldstein 2001, p. 836).

tshem tshem (ཚེམ་ཚེམ་). Archaic term for armor (Goldstein 2001, p. 884). The use of the term *tshem* (ཚེམ་), which relates to sewing, suggests that this and the following two entries may have once referred to armor made predominantly of textile. See also *tshem zhu* (ཚེམ་ཞུ་) and *tshem zhva* (ཚེམ་ཞྭ་).

tshem zhu (ཚེམ་ཞུ་). Archaic term for helmet (Goldstein 2001, p. 884). See also *tshem tshem* (ཚེམ་ཚེམ་) and *tshem zhva* (ཚེམ་ཞྭ་).

tshem zhva (ཚེམ་ཞྭ་). Archaic term for helmet (Goldstein 2001, p. 884). See also *tshem tshem* (ཚེམ་ཚེམ་) and *tshem zhu* (ཚེམ་ཞུ་).

mtshon skyob (མཚོན་སྐྱོབ་). Body armor (*bod rgya*, p. 2323).

mtshon 'gog (མཚོན་འགོག་). Something that protects against weapons, e.g., armor (Goldstein 2001, p. 897).

mtshon g.yol (མཚོན་གཡོལ་). An amulet that protects the wearer against weapons (Goldstein 2001, p. 898). For an example, see Waddell 1905, p. 174.

mdze rmog (མཛེ་རྨོག་). A kind of helmet (Das 1902b, p. 1050, citing *Jig* 31).

zhub (ཞུབ་) or **zhub pa** (ཞུབ་པ་). Armor. Same as *go cha* (གོ་ཆ་), *go khrab* (གོ་ཁྲབ་), or *lcags gos* (ལྕགས་གོས་) (Das 1902b, p. 1074, citing *Mngon; bod rgya*, p. 2397; Goldstein 2001, p. 935).

zhub can (ཞུབ་ཅན་). A person wearing armor, armored (*bod rgya*, p. 2397; Goldstein 2001, p. 935).

zhva gdan (ཞྭ་གདན་). A cap worn under a helmet (Goldstein 2001, p. 939). See also *rmog tshangs* (རྨོག་ཚངས་) and *rmog stan* (རྨོག་སྟན་).

zhva mo'i tog (ཞྭ་མོའི་ཏོག་). The point of a helmet or of a Chinese cap (Das 1902b, p. 519, under ཏོག་).

zhva rmog (ཞྭ་རྨོག་). 1: A helmet in the Central Asian or Mongolian style (*bod rgya*, p. 2409). 2: Military helmet (Goldstein 2001, p. 939).

gzha' ma (གཞའ་མ་). A kind of helmet (Das 1902b, p. 1077, citing *Yig* [*Jig?*]) 31).

gzha'i li (གཞའི་ལི་). Helmet made of bell-metal (Das 1902b, p. 1077, under གཞའ་མ་, citing *Yig* [*Jig?*]) 31).

ya lad (ཡ་ལད་). Corselet [i.e., body armor] and helmet, mail, armor: *ya lad bgos* (ཡ་ལད་བགོས་), equipped with armor; *ya lad gyon* (ཡ་ལད་གྱོན་), put on the coat of mail [i.e., armor] (Das 1902b, p. 1125); armor and helmet (*bod rgya*, p. 2544).

g.yul gyi chas zhugs pa (གཡུལ་གྱི་ཆས་ཞུགས་པ་). To dress in coat of mail, to be in full armor. Same as *go cha gyon pa* (གོ་ཆ་གྱོན་པ་) (Das 1902b, p. 1154, under གཡུལ་བ་, to fight, to make battle, etc.).

re lde (རེ་ལྡེ་). A kind of buckler [i.e., shield] manufactured in Tsang (Das 1902b, p. 1190, citing *Jig* 32). Also defined as a coarse material woven from yak hair and as a bamboo basket (Goldstein 2001, p. 1046), suggesting that shields of this type may have been of wickerwork construction. See also *phub* (ཕུབ་).

sring bal khrab (སྲིང་བལ་ཁྲབ་). According to Das (1902b, p. 169, under ཁྲབ་), the common quilted armor used in Mongolia and China (in Mongolia, called "dasa").

bse ko (བསེ་ཀོ་). 1: Rhinoceros hide of which shields are made (Das 1902b, p. 1319). 2: Rhinoceros hide, or varnished/lacquered hide (Goldstein 2001, p. 1167; *bod rgya*, p. 3048). Similar to (གོ་བསེ་), varnished leather (Goldstein 2001, p. 9). See also *phub* (ཕུབ་).

bse khrab (བསེ་ཁྲབ་). 1: Armor made from varnished or painted leather (*bod rgya*, p. 3048). 2: A shield made from rhinoceros hide (Das 1902b, p. 1319, under བསེ་). See also *phub* (ཕུབ་)

bse phub (བསེ་ཕུབ་). A shield of rhino leather (Nebesky-Wojkowitz 1975, p. 8).

a khrab (ཨ་ཁྲབ་). Mail, a type of armor made of interlocking iron rings. See *a lung gi khrab* (ཨ་ལུང་གི་ཁྲབ་), of which this is an abbreviation, and *lcags long sbrel khrab* (ལྕགས་ལོང་སྦྲེལ་ཁྲབ་).

a lung gi khrab (ཨ་ལུང་གི་ཁྲབ་). Mail, a type of armor made of interlocking iron rings. According to Das (1902b, p. 169, under ཁྲབ་), a type of armor which is made or iron rings or scales, but note that it literally means "armor of rings," and is almost certainly the specific Tibetan term for mail armor, as opposed to lamellar or scale armor. See also *a khrab* (ཨ་ཁྲབ་) and *lcags long sbrel khrab* (ལྕགས་ལོང་སྦྲེལ་ཁྲབ་).

II. Hand-Held Weapons (མཚོན་ཆ་), Non-Projectile

kong mdung (ཀོང་མདུང་). A kind of spear manufactured in Kong po, a province southeast of Lhasa (Das 1902b, p. 36, under ཀོང་པོ་, citing *Jig* 32). See also sec. I, under *kong bzo* (ཀོང་བཟོ་).

kha chag (ཁ་ཆག་). Defect in the blade of a weapon (Das 1902b, p. 126).

kha gsar (ཁ་གསར་). An edge or a blade just sharpened (Das 1902b, p. 1304, under གསར་བ་).

khu tshur (ཁུ་ཚུར་). The place on a weapon that is grasped by the hand, so that a fist results; the handle, etc., of a weapon (*Illuminator*). See also *yu ba* (ཡུ་བ་).

'khor lo (འཁོར་ལོ་). In addition to the more common usage of the term in reference to wheels, mandalas, etc., this may also refer to a chakra, a circular throwing weapon (known as a quoit in English) often mentioned in the ancient Indian epics and, as an extant symbolic weapon, among the Sikhs. Das (1902b, p. 191, def. 1, citing *Mngon*) includes the term in a list of weapons of war. See also *be rdo* (བེ་རྡོ་).

gu zi (གུ་ཟི་). See *dgu zi* (དགུ་ཟི་).

go mtshon (གོ་མཚོན་) or **go mtshon rdzas mdel** (གོ་མཚོན་རྫས་མདེལ་). Weapons, arms (Goldstein 2001, p. 187). The second term means literally "weapons, powder, and shot."

gri (གྲི). Knife or sword. Under *gri* (གྲི) Das also lists the following weapons: *chu gri* (ཆུ་གྲི), *gri thung* (གྲི་ཐུང), *ral gri'i bu* (རལ་གྲིའི་བུ), *gri gug* (གྲི་གུག), *gri 'khyog po* (གྲི་འཁྱོག་པོ), *dgra sta* (དགྲ་སྟ), *sta ri* (སྟ་རི), *ral gri'i 'khrul 'khor* (རལ་གྲིའི་འཁྲུལ་འཁོར), *gri sgur* (གྲི་སྒུར), *sa rang* (ས་རང); and the following syn.: *shang lang* (ཤང་ལང), *brdeg cha* (བརྡེག་ཆ), *rjes su gcod* (རྗེས་སུ་གཅོད), *lag skyong* (ལག་སྐྱོང), *zla ba 'dzum byed* (ཟླ་བ་འཛུམ་བྱེད), *dpal gyi snying po* (དཔལ་གྱི་སྙིང་པོ), *gcod byed* (གཅོད་བྱེད), *sha ma ka* (ཤ་མ་ཀ) (Das 1902b, p. 243, citing *Mngon* for the synonyms).

gri kha (གྲི་ཁ) or **gri so** (གྲི་སོ). 1: The edge of a knife (Das 1902b, p. 243). 2: Blade (Kazi 1919, p. 92). See also *gri dngo* (གྲི་དངོ), *gri'i kha* (གྲིའི་ཁ), *gri'i so* (གྲིའི་སོ), *lce* (ལྕེ), *gzang* (གཟང), *ral kha* (རལ་ཁ), *ral so* (རལ་སོ), and *ral gri'i 'dab ma* (རལ་གྲིའི་འདབ་མ).

gri kha 'gran (གྲི་ཁ་འགྲན). To fence with swords (Goldstein 2001, p. 200). See also *gri rtsed rtse* (གྲི་རྩེད་རྩེ).

gri kha gnyis ma (གྲི་ཁ་གཉིས་མ) or **gri so gnyis ma** (གྲི་སོ་གཉིས་མ). Double-edged knife or sword (Goldstein 2001, p. 200, 201).

gri gu chung (གྲི་གུ་ཆུང). Small knife (Das 1902b, p. 244).

gri gug (གྲི་གུག). 1: A short crooked sword (Das 1902b, p. 244). 2: A curved knife, a chopper shaped like a crescent moon, held by certain deities; an ancient weapon (ETED, p. 523).

gri mgo (གྲི་མགོ) or **gri 'go** (གྲི་འགོ). Handle [hilt] of a knife or sword (Goldstein 2001, p. 200). See also *yu ba* (ཡུ་བ).

gri dngo (གྲི་དངོ). The cutting edge of a knife or sword (Goldstein 2001, p. 200). See also *gri kha* (གྲི་ཁ).

gri dngo 'don (གྲི་དངོ་འདོན). To unsheathe a sword or knife (Goldstein 2001, p. 200).

gri lcag (གྲི་ལྕག). The flat of a sword or knife; or the unsharpened back edge of a single-edged blade (*bod rgya*, p. 398). See also *gri ltag* (གྲི་ལྟག).

gri bton (གྲི་བཏོན). Unsheathed sword or knife (Goldstein 2001, p. 200).

gri ltag (གྲི་ལྟག) or **gri'i ltag pa** (གྲིའི་ལྟག་པ). The unsharpened back edge of a single-edged sword or knife (*bod rgya*, p. 398). See also *gri lcag* (གྲི་ལྕག).

gri thung (གྲི་ཐུང). Knife or short sword (Das 1902b, p. 243, under གྲི; *bod rgya*, p. 2667, under རལ་གྲི).

gri mdur (གྲི་མདུར). The oblique edge of a sword or knife point, *gri rtse'i gseg kha* (གྲི་རྩེའི་གསེག་ཁ) (*bod rgya*, p. 398). This term may refer specifically to the distinctive sloped edge of the tip of a traditional single-edged Tibetan sword.

gri ldebs (གྲི་ལྡེབས). The flat of a blade, i.e., the sides (Schmidt 1841, p. 76).

gri dpa' dam (གྲི་དཔའ་དམ). A long sword (Goldstein 2001, p. 200), or a long knife worn at the waist (ETED, p. 524). See also *dpa' dam* (དཔའ་དམ).

gri bya gag gi gshog pa lta bu (གྲི་བྱ་གག་གི་གཤོགས་པ་ལྟ་བུ). A knife in the shape of the wings of a cock (Das 1902b, p. 244).

gri bya rog gi mchu (གྲི་བྱ་རོག་གི་མཆུ). A knife in the shape of a crow's bill (Das 1902b, p. 244).

gri dmar (གྲི་དམར). Knife of superior quality manufactured in Tibet (Das 1902b, p. 244).

gri rtsal (གྲི་རྩལ). The art of swordsmanship (Goldstein 2001, p. 200). See also *ral gri'i thabs* (རལ་གྲིའི་ཐབས).

gri rtse (གྲི་རྩེ). Point of a knife (Das 1902b, p. 1012, under རྩེ).

gri rtsed (གྲི་རྩེད). Fencing (Goldstein 2001, p. 200). See also *ral gri'i thabs* (རལ་གྲིའི་ཐབས).

gri rtsed rtse (གྲི་རྩེད་རྩེ). To fence with swords (Goldstein 2001, p. 200).

gri mtshon (གྲི་མཚོན). Weapons; same as *gri ring* (གྲི་རིང), sword (Goldstein 2001, p. 200).

gri yu (གྲི་ཡུ). Haft of a knife (Das 1902b, p. 1138, under ཡུ་བ, general term for handle). Possibly a term that could also be used to refer to a sword hilt. See also *yu ba* (ཡུ་བ).

gri ring (གྲི་རིང). Sword or long knife (Goldstein 2001, p. 200; *bod rgya*, p. 2667, under རལ་གྲི).

gri shubs (གྲི་ཤུབས). Sheath or scabbard (Goldstein 2001, p. 201).

gri so (གྲི་སོ). See *gri'i so* (གྲིའི་སོ).

gri'i kha (གྲིའི་ཁ). The blade of a knife [or sword] (Das 1902b, p. 126, under ཁ་ཚག). See also *gri kha* (གྲི་ཁ).

gri'i ltag pa (གྲིའི་ལྟག་པ). Back of a knife [or sword] (Das 1902b, p. 542, under ལྟག་པ).

gri'i rtse mo (གྲིའི་རྩེ་མོ). The point of a scimitar [a curved sword] or sword (Das 1902b, p. 244).

gri'i so (གྲིའི་སོ). Sharp edge of a knife (Das 1902b, p. 244). Also defined as the blade of a knife (Das 1902b, p. 126, under ཁ་ཚག). See also *gri kha* (གྲི་ཁ).

gri'u (གྲིའུ). A small knife (Das 1902b, p. 244).

glo gri (གློ་གྲི་). Dagger (Goldstein 2001, p. 211); sheath knife worn at the side (ETED, p. 564).

dgu zi (དགུ་ཟི་). According to Tibetan historical literature, one of the five principal types of swords, specifically that which was used in Tibet and originated in the time of the legendary ancient king Trigum Tsenpo (*gri gum btsan po*). See "Swords," the introduction to the sword section of this catalogue, and the appendix "Excerpts from *A Treatise on Worldly Traditions*" for further comments. Cited in *brda dkrol* (p. 103).

dgu zi glang po sna (དགུ་ཟི་གླང་པོ་སྣ་). Defined by Das (1902b, p. 267) as the name of the enchanted sword of Trigum Tsenpo (*gri gum btsan po*), one of the early kings of Tibet.

dgra chas (དགྲ་ཆས་). The equipment of war; weapons; arms (Das 1902b, p. 277).

dgra sta (དགྲ་སྟ་). An ax, the blade of which is semicircular; a sector like a disk; a weapon of war (Das 1902b, p. 278).

mgar zog (མགར་ཟོག). A name for a dagger (Kazi 1919, p. 194).

rgya gri (རྒྱ་གྲི་). A knife from China (*bod rgya*, p. 530).

rgya lu'i gri (རྒྱ་ལུའི་གྲི་). Knife worn by an official as part of a traditional ceremonial costume (ETED, p. 712).

sgro mdung (སྒྲོ་མདུང་). Spear with feathers attached to it (Goldstein 2001, p. 287).

sgro zur ma (སྒྲོ་ཟུར་མ་). A name for a dagger (Kazi 1919, p. 194).

gcod byed (གཅོད་བྱེད་). Metaphor for knife [or sword] (Das 1902b, p. 390; *bod rgya*, p. 2667, under རལ་གྲི་).

lcags kyu (ལྕགས་ཀྱུ་). Iron pin to guide and punish elephants [i.e., an elephant goad or *ancus*] (Das 1902b, p. 397).

lcags zhol (ལྕགས་ཞོལ་). Name of a weapon (Das 1902b, p. 398).

lcags ril thag sbrags (ལྕགས་རིལ་ཐག་སྦྲགས་). Weapon composed of an iron ball with a rope attached (Goldstein 2001, p. 345).

lcang gri (ལྕང་གྲི་). A type of sword (Goldstein 2001, p. 346).

lcugs (ལྕུགས་). The sharp point of a knife or sword (*bod rgya*, p. 768).

lce (ལྕེ་). The blade of a knife or sword [lit. tongue] (Das 1902b, p. 1170, under རལ་གྲི་; Schmidt 1841, p. 76). See also *gri kha* (གྲི་ཁ་) and *ral gri'i 'dab ma* (རལ་གྲིའི་འདབ་མ་).

'chang ba (འཆང་བ་). Handle, also the grip of a sword, equivalent to *yu ba* (ཡུ་བ་) (*bod rgya*, p. 859). See also *yu ba* (ཡུ་བ་).

'ja' ral (འཇའ་རལ་). According to Tibetan historical literature, one of the five principal types of swords, specifically that which was used in the southern borderlands of Tibet (*lho mon*). See "Swords," the introduction to the sword section of this catalogue, and the appendix "Excerpts from *A Treatise on Worldly Traditions*" for further comments. Cited in *brda dkrol* (p. 197).

rjes su gcod (རྗེས་སུ་གཅོད་). Metaphor for knife [or sword] (Das 1902b, p. 466; *bod rgya*, p. 2667, under རལ་གྲི་).

rta mdung (རྟ་མདུང་). A type of short spear used on horseback (Goldstein 2001, p. 458).

sta gri (སྟ་གྲི་). See *sta re* (སྟ་རེ་).

sta dngo (སྟ་དངོ་). The blade of an ax (Goldstein 2001, p. 469).

sta re (སྟ་རེ་), same as *sta gri* (སྟ་གྲི་), frequently **sta ri** (སྟ་རི་). Ax, hatchet (Das 1902b, p. 547). See also *dgra sta* (དགྲ་སྟ་), ax with a crescentic blade.

sta re'i ltag pa (སྟ་རེའི་ལྟག་པ་). Back of an ax (Das 1902b, p. 542, under ལྟག་པ་). See also *star ltag* (སྟར་ལྟག).

sta so (སྟ་སོ་) or **star so** (སྟར་སོ་). Edge of an ax blade (Goldstein 2001, pp. 469, 471). See also *ste kha* (སྟེ་ཁ་).

star ltag (སྟར་ལྟག). The blunt side of an ax (Goldstein 2001, p. 471). See also *sta re'i ltag pa* (སྟ་རེའི་ལྟག་པ་).

star yu (སྟར་ཡུ་). Ax shaft or handle (Goldstein 2001, p. 471). See also *ste yu* (སྟེ་ཡུ་).

ste kha (སྟེ་ཁ་). Edge of an ax blade (Das 1902b, p. 550, under སྟེ་བོ་). See also *sta so* (སྟ་སོ་).

ste yu (སྟེ་ཡུ་). Ax handle (Das 1902b, p. 550, under སྟེ་བོ་).

thag mdung (ཐག་མདུང་). A rope that is attached to a short spear (Goldstein 2001, p. 485).

mda' mo che (མདའ་མོ་ཆེ་). An iron club or crow; a lance (Das 1902b, p. 673).

mdung (མདུང་). Lance spear, pike; *mdung ba* (མདུང་བ་) or *mdung brgyab pa* (མདུང་བརྒྱབ་པ་), to sting, to pierce with a spear; *mdung bskor ba* (མདུང་བསྐོར་བ་), to brandish, to whirl a spear; *thag mdung* (ཐག་མདུང་), a spear attached to a sling (Das 1902b, p. 674).

mdung khyim (མདུང་ཁྱིམ་). A frame to lean spears against (also an improvised tent or sunshade using spears as supports) (Das 1902b, p. 674).

mdung mkhan (མདུང་མཁན་). Spearman (Goldstein 2001, p. 568). See also *mdung thogs* (མདུང་ཐོགས་) and *mdung pa* (མདུང་པ་).

mdung lcags kyu ma (མདུང་ལྕགས་ཀྱུ་མ་). A spear with a hook on it (Goldstein 2001, p. 568).

mdung thung (མདུང་ཐུང་). 1: A type of short spear (Goldstein 2001, p. 568). 2: Javelin (Kazi 1919, p. 414).

mdung thogs (མདུང་ཐོགས་). A spearman, lancer (also an epithet of Mahadeva; Das 1902b, p. 674, citing *Mngon*). See also *mdung mkhan* (མདུང་མཁན་) and *mdung pa* (མདུང་པ་).

mdung dar (མདུང་དར་). A lance with a little flag on top (Das 1902b, p. 674). A banner tied to the head of a spear (Goldstein 2001, p. 568; *bod rgya*, p. 1378).

mdung pa (མདུང་པ་). Spearman (Goldstein 2001, p. 568). See also *mdung mkhan* (མདུང་མཁན་) and *mdung thogs* (མདུང་ཐོགས་).

mdung mo rtse gsum (མདུང་མོ་རྩེ་གསུམ་). Trident (Goldstein 2001, p. 568). See also *mdung rtse* (མདུང་རྩེ་) and *mdung rtse gsum pa* (མདུང་རྩེ་གསུམ་པ་).

mdung rtse (མདུང་རྩེ་). 1: A spearhead, point of a spear, top of a spear or lance. 2: The religious trident (Das 1902b, p. 674). See also *mdung mo rtse gsum* (མདུང་མོ་རྩེ་གསུམ་) and *mdung rtse gsum pa* (མདུང་རྩེ་གསུམ་པ་).

mdung rtse gsum pa (མདུང་རྩེ་གསུམ་པ་). Trident (Goldstein 2001, p. 568; *bod rgya*, p. 1378). See also *mdung mo rtse gsum* (མདུང་མོ་རྩེ་གསུམ་) and *mdung rtse* (མདུང་རྩེ་).

mdung 'dzar (མདུང་འཛར་). A tassel attached to a spear (Goldstein 2001, p. 568).

mdung zhags (མདུང་ཞགས་). A throwing spear with a long rope attached to the shaft (*bod rgya*, p. 1378).

mdung zla tshes ma (མདུང་ཟླ་ཚེས་མ་). A crescent- or sickle-shaped spearhead (Goldstein 2001, p. 568; *bod rgya*, p. 1378).

mdung bzo pa (མདུང་བཟོ་པ་). A maker of lances (Das 1902b, p. 674).

mdung yu (མདུང་ཡུ་). Spear shaft (*bod rgya*, p. 1379).

mdung shing (མདུང་ཤིང་). Wooden spear shaft (*bod rgya*, p. 1379).

'debs byed (འདེབས་བྱེད་). Metaphor for knife [or sword] (*bod rgya*, p. 2667, under རལ་གྲི་).

rdung byed (རྡུང་བྱེད་), same as *dbyug po* (དབྱུག་པོ་). A stick, a striker (Das 1902b, p. 700, listed as a type of weapon under འཕོར་ལོ་).

rdeg cha (རྡེག་ཆ་). Metaphor for knife [or sword] (*bod rgya*, p. 2667, under རལ་གྲི་; and as བརྡེག་ཆ་ in Das 1902b, p. 243, under གྲི་). See also *brdeg cha* (བརྡེག་ཆ་).

brdeg cha (བརྡེག་ཆ་). A general name for a striking weapon (*bod rgya*, p. 1486; Goldstein 2001, p. 598), but included by Das (1902b, pp. 243, 724) as syn. for knife or sword. See also *rdeg cha* (རྡེག་ཆ་).

pa tam (པ་ཏམ་). See *dpa' dam* (དཔའ་དམ་).

dpa' dam (དཔའ་དམ་). A long Tibetan sword (Goldstein 2001, p. 647; Goldstein 1999a, p. 302, under "sword"), but also defined as a long belt knife (*sked gri ring po* [སྐེད་གྲི་རིང་པོ་], in *bod rgya*, p. 1624). Given by Das (1902b, p. 788) as *dpa' gdam* (དཔའ་གདམ་), equaling *gri ring* (གྲི་རིང་), long knife or sword. Also spelled *pa tam* (པ་ཏམ་) in Kazi (1919, pp. 107 under "broad sword," 193 under "cutlass"). This may be the common name for the type of Tibetan sword with a straight blade, single edge, and oblique tip. See also *ral gri* (རལ་གྲི་).

dpa' lung (དཔའ་ལུང་). The strap attached to the hilt of a sword [or the ring to which the strap is attached] (*bod rgya*, p. 1627). Usually found on the back of the pommel.

dpal gyi snying po (དཔལ་གྱི་སྙིང་པོ་). Metaphor for sword (*bod rgya*, pp. 1628, 2667 under རལ་གྲི་).

'phang mdung (འཕང་མདུང་). 1: A sling-hook or spearhead to which a string is tied and, being held fast, the spearhead is flung at a fish or bird (Das 1902b, p. 847, but on p. 191, listed as a weapon under འཕོར་ལོ་). 2: A spear with a rope attached, which can be thrown and then pulled back (*bod rgya*, p. 1778). 3: Throwing spear, javelin, harpoon (Goldstein 2001, p. 703).

be mdung (བེ་མདུང་). A spear or javelin [with a shaft] made of oak wood (Das 1902b, p. 875).

be rdo (བེ་རྡོ་). According to Das (1902b, p. 875), a quoit or discus, but according to other sources, this term means a type of tree, particularly the oak tree (Goldstein 2001, p. 724; *bod rgya*, p. 1838). See also *'khor lo* (འཁོར་ལོ་).

dbyig pa (དབྱིག་པ་). A walking staff, wand, or stick (Das 1902b, p. 914, but on p. 191, listed as a weapon under འཕོར་ལོ་).

dbyug pa (དབྱུག་པ་). A stick, cudgel, staff (Das 1902b, p. 915; also listed, p. 191, as a weapon under འཕོར་ལོ་).

dmag gri (དམག་གྲི་). Military sword (Goldstein 2001, p. 824).

rtse rgod (རྩེ་རྒོད་). A sharply pointed knife (Das 1902b, p. 1012, under རྩེ་).

rtse mdung (རྩེ་མདུང་). Spear (Goldstein 2001, p. 862).

rtse gsum (རྩེ་གསུམ་). A trident, a weapon attribute of *tshogs bdag* (ཚོགས་ བདག་, Ganesha), *mgon po phyag drug pa* (མགོན་པོ་ཕྱག་དྲུག་པ་, Six-Armed Mahakala), and *dpal 'khor lo sdom pa* (དཔལ་འཁོར་ལོ་སྡོམ་པ་, a form of Samavara) (Das 1902b, p. 1013).

mtshon khar sra (མཚོན་ཁར་སྲ་). Proof against cut and thrust [i.e., effective protection against edged weapons] (Das 1902b, p. 1386, under སྲ་). Note that this phrase occurs in the armor chapter of the Tashi Namgyal texts (e.g., Burmiok Athing, fol. 27b; British Library Or 11,374, fol. 84a).

mtshon sgrom (མཚོན་སྒྲོམ་). A stand or frame on which weapons are placed (Goldstein 2001, p. 897).

mtshon cha (མཚོན་ཆ་). Any pointed or sharp cutting instrument, a sword, weapons (Das 1902b, p. 1041, under མཚོན་). Das (1902b, p. 191, under འབོར་ལོ་, def. 1, citing *Mngon*) gives the following list of examples: *g.yul du 'dzin pa* (གཡུལ་དུ་འཛིན་པ་), *tho ba* (ཐོ་བ་), *rdung byed* (རྡུང་བྱེད་), *'dzom byed* (འཛོམ་བྱེད་), *dbyug pa* (དབྱུག་པ་), *lcags bcings* (ལྕགས་བཅིངས་), *dbyig ba* (དབྱིག་བ་), *'phang mdung* (འཕང་མདུང་), *shang lang* (ཤང་ལང་), *gsor mdung* (གསོར་མདུང་), *tsa kra* (ཙ་ཀྲ་), and *'khor lo* (འཁོར་ལོ་).

mtshon cha mkhan (མཚོན་ཆ་མཁན་). Both Das (1902b, p. 1042, def. 2) and *bod rgya* (p. 2322) define this as equivalent to *mgar ba* (མགར་བ་), a blacksmith, but the term may once have referred more specifically to one who makes weapons.

mtshon cha rnam pa bzhi (མཚོན་ཆ་རྣམ་པ་བཞི་). The four kinds of weapons: sword, spear, dart, and arrow (Das 1902b, pp. 1041–42, under མཚོན་).

mtshon cha rno ngar can (མཚོན་ཆ་རྣོ་ངར་ཅན་) or **mtshon cha rno po** (མཚོན་ཆ་རྣོ་པོ་). Sharp-edged weapons (Goldstein 2001, p. 897). Possibly the equivalent to the English term "edged weapons," which is used collectively to refer to any hand-held weapons with a point or a cutting edge. Literally, the terms mean "weapons that are tempered and sharp," and "sharp weapons."

mtshon cha'i gtso (མཚོན་ཆའི་གཙོ་). Literally, foremost or chief of weapons, a metaphor for *mda'* (མདའ་), arrow (Das 1902b, p. 1042, under མཚོན་ཆ་མཁན་, citing *Mngon*).

mtshon cha'i gzhi (མཚོན་ཆའི་གཞི་). Literally, foundation or source of weapons, a metaphor for sword or knife (Das 1902b, p. 1042, under མཚོན་ཆ་མཁན་, citing *Mngon*).

mtshon rtse (མཚོན་རྩེ་). Spearhead (Goldstein 2001, p. 898).

mtshon rtse gcig (མཚོན་རྩེ་གཅིག་). A weapon with one point, like an arrow or spear (Das 1902b, p. 1042, under མཚོན་).

zhang rtags (ཞང་རྟགས་). A kind of long knife manufactured in Zhang. (Das 1902b, p. 1065, under ཞང་, citing *Jig* 31).

zhang ma (ཞང་མ་). According to Tibetan historical literature, one of the five principal types of swords, which is said variously to have originated in the land of Zhang Zhung (a semi-legendary kingdom in western Tibet) or in the land of the uncle (*zhang*) of the Chinese emperor Taizong (r. 626–49). See "Swords," the introduction to the sword section of this catalogue, and the appendix "Excerpts from *A Treatise on Worldly Traditions*" for further comments. Cited in *brda dkrol* (p. 761).

zor (ཟོར་). Reaping hook, a sickle, a knife, especially the weapons employed in combating the evil spirits in the *gtor ma* (གཏོར་མ་), such as knife, sword, sling, bow and arrows (Das 1902b, p. 1098).

zla ba 'dzum byed (ཟླ་བ་འཛུམ་བྱེད་). Metaphorically, a sword (Das 1902b, p. 1100). If the allusion is to a crescent moon, then this may indicate a curved sword or type of saber.

gzang (གཟང་). Point, tip, edge, of a blade (Goldstein 2001, p. 966, def. 1). See also *gri kha* (གྲི་ཁ་).

yu ba (ཡུ་བ་). Stick, handle, or grip in general, but also the grip or hilt of a knife or sword, and the haft of an ax or other weapons (*Illuminator*; Das 1902b, p. 1138; *bod rgya*, p. 2482). See also *khu tshur* (ཁུ་ ཚུར་), *gri mgo* (གྲི་མགོ་), *gri yu* (གྲི་ཡུ་), and *'chang ba* (འཆང་བ་).

g.yul du 'dzin (གཡུལ་དུ་འཛིན་). Metaphorically, a knife or sword (Das 1902b, p. 1154).

ral kha (རལ་ཁ་) or **ral so** (རལ་སོ་). 1: Sword edge (Das 1902b, p. 1170, under རལ་གྲི་). 2: Blade of a sword (Goldstein 2001, p. 1031). See also *gri kha* (གྲི་ཁ་).

ral gyi (རལ་གྱི་). Archaic form of *ral gri* (རལ་གྲི་) (*bod rgya*, p. 2667).

ral gri (རལ་གྲི་). Sword (Goldstein 2001, p. 1031; *bod rgya*, p. 2667; Kazi 1919, p. 794), but according to Das (1902b, p. 1170), a sword, spear, rapier, hunting knife, or dagger. However, sword appears to be the principal meaning of the term. It may also be the common name for the type of Tibetan sword with a straight blade and a pointed or acute tip, as opposed to the type with an oblique tip. See also *dpa' dam* (དཔའ་དམ་).

ral gri nye ba'i rin po che (རལ་གྲི་ཉེ་བའི་རིན་པོ་ཆེ་). The enchanted sword considered as a secondary gem (Das 1902b, p. 1170, under རལ་གྲི་). One of the set of auspicious symbols known as the Seven Secondary Jewels.

ral gri 'dzam (རལ་གྲི་འཛམ). A broad-bladed knife (Das 1902b, p. 1170, under རལ་གྲི, citing *Rtsii*).

ral gri'i 'khrul 'khor (རལ་གྲིའི་འཁྲུལ་འཁོར). The magical flourish of an enchanted sword (Das 1902b, p. 1170, under རལ་གྲི, citing *Mngon*).

ral gri'i dngos grub (རལ་གྲིའི་དངོས་གྲུབ). The enchanted sword; one of the *thun mong gi dngos grub* (ཐུན་མོང་གི་དངོས་གྲུབ), the eight common accomplishments (Das 1902b, p. 359).

ral gri'i thabs (རལ་གྲིའི་ཐབས). Fencing, skill in swordmanship, one of the *sgyu rtsal drug cu re bzhi* (སྒྱུ་རྩལ་དྲུག་ཅུ་རེ་བཞི), the Sixty-four Arts (*bod rgya*, p. 2668). See also *gri rtsal* (གྲི་རྩལ) and *gri rtsed* (གྲི་རྩེད).

ral gri'i 'dab ma (རལ་གྲིའི་འདབ་མ). Blade of a sword (Das 1902b, p. 1170, under རལ་གྲི). See also *lce* (ལྕེ) and *gri kha* (གྲི་ཁ).

ral gri'i bu (རལ་གྲིའི་བུ) or **ral chung** (རལ་ཆུང). Small knife [or short sword?] (Das 1902b, p. 1170, under རལ་གྲི, citing *Mngon*).

ral gri'i rtse (རལ་གྲིའི་རྩེ). The sword point (Das 1902b, p. 1170, under རལ་གྲི).

ral gri'i shubs (རལ་གྲིའི་ཤུབས). Scabbard of a sword (Das 1902b, p. 1170, under རལ་གྲི).

ral gri'i so (རལ་གྲིའི་སོ). Edge of a sword (Das 1902b, p. 1170, under རལ་གྲི). See also *gri kha* (གྲི་ཁ).

lag skyong (ལག་སྐྱོང). Metaphor for knife [or sword] (*bod rgya*, p. 2667, under རལ་གྲི; Das 1902b, pp. 1203, 243 under གྲི).

lag cha (ལག་ཆ). Knife, tool, weapon (*bod rgya*, p. 2667, under རལ་གྲི; Goldstein 2001, p. 1059).

lag mdung (ལག་མདུང). A short spear easily carried in one hand (*bod rgya*, p. 2751).

lag srung (ལག་སྲུང). Metaphor for knife [or sword] (*bod rgya*, p. 2667, under རལ་གྲི).

shag ti (ཤག་ཏི). A type of sword (*bod rgya*, p. 2831; Goldstein 2001, p. 1093; *brda dkrol*, pp. 930–31); a weapon such as a spear, sword, or trident (Das 1902b, p. 1229, citing Csoma 1834).

shang lang (ཤང་ལང). A single-edged sword or knife (*bod rgya*, p. 2832; Goldstein 2001, p. 1093). The term appears, however, to refer specifically to a curved sword, which in English would be called a saber, and is called such by Nebesky-Wojkowitz (1975, p. 15). Das equates it with *gri gug* (གྲི་གུག), which implies a curved blade, and defines it as a saber, sword, or knife (Das 1902b, p. 1230, citing *Mngon*; also included in the list of weapons under འཚོར་ལོ, Das 1902b, p. 191).

shog lang (ཤོག་ལང). Sword, according to Kazi (1919, p. 794).

so (སོ). Blade of a sword or knife (Goldstein 2001, p. 1133). Edge of a blade (*bod rgya*, p. 2952, under སོ, def. 1, pt. 3). See also *gri kha* (གྲི་ཁ) and *gri'i so* (གྲིའི་སོ).

sog po (སོག་པོ). According to Tibetan historical literature, one of the five principal types of swords, specifically that which was used by the eponymous *sog po* (Mongols). See "Swords," the introduction to the sword section of this catalogue, and the appendix "Excerpts from *A Treatise on Worldly Traditions*" for further comments.

gsor mdung (གསོར་མདུང). Included by Das (1902b, p. 191) in the list of weapons under འཚོར་ལོ, but not defined. Probably a kind of spear with a spikelike head, as in the Tibetan spear MMA 36.25.1960 (cat. no. 76), in the sense of *gsor* (གསོར) referring to sharp narrow blade, or tool such as an awl, punch, or gimlet (*bod rgya*, p. 3033, under གསོར, def. 2; Das 1902b, p. 1314).

hu bde (ཧུ་བདེ). A type of sword used by the Mongols (Das 1902b, p. 1328, citing *Jig* 31). But note that this term is spelled *hu phed* (ཧུ་ཕེད) in the sword chapter of the *rgya bod yig tshang chen mo* (རྒྱ་བོད་ཡིག་ཚང་ཆེན་མོ) (Palchor Zangpo, pp. 232–39), and appears elsewhere as *hu bed* (ཧུ་བེད) and *hu wed* (ཧུ་ཝེད). See "Swords," the introduction to the sword section of this catalogue, and the appendix "Excerpts from *A Treatise on Worldly Traditions*" for further comments.

hu phed (ཧུ་ཕེད). According to Palchor Zangpo (pp. 232–39) the name of the principal type of sword used by the Hor (ཧོར). One of the five main categories of classic sword types recorded in Tibetan literature. See also *hu bde* (ཧུ་བདེ) re spelling variations.

am gri (ཨམ་གྲི). Dagger (Goldstein 2001, p. 1192; Kazi 1919, p. 194).

III. Archery Equipment (འཕོང་སྒྲུང) and Projectile Weapons (འཕེན་མཚོན), other than Firearms

krad (གྲད). Bowstring made of leather (Goldstein 2001, p. 11). See also *gzhu krad* (གཞུ་གྲད).

krad kor (གྲད་ཀོར). An archer's thumb ring (Goldstein 2001, p. 11).

dkar thag (དཀར་ཐག). The string of a bow (Das 1902b, p. 51). See also *krad* (གྲད) and *gzhu rgyud* (གཞུ་རྒྱུད).

rked pa (རྐེད་པ) or **sked pa** (སྐེད་པ). Usually meaning "waist," but according to Das also meaning the ends or notches of the bow [i.e., the nocks], which hold the string, and citing the phrase *gzhu'i 'chang bzung* (གཞུའི་འཆང་བཟུང) (Das 1902b, p. 77, under རྐེད་པ). But see also *gzhu* *mchog* (གཞུ་མཆོག་) and *gzhu'i 'chang bzung* (གཞུའི་འཆང་བཟུང་) for further comment.

gro ga (གྲོ་ག་) or **gro kha** (གྲོ་ཁ་). White birch bark sometimes used for ornamenting bows (Das 1902b, p. 249, citing Jäschke 1881).

sgu rdo (སྒུ་རྡོ་), also **'ur rdo** (འུར་རྡོ་). According to Das, sling-string, explained as *'ur rdo 'phan byed kyi thag pa* (འུར་རྡོ་འཕན་བྱེད་ཀྱི་ཐག་པ་), the string that is coiled round a stone for flinging it; a sling (Das 1902b, p. 321; see also Kazi 1919, p. 724). Described by Stone (1934, under "Gudo, Orta," pp. 254–55 and fig. 313) as "made of a square-braided cord with a loop at one end and a broad pocket of woven material in the middle. The end with the loop is shorter than the other. It is woven of a mixture of wool and hair, and is used as a whip when driving sheep or cattle. The Tibetan tent dwellers, both men and women, always carry one and are very expert in its use." See also *'ur rdo* (འུར་རྡོ་).

sgro gu rten pa (སྒྲོ་གུ་རྟེན་པ་). The steel point of an arrow to which a feather is attached (Das 1902b, p. 337, under སྒྲོ་གུ་).

sgro ldan (སྒྲོ་ལྡན་). Metaphorically, an arrow (lit. feather bearing; also a general name for birds; Das 1902b, p. 336, under སྒྲོ་).

lcags mda' (ལྕགས་མདའ་). 1: An iron arrow; steel pointed arrow; steel arrow (Das 1902b, p. 398). 2: A ramrod (Das 1902b, p. 672, under མདའ་).

lcags mda' sgra can (ལྕགས་མདའ་སྒྲ་ཅན་), or **lcags sbubs can** (ལྕགས་སྦུབས་ཅན་). A kind of steel-tipped arrow from which when flung a whizzing sound came forth (Das 1902b, p. 398, citing *Mngon*). This appears to be the term for a whistling arrow. Compare with a whistling arrowhead, MMA 1999.32 (cat. no. 98).

lcags gzhu (ལྕགས་གཞུ་). Crossbow (Kazi 1919, p. 51, under "arbalist"). See also *'phrul gzhu* (འཕྲུལ་གཞུ་).

'chi gu (འཆི་གུ་). 1: Sling, string weapon (Das 1902b, p. 443). 2: A bow-like implement for hurling small stones and similar projectiles (*bod rgya*, p. 863). 3: A slingshot (Goldstein 2001, p. 384). It is unclear if these definitions apply to a sling, a slingshot, or a pellet bow.

ljong dar (ལྗོང་དར་). A scarf that is used to cover a quiver (Das 1902b, p. 470).

nyag phran (ཉག་ཕྲན་). Equivalent to *mda'* (མདའ་), an arrow (Das 1902b, p. 474).

ltong ka (ལྟོང་ཀ་) or **ltong ga** (ལྟོང་ག་). The notch at the end of an arrow where the bowstring is placed [i.e., the nock] (Das 1902b, p. 546; Goldstein 2001, p. 469). See also *mda' ltong* (མདའ་ལྟོང་).

stag dong (སྟག་དོང་) or **mda' dong** (མདའ་དོང་). A quiver; *stag dong gzig shubs* (སྟག་དོང་གཟིག་ཤུབས་), a quiver for arrows lined with leopard skin (Das 1902b, p. 547, citing *Rtsii*), or a quiver made from tiger skin (Goldstein 2001, p. 469; Nebesky-Wojkowitz 1975, p. 8). See also *dong pa* (དོང་པ་) and *gzig shubs* (གཟིག་ཤུབས་).

dar tshon sna lnga btags pa'i mda' (དར་ཚོན་སྣ་ལྔ་བཏགས་པའི་མདའ་). Arrow with five pieces of silk, each of a different color, attached to it (Goldstein 2001, p. 529). See *mda' dar* (མདའ་དར་).

dong pa (དོང་པ་). A quiver or sheath for arrows (Goldstein 2001, p. 543; *bod rgya*, p. 1299). Spelled *dong ba* (དོང་བ་) by Das (1902b, p. 642, def. 2). See also *stag dong* (སྟག་དོང་), *mda' grong* (མདའ་གྲོང་), *mda' dong* (མདའ་དོང་), *mda' snod* (མདའ་སྣོད་), *mda' 'dzin* (མདའ་འཛིན་), *mda' shubs* (མདའ་ཤུབས་), *gzig shubs* (གཟིག་ཤུབས་), *brtsang rtsa* (བརྩང་རྩ་), *lo dong* (ལོ་དོང་), *sag thag* (སག་ཐག་), and *bse dong* (བསེ་དོང་).

mda' (མདའ་). An arrow: *mda' rgyab pa* (མདའ་རྒྱབ་པ་), to shoot an arrow; *myug mda'* (མྱུག་མདའ་), an arrow of reed or bamboo; *lcags mda'* (ལྕགས་མདའ་), an iron arrow; *dug mda'* (དུག་མདའ་), a poisoned arrow (Das 1902b, p. 672). Syn.: *nyag phran* (ཉག་ཕྲན་), *drang 'gro* (དྲང་འགྲོ་), *mi 'khyog 'gro* (མི་འཁྱོག་འགྲོ་), *sha ra 'bigs byed* (ཤ་ར་འབིགས་བྱེད་), *'dab ldan mtshon* (འདབ་ལྡན་མཚོན་), *sgro ldan* (སྒྲོ་ལྡན་), *stong can* (སྟོང་ཅན་), *rtse mo can* (རྩེ་མོ་ཅན་), *'ben bsnun* (འབེན་བསྣུན་), *mda' mo* (མདའ་མོ་), *lcags mda' sgra can* (ལྕགས་མདའ་སྒྲ་ཅན་), *lcags sbubs can* (ལྕགས་སྦུབས་ཅན་), *'ur sgra can* (འུར་སྒྲ་ཅན་), *mtshon cha'i gtso* (མཚོན་ཆའི་གཙོ་), *dug gi byug pa can* (དུག་གི་བྱུག་པ་ཅན་), *lo sta ka* (ལོ་སྟ་ཀ་).

mda' khur can (མདའ་ཁུར་ཅན་). Archer, person carrying a bow and arrow (Goldstein 2001, p. 567).

mda' mkhan (མདའ་མཁན་). An archer, an arrow maker (Das 1902b, p. 673, def. 2; also name of a low caste in ancient India). According to Goldstein (2001, p. 567), also a maker of bows as well as arrows.

mda' grong (མདའ་གྲོང་). A quiver for arrows (Das 1902b, p. 673). See also *dong pa* (དོང་པ་).

mda' rgyang (མདའ་རྒྱང་). The range of an arrow shot (Das 1902b, p. 673).

mda' rgyan (མདའ་རྒྱན་). Decoration for an arrow (Goldstein 2001, p. 567, def. 2).

mda' rgyud (མདའ་རྒྱུད་). The bowstring (Das 1902b, p. 673). See also *gzhu rgyud* (གཞུ་རྒྱུད་).

mda' sgro (མདའ་སྒྲོ་). The feathers attached to an arrow (Das 1902b, p. 673).

mda' lcags (མདའ་ལྕགས་). Iron arrowhead (Goldstein 2001, p. 567). See also *mde'u* (མདེའུ་).

mda' che (མདའ་ཆེ་) or **mda' bo che** (མདའ་བོ་ཆེ་). A very powerful and effective arrow or lance (Das 1902b, p. 673).

mda' chen (མདའ་ཆེན་). A long arrow (Goldstein 2001, p. 567). See also *mda' bo che* (མདའ་བོ་ཆེ་).

mda' snyug (མདའ་སྙུག་). Bamboo for making arrows (Goldstein 2001, p. 567).

mda' ltong (མདའ་ལྟོང་). The notch at the end of an arrow, which is placed against the bowstring [i.e., the nock] (Goldstein 2001, p. 567; *bod rgya*, p. 1376). Spelled *mda' stong* (མདའ་སྟོང་) by Das (1902b, p. 673). See also *ltong ka* (ལྟོང་ཀ་).

mda' stan (མདའ་སྟན་). Metaphor for the bow for shooting an arrow (Goldstein 2001, p. 567).

mda' dar (མདའ་དར་). According to Goldstein (2001, p. 567), a ceremonial arrow having ribbons of different colors attached to it. According to Das, a lance; also a flag attached to an arrow with silk ribbons of five different colors, by hooking which arrow into the collar of a bride the matchmaker draws her forth from among her maiden companions. Also an arrow wrapped in a scarf, with which the head of the bride is touched during a marriage ceremony (Das 1902b, p. 673). Compare this with an arrow in the Royal Museum, National Museums of Scotland, which is braided with five colored scarves (part of a full set of quiver and arrows; NMS A.1927.321A–O [cat. no. 96]). See also *dar tshon sna lnga btags pa'i mda'* (དར་ཚོན་སྣ་ལྔ་བཏགས་པའི་མདའ་).

mda' dar rtse lnga (མདའ་དར་རྩེ་ལྔ་). See *mda' dar* (མདའ་དར་).

mda' dong (མདའ་དོང་). A quiver, generally made of bamboo, according to Das (1902b, pp. 642 under དོང་པོ་, 673; *bod rgya*, p. 1299). See also *dong pa* (དོང་པ་).

mda' mdong (མདའ་མདོང་). A bow-holder (Goldstein 1999a, p. 37). Equivalent to *gzhu shubs* (གཞུ་ཤུབས་)?

mda' mde'u (མདའ་མདེའུ་). Metal arrowhead (*bod rgya*, p. 1376). See also *mde'u* (མདེའུ་).

mda' snod (མདའ་སྣོད་). A quiver for arrows (Das 1902b, p. 673, under མདའ་དོང་). See also *dong pa* (དོང་པ་).

mda' snod sgam (མདའ་སྣོད་སྒམ་). Box for keeping arrows (Goldstein 2001, p. 567).

mda' pa (མདའ་པ་). Archer (Goldstein 2001, p. 567).

mda' phyed byas pa (མདའ་ཕྱེད་བྱས་པ་). An arrow with a sharp semicircular disk at the top end (Das 1902b, p. 673). Note that this probably refers to a type of arrowhead intended for hunting, comparable with forms found in India, the Middle East, and Europe.

mda' bo che (མདའ་བོ་ཆེ་) or **mda' mo che** (མདའ་མོ་ཆེ་). A long arrow (Goldstein 2001, p. 567). See also *mda' chen* (མདའ་ཆེན་).

mda' mo (མདའ་མོ་). Arrow (Goldstein 2001, p. 567). Arrow-lot, a kind of fortune-telling by shooting arrows (Das 1902b, p. 673).

mda' rtse (མདའ་རྩེ་). Arrowhead (Goldstein 2001, p. 567). See also *mde'u* (མདེའུ་).

mda' tsha (མདའ་ཚ་). Archery (Kazi 1919, p. 52). See also *'phong* (འཕོང་).

mda' tsho (མདའ་ཚོ་). A company of archers (Schmidt 1841, p. 267).

mda' tshad ma (མདའ་ཚད་མ་). The length of an arrow, or something measured in arrow lengths (*bod rgya*, p. 1377).

mda' tshan chen po (མདའ་ཚན་ཆེན་པོ་). A skilled archer (*bod rgya*, p. 1377).

mda' 'dzin (མདའ་འཛིན་). A quiver for arrows (*bod rgya*, p. 1376). See also *dong pa* (དོང་པ་).

mda' zhar (མདའ་ཞར་). Mounted archery competition (Goldstein 2001, p. 567).

mda' gzhu (མདའ་གཞུ་). Bow and arrow (Goldstein 2001, p. 567).

mda' bzo ba (མདའ་བཟོ་བ་). Arrow maker (*bod rgya*, p. 1377). Maker of bows and arrows (Goldstein 2001, p. 568).

mda' yab (མདའ་ཡབ་). According to Schmidt (1841, p. 267), a breastwork or parapet for protection against arrows.

mda' shubs (མདའ་ཤུབས་). A case or cover for keeping arrows; a quiver (Das 1902b, p. 672, under མདའ་). See also *dong pa* (དོང་པ་).

mde'u (མདེའུ་) or **mda'i mde'u** (མདའི་མདེའུ་). 1: According to Das (1902b, p. 675), the pointed arrowhead made of steel in Tibet and Mongolia; the arrowhead is made of various designs, some with three points, others like a miniature pickax: *mde'u be'u'i so 'dra ba* (མདེའུ་བེའུའི་སོ་འདྲ་བ་), arrowhead like a calf's teeth; *mde'i byi'u snying ma* (མདེའི་བྱིའུ་སྙིང་མ་), arrowhead like a bird's heart; *mde'u zur bzhi pa* (མདེའུ་ཟུར་བཞི་པ་), an arrow with four-bladed head. 2: Musket ball or arrowhead (*bod rgya*, p. 1380). See also *mda' lcags* (མདའ་ལྕགས་) and *mda' rtse* (མདའ་རྩེ་).

rdel mda' (རྡེལ་མདའ་). 1: Stone projectile used in a sling (Goldstein 2001, p. 586). 2: Hurling a stone from a sling like an arrow (*bod rgya*, p. 1436).

rna sgrang (རྣ་སྒྲང་). According to Das (1902b, p. 765), equivalent to *mda'i mde'u* (མདའི་མདེའུ་), a bullet, a buzzing arrow.

'phong (འཕོང་) or **'phong spyod** (འཕོང་སྤྱོད་). Archery (Das 1902b, p. 850). See also *mda' tsha* (མདའ་ཚ་).

'phong skyen pa (འཕོང་སྐྱེན་པ་). Skilled archer, bowman (Goldstein 2001, p. 705).

'phong gi dbye ba lnga (འཕོང་གི་དབྱེ་བ་ལྔ་) or **'phong rkyen** (འཕོང་རྐྱེན་). According to Das (1902b, p. 850, under འཕོང་), the five distinguishing features in archery: 1. to hit from a great distance, *rgyang ring nas 'phog pa* (རྒྱང་རིང་ནས་འཕོག་པ་); 2. to hit without perceiving it, *mi 'tshor bar 'phog pa* (མི་འཚོར་བར་འཕོག་པ་); 3. to hit with great force, *tshabs che bar 'phog pa* (ཚབས་ཆེ་བར་འཕོག་པ་); 4. to hit at the main point, or object, *gnad du 'phog pa* (གནད་དུ་འཕོག་པ་); 5. to hit an object with a sound, *sgra grags par 'phog pa* (སྒྲ་གྲགས་པར་འཕོག་པ་).

'phong rgyug (འཕོང་རྒྱུག་). Shooting arrows while galloping on horseback (Goldstein 2001, p. 705).

'phong spyad (འཕོང་སྤྱད་). Archery equipment (Goldstein 2001, p. 705; *bod rgya*, p. 1785).

'phrul gzhu (འཕྲུལ་གཞུ་). Crossbow (Goldstein 2001, p. 709). See also *lcags gzhu* (ལྕགས་གཞུ་).

'ben (འབེན་). Target, goal [in the sense of archery target] (Das 1902b, p. 921).

'ben bsnun (འབེན་བསྣུན་). Metaphorically, an arrow; equivalent to *mda'* (མདའ་) or *mda' mo* (མདའ་མོ་) (Das 1902b, p. 921, under འབེན་, citing *Mngon*).

me 'bar mda' mo (མེ་འབར་མདའ་མོ་). Fire arrow, used in warfare (Goldstein 2001, p. 817).

myag phran (མྱག་ཕྲན་). Archaic spelling of *nyag phran* (ཉག་ཕྲན་), arrow (*Illuminator*).

smyug mda' (སྨྱུག་མདའ་). An arrow made of cane or reed (Schmidt 1841, p. 267). An arrow made from bamboo (Goldstein 2001, p. 841).

rtse lcags (རྩེ་ལྕགས་). Iron arrowhead (Goldstein 2001, p. 862).

brtsang rtsa (བརྩང་རྩ་). A quiver for arrows (*bod rgya*, p. 1299, under དོང་པ་). See also *dong pa* (དོང་པ་).

gzhu (གཞུ་). Bow for shooting arrows (Das 1902b, p. 1081, citing *Mngon* for syn.). Syn.: *mda' 'phen byed* (མདའ་འཕེན་བྱེད་), *mda' za* (མདའ་ཟ་), *mda' zas can* (མདའ་ཟས་ཅན་), *mda' bskyo* (མདའ་བསྐྱོ་), *mda' rten* (མདའ་རྟེན་), *mda' lto ba* (མདའ་ལྟོ་བ་), *mda' snun byed* (མདའ་སྣུན་བྱེད་), *gnam ru* (གནམ་རུ་).

gzhu krad (གཞུ་གྲད་). The bowstring (Goldstein 2001, p. 943; *bod rgya*, p. 2425). See also *gzhu rgyud* (གཞུ་རྒྱུད་).

gzhu mkhan (གཞུ་མཁན་). Bow maker (Das 1902b, p. 1081).

gzhu gar ma (གཞུ་གར་མ་). A strong or tough bow (Goldstein 2001, p. 943).

gzhu 'gugs pa (གཞུ་འགུགས་པ་). To bend the bow in order to string it (Schmidt 1841, p. 496; Das 1902b, p. 1081, under གཞུ་). Opposite of *gzhu 'bud pa* (གཞུ་འབུད་པ་).

gzhu rgyud (གཞུ་རྒྱུད་). Bowstring (Das 1902b, p. 1081). See also *krad* (གྲད་), *dkar thag* (དཀར་ཐག་), *mda' rgyud* (མདའ་རྒྱུད་), *gzhu krad* (གཞུ་གྲད་), and *gzhu thag* (གཞུ་ཐག་).

gzhu rgyud spring ba (གཞུ་རྒྱུད་སྤྲིང་བ་). According to Schmidt (1841, p. 496), the sound produced by means of a bowstring under tension.

gzhu sgra (གཞུ་སྒྲ་). The buzzing sound of the bowstring (Das 1902b, p. 1081).

gzhu can (གཞུ་ཅན་). Bowman, archer (Das 1902b, p. 1081).

gzhu mchog (གཞུ་མཆོག་). 1: The bow end, the two ends of the bow [i.e., the nocks] (Das 1902b, p. 1081; *bod rgya*, p. 2425, def. 2). 2: A bow of excellent quality (Goldstein 2001, p. 944; *bod rgya*, p. 2425, def. 1). See also *gzhu mchog 'dzug pa* (གཞུག་མཆོག་འཛུག་པ་) and *gzhu'i mchog ma* (གཞུའི་མཆོག་མ་).

gzhu mchog dkar (གཞུ་མཆོག་དཀར་). A bow of excellent quality (Goldstein 2001, p. 944).

gzhu mchog 'dzug pa (གཞུག་མཆོག་འཛུག་པ་). To set the string to the bow (Das 1902b, p. 1081).

gzhu thag (གཞུ་ཐག་). Bowstring (Kazi 1919, p. 101). See also *gzhu rgyud* (གཞུ་རྒྱུད་).

gzhu thung (གཞུ་ཐུང་). A short bow (Goldstein 2001, p. 944).

gzhu ldan (གཞུ་ལྡན་). Furnished with a bow (Das 1902b, p. 1081).

gzhu 'bud pa (གཞུ་འབུད་པ་). To unstring the bow (Schmidt 1841, p. 496; Das 1902b, p. 1081, under གཞུ་). Opposite of *gzhu 'gugs pa* (གཞུ་འགུགས་པ་).

gzhu mo (གཞུ་མོ་). A bow. Same as *gzhu* (གཞུ་) (Goldstein 2001, p. 944).

gzhu ring (གཞུ་རིང་). A longbow (Goldstein 2001, p. 944).

gzhu shubs (གཞུ་ཤུབས་). Bow case or sheath (Goldstein 2001, p. 944).

gzhu'i mchog ma (གཞུའི་མཆོག་མ་). The two ends of a bow [i.e., the nocks] (Schmidt 1841, p. 496). See also *gzhu mchog* (གཞུ་མཆོག་).

gzhu'i 'chang bzung (གཞུའི་འཆང་བཟུང་). Defined by Schmidt (1841, p. 496) as the grip in the middle of a bow, but according to Das

(1902b, p. 77, under ཀེད་པ་) this is a synonym for *rked pa* (རྐེད་པ་) or *sked pa* (སྐེད་པ་), when those terms mean the ends or notches of a bow [i.e., the nocks], which hold the bowstring. The primary meaning of *'chang bzung* (འཆང་བཟུང་), handle or fist, corresponds with Schmidt's definition. However, the slightly different spelling *'chang zungs* (འཆང་ཟུངས་), meaning the crook of a stick, would make sense in relation to Das's definition as a term for the nocks of a bow. See also *rked pa* (རྐེད་པ་) and *gzhu mchog* (གཞུ་མཆོག་).

gzig shubs (གཟིག་ཤུབས་). 1: Quiver made from or covered with leopard skin (Goldstein 2001, p. 968; *bod rgya*, p. 2495). 2: Leopard-skin case for a bow (Das 1902b, p. 1104, under གཟིག་, citing *Rtsii*; Nebesky-Wojkowitz 1975, p. 8). See also *dong pa* (དོང་པ་).

'ur sgra can (ཨུར་སྒྲ་ཅན་). Arrow that flies buzzing (Das 1902b, p. 1116, under ཨུར་, citing *Mngon*). This may refer to the sound of a whistling arrow, or simply to the whirring sound made by any arrow in flight, and perhaps also to that of a sling-stone.

'ur rdo (ཨུར་རྡོ་), also **sgu rdo** (སྒུ་རྡོ་). A sling (Das 1902b, p. 1116, under ཨུར་; Kazi 1919, p. 724). The traditional Tibetan sling, carried by both men and women in nomadic areas. It is made from braided yak or horsehair, wool, and felt, and can be used to herd animals, drive off predators, for hunting, and as a weapon. See Rockhill 1895, p. 714, and Olson 1950–71, vol. 5, p. 18. See also *sgu rdo* (སྒུ་རྡོ་).

'ur rdo chu mig dgu sgril (ཨུར་རྡོ་ཆུ་མིག་དགུ་སྒྲིལ་). A type of sling braided with dyed fibers to form a pattern with nine eyelike designs (Goldstein 2001, p. 981; *bod rgya*, p. 2524).

'ur rdo 'phen pa (ཨུར་རྡོ་འཕེན་པ་). To throw with a sling (Das 1902b, p. 1116, under ཨུར་).

'ur rdo'i tshar lce (ཨུར་རྡོའི་ཚར་ལྕེ་). The end of the sling, which can be cracked like a whip when driving animals (Goldstein 2001, p. 981).

ral shubs (རལ་ཤུབས་). According to Schmidt (1841, p. 542), a bow case, but possibly an abbreviated term for a sword scabbard. Compare with *ral gri'i shubs* (རལ་གྲིའི་ཤུབས་) in sec. II above.

rva gzhu (ར་གཞུ་). A bow made from horn (Goldstein 2001, p. 1051).

lo dong (ལོ་དོང་). A kind of quiver manufactured in Lo country (Das 1902b, p. 1221, citing *Rtsii*). See also *dong pa* (དོང་པ་).

sa mda' chu sgro ma (ས་མདའ་ཆུ་སྒྲོ་མ་). A sharp pointed arrow having a feather at its end, which is shot to pierce the earth and also through water (Das 1902b, p. 1258, citing *Rtsii*).

sag thag (སག་ཐག་). 1: A quiver for arrows (Goldstein 2001, p. 1121). 2: The quiver for arrows and the sheath or case for the bow (*bod rgya*, p. 2912). See also *dong pa* (དོང་པ་).

bse dong (བསེ་དོང་). A quiver for arrows, made of lacquered or varnished leather (Goldstein 2001, p. 1167; *bod rgya*, p. 3048). See also *dong pa* (དོང་པ་).

IV. Firearms (མེ་མདའ་) and Accessories (མེ་མདའ་ཆས་), Ordnance (སློག་ས་)

krob mda' (ཀྲོབ་མདའ་). Musket, equivalent to *me mda'* (མེ་མདའ་), but note that this term was found only in Kazi (1919, p. 507).

kha'i tshang thig (ཁའི་ཚང་ཐིག་). Bore, caliber of a gun (Goldstein 2001, p. 118). See also *zheng tshad* (ཞེང་ཚད་).

gag (གག). Wad; wadding for loading muskets (Das 1902b, p. 207, citing Jäschke 1881).

gung shing (གུང་ཤིང་). Gunstock (Kazi 1919, p. 337). See also *sgum mda'* (སྒུམ་མདའ་).

sgum mda' (སྒུམ་མདའ་). The butt of a gun; gunstock (Das 1902b, p. 322). Note, however, that another meaning of this term appears to be slingshot (Goldstein 2001, p. 275; *bod rgya*, p. 589). See also *gung shing* (གུང་ཤིང་), *sgum shing* (སྒུམ་ཤིང་) *bya gzhug* (བྱ་གཞུག་), and *me mda'i bya gzhug* (མེ་མདའི་བྱ་གཞུག་).

sgum shing (སྒུམ་ཤིང་). Stock of a gun, gun butt, catapult (Goldstein 2001, p. 275). See also *gung shing* (གུང་ཤིང་), *sgum mda'* (སྒུམ་མདའ་), *bya gzhug* (བྱ་གཞུག་), and *me mda'i bya gzhug* (མེ་མདའི་བྱ་གཞུག་).

sgyog (སློག). Catapult (Kazi 1919, p. 126). See also *sgyogs mda'* (སློགས་མདའ་).

sgyogs (སློགས་) or **sgyogs kyi 'phrul 'khor** (སློགས་ཀྱི་འཕྲུལ་འཁོར་). Cannon, mortar, a warlike engine to shoot darts or fling stones (Das 1902b, p. 330; Goldstein 2001, p. 282).

sgyogs mda' (སློགས་མདའ་). Catapult (Das 1902b, p. 330). See also *sgyog* (སློག).

sgyogs rdo (སློགས་རྡོ་). The stone flung from a catapult, mortar, or cannon (Das 1902b, p. 330, under སློགས་).

lcags mda' (ལྕགས་མདའ་). 1: A ramrod (Das 1902b, p. 672, under མདའ་). See also *rdzong thur* (རྫོང་ཐུར་). 2: An iron arrow; steel-pointed arrow; steel arrow (Das 1902b, p. 398).

lcags sbugs (ལྕགས་སྦུགས་). A matchlock made (formerly) in India (Das 1902b, p. 398). Literally, iron tube.

tho chung (ཐོ་ཆུང་). The cock or hammer of a gun [part of the firing mechanism] (Das 1902b, p. 589, under ཐོ་བ་). Literally, small hammer. See also *me skam* (མེ་སྐམ་).

mde'u (མདེའུ་). Bullet or arrowhead (*bod rgya*, p. 1380). See also *rde'u* (རྡེའུ་).

mde'u khug (མདེའུ་ཁུག་) or **mdel khug** (མདེལ་ཁུག་). A flask or pouch for holding bullets (Goldstein 2001, p. 569; *bod rgya*, p. 1380). See also *mdel shubs* (མདེལ་ཤུབས་).

mdel (མདེལ་). Bullets (Goldstein 2001, p. 569).

mdel par (མདེལ་པར་). Mold for casting musket balls (*bod rgya*, pp. 1380–81). See also *rde'u par* (རྡེའུ་པར་).

mdel ril (མདེལ་རིལ་). Musket ball made of lead, for a traditional Tibetan musket (*bod rgya*, p. 1381).

mdel shubs (མདེལ་ཤུབས་) or **mde'u shubs** (མདེའུ་ཤུབས་). Container for bullets (*bod rgya*, p. 1381). See also *mde'u khug* (མདེའུ་ཁུག་).

rde'u (རྡེའུ་) or **rdel po** (རྡེལ་པོ་). Diminutive for *rdo* (རྡོ་), stone; a musket ball, or bullet (Das 1902b, p. 702, def. 3). See also *mde'u* (མདེའུ་) and *mdel* (མདེལ་).

rde'u par (རྡེའུ་པར་). A bullet font or bullet mold (Das 1902b, p. 702, under རྡེའུ་). Compare with Tibetan bullet mold and case MMA 36.25.2459a–c (cat. no. 109). See also *mdel par* (མདེལ་པར་).

rdo sgyogs (རྡོ་སྒྱོགས་). Cannon. Also, according to Das (1902b, p. 330, under སྒྱོགས་), a stone thrower used in Bhutan. See also *sgyogs* (སྒྱོགས་) and *me sgyogs* (མེ་སྒྱོགས་).

rna mchog (རྣ་མཆོག་). Usually "ear," but in reference to a matchlock gun it appears to refer to the priming pan (Jäschke 1881, p. 312, under རྣ་བ་). This is the small panlike protrusion, shaped roughly like an ear in silhouette, affixed to the right side of the barrel at its base, just beneath the touchhole, or *rdzas khung* (རྫས་ཁུང་). The priming pan has a shallow recess to hold the priming powder, or *rna rdzas* (རྣ་རྫས་).

rna rdzas (རྣ་རྫས་). Defined by Goldstein (2001, p. 629) as the gunpowder used to ignite a Tibetan matchlock gun. This appears to refer specifically to the priming powder, i.e., the gunpowder put in the priming pan, which, when ignited by the match cord, sets off the charge in the barrel, firing the gun. Compare this with the term *rna mchog* (རྣ་མཆོག་), signifying the priming pan. See also *me len gyi rdzas* (མེ་ལེན་གྱི་རྫས་).

pho brang (པོ་བྲང་). Usually "palace," but in the sense of "chamber" it can refer to the breech, or chamber, of a gun barrel (*bod rgya*, p. 1726,

def. 4). The barrel of a gun (Goldstein 2001, p. 685). See also *me mda'i pho brang* (མེ་མདའི་པོ་བྲང་).

pho rva (པོ་ར་). A gunpowder flask made of horn, used with a traditional Tibetan matchlock gun (*bod rgya*, p. 1731).

'phen rdo (འཕེན་རྡོ་). Cannonball (Goldstein 2001, p. 705).

bal mda' (བལ་མདའ་). Matchlock guns manufactured in Nepal and imported into Tibet (Das 1902b, p. 868, under བལ་པོ་, citing *Rtsii* 50).

bir thig (བིར་ཐིག་). Slow-burning match cord that is used to ignite a matchlock gun (*bod rgya*, p. 1827). See also *sbi sdi* (སྦི་སྡི་) and *me len skud pa* (མེ་ལེན་སྐུད་པ་). In Western firearms terminology this is referred to as the match, match cord, or slow match.

bir shubs (བིར་ཤུབས་). Container for the match cord of a matchlock gun. In Amdo, generally called *bir lto* (བིར་ལྟོ་) (*bod rgya*, p. 1827). This may refer to the narrow rectangular leather pouch that is usually affixed to the outside of the butt of the stock of a Tibetan matchlock, and in which the spare match cord is stored.

bod mda' (བོད་མདའ་). A traditional muzzle-loading Tibetan matchlock gun (*bod rgya*, p. 1848). See also *me mda'* (མེ་མདའ་).

bya gzhug (བྱ་གཞུག་). The butt of a gunstock (Goldstein 2001, 731, def. 2). See also *gung shing* (གུང་ཤིང་), *sgum mda'* (སྒུམ་མདའ་), *sgum shing* (སྒུམ་ཤིང་), and *me mda'i bya gzhug* (མེ་མདའི་བྱ་གཞུག་).

sbi sdi (སྦི་སྡི་). Slow-burning match cord that is used to ignite a matchlock gun (*bod rgya*, p. 2016; Goldstein 2001, p. 777, with alternative spellings: *sbi ti* སྦི་ཏི་, *sbi sti* སྦི་སྟི་, and *sbi thi* སྦི་ཐི་). See also *bir thig* (བིར་ཐིག་) and *me len skud pa* (མེ་ལེན་སྐུད་པ་).

me skam (མེ་སྐམ་). The hammer or cock of a gun (Das 1902b, p. 970, under མེ་). Also *me mda'i skam pa* (མེ་མདའི་སྐམ་པ་) (Goldstein 1999a, p. 136, under "hammer"). On a matchlock musket, such as the traditional *me mda'* (མེ་མདའ་) used in Tibet, this is a curved iron arm, which holds the match cord above the priming pan, ready to ignite the powder and fire the gun. It is not a hammer, in the sense of later firearms. The correct English equivalent for this part of the matchlock mechanism would be match-holder, cock, or serpentine. Note that Goldstein later (2001, pp. 815, 817) defined *me skam* (མེ་སྐམ་) and *me mda'i skam pa* (མེ་མདའི་སྐམ་པ་) as meaning the trigger of a gun, but the meaning of match-holder seems to be the correct one, at least for traditional matchlock guns. The confusion may arise from the fact that while on later firearms the trigger and the cock or hammer are two distinct pieces, on rudimentary matchlock mechanisms (such as are often found in Tibet), the match-holder and trigger can be one continuous piece of S-shaped metal: the upper portion protrudes above the stock and is where the end of the match is held; the lower portion protrudes below the stock and serves as the trigger.

me sgyogs (མེ་སྒྱོགས་). Cannon, artillery (Goldstein 2001, p. 815). According to Das (1902b, p. 330, under སྒྱོགས་), then called a *dob* (དོབ་) in Tibet. See also *sgyogs* (སྒྱོགས་) and *rdo sgyogs* (རྡོ་སྒྱོགས་). Spelled *me sgyog* (མེ་སྒྱོག་) by Kazi (1919, p. 56, under "artillery").

me mda' (མེ་མདའ་). This is the most usual term for the traditional Tibetan style of matchlock gun. Defined by Das (1902b, p. 672, under མདའ་) as gun, firelock, or any straight and thin pole or piece of wood, e.g., the tube of a tobacco pipe. Now a generic word for firearm. See also *bod mda'* (བོད་མདའ་). Included in Stone (1934, p. 443) under the phonetic spelling, *me-da*.

me mda'i skam pa (མེ་མདའི་སྐམ་པ་). See *me skam* (མེ་སྐམ་).

me mda'i kha (མེ་མདའི་ཁ་). Muzzle of a gun (Goldstein 2001, p. 817).

me mda'i kha rdzas (མེ་མདའི་ཁ་རྫས་). Priming (in reference to gunpowder) (Kazi 1919, p. 609). Note, however, that this term appears to refer to the gunpowder for the main charge, which is loaded through the muzzle, *me mda'i kha* (མེ་མདའི་ཁ་). Priming powder should refer specifically to the gunpowder put in the priming pan, *rna mchog* (རྣ་མཆོག་). See also *rna rdzas* (རྣ་རྫས་).

me mda'i sgum shing (མེ་མདའི་སྒུམ་ཤིང་). Gunstock, rifle butt (Goldstein 2001, p. 817). See also *gung shing* (གུང་ཤིང་), *sgum mda'* (སྒུམ་མདའ་), *sgum shing* (སྒུམ་ཤིང་), *bya gzhug* (བྱ་གཞུག་), and *me mda'i bya gzhug* (མེ་མདའི་བྱ་གཞུག་).

me mda'i bya gzhug (མེ་མདའི་བྱ་གཞུག་). The butt of a gun stock, which flares out like a bird's tail (*bya gzhug*) (*bod rgya*, p. 2111). See also *gung shing* (གུང་ཤིང་), *sgum mda'* (སྒུམ་མདའ་), *sgum shing* (སྒུམ་ཤིང་), and *bya gzhug* (བྱ་གཞུག་).

me mda'i pho brang (མེ་མདའི་པོ་བྲང་). The breech, or chamber, of a gun barrel (Goldstein 2001, p. 817). See also *pho brang* (པོ་བྲང་).

me mda'i tsha kha (མེ་མདའི་ཚ་ཁ་). Gun sight (Goldstein 2001, p. 817). Perhaps referring to the bead sight or the leaf sight found on the top of the muzzle of a gun barrel. See also *so kha* (སོ་ཁ་).

me mda'i ru (མེ་མདའི་རུ་). Gun rest made of two prongs attached to the gun stock near the muzzle (*bod rgya*, p. 2111). See also *me mda'i rva co* (མེ་མདའི་རྭ་ཙོ་) and *ru kha* (རུ་ཁ་).

me mda'i rva co (མེ་མདའི་རྭ་ཙོ་). Gun rest, as in *me mda'i ru* (མེ་མདའི་རུ་), in which the prongs, or the tips of the prongs, are made of horn. See also *ru kha* (རུ་ཁ་).

me rdel (མེ་རྡེལ་). Bullet, cartridge, shell (Goldstein 2001, p. 817).

me rdzas (མེ་རྫས་). Gunpowder (Goldstein 2001, p. 818). See also *rdzas* (རྫས་).

me zhar (མེ་ཞར་). Shooting a gun from horseback (Goldstein 2001, p. 818).

me rub (མེ་རུབ་). Musketry (Kazi 1919, p. 507).

me len skud pa (མེ་ལེན་སྐུད་པ་). The slow match, or match cord, which is used to ignite the gunpowder in the priming pan and fire a matchlock gun (Goldstein 2001, p. 818). See also *bir thig* (བིར་ཐིག་) and *sbi sdi* (སྦི་སྡི་).

me len gyi rdzas (མེ་ལེན་གྱི་རྫས་). Gunpowder used to ignite a matchlock gun (Goldstein 2001, p. 818). This may also refer specifically to the priming powder, which is put in the priming pan at the breech of the barrel, suggested by the term *me len* (མེ་ལེན་), meaning "fire tongs," probably indicating the match-holder. See also *rna rdzas* (རྣ་རྫས་).

'dzam bur (འཛམ་བུར་). A gun, cannon (Das 1902b, p. 1053, citing Jäschke 1881).

rdzas (རྫས་). Gunpowder (Goldstein 2001, p. 913). See also *me rdzas* (མེ་རྫས་).

rdzas khug (རྫས་ཁུག་). A container to hold gunpowder for a matchlock musket (*bod rgya*, p. 2353), i.e., in Western firearms terminology, a powder horn or powder flask.

rdzas khung (རྫས་ཁུང་). The touchhole. On a matchlock gun this is the small hole or vent at the base of the barrel on the right side of the breech (*pho brang* [པོ་བྲང་]) through which a spark touched off in the priming pan (*rna mchog* [རྣ་མཆོག་]) by the match cord (*sbi sdi* [སྦི་སྡི་]) ignites the powder in the breech and thereby fires the gun (Goldstein 2001, pp. 913–14; *bod rgya*, p. 2353, with slightly different definitions).

rdzas gri (རྫས་གྲི་). Small wooden knife used for grinding gunpowder (Goldstein 2001, p. 914).

rdzas mda' (རྫས་མདའ་) or **rdzas me mda'** (རྫས་མེ་མདའ་). A matchlock gun (Goldstein 2001, p. 914).

rdzas mdel (རྫས་མདེལ་) or **rdzas mde'u** (རྫས་མདེའུ་). Bullet and gunpowder, ammunition (Goldstein 2001, p. 914).

rdzas ru (རྫས་རུ་) or **rdzas rva** (རྫས་རྭ་). Powder horn. Container for gunpowder made from an animal horn (*bod rgya*, p. 2354).

rdzong thur (རྫོང་ཐུར་). The ramrod of a Tibetan matchlock gun, made of wood or iron (*bod rgya*, p. 2362; Goldstein 2001, p. 916). See also *lcags mda'* (ལྕགས་མདའ་), *sin ti* (སིན་ཏི་), *sin 'bi* (སིན་འབི་), *sin 'bid* (སིན་འབིད་), *sin 'ben* (སིན་འབེན་), and *sim 'big* (སིམ་འབིག་).

zheng tshad (ཞེང་ཚད་). Bore, caliber of a gun (Goldstein 2001, p. 937, def. 2). See also *kha'i tshang thig* (ཁའི་ཚང་ཐིག་).

zi ling lcags khra (ཟི་ལིང་ལྕགས་ཁྲ་). A specific type of Tibetan matchlock gun (Goldstein 2001, p. 958; *bod rgya*, p. 2458).

rin di (རིན་དི་). Musket ball (Das 1902b, p. 1183, def. 2). See also *rde'u* (རྡེའུ་).

ru kha (རུ་ཁ་). The horn brace of a Tibetan gun (Goldstein 2001, p. 1042). See also *me mda'i ru* (མེ་མདའི་རུ་) and *me mda'i rva co* (མེ་མདའི་རྭ་ཚོ་).

sin ti (སིན་ཏི་). The ramrod of a Tibetan matchlock gun (Goldstein 2001, p. 1123). See also *rdzong thur* (རྫོང་ཐུར་).

sin 'bi (སིན་འབི་). Ramrod. Same as *sin ti* (སིན་ཏི་) (Goldstein 2001, p. 1123). See also *rdzong thur* (རྫོང་ཐུར་).

sin 'bid (སིན་འབིད་). Ramrod (Kazi 1919, p. 640, under "rammer" and "ramrod"). See also *rdzong thur* (རྫོང་ཐུར་).

sin 'ben (སིན་འབེན་). Ramrod. Same as *sin 'bi* (སིན་འབི་) (Goldstein 2001, p. 1123). See also *rdzong thur* (རྫོང་ཐུར་).

sim khung (སིམ་ཁུང་). The groove, slot, or hollow recess in the fore-stock, beneath the barrel of a Tibetan matchlock gun, in which the ramrod is kept (*bod rgya*, p. 2923; Goldstein 2001, p. 1123).

sim 'big (སིམ་འབིག་). Ramrod (Goldstein 1999a, p. 248, under "ramrod"). See also *rdzong thur* (རྫོང་ཐུར་).

so kha (སོ་ཁ་). Gunsight (Goldstein 2001, p. 1133). See also *me mda'i tsha kha* (མེ་མདའི་ཚ་ཁ་).

V. Equestrian Equipment, including Saddles and Tack (སྒ་ཆས་), and Horse Armor (རྟ་གོ་)

kha mur (ཁ་མུར་). According to Das (1902b, p. 133), bit of a bridle. However, the primary term for this is *srab lcags* (སྲབ་ལྕགས་).

khyud mo (ཁྱུད་མོ་). According to Das (1902b, p. 164), equivalent to *rta chas* (རྟ་ཆས་), the equipment of a horse.

gong (གོང་) or **gong thag** (གོང་ཐག་). The breast collar of a horse harness (Goldstein 2001, p. 118).

glo (གློ་). The cinch or girth strap of a saddle (Goldstein 2001, p. 211, def. 3; ETED, p. 564, def. 3). See also *sga glo* (སྒ་གློ་).

glo chung (གློ་ཆུང་). See *phyi glo* (ཕྱི་གློ་).

glo thag (གློ་ཐག་). The cinch strap (Goldstein 2001, p. 212; *bod rgya*, p. 430).

glo len (གློ་ལེན་). Strap for tightening the cinch (*bod rgya*, p. 433). According to Goldstein (2001, p. 212), same as *glo thag* (གློ་ཐག་).

sga (སྒ་), also spelled **lga** (ལྒ་). Saddle, a saddle for a horse. Honorific form: *chibs sga* (ཆིབས་སྒ་); *chib sga bstad pa* (ཆིབ་སྒ་བསྟད་པ་), to lay the saddle on, to saddle (Das 1902b, p. 319).

sga khebs (སྒ་ཁེབས་). The covering on top of a saddle (*bod rgya*, p. 583).

sga khog (སྒ་ཁོག་). The interior space or underside of the saddle (*bod rgya*, p. 583).

sga khongs (སྒ་ཁོངས་). The middle part of a saddle (Csoma 1834, p. 313; Schmidt 1841, p. 113). Compare with *sga nyag* (སྒ་ཉག་).

sga 'khor bcas (སྒ་འཁོར་བཅས་). A complete set of saddle furniture (*bod rgya*, p. 583).

sga glo (སྒ་གློ་). The cinch or girth of a saddle (Das 1902b, p. 319).

sga glo gsum ma (སྒ་གློ་གསུམ་མ་). A saddle with three cinches, or girths (Goldstein 2001, p. 273).

sga rgyun (སྒ་རྒྱུན་). Leather straps on a saddle (*bod rgya*, p. 583). Similar to *sga thag* (སྒ་ཐག་).

sga chas (སྒ་ཆས་). Saddle furniture, tack (*bod rgya*, p. 583).

sga nyag (སྒ་ཉག་). The open space on the top of a saddle, between the pommel and the cantle (*bod rgya*, p. 584). The part of the saddle where the rider sits (Goldstein 2001, p. 273). Compare with *sga khongs* (སྒ་ཁོངས་).

sga stan (སྒ་སྟན་) or **sga gdan** (སྒ་གདན་). Saddle rug; saddle and saddle rug (Goldstein 2001, p. 273).

sga stan srab gsum (སྒ་སྟན་སྲབ་གསུམ་). Collective name for the three items: saddle, saddle rug, and bridle (*bod rgya*, p. 584).

sga thag (སྒ་ཐག་). Ropes or straps used in adjusting a saddle (Das 1902b, p. 320).

sga thod lo (སྒ་ཐོད་ལོ་). A type of saddle, the pommel and cantle of which have a rounded form (*bod rgya*, p. 584).

sga mthongs (སྒ་མཐོངས་). The outer surface of the pommel and cantle (*bod rgya*, p. 584).

sga gdan (སྒ་གདན་). See *sga stan* (སྒ་སྟན་).

sga ldebs (སྒ་ལྡེབས་). The sideboards, or bars, of a saddletree; the horizontal structural members on either side of the saddletree, to which the pommel and cantle are attached (*bod rgya*, p. 584). See also *sga gshog* (སྒ་གཤོག་).

sga 'phong (སྒ་འཕོང་). The cantle of a saddletree; equivalent to *sga'i phyi ru* (སྒའི་ཕྱི་རུ་) (Dagyab 1989, p. 158).

sga dbrag (སྒ་དབྲག་). The space between the underside of the saddletree and the saddle rug (Goldstein 2001, p. 273).

sga 'bor (སྒ་འབོར་). Ornamental bosses or studs, with flat or hemispherical heads, made of gold, silver, or other materials, by which the cushioned seat is laced to the top of the saddletree (*bod rgya*, p. 584).

sga 'bol (སྒ་འབོལ་). The seat cushion attached to the top of the saddletree (*bod rgya*, p. 584).

sga mig (སྒ་མིག་). 1: The hollow space beneath the arch of the pommel and cantle (*bod rgya*, p. 584); or 2: the holes by which the front and back of the saddle are held together (Goldstein 2001, p. 273).

sga tshang (སྒ་ཚང་). The hollow space between the sideboards of the saddletree (*bod rgya*, p. 584).

sga yag (སྒ་ཡག་). The tips of the sideboards of the saddletree, which extend beyond the pommel in the front and the cantle in the rear (*bod rgya*, p. 584). In Western saddle terminology, the extensions in the front are referred to as the bur, and those in the rear as the fan of the sideboard or bar. In this catalogue they are referred to as the end-boards.

sga ru (སྒ་རུ་). See *snga ru* (སྔ་རུ་) and *phyi ru* (ཕྱི་རུ་).

sga lag (སྒ་ལག་). Frame of the saddle; saddlebow; saddletree (Das 1902b, p. 320, citing Csoma 1834).

sga sha (སྒ་ཤ་), also **sha stag** (ཤ་སྟག་). Straps for fastening the traveling baggage to the saddle (Das 1902b, p. 320; Schmidt 1841, p. 113).

sga shan (སྒ་ཤན་). Fittings or reinforcing borders for the edges of a saddle, which are made of gold, silver, and other materials (*bod rgya*, p. 585).

sga shing (སྒ་ཤིང་). Bent-wood form, used in making saddles (*bod rgya*, p. 585).

sga gshog (སྒ་གཤོག་). The two flat wooden boards, shaped like wings, which are the sideboards, or bars, of the saddletree (*bod rgya*, p. 585). See also *sga ldebs* (སྒ་ལྡེབས་).

sga srab (སྒ་སྲབ་). Collective term for saddle and bridle (*bod rgya*, p. 585).

sga'i snga ru (སྒའི་སྔ་རུ་). See *snga ru* (སྔ་རུ་).

sga'i mdun ru (སྒའི་མདུན་རུ་). The front saddle arch [i.e., the pommel] (Csoma 1834, p. 313; Schmidt 1841, p. 113). See *snga ru* (སྔ་རུ་).

sga'i phyi ru (སྒའི་ཕྱི་རུ་). See *phyi ru* (ཕྱི་རུ་).

sga'i rmed (སྒའི་རྨེད་). See *rmed* (རྨེད་).

sga'i am cog (སྒའི་ཨམ་ཅོག་). Literally, ears of the saddle. The pair of flaps or fenders, usually of leather, which hang from either side of a saddle (ETED, p. 776, under སྒ).

snga ru (སྔ་རུ་). The pommel of a saddle, the front arch (lit. front horn) (*bod rgya*, pp. 707, 583 under སྒ).

snga sha (སྔ་ཤ་). Das (1902b, p. 372) defines as "straps for binding things to a saddle," but equates the term to *rta sga'i snga ru* (རྟ་སྒའི་སྔ་རུ་), which means "the pommel [front] of a saddle." According to Goldstein (2001, p. 322) and *bod rgya* (p. 707) the term is equivalent to *snga ru* (སྔ་རུ་), i.e., the pommel of a saddle. Das may have confused the term with *sga sha* (སྒ་ཤ་) or *sha stag* (ཤ་སྟག་), which he defines as straps for tying things such as baggage to a saddle. Accepting the Goldstein and *bod rgya* definitions, by extension the term *phyi sha* (ཕྱི་ཤ་), when used specifically in reference to saddles, would be equivalent to *phyi ru* (ཕྱི་རུ་), i.e., the cantle. See also *snga sha phyi sha* (སྔ་ཤ་ཕྱི་ཤ་).

snga sha phyi sha (སྔ་ཤ་ཕྱི་ཤ་). The front and back of a saddle [i.e., the pommel and cantle] (Goldstein 2001, p. 322). This appears to be equivalent to *snga ru* (སྔ་རུ་) and *phyi ru* (ཕྱི་རུ་). See also *snga sha* (སྔ་ཤ་).

lcag tshan (ལྕག་ཚན་) or **rta lcag** (རྟ་ལྕག་). A whip in general; a horse whip (Das 1902b, p. 396).

lceg (ལྕེག་). An apparently rare term defined by Das (1902b, p. 401) and Jäschke (1881, p. 150) as "a coat of mail for a horse," both citing Schmidt 1841 and translating verbatim into English Schmidt's original definition. Note, however, that Schmidt (p. 154) used the word *Panzer*, which here probably should be translated as "armor" in a general sense, and not "coat of mail" specifically. See also *rta khrab* (རྟ་ཁྲབ་).

chibs (ཆིབས་) or **chibs pa** (ཆིབས་པ་). Honorific term for *rta* (རྟ་), a horse; generally a riding horse; a saddle horse (Das 1902b, p. 412).

chibs sga (ཆིབས་སྒ་). Honorific term for *sga* (སྒ་), saddle (Das 1902b, p. 413).

chibs lcag (ཆིབས་ལྕག་). Honorific term for whip (Das 1902b, p. 413).

chibs chas (ཆིབས་ཆས་). Honorific term for a horse's furniture, harness; the equipment of a horse (Das 1902b, p. 413).

chibs chen (ཆིབས་ཆེན་). A charger; the best horse in the stable (Das 1902b, p. 413).

chibs thur (ཆིབས་ཐུར་). Honorific term for a horse's headpiece [i.e., bridle or headstall] (Das 1902b, p. 413).

snying dom (སྙིང་དོམ་). Red tassel indicating rank or status, which hangs from the breast collar of a horse or mule (Goldstein 2001, p. 436; *bod rgya*, p. 1005). See also *dom dom* (དོམ་དོམ་).

rta ka (རྟ་ཀ་) or **rtar ka** (རྟར་ཀ་). Horseshoe (Das 1902b, p. 530). See also *rta lcags* (རྟ་ལྕགས་) and *rmig lcags* (རྨིག་ལྕགས་).

rta khrab (རྟ་ཁྲབ་). Horse armor (Goldstein 2001, p. 456). See also *rta go* (རྟ་གོ་) and *lceg* (ལྕེག་).

rta go (རྟ་གོ་) or **rta'i khrab cha tshang** (རྟའི་ཁྲབ་ཆ་ཚང་). Coat of mail for a horse [i.e., horse armor, not specifically made of mail]; *de dmag dpon rnams kyi rta chas yin* (དེ་དམག་དཔོན་རྣམས་ཀྱི་རྟ་ཆས་ཡིན་), the horse equipment for generals (Das 1902b, p. 530, citing *Rtsii*). See also *rta khrab* (རྟ་ཁྲབ་).

rta gal (རྟ་གལ་). Saddlebag (Das 1902b, p. 530).

rta gral (རྟ་གྲལ་). A row of horses, in the sense of *rta mang po gral sgrigs nas bzhag pa* (རྟ་མང་པོ་གྲལ་སྒྲིགས་ནས་བཞག་པ་), a line of horses in martial array (Das 1902b, p. 530).

rta gras (རྟ་གྲས་) or **rta ra** (རྟ་ར་). Stable for horses (Das 1902b, p. 530).

rta rgyug mda' 'phen (རྟ་རྒྱུག་མདའ་འཕེན་). Contest involving riders shooting arrows from horseback (Goldstein 2001, p. 457).

rta rgyug zhar 'phen (རྟ་རྒྱུག་ཞར་འཕེན་). 1: Contest involving riding a horse at full gallop and firing a rifle at a target, then shooting an arrow at the next target, then thrusting a spear at a third target (Goldstein 2001, p. 457). 2: Contest held mostly in the summertime in connection with various festivals, which involves shooting an arrow at a target from a galloping horse (*bod rgya*, p. 1057).

rta sga (རྟ་སྒ་) or **rta'i sga** (རྟའི་སྒ་). Horse saddle (Das 1902b, p. 530).

rta sga 'khor (རྟ་སྒ་འཁོར་) or **rta sga 'khor cha 'grig** (རྟ་སྒ་འཁོར་ཆ་འགྲིག་). The equipment of a riding horse (Das 1902b, p. 530, citing *Rtsii*). See also *rta chas* (རྟ་ཆས་) and *srab sga stan cha tshang* (སྲབ་སྒ་སྟན་ཆ་ཚང་).

rta sgam (རྟ་སྒམ་). Large trunk or chest generally carried on horseback (Das 1902b, p. 531).

rta lcag (རྟ་ལྕག་). Horse whip; whip in general (Das 1902b, p. 531).

rta lcags (རྟ་ལྕགས་). Horseshoe (Goldstein 2001, p. 457). See also *rta ka* (རྟ་ཀ་) and *rmig lcags* (རྨིག་ལྕགས་).

rta chas (རྟ་ཆས་). Equipment of a riding horse (Das 1902b, p. 531). See also *rta sga 'khor* (རྟ་སྒ་འཁོར་) and *khyud mo* (ཁྱུད་མོ་).

rta stan (རྟ་སྟན་). Saddle rug (Goldstein 2001, p. 457). See also *sga stan* (སྒ་སྟན་).

rta mthur (རྟ་མཐུར་). See *mthur* (མཐུར་).

rta mda' 'phen (རྟ་མདའ་འཕེན་). 1: To shoot an arrow while galloping on horseback (Goldstein 2001, p. 458). 2: Horseback archery contest at the time of the summer farming festival (*'ong skor* [འོང་སྐོར་]) (*bod rgya*, p. 1059).

rta sna (རྟ་སྣ་). A mounted competition with bow, spear, and gun that is held in front of government officials of the fourth rank and higher during the *drung 'khor rtsal rgyugs* (དྲུང་འཁོར་རྩལ་རྒྱུགས་) ceremony (Goldstein 2001, pp. 458, 554). See also *rdzong rgyab zhabs 'bel* (རྫོང་རྒྱབ་ཞབས་འབེལ་) and *rdzong rgyab gzhar 'phen* (རྫོང་རྒྱབ་གཞར་འཕེན་).

rta pa (རྟ་པ་). A horseman, a rider; *rkang thang rta pa* (རྐང་ཐང་རྟ་པ་), infantry and cavalry (Das 1902b, p. 531). Other terms signifying a horseman are: *rta la zhon pa* (རྟ་ལ་ཞོན་པ་), *skyes bu can* (སྐྱེས་བུ་ཅན་), *rnam par gnon* (རྣམ་པར་གནོན་) (Das 1902b, p. 531, citing *Mngon*).

rta pa'i dpung (རྟ་པའི་དཔུང་). Cavalry (Das 1902b, p. 532).

rta bon pa (རྟ་བོན་པ་). Mare (Das 1902b, p. 532).

rta dmag (རྟ་དམག་). Cavalry (Das 1902b, p. 532).

rta gzhung (རྟ་གཞུང་). The list of ancient cavalry displayed after their procession in the Monlam Chenmo (Great Prayer Festival) (Goldstein 2001, p. 459). Part of the 23rd day of the Monlam Chenmo, known as the *gra phyi rtsis bsher* (གྲ་ཕྱི་རྩིས་བཤེར་), the review at Trapchi (Richardson 1993, pp. 34–37).

rta srab (རྟ་སྲབ་). See *srab* (སྲབ་).

rting lcags (རྟིང་ལྕགས་). 1: Spurs (Das 1902b, p. 535). 2: Shoes for horse or mule (*bod rgya*, p. 1017).

mthur (མཐུར་), also **mthur mgo** (མཐུར་མགོ་) or **rta'i mthur** (རྟའི་མཐུར་). Halter (without a bit); *mthur mda'* (མཐུར་མདའ་), or *mthur thag* (མཐུར་ཐག་), a halter, rope tied to the muzzle of a horse; *mthur mog* (མཐུར་མོག་), reins (Das 1902b, p. 601).

dom dom (དོམ་དོམ་). Red tassels suspended from the neck and chest harness of horses or mules of high-ranking traditional officials (Goldstein 2001, p. 547; *bod rgya*, p. 1309). See also *snying dom* (སྙིང་དོམ་), *dom dom nyis brtsegs* (དོམ་དོམ་ཉིས་བརྩེགས་), and *aog dom* (ཨོག་དོམ་).

dom dom nyis brtsegs (དོམ་དོམ་ཉིས་བརྩེགས་). Two red tassels suspended from the neck and chest harness of horses or mules of officials of the fourth rank or higher (Goldstein 2001, p. 547; *bod rgya*, p. 1309). See also *snying dom* (སྙིང་དོམ་), *dom dom* (དོམ་དོམ་), and *aog dom* (འོག་དོམ་).

phyi glo (ཕྱི་གློ་). The rear or primary cinch of a saddle with two cinches (*bod rgya*, p. 1739).

phyi ru (ཕྱི་རུ་). The cantle of a saddle [lit. rear horn] (*bod rgya*, pp. 1746, 582 under སྒ་).

phyi sha (ཕྱི་ཤ་). When used specifically in reference to saddles this term appears to be equivalent to *phyi ru* (ཕྱི་རུ་), the cantle. See discussion under *snga sha* (སྔ་ཤ་).

phying gzar (ཕྱིང་གཟར་). Cushion made of felt, which is placed beneath the saddle (*bod rgya*, p. 1747). A saddle pad.

dbang sga (དབང་སྒ་). Defined as a royal saddle (ETED, p. 776, under སྒ་), and simply as a particular type of saddle (*bod rgya*, p. 1930; Goldstein 2001, p. 750). This seems to be a term for a very elaborately decorated saddle appropriate for a person of high rank.

sbal sga (སྦལ་སྒ་). A type of saddle that is covered with frog skin (Goldstein 2001, p. 776).

rmig lcags (རྨིག་ལྕགས་). Horseshoe. See also *rta ka* (རྟ་ཀ་) and *rta lcags* (རྟ་ལྕགས་).

rmed (རྨེད་). Crupper attached to a saddle, *rta sga'i rmed* (རྟ་སྒའི་རྨེད་); crupper of a horse's saddle (Das 1902b, p. 986; *bod rgya*, p. 2155). This refers to the harness straps behind the saddle and on top of the horse's rump.

rmed sgrogs (རྨེད་སྒྲོགས་). Same as *rmed* (རྨེད་) (Goldstein 2001, p. 835).

rmed thag (རྨེད་ཐག་). Same as *rmed* (རྨེད་) (*bod rgya*, p. 2155).

rmed gdan (རྨེད་གདན་). Cushion underlying the crupper (*bod rgya*, p. 2155). This may refer specifically to the small square cushion attached to the underside of the crosspiece of a crupper, which sits atop the center of the horse's rump.

rmed phying (རྨེད་ཕྱིང་). The felt of the crupper pad (*bod rgya*, p. 2155).

rmed 'dzar (རྨེད་འཛར་). Piece of red cloth attached to the crupper (Goldstein 2001, p. 835). This probably refers to the shaped cloth flaps often found on the sides of the rear crupper straps or on either side of the tail pad.

rmed hril (རྨེད་ཧྲིལ་). The padded band attached to the ends of the crupper straps, which fits under the tail (*bod rgya*, p. 2155).

rdzong rgyab zhabs 'bel (རྫོང་རྒྱབ་ཞབས་འབེལ་). An equestrian contest known as "the gallop behind the fort," held during the Great Prayer Festival in Lhasa (Richardson 1993, p. 56). See also *rta sna* (རྟ་སྣ་).

rdzong rgyab gzhar 'phen (རྫོང་རྒྱབ་གཞར་འཕེན་). An equestrian contest known as "shooting in succession behind the fort," held during the Great Prayer Festival in Lhasa (Richardson 1993, p. 56). See also *rta sna* (རྟ་སྣ་).

gzang (གཟང་). A leather piece used under a saddle (Goldstein 2001, p. 966, def. 2).

'ob (འོབ་). Alternative spelling of *yob* (ཡོབ་), stirrups (Jäschke 1881, p. 516; Das 1902b, p. 1148).

yob (ཡོབ་). Stirrups (*bod rgya*, p. 2610; Das 1902b, p. 1148, def. 2).

yob rkang (ཡོབ་རྐང་). The arms or branches on either side of the stirrup, which run from the tread at the bottom to the slot for the stirrup leathers at the top (Tashi Namgyal, chapter on stirrups; see the appendix "Excerpts from *A Treatise on Worldly Traditions*"). See also *yob long* (ཡོབ་ལོང་).

yob rgyan (ཡོབ་རྒྱན་). The designs or various types of decoration on stirrups (*bod rgya*, p. 2610).

yob chen (ཡོབ་ཆེན་). Stirrups. Same as *yob* (ཡོབ་) (Goldstein 2001, p. 1009; Jäschke 1881, p. 516).

yob stan (ཡོབ་སྟན་). Pad made of felt, or other materials, to protect the horse's coat from abrasion by the stirrups (*bod rgya*, p. 2610).

yob thag (ཡོབ་ཐག་). Stirrup leather (Das 1902b, p. 1148, under def. 2). The straps by which the stirrups are suspended on either side of a horse.

yob mthil (ཡོབ་མཐིལ་). The part of the stirrup where the bottom of the foot rests (*bod rgya*, p. 2610), i.e., the tread.

yob lung (ཡོབ་ལུང་). 1: The stirrup leather, or *yob thag* (ཡོབ་ཐག་). 2: The ring or slot at the top of a stirrup, through which the stirrup leather passes (Goldstein 2001, p. 1009; *bod rgya*, p. 2610; Schmidt 1841, p. 533).

yob long (ཡོབ་ལོང་). According to Jäschke (1881, p. 516, citing Schmidt 1841), the hoop of the stirrup. This presumably refers to the arms on either side, through which the foot is passed. Schmidt (1841, p. 533) used the term *Reif*, literally hoop. See also *yob rkang* (ཡོབ་རྐང་).

sha stag (ཤ་སྟག). See *sga sha* (སྒ་ཤ).

srab (སྲབ) or **rta'i srab** (རྟའི་སྲབ). Bridle, i.e., bit and headstall (Das 1902b, p. 1287; Goldstein 2001, p. 1138). See also *kha mur* (ཁ་མུར).

srab kyi kha dur (སྲབ་ཀྱི་ཁ་དུར). The bridle or the reins (*bod rgya*, p. 2971).

srab kyi lce mdud (སྲབ་ཀྱི་ལྕེ་མདུད). The rings attaching the bit to the head stall of a bridle (Goldstein 2001, p. 1138; *bod rgya*, p. 2971). See also *srab sgor* (སྲབ་སྒོར).

srab skyog (སྲབ་སྐྱོག) or **srab kyogs** (སྲབ་ཀྱོགས). The reins (Das 1902b, p. 1287, under སྲབ). See also *srab mda'* (སྲབ་མདའ).

srab gor (སྲབ་གོར). Alternative spelling of *srab sgor* (སྲབ་སྒོར).

srab sga stan cha tshang (སྲབ་སྒ་སྟན་ཆ་ཚང). The complete set of equipment for a horse or mule, including bridle, saddle, and saddle rug (*bod rgya*, p. 2972). See also *rta sga 'khor* (རྟ་སྒ་འཁོར) and *rta chas* (རྟ་ཆས).

srab sgor (སྲབ་སྒོར). Two iron rings, one on each side of the bridle (*bod rgya*, p. 2972). These rings are where the bit, the headstall, and the reins are attached together. According to Goldstein (2001, p. 1138), same as *srab kyi lce mdud* (སྲབ་ཀྱི་ལྕེ་མདུད).

srab lcags (སྲབ་ལྕགས). Bit for a horse (Das 1902b, p. 1287, under སྲབ).

srab thag (སྲབ་ཐག). Reins (Goldstein 2001, p. 1138).

srab mthur (སྲབ་མཐུར). Bit and halter, i.e., bridle (Das 1902b, p. 1287, under སྲབ).

srab mda' (སྲབ་མདའ). Reins (Das 1902b, p. 1287, under སྲབ). See also *srab skyog* (སྲབ་སྐྱོག).

srab gzer (སྲབ་གཟེར). According to *bod rgya* (p. 2972), tacks or small nails used to attach the bit. According to Goldstein (2001, p. 1139), the nail that is used to attach the reins to the bridle.

gser sga (གསེར་སྒ). A saddle decorated with gold (*bod rgya*, p. 3023). Gilded saddle, gold saddle (Goldstein 2001, p. 1159).

gser srab (གསེར་སྲབ). A horse bridle decorated with gold (*bod rgya*, p. 3027). Literally, gold bridle.

bse sga (བསེ་སྒ). A saddle that is covered with hide (Goldstein 2001, p. 1167).

aog dom (ཨོག་དོམ). Red tassel tied to the harness beneath the chin of the horse as a sign of rank for lay and religious government officials (Goldstein 2001, p. 1194; *bod rgya*, p. 3144). See also *snying dom* (སྙིང་དོམ), *dom dom* (དོམ་དོམ), and *dom dom nyis brtsegs* (དོམ་དོམ་ཉིས་བརྩེགས).

Radiocarbon Dating Results

compiled by Edward H. Hunter

Catalogue number	Accession number	Object and type of sample	Material of sample	Date range (95% probability)	Date range (65% probability)
1	NMS A1909.406	Lamellar armor: leather lacing integral to interior	leather	cal A.D. 1630–1690, 1730–1810	1640–1670, 1780–1800s
6	MMA 2001.318	Lamellar armor: leather lacing integral to interior	leather	cal A.D. 1480–1660	1520–1590, 1620–1650
9	MMA 1999.158	Lamellar helmet: leather lacing from interior	leather	cal A.D. 1271–1431	1288–1412
10	MMA 2001.183	Lamellar helmet: leather lacing from interior	leather	cal A.D. 1440–1640	1460–1530, 1560–1630
27	MMA 2004.402	Shaffron: leather lacing integral to interior	leather	cal A.D. 1450–1650	1470–1530, 1550–1630
30	MMA 1997.242a	Horse armor, crinet: hard leather substrate	leather	cal A.D. 1475–1665	1515–1585, 1625–1650
30	MMA 1997.242b	Horse armor, crinet: varnish coating	tung oil	cal A.D. 1455–1640	1475–1525, 1560–1630
30	MMA 1997.242c	Horse armor, peytral: soft strap integral to interior	leather	cal A.D. 1435–1640	1450–1515, 1585–1625
31	MMA 1999.36	Horse armor, peytral: hard leather substrate	leather	cal A.D. 1402–1520, 1574–1626	1423–1474
34	MMA 1998.1	Leather helmet: hard leather substrate	leather	cal A.D. 1417–1654	1438–1632
39	MMA 2001.268	Leather lamellar armor: hard leather from lamella	leather	cal A.D. 1440–1640	1450–1520, 1590–1620
91	MMA 2001.65a	Quiver: leather from exterior back	leather	cal A.D. 1290–1410	1300–1400

Bibliography

Ainscough 1914
Ainscough, Thomas M. "The Marches of Chinese Tibet." *Journal of the Manchester Geographical Society*, 1914, pp. 7–21.

Alexander 1992
Alexander, David. *The Arts of War: Arms and Armour of the 7th to 19th Centuries.* Nasser D. Khalili Collection of Islamic Art Series, vol. 21. London and New York, 1992.

Allan 1982
Allan, James W. *Islamic Metalwork: The Nuhad Es-Said Collection.* London, 1982.

Allen 2004
Allen, Charles. *Duel in the Snows: The True Story of the Younghusband Mission to Lhasa.* London, 2004.

Anninos 2000
Anninos, Tony. "Tibetan Leather Boxes." *Arts of Asia* 30, no. 1 (January–February 2000), pp. 101–17.

Arendt 1935
Arendt, Wsewolod. "Der Nomadenhelm des frühen Mittelalters in Osteuropa." *Zeitschrift für historische Waffen- und Kostümkunde*, n.s. 5 (1935–36), pp. 26–34.

Aris 1979
Aris, Michael. *Bhutan, the Early History of a Himalayan Kingdom.* Warminster, 1979.

Aris 1992
Aris, Michael, with the assistance of Patrick Booz and contributions by S. B. Sutton and Jeffrey Wagner. *Lamas, Princes, and Brigands: Joseph Rock's Photographs of the Tibetan Borderlands of China.* Exh. cat., China House Gallery. New York, 1992.

Backus 1981
Backus, Charles. *The Nan-Chao Kingdom and T'ang China's Southwestern Frontier.* Cambridge, 1981.

Bacot et al. 1946
Bacot, Jacques, Frederick William Thomas, and Gustave Charles Toussaint. *Documents de Touen-houang relatifs à l'histoire du Tibet.* Paris, 1946.

Bailey 2002
Bailey, F. M. *Mission to Tashkent.* London, 1946; Oxford, 2002.

Beasley 1938
Beasley, H. G. "Tibet: Notes on Laminated Armour." *Ethnologia Cranmorensis* 2 (1938), pp. 18–22.

Beazley 1903, 1967
Beazley, C. Raymond. *The Texts and Versions of John de Plano Carpini and William de Rubruquis.* London, 1903; reprint, Nendeln, Liechtenstein, 1967.

Beckwith 1977
Beckwith, Charles I. "Tibet and the Early Medieval Florissance in Eurasia: A Preliminary Note on the Economic History of the Tibetan Empire." *Central Asiatic Journal* 21, no. 2 (1977), pp. 89–104.

Beckwith 1987, 1993
Beckwith, Christopher I. *The Tibetan Empire in Central Asia: A History of the Struggle for Great Power among Tibetans, Turks, Arabs, and Chinese during the Early Middle Ages.* Princeton, 1987; paperback ed., Princeton, 1993.

Beer 1999
Beer, Robert. *The Encyclopedia of Tibetan Symbols and Motifs.* Boston, 1999.

Beinecke
Tashi Namgyal (*bkra shis rnam rgyal*). *'jig rten lugs kyi bstan bcos las dpyad don gsal ba'i sgron me zhes grags pa bzhugs so* (A Treatise on Worldly Traditions, known as the Shining Lamp of Analysis), 1524. Tibetan manuscript in the Beinecke Library, Yale University, New Haven. For more information, see the appendix "Excerpts from *A Treatise on Worldly Traditions*," no. 1.

Bell 1946, 1987
Bell, Sir Charles. *Portrait of a Dalai Lama: The Life and Times of the Great Thirteenth.* London, 1946; reprint, London, 1987.

Blackmore 1961
Blackmore, Howard L. *British Military Firearms, 1650–1850.* London, 1961.

bod rgya
Zhang, Yisun, et al., eds. *bod rgya tshig mdzod chen mo* (The Large Tibetan-Chinese Dictionary). Compact ed., 2 vols. Beijing, 1996.

Bonvalot 1891
Bonvalot, Gabriel. *Across Tibet; being a translation of "De Paris au Tonkin à travers le Tibet inconnu."* Translated by C. B. Pitman. 2 vols. London, 1891.

Boots 1932

Boots, John L. *Korean Weapons and Armor.* [Seoul?], 1932.

Boston 1992

Selected Masterpieces of Asian Art: Museum of Fine Arts, Boston. Boston, 1992.

Bosworth and Asimov 1998–2000

Bosworth, C. E., and M. S. Asimov, eds. *History of Civilizations of Central Asia.* Vol. 4, *The Age of Achievement: A.D. 750 to the End of the Fifteenth Century.* Pt. 1, *The Historical, Social and Economic Setting.* Pt. 2, *The Achievements.* Paris, 1998–2000.

brda dkrol

btsan lha ngag dbang tshul khrims. *brda dkrol gser gyi me long zhes bya ba bzhugs so* (A Golden Mirror of Symbols). Beijing, 1997.

Brentjes 1996

Brentjes, Burchard. *Arms of the Sakas (and Other Tribes of the Central Asian Steppes).* Varanasi, 1996.

British Library Or 11,374

rin po che bzo yi las kyi bsgrub pa'i rgyud dang ja dang dar gos chen dang rta rgyud tshugs bzang ngan gyi rtag pa bzhugs so (The Continuum of Precious Things Accomplished by the Crafts, and the Analysis of the Quality and Forms of Tea, Silk Brocades, and Horse Breeds). Unsigned and undated Tibetan manuscript in the Oriental and India Office Collections, British Library, London, Or 11,374. For more information, see the appendix "Excerpts from *A Treatise on Worldly Traditions,*" no. 3.

Burmiok Athing

'jig rten lugs kyi bstan bcos las dpyad don gsal ba'i sgron me zhes grags pa bzhugs so (A Treatise on Worldly Traditions, known as the Shining Lamp of Analysis). Photocopy of a Tibetan manuscript formerly in the library of Rai Bahadur Burmiok Athing (1902–1988), Sikkim. For more information, see the appendix "Excerpts from *A Treatise on Worldly Traditions,*" no. 2.

Cammann 1952

Cammann, Schuyler V. R. *China's Dragon Robes.* New York, 1952.

Candler 1905

Candler, Edmund. *The Unveiling of Lhasa.* London, 1905.

Carter 1998

Carter, Martha L. "Three Silver Vessels from Tibet's Earliest Historical Era: A Preliminary Study." *Cleveland Studies in the History of Art* 3 (1998), pp. 22–47.

Chan 1994

Chan, Victor. *Tibet Handbook: A Pilgrimage Guide.* Chico, Calif., 1994.

Clarke 1995

Clarke, John. "A Regional Survey and Stylistic Analysis of Tibetan Metalworking, 1850–1959." 2 vols. PhD diss., School of African and Oriental Studies, London, 1995.

Clarke 2002

Clarke, John. "Metalworking in dBus and gTsang, 1930–1977." *Tibet Journal* 27, nos. 1–2 (spring–summer 2002), pp. 113–52.

Clarke 2004

Clarke, John. *Jewellery of Tibet and the Himalayas.* London, 2004.

Craddock and Lang 2003

Craddock, P. T., and Janet Lang, eds. *Mining and Metal Production through the Ages.* London, 2003.

Csoma 1834, 1973

Csoma de Körös, Alexander. *Essay towards a Dictionary, Tibetan and English.* Calcutta, 1834; reprint, New Delhi, 1973.

Dagyab 1977

Dagyab, Loden Sherap. *Tibetan Religious Art.* 2 vols. Wiesbaden, 1977.

Dagyab 1989

Dagyab, Loden Sherap. *bod brda'i tshig mdzod* (A Dictionary of Tibetan Terms). Dharamsala, 1989.

Dagyab 1995

Dagyab, Loden Sherap Rinpoche. *Buddhist Symbols in Tibetan Culture: An Investigation of the Nine Best-Known Groups of Symbols.* Translated by Maurice Walshe. Boston, 1995.

Daoulas 1998

Jean-Yves Cozan et al. *Entre Inde et Tibet: Le royaume du Bhoutan.* Exh. cat., Abbaye de Daoulas. Daoulas, 1998.

Das 1902a, 1904, 2001

Das, Sarat Chandra. *Journey to Lhasa and Central Tibet.* London, 1902; new ed., London, 1904; reprint, Delhi, 2001.

Das 1902b, 1998

Das, Sarat Chandra. *A Tibetan-English Dictionary.* Calcutta, 1902; reprint, Delhi, 1998.

Das 1904. See Das 1902a

Demiéville 1952, 1987
Demiéville, Paul. *Le concile de Lhasa: Une controverse sur le quiétisme entre bouddhistes de l'Inde et de la Chine au VIIIe siècle de l'ère chrétienne.* Paris, 1952; Paris, 1987.

Dien 2000
Dien, Albert E. "A Brief Survey of Defensive Armor across Asia." *Journal of East Asian Archaeology* 2, nos. 3–4 (2000), pp. 1–22.

Dudjom Rinpoche 1991
Dudjom Rinpoche. *The Nyingma School of Tibetan Buddhism: Its Fundamentals and History.* Translated and edited by Gyurme Dorje and Matthew Kapstein. 2 vols. Boston, 1991.

***dung dkar* 2002**
mkhas dbang dung dkar blo bzang 'phrin las mchog gis mdzad pa'i bod rig pa'i tshig mdzod chen mo shes bya rab gsal zhes bya ba bzugs so / Dungkar Tibetological Great Dictionary. Beijing, 2002.

Dunlop 1973
Dunlop, D. M. "Arab Relations with Tibet in the 8th and Early 9th Centuries A.D." *Islâm Tetkikleri Enstitüsü Dergisi* (Review of the Institute of Islamic Studies) 4–5 (1964–73), pp. 301–18.

Elgood 1979
Elgood, Robert, ed. *Islamic Arms and Armour.* London, 1979.

Elverskog 2003
Elverskog, Johan. *The Jewel Translucent Sūtra: Altan Khan and the Mongols in the Sixteenth Century.* Leiden, 2003.

***Encyclopedia of Islam* IV**
Encyclopedia of Islam. Vol. IV. Edited by E. van Donzel, B. Lewis, Ch. Pellat, et al. Leiden, 1978.

ETED
An Encyclopaedic Tibetan-English Dictionary / bod dbyin tshig mdzod chen mo. Beijing and London, 2001.

Francke 1914–26
Francke, August Hermann. *Antiquities of Indian Tibet.* 2 vols. Calcutta, 1914–26.

Francke 1999
Francke, August Hermann. *A History of Western Tibet: One of the Unknown Empires.* London, 1907; reprint, Delhi, 1999.

French 1995
French, Patrick. *Younghusband: The Last Great Imperial Adventurer.* London, 1994; paperback ed., London, 1995.

Gangtok 1981
Hūṃkaradzaya. *legs par bshad pa padma dkar po'i chun po: A Treatise Describing the Qualities and Criteria for Appraisal and Appreciation of Omens, Precious Objects, Weapons, and Other Possessions . . . reproduced from a rare manuscript belonging to Jokhang Lama Gyaltsen.* Gangtok, 1981.

Gluckman 2004
Gluckman, Dale. "A Multi-Faceted Relationship: Textiles and Tibetan Painted Furniture." In Kamansky 2004, pp. 71–87.

Goldstein 1999a
Goldstein, Melvyn C., with Ngawangthondup Narkyid. *English-Tibetan Dictionary of Modern Tibetan.* Rev. ed. Dharamsala, 1999.

Goldstein 1999b
Goldstein, Melvyn C. *The Snow Lion and the Dragon: China, Tibet, and the Dalai Lama.* Berkeley, 1997; paperback ed., Berkeley, 1999.

Goldstein 2001
Goldstein, Melvyn C., ed.; T. N. Shelling and J. T. Surkhang, asst. eds., with Pierre Robillard. *The New Tibetan-English Dictionary of Modern Tibetan.* Berkeley, 2001.

Gorelik 1979
Gorelik, Michael V. "Oriental Armour of the Near and Middle East from the Eighth to the Fifteenth Centuries as Shown in Works of Art." In Elgood 1979, pp. 30–63.

Grancsay 1959
Grancsay, Stephen V. "A Viking Chieftain's Sword." *The Metropolitan Museum of Art Bulletin,* n.s. 17 (March 1959), pp. 173–81.

***Guge* 1991**
gu ge'i gna' grong rdzes shul / Guge gu cheng / The Site of the Ancient Guge Kingdom (text in Chinese with Tibetan and English synopses). 2 vols. Beijing, 1991.

Guise 1988
Guise, Anthony, ed. *The Potala of Tibet.* London and Atlantic Highlands, N.J., 1988.

Gulati 2003
Gulati, M. N. *Tibetan Wars through Sikkim, Bhutan, and Nepal.* New Delhi, 2003.

Gutowski 1997
Gutowski, Jacek. *Broń i uzbrojenie Tatarów / Tartar Arms and Armour.* Warsaw, 1997.

Haider 1991

Haider, Syed Zafar. *Islamic Arms and Armour of Muslim India*. Lahore, 1991.

Harrer 1992

Harrer, Heinrich. *Lost Lhasa: Heinrich Harrer's Tibet*. New York, 1992.

Harris and Shakya 2003

Harris, Clare, and Tsering Shakya, eds. *Seeing Lhasa: British Depictions of the Tibetan Capital, 1936–1947*. Chicago, 2003.

Heller 1992

Heller, Amy. "Historic and Iconographic Aspects of the Protective Deities Srung-ma dmar-nag." In Shoren Ihara and Zuiho Yamaguchi, eds., *Tibetan Studies: Proceedings of the 5th Seminar of the International Association for Tibetan Studies, Narita, 1989*, pp. 479–92. Narita, 1992.

Heller 1997

Heller, Amy. "Notes on the Symbol of the Scorpion in Tibet." In Samten Karmay and Philippe Sagant, eds., *Les habitants du toit du monde: Études recueillies en hommage à Alexander W. MacDonald*, pp. 283–97. Nanterre, 1997.

Heller 1998

Heller, Amy. "Two Inscribed Fabrics and Their Historical Context: Some Observations on Esthetics and the Silk Trade in Tibet, 7th to 9th Century." In Karel Otavsky, ed., *Entlang der Seidenstrasse: Frühmittelalterliche Kunstzwischen Persien und China in der Abegg-Stiftung*, pp. 95–118. Riggisberger Berichte 6. Riggisberg, 1998.

Heller 1999

Heller, Amy. *Tibetan Art: Tracing the Development of Spiritual Ideals and Art in Tibet, 600–2000 A.D.* Milan, 1999.

Henss 1997

Henss, Michael. "The Woven Image: Tibeto-Chinese Textile Thangkas of the Yuan and Early Ming Dynasties." *Orientations* 28 (November 1997), pp. 26–39.

Hong Kong 1995

Jin xiu luo yi qiao tian gong / Heaven's Embroidered Cloths: One Thousand Years of Chinese Textiles. Exh. cat., Hong Kong Museum of Art. Hong Kong, 1995.

Hummel 1954

Hummel, Siegbert. *Tibetisches Kunsthandwerk in Metall*. Leipzig, 1954.

Huntington 1975

Huntington, John C. *The Phur-pa, Tibetan Ritual Daggers*. Ascona, 1975.

Huntington and Bangdel 2003

Huntington, John C., and Dina Bangdel. *The Circle of Bliss: Buddhist Meditational Art*. Exh. cat., Los Angeles County Museum of Art and Columbus Museum of Art. Columbus and Chicago, 2003.

Illuminator

Duff, Tony, ed. *The Illuminator Tibetan-English Dictionary*. CD-ROM. Padma Karpo Translation Committee.

Jackson 1996

Jackson, David Paul. *A History of Tibetan Painting: The Great Tibetan Painters and Their Traditions*. Vienna, 1996.

Jäschke 1881, 1998

Jäschke, H. A. *A Tibetan-English Dictionary*. London, 1881; reprint, Richmond, Surrey, 1998.

Jaubert 1975

Jaubert, P.-A., trans. and ed. *La géographie d'Édrisi*. Paris, 1836–40; reprint, Amsterdam, 1975.

Jig. See Tashi Namgyal

Jing 1994

Jing, Anning. "The Portraits of Khubilai Khan and Chabi by Anige (1245–1306), a Nepali Artist at the Yuan Court." *Artibus Asiae* 54, nos. 1–2 (1994), pp. 40–86.

Jones 1996

Jones, Schuyler. *Tibetan Nomads: Environment, Pastoral Economy, and Material Culture*. Copenhagen, London, and New York, 1996.

Kamansky 2004

Kamansky, David, ed. *Wooden Wonders: Tibetan Furniture in Secular and Religious Life*. Exh. cat., Pacific Asia Museum, Pasadena. Chicago, 2004.

Karmay 1975

Karmay, Heather. *Early Sino-Tibetan Art*. Warminster, 1975.

Karsten 1983

Karsten, Joachim. "A Note on *ya sor* and the Secular Festivals Following the *smon lam chen mo*." In Ernst Steinkellner and Helmut Tauscher, eds., *Contributions on Tibetan Language, History and Culture*. Vol. 1 of *Proceedings of the Csoma de Körös Symposium, Held at Velm-Vienna, Austria, 13–19 September 1981*, pp. 117–49. Vienna, 1983.

Kazi 1919, 1990

Kazi, Lama Dawasamdup. *An English Tibetan Dictionary*. Calcutta, 1919; reprint, New Delhi, 1990.

Kerr 1991
Kerr, Rose, et al. *Chinese Art and Design: The T. T. Tsui Gallery of Chinese Art*. London, 1991.

Kidd 1975
Kidd, David. "Tibetan Painting in China: New Light on a Puzzling Group of Dated Tangkas." *Oriental Art*, n.s. 21, no. 1 (spring 1975), pp. 56–60.

Kolmas 1968
A Genealogy of the Kings of Derge, sde dge'i rgyal rabs. Tibetan text edited with historical introduction by Josef Kolmas. Prague, 1968.

Komaroff and Carboni 2002
Komaroff, Linda, and Stefano Carboni, eds. *The Legacy of Genghis Khan: Courtly Art and Culture in Western Asia, 1256–1353*. Exh. cat., The Metropolitan Museum of Art and Los Angeles County Museum of Art. New York, 2002.

Kubarev 1997
Kubarev, Gleb V. "Der Panzer eines alttürkischen Ritters aus Balyk-Sook." *Eurasia Antiqua* 3 (1997), pp. 629–45.

Lang, Craddock, and Simpson 1998
Lang, J., P. T. Craddock, and St. J. Simpson. "New Evidence for Early Crucible Steel." *Journal of the Historical Metallurgy Society* 32, no. 1 (1998), pp. 7–14.

LaRocca 1995
LaRocca, Donald J. "Sword." In *Recent Acquisitions: A Selection, 1994–1995. The Metropolitan Museum of Art Bulletin* 53, no. 2 (fall 1995), p. 77.

LaRocca 1996
LaRocca, Donald J. *The Gods of War: Sacred Imagery and the Decoration of Arms and Armor*. Exh. cat., The Metropolitan Museum of Art. New York, 1996.

LaRocca 1997
LaRocca, Donald J. "Helmet." In *Recent Acquisitions: A Selection, 1996–1997. The Metropolitan Museum of Art Bulletin* 55, no. 2 (fall 1997), p. 90.

LaRocca 1998
LaRocca, Donald J. "Elements of a Ceremonial Horse Armor." In *Recent Acquisitions: A Selection, 1997–1998. The Metropolitan Museum of Art Bulletin* 56, no. 2 (fall 1998), p. 79.

LaRocca 1999a
LaRocca, Donald J. "An Approach to the Study of Arms and Armour from Tibet." *Royal Armouries Yearbook* 4 (1999), pp. 113–32.

LaRocca 1999b
LaRocca, Donald J. Introduction to the Dover reprint of Stone 1934, pp. v–vi. New York, 1999.

LaRocca 1999c
LaRocca, Donald J. "Fittings for a Ceremonial Saddle." In *Recent Acquisitions: A Selection, 1998–1999. The Metropolitan Museum of Art Bulletin* 57, no. 2 (fall 1999), pp. 76–77.

LaRocca 2001
LaRocca, Donald J. "Cane Shield with Iron Fittings." In *Recent Acquisitions: A Selection, 2000–2001. The Metropolitan Museum of Art Bulletin* 59, no. 2 (fall 2001), p. 83.

Laufer 1914
Laufer, Berthold. *Chinese Clay Figures, Part I: Prolegomena on the History of Defensive Armor*. Field Museum of Natural History Publication 177, Anthropological Series, vol. 13, no. 2. Chicago, 1914.

Lavin 1997
Lavin, James D., with an essay by Ramiro Larrañaga. *The Art and Tradition of the Zuloagas: Spanish Damascene from the Khalili Collection*. Exh. cat., Victoria and Albert Museum. [London?], 1997.

Lebedynsky 2001
Lebedynsky, Iaroslav. *Armes et guerriers barbares au temps des grandes invasions (IVe au VIe siècle apr. J.-C.)*. Paris, 2001.

Le Strange 1930
Le Strange, G. *The Lands of the Eastern Caliphate: Mesopotamia, Persia, and Central Asia, from the Moslem Conquest to the Time of Timur*. Cambridge, 1905; Cambridge, 1930.

Lhasa 1990
chab spel tshe brtan phun tshogs, ed. *bzo rigs nyer mkho bdams bsgrigs* (A Compilation of Selected Texts on Important Crafts). Lhasa, 1990.

Liu 1988
Liu, Lizhong. *Buddhist Art of the Tibetan Plateau*. Edited and translated by Ralph Kiggell. Hong Kong and San Francisco, 1988.

Lo Bue 1981
Lo Bue, Erberto. "Statuary Metals in Tibet and the Himalayas: History, Tradition and Modern Use." In W. A. Oddy and W. Zwalf, eds., *Aspects of Tibetan Metallurgy*. British Museum Occasional Paper, no. 15. London, 1981.

Lo Bue 1997
Lo Bue, Erberto. "Sculptural Styles According to Pema Karpo." In

Jane Casey Singer and Philip Denwood, eds., *Tibetan Art: Towards a Definition of Style*, pp. 242–53, 302–4. London, 1997.

Lowry 1973
Lowry, John. "Tibet, Nepal or China? An Early Group of Dated Tangkas." *Oriental Art*, n.s., 19, no. 3 (autumn 1973), pp. 306–15.

Martin 1997
Martin, Dan, in collaboration with Yael Bentor. *Tibetan Histories: A Bibliography of Tibetan-Language Historical Works*. London, 1997.

McKay 1997
McKay, Alex. *Tibet and the British Raj: The Frontier Cadre, 1904–1947*. Richmond, Surrey, 1997.

Mikami 1981
Mikami, Tsugio. *Ryō, Kin, Gen / Liao, Chin and Yüan Dynasties*. Sekai Tōji Zenshū / Ceramic Art of the World, vol. 13. Tokyo, 1981.

Minorsky 1937
Hudud al-ʿAlam / "The Regions of the World": A Persian Geography, 372 A.H.–982 A.D. Translated and explained by Vladimir Minorsky. London, 1937.

Mngon
ngag dbang ʾjigs med grags pa. *mngon brjod mkhas paʾi rna rgyan* (The Scholar's Earring of Synonyms). A text often cited in Das 1902b in relation to arms and armor terms.

Moore 1995
Moore, Oliver. "Arms and Armour in Late Imperial China: Examples of A.D. 1600–1900 in the British Museum." *Apollo*, n.s. 141 (February 1995), pp. 16–19.

Moriyasu 1980
Moriyasu, Takao. "La nouvelle interprétation des mots Hor et Ho-yo-hor dans le manuscrit Pelliot tibétain 1283." *Acta Orientalia Academiae Scientiarum Hungaricae* 34, nos. 1–3 (1980), pp. 171–84.

Mullin 1996
Mullin, Glenn H., et al. *The Mystical Arts of Tibet: Featuring Personal Sacred Objects of H.H. the Dalai Lama*. Atlanta, 1996.

Mullin 2001
Mullin, Glenn H. *The Fourteen Dalai Lamas: A Sacred Legacy of Reincarnation*. Santa Fe, N.M., 2001.

Musée de Tzarskoe-Selo 1853
Musée de Tzarskoe-Selo, ou collection d'armes de sa majesté l'empereur de toutes les Russies: Ouvrage composé de 180 planches lithographiées par Asselineau d'après les dessins originaux de A. Rockstuhl. Saint Petersburg, 1853.

Nebesky-Wojkowitz 1975
Nebesky-Wojkowitz, René de. *Oracles and Demons of Tibet: The Cult and Iconography of the Tibetan Protective Deities*. The Hague, 1956; reprint, Graz, 1975.

Needham 1971
Needham, Joseph, with contributions by Lu Gwei-Djen and Ling Wang. *Civil Engineering and Nautics*. Pt. 3 of *Physics and Physical Technology*. Vol. 4 of *Science and Civilisation in China*. Cambridge, 1971.

Nicolle 1995
Nicolle, David. *Medieval Warfare Source Book*. London, 1995.

Nicolle 1999
Nicolle, David. *Arms and Armour of the Crusading Era, 1050–1350: Western Europe and the Crusader States*. London and Mechanicsburg, Pa., 1999.

Nicolle 2002
Nicolle, David, ed. *A Companion to Medieval Arms and Armour*. Woodbridge, England, 2002.

Norbu and Turnbull 1968
Norbu, Thubten Jigme, and Colin M. Turnbull. *Tibet: An Account of the History, the Religion, and the People of Tibet*. New York, 1968.

Norwick 2003
Norwick, Braham. "Reading Magic Writing: *Bija* and *Lantsha*." *Archiv Orientální* 71, no. 3 (August 2003), pp. 395–408.

'od zer 1989
bkra shis ʾod zer. *bod kyi lag shes bzo las kyi ya gyal mgar gyi lag rtsal dang shes byaʾi skor gyi bstan bcos mdor bsdus blo gsal gzhon nuʾi mgul rgyan pad ma kdar poʾi ʾphreng ba zhes bya ba bzhugs so* (A Concise Treatise on What Should Be Known Concerning the Craft of Smithing, among the Arts and Crafts of Tibet, called the White Lotus Garland Necklace of Intelligent Youth). Beijing, 1989.

Olson 1950–71
Olson, Eleanor. *Catalogue of the Tibetan Collection and Other Lamaist Articles in the Newark Museum*. 5 vols. Newark, N.J., 1950–71.

Palchor Zangpo
Palchor Zangpo (*dpal ʾbyor bzang po*). *rgya bod yig tshang chen mo* (The Great Chinese-Tibetan Compendium). 1434; Chengdu, 1985.

Pant 1982
Pant, G. N. *Indian Shield*. New Delhi, 1982.

Peers 1992

Peers, C. J. *Medieval Chinese Armies, 1260–1520.* Illustrated by David Sque. Osprey Men-at-Arms Series, no. 251. London, 1992.

Petech 1950

Petech, Luciano. *China and Tibet in the Early 18th Century: History of the Establishment of the Chinese Protectorate in Tibet.* Leiden, 1950.

Petech 1983

Petech, Luciano. "Tibetan Relations with Sung China and with the Mongols." In Morris Rossabi, ed., *China among Equals: The Middle Kingdom and Its Neighbors, 10th–14th Centuries,* pp. 173–203. Berkeley, 1983.

Petech 1999

Petech, Luciano. *A Study on the Chronicles of Ladakh (Indian Tibet).* Calcutta, 1939; Delhi, 1999.

Pyhrr, LaRocca, and Breiding 2005

Pyhrr, Stuart W., Donald J. LaRocca, and Dirk H. Breiding. *The Armored Horse in Europe, 1480–1620.* Exh. cat., The Metropolitan Museum of Art. New York, 2005.

Pyhrr, LaRocca, and Ogawa 2002

Phyrr, Stuart W., Donald J. LaRocca, and Morihiro Ogawa. *Arms and Armor: Notable Acquisitions 1991–2002.* Exh. cat., The Metropolitan Museum of Art. New York, 2002.

Rapten 2001

Rapten, Phuntsho. "Patag—The Symbol of Heroes." *Journal of Bhutan Studies* 5 (winter 2001), pp. 94–112.

Rauber-Schweizer 1976

Rauber-Schweizer, Hanna. *Der Schmied und sein Handwerk im traditionellen Tibet.* PhD diss., Universität Zürich, 1976; Rikon, 1976.

Reynolds 1999

Reynolds, Valrae, with contributions by Janet Gyatso, Amy Heller, and Dan Martin. *From the Sacred Realm: Treasures of Tibetan Art from the Newark Museum.* Exh. cat., Newark Museum. Munich, London, New York, 1999.

rgyal rtse rnam rgyal dbang 'dud 1976

rgyal rtse rnam rgyal dbang 'dud. *bod ljongs rgyal khab chen po'i srid lugs dang 'brel ba'i drag po'i dmag gi lo rgyus rags bsdus* (An Outline of Military Organization under the Traditional Government of Central Tibet). Dharmsala, 1976.

Richardson 1985

Richardson, Hugh. *A Corpus of Early Tibetan Inscriptions.* [London], 1985.

Richardson 1993

Richardson, Hugh. *Ceremonies of the Lhasa Year.* London, 1993.

Richardson 1998

Richardson, Hugh. *High Peaks, Pure Earth: Collected Writings on Tibetan History and Culture.* London, 1998.

T. Richardson 1996

Richardson, Thom. "The Ming Sword." *Royal Armouries Yearbook* 1 (1996), pp. 95–99.

Rituels tibétains 2002

Rituels tibétains: Visions secrètes du Ve Dalaï Lama. Edited by Nathalie Bazin. Exh. cat., Musée National des Arts Asiatiques–Guimet. Paris, 2002.

Robinson 1967, 1995

Robinson, H. Russell. *Oriental Armour.* London, 1967; reprint, New York, 1995.

Rock 1955

Rock, Joseph F. "The D'a Nv Funeral Ceremony with Special Reference to the Origin of Na-Khi Weapons." *Anthropos* 50, nos. 1–3 (1955), pp. 1–31.

Rockhill 1891

Rockhill, William Woodville. *The Land of the Lamas: Notes of a Journey through China, Mongolia, and Tibet.* London, 1891.

Rockhill 1894/2001

Rockhill, William Woodville. *Diary of a Journey through Mongolia and Tibet in 1891 and 1892.* Washington, 1894; reprint, n.p.: Elibron, 2001.

Rockhill 1895

Rockhill, William Woodville. "Notes on the Ethnology of Tibet: Based on the Collections of the United States National Museum." In *Annual Report of the Board of Regents of the Smithsonian Institution . . . for the Year Ending 1893: Report of the U.S. National Museum,* pp. 665–747. Washington, 1895.

Roerich 1931

Roerich, George N. *Trails to Inmost Asia: Five Years of Exploration with the Roerich Central Asian Expedition.* New Haven, 1931.

Roerich 1959

Roerich, George. *Biography of Dharmasvamin (Chag lo tsa ba Chos rje dpal), a Tibetan Monk Pilgrim.* Patna, 1959.

Ronge 1978

Ronge, Veronika. *Das tibetische Handwerkertum vor 1959.* Wiesbaden, 1978.

Rtsii

rtsis gzhi phyogs bsgrigs (Arrangements of Accounts). A work often cited in Das 1902b in relation to arms and armor terms and defined by Das (p. 1012) as "the name of the standard work on the subsidies, pensions, allowances, etc., that the government of Lhasa makes."

Sandberg 1906

Sandberg, Graham. *Tibet and the Tibetans*. London, 1906.

Schafer 1963

Schafer, Edward H. *The Golden Peaches of Samarkand: A Study of T'ang Exotics*. Berkeley, 1963.

Schmidt 1841

Schmidt, I. J. *Tibetisch-deutsches Wörterbuch nebst deutschem Wortregister*. Saint Petersburg, 1841.

Selby 2000

Selby, Stephen. *Chinese Archery*. Hong Kong, 2000.

Shakabpa 1967

Shakabpa, Tsepon W. D. *Tibet: A Political History*. New Haven, 1967.

Shakya 1999

Shakya, Tsering. *The Dragon in the Land of Snows: A History of Modern Tibet since 1947*. New York, 1999.

Shuguba 1995

Shuguba, Tsipon (*rtsi dpon shud khud 'jam dbyangs mkhas grub*), with Sumner Carnahan. *In the Presence of My Enemies: Memoirs of Tibetan Nobleman Tsipon Shuguba*. Santa Fe, N.M., 1995.

Sinor 1990

Sinor, Denis, ed. *The Cambridge History of Early Inner Asia*. Cambridge, 1990.

Sinor, Shimin, and Kychanov 1998–2000

Sinor, D., G. Shimin, and Y. Kychanov. "The Uighurs, the Kyrgyz, and the Tangut (8th to 13th Century)." In Bosworth and Asimov 1998–2000, pt. 1, pp. 191–214.

Skorupski 1983

Skorupski, Tadeusz. *Tibetan Amulets*. Bangkok, 1983.

Smith 1960

Smith, Cyril Stanley. *A History of Metallography: The Development of Ideas on the Structure of Metals before 1890*. Chicago, 1960.

Smith 1996

Smith, Warren W., Jr. *Tibetan Nation: A History of Tibetan Nationalism and Sino-Tibetan Relations*. Boulder, 1996.

Snellgrove and Richardson 1995

Snellgrove, David, and Hugh Richardson. *A Cultural History of Tibet*. New York, 1968; rev. ed., Boulder, 1980; reprint, Boston, 1995.

Sotheby's 1985

Indian, Himalayan, South-East Asian Art and Indian Minatures. Sale cat. Sotheby's, New York, September 20–21, 1985.

Spring 1993

Spring, Christopher. *African Arms and Armour*. London, 1993.

Stein 1972

Stein, R. A. *Tibetan Civilization*. Translated from the French by J. E. Stapleton Driver. Stanford, 1972.

Stone 1934, 1999

Stone, George Cameron. *A Glossary of the Construction, Decoration, and Use of Arms and Armor in All Countries and in All Times*. Portland, Maine, 1934; reprint, New York, 1999.

Świętosławski 1999

Świętosławski, Witold. *Arms and Armour of the Nomads of the Great Steppe in the Times of the Mongol Expansion (12th–14th Centuries)*. Translated by Maria Abramowicz. Łódź, Poland, 1999.

Tashi Namgyal

Tashi Namgyal (*bkra shis rnam rgyal*). *'jig rten lugs kyi bstan bcos las dpyad don gsal ba'i sgron me zhes grags pa bzhugs so* (A Treatise on Worldly Traditions, known as the Shining Lamp of Analysis), 1524. See appendix "Excerpts from *A Treatise on Worldly Traditions*" for various versions. An unspecified version is cited as *Jig* in Das 1902b.

Tashi Tsering 1979

Tashi Tsering, ed. *Brtag thabs padma dkar po'i 'chun po: A Reproduction of an Incomplete Mansucript of a Verse Work on the Appraisal and Appreciation of Omens, Precious Objects, Weapons, and Other Possessions, by Snags-'chan Hūṃ-ka-ra-dza-ya*. Delhi, 1979.

Tavard 1975

Tavard, Christian-H. *L'habit du cheval: Selle et bride*. Paris, 1975.

Teichman 1922

Teichman, Eric. *Travels of a Consular Officer in Eastern Tibet: Together with a History of the Relations between China, Tibet and India*. Cambridge, 1922.

Thimphu 1975

'jig rten lugs kyi bstan bcos las dpyad don gsal ba'i sgron me bzhugs so (A Treatise on Worldly Traditions, known as the Shining Lamp of Analysis). Thimphu, Bhutan, 1975. For further information, see the appendix "Excerpts from *A Treatise on Worldly Traditions*," no. 5.

Thinley 1980
Karma Thinley, Lama Wangchhim. *The History of the Sixteen Karmapas of Tibet*. Boulder, 1980.

Thordeman 1939–40
Thordeman, Bengt, in collaboration with Poul Nørlund and Bo E. Ingelmark. *Armour from the Battle of Wisby, 1361*. 2 vols. Stockholm, 1939–40.

Thurman and Weldon 1999
Thurman, Robert A. F., and David Weldon. *Sacred Symbols: The Ritual Art of Tibet*. Exh. cat. New York, 1999.

Tibet 1981
Nagpo Ngawang Jigmei et al. *Tibet*. Belgrade, Shanghai, and London, 1981.

Tokya-Fuong 1997
Tokya-Fuong, Ursula. "Reflections of Heavenly Bliss." *Christie's International Magazine* 14 (November 1997), p. 30.

Tom 2001
Tom, Philip M. W. "Some Notable Sabers of the Qing Dynasty at The Metropolitan Museum of Art." *Metropolitan Museum Journal* 36 (2001), pp. 207–22.

Tsai 2001
Tsai, Shih-shan Henry. *Perpetual Happiness: The Ming Emperor Yongle*. Seattle, 2001.

Tucci 1959
Tucci, Giuseppe. "A Tibetan Classification of Buddhist Images, According to Their Style." *Artibus Asiae* 22, nos. 1–2 (1959), pp. 179–87.

Tung 1980, 1996
Tung, Rosemary Jones. *A Portrait of Lost Tibet*. Photographs by Ilya Tolstoy and Brooke Dolan. New York, 1980; reprint, Berkeley, 1996.

Turnbull 1980
Turnbull, S. R., and Angus McBride. *The Mongols*. Osprey Men-at-Arms Series, no. 105. Oxford, 1980.

Untracht 1975
Untracht, Oppi. *Metal Techniques for Craftsmen: A Basic Manual for Craftsmen on the Methods of Forming and Decorating Metals*. Garden City, N.Y., 1975.

Uray-Köhalmi 1989
Uray-Köhalmi, Käthe. "Grob und Feinschmiedearbeit." In Walther Heissig and Claudius C. Müller, eds., *Die Mongolen*, vol. 2, pp. 187–91.

Exh. cat., Haus der Kunst München. Innsbruck and Frankfurt am Main, 1989.

UVA
The Online Tibetan to English Translation/Dictionary Tool, University of Virginia. http://www.people.virginia.edu/~am2zb/tibetan.

Vitali 1990
Vitali, Roberto. *Early Temples of Central Tibet*. London, 1990.

Waddell 1905, 1906, 1988
Waddell, L. A. *Lhasa and Its Mysteries, with a Record of the [British Tibetan] Expedition of 1903–1904*. London and New York, 1905; 3rd ed., London and New York, 1906; reprint of New York, 1905 ed., New York, 1988.

Wagner 2001
Wagner, Donald B. *The State and the Iron Industry in Han China*. Copenhagen, 2001.

Wagner forthcoming
Wagner, Donald B. *Ferrous Metallurgy*. Vol. 5, pt. N, sec. 36c of *Science and Civilisation in China*. Cambridge, forthcoming.

Watt 2004
Watt, James C. Y., et al. *China: Dawn of a Golden Age, 200–750 A.D.* Exh. cat., The Metropolitan Museum of Art. New York, 2004.

Watt and Leidy 2005
Watt, James C. Y., and Denise Patry Leidy. *Defining Yongle: Imperial Art in Early Fifteenth-Century China*. Exh. cat., The Metropolitan Museum of Art. New York, 2005.

Weldon 1996
Weldon, David. "The Perfect Image: The Speelman Collection of Yongle and Xuande Buddhist Icons." *Arts of Asia* 26, no. 3 (May–June 1996), pp. 64–73.

Weldon and Singer 1999
Weldon, David, and Jane Casey Singer. *The Sculptural Heritage of Tibet: Buddhist Art in the Nyingjei Lam Collection*. Exh. cat., Ashmolean Museum, Oxford. London, 1999.

White 1909
White, J. Claude. *Sikhim and Bhutan: Twenty-One Years on the North-East Frontier, 1887–1908*. London, 1909.

Whitfield 1982–85
Whitfield, Roderick. *The Art of Central Asia: The Stein Collection in the British Museum*. 3 vols. Tokyo, 1982–85.

Wilson 2000

Wilson, Guy M. "Short Notes: A Taste of One's Own Medicine." *Royal Armouries Yearbook* 5 (2000), pp. 194–96.

Wimmel 2003

Wimmel, Kenneth. *William Woodville Rockhill: Scholar-Diplomat of the Tibetan Highlands*. Bangkok, 2003.

Wissing 2004

Wissing, Douglas A. *Pioneer in Tibet: The Life and Perils of Dr. Albert Shelton*. New York, 2004.

Yang Hong 1992

Yang Hong, ed. *Weapons in Ancient China*. New York, 1992.

Yang Hong 2000

Yang Hong. "Lamellar Armor and Horse Bardings in Yamato and Koguryo and Their Connections with China." *Journal of East Asian Archaeology* 2, nos. 3–4 (2000), pp. 123–37.

Yi 1987

Yi, Kang-chil. *Han'guk ŭi kapchu* (Korean armor). Seoul, 1987.

Yoshinobu 1983

Yoshinobu, Shiba. "Sung Foreign Trade." In Morris Rossabi, ed., *China among Equals: The Middle Kingdom and Its Neighbors, 10th–14th Centuries*, pp. 89–115. Berkeley, 1983.

***Younghusband* 1999**

The British Invasion of Tibet: Colonel Younghusband, 1904. London, 1999.

Zeki Validi 1936

Zeki Validi [Togan], A. "Die Schwerter der Germanen, nach arabischen Berichten des 9.–11. Jahrhunderts." *Zeitschrift der deutschen Morgenländischen Gesellschaft* 90, n.s. 15 (1936), pp. 1–37.

Zwalf 1981

Zwalf, W. *Heritage of Tibet*. London, 1981.

Zwalf 1985

Zwalf, W. *Buddhism: Art and Faith*. London, 1985.

Index

bullet pouches (*mde'u khug, mdel khug,* or *mdel shubs*), 199.
    See also bandoliers
    Tibetan, 19th century (cat. no. 107), 199, 211, *211*
    Tibetan, 19th century (cat. no. 110), 213, *213*
burial rituals, 36, 41n.9
Buriats, a Mongol people, 23

Candler, Edmund, 67
cane, 15, 187, 188. *See also* shields
cantles (*phyi ru*), 214. *See also* saddles
cavalry, armored (figs. 3, 6, 7, 45), *4, 7,* 199
    complete set of equipment for, 6, 126
        armor for man and horse, Tibetan or Mongolian,
            and Bhutanese, mainly 15th–17th century (cat.
            no. 26), 10, 96, 97–100, *99, 102*
        Tibetan, and possibly Bhutanese and Nepalese, 18th–
            19th century (cat. no. 46), 6, 9, 126, 134, *134–37*
Central Asia, 10, 51
    armor from, 126. *See also* cat. no. 41
    Buddhist iconography in, 35
    helmets in style of, 70. *See also* cat. nos. 21–23
    leather armor in, 116
    metallurgical skills in, 21–22, 23, 32n.23
    saddles in, 214
ceramics, 27
Chaglotsapa Dharmasvami (*chos rje chag lotsawa,* 1197–1264),
    49
chakras (*'khor lo* or *be rdo,* quoits), 186
    Tibetan, 15th–18th century (?) (cat. no. 90), 16, 174, 186,
        186
Chakzam (*lchag zam*), bridge, 24
Chakzampa. *See* Tangtong Gyalpo
Chamdo (*chab mdo*), 29, 30, 31
Changchub Gyaltsen (*byang chub rgyal mtshan,* 1302–1364), 8
chape, of scabbard fittings, 147
    objects with, cat. nos. 67, 69, 72, 74, 124
Chapman, Frederick Spencer (1907–1971), 6
    photograph by (fig. 5), *5*
chasing, in metalwork, 15, 31
China, 8–9, 10–11, 14, 15, 21, 22, 23, 29, 38, 51, 53. *See also*
    specific dynasties
    archery equipment from. *See* cat. nos. 97, 98
    armor from, 116. *See also* cat. nos. 47, 54
    ax head from. *See* cat. no. 89
    Buddhist iconography in, 35
    delineation of claws on dragons in, 233n.4
    domed cane shields from, 92
    firearms in, 198, 208
    helmets from, 6, 68, 80, 90. *See also* cat. nos. 11, 18–20
    horse armor in, 96
    metallurgical skills in, 21, 30, 31
    missions and gift givings between Tibet and, 26–27,
        32n.58, 33n.70
    saddles and stirrups from, 214, 215n.1, 244. *See also* cat.
        nos. 111, 118–123
    Sino-Tibetan ritual art of early 15th century and, 24–27
    spearheads from, 174. *See also* cat. nos. 86–88
    swords from, 146, 147, 148n.8, 172–73, 238. *See also* cat.
        nos. 55–57, 60, 71, 72
    textiles of, 27, 28
    Tibetan motifs borrowed from, 27–29
chiseling, metalworking technique, 15. *See also* punches and
    chisels
Chödrak Gyatso (*chos grags rgya mtsho,* 1454–1506), Seventh
    Karmapa, 24

choppers, ritual (fig. 21), 24, *25,* 31
    object with, cat. no. 16
chos skyong bse khrab pa (main protector of Likir Monastery),
    43, 45–47
    chants in propitiation of, 45–46
    divination by means of, 47
    Dorje Setrap (*rdo rje bse khrab*), *tangka* depicting (fig. 41), *45*
    religious dances (*'chams*) of, 47
Christie's, London, 201
Christie's, New York, 219
Chronicles of Ladakh (*la dvags rgyal rabs*), 200
Chungriboche (*chung ri bo che*), bridge, 24
Chusul (*chu shul*) ferry, bridge at, 24
Chuwori (*chu bo ri*), bridge at, 24
cinch or girth straps for horses (*sga glo*), 214
Cleveland Museum of Art, iron ritual objects at, 24, 27
clouds, stylized (*sprin ris,* fig. 26), 16, 24, 27, 28, *28*
    objects with, cat. nos. 18, 23, 26, 31, 33, 36, 73, 78, 88, 94,
        95, 98, 118–20, 122
cloud scrolls (*ju'i*), 38
    objects with, cat. nos. 27, 67, 87, 92, 123, 133
coat of plates (figs. 11, 14), 8, *12, 13,* 14, 18n.18
coin motif, objects with, cat. nos. 36, 41, 88
collections of Tibetan material culture, 10–11
composite iron (*sna 'dus lcags*), 146, 168
concentric circles and spirals, objects with, cat. nos. 11, 57,
    100, 111, 129, 133–135
conch shell (*dung*), 16
    objects with, cat. nos. 31, 88, 96, 122
constellation, object with depiction of, cat. no. 88
copper, metalworking techniques with, 15
copper armor (*zangs kyi beg tse*), 39
coral, 15, 146, 147
    objects with, cat. nos. 62–67, 69, 122
Cranmore Museum, Chiselhurst, Kent, 62, 92n.7
crescent moon, object with, cat. no. 88
crinets (neck defenses of horse armor), 96
    Tibetan or Mongolian, 15th–17th century (Metropolitan
        Museum, cat. no. 30), 11, 15, 96, 98, 100, 102, 105–7,
        106, 107, 118, 120
    Tibetan or Mongolian, 15th–17th century (Royal
        Armouries Museum, cat. no. 26), 98, *99*
    Tibetan or Mongolian, 16th–17th century (Victoria and
        Albert Museum, cat. no. 33), 98, 100, 114, *114, 115*
cross motifs, 192
crupper (*rmed*), 214. *See also* tack
    armored cavalryman, Tibetan, and possibly Bhutanese
        and Nepalese, 18th–19th century (cat. no. 46), 6,
        134, *134–37*
    bridle and and matching crupper straps, Tibetan, 15th–17th
        century (cat. no. 134), 15, 74, 148, *248, 248–49, 249*
    decorative fitting from, eastern Tibetan or Chinese for
        the Tibetan market, 17th–18th century (cat. no.
        121), 15, 230, *230*
    Tibetan, probably 19th–early 20th century (cat. no. 124),
        234, *237,* 238
crupper panels (flank, thigh, and rump defenses for horse
    armor), 96
    Tibetan or Mongolian, 15th–17th century (Royal Museum,
        Edinburgh, cat. no. 32), 96, 110, 111, *111–13, 113*
    Tibetan or Mongolian, 15th–17th century (Victoria and
        Albert Museum, cat. no. 26), 98, *99*
Cultural Revolution, 11, 218
cup case, eastern Tibetan, 15th century (fig. 19, cat. no. 113),
    20, 27, 30–31, 167, 172, 220, *220*

curling tendril motifs, 177, 178
Curzon, Lord (George Nathaniel Curzon, first Marquess
    Curzon of Kedleston, 1859–1925), 164
cushions, for saddles (*sga 'bol*), 214. *See also* saddles

daggers, 29–30, 31, 37
    Tibetan, 19th century (cat. no. 110), 213, *213*
Dakinis (*mkha' 'gro ma*), object with, cat. no. 16
Dalai Lama, 6, 9–10, 40
    origin of term, 9
    Third Dalai Lama, Sonam Gyatso (*bsod nams rgya mtsho,*
        1543–1588), 9
    Fourth Dalai Lama, Yonten Gyatso (*yon tan rgya mtsho,*
        1589–1617), 9, 181
    Fifth Dalai Lama, Nawang Losang Gyatso (*ngag dbang
        blo bzang rgya mtsho,* 1617–1682), 9, 23, 28, 40, 52,
        200, 230
    Sixth Dalai Lama, Tsangyang Gyatso (*tsangs dbyangs rgya
        mtsho,* 1683–1706), 239n.4
    Seventh Dalai Lama, Kalzang Gyatso (*skal bzang rgya
        mtsho,* 1708–1757), 9
    Eighth Dalai Lama, Jampal Gyatso (*'jam dpal rgya mtsho,*
        1758–1804), 9, 10
    Thirteenth Dalai Lama, Thubten Gyatso (*thub bstan rgya
        mtsho,* 1876–1933), 10, 18–19n.23, 97, 100, 114, 234, 239
    Fourteenth Dalai Lama, Tenzin Gyatso (*bstan 'dzin rgya
        mtsho,* b. 1935), 10, 230, 242
Dalmahoy, Captain and Miss, 194
damascening (also called overlay), decorative technique in
    metalworking, 15, 29, 31, 33n.64, 80, 85
    with flat strips of gold instead of gold wire. *See* cat.
        nos. 18, 23, 27, 47, 127
    origins of, in Tibet, 22–23
    in Sino-Tibetan style of early 15th century (figs. 21–24),
        24, 25, 26
Damascus barrel, 208
dances, religious (*'chams*), 47
Darjeeling, 10, 213
Das, Sarat Chandra (1849–1917), 12, 23, 155
dastana (Indian arm defenses), 143
Dayap (*brag g.yab*), in Kham, 29
dbu can (Tibetan script), 16
    objects inscribed with, cat. nos. 3, 4, 7, 16, 45, 46, 58, 77,
        80, 85, 90, 103, 104
dbu med (Tibetan cursive script), 51
    objects inscribed with, cat. nos. 4, 5, 112
decorative motifs, 15–16. *See also specific motifs*
deer, objects with, cat. nos. 42, 116, 125
Demiéville, Paul, 36–37
Derge (*sde dge*), in Kham, 5, 22–23, 24, 26, 27, 29–30, 31, 147,
    164, 218, 242
Deshin Shekpa (*de bzhin gshegs pa,* 1384–1415), Fifth Karmapa,
    26–27
Dharma, one of the Three Jewels, 43
Dharmasvami (*chos rje chag lotsawa,* 1197–1264), 49
dhotis, 38
divination, 209. *See also* oracles
    by means of *bse khrab pa,* 47
Dolan, Brooke, 6, 12–14
    photographs by (figs. 7, 10), *7, 11*
Dongtse Monastery, 12
door fittings (figs. 25–28), 27–29, *28*
    Tibetan, probably 15th–16th century (cat. no. 114), 167,
        221, *221*
Dorje Setrap (*rdo rje bse khrab*), *tangka* depicting (fig. 41), *45*

Tibetan or Central Asian, possibly 15th–17th century
(cat. no. 23), 16, 68, 83, 84, 90, 90, 91
as votive objects (figs. 9, 11, 13–15, 34, 37), 11–13, 14, 38, 39, 40
Waddell's description of, 3–4
with wax seals, 52. See also cat. nos. 3, 9
western Tibetan or Central Asian, possibly 14th–16th
century (cat. no. 22), 68, 88, 89
Hemis Monastery, Ladakh (fig. 16), 13, 14
hilts. See swords
Hinduism, 43, 186
honeycomb or tortoiseshell pattern, objects with, cat.
nos. 38, 60, 73, 94, 95, 104
Hongwu, Chinese emperor (r. 1368–98), 24, 148, 216
Hongwu-Yongle iron ritual objects (figs. 21, 23, 24), 24, 25, 26,
32n.54, 148–50, 151, 152, 216
Hor, a Mongol people, 14, 22, 147
hor, use of word, 22, 32n.30, 215n.7
Horpo (hor po), 22–23, 27, 29–30
horse, object with, cat. no. 33
horse armor (figs. 3, 9; cat. nos. 26–33), 4, 4, 5, 8, 11, 11, 15, 21,
36, 96–114
armor for man and horse, Tibetan or Mongolian, mainly
15th–17th century (cat. no. 26), 10, 96, 97–100, 99, 102
crinets (neck defenses), 96
Tibetan or Mongolian, 15th–17th century
(Metropolitan Museum, cat. no. 30), 11, 15, 96,
98, 100, 102, 105–7, 106, 107, 118, 120
Tibetan or Mongolian, 15th–17th century (Royal
Armouries Museum, cat. no. 26), 98, 99
Tibetan or Mongolian, 16th–17th century (Victoria
and Albert Museum, cat. no. 33), 98, 100, 114,
114, 115
crupper panels (flank, thigh, and rump defenses), 96
Tibetan or Mongolian, 15th–17th century (Royal
Museum, Edinburgh, cat. no. 32), 96, 110, 111,
111–13, 113
Tibetan or Mongolian, 15th–17th century (Victoria
and Albert Museum, cat. no. 26), 98, 99
decoration of leather panels in, 96, 97, 98, 116
flanchards (side panels, cat. no. 26), 96
Tibetan or Mongolian, 15th–17th century (cat. no. 26),
98, 99, 116
four matching elements of, Tibetan or Mongolian, 15th–
17th century (cat. no. 32), 54, 56, 58, 96, 110–13, 110–13
loin defenses, 96
Tibetan or Mongolian, 15th–17th century (cat. no. 26),
98, 99
of Mongols, 96–97, 107. See also cat. nos. 26–33
peytrals (breast defenses, cat. nos. 30–32), 96, 105–11,
113n.2
Tibetan or Mongolian, 15th–17th century (cat. no. 30),
11, 15, 96, 100, 105–7, 106, 120
Tibetan or Mongolian, 15th–17th century (cat. no. 31),
11, 96, 98, 100, 108, 108, 109
Tibetan or Mongolian, 15th–17th century (Royal
Museum, Edinburgh, cat. no. 32), 96, 110, 110–11
Tibetan or Mongolian, 15th–17th century (Victoria
and Albert Museum, cat. no. 26), 98, 99
shaffrons (head defenses, cat. nos. 27–29), 96, 100–105
Tibetan or Mongolian, 15th–17th century
(Metropolitan Museum, cat. no. 27), 83, 96, 100,
100, 101, 140
Tibetan or Mongolian, 15th–17th century
(Metropolitan Museum, cat. no. 28), 100, 102,
102, 103, 140

Tibetan or Mongolian, 15th–17th century (Victoria
and Albert Museum, cat. no. 26), 97–98, 99, 102
Tibetan or Mongolian, probably 15th–17th century
(Victoria and Albert Museum, cat. no. 29), 104,
104–5, 139, 140
tailpiece, 96
Tibetan or Mongolian, 15th–17th century (Royal
Museum, Edinburgh, cat. no. 32), 110, 112, 113
Tibetan or Mongolian, 15th–17th century (Victoria
and Albert Museum, cat. no. 26), 98, 99
of Tsaparang-Phyang type, 96
as votive objects (fig. 15), 13, 14
horseback target-shooting contests (fig. 45), 6, 174, 199, 200, 242
Hôtel Drouot, Paris, 209
Huangchao Liqi Tushi (Illustrated Regulations for the
Ceremonial Regalia of the Present Dynasty, fig. 44),
144, 144, 197
Hūṃkaradazaya (dates unknown, but possibly 18th century),
68, 126, 147, 187. See also Lotus Bouquet of Analytical
Methods
Hyslop, Captain, 144

India, 8, 10, 14, 21, 23, 30, 45, 53, 185
armor of, 140, 143. See also cat. nos. 40, 53
Buddhist iconography in, 35, 37, 38, 40
chakras of Sikhs in, 186
firearms of, 198, 208
four mirrors in, 126
horse armor of Mughals in, 96
leather shields from, 6, 92
mail imported from, 5
metallurgy in, 22, 32n.19
swords of, 146, 148n.8. See also cat. no. 74
Indian ricasso, 172
infantry, armored (figs. 2, 4, 5), 2, 4, 5, 6, 11–12, 94
ingot, object with, cat. no. 88
inlaying, decorative technique in metalworking, 15, 31. See
also encrustation
origins of, in Tibet, 23
Inner Mongolia, 214
inscriptions:
with Chinese characters, 230, 230n.3
dual-language, in Tibetan and Mongolian (cat. no. 85),
16, 181, 181
inventory numbers, 11, 52, 54n.5, 232. See also cat. nos. 3–
7, 26, 122
Islamic (cat. no. 74), 172
mantras, objects with, cat. nos. 16, 34, 58
objects with. See cat. nos. 3–7, 16, 26, 28, 34, 45, 55, 58, 68,
74, 77, 80, 85, 90, 103, 104, 112, 120
poetry, 186. See also cat. no. 90
Iran, 22, 23, 96
helmet possibly from. See cat. no. 21
iron chain suspension bridges (fig. 20), 21, 23–24, 24, 36
ironworking, 21–33
decorative motifs and dating of, 27–29
in early period, 7th–12th centuries, 21–23
guild system and, 23
Hongwu-Yongle ritual objects, 148–50, 151, 152
monastic patronage and, 23
in 19th and 20th centuries, 29–31
raw materials and techniques in, 15, 19n.45, 30–31, 85. See
also damascening; inlaying; mercury gilding;
pierced iron decoration
Sino-Tibetan ritual art of early 15th century and, 24–27

steel production and, 22, 30, 31, 32nn. 16, 19
wrought iron and, 21, 30, 31, 32n.10
Islands of the Immortals, decorative motif, 182, 183, 225, 227,
233

Jamchen Chojey (byams chen chos rje shakya ye shesi, 1352–
1435), 26
Jampal Gyatso ('jam dpal rgya mtsho, 1758–1804), Eighth
Dalai Lama, 9, 10
funerary chapel of (fig. 27), 28, 29
Jamyang Namgyal, Ladakhi king (r. ca. 1580–90), 14
Japan, 15
jewel tray (gzhong pa rin po che), object with, cat. no. 125
Jokhang Temple, Lhasa, 6, 12, 32n.58
ju'i. See cloud scrolls

Kadam (bka' gdams), Tibetan Buddhist sect, 8
Kagyu (bka' brgyud), Tibetan Buddhist sect, 8
Kalmuks, a Mongol people, 23
Kalzang Gyatso (skal bzang rgya mtsho, 1708–1757), Seventh
Dalai Lama, 9
Kandze (dkar mdzes), 31
Kangxi, Chinese emperor (1662–1722), 9
Kangyur (bka' 'gyur), 62
Karluks (gar log), 22, 32n.25
Karma Kagyu, 9
Karma (ka rma), Tibetan Buddhist sect, 8, 27
Karma Tenkyong (kar ma btsan skyong), Tsang king, 9
khadgaratna, or Precious Sword (Tibetan ral gri rin po che),
150
Khalili Collection, London, 23
Kham (khams), 9, 27, 29, 30, 31, 32n.30, 52, 124, 164, 202, 218
Khampas, 146
khatvanga (ritual staff, fig. 24), 24, 25, 26, 27
king's earrings motif, object with, cat. no. 130
kinnara (mi'am ci, half-bird half-human creature), objects
with, cat. no. 125
Kirghiz, 22
kirttimukha. See tsi pa ṭa or kirttimukha masks
knee defenses:
possibly Mongolian or Chinese, 13th–15th century (cat.
no. 47), 25–26, 83, 138, 138
Tibetan or Mongolian, probably 15th–17th century (cat.
nos. 48, 49), 139, 139
Kocho, 22
Korea, helmet in style of (cat. no. 17), 8, 82, 82
Kronos Collections: sword guard, Tibetan or Chinese, 14th–
15th century (cat. no. 56), 147, 150–51, 151
Kublai Khan (1215–1294), 8
Kunga Gyaltsen (kun dga' rgyal mtshan, 1182–1251, known as
Sakya Pandita), 8, 26
Kunga Tashi Gyaltsen (kun dga' bkra shis rgyal mtshan,
b. 1349), 26–27
Kuqa, 21, 22, 32n.25
Kyentse (mkhyen brtse, fig. 36), 39, 39

Labre, Gérard, 209
Ladakh, 9, 43
firearms in, 199–200
Hemis Monastery in (fig. 16), 13, 14
Lamayuru Monastery in (fig. 17), 14, 14
Likir Monastery in (figs. 39, 40), 14, 42, 43–49, 44
Phyang Monastery in (figs. 9, 15), 11, 14, 92, 96
Stok Palace Museum in, 143
ladle, ritual, for Fire Offering ceremony (fig. 23), 24, 26